JOURNAL FOR THE STUDY OF THE OLD TESTAMENT
SUPPLEMENT SERIES
141

JSOT Press
Sheffield

Debt-Slavery in Israel and the Ancient Near East

HT
915
.C44
1993
sed b

Gregory C. Chirichigno

Journal for the Study of the Old Testament
Supplement Series 141

Published by JSOT Press
JSOT Press is an imprint of
Sheffield Academic Press Ltd
343 Fulwood Road
Sheffield S10 3BP
England

Typeset by Sheffield Academic Press
and
Printed on acid-free paper in Great Britain
by Biddles Ltd
Guildford

British Library Cataloguing in Publication Data

Chirichigno, Gregory C.
   Debt Slavery in Israel and the Ancient
   Near East — (JSOT Supplement Series,
   ISSN 0309-0708; No. 141)
   I. Title II. Series
   221.9

   ISBN 1-85075-359-8

CONTENTS

The origin of the present work lies in my unpublished doctoral thesis (1989) which was undertaken at the Cheltenham & Gloucester College of Higher Education (formally known as the College of St Paul & St Mary) and the Oxford Centre for Post Graduate Hebrew Studies, England. While the present work does not differ greatly from its predecessor, I have nevertheless endeavoured to bring the discussions contained herein up to date with the current state of scholarship, with perhaps the exception of the study of the early history of Israel which continues to evoke much scholarly discussion from all fields. My main aim has been to provide an exhaustive treatment of the biblical manumission laws in the light of parallel ancient Near Eastern social and legal institutions. To this end I have not attempted to abridge significantly any of the original references or excurses found in the text or footnotes. However, three articles by R. Westbrook that appear in this work have now been included in a single work entitled *Property and the Family in Biblical Law* (JSOTSup, 113; Sheffield: JSOT Press, 1991). These articles have been marked with an (*) in the Bibliography.

My initial interest in the biblical manumission laws originated in my research on the literary structure of the Covenant Code. I have always been intrigued by the special treatment given by the compiler(s) of the Covenant Code to these and the other slave laws that occur there, especially since they occur at the beginning of each major legal discussion.

While there are many people to whom I owe my gratitude, I would especially like to thank Dr Gordon J. Wenham, who was my director of study, for his careful and insightful direction throughout the course of my work and for continuing to provide valuable direction. I also would like to thank the editors at JSOT Press for including my work in their valuable series.

Sunnyvale, CA, December 1992

Greg Chirichigno

ראשית חכמה קנה חכמה
ובכל־קנינך קנה בינה
Prov. 4.7

ABBREVIATIONS

AA	*American Anthropologist*
AASOR	Annual of the American Schools of Oriental Research
AB	Anchor Bible
AbhBAW	*Abhandlungen der Bayerischen Akademie der Wissenschaften philosophisch-historische Klasse* N.F.
AbrN	*Abr-Nahrain*
ADSNS	*Annali della Scuola Normale Superiore*
AHDO	*Archives d'Histoire du Droit Oriental*
AHR	American Historical Review
AJA	*American Journal of Archaeology*
AJSL	*American Journal of Semitic Languages and Literature*
ALCRDS	The Ayers Lectures of the Colgate-Rochester Divinity School
AnBib	Analecta biblica
ANESTP	J.B. Pritchard (ed.), *Ancient Near East Supplementary Texts and Pictures*
ANET	J.B. Pritchard (ed.), *Ancient Near Eastern Texts*
AnOr	Analecta orientalia
Anton	*Antonianum*
AOAT	Alter Orient und Altes Testament
AOS	American Oriental Series
ARA	*Annual Review of Anthropology*
ARM	Archives royales de Mari
ArOr	*Archiv orientálni*
ARU	J. Kohler and A. Ungnad, *Assyrische Rechtsurkunden*
A-s	Ammisaduqa's Edict
AS	Assyriological Studies
ASAR	Association of Social Anthropologists Research Methods in Social Anthropology
ASAW	Abhandlungen der Sächsischen Akademie der Wissenschaften
ASORSVS	American Schools of Oriental Research Special Volume Series
ASSt	All Souls Studies
ATANT	Abhandlungen zur Theologie des Alten und Neuen Testaments
BA	*Biblical Archaeologist*
BARev	*Biblical Archaeology Review*
BASOR	*Bulletin of the American Schools of Oriental Research*
BAWPHKA	Bayerische Akademie der Wissenschaften Philosphisch-Historische Klasse Abhandlungen, N.F.

BBB	Bonner biblische Beiträge
BBVO	Berliner Beiträge zum Vorderen Orient
BDB	F. Brown, S.R. Driver, C.A. Briggs, *Hebrew and English Lexicon of the Old Testament*
BETL	Bibliotheca ephemeridum theologicarum lovaniensum
BHS	*Biblia Hebraica Stugartensia*
Bib	*Biblica*
BibN	*Biblische Notizen*
BibRev	*Bible Review*
BJRL	*Bulletin of the John Rylands University Library of Manchester*
BKAT	Biblischer Kommentar: Altes Testament
BJS	Brown Judaic Studies
BM	*Beth Mikra*
BM	British Museum
BO	*Bibliotheca Orientalis*
BSC	Bible Students Commentary
BSO(A)S	*Bulletin of the School of Oriental (and African) Studies*
BT	*The Bible Translator*
BTB	*Biblical Theology Bulletin*
BWANT	Beiträge zur Wissenschaft vom Alten und Neuen Testaments
BZAW	Beihefte zur *ZAW*
CAD	The Assyrian Dictionary of the Oriental Institute of the University of Chicago
CAH	Cambridge Ancient History
CahRB	Cahiers de la Revue Biblique
CahSA	Cahiers de la Société Asiatique
CB	Century Bible
CBC	Cambridge Bible Commentary
CBQ	*Catholic Biblical Quarterly*
CBSC	Cambridge Bible for Schools and Colleges
CFTL	Clark's Foreign Theological Library ns
Comm	*Communio*
ConBOT	Coniectanea biblica, Old Testament
CT	*Cuneiform Texts from Babylonian Tablets in the British Museum*
CTA	A. Herdner (ed.), *Corpus des tablettes en cunéiformes alphabétiques*
DAK	B. Kienast (ed.), *Das Altassyrische Kaufvertragsrecht*
DBHOT	De Boeken van het Oude Testament
DHSAT	Die Heilige Schrift des Alten Testaments
DZZ	*Die Zeichen der Zeit*
EA	Amarna Letters
EF	Erträge der Forschung
Enc	*Encounter*

EncJud	*Encyclopaedia Judaica*
ERC	Editions Recherche sur les Civilisations
EstBíb	*Estudios bíblicos*
EvQ	*Evangelical Quarterly*
EvT	*Evangelische Theologie*
ExpTim	*Expository Times*
FAS	Freiburger Altorientalische Studien
GBS	Guides to Biblical Scholarship
GKC	*Gesenius' Hebrew Grammar*, ed. E. Kautzsch, trans. A.E. Cowley
GPIT	Growing Points in Theology
HALAT	W. Baumgartner *et al.*, *Hebräisches und aramäisches Lexikon zum Alten Testament*
HAR	*Hebrew Annual Review*
HKAT	Handkommentar zum Alten Testament
HL	Hittite Laws
HOr	Handbuch der Orientalistik
HSM	Harvard Semitic Monographs
HSS	Harvard Semitic Studies
HTR	*Harvard Theological Review*
HUCA	*Hebrew Union College Annual*
HWS	History Workshop Series
ICC	International Critical Commentary
IDB	G.A. Buttrick (ed.), *Interpreter's Dictionary of the Bible*
IDBSup	*IDB*, Supplementary Volume
IEJ	*Israel Exploration Journal*
ILR	*Israel Law Review*
Int	*Interpretation*
IOA	Iura Orientis Antiqui
ISBE	G.W. Bromiley (ed.), *International Standard Bible Encyclopedia* (Grand Rapids: Eerdmans, 1979–88)
JA	*Journal asiatique*
JAOS	*Journal of the American Oriental Society*
JBL	*Journal of Biblical Literature*
JCR	*The Journal of Conflict Resolution*
JCS	*Journal of Cuneiform Studies*
JEN	Joint Expedition with the Iraq Museum at Nuzi
JESHO	*Journal of the Economic and Social History of the Orient*
JETS	*Journal of the Evangelical Theological Society*
JHI	*Journal of the History of Ideas*
JJS	*Journal of Jewish Studies*
JNES	*Journal of Near Eastern Studies*
JNSL	*Journal of Northwest Semitic Languages*
JPOS	*Journal of the Palestine Oriental Society*

JQR	*Jewish Quarterly Review* New Series
JRAI	*Journal of the Royal Anthropological Institute*
JRL	Textes Cunéiformes. Musée du Louvre
JSOT	*Journal for the Study of the Old Testament*
JSOTSup	Journal for the Study of the Old Testament Supplements Series
JSS	*Journal of Semitic Studies*
Jud	*Judaism*
JWH	*Journal of World History*
KAJ	E. Ebeling, *Keilschrifttexte aus Assur juristischen Inhalts.*
KH	Kurzgefasstes exegetisches Handbuch zum Alten Testament
KHAT	Kürzer Handkommentar zum Alten Testament
Kish	Tablets excavated at Kish, in the collection of the Ashmolean Museum, Oxford
KlF	*Kleinasiatische Forschungen*
LAPO	Littératures Anciennes du Proche-Orient
LE	Laws of Eshnunna
LH	Laws of Hammurabi
LI	Lipit-Ishtar's Legal Collection
LU	Ur-Nammu's Legal Collection
MAL	Middle Assyrian Laws
MANE	Monographs on the Ancient Near East
MANT	Monographien zum Alten und Neuen Testament
MB	Middle Babylonian Period
MCAAS	*Memoirs of the Connecticut Academy of Arts & Sciences*
NA	Neo-Assyrian Period
NASB	New American Standard Bible
NB	Neo-Babylonian Period
NBL	Neo-Babylonian Laws
NCBC	New Century Bible Commentary
NICOT	The New International Commentary of the Old Testament
NIVNO	Nederlands Instituut voor het Nabije Oosten Studia Francisci Scholten Memoriae Dicata
OA	Old Assyrian Period
OB	Old Babylonian Period
OBO	Orbis Biblicus et Orientalis
OLA	Orientalia Lovaniensia Analecta
OPSEA	Occasional Papers in Social and Economic Administration
Or	*Orientalia*
OrAnt	*Oriens antiquus*
OrLit	*Orientalische Literaturzeitung*
OrN	*Orientalia Neerlandica*
OTL	Old Testament Library
OTS	*Oudtestamentische Studiën*
OTWSA	*Ou Testament Werkgemeenskap in Suid-Afrika*

Pal	Palaeologia
PB	The Polychrome Bible
PBS	Publications of the Babylonian Section, University Museum, University of Pennsylvania
PEQ	Palestine Exploration Quarterly
PFGUC	Publicazioni della Facoltà di Giurisprudence, Università di Catania
PPFBR	Publication of the Perry Foundation for Biblical Research in the Hebrew University of Jerusalem
PRIA	Proceedings of the Royal Irish Academy
PRU	Le palais royal d'Ugarit.
RA	Revue d'assyriologie et d'archéologie orientale
RAS	Regional Anthropology Series
RB	Revue biblique
RechBib	Recherches bibliques
ResQ	Restoration Quarterly
RevSI	Revista storica italiana
RGG	H. Campenhausen et al. (eds.), Die Religion in Geschichte und Gegenwart
RIDA	Revue internationale des droits de l'antiquité
RS	Ras Shamra
RSO	Revista degli studi orientali
SB	Sources bibliques
SBLDS	SBL Dissertation Series
SBLI	SBL: The Bible and Its Modern Interpreters
SBLMS	Society of Biblical Literature Monograph Series
SBTSS	Studies in Biblical Theology Second Series
SDE	Social Dimensions of Economics
SDOAP	Studia et Documenta Ad Iura Orientis Antiqui Pertinentia
SGKAO	H. Klengel (ed.), Schriften zur Geschichte und Kultur des Alten Orients
SJA	Southwestern Journal of Anthropology
SJLA	Studies in Judaism in Late Antiquity
SLBA	The Schweich Lectures of the British Academy
SPSH	Scholars Press Studies in the Humanities
SPSME	Social and Political Studies of the Middle East
SS	Studi Semitici
SSN	Studia Semitica Neerlandica
SCath	Studia catholica
ST	Studia theologica
StudOr	Studia orientalia
SWBAS	The Social World of Biblical Antiquity Series
SZ	Zeitschrift der Savigny-Stiftung für Rechtsgeschichte
TAPS	Transactions of the American Philosophical Society

TynBul	*Tyndale Bulletin*
TCL	Textes cunéiformes du Musée du Louvre
TDNT	G. Kittel and G. Friedrich (eds.), *Theological Dictionary of the New Testament*
TDOT	G.J. Botterweck and H. Ringgren (eds.), *Theological Dictionary of the Old Testament*
TESG	*Tijdschrift voor economische en sociale geografie*
TextsS	Texts and Studies
ThA	Theologische Arbeiten
ThViat	*Theologia Viatorum*
ThWat	G.J. Botterweck and H. Ringgren (eds.), *Theologisches Wörterbuch zum Alten Testament*
TOTC	Tyndale Old Testament Commentaries
TSTS	Toronto Semitic Texts and Studies
TTQ	*Tübinger Theologische Quartalschrift*
TUAT	R. Borger *et al.* (eds.), *Texts aus der Umwelt des Alten Testaments*
TynBul	*Tyndale Bulletin*
UET	Ur Excavations, Texts
UF	*Ugarit-Forschungen*
UNHAII	Uitgaven van het Nederlands Historisch-Archaeologisch Instituut to Instanbul
UT	C.H. Gordon, *Ugaritic Textbook* (AnOR, 38; Rome: Pontifical Biblical Institute, 1967)
VAB5	M. Schorr, *Urkunden des altbabylonischen Zivil-und Prozessrechts*, 1913
VAS	Vorderasiatische Schriftdenkmäler tablets in the Collections of the Staatliche Museen, Berlin
Vg	Vulgate
VicOr	*Vicino Oriente*
VS	Verbum salutis
VT	*Vetus Testamentum*
VTSup	Vetus Testamentum, Supplements
WB	*Wittenburg Bulletin*
WBC	Word Biblical Commentary
WCom	Westminster Commentaries
WD	*Wort und Dienst*
WMANT	Wissenschaftliche Monographien zum Alten und Neuen Testament
WO	*Die Welt des Orients*
YNER	Yale Near Eastern Researches
YOS	Yale Oriental Series
ZA	*Zeitschrift für Assyriologie*
ZAW	*Zeitschrift für die alttestamentliche Wissenschaft*

ZDMG	*Zeitschrift der deutschen morgenländischen Gesellschaft*
ZDPV	*Zeitschrift des deutschen Palästina-Vereins*
ZEE	*Zeitschrift für Evangelisches Ethik*
ZKM	*Zeitschrift für die Kunde des Morgenlandes*
ZSSR	*Zeitschrift der Savigny-Stiftung für Rechtsgeschichte, romnistische Abteilung*

Chapter 1

INTRODUCTION

Aim and Scope

This book aims to clarify the meaning and *Sitz im Leben* of the manumission laws that are found in Exod. 21.2-6, 7-11 and Deut. 15.12-18 and in Lev. 25.39-54. While these laws have been the subject of various studies throughout the years, a synopsis of which I will present below, there has yet to be a consensus of opinion concerning them. It is for this reason that I decided to adopt a comparative approach, first looking at the social and legal background to debt-slavery in Mesopotamia. This comparative investigation will concentrate on those social structures, laws and institutions that have a particular bearing on the interpretation of the biblical manumission laws. Secondly, I will investigate the social and legal background to debt-slavery in Israel. While the main concern of the latter analysis will be the biblical manumission laws, I will also take a look at the Fallow, Sabbatical and Jubilee year institutions, all of which are associated with and literarily connected to the various biblical manumission laws.

History of Investigation

The discussion of the biblical manumission laws in the books of Exodus, Deuteronomy and Leviticus has been greatly influenced, on the one hand, by the discovery of the references to the *ḫabiru* in the Amarna letters (EA) and other extant documents, and on the other by the continuing debate concerning the relative dating of the sources JE, D and P, in which the manumission laws are found. The discovery of the references to the *ḫabiru* in the EA and other extant documents gave rise to the comparison of the *ḫabiru* with the biblical (עברי(ם) who are mentioned in both of the manumission laws in Exod. 21.2-6 and Deut. 15.12-18, and elsewhere in the Old Testament. For example, Alt[1] suggested that the biblical manumission laws in Exod. 21.2-6 and Deut. 15.12-18 referred to Israelites who belonged to a lower social class in Israel, although he noted that the use of the term עברי in these laws tells us little about anyone's nationality or legal status. However, Lewy,[2] who was probably the first scholar to discuss thoroughly the biblical manumission laws in Exod. 21.2-6 and Deut. 15.12-18 in the light of the Nuzi *ḫabiru* service contracts, suggested that these laws concerned the manumission of foreign slaves. However, while many scholars continue to compare these two biblical manumission laws with the Nuzi service contracts, they have generally followed Alt in suggesting that the biblical laws refer to a lower social class of Israelites. This view is particularly evident in Weippert's[3] study of the *ḫabiru*, and Paul's[4] thorough study of the laws in the Book of the Covenant, in which he suggests that the עבד עברי was a *ḫabiru*-type 'slave', although he suggests that in Deut. 15.12-18 the עבד עברי clearly refers to an Israelite. Paul's position has been adopted by many scholars, such as Wright,[5] although Wright, who follows the earlier work of Ellison,[6] suggests that the manumission laws in Exod. 21.2-6 and Deut. 15.12-18 refer specifically to a class of *landless* Israelites in order to harmonize these laws with the manumission law in Lev. 25.39-54, which does not use the designation עברי(ם). Similarly, both Riesener[7] and Kaufman[8] suggest that these

---

1. A. Alt, 'The Origin of Israelite Law', in *Essays on Old Testament History and Religion* (Oxford: Oxford University Press, 1966), pp. 93-96 = *Kleine Schriften zur Geschichte des Volkes Israel*, I (Munich: Beck, 1959), pp. 278-332.

2. J. Lewy, 'Ḥabiru and Hebrews', *HUCA* 14 (1939), pp. 587-623; cf. also 'A New Parallel between Ḥabiru and Hebrews', *HUCA* 15 (1940), pp. 47-58; 'Origin and Signification of the Biblical Term "Hebrew"', *HUCA* 28 (1957), pp. 2-13.

3. M. Weippert, *The Settlement of the Israelite Tribes in Palestine* (SBTSS, 21; London: SCM Press, 1971), pp. 85-87.

4. S.M. Paul, *Studies in the Book of the Covenant in the Light of Cuneiform and Biblical Law* (VTSup, 18; Leiden: Brill, 1970), pp. 45-52.

5. C.J.H. Wright, 'What Happened Every Seven Years in Israel? Old Testament Sabbatical Institutions for Land, Debts and Slaves, Part I', *EvQ* 56 (1984), pp. 193-201.

6. H.L. Ellison, 'The Hebrew Slave; A Study in Early Israelite Society', *EvQ* 45 (1955), pp. 30-35.

7. I. Riesener, *Der Stamm עבד im Alten Testament: Eine Wortuntersuchung unter Berücksichtigung neuerer sprachwissenschaft-licher Methoden* (BZAW, 149;

iblical manumission laws refer to a class of *landless* Israelites, though neither compare these laws with the Nuzi service contracts.)n the contrary, Riesener, who suggests that the term עברי(ם) is an thnic designation that has an entirely different origin from the term abiru, notes that these biblical manumission laws are more similar to he manumission law in LH §117, which stipulates the release of debt-laves in the third year of service. However, the strongest objection to 'aul's comparative study of Exod. 21.2-6 is found in Cardellini's[1] xhaustive comparative treatment of slavery in the ancient Near East nd Israel. He argues that the biblical manumission laws in Exod. 1.2-6 and Deut. 15.12-18 were not similar to the Nuzi service ontracts, although he still follows Alt in asserting that the biblical xpression עבד עברי refers to a lower social class of Israelites.

While the meaning and *Sitz im Leben* of Exod. 21.2-6 have generally been determined by the way in which scholars view the meaning of the term עברי(ם), the meaning and *Sitz im Leben* of Deut. 15.12-18, and of Lev. 25.39-54, in which the term עברי(ם) does not appear, have been greatly influenced by the discussion of the dating of he sources JE, D and P. The classic exposition of the documentary heory can be found in the important work of Wellhausen,[2] who argued that the source D, which he associated with Josiah's reform, was later than the source JE and earlier than the priestly source P. It was Wellhausen's belief that the centralization of worship appears for the first time in Deuteronomy, and that this reform is presupposed in P. However, Wellhausen recognized that certain parts of Deuteronomy, particularly chs. 12–16 which contain various laws (*Urdeuteronomium*), could not have been composed during the time of Josiah, although he still contended that Deuteronomy could be seen as the basis of Josiah's reform, which was essentially a programme for

Berlin: de Gruyter, 1979), pp. 115-35.

8. S.A. Kaufman, 'A Reconstruction of the Social Welfare Systems of Ancient Israel', in *The Shelter of Elyon: Essays on Ancient Palestinian Life and Literature in Honor of G.W. Ahlström* (ed. W.B. Barrick and J.R. Spencer; JSOTSup, 31; Sheffield: JSOT Press, 1984), pp. 277-86.

1. I. Cardellini, *Die biblischen 'Sklaven'-Gesetze im Lichte des keilschriftlichen Sklaven rechts: Ein Beitrag zur Tradition, Überlieferung und Redaktion der alttestamentlichen Rechtstexte* (BBB, 55; Bonn: Peter Hanstein, 1981), pp. 243-51, 337-44.

2. J. Wellhausen, *Prolegomena to the History of Ancient Israel* (Edinburgh: T. & T. Clark, 1885), pp. 29-36.

cult-centralization. However, in the wake of various commentaries
and monographs on Deuteronomy, the general scholarly consensus is
that the origins of Deuteronomy should be divorced from Josiah's or
Hezekiah's reform, although instances of the altar-law—those laws
that demanded that sacrifices should be brought to 'the place which the
Lord will choose'—were later additions which can be identified as a
separate stratum within the *Urdeuteronomium*.[1] This view is
particularly evident in Weinfeld's[2] analysis of Deut. 15.17-18, which,
he argues, has been changed from a sacred rite performed at the
sanctuary (cf. Exod. 21.5-6) into a secular rite performed at the
master's house, since it was more practical for the master to perform
this rite at his house rather than at the central sanctuary. Similar
deuteronomic revisions have been noted in Deut. 15.12-18 by Driver[3]
and Mayes,[4] both of whom argue that certain economic and social
conditions envisaged in Exod. 21.2-6, 7-11 no longer applied to the
period during which changes were made to the manumission law in
Deuteronomy. However, it is not assured that the deuteronomist
altered the manumission law in Deuteronomy significantly, since
Hengstenberg,[5] Boecker,[6] Phillips[7] and Jackson[8] have argued that

1. For example, see M. Weinfeld, 'Cult Centralization in Israel in the Light of a
Neo-Babylonian Analogy', *JNES* 23 (1964), p. 204; G. Seitz, *Redaktions-
geschichtliche Studien zum Deuteronomium* (BWANT, 13; Stuttgart: Kohlhammer,
1971), pp. 187-212; R.P. Merendino, *Das deuteronomische Gesetz: Eine literarkritische gattungs- und überlieferungsgeschichtliche Untersuchung zu Dt 12-16*
(BBB, 31; Bonn, 1969), p. 122; cp. F. Dumermuth, 'Zur deuteronomischen
Kulttheologie und ihren Voraussetzungen', *ZAW* 70 (1958), p. 61; and
A.D.H. Mayes, *Deuteronomy* (NCBC; Grand Rapids: Eerdmans; London: Morgan
& Scott , 1979), p. 61, both of whom argue that the altar-law(s) is a fundamental
feature of Deuteronomy and therefore cannot be treated as a late redactional layer.
2. M. Weinfeld, *Deuteronomy and the Deuteronomic School* (Oxford: Oxford
University Press, 1972), pp. 233, 282-83.
3. S.R. Driver, *A Critical and Exegetical Commentary of Deuteronomy* (ICC;
Edinburgh: T. & T. Clark, 1902), pp. 181-85.
4. Mayes, *Deuteronomy*, pp. 251-52.
5. E.W. Hengstenberg, *Beiträge zur Einleitung ins AT* (Berlin, 1831-39), III,
p. 439 = *Dissertations on the Genuineness of the Pentateuch* (Edinburgh: T. & T.
Clark, 1847). Cf. Driver, *Deuteronomy*, p. 182, who refers to this view.
6. H.J. Boecker, *Law and the Administration of Justice in the Old Testament and
Ancient East* (Minneapolis: Augsburg Press, 1980), pp. 181-82.
7. A. Phillips, 'The Laws of Slavery: Exodus 21:2-11', *JSOT* 30 (1984), p. 56.
8. B.S. Jackson, 'Some Literary Features of the Mishpatim', in *Wünschet*

some of the differences between the manumission laws in Exodus and Deuteronomy can be successfully harmonized.

Similarly, the study of the manumission law in Lev. 25.39-54 has been greatly influenced by Wellhausen's view that D is earlier than P—viz., the manumission law in Lev. 25.39-54 replaced or abolished the previous legislation in Exod. 21.2-6, 7-11 and Deut. 15.12-18, since the former law stipulates a fiftieth-year release while the latter laws stipulate a seventh-year release, and it appears to grant a higher status to the Israelite debt-slave not envisaged in the laws in Exodus or Deuteronomy (cf. Lev. 25.39-40). However, the manumission law in Lev. 25 belongs to the complex of laws called the 'Holiness Code' (H: chs. 17–26)[1] which, like the *Urdeuteronomium*, most likely contains many laws dating to an early period of Israel's legal history. It is therefore possible that the manumission law in Lev. 25.39-54 could be dated to an earlier period. However, according to the standard critical view, the source P, which contains the narrative elements in Leviticus (chs. 8–10; 16) and is usually given a date near the exilic period, has edited and altered many aspects of H, although there is much disagreement about what material belongs to H and what to the reworking of P. Although H contains many early laws, the majority of critical scholars nonetheless date the final composition of H either to the exilic period (later than D; e.g., Eissfeldt[2] and Fohrer[3]), based on the literary affinities between H and the prophet Ezekiel (contemporaneous with P), or earlier (before D; e.g., Elliot-Binns).[4] However, the views that P is late, and that one can successfully separate the older regulations belonging to H from P's

1. Cf. A. Klostermann, *Der Pentateuch*, I (Leipzig: Deichert, 1893), pp. 368-418, esp. 378, who was the first to coin the name 'Holiness Code'. He noted that these chapters contained several motivation clauses and parenetic statements calling for the people of Israel to be holy; e.g. 'you are to be holy, for I, Yahweh, your God, am holy' (cf. 19.2; 20.7, 8, 26; 21.6, 8, 15, 23; 22.9, 16, 32).

2. O. Eissfeldt, *The Old Testament: An Introduction* (Oxford: Basil Blackwell, 1966), pp. 233-39.

3. G. Fohrer, *Die Hauptprobleme des Buches Ezekiel* (BZAW, 72; Berlin: de Gruyter, 1952), pp. 144-48.

4. L.E. Elliot-Binns, 'Some Problems of Holiness Code', *ZAW* 67 (1955), pp. 26-40.

additions and amplifications, have not gone unchallenged.

For example, regarding the date of P, Kaufmann[1] has advanced important arguments in support of the pre-exilic dating of the Priestly Source by noting how P's conception of holiness and the ritual regulations are of great antiquity in the ancient Near East. Furthermore, Weinfeld[2] has noted that both the books of Deuteronomy and Joshua quote Leviticus, but not *vice versa*, which suggests that P was written before Deuteronomy. Lastly, Hurvitz[3] has demonstrated that the apparent similarities of P and Ezekiel are superficial and even misleading in demonstrating their origin in the same period. For example, he has demonstrated that the two sources are *linguistically* distinct and that *literarily*, only P can be said to employ expressions and idioms belonging exclusively to classical Hebrew (Ezekiel contains late Hebrew elements).[4] He therefore concludes that Eissfeldt's argument that H must 'no doubt' be assigned to the exilic period is highly questionable.[5]

Regarding the dating of the regulations in H, I noted above that although scholars generally date the final composition of H to the exilic period, many of its laws date to an earlier period. This is particularly true for the Sabbatical and Jubilee year regulations in Leviticus 25, which scholars have subjected to both literary and stylistic analyses in order to assist them in determining the date of these different regulations. Nevertheless, the task of separating the older regulations belonging to H from the later additions and amplifications of P has proved to be very troublesome. As we saw

---

1. Y. Kaufmann, *The Religion of Israel* (London: Allen & Unwin, 1961), p. 178; cf. also E.A. Speiser, 'Leviticus and the Critics', in *Oriental and Biblical Studies* (Philapdelphia: University of Pennsylvania Press, 1967), pp. 123-42; M. Douglas, *Implicit Meanings* (London: Routledge & Kegan Paul, 1975), pp. 315-17; G.J. Wenham, *The Book of Leviticus* (NICOT; Grand Rapids: Eerdmans, 1979), pp. 11-13.

2. Weinfeld, *Deuteronomy*, pp. 179-85; cf. also *Getting at the Roots of Wellhausen's Understanding of the Law of Israel on the 100th Anniversary of the Prolegomenon* (Jerusalem: Institute for Advanced Hebrew Studies, 1979).

3. A. Hurvitz, *A Linguistic Study of the Relationship Between the Priestly Source and the Book of Ezekiel: A New Approach to an Old Problem* (CahRB, 20; Paris: Gabalda, 1982), pp. 143-55; cf. also his earlier work, 'The Evidence of Language in Dating the Priestly Code', *RB* 81 (1974), pp. 24-57.

4. Hurvitz, *Priestly Source and the Book of Ezekiel*, p. 154.

5. Hurvitz, *Priestly Source and the Book of Ezekiel*, p. 144.

above, a similar limitation has complicated the task of recognizing the later redactions of the deuteronomist within the regulations of the *Urdeuteronomium*. Scholars, therefore, have generally determined the date of individual regulations on the basis of whether a regulation can be traced to an early practice (and is thus practical) or is idealistic (and thus impractical) and therefore late.[1] This situation has led, therefore, to the widespread disagreement among scholars over the dating and the interpretation of the Sabbatical and especially the Jubilee year regulations.[2]

For example, Wellhausen[3] argued that the cultic regulations concerning the Sabbatical and Jubilee years in Leviticus 25 were idealistic and late (i.e., post-exilic) compared to the so-called non-cultic fallow law of Exod. 23.10-11, which dates to an early period in Israel's history. This view is still held by many scholars, including Snaith,[4] Westbrook,[5] Porter,[6] Lemche[7] and Gnuse.[8] However, Driver[9] already noted long ago that the redistribution of land in Lev. 25.8-16 was also practised among the other ancient nations, which led him to conclude that these regulations were not idealistic and that they were probably early (and thus belonged to H). However, he argued that the slave law found in

1. Cf. R. North, *Sociology of the Biblical Jubilee* (AnBib, 4; Rome: Pontifical Biblical Institute, 1954), pp. 197-205.

2. Cf. W. Thiel, 'Erwägungen zum Alter des Heiligkeitsgesetzes', *ZAW* 81 (1969), p. 61, who writes: 'Besonders die Institution des Jobeljahrs, die im Alten Testament nur hier belegt ist, hat zu einem scharfen Dissens in der Forschung geführt.'

3. Wellhausen, *Prolegomena*, pp. 116-20; cf. also G. Robinson, *The Origin and Development of the Old Testament Sabbath* (Beiträge zur biblischen Exegese und Theologie, 21; New York: Peter Lang, 1988), for a recent form-critical analysis of the Sabbath and Sabbatical Year (cf. esp. pp. 218-20 for Lev 25.1-8).

4. N.H. Snaith, *Leviticus and Numbers* (CB; London: Nelson, 1967), p. 163.

5. R. Westbrook, 'Jubilee Laws', *ILR* 6 (1971), pp. 220-21.

6. J.R. Porter, *Leviticus* (CBC; Cambridge: Cambridge University Press, 1976), pp. 196-98.

7. N.P. Lemche, *Early Israel: Anthropological and Historical Studies on the Israelite Society before the Monarchy* (VTSup, 37; Leiden: Brill, 1985), pp. 260-61, 344-45.

8. R. Gnuse, 'Jubilee Legislation in Leviticus: Israel's Vision for Social Reform', *BTB* 15 (1985), p. 46.

9. S.R. Driver, *An Introduction to the Literature of the Old Testament* (repr. Gloucester: Peter Smith, 1972 [1897]), p. 57.

vv. 39-55 was to be attributed to P[1], since this law and that in Deut. 15.12-18 could hardly have been operative at the same time—viz., Lev. 25.39-55 postdated Deut. 15.12-18. However, despite the fact that Lev. 25.39 stipulates a different period of service, scholars such as Keil,[2] Elliger,[3] Allis[4] and Cole[5] argue that the seventh-year release was granted unless the Jubilee came first, in which case the debt-slave was released earlier. Furthermore, Wenham,[6] Wright[7] and Japhet,[8] all of whom date P prior to D, suggest that Lev. 25.39-54 is prior to Deut. 15.12-18, although their interpretations of these manumission laws vary greatly.

Nonetheless, Driver's uncertainty about the dating of the various regulations in Leviticus 25 is also reflected in modern specialized studies,[9] in which a consensus has still not been reached concerning the scope, source, or date of the various literary strata and legal regulations in Leviticus 25.[10] Reventlow,[11] for example, suggests that

---

1. Driver, *Introduction*, p. 57. Driver assigned the earlier land regulations to H (vv. 2b-7, 8-9a, 10a, 13-15, 17-22, 24-25, 35-40a, 43, 47, 53, 55) and the later regulations concerning the redemption of people to P (i.e. vv. 40b-42, 44-46, 48-52, 54).

2. C.F. Keil, *Commentary of the Old Testament in Ten Volumes*. I. *The Pentateuch* (repr. Grand Rapids: Eerdmans, 1981 [n.d.]), pp. 464-65.

3. K. Elliger, *Leviticus* (HKAT, 4; Tübingen: Mohr, 1966), pp. 358-60.

4. O.T. Allis, 'Leviticus', in *New Bible Commentary Revised* (ed. D. Guthrie, J.A. Motyer, A.M. Stibbs and D.J. Wiseman; Leicester: Inter-Varsity Press, 1970), p. 165.

5. R.A. Cole, *Exodus: An Introduction and Commentary* (TOTC; Downers Grove: Inter-Varsity Press, 1973), p. 165.

6. Wenham, *Leviticus*, p. 12.

7. Wright, 'What Happened Every Seven Years, I,' p. 133 and n. 9.

8. S. Japhet, 'The Relationship Between the Legal Corpora in the Pentateuch in Light of Manumission Laws', in *Studies in Bible 1986* (ed. S. Japhet; Scripta Hierosolymitana, 31; Jerusalem: Magnes Press, 1986), pp. 63-89.

9. For a survey of the literature from 1970–1984, see H. Schmid, *Die Gestalt des Mose: Probleme alttestamentlicher Forschung unter Berücksichtigung der Pentateuchkrise* (EF, 237; Darmstadt: Wissenschaftliche Buchgesellschaft, 1986), pp. 27-28.

10. This observation is also made by Japhet, 'The Relationship Between the Legal Corpora', p. 75 and n. 33.

11. H.G. Reventlow, *Das Heiligkeitsgesetz formgeschichtlich untersuch* (WMANT, 6; Neukirchen–Vluyn: Neukirchener Verlag, 1961), pp. 125-50, esp.

Leviticus 25 contains three originally independent units. The first unit, which includes vv. 1-24, contains two older traditions concerning the Sabbatical and the Jubilee year which date to the Settlement Period.[1] The last section, which includes vv. 25-55, is composed of the so-called מוך rules (cf. vv. 25, 35, 39, 47 כי־ימוך אחיך), which were social regulations to aid the impoverished sections of the Israelite population. According to Reventlow, these regulations were combined with the other Jubilee regulations at a later stage, including parenetic commentaries that were added by a 'Prediger'. Similarly, Cholewiński[2] who is followed by Cardellini[3] and Kaufman,[4] proposes that Leviticus 25 should be arranged according to 'drei Inclusionen', that belong to the earliest Hg-redaction (i.e., vv. 2ab-19.23-28.39-55), the last of which postdates the slave law in Deut. 15.12-18.[5] Lastly, Feucht,[6] who attempts to isolate the so-called original short casuistic formulations in Leviticus 25 that were then expanded and amplified by later redactors, suggests that the slave stipulations in vv. 39, 47-49 belong to an original core/nucleus of regulations that played a meaningful role in ancient Israel (cf. Jer. 32.6-7; Ruth 4.1; 1 Kgs 21) and were then introduced into the Jubilee legislation by the source H[2].

However, despite the effort of these scholars and others to isolate the 'original' sources and regulations from the latter additions within

---

125, 133ff.; cf. also the discussion in N.P. Lemche, 'The Manumission of Slaves–The Fallow Year–The Sabbatical Year–The Jobel Year', *VT* 26 (1976), pp. 47, 49-50; Thiel, 'Heiligkeitsgesetzes', p. 61.

1. Cf. A. Jirku, 'Das israelitische Jobeljahr', *Reinhold-Seeberg-Festschrift II* (Leipzig, 1929), pp. 169-79; E. Neufeld, 'Socio-Economic Background of *Yōbēl and Šemiṭṭā*', *RSO* 33 (1958), p. 65.

2. S.I. Cholewincski, *Heiligkeitsgesetz und Deuteronomium: Eine vergleichende Studie* (AnBib, 66; Rome: Biblical Institute Press, 1976), pp. 100-14, esp. 113-14.

3. Cardellini, *Die biblischen 'Sklaven'-Gesetze*, pp. 281-305, esp. 281.

4. S.A. Kaufman, 'Deuteronomy 15 and Recent Research on the Dating of P', in *Das Deuteronomium: Entstehung, Gestalt und Botschaft.* [*Deuteronomy: Origin Form and Message*] (ed. N. Lohfink; BETL, 68; Leuven: Leuven University Press, 1985), pp. 273-76; 'Social Welfare Systems of Ancient Israel,' pp. 283-84.

5. Cf. also Elliger, *Leviticus*, pp. 338-39, 347, who assigns this redaction to the earliest editor Ph1.

6. C. Feucht, *Untersuchungen zum Heiligkeitgesetz* (ThA, 20; Berlin, 1964), pp. 49-51, 72-75; cf. also W. Kornfeld, *Studien zum Heiligkeitsgesetz (Lev 17-26)* (Wien: Herder, 1952), pp. 33-68, 135-38; H. Schmökel, '"Biblische Du sollst"-Gebote und ihr historischer Ort', *ZSSR* 36 (1950), pp. 365-90; Jirku, 'Das israelitische Jobeljahr', pp. 169-79.

Leviticus 25 by means of linguistic and stylistic analyses, there are others who suggest that the original sources and regulations are not likely to be separated successfully. For example, Thiel[1] suggests that the relationship between the texts concerning the Sabbatical and Jubilee year regulations are so complex that one cannot merely peel off (*herausschälen*) the older forms. Furthermore, Whybray[2] suggests that the criteria by which documents have been identified, such as language and style (e.g., choice of words, stylistic characteristics) are not useful in distinguishing separate documents. For example, he points out that the source P, like the other supposed 'documents', has no distinctive style of its own.[3] Lastly, attempts to isolate the so-called original (casuistic) regulations from their present contexts, which contain much legal parenesis, also face difficulties in view of the parallel stylistic devices found in Ammiṣaduqa's Edict (A-s) and elsewhere.[4]

The Problem

As the above brief delineation of the various views of the manumission law in Exod. 21.2-6 shows, the central problem regarding the interpretation of this law is whether the biblical (ם)עברי should be compared to the cuneiform *ḫabiru*. It is this identification that has helped to strengthen the view that the manumission law in Deut. 15.12-18 has abolished many of the practices envisaged in the manumission laws in Exod. 21.2-6, 7-11. Furthermore, the above delineation of the various views of the manumission laws in Deut.

1. Thiel, 'Heiligkeitsgesetzes', pp. 60-61.
2. R.N. Whybray, *The Making of the Pentateuch: A Methodological Study* (JSOTSup, 53; Sheffield: JSOT Press, 1987), pp. 35-131, esp. 35-36, 55-61.
3. Whybray, *Making of the Pentateuch*, pp. 59-61.
4. Cf. R. Hentschke, 'Erwägungen zur israelitischen Rechtgeschichte', *ThViat* 10 (1965/66), pp. 108-33; cf. also G. Liedke, *Gestalt und Bezeichnung alttestamentlicher Rechtssätze: Eine formgeschichtlich-terminologische Studie* (WMANT, 39; Neukirchen–Vluyn: Neukirchener Verlag, 1971), pp. 126-27; N.P. Lemche, 'The "Hebrew Slave": Comments on the Slave Law Ex. xxi 2-11', *VT* 25 (1975), pp. 130-31 and ns. 3, 8; Wenham, *Leviticus*, pp. 6-7; and S. Gevirtz, 'West Semitic Curses and the Problem of the Origins of Hebrew Law', *VT* 11 (1961), pp. 137-58, who notes that changes from second to third person speech is common in northwest Semitic curses. Furthermore, he suggests that casuistic law was strictly obeyed, while apodictic law was used for laws that were hard to enforce (p. 157).

15.12-18 and Lev. 25.39-54 shows that the central problem regarding the interpretation of these laws is whether it is possible to distinguish between the older *Urdeuteronomium* and H regulations, and the so-called additions and amplifications of D and P respectively. For example, does the absence from Deut. 15.12-18 of an explicit reference to the sacral rite, which seems to be stipulated in Exod. 21.5-6, argue in favour of the view that this rite was abolished by the deuteronomist? Furthermore, does the fact that Lev. 25.39-54 stipulates a fiftieth-year release, while Deut. 15.12-18 stipulates a seventh-year release, demonstrate that the former law abrogated the previous law or *vice versa*?

It is my contention that the comparative analysis of biblical and cuneiform texts, and the delimitation of older regulations from their respective literary framework, are beset by two interrelated problems. On the one hand, both analyses suffer from not being prefaced by an adequate discussion of the social and legal background to debt-slavery (and other relevant social and legal institutions), since biblical scholars have often misunderstood the ancient Near Eastern background to this important social phenomenon. While the legal background to various aspects of debt-slavery has been treated by scholars such as Mendelsohn[1] and Cardellini,[2] these studies generally suffer from being too general in their approach, since they deal mostly with the institution of chattel-slavery. On the other hand, there is a tendency among scholars to base their interpretation of the biblical manumission laws in accordance with the view that they arose in certain historical circumstances—viz., the biblical manumission laws are felt to have a *Sitz im Leben* in the events surrounding the composition of the various sources in which they are found. This interpretational problem has also been observed by Muilenberg,[3] Knight,[4] and McConville,[5] all of whom note the danger of too readily assigning

---

1. I. Mendelsohn, *Slavery in the Ancient Near East: A Comparative Study of Slavery in Babylonia, Assyria, Syria, and Palestine from the Middle of the Third Millennium to the End of the First Millennium* (New York: Oxford University Press, 1949).

2. Cardellini, *Die biblischen 'Sklaven'-Gesetze.*

3. J. Muilenburg, 'Form Criticism and Beyond', *JBL* 88 (1969), p. 11.

4. D.A. Knight, 'The Understanding of "Sitz im Leben" in Form Criticism', *SBL Seminar Papers 1974*, I (Cambridge, MA: SBL Press, 1974), pp. 107-13.

5. J.G. McConville, *Law and Theology in Deuteronomy* (JSOTSup, 33; Sheffield: JSOT Press, 1984), p. 7.

texts to a particular *Sitz im Leben*. Furthermore, attempts to determine the *Sitz im Leben* of the biblical manumission laws, and the Sabbatical and Jubilee regulations, have also suffered from a general misunderstanding of the ancient Near Eastern social and legal background to these regulations and related practices.

Method and Procedure

What I have said above does not imply that I have no interest in the historical background to the biblical manumission laws. On the contrary, my discussion of the biblical manumission laws begins with a comprehensive comparative investigation of the social background to debt-slavery in Mesopotamia in order that we may gain a better understanding of the ancient Near Eastern institution of debt-slavery (or slavery in general) and the alienation of land, both of which were caused by varying degrees of insolvency (Chapter 2). This discussion will provide the necessary background to the comparative investigation of the legal background to debt-slavery in Mesopotamia (Chapter 3). In this chapter I will limit the discussion to those laws, contracts and edicts that have a particular bearing on the interpretation of the biblical manumission laws and the Sabbatical and Jubilee year regulations that are closely connected with these biblical laws. I am aware, however, that a comparative investigation of this sort poses many methodological problems, although it is my contention that such a comparative investigation is the only way in which to attempt to clarify the meaning and *Sitz im Leben* of the biblical manumission laws.[1] Therefore, in Chapters 2 and 3 I will attempt to bring out just the consensus view of Assyriologists and other scholars who specialize in the various areas of ancient Near Eastern studies. I do not claim to add anything new to the study of these very difficult pursuits, although where there are significant differences of opinion I have followed those opinions that I have deemed to be the most convincing. Following this comparative study, I will investigate the social background to debt-slavery in Israel (Chapter 4) in order to provide a suitable historical background to the institution of debt-slavery in Israel.

These three chapters, therefore, provide the necessary social and legal background upon which I will base the investigation of the biblical manumission laws in Chapters 5–8. In Chapter 5 I will

---

1. Cf. Boecker, *Law and the Administration of Justice*, pp. 14-19.

investigate the various slave laws that appear within the Pentateuchal legal collections in order to delimit the chattel-slave laws from the debt-slave laws. I will look, in particular, at the slave law in Exod. 21.20-21, which remains a *crux interpretum* to the discussion of the various slave laws that appear in the Covenant Code, including of course the manumission laws in 21.2-6, 7-11. I will then move on to investigate the manumission laws that are found in Exod. 21.2-6, 7-11 (Chapter 6), Deut. 15.12-18 (Chapter 7) and Lev. 25.39-54 (Chapter 8). In these chapters I will approach the different manumission laws in a more or less consistent way. Chapter 6 will begin with an investigation of the setting, form and structure of the manumission laws in Exod. 21.2-6, 7-11. I will follow with an exegesis of these laws, paying particular attention to those problematic areas pointed out briefly above. Similarly, Chapter 7 will begin with an investigation of the setting and form of the manumission law in Deut. 15.12-18, although rather than looking at the structure of this law I will investigate the שמחה 'release' in Deut. 15.1-11 which is closely connected to the manumission law. I will follow with an exegesis of this law, again paying close attention to those problematic areas pointed out above. Chapter 8, however, will begin with an investigation of the Fallow and Jubilee years, both of which are closely connected to the manumission law in Lev. 25.39-54. I will follow this with an investigation of the structure of the Jubilee regulations, and lastly by an exegesis of the manumission law in Lev. 25.39-54, paying particular attention to its relationship to the manumission laws in Exodus and Deuteronomy.

It is my hope, therefore, that this sort of investigation into the biblical manumission laws will contribute, in a small way, to the clarification of the meaning and *Sitz im Leben* of these laws. Although it is not my main intention to determine the exact date of the biblical manumission laws, since such a task lies outside the scope of this book, I hope nevertheless that this investigation will lead to a clarification of the relationship of these laws to each other, as well as providing a historical and interpretational framework from which to date these laws, especially in relation to the literary sources in which they appear.

Chapter 2

THE SOCIAL BACKGROUND TO DEBT-SLAVERY IN MESOPOTAMIA

From a sociological perspective, scholars generally agree that debt-slaves can be categorized as *temporary slaves*—those who probably retained a right to redemption—while foreign chattel-slaves can be categorized as *permanent slaves*—those who had no individual right of redemption.[1] However, Gelb[2] has noted that such a categorization, which is based on the criterion of freedom, does not identify clearly the types or classes of people who could belong to these two groups of slaves. Furthermore, such a categorization does not take into account the various socio-economic factors that might have encouraged the rise of debt-slavery in Mesopotamia. For example, Gelb[3] writes:

> . . . it is impossible to analyze and understand individual aspects of society without placing them within the total framework of that society. Such terms, as for instance 'unfree' or 'slave' are meaningless by themselves. They become meaningful only when contrasted with other terms involved in social stratification,[4] such as 'semi-free' and 'free'.

1. For example, see R. Thurnwald, 'Sklave', in *Reallexikon der Vorgeschichte, XII* (ed. M. Ebert; Berlin, 1928), pp. 210-12, who differentiates between the full chattel 'Sklaverei' and the household 'Knechtschaft'; and B.J. Siegel, 'Some Methodological Considerations for a Comparative Study of Slavery', NS *AA* 49 (1976), pp. 388-89.

2. I.J. Gelb, 'Definition and Discussion of Slavery and Serfdom', *UF* 11 (1980), p. 284; cf. also, Quantitative Evaluation of Slavery and Serfdom', in *Kramer Anniversary Volume* (AOT, 25; Neukirchen–Vluyn: Neukirchener Verlag, 1976), p.195-207.

3. I.J. Gelb, 'Approaches to the Study of Ancient Society', *JAOS* 87 (1967), p. 4.

4. For a review of the Marxist, quasi-Marxist and non-Marxist approaches to the study of social stratification, see F. Cancian, 'Social Stratification', *ARA* 5 (1976), pp. 227-48.

Therefore, in order that we may gain a better understanding of the institution of slavery (both debt- and chattel-slavery) and the alienation of land, both of which were caused by varying degrees of insolvency, I will examine the social and economic structures under which both conditions were able to develop and increase, structures which have been illuminated by the important work of historians, archaeologists, anthropologists, sociologists and ethnographers.[1]

The Formation of the City-States of Mesopotamia[2]

Urbanism in lowland Mesopotamia developed in the fifth–third millennium BCE, beginning with the formation of temple-towns in the lowlands (ca. 5300–2900 BCE).[3] It culminated in the formation of the

---

1. Cf. G.A. Herion, 'The Impact of Modern and Social Science Assumptions on the Reconstruction of Israelite History', *JSOT* 34 (1986), pp. 3-33; J.W. Rogerson, *Anthropology and the Old Testament* (GPIT; Oxford: Basil Blackwell, 1978), pp. 17-18; and F.S. Frick, *The Formation of the State in Ancient Israel* (SWBAS, 4; Sheffield: Almond Press, 1985), pp. 17-25, who note that the study of ancient Near Eastern life using the methods of cultural anthropologists and ethnographers is essential if we are to understand properly the history of Israel.

2. In this discussion I am concerned primarily with the course of development of the city and national states of Mesopotamia. While anthropologists and biblical scholars continue to be interested in the causes or origins of the formation of the state, it is beyond the scope of my present discussion to elaborate on this aspect of state formation. For surveys of the current views of state origin, see R. Cohen, 'State Origins: A Reappraisal', in *The Early State* (ed. H.J.M. Claessen and P. Skalnik; The Hague: Mouton, 1978), pp. 31-75; *idem*, 'Introduction', in *Origins of the State: The Anthropology of Political Evolution* (ed. R. Cohen and E.R. Service; Philadelphia: Institute for the Study of Human Issues, 1978), pp. 1-20; E.R. Service, 'Classical and Modern Theories of the Origins of Government', in Cohen and Service (eds.), *Origins of the State*, pp. 21-34; H.T. Wright, 'Recent Research on the Origin of the State', *ARA* 6 (1977), pp. 379-97; *idem*, 'Toward an Explanation of the Origin of the State', in Cohen and Service (eds.), *Origins of the State*, pp. 49-68; cf. also Frick, *The Formation of the State in Ancient Israel*, pp. 29-44; *idem*, 'Social Science Methods and Theories of Significance for the Study of the Israelite Monarchy: A Critical Review Essay', *Semeia* 37 (1986), pp. 17-26; R.B. Coote and K.W. Whitelam, 'The Emergence of Israel: Social Transformation and State Formation Following the Decline in Late Bronze Age Trade', *Semeia* 37 (1986), pp. 128-31; *idem, The Emergence of Early Israel in Historical Perspective* (SWBAS, 5; Sheffield: Almond Press, 1987), pp. 143-51.

3. For a discussion of the temple cities that existed during this period, see

city-states of Sumer which developed in the river-valleys and main water canals of Middle and Northern Mesopotamia in the third millennium BCE (ca. 2700 BCE).[1] During the second half of the third millennium the city-states of Agade (i.e. the Akkadian empire: ca. 2340–2200 BCE) and Ur (i.e. the Ur III dynasty: ca. 2111–2003 BCE) contributed significant cultural and political achievements.[2]

The social organization of most of the tribal and non-urban populations that lived within the Mesopotamian and other ancient Near Eastern city-states was based on the concept of real or fictitious kinship, which anthropologists usually call *lineage systems*. Scholars generally distinguish three stages of kinship: (1) minimal lineage (i.e. nuclear family); (2) lineage proper (e.g. clan); (3) maximal lineage (e.g. tribe).[3] In pre-state societies, the tribe was responsible for the

A. Falkenstein, *The Sumerian Temple City* (MANE, 1.1; Los Angeles: Undena Publications, 1974); cp. B. Foster, 'A New Look at the Sumerian Temple State', *JESHO* 24 (1981), pp. 225-41.

1. C.L. Redman (*The Rise of Civilization: From Early Farmers to Urban Society in the Ancient Near East* [San Francisco: W.H. Freeman, 1978], p. 221) notes, however, that this path of development varied in different parts of the ancient Near East. He writes: 'For example, in the upland regions of the northern Near East, large urban centers did not develop early but towns and townships did. In Egypt, the developments did not lead to cities as large population centers, but rather to moderate population centers, each with far-reaching administrative and religious responsibilities. The rate of development in Egypt was more rapid than in Mesopotamia . . . [it] went almost directly from temple-towns to a unified national state.' See also the more recent discussion of the rise of civilization in Mesopotamia in H.J. Nissen, *The Early History of the Ancient Near East* (Chicago: University of Chicago Press, 1988).

2. For discussions concerning the formation of the city and national states of Mesopotamia, see Redman, *The Rise of Civilization*, pp. 214-309, esp. 221, 286-308; Nissen, *The Early History of the Ancient Near East*; H.W.F. Saggs, *The Might That Was Assyria* (Sidgwick & Jackson Great Civilizations Series; London: Sidgwick & Jackson, 1984), pp. 2-45; cf. also Falkenstein, *The Sumerian Temple City*, pp. 10-21, who discusses the development of the temple cities into the early dynastic city-states.

3. Cf. M. Forte and E.E. Evans-Pritchard, 'Introduction', in *African Political Systems* (ed. M. Forte and E.E. Evans-Pritchard; London: Oxford University Press, 1940), pp. 1-23; M. Forte, 'The Structure of Unilineal Descent Groups' *AA* 55 (1953), pp. 17-41; *idem, Kinship and Social Order* (Chicago: Aldine, 1969); M.H. Fried, 'The Classification of Corporate Unilineal Descent Groups', *JRAI* 87 (1957), pp. 1-29; M.G. Smith, 'On Segmentary Lineage Systems', *JRAI* 86

protection of the social and territorial rights of its local inhabitants. Furthermore, as Diakonoff[1] points out, the Sumerian tribes (or territorial communes) had their own collective bodies of self-government (i.e. council of elders and general assembly of free male adults). This self-government or 'primitive democracy', which is discussed at length by Jacobsen,[2] was most likely an important feature

(1956), pp. 39-80; J. Middleton and D. Tait, 'Introduction', in *Tribes without Rulers* (ed. J. Middleton and D. Tait; London: Routledge & Kegan Paul, 1958), pp. 1-31; J. Beatie, *Other Cultures: Aims, Methods and Achievements in Social Anthropology* (London: Paul & Kegan, 1964); R. Patai, 'The Structure of Endogamous Unilineal Descent Groups', *SJA* 21 (1965), pp. 325-50; A. Bernard and A. Good, *Research Practices in the Study of Kinship* (ASAR, 2; London: Academic Press, 1984); cf. also the discussions of Lemche, *Early Israel*, pp. 209-44; R.R. Wilson, *Genealogy and History in the Biblical World* (New Haven: Yale University Press, 1977), pp. 18-37; *idem, Sociological Approaches to the Old Testament* (GBS; Philadelphia: Fortress Press, 1984), pp. 40-46; B.F. Batto, 'Land Tenure and Women at Mari', *JESHO* 23 (1980), p. 210; M. Liverani, 'Communautés de village et palais royal dans la Syrie du IIème Millénaire', *JESHO* 18 (1975), pp. 156-59; I.M. Diakonoff, 'The Rural Community in the Ancient Near East', *JESHO* 18 (1975), p. 125; G. Buccellati, *Cities and Nations of Ancient Syria: An Essay on Political Institutions with Special Reference to the Israelite Kingdoms* (SS, 26: Rome: University of Rome, 1967), pp. 12-15, 83-92.

1. I.M. Diakonoff, 'Socio-Economic Classes in Babylonia and the Babylonian Concept of Social Stratification', *AbhBAW* 75 (1972), pp. 44-45; *idem*, 'The Rise of the Despotic State in Ancient Mesopotamia', in *Ancient Mesopotamia Socio-Economic History: A Collection of Studies by Soviet Scholars* (ed. I.M. Diakonoff; USSR Academy of Sciences Institute of the Peoples of Asia; Moscow: 'Nauka', 1969), pp. 179-84; *idem*, 'Slaves, Helots and Serfs in Early Antiquity', in *Wirtschaft und Gesellschaft im alten Vorderasien* (ed. J. Harmatta and G. Komoróczy; Budapest: Akadémiai Kiadó, 1976), pp. 47-50; cf. also L. Epsztein, *Social Justice in the Ancient Near East and the People of the Bible* (London: SCM Press, 1986), p. 3.

2. T. Jacobsen, 'Primitive Democracy in Ancient Mesopotamia', *JNES* 2 (1946), pp. 159-72; *idem*, 'Early Political Development in Mesopotamian Assemblies', *ZA* 52 (1957), pp. 91-104; *idem*, 'Note sur le rôle de l'opinion publique dans l'ancienne Mésopotamie', *RA* 58 (1964), pp. 157-58. Cf. also G. Evans, 'Ancient Mesopotamian Assemblies', *JAOS* 78 (1958), pp. 1-11; S.N. Kramer, '"Vox Populi" and the Sumerian Literary Documents', *RA* 58 (1964), pp. 148-56; J. Milgrom, 'The Priestly Terminology and the Political and Social Structure of Pre-Monarchic Israel', in *Studies in Cultic Theology and Terminology* (SJLA, 36; Leiden: Brill, 1983), pp. 1f.; D.J. Wiseman, 'Law and Order in Old Testament Times', *Vox Evangelica* 8 (1976), pp. 13-14; P. Artzi, '"Vox populi" in the El

of the early Sumerian city-states (ca. 2700 BCE). For example, during the Early-Royal period of the Sumerian city-states the king often consulted the council of elders who, in turn, consulted the popular assembly of free male adults whenever the king undertook wars or made other important decisions, although he could ignore their advice. This sort of *vox populi* or classical democracy had an important influence upon the decisions of the king, which is clearly expressed in the early Sumerian legal collections, although as the central bureaucracy grew in scope 'public opinion'[1] became effective only in local issues.[2] Nevertheless, while the tribal government lost much of its political influence in state societies, tribal representatives continued to operate as local administrators during most periods.[3]

However, while city- and national states, that were composed of the state (temple and palace households) and private sectors,[4] held many

Amarna Tablets', *RA* 58 (1964), pp. 159-66. It should be pointed out, though, that much of the evidence used to substantiate the existence of 'primitive democracy', particulary in Jacobsen's work, is confined to literary sources.

1. For a discussion of the importance of 'public opinion' among the elders and public in reference to the decisions of the king, see J.J. Finkelstein, 'Early Mesopotamia, 2500–1000 BC', in *Propaganda and Communication in World History. I. The Symbolic Instrument in Early Times* (ed. H.D. Lasswell, D. Lerner and H. Speier; Honolulu: The University Press of Hawaii, 1979), pp. 54-58; L. Epsztein, *Social Justice*, pp. 3-6, 13-16.

2. For a discussion of the process by which kinship groups lost their political influence, see H.J. Claessen and P. Skalník, 'The Early State: Theories and Hypotheses', in *The Early State* (ed. H.J. Claessen and P. Skalník; The Hague: Mouton, 1978), pp. 22-24; and Frick, 'Theories of Significance for the Study of the Israelite Monarchy', pp. 20-21, who discusses the views of Claessen and Skalník.

3. For discussions about the role of local governmental adminstrators (and councils) who were often affiliated with local tribes, see M. Stol, *Studies in Old Babylonian History* (UNHAII, 40; Leiden: Instituut voor het Nabije Oosten Noordeindsplein, 1976), pp. 73-93; *idem*, 'A Cadastral Innovation by Hammurabi', in *ZIKIR ŠUMIM: Assyriological Studies Presented to F.R. Kraus on the Occasion of his Seventieth Birthday* (ed. G. van Driel, Th.J.H. Krispijn, M. Stol and K.R. Veenhof; NIVNO, V; Leiden: Brill, 1982), pp. 351-58; cf. also Diakonoff, 'The Rise of the Despotic State', pp. 183-84; and M.A. Dandamayev, 'The Neo-Babylonian Elders', in *Societies and Languages of the Ancient Near East in Honour of I.M. Diakonoff* (ed. M.A. Dandamayev, I. Gerschevitch, H. Klengel, G. Komoróczy, M.T. Larsen and J.N. Postgate; Warminster: Aris & Phillips, 1982), pp. 38-41.

4. Cf. I.J. Gelb, 'Alleged Temple and State Economies in Ancient Mesopotamia',

advantages over other smaller independent groups, one of the negative results of the process of centralization that took place among city- and national states was an increase in social stratification, characterized by an increase in debt-slavery and the alienation of land among free citizens. While there is some debate whether citizens in the private sector owned their own land, most scholars acknowledge that private ownership of land is attested in most periods,[1] particularly in Mari and Ugarit where land transfer was accomplished by real or fictitious inheritance,[2] although a small percentage of citizens owned some

in *Studi in Onore di Eduardo Volterra*, VI (Milan, 1969), pp. 137-54.

1. Cf. I.J. Gelb, 'Alleged Temple and State Economies in Ancient Mesopotamia', pp. 137-54; Saggs, *The Might That Was Assyria*, pp. 131-34; Finkelstein, 'Early Mesopotamia', pp. 52-53; W.F. Leemans, 'The Rôle of Landlease in Mesopotamia in the Early Second Millennium BC', *JESHO* 18 (1975), pp. 135-37; Liverani, 'Communautés de village et palais royal', pp. 145-47, 56; J.N. Postgate, 'ILKU and Land Tenure in the Middle Assyrian Kingdom–A Second Attempt', in Dandamayev *et al.* (eds.), *Societies and Languages*, pp. 309-12; A.L. Oppenheim, *Ancient Mesopotamia: A Portrait of a Dead Civilization* (Chicago: University of Chicago Press, rev. edn, 1977), pp. 95-109; *idem*, 'A Bird's Eye View of Mesopotamian Economic History', in *Trade and Market in the Early Empires* (ed. K. Polanyi; Glencoe, 1957), pp. 27-37; F.I. Andersen, 'The Early Sumerian City-State in Recent Soviet Historiography', *AbrN* 1 (1960), pp. 56, 61; Diakonoff, 'Socio-Economic Classes in Babylonia', pp. 43-44; *idem*, 'The Rise of the Despotic State', p. 180; *idem*, 'On the Structure of the Old Babylonian Society', in *Beiträge zur sozialen Struktur des Alten Vorderasien* (ed. H. Klengel; SGKAO, 1; Berlin: Akademie-Verlag, 1971), pp. 15-31; *idem*, 'Slaves, Helots and Serfs in Early Antiquity', pp. 46-52; W.F. Albright, *From the Stone Age to Christianity* (Garden City, NY: Doubleday, 2nd edn, 1957), pp. 189-90; M. Silver, *Economic Structures of the Ancient Near East* (London: Croom Helm, 1985), pp. 57-60. Cp. J. Renger, 'Interaction of Temple, Palace, and "Private Enterprise"', in *State and Temple Economy in the Ancient Near East, I, II: Proceedings of the International Conference Organized by the Katholieke Iniversiteit Leuven from the 10th to the 14th of April 1978* (ed. E. Lipiński; OLA, 5; Leuven: Dept. Oriëntalistiek, 1979), pp. 250-51, who suggests that in the OB period there is little evidence of private ownership of land in southern Mesopotamia. However, Diakonoff, 'Slaves, Helots and Serfs in Early Antiquity', pp. 48-51 disagrees with Renger and presents evidence from LH and other sources to demonstrate that private ownership of land did exist in southern Mesopotamia.

2. Cf. A. Malamat, 'Mari and the Bible: Some Patterns of Tribal Organization and Institutions', *JAOS* 82 (1962), pp. 147-50; *idem*, 'Pre-Monarchical Social Institutions in Israel in the Light of Mari', in *Congress Volume, Jerusalem 1986* (ed. J.A. Emerton; VTSup, 40; Leiden: Brill, 1988), pp. 172-76; Buccellati, *Cities and*

other means of production (e.g. weaving, carpentry, metallurgy, etc.). In the following sections I will discuss the composition of these state and private households and those factors that contributed to the increase of debt-slavery and the alienation of land among free citizens.

Composition of the State and Private Sector Households

State Sector Households

The state sector maintained large land holdings, which Diakonoff[1] suggests were probably originally owned by the community. The main economic activities of the state sector included cereal agriculture, date palm cultivation, animal husbandry and other assorted 'industries'.[2] These resources were then manufactured into goods and distributed and traded by the merchants (Sum. *dam-gar*, Bab. *tamkārum*) who worked for the temple and palace. One of the important functions of the temple and palace was to create a fund from which the state could protect the community in emergencies, such as war or famine, and to fund large-scale projects that were beyond the means of the individual, such as building dikes and dredging the silted-up canals.[3] However, the size and composition of the households of the temple

Nations of Ancient Syria, pp. 90-92; K.W. Whitelam, *The Just King: Monarchical Judicial Authority in Ancient Israel* (JSOTSup, 12; Sheffield: JSOT Press, 1979), p. 174; cp. Batto, 'Land Tenure and Women at Mari', pp. 210, 225-26, who, although he acknowledges the existence of private land, suggests that the supposed meaning of patrimony at Mari was actually a royal land grant.

1. Diakonoff, 'The Rise of the Despotic State', pp. 178-79; *idem*, 'Slaves, Helots and Serfs in Early Antiquity', pp. 44-78, who notes that during the Early Dynastic Period (ca. 2800–2400 BCE) land belonging to free members of the community was either bought or taken over by the Crown. In addition, during this period the temple land was composed of community land.

2. Cf. Oppenheim, *Ancient Mesopotamia*, pp. 95-96; Renger, 'Interaction of Temple, Palace, and "Private Enterprise"', pp. 252-53; Gelb, 'Approaches to the Study of Ancient Society', p. 6.

3. Cf. Oppenheim, *Ancient Mesopotamia*, pp. 84-85; S.N. Kramer, 'Aspects of Mesopotamian Society: Evidence from the Sumerian Literary Sources', in *Beiträge zur sozialen Struktur des Alten Vorderasien* (ed. H. Klengel; SGKAO, 1; Berlin: Akademie-Verlag, 1971), pp. 6-7; Diakonoff, 'Socio-Economic Classes in Babylonia', p. 43; Finkelstein, 'Early Mesopotamia', p. 65; R. Gnuse, *You Shall Not Steal: Community and Property in the Biblical Tradition* (Maryknoll: Orbis Books, 1985), pp. 55-57.

and palace, which maintained the land and supervised the labour and administration, differed from period to period. To the composition of these households we now turn.

The temple households. The temple household was the first state sector to develop into a large agricultural concern employing a large labour force.[1] While the temple household remained an important economic force during most periods, its economic and political authority began to be taken over by the palace of the city- and national states from the third millennium onwards.[2] Based on the administrative texts from Lagash during the Ur III period (ca. 2050–1955 BCE), Gelb[3] discusses the composition of the households that maintained the temple lands and herds and those households that specialized in the production of cloth, flour, oil and so on.[4] He suggests that such a description can serve as a paradigm for other temple households in early Mesopotamian times, as well as the palace households in OB times (ca. 1830–1530 BCE).[5]

In his discussion, Gelb[6] isolates four different types of personnel found in the individual temple households[7], which were made up of

1. Cf. Redman, *The Rise of Civilization*, pp. 256-57.
2. Cf. Finkelstein, 'Early Mesopotamia', pp. 58-59; Renger, 'Interaction of Temple, Palace, and "Private Enterprise"', p. 250; Falkenstein, *The Sumerian Temple City*, p. 7; Oppenheim, *Ancient Mesopotamia*, p. 105.
3. I.J. Gelb, 'Household and Family in Early Mesopotamia', in Lipiński (ed.), *State and Temple Economy*, pp. 11-24; *idem*, 'Approaches to the Study of Ancient Society', pp. 6-7; cf. also Falkenstein, *The Sumerian Temple City*, pp. 8-9.
4. For discussions about the temple economy during the Ur III and OB period, see Falkenstein, *The Sumerian Temple City*; Renger, 'Interaction of Temple, Palace, and "Private Enterprise"', pp. 251-52; V.V. Struve, 'The Problem of the Genesis, Development and Disintegration of the Slave Societies in the Ancient Orient', in Diakonoff (ed.), *Ancient Mesopotamia*, pp. 29-34, 36-40, who discusses the temple economy during the period of Urukagina of *Lagaš* (ca. 2375 BCE); K. Butz, 'Ur in altbabylonischer Zeit als Wirtschaftsfaktor', in Lipiński (ed.), *State and Temple Economy*, pp. 257-409.
5. Gelb applies this paradigm to OB state households in his critique of Diakonoff's views as expressed in 'Socio-Economic Classes', pp. 49-50.
6. Gelb, 'Household and Family in Early Mesopotamia', p. 7, who notes that different households were linked to each other forming a larger 'household' that eventually was linked to the household of the temple or palace.
7. Cf. Diakonoff, 'The Rise of the Despotic State', p. 176, who notes that during

mainly native impoverished classes: (1) officials and supervisors; (2) craftspeople and persons with various occupations; (3) workers/ soldiers; (4) women and children without family and other 'rejects of society'.

The officials, who were called the 'elders' (Sum. *ab-ba-ab-ba*, which designates seven high offices including the priest[1]), and the supervisors, who supervised agricultural activities (Sum. *engar nubanda gud-me*), worked full-time for the household.[2] Many of these officials and supervisors were presented with temple land, from which they sustained themselves, although they also frequently received additional rations which they could use in whatever manner they liked.[3] As we saw above, one of the more important officials of the temple and palace households was the 'merchant' (Sum. *dam-gar*, Bab. *tamkārum*) who traded on their behalf.[4] Trade, which remained an important part of the temple and palace economy in most periods, was essential for the distribution of products.[5] Furthermore, Silver[6] notes

the Early Dynastic Period (ca. 2800–2400 BCE) the temple land in *Lagaš* was divided into three categories: (1) *níg-en-(n)a*-land reserved for the maintenance of the temple; (2) *gán-kur₆*-land divided into non-hereditary and interchangeable, strictly individual parcels allotted for their service to those working on *níg-en-(n)a*-land and to temple artisans and administrative personnel; (3) *gán-uru₄-lal*-land allotted against a share in the crop to different persons—mostly to members of the temple personnel as a supplement to what they got of *gán-kur₆*-land.

1. Gelb, 'Household and Family in Early Mesopotamia', pp. 15-16.

2. Officials of the Assyrian Temple were similar in many respects to those in Babylonia; cf. Saggs, *The Might That Was Assyria*, pp. 209-12.

3. For a discussion of the ration system employed in ancient Mesopotamia, see I.J. Gelb, 'The Ancient Mesopotamian Ration System', *JNES* 24 (1965), pp. 230-34.

4. For a discussion of the role of the *dam-gar* in the temple and palace during the Ur III period, see T. Fish, 'Aspects of Sumerian Civilisation in the Third Dynasty of Ur', *BJRL* 22 (1938), pp. 160-74; W.W. Hallo, 'God, King, and Man at Yale', in Lipiński (ed.), *State and Temple Economy*, pp. 103-104.

5. For discussions about the role of trade in the state sector, see N. Yoffee, *Explaining Trade in Ancient Western Asia* (MANE, 2.2; Los Angeles: Undena Publications, 1981); J. Gledhill and M.T. Larsen, 'The Polanyi Paradigm and a Dynamic Analysis of Archaic States', in *Theory and Explanation in Archaeology: The Southampton Conference* (ed. C. Renfrew, M.J. Rowlands and B.A. Seagraves; New York: Academic Press, 1982), pp. 197-226; M. Silver, *Prophets and Markets: The Political Economy of Ancient Israel* (SDE; Boston : Kluwer-Nijhoff Publishing, 1983), pp. 73-77, 259-63; *idem*, *Economic Structures of the*

that with the introduction of new agricultural products which were traded among the neighbouring nations, the consolidation of land ownership by the state increased. Silver[1] further notes that this process was already evident in Lagash as demonstrated by one tablet which appears to show a priest purchasing fields from a number of sellers. Although it was once thought that the merchants were the exclusive agents of the temple and palace, it has now been shown that as early as the Sumerian period merchants who worked as agents of the temple also engaged in private enterprises, just like certain employees of the British government who also work for the private sector (e.g. McGregor, who while he was the head of British Coal, which was a government-owned industry in the UK, also retained his position at a private bank).[2] However, during the OB period[3] and

---

Ancient Near East; Falkenstein, *The Sumerian Temple City*, p. 9; Saggs, *The Might That Was Assyria*, pp. 27-33, 170-79; W.F. Leemans, *Foreign Trade in the Old Babylonian Period* (Leiden: Brill, 1960); *idem*, 'The Importance of Trade: Some Introductory Remarks', *Iraq* 39 (1977), pp. 2-10. That trade was an important source of income for the early temple is demonstrated by the epithet of Enlil—the chief god of Nippur—which reads 'trader of the wide world'. Furthermore, his spouse was called 'merchant of the world' (cf. Falkenstein, p. 9).

6. Silver, *Prophets and Markets*, pp. 259-63; *idem, Economic Structures of the Ancient Near East*, pp. 147-57.

1. Silver, *Economic Structures of the Ancient Near East*, p. 147. This tablet dates ca. 2570 BCE, although Silver does not specify the tablet reference.

2. Cf. Gelb's response in Diakonoff, 'Socio-Economic Classes in Babylonia', p. 50; Renger, 'Interaction of Temple, Palace, and "Private Enterprise"', p. 251; cp. Diakonoff, 'Socio-Economic Classes in Babylonia', pp. 44-48, who does not distinguish between the citizens who own land in the private sector and the state 'officials' who own land. Cf. also Oppenheim, *Ancient Mesopotamia*, p. 91, who is not clear about the merchant's freedom of disposition and individual financial responsibility.

3. Cf. W.F. Leemans, *The Old-Babylonian Merchant: His Business and His Social Position* (SDOAP, 3; Leiden: Brill, 1950), pp. 11, 64-70, 113-15, for an account of the merchant Balmunamhe from OB Larsa, who is mentioned in many documents; cf. also B.L. Eichler, *Indenture at Nuzi: The Personal* tidennutu *Contract and its Mesopotamian Analogues* (YNER, 5; New Haven: Yale University Press, 1973), p. 46, for a description of merchant/lender Tehib-tilla son of Puhi-senni, who was one of the most economically influential people in Nuzi; and M.T. Larsen, 'Your Money or Your Life! A Portrait of an Assyrian Businessman', in Dandamayev *et al.* (eds.), *Societies and Languages*, pp. 214-44, who describes the nineteenth-century BC businessman called Imdi-ilum; Struve, 'The Problem of the Genesis',

later[1] it is likely that many merchants worked independently of the state.[2] Both the private and state-connected merchants and priests engaged in private commercial activities, such as trade and lending, which allowed them to accumulate both land and wealth. While merchants or money-lenders remained the most prominent acquirers of private sector land during all periods, during the NA period state officials become the most prominent acquirers of land.[3]

The craftspeople and workers/soldiers fell into two groups: the first group included those who worked full-time for the temple household and received rations throughout the year; the second group included those who had means of production of land and received rations only when they worked for the household (e.g. like the soldiers who would receive rations when they were away from home on military campaigns). Lastly, those who had no family worked full-time in a household and received rations throughout the year. After the Ur III period the temple also began to employ 'hired labour(ers)' (Sum. *hun-gá*) who worked for wages (Sum. *á*) instead of rations.[4]

As Gelb[5] and Oppenheim[6] have shown, part of the temple's labour

pp. 34-35; M.A. Dandamayev, 'Die Rolle des *tamkārum* in Babylonien im 2. und 1. Jahrtausend v.u.Z', in *Beiträge zur sozialen Struktur des Alten Vorderasien* (ed. H. Klengel; SGKAO, 1; Berlin: Akademie-Verlag, 1971), pp. 69-78.

1. Cf. M. Elat, 'The Monarchy and the Development of Trade in Ancient Israel', in Lipiński (ed.), *State and Temple Economy*, pp. 527-46.

2. Cf. Leemans, *The Old-Babylonian Merchant*, p. 113; A. Goetze, *The Laws of Eshnunna* (AASOR, 31; New Haven: American Schools of Oriental Research, 1956), pp. 56-57; Silver, *Economic Structures of the Ancient Near East*, pp. 132-36; Hallo, 'God, King, and Man at Yale', p. 103, who reports the findings of D.C. Snell, 'Ledgers and Prices: Ur III Silver Balanced Accounts' (PhD disseration, Yale University, 1975); cf. also Fish, 'Aspects of Sumerian Civilisation in the Third Dynasty of Ur', p. 166, who notes that the only evidence for the function of the *dam-gar* comes from temple records, but he suggests that there is the possibility that even during the early periods of Sumerian civilisation that the *dam-gar* may have been independent traders with no association with the temple or palace.

3. Cf. Saggs, *The Might That Was Assyria*, pp. 133-34.

4. Cf. Gelb, 'Approaches to the Study of Ancient Society', p. 7.

5. Gelb, 'Household and Family in Early Mesopotamia', p. 23; 'The Arua Institution', *RA* 66 (1972), pp. 10-13.

6. Oppenheim, *Ancient Mesopotamia*, pp. 107-108; cf. also Mendelsohn, *Slavery in the Ancient Near East*, p. 103, who notes that orphans and poor children were often dedicated to the sanctuary as slaves.

supply was originally obtained through 'charitable' acts such as supplying refuge for the outcasts of society, including the poor, the indigent, the crippled and the orphan and widow. The temple also provided ransom for citizens who were captured by the enemy (cf. also LH §32, which notes that ransom was provided by oneself (family), the temple, or palace) and loans to those who were in need. However, according to one Lagash text, the temple also used individuals (homeless or poor?) who were seized in the street and forced to render service for a temple household (Sum. *dumu-da-ba* or *dumu-dab5-ba*; literally 'seized child').[1] Therefore, while there is evidence that suggests that the temple originally engaged in 'charitable' acts, it is nevertheless likely that the temple often coerced citizens into service, especially when it was difficult to obtain workers by any other means.[2] Furthermore, it is questionable whether the temple's creditor relationship with the private sector was entirely a charitable one, since such transactions could lead to the loss of dependents or land if the loan was foreclosed, both of which were vital to the economy of the temple.[3] This is particularly true for those merchants and state officials who often engaged in private transactions in order to increase their own property and wealth.[4]

While the temple used mainly citizens in its agricultural and industrial activities,[5] the temple also used foreign captives, who during most periods were often presented to the temple by the palace.[6]

1. Gelb, 'Household and Family in Early Mesopotamia', p. 21.
2. While Oppenheim, *Ancient Mesopotamia*, pp. 96-97, refuses to attribute the presence of a large semi-free population in the temple households to acts of coercion, Marxist scholars, such as Diakonoff, 'Socio-Economic Classes in Babylonia', pp. 43-44, and Gnuse, *You Shall Not Steal*, pp. 55-56, suggest that the temple (and palace) coerced impoverished citizens to work on its land.
3. Cf. Leemans, 'The Rôle of Landlease in Mesopotamia', pp. 134-45, who notes that landless people are attested in the Ur III period, and that after this period landless people become more common.
4. Cf. Gledhill and Larsen, 'The Polanyi Paradigm', pp. 219-20, who note that although the market system permitted the state to redistribute goods within the state, which was essential for the livelihood of its citizens, it also permitted the private accumulation of wealth outside the state sectors of the economy.
5. Cf. Mendelsohn, *Slavery in the Ancient Near East*, p. 106.
6. Cf. Mendelsohn, *Slavery in the Ancient Near East*, pp. 101-102; I.J. Gelb, 'Prisoners of War in Early Mesopotamia', *JNES* 32 (1973), pp. 95-96; B. Oded, *Mass Deportations and Deportees in the Neo-Assyrian Empire* (Wiesbaden:

During the early periods chattel-slaves were not generally used in the agricultural activities of the temple, but rather were used for the more menial jobs such as maintaining irrigation canals. However, in the later periods they were often used in various activities, although they were generally treated more harshly than privately-owned chattel-slaves.[1] Lastly, high officials of the palace and private citizens dedicated slaves to the temple in most periods in hope of securing favours from the gods.[2]

Gelb[3] has also shown that the individual temple households were most likely composed of nuclear-type families. While nuclear families were members of higher (or broader) kinship groups in the private sector, such kinship ties are not evident in the temple households.[4] For example, while citizens of the private sector are identified within (or over) several generations (as many as six), citizens of the public sector are identified within (or over) one or two generations.[5] However, in many cases semi-free citizens simply bear a patronymic (e.g. son of PN),[6] while chattel-slaves are known only by their single name,[7]

Dr Ludwig Reichert, 1979), pp. 110-15; M.A. Dandamayev, *Slavery in Babylonia: From Nabopolassar to Alexander the Great (626–331 BC)* (DeKalb: Northern Illinois University Press, rev. edn, 1984), p. 472.

1. Cf. Mendelsohn, *Slavery in the Ancient Near East*, p. 104; Dandamayev, *Slavery in Babylonia*, pp. 547-57, esp. 555.

2. Cf. Mendelsohn, *Slavery in the Ancient Near East*, pp. 102-103; Dandamayev, *Slavery in Babylonia*, pp. 472-76.

3. Gelb 'Household and Family in Early Mesopotamia', pp. 5-21, 68. Gelb uses administrative texts of the temple households dating from the Pre-Sargonic (ca. before 2300 BCE), Sargonic (ca. 2334–2279 BCE), Ur III (ca. 2050–1955 BCE), and OB periods (ca. 1830–1530 BCE); and the Votive Inscriptions from the Pre-Sargonic and Sargonic periods.

4. Gelb, 'Household and Family in Early Mesopotamia', pp. 75-76, states that in the early Sumerian periods a nuclear family existed only within the frame of higher kinship groupings.

5. Cf. Gelb, 'Household and Family in Early Mesopotamia', pp. 26-28.

6. Cf. Gelb, 'Household and Family in Early Mesopotamia', p. 26; 'From Freedom to Slavery', in *Gesellschaftsklassen im Alten Zweistromland und den angrenzenden Gebeiten -XVIII: Recontre assyriologique internationale, München, 29. Juni bis 3. Juli 1970* (ed. D.O. Edzard; BAWPHKA, 75; Munich: Verlag der Bayerischen Akademie der Wissenschaften, 1972), p. 87, which notes that serfs rarely bear a metronymic; cf. also Diakonoff, 'Slaves, Helots and Serfs in Early Antiquity', pp. 59, 62.

7. Cf. Mendelsohn, *Slavery in the Ancient Near East*, p. 34.

although during the NB period Babylonian slaves were often identified by a patronymic, which attests to the relatively higher status chattel-slaves achieved during this period.[1] Drawing on Alt's[2] study on the use of the patronymic among semi-free citizens, Gelb[3] suggests that individuals who were referred to in this manner had worked for the state for several generations, during which time their positions and occupations were passed down from father to son.

The palace households. In contrast to the temple households, relatively little is known about the palace households in early Mesopotamia. Gelb[4] suggests that the reason for this lies partly in the lower level of literacy of the palace bureaucracy as compared with that of the temple, and partly in the composition of the labour forces in the two households. As we saw above, the temple employed a permanent work force mainly composed of impoverished citizens. Gelb therefore suggests that the main work force of the palace during early Mesopotamia may have been foreign captives, a point supported by the absence of records, since administrators would be less likely to keep records of a work force that was cheaply acquired and easily replenished. There are, in fact, many texts from early Mesopotamia that list large numbers of foreign captives taken from military campaigns which support Gelb's view, although the use of foreign captives in both the temple and palace households is attested in most periods.[5] For the most part, these foreign captives would be put to work in corvées that maintained the irrigation systems, constructed roads, erected city walls and so on. This type of labour likely supplemented the mainly civilian corvées that are attested during the reign of Urukagina of Lagash (ca. 2370 BCE) and later.[6]

1. Cf. Dandamayev, *Slavery in Babylonia*, pp. 402-403.
2. A. Alt, 'Menschen ohne Namen', *ArOr* 18 (1950), pp. 9-24.
3. Gelb, 'Household and Family in Early Mesopotamia', p. 33.
4. Gelb, 'Household and Family in Early Mesopotamia', p. 12. Gelb suggests that in the case of Lagash the reason why no palace records exist is that Lagash was dominated by temples and priests.
5. For a discussion of the relevant texts concerning prisoners of war in ancient Mesopotamia, see Gelb, 'Prisoners of War in Early Mesopotamia', pp. 70-98; Mendelsohn, *Slavery in the Ancient Near East*, pp. 1-2.
6. Cf. Mendelsohn, *Slavery in the Ancient Near East*, pp. 98-99; and G. Komoróczy, 'Work and Strike of Gods: New Light on the Divine Society in the

However, while the palace continued to use foreign captives in its work force in most periods, the composition of the palace households did change as the palace household became more active in the agricultural economy of the state. For example, Diakonoff[1] identifies the same sort of labour force in the OB palace households that Gelb identifies among the temple households in the Ur III period. During the OB period Hammurabi placed the temple administration under the control of the palace administrators, which possibly accounts for the similarity in composition of both state households.[2] Furthermore, during this period there was apparently a particular need for civilian labour, which was supplied from the private sector, and included both impoverished and other types of citizens.[3] In order to meet the labour demands the palace often used corvées, which were composed of private sector slaves and some citizens, on state projects when there were not enough labourers.[4] Another important source of labour found in the palace households were groups of palace dependents or semi-free citizens, such as the *muškēnu* who are encountered in texts from the Sumerian period onwards. Lastly, during this period the palace began to rent out palace and temple lands to the private sector who, in turn, paid rent to the palace (i.e. tenants).[5]

Sumero-Akkadian Mythology', *Oikumene* 1 (1976), p. 33, who notes that the law collection of Lipit-Ishtar (ca. 1950 BCE) fixes a maximum compulsory labour for married and single men at 70 and 120 days respectively.

1. Diakonoff, 'Socio-Economic Classes in Babylonia', pp. 43-44; cf. also M. Heltzer, 'Royal Economy in Ancient Ugarit', in Lipiński (ed.), *State and Temple Economy*, pp. 459-96, whose description of the employees of palace and temple households of Ugarit resembles those during the Ur III period.

2. Cf. Renger, 'Interaction of Temple, Palace, and 'Private Enterprise'', p. 252; R. Harris, 'On the Process of Secularization under Hammurabi', *JCS* 15 (1961), pp. 117-20.

3. Cf. Mendelsohn, *Slavery in the Ancient Near East*, p. 5, who remarks that captives of war and foreign slaves did not make up the bulk of Babylonian and Assyrian slaves, who were obtained from the ranks of the impoverished native population.

4. Cf. Mendelsohn, *Slavery in the Ancient Near East*, pp. 92, 98-99 and n. 41.

5. Cf. Renger, 'Interaction of Temple, Palace, and "Private Enterprise"', p. 253; F.R. Kraus, *Ein Edikt des Königs Ammi-Saduqa von Babylon* (SDOAP, 5; Leiden: Brill, 1958), pp. 75-78, both of whom suggest that the palace rented out fields to other individuals (Bab. *iššakkum*); cf. also G.R. Driver and C.J. Miles, *The Babylonian Laws*, I (Oxford: Clarendon Press, 1956), pp. 131-36; Diakonoff,

During the MB period (ca. 1530–1200 BCE), several texts illustrate that the palace still maintained a large number of forced foreign labourers, although citizens (Akkadians and Kassites) who were forced into service, either by physical force or on account of debt, also made up a large portion of the work force.[1] Furthermore, during the NA period (ca. 1100–612 BCE) there are several documents which illustrate that many Babylonians were enslaved and used by the Assyrian palace to build public works (corvées), and distributed by the king among palace and temple households, just as captives were used in earlier periods.[2] Lastly, during the NB period (ca. 612–525 BCE) the palace often used foreign captives,[3] but in addition several types of semi-free citizens were also utilized on palace lands, including the *errēšu, ikkaru, sušanū* and the *muškēnu*.[4]

Private Sector Households

In comparison to the state households, there is relatively little known about the composition of the households of the private sector, which included free citizens who owned land or some other means of production independent of state control. Gelb[5] and Oppenheim[6] suggest that this discrepancy is probably due to the fact that administrative accounts were more likely to be kept in the larger-scale households of the palace and temple than in the relatively smaller households of private individuals and higher kinship groups. Furthermore, due to the lack of textual evidence, it is almost

'Socio-Economic Classes in Babylonia', p. 48; *idem*, 'The Rise of the Despotic State', p. 197; cp Stol, *Studies in Old Babylonian History*, pp. 93-94, who suggests that the *iššakku* was a manager of arable public (Crown) lands.

1. Cf. J.A. Brinkman, 'Forced Laborers in the Middle Babylonian Period', *JCS* 32 (1980), pp. 17-22, esp. 20-21; cf. also 'Sex, Age, and Physical Condition Designations for Servile Laborers in the Middle Babylonian Period: A Preliminary Survey', in van Driel *et al.* (eds.), *ZIKIR ŠUMIM*, pp. 1-8, although he is not certain about the identity (citizen or foreigner) or class (free, semi-free, unfree) of these labourers.

2. Cf. Oded, *Mass Deportations and Deportees*, pp. 109-15.

3. Cf. Dandamayev, *Slavery in Babylonia*, pp. 559-60, who notes that large numbers of foreign captives were used in the palace corvées from the time of the reign of Nebuchadnezzar II (605–562 BCE).

4. Cf. Dandamayev, *Slavery in Babylonia*, pp. 585-615, 626-46.

5. Gelb, 'Household and Family in Early Mesopotamia', p. 11.

6. Oppenheim, *Ancient Mesopotamia*, p. 84.

impossible to come to any firm conclusions about the relative size of the state and private sector, although it probably fluctuated greatly according to the period, the region and the condition of the soil.[1] Nevertheless, based on the sale contracts that date from the Fara, Pre-Sargonic, Sargonic and Ur III periods Gelb has been able to illustrate some characteristics of private sector households.[2]

In the sale contracts dated from the Fara and Pre-Sargonic periods, Gelb[3] has shown that sales of fields and houses involve either a single seller or many large numbers of sellers (i.e. seven, eight and nine, with as many as 27 sellers). However, in the Sargonic- and Ur III-period contracts the number of sellers varies between one and four; the majority of Ur III contracts list a single seller. Gelb also notes that the size of the house being sold by either single or multiple sellers was most likely a nuclear-type dwelling.[4] Therefore, those contracts that

---

1. Oppenheim, *Ancient Mesopotamia*, p. 84.
2. The criterion 'land ownership' is also used by Diakonoff, 'Socio-Economic Classes in Babylonia', p. 47, to define the different socio-economic classes during the OB period.
3. Gelb, 'Household and Family in Early Mesopotamia', pp. 68-71; cf. also Diakonoff, 'The Rise of the Despotic State', pp. 176-81, 193.
4. For the various types of family households that might be related to dwellings, we will adopt the definitions proposed by P. Laslett and R. Wall, *Household and Family in Past Time: Comparative Studies in the Size and Structure of the Domestic Group over the Last Three Centuries in England, France, Serbia, Japan, and Colonial North America with Further Material from Western Europe* (Cambridge: Cambridge University Press, 1972), which is cited in L.E. Stager, 'The Archaeology of the Family in Ancient Israel', *BASOR* 260 (1985), p. 29; cf. also Gelb, 'Household and Family in Early Mesopotamia', pp. 25-31, who offers similar definitions:

   (1) *Nuclear Family (conjugal, simple family):* includes father, mother, their children and live-in 'servants'.
   (2) *Extended Family:* includes the nuclear family plus married relatives and 'servants'. This type may extend 'upwards' to include widowed grandmothers, uncles or aunts, 'downwards' to the grandchildren of the head of the household, or 'laterally' to the brothers or sisters of the household head. But only one married couple lives in the household at any one time.
   (3) *Multiple Family:* includes two or more nuclear families. This type has many variants, such as 'stem' families common to Eastern Europe or 'joint' families common in the Middle East.

While the extended-type family has usually been considered to be the typical Middle Eastern family, anthropologists and ethnographers have demonstrated that the nuclear family was the most dominant kinship grouping, although the extended family

list larger numbers of sellers, including both the primary sellers (who received both the price of the property and gifts) and the secondary sellers or primary witnesses (who received only gifts), probably posit a large kinship grouping who most likely lived in either separate nuclear dwellings or in joint compounds (e.g. proper lineage).[1] Gelb notes that people who belonged to a higher kinship grouping shared jointly the right to land, even though they did not live together in a single dwelling. This sort of 'solidarity' which existed between families prevented one family from selling property without the consent of the others. If one family was having financial problems the other families could pitch in and help the family to retain its land or prevent it from being removed from the control of the proper lineage (or clan). Furthermore, the sale of large amounts of kinship land probably needed the approval of the local popular assemblies.[2]

However, Gelb[3] suggests that during the later periods the nuclear

averaged between 10 and 30 per cent in both urban and non-urban societies; cf. J. Gulick, *The Middle East: An Anthropological Perspective* (Goodyear RAS: Pacific Palisades, 1976), pp. 128-30; L.E. Stager, 'The Archaeology of the Family in Ancient Israel', p. 20; cf. also M. Heltzer, *The Rural Community in Ancient Ugarit* (Wiesbaden Rachert, 1976), pp. 102-12, who notes that the average family at Ugarit contained 6.5 people; and Liverani, 'Communautés de village et palais royal', p. 152.

1. Gelb, 'Household and Family in Early Mesopotamia', p. 71. However, Gelb does acknowledge that there may have not been any legal obligation to name all the sellers, which suggests that contracts that name only a single seller may, in fact, represent a sale that was represented by a single person in the name of a larger family grouping.

2. Cf. Diakonoff, 'The Rise of the Despotic State', p. 177, who suggests that the sale of large tracts of communal land during the Early Dynastic (ca. 2800–2400 BC) and Akkadian periods (ca. 2300 BC) probably needed the approbation of the Popular Assembly of the rural community; cf. also R.McC. Adams, 'Property Rights and Functional Tenure in Mesopotamian Rural Communities', in Dandamayev *et al.* (eds.), *Societies and Languages*, pp. 1-13; and Postgate, 'Land Tenure in the Middle Assyrian Kingdom', pp. 309-10, who suggests that during the MA period land could not be sold without the co-operation of others. Lemche, *Early Israel*, pp. 248-49, notes that in many modern Middle East villages when a member of a *humula* (a type of 'clan') attempts to sell land to a foreigner the other members of the 'clan' step in on behalf of the family to redeem the land, since the land is regarded as the communal property of all members of the 'clan'.

3. Gelb, 'Household and Family in Early Mesopotamia', pp. 57, 72, 75-76. Cp. C.A.O. vanNieuwenhuijze, *Sociology of the Middle East: A Stocktaking and*

family, as evidenced by the majority of single-seller contracts, no longer existed within higher kinship groupings (lineages). However, while it is true that many sedentary tribes eventually disintegrated under the influence of the state,[1] it is most likely that the lower kinship groupings (minimal and proper lineages) remained intact, although these kinship groups could no longer give the same type of communal assistance or exercise the same sort of coparcenary rights on property as they once were able to do.[2] Furthermore, Jankowska[3]

Interpretation (SPSME, 1; Leiden: Brill, 1971), p. 386; C.H.J. de Geus, *The Tribes of Israel: An Investigation into Some of the Presuppositions of Martin Noth's Amphictyony Hypothesis* (SSN, 18; Assen, 1976), p. 136; Renger, 'Interaction of Temple, Palace, and "Private Enterprise"', pp. 250-51; Diakonoff, 'Socio-Economic Classes in Babylonia', p. 44; *idem*, 'The Rise of the Despotic State', p. 193, who suggest that the increase in the number of nuclear families is attributed to the breakdown of extended families (multi-generational).

1. Cf. G.E. Dole, 'Tribe as the Autonomous Unit', in *Essays on the Problem of Tribe* (ed. J. Helm; Proceedings of the 1967 Annual Spring Meeting of the American Ethnological Society; Seattle, 1968), pp. 91-94; cf. also Gelb, 'From Freedom to Slavery', pp. 81-82, who suggests that the tribal leaders eventually became the ruling classes.

2. Cf. Gelb, 'Household and Family in Early Mesopotamia', pp. 56-58, 71; Patai, 'The Structure of Endogamous Unilineal Descent Groups', pp. 325-50; Renger, 'Interaction of Temple, Palace, and "Private Enterprise"', pp. 250-51; Lemche, *Early Israel*, pp. 242-44; V.A. Jakobson, 'Some Problems Connected with the Rise of Landed Property (Old Babylonian Period)', in *Beiträge zur sozialen Struktur des Alten Vorderasien* (ed. H. Klengel; SGKAO, 1; Berlin: Akademie-Verlag, 1971), pp. 33-37; and Diakonoff, 'Socio-Economic Classes in Babylonia', p. 44. Cp. M.B. Rowton, 'Dimorphic Structure and the Problem of the *'Apiru-'Ibrîm*', *JNES* 35 (1976), p. 14; *idem*, 'Dimorphic Structure and the Parasocial Element', *JNES* 36 (1977), p. 183, who suggests that 'detribalization' takes place in urban communities. However, K.A. Kamp and N. Yoffee, 'Ethnicity in Ancient Western Asia during the Early Second Millennium BC: Archaeological Assessments and Ethno-archaeological Prospectives', *BASOR* 237 (1980), pp. 93-94, note that recent ethnoarchaeological studies suggest that ethnic identity is often maintained and may actually increase within cities; cf. also A.R.W. Green, 'Social Stratification and Cultural Continuity at Alalakh', in *The Quest for the Kingdom of God: Studies in Honor of G.E. Mendenhall* (ed. H.B. Huffmon, F.A. Spina and A.R.W. Green; Winona Lake, IN: Eisenbrauns, 1983), pp. 181-203.

3. N.B. Jankowska, 'Extended Family Commune and Civil Self-Government in Arrapha in the Fifteenth–Fourteenth Century BC', in Diakonoff (ed.), *Ancient Mesopotamia*, pp. 235-52; *idem*, 'Communal Self-Government and the King of Arrapha', *JESHO* 12 (1968), pp. 233-82; cf. also M.A. Dandamayev, 'Social

notes that, originally, transfer of land was only possible between relatives, but as credit and loan transactions increased, demanding the pledging of persons and property, the creditor's rights were recognized by the state as prevailing over the claims of heirs by kins. This trend appears to be checked in certain laws that enabled a person to retain a right to redemption on property (cf. LE §39), although as we will see in Chapter 3 the application of such laws to real cases remains unclear.

Lastly, some overlapping did occur between the state and public sectors. On the one hand, Gelb[1] notes that a family or individual who owns its own patrimonial land may at the same time have the right of usufruct in public land. On the other, officials (including rulers) could appropriate public land for their own use so that the public land became *de facto* private.[2] Further, I have already pointed out above that merchants who worked for the state engaged in private enterprises and as a result acquired their own lands. While it is difficult to assess the importance of private citizens using state land it is clear that officials who became large private landowners had a significant impact on the private sector.

Social Stratification in Mesopotamia

As the above discussions show, there was a high degree of social stratification in Mesopotamian society, in which three social classes can be distinguished: (1) free citizens; (2) semi-free citizens; (3) unfree chattel-slaves. The first (1) category includes the priests, nobility, officials, merchants and the kinship families who owned land or some other means of production. The second (2) category includes all those citizens who worked for the state (temple and palace) households but who did not own their own means of production (e.g. Sum. *guruš*, Akkad. *muškēnum*, etc.), although it should be pointed out that the *muškenum* could own slaves (cf. LH §175, §219). The third (3) category includes the foreign captives, who were utilized in

Stratification in Babylonia (7th–4th Centuries BC)', in Harmatta and Komoróczy (eds.), *Wirtschaft und Gesellschaft im alten Vorderasien*, pp. 433-44; Diakonoff, 'Slaves, Helots and Serfs in Early Antiquity', pp. 47-48.

1. Gelb, 'Household and Family in Early Mesopotamia', p. 5; Diakonoff, 'Socio-Economic Classes in Babylonia', p. 50.

2. Cf. Struve, 'The Problem of the Genesis', p. 36.

the state households,[1] and chattel-slaves—either those who were bought in foreign and domestic markets or who were born in the house of their master—who were used mostly by the free citizens in their households.[2] I will discuss this last category in more detail below.

Although I have adopted the criterion 'freedom' in my description of the different social classes, we have already seen that such a criterion is not adequate in evaluating the social classes of Mesopotamia and the ancient Near East, since free citizens could easily become semi-free citizens if they lost their means of production (e.g. their land). Noting the mobility that exists between the three social classes, Gelb suggests that in an economic sense two classes can be distinguished. He writes.[3]

> In the economic sense, we may very well distinguish not three, but two classes, the master class and the rest of the population. The latter would include all dependent labor, composed not only of serfs [semi-free] and slaves [chattel-slaves], but also of the so-called free peasantry [citizens] and craftsmen, who, while theoretically free and independent, sooner or later became dependent on the large landowners for water, draft animals, plows, seed grain, and other means of production.

From an economic point of view, therefore, social stratification can be seen as the result of a process by which free citizens eventually lost

1. Cf. Gelb, 'Definition and Discussion of Slavery', pp. 293-94; *idem*, Gelb's response in Diakonoff, 'Socio-Economic Classes in Babylonia', p. 50; Diakonoff, 'Socio-Economic Classes in Babylonia', pp. 45-46; cf. also Driver and Miles, *Babylonian Laws*, I, pp. 106-107; J.J. Finkelstein, 'Ammiṣaduqa's Edict and the Babylonian "Law Codes"', *JCS* 15 (1961), p. 97, both of whom suggest that chattel-slaves were employed by semi-free citizens (*muškēnum*).

2. Cf. Mendelsohn, *Slavery in the Ancient Near East*, pp. 3-4; Driver and Miles, *Babylonian Laws*, I, pp. 221-22; Gelb, 'Definition and Discussion of Slavery', pp. 294-95.

3. Gelb, 'From Freedom to Slavery', p. 92; cf. also J. Renger, 'Flucht as soziales Problem in der altbabylonischen Gesellschaft', in *Gesellschaftsklassen im Alten Zweistromland und den angrenzenden Gebeiten-XVIII: Recontre assyriologique internationale, Munich, 29. Juni bis 3. Juli 1970* (ed. D.O. Edzard; BAWPHKA, 75; Munich: Verlag der Bayerischen Akademie der Wissenschaften, 1972), pp. 167-82; and G. Giorgadze, 'Die Begriffe "freie" und "unfreie" bei den Hethitern', in Harmatta and Komoróczy (eds.), *Wirtschaft und Gesellschaft*, pp. 299-308, who notes the mobility between free and semi-/unfree classes among the Hittites.

control over their means of production, on account of their growing dependency upon the large landowners (and merchants) and state for resources. Once this dependency was established the small landowners were often forced into procuring loans which often included high interest rates. If their crop(s) failed or was below expectation, then the debtors would be hard-pressed to pay back the loan.[1] Therefore, many of these small landowners were likely to become insolvent, since they were able to engage only in subsistence farming. As a result of their insolvency farmers were forced to sell or surrender dependents into debt-slavery. Furthermore, they would eventually be forced to sell their land (means of production), themselves and their families. Although kinship groups attempted to prevent the sale of land by offering political or economic support, it is clear that such groups could not always prevent the sale of land on account of insolvency. The landless poor most likely had no other option than to enter into the service of the state households[2] or become sharecroppers or tenants on land owned by the state or the large landowning elite. The latter situation demonstrates the mobility that existed between the free and semi-free classes, while the former demonstrates the mobility between the free and unfree classes, since in many cases debtors were unlikely to be able to redeem their dependents.[3]

Free citizens who were dependent upon the ruling elite for resources and loans could also become 'indentured servants'. For example, large landowners often secured labour through the use of the *tidennu* (Nuzi) and *mazzazānu* (OB and OA) loan contracts, which required a pledge of the debtor to work on the creditor's land. In many cases these pledges served from several years to a lifetime. These 'indentured servants' generally proved to be a useful source of labour for the large landowners, especially when an alternative source

---

1. Cf. LH §48 and the discussion of this law in Driver and Miles, *Babylonian Laws*, I, pp. 144-45.

2. Cf. Gelb, 'From Freedom to Slavery', p. 87; Diakonoff, 'Slaves, Helots and Serfs', pp. 58-63, both of whom suggest that the economic characteristics and the servant-master relationship of both semi-free citizens and chattel-slaves are similar; cf. also Gelb, 'Definition and Discussion of Slavery', pp. 292-94; *idem*, 'Household and Family in Early Mesopotamia', pp. 23ff.

3. Cf. also Dandamayev, *Slavery in Babylonia*, pp. 179-80, 648.

of labour could not be found.[1] I will discuss these contracts in more detail below in Chapter 3.

The relationship that the large landowners and merchants had with the rest of the free and semi-free population is considered by Diakonoff[2] to be one of exploitation. This process of exploitation, which Bobek[3] calls *Rentenkapitalismus* (rent capitalism), probably accounts for much of the latifundia that existed within many city- and national states in the ancient Near East. Lastly, Lenski[4] suggests that the ruling elite of agrarian monarchies, who comprised no more than two per cent of the population, controlled up to half or more of goods and services.

In comparison to the mobility that existed among free citizens, chattel-slaves were able to attain the status of semi-free or free citizens under special circumstances. For example, LH §§170-171 stipulated that the children of a houseborn slave whose father is the master could be made legitimate, but even if they were not made legitimate both the mother (who could be a foreign-bought slave or

1. Cf. Mendelsohn, *Slavery in the Ancient Near East*, p. 5; and Dandamayev, *Slavery in Babylonia*, p.103, both of whom suggest that the bulk of slaves in Mesopotamia (including Babylonia) came from the ranks of the native population.

2. Diakonoff, 'Socio-Economic Classes in Babylonia', pp. 47-48; 'Slaves, Helots and Serfs', pp. 52-68.

3. H. Bobek, 'Zum Konzept des Rentenkapitalismus', *TESG* 65 (1974), pp. 73-77; *idem*, 'Rentenkapitalismus und Entwicklung im Iran', in *Interdisziplinäre Iran-Forschung* (ed. G. Schweizer; Wiesbaden, 1979), pp. 113-24; Cf. also E.R. Wolf, *Peasants* (Englewood Cliffs, NJ: Prentice-Hall, 1966), pp. 55-56; R.B. Coote, *Amos Among the Prophets: Composition and Theology* (Philadelphia: Fortress Press, 1981), pp. 26-32; and B. Lang, 'The Social Organization of Peasant Poverty in Biblical Israel', *JSOT* 24 (1982), pp. 48-51, who cites Bobek. The process by which large landowners, who were often local officials or merchants, could procure income and land from free citizens through the monopolization of resources is called the *mercantile system*, which is also known as *rent capitalism* (*Rentenkapitalismus*). Furthermore, in many societies the king, who had domain over the land, gave land grants to officials who controlled the income (*prebend*) generated from these lands (*prebendal system*). Officials could also be granted *patrimonial domain* over lands controlled by the king. Both of these types of domains were maintained by peasants. Those lands acquired by officials from free citizens would be added to their prebendal or patrimonial domain.

4. G.E. Lenski, *Power and Privilege: A Theory of Social Stratification* (New York: McGraw-Hill, 1966), pp. 189-296.

even a captive) and her children were given their freedom after the death of their master (cf. also §§175-176).[1] Further, during the OB period and later, when the number of chattel-slaves increased dramatically, chattel-slaves became artisans and agents, who received a *peculium* from their masters and who often owned their own land and slaves.[2]

While the above examples illustrate that free citizens could attain a status similar to that of a chattel-slave, and that chattel-slaves could attain the status of free or semi-free citizens, a clear distinction was nevertheless maintained between chattel- and debt-slaves.[3] For example, chattel-slaves did not have individual rights to redemption, although they were sometimes released by their masters.[4] However, the majority of these slaves remained the property of their owners, even during the NB period when they engaged in many professional activities normally attributed to free citizens.[5] Furthermore, chattel-slaves are clearly distinguished from debt-slaves in the ancient Near Eastern legal collections and in the *mēšarum* edicts, in which the term *wardum* is never used to designate debt-slaves, and in which chattel-slaves are never released except under special circumstances.[6]

---

1. Cf. Driver and Miles, *Babylonian Laws*, I, pp. 222, 350-52.

2. Cf. Mendelsohn, *Slavery in the Ancient Near East*, pp. 66-69; Driver and Miles, *Babylonian Laws*, I, pp. 353-56, esp. 355; Dandamayev, 'The Economic and Legal Character of the Slaves' Peculium in the Neo-Babylonian and Achaemenid Periods', *AbhBAW* 75 (1972), pp. 35-39; *idem*, *Slavery in Babylonia*, pp. 320-44.

3. Cf. also Diakonoff, 'Slaves, Helots and Serfs in Early Antiquity', pp. 74-77.

4. For a discussion of the different ways in which a slave could be set free, see Mendelsohn, *Slavery in the Ancient Near East*, pp. 66-91; Driver and Miles, *Babylonian Laws*, I, pp. 221-30; Dandamayev, *Slavery in Babylonia*, pp. 463-68; cf. also K.R. Veenhof, 'A Deed of Manumission and Adoption from the Later Old Assyrian Period: Its Writing, Language, and Contents in Comparative Perspective', in van Driel *et al.* (eds.), *ZIKIR ŠUMIM*, pp. 359-85, esp. 373-79, a discussion of an OA manumission document that uses terminology found in many OB manumission documents.

5. Cf. Dandamayev, *Slavery in Babylonia*, pp. 463-68, 648-49.

6. Cf. B.S. Jackson, 'Biblical Laws of Slavery: a Comparative Approach', in *Slavery and Other Forms of Unfree Labour* (ed. L. Archer; HWS; London: Routledge, 1988), p. 96; Struve, 'The Problem of the Genesis', p. 55; and J.R. Ziskind, 'Legal Observations on the Enslavement of the Native and Foreign Born in the Ancient Near East in the Second and Early First Millennium BC', *Pal* 15 (1969), pp. 159-62, who writes: 'The evidence... shows that throughout the ancient

Therefore, while chattel-slaves attained a position similar to that of semi-free or free citizens in exceptional cases, they were nevertheless clearly distinguished from free citizens who became debt-slaves (cf. LH §§15-20, 156, 175-196, 215-223, 226-227).[1]

Summary and Conclusions

To sum up, the rise of debt-slavery and the alienation of land in the Mesopotamian city states can be attributed to insolvency among free citizens caused by various interrelated socio-economic factors, including taxation, the monopoly of resources and services among the state and private elite (i.e. rent capitalism), high-interest loans and the economic and political collapse of higher kinship groups. Debt-slavery became a serious problem as early as the Ur III period (ca. 2050–1955 BCE) and continued to be a major problem throughout the history of the ancient Near East. That debt-slavery was a major problem confronting the various ancient Near Eastern city-states is further suggested by the existence of various laws and edicts that attempted to curb its rise.

Near East there existed a legal discrimination in favor of the enslaved native and against the foreign born slaves...' (p. 162).

1. LH §54, however, states that a man who does not maintain his river-bank can be sold as a slave. Driver and Miles, *Babylonian Laws*, I, p. 153 and n. 1, suggest that this man could have been either a tenant or a landowner whose property could not be sold since it was the inheritance of the family. However, there is no indication whether this sale was permanent, in which case he is released according to §117, or whether the man was surrendered for service until he paid for the damage.

Chapter 3

THE LEGAL BACKGROUND TO DEBT-SLAVERY IN MESOPOTAMIA

Within the various legal collections and royal edicts of the ancient Near East there are several laws and decrees that deal with the treatment and manumission of debt-slaves as well as various aspects of the institution of lending that was often responsible for debt-slavery. While it is beyond the scope of my investigation to engage in a comprehensive survey of this diverse legislation, I will nevertheless discuss briefly the various laws, royal decrees, loan transactions and service contracts that have a particular bearing on the interpretation of the biblical manumission laws. However, before I begin this survey I will present a brief survey of the role of justice in the Mesopotamian legal collections and edicts.

The Role of Justice in the Mesopotamian Legal Collections and Edicts[1]

In Chapter 1 we saw that with the advent of the city-states and their respective temple and palace economies during the latter half of the third millennium BCE several social problems developed including debt-slavery and the alienation of land.[2] These problems eventually provoked the enactment of certain types of legislation by several kings, including king Urukagina[3] of the city-state Lagash (ca. 2370

1. For similar comparative analyses of social justice in the ancient Near East, see L. Epsztein, *Social Justice in the Ancient Near East*, pp. 3-42; J.L. Sicre, *'Con los Pobres de la Tierra': La Justicia Social en Los Profetas de Israel* (Madrid: Ediciones Christiandad, 1984), pp. 19-47.

2. Cf. B.J. Siegel, 'Slavery during the Third Dynasty of Ur', *AA* 49/1/2 (1976), pp. 13-25; Mendelsohn, *Slavery in the Ancient Near East*, pp. 6-8; Cardellini, *Die biblischen 'Sklaven'-Gesetze*, p. 26.

3. Cf. W.G. Lambert, 'The Reading of the Name Uru.Ka.gi.na', *Or* 39 (1970), p. 41, who suggests that Urukagina should be read as Uruinimgina. In this book, though, I will continue to use the more common reading Urukagina.

BCE), who is said to have *ama.gi₄ e-gar* 'established the freedom'
(= Akkadian *andurāram šakānum*) of the people of Lagash,[1]
including debtors and their families, widows and orphans, all of
whom were exploited by the rich.[2] Similar legislation is also found in
the Sumerian law collections of king Ur-Nammu (LU), who was the
founder of the second major Mesopotamian national state (ca. 2112–
2094 BCE: Ur III dynasty),[3] and king Lipit-Ishtar (LI), who was the
fifth king of the dynasty of Isin (ca. 1950 BCE).[4] Both of these law
collections, like the legislation of Urukagina,[5] contain references to

1. Cf. Finkelstein, 'Ammiṣaduqa's Edict', pp. 103-104; cf. also M. Lambert,
'L'Expansion de Lagash au temps d'Entéména', *RSO* 47 (1972), pp. 1-22, who
cites a text that demonstrates that King Entemena, 50 years before Urukagina's
reform, also boasted about liberating the inhabitants of Lagash.

2. For a discussion of the so-called reforms of Urukagina, see M. Lambert, 'Les
"Réformes" d'Urukagina', *RA* 50 (1965), pp. 169-84; I.M. Diakonoff, 'Some
Remarks on the "Reforms" of Urukagina', *RA* 52 (1958), pp. 1-15; B. Hruška,
'Die Reformstexte Urukaginas', in *Le Palais et la royauté: XIX recontre
assyriologique international 1971* (Paris, 1974), pp. 151-61; *idem*, 'Die innere
Struktur der Reformtexte Urukaginas von Lagaš', *ArOr* 41 (1973), pp. 4-13, 104-
32; J.S. Cooper, *Sumerian and Akkadian Royal Inscriptions*, I (New Haven:
American Oriental Society, 1986), pp. 70ff.; R. Westbrook, *Studies in Biblical and
Cuneiform Law* (CahRB, 26; Paris: Gabalda, 1988), pp. 11-12; Cardellini, *Die
biblischen 'Sklaven'-Gesetze*, pp. 5-10.

3. Cf. S.N. Kramer and A. Falkenstein, 'Ur-Nammu Law Code', *Or* ns 23
(1954), pp. 40-51; E. Szlechter, 'A propos du code d'Ur-Nammu', *RA* 47 (1953),
pp. 1-10; *idem*, 'Le Code d'Ur-Nammu', *RA* 49 (1955), pp. 169-77; *idem*,
'Nouveaux textes législatifs sumériens', *RA* 61 (1967), pp. 105-26; V. Korošec,
'Keilschriftrecht', in *Orientalisches Recht* (HOr, III; Leiden: Brill, 1964), pp. 67-73;
J.J. Finkelstein, 'The Laws of Ur-Nammu', *JCS* 22 (1968/69), pp. 66-82;
Westbrook, *Studies in Biblical and Cuneiform Law*, pp. 11-12; Cardellini, *Die
biblischen 'Sklaven'-Gesetze*, pp. 15-19.

4. Cf. F.R. Steele, 'Lipit-Ishtar Law Code', *AJA* 51 (1947), pp. 138-64; 52
(1948), pp. 425-50; M. San Nicoló, 'Das Gesetzbuch Lipit-Ištar II,
Rechtsgeschichtliches zum Gesetzbuch', *Or* 19 (1950), pp. 111-18; E. Szlechter,
'Le Code de Lipit-Ištar', *RA* 51 (1957), pp. 57-82, 177-96; *idem*, 'Les anciennes
codifications en Mésopotamie', *RIDA* 4 (1957), pp. 74-90; J. Klíma, 'Über neuer
Studien auf dem Gebiete des Keilschriftrechts', *ArOr* 18 (1950), pp. 525-38;
M. Civil, 'New Sumerian Law Fragments', *AS* 16 (1965), pp. 1-12; Korošec,
'Keilschriftrecht', pp. 74-84; Cardellini, *Die biblischen 'Sklaven'-Gesetze*,
pp. 31-39.

5. Cf. Finkelstein, 'Ammiṣaduqa's Edict', p. 104; D.O. Edzard, ' "Social
Reformen" in Zweistromland bis ca. 1600 v. Chr.: Realität oder literarischer

the role of justice (e.g., *níg.si.sá gar* [= Bab. *mēšarum šakānum*] 'establish justice' in the land),[1] and follow a tripartite division: a prologue, legal corpus, and epilogue.[2]

This Babylonian and Sumerian tradition of justice, according to which a king was called upon by his god(s) to institute justice in the land, can also be found in the Akkadian legal collection (LH) of Hammurabi (ca. 1758 BCE) who brought all of Mesopotamia under one rule[3]. LH contains various legal precedents[4] that attempted to curb some of the abuses prevalent in Babylon, including LH §§114-116, 117-119 which I will discuss in some detail below. Similar laws can also be found in the Akkadian legal collection LE from Eshnunna (ca. 1790 BCE)[5] and in MAL (ca. 1450–1250 BCE), neither of which contains a prologue or epilogue.

In addition to the promulgation of legal collections, various OB kings including Hammurabi effected judicial control in the land by proclaiming *mēšarum* edicts during their regnal year. These edicts, which I will also discuss in more detail below, sought to establish economic order by instituting various economic reforms, including the cancellation of various debts and the sale of land caused by insolvency, although these edicts were more restricted in scope than the legal collections. Nevertheless, these edicts exemplified the same

---

Topos?', in Harmatta and Komoróczy (eds.), *Wirtschaft und Gesellschaft*, pp. 149-51, both of whom note that these two Sumerian law collections share common elements with Urukagina's reform.

1. Cf. LU ll.104-113 (*TUAT* I/1: 18; *ANET*, p. 523); and LI Col. I: ll.39-55 (*TUAT* I/1: 24; *ANET*, p. 159).

2. For a discussion of the nature of the tripartite structure of the ancient Near East law collections, see Paul, *Book of the Covenant*, pp. 3-26.

3. Cf. the prologue to LH, col. ia, ll.30-49; and col. ia, ll.50-65; col. iia, ll.1-65 (G.R. Driver and C.J. Miles, *The Babylonian Laws. II. Transliterated Text, Translation, Philological Notes, Glossary* [Oxford: Clarendon Press, 1956], p. 7); *TUAT* I/1: 40; cf. also the discussions in J. Bottéro, 'Le "Code" de Ḥammūrabi', *ADSNS* 12 (1982), pp. 413-14; Boecker, *Law and the Administration of Justice*, pp. 74-77; Paul, *Book of the Covenant*, pp. 5-10; Wiseman, 'Law and Order in Old Testament Times', pp. 5-8.

4. Cf. Wiseman, 'Law and Order in Old Testament Times', pp. 9-10.

5. For a discussion of the dating of LE, see E. Szlechter, 'Les Lois d'Eshnunna', *RIDA* 25 (1978), pp. 109-10; R. Yaron, *The Laws of Eshnunna* (Jerusalem: Magnes; Leiden: Brill, 2nd edn, 1988), pp. 20-21; Driver and Miles, *Babylonian Laws*, I, pp. xxiv-xxv, 34-36.

Sumerian tradition of establishing justice in the land. Westbrook writes:[1]

> By ordaining 'justice' for the land, particularly at the opening of his reign, a king demonstrated his quality as a ruler according to the law (*šar mēšarim*) 'instituting the misharum for *Šamaš* who loves him' [Ammisaduqa: I.3]. It is worth comparing the activity of these same kings in drawing up 'law-codes', whose primary purpose was to lay before the public, posterity, future kings and above all, the gods, evidence of the king's execution of his divinely ordained mandate: to have been the *re'um* [cf. LH col.xxivb 43; written SIBA] (lit. 'shepherd'—a king who makes just laws) and the *šar mīsarim* [cf. LH xxivb 75; written LUGAL *mīsarim*].'

It was therefore the duty of all Mesopotamian kings to establish (or re-establish) justice by promulgating decrees and publishing legal collections in order to deal with various social problems, including debt-slavery and land alienation.

However, while it is generally acknowledged that the OB *mēšarum* edicts were written records of actual regal proclamations, the practical role of the various ancient Near Eastern legal collections remains unclear. For example, it has long been recognized by scholars that these legal collections were not to be comprehensive in their treatment of law. The term 'code', therefore, has been avoided in many treatments of ancient Near Eastern legal collections. Nevertheless, while Driver and Miles[2] suggest that LH should be regarded as 'a series of amendmen᷄   d restatements of parts of the law in force', others such as Finkelstein[3] and Kraus,[4] who question the

---

1. Westbrook, 'Jubilee Laws', p. 218.

2. Driver and Miles, *Babylonian Laws*, I, p. 45.

3. Finkelstein, 'Ammisaduqa's Edict', pp. 91-104; *idem*, 'On Some Recent Studies in Cuneiform Law', *JAOS* 90 (1970), pp. 255-56; cf. also W.F. Leemans, 'King Hammurabi as Judge', in *Symbolae juridicae et historicae M. David dedicatae*, II (ed. J.A. Ankum, R. Feenstra and W.F. Leemans; IOA; Leiden: Brill, 1968), pp. 107-109; Paul, *Book of the Covenant*, pp. 25-26; and Bottéro, 'Le "Code" de Ḥammūrabi', p. 444; and B.L. Eichler, 'Literary Structure in the Laws of Eshnunna', in *Language, Literature, and History: Philological and Historical Studies Presented to Erica Reiner* (ed. F. Rochberg-Halton; AOS, 67; New Haven: American Oriental Society, 1987), pp. 81-84, who, based on his study of the structure of LE, concludes that much of LH that parallels LE is the result of scholastic endeavours to comment on LE's laws.

4. F.R. Kraus, 'Ein zentrales Problem des altmesopotamischen Rechtes: Was ist

practicality of LH, suggest that LH was merely a literary work or royal apologia that was composed by scribal schools rather than by jurists. This latter argument is strengthened by the fact that while Hammurabi declared various *mēšarum* edicts during his reign, his legal collection was not composed until the end of his reign.[1] Nevertheless, Westbrook[2] has recently offered a mediating position in which he suggests that LH and other legal collections were used as reference works by royal judges in deciding difficult legal decisions.[3] He notes that the Hittite legal collection (HL), for example, which was originally part of the royal archives, was recopied over several centuries, but that subsequent copies show not only evidence of an updating of language but also of substantive law.[4] While Westbrook concedes that legal collections could have been used only as a scribal exercise by other societies, he suggests nevertheless that an earlier legal collection could have been as a model by other societies who shared a common legal tradition. Westbrook[5] concludes therefore that various legal collections such as MAL or HL began as an oral tradition and gradually became a systematic written corpus. However, such collections could be adopted to other secondary purposes: i.e., (1) royal inscriptions designed to praise the king's activity as a judge,

---

der Codex Hammu-rabi?', *Geneva* 8 (1960), pp. 183-96; cf. also B.S. Jackson, 'Reflections on Biblical Criminal Law', in *Essays in Jewish and Comparative Legal History* (SJLA, 10; Leiden: Brill, 1975), pp. 26-29 and n. 12.

1. Cf. G. Cardascia, 'Les Droits cunéiformes', in *Histoire des institutions et des faits sociaux des origines à l'aube du Moyen Age* (ed. R. Monier, G. Cardascia and J. Imbert; Paris, 1956), p. 40, who suggests that Hammurabi did not have enough time to implement his 'code'.

2. R. Westbrook, 'Biblical and Cuneiform Law Codes', *RB* 92 (1985), pp. 247-64.

3. Cf. also the earlier discussions of J. Klíma, 'La Perspective historique des lois hamourabiennes', in *Comptes Rendues de l'Académie des Inscriptions et Belles-Lettres* (1972), pp. 297-317 (who is cited by Epsztein, *Social Justice in the Ancient Near East*, p. 15); *idem*, 'Zur gesellschaftlichen Relevanz der Hammurapischen Gesetze', in Dandamayev *et al.* (eds.), *Societies and Languages*, pp. 174-95; G. Cardascia, 'La Transmission des sources cunéiformes', *RIDA* 7 (1960), p. 47; D.J. Wiseman, 'The Laws of Hammurabi Again', *JSS* 7 (1962), pp. 161-68; R. de Vaux, *Ancient Israel: Its Life and Institutions* (London: Darton, Longman & Todd, 1961), p. 145.

4. Westbrook, 'Biblical and Cuneiform Law Codes', pp. 255-56.

5. Westbrook, 'Biblical and Cuneiform Law Codes', p. 258.

which were characterized by the addition of a prologue and epilogue (LU, LI, LH); (2) school texts that would take on an independent existence as part of the scribal curriculum (LU, LI, LH, LE,[1] NBL); and (3) part of a religio-historical narrative (Covenant Code and Deuteronomic legal collection) where the deity replaces the king as the source of law. Similarly, Wiseman,[2] in response to the claim that the ancient Near Eastern legal collections were not practical, suggests that LH sought to preserve law and order as a living and continuing tradition for future kings. As I will argue below, this aspect is particularly evident in LH §117, which sought to establish a periodic release of debt-slaves, something that was only attained through the sporadic proclamation of the *mēšarum* edicts.[3] Nevertheless, the fact that *mēšarum* edicts continued to be proclaimed after Hammurabi's reign suggests that LH §117 was not put into practice.[4]

---

1. Cp. Yaron, *Laws of Eshnunna*, pp. 121-26, 292-94, who suggests that LE is composed of both 'decrees of the king' (cf. LE §58) and court decisions which have a long history (e.g. LE §53, 'goring ox').

2. Wiseman, 'The Laws of Hammurabi Again', pp. 162-67.

3. While it may remain a moot point whether the legal collections of the ancient Near East were used as practical guides to judges, it is generally acknowledged that the OB *mēšarum* edicts were written records of actual regal proclamations. These so-called economic reforms can be compared with the earlier legislation of Urukagina, although it is difficult to demonstrate whether Urukagina's proclamation had any practical application. For a comparison of the edicts to Urukagina's legislation, see J. Bottéro, 'Désordre économique et annulation des dettes en Mésopotamie à l'époque paléo-babylonienne', *JESHO* 4 (1961), p. 163; and W.G. Lambert, 'Book Review of F.R. Kraus *Königliche Verfügungen in altbabylonischer Zeit*', *BSO(A)S* 51 (1988), pp. 119-20, who notes that the reform texts of Urukagina are the closest thing from ancient Mesopotamia to the OB *mēšarum* edicts. For a discussion of the practical application of Urukagina's proclamation, see Edzard, 'Social Reformen', pp. 145-56, esp. 145-49, 155-56.

4. Cf. Mendelsohn, *Slavery in the Ancient Near East*, pp. 75-76, who mentions a case in which a free man called Warad-Bunene (First Dynasty of Babylon) escaped after being sold into a foreign country by his creditor. Upon his return the elders of the city tried to force him to serve in the army, but he was released in accordance to LH §280, which forbids the sale of native-born slaves into foreign countries and guarantees his freedom. However, Mendelsohn suggests that he should have been freed in accordance with LH §117, which limits the time of service to three years for pledges. Mendelsohn concludes, therefore, that LH §117 was merely 'a pious wish of the well-meaning lawgiver'(p. 76).

The Distraint and Voluntary Surrender or Sale of Dependents in LH

The laws in LH §§114-116 concern the taking of human distraints by a creditor, while those in §§117-119 concern the voluntary sale or surrender of dependents by a debtor. Both groups of laws envisage the defaulting of a *ḫubullûm* loan, which is defined by Driver and Miles[1] as an 'advance for some commercial purpose such as a loan of money or grain to enable a farmer to sow his land for the following harvest'. The fact that the *ḫubullûm* loans were given to farmers suggests strongly that those laws dealing with this type of loan transaction applied to landed free men (*awīlum*; cf. LH §48 which refers specifically to a landed farmer). This conclusion is further supported by the presence of laws restricting the taking of an ox or grain as a pledge (LH §§113, 241; cf. also *PRU* III: 101 [Ugarit]; ARM VII [Mari]). The creditor in these laws is called the *tamkārum* 'merchant', whom Driver and Miles[2] define as a 'typical money-lender'. As we saw in Chapter 2, various people engaged in lending, including free-citizens of the private sector, priests and officials (including the *tamkārum*) of the temple and palace households.

The *ḫubullûm* loans were usually in grain (LH §48), silver (LH §§A, M), silver or grain (LH §§L, N-Q), dates and sesame.[3] However, there is a question whether there was any fixed time at which the loan and interest were to be repaid by the debtor to the creditor. While the amount of interest is mentioned in some contracts and legislation (cf. LH §L), most documents do not mention the amount of interest paid.[4] Further, in LH the duration of the loan and the time of its repayment together with the interest is fixed indefinitely (note that LH §L refers to the amount of interest charged, it does not indicate when the loan or interest was to be paid). Driver and Miles[5] suggest, therefore, that

1. Driver and Miles, *Babylonian Laws*, I, pp. 209-10.
2. Driver and Miles, *Babylonian Laws*, I, p. 210.
3. All of these were staple commodities by which the economy and inflation were judged.
4. Cp. LE §18A: 20-21, all of which mention the amount of interest paid.
5. Driver and Miles, *Babylonian Laws*, I, pp. 174-76; cp. Yaron, *The Laws of Eshnunna*, pp. 236ff., who suggests that in regards to LE §19, which does not mention the payment of interest, interest could have been collected at the beginning of the loan.

usually Babylonians and sometimes Assyrians paid a single sum of interest when the original loan was repaid. Thus in normal agricultural loans, which were the most common type of loans, the loan would run from seed-time to harvest and the interest would be paid when the original capital was repaid.[1] While the interest rates mentioned in LH are generally representative of the rates found in OB documents and in documents from other periods (cf. LH §L: 33.3% for loans of grain and 20% for loans of money; cf. also LE §§18A, 20-21), these rates did fluctuate depending on various socio-economic factors such as famine and economic instability.[2] Furthermore, it seems likely that in the ancient Near East interest was probably one of the principal causes of default, which could lead to the enslavement of dependents or of the debtors themselves.[3]

LH §§114-116[4]

[§114] 17-21 If a man has [a claim to] corn or silver against a man and has distrained his distraint (*ana niputim*), 22-25 for each distress he shall pay 1/3 maneh of silver.

[§115] 26-30 If a man has [a claim to] corn or silver against a man and has distrained his distraint 31-34 [and] the distress dies a natural death in the house of him who has taken him as his distrainor, 35-37 that lawsuit has not a claim.

[§116] 38-42 If the distress dies in the house of him who has taken his distrainor from striking him or from ill-treating [him], 43-50 the owner of the distress shall convict his creditor and, if [he is] a [free] man's son, his son shall be put to death or, if [he is] a [free] man's slave, he shall weigh 1/3 maneh of silver 51-53 and forfeits anything whatsoever that he has lent.

1. Cf. also Yaron, *The Laws of Eshnunna*, p. 242; cp. Mendelsohn, *Slavery in the Ancient Near East*, p. 25, who suggests that during the time of Hammurabi interest was paid by the month.

2. Cf. Driver and Miles, *Babylonian Laws*, I, pp. 176-77; Mendelsohn, *Slavery in the Ancient Near East*, pp. 25-26; Yaron, *The Laws of Eshnunna*, pp. 235, 241-43; Dandamayev, *Slavery in Babylonia*, p. 140.

3. Cf. Mendelsohn, *Slavery in the Ancient Near East*, pp. 23-33, esp. 23-24; cf. also D.I. Owen, ' "Death for Default" ', *MCAAS* 19 (1977), pp. 159-61, who notes an extreme case in which a defaulted loan resulted in the death of the debtor.

4. This translation is taken from Driver and Miles, *Babylonian Laws*, II, p.47.

Sections 114-116 deal with the taking of a human *nipûtum*[1] 'distraint' or 'pledge' who was apparently seized by the creditor when a loan was defaulted in order to compel the debtor to pay the loan.[2] In most cases the seizure (verb *nepûm*)[3] was a form of 'self-help',[4] although in some cases officials seized the distraint on behalf of the creditor. Aspects of this type of seizure is elucidated in many OB letters.[5] For example, a distraint is seized in one case by the *rēdûtum* 'sheriff and his men' (*CT* VIII 17c), and in another by the *šāpir mātim* 'commissioner of the land' (JRL 885). The distraint is usually taken to the creditor's house (JRL 893; *TCL* I 15; UET V 6) but in one case the distraint is taken to jail (Kish D 39). The detention of the distraint was not supposed to last long; in two cases the duration of incarceration was five days (*CT* XXIX 23; *TCL* I 15). However, in one case five months is mentioned (PBS VII 106), although this was considered an unreasonable amount of time. These later documents illustrate that the *nipûtum* 'distraint' who worked in the creditor's house did not pay the debt,[6] although the 'distraint' probably worked in the creditor's house

---

1. Cf. *nipûtu*, s. fem. in *CAD* 11/2, cols. 249-51.

2. Cf. Driver and Miles, *Babylonian Laws*, I, p. 210; Eichler, *Indenture at Nuzi*, p. 82; Goetze, *Laws of Eshnunna*, pp. 69-75; Yaron, *The Laws of Eshnunna*, pp. 246-47; B.S. Jackson and T.F. Watkins, 'Distraint in the Laws of Eshnunna and Hammurabi', in *Studi in onore di desare San Filippo*, V (ed. A. Giuffré; PFGUC, 96; Milan, 1984), pp. 411-19.

3. Cf. *CAD* 11/2, cols. 171-72.

4. Cf. Driver and Miles, *Babylonian Laws*, I, p. 210; Yaron, *Laws of Eshnunna*, pp. 163-64; F.R. Kraus, *Königliche Verfügungen in altbabylonischer Zeit* (SDOAP, XI; Leiden: Brill, 1984), pp. 277-78.

5. For a discussion of these letters and their contents, see Goetze, *Laws of Eshnunna*, pp. 69-72; cf. also *CAD* 11/2, cols. 170-72, 249-51.

6. Cf. PBS 7 106: 23; 35ff. (*CAD* 11/2, col. 250), which reads: 'send (fem.) the woman, the distress, I will send you the barley—(during the time) I have been holding the woman, the distress from him (he has not sent the barley)... (let the judges order PN) to send the barley and I will send him the woman in distress for him, *for five months I have provided the distress with food, should I release the distress to one who did not bring the barley?*'. Cf. also Yaron, *Laws of Eshnunna*, pp. 246-47; Goetze, *Laws of Eshnunna*, pp. 69-73; and Jackson and Watkins, 'Distraint in the Laws of Eshnunna and Hammurabi', pp. 417-18, who also note the importance of PBS 106 in the interpretation of the institution of the *nipûtum*; cp. Driver and Miles, *Babylonian Laws*, I, p. 210.

in order to pay maintenance and additional interest accrued on the overdue loan.[1]

However, in other documents distraints are seized as pledges who perform substitute work for people under work obligations, although these cases are clearly different from loan transactions.[2] Furthermore, Finet[3] and Kraus[4] suggest that the institution of the *nipûtum* was similar to the institution of the *kiššātum*, a method by which a creditor obtained satisfaction of the debt by forcing the debtor or members of the debtor's family to work in the creditor's house.[5] Therefore, Kraus[6] suggests that in certain cases a *nipûtum* 'distraint' was seized by a creditor and forced to work in order to pay the debt, although the extant documents do not illustrate such a practice clearly. However, if such a method of payment was envisaged in the institution of the *nipûtum*, the question remains as to why such a practice is demonstrated clearly in the institution of the *kiššātum* but not in the institution of the *nipûtum* —viz., was it an accepted norm (customary or legal) for creditors to seize 'distraints' (i.e., self-help) and force them to work in their house (as with the *kiššātum*)?

In an attempt to clarify the institution of the *nipûtum*, Jackson and Watkins[7] suggest that although the *nipûtum* did work in the house of the creditor in order to pay maintenance and the accumulated interest on the loan, the distraint most likely did not work off the capital and initial interest. They suggest, therefore, that the institution of the *nipûtum* was less rigorous than the transfer *ana kiššātim* or sale *ana kaspim*, both of which I will discuss in greater detail below. Based on

1. Cf. Jackson and Watkins, 'Distraint in the Laws of Eshnunna and Hammurabi', pp. 418-19.

2. Cf. *CAD* 11/2, cols. 250-51; 271-72; and Goetze, *Laws of Eshnunna*, pp. 70, 73.

3. A. Finet, 'Le "Gage" et la "sujetion" (*nipûtum* et *kiššatum*) dans les Textes de Mari et le Code de Hammurabi', *Akkadica* 8 (1978), pp. 12-18.

4. Kraus, *Königliche Verfügungen*, pp. 266-77.

5. Cf. also R. Harris, 'The Archive of the Sin Temple in Khafajah (Tutub) (Conclusion)', *JCS* 9 (1955), p. 98.

6. Kraus, *Königliche Verfügungen*, pp. 275-76; cf. also Driver and Miles, *Babylonian Laws*, I, p. 210; and Yaron, *Laws of Eshnunna*, p. 247, who suggests nevertheless that such a method of repayment would have been impractical in cases where a large debt was accrued.

7. Jackson and Watkins, 'Distraint in the Laws of Eshnunna and Hammurabi', pp. 409-19.

the available evidence, therefore, it appears that *nipûtum* was only used by the creditor to force the debtor to pay the loan. Nevertheless, as Kraus[1] points out, much of the difficulty in understanding the various institutions (e.g., *nipûtum, kiššātum*) lies in understanding the creditor–debtor relationship, something about which the extant documents give no more information.

Although it is clear that the creditor had the right to secure a distraint in order to force a debtor to pay the loan, both LH and LE include sample cases in which creditors were restricted in their power over debtors in regard to the payment of loans and the taking of a *nipûtum* 'distraint'. For example, LH §48 stipulates that if a debtor should lose a crop on account of heavy rain or floods, the debtor does not have to pay the interest for that year, although it is assumed that the debtor is still liable for the principal.[2] Furthermore, LH forbids a creditor from taking an ox (§241) as a *nipûtum* 'distraint', although it does allow the creditor to take a dependent of the debtor (§§115-116).[3] However, a creditor was not allowed to ill-treat a *nipûtum* 'distraint'. For example, in LH §116 it stipulates that if a creditor kills a distraint the creditor's own son is to be put to death. The phrase *bêl nipûtim* 'owner of the distress' in §116 l.43 indicates that the distraint is still the property of the debtor. Similarly, LE §23 stipulates that if a slave woman dies in the house of a creditor, who has legally distrained her but who nonetheless did not release her when the debt was paid, the creditor shall give as replacement two slave women to the owner of the slave woman.[4] Further, in LE §24 it stipulates that if creditors

---

1. Kraus, *Königliche Verfügungen*, p. 277.
2. Cf. Driver and Miles, *Babylonian Laws*, I, pp. 144-45. While the previous sections §§45-48 concern a farmer who tills another's land (Bab. *irrīšum*), §48 refers to an *awīlum*, in order that the law should apply to those who till their own land (p. 144).
3. Cf. Driver and Miles, *Babylonian Laws*, I, pp. 208-209; cf. also Szlechter, 'Les Lois d'Eshnunna', pp. 213-19, who suggests that there are three types of distraint dealt with in LH: LH §§115-119 deals with 'saisie légale'; LH §113 deals with 'saisie arbitraire'; and LH §114 deals with 'saisie illégale'. However, Jackson and Watkins, 'Distraint in the Laws of Eshnunna and Hammurabi', pp. 411-14, suggest that LH §113 does not deal with the institution of *nipûtum* but with the illegal seizure of corn in *satisfaction* of the loan. This accounts for the absence of the verb *nepûm* or the noun *nipûtum* in this stipulation.
4. Cf. E. Szlechter, 'La saisie illégale dans les lois d'Ešnunna et dans le code de Hammurabi', in *Studi in Onore di P. De Francisci*, I (Milan, 1956), pp. 273-74 (see

kill the distress (the wife or son of a *muškênum*)[1] in their house then their lives are forfeit (talion). In this case the creditors forfeit their own lives, which is different from LH §116 which only requires vicarious substitution. However, the two cases are dissimilar in that while LH §116 concerns the lawful distraint of a person, LE §24 deals with the unlawful distraint of a person.[2] Lastly, MAL A §48 states that a creditor is not allowed to give in marriage a daughter of a debtor who is dwelling as a pledge (Bab. *ki ḫubulli*) without the consent of the debtor. Since this loan is a *ḫubullûm* loan, the woman is being held in distraint by the creditor until the debt is paid by the debtor.[3]

Many aspects of the above stipulations are reflected in several OB letters, although it must be stressed that, while the above laws were carried out in some cases, the existence of such stipulations suggest that creditors often ill-treated distraints. One letter, for example, mentions that persons who are not the debtor's full property are not to be seized (VAS XVI 41), though members of the family of the debtor can be seized. However, it appears that persons whose services were vital could not be seized (*CT* XXIX 23). Similarly, the creditor was prevented from taking property that was deemed essential to the existence of the debtor and the debtor's family (cf. also Deut 24.6, 12-13; cp. Job. 24.3 in which an ox is taken as a pledge).[4]

more recently Szlechter, 'Les Lois d'Eshnunna', pp. 215-19); and W. von Soden, 'Kleine Beiträge zum Verständnis der Gesetze Hammurabis und Bilalamas', *ArOr* 17 (1949), p. 370; cf. also Cardellini, *Die biblischen 'Sklaven'-Gesetze*, pp. 52-54. Cp. Yaron, *Laws of Eshnunna*, pp. 275-78, who suggests that Szlechter's view is too narrow and that the case in question simply deals with an illegal distraint.

1. The identity of the *muškênum* is still unclear. For a discussion of this term in LE and LH, see Yaron, *Laws of Eshnunna*, pp. 132-46; cf. also Szlechter, 'La saisie illégale dans les lois d'Ešnunna', pp. 215-19.

2. Cf. Yaron, *The Laws of Eshnunna*, p. 267.

3. Cf. G.R. Driver and C.J. Miles, *The Assyrian Laws* (Oxford: Clarendon Press, 1935), pp. 277-79; G. Cardascia, *Les lois assyriennes: introduction, traduction, commentaire* (LAPO, 2; Paris: Cerf, 1969), pp. 237-38.

4. Cf. Driver and Miles, *Babylonian Laws*, I, p. 215; Yaron, *Laws of Eshnunna*, pp. 246-47.

LH §§117-119[1]

[§117] 54-60 If a liability has become due against a man and he has sold (Bab. *ana kaspim*) his wife his son or his daughter or bound [them, or each of them, or himself] (Bab. *it-ta-an-di-in*) over into servitude (Bab. *ana kiššātim*), 61-67 for 3 years they shall do work in the house of him who has bought them or taken them in servitude; in the fourth year their release shall be reestablished.

[§118] 68-70 If he gives a slave or a slave-girl who was bound over into servitude, 71-72 the merchant shall let [the period of redemption] expire [and] shall sell [him]; 73 he or she cannot be [re]claimed.

[§119] 74-79 If an obligation becomes due against a man and he sells (the services of?) his slave-girl who has borne him children, the owner of the slave-girl may pay the money that the merchant has given [for her] and thus shall redeem his slave-girl.

The laws in LH §§117-119 differ from those in §§114-116, which deal with the taking of a distraint, in that here the debtor raises money to pay a foreclosed loan by selling or surrendering a dependent.[2] As we saw above, the creditor in §§114-116 had the option to take a distress without court approval. Furthermore, the creditor also had the option to arrest the debtors who therefore had to pay the debt or be imprisoned. This latter option was widely exercised during the MB and NB periods, when debtors who were unable to pay a loan could be placed in 'prisons' or 'workhouses', owned by the state, temple and the wealthy private persons in order to work off their debts.[3] In order to prevent such circumstances from occurring debtors apparently had the option of selling either a wife, child (§117) or slave (§119) *ana kaspim* 'for money' or surrendering them (§117) *ana kiššātim* 'into control' or 'bondage'. In these stipulations the *tamkārum* 'merchant', to whom the debtor sells or surrenders dependents, probably is not the original creditor, but there is no reason why the original creditor could not accept such a transaction.[4]

---

1. This translation is based on one given by D.J. Wiseman in private correspondence.

2. For a discussion of these laws, see Driver and Miles, *Babylonian Laws*, I, pp. 217-21; Cardellini, *Die biblischen 'Sklaven'-Gesetze*, pp. 79-80; Cardascia, *Les lois assyriennes*, p. 297.

3. Cf. Driver and Miles, *Babylonian Laws*, I, p. 216 and n. 8; Dandamayev, *Slavery in Babylonia*, pp. 159-64.

4. Cf. Driver and Miles, *Babylonian Laws*, I, p. 217; cf. also R. Yaron, 'Redemption of Persons in the Ancient Near East', *RIDA* 6 (1959), pp. 158-59; and

While it is clear that this stipulation envisages the amortization of the debt by the service rendered by the dependents (*Kapitalantichrese*), it is not clear whether the two transactions *ana kaspim* or *ana kiššātim* originally envisaged this method of payment. For example, the transaction *ana kaspim* was commonly used for the sale of various items, including property and slaves, and envisaged the transfer of these from the seller to the buyer. Further, we saw above that in the case of the institution of the *kiššātum* a creditor was able to force a defaulting debtor, or a member of the debtor's family, to serve in the creditor's house in order to pay the debt. The institution of the *kiššātim* was also employed by the court as punishment for criminal offenses, such as theft.[1] In contrast to the institution of the *niputum*, the creditor could force the debtor into debt-slavery, although I will argue below that LH §117 most likely does not envisage this. However, there is some question whether the *kiššātum* was a mere pledge, who worked for the debt, or whether the creditor took possession of the *kiššātum*, since LH §118 states that the debtor had only a limited period of time to redeem a slave surrendered to the creditor. Various interpretations have been proposed concerning the relationship between the *ana kaspim* and *ana kiššātim* transactions. To these interpretations we now turn.

For example, on the basis of the stipulation in §119, Driver and Miles[2] suggest that when debtors sell slaves *ana kaspim* they are not able to redeem the slaves once this transaction is completed. However, on the basis of the stipulation in §118, they suggest that when debtors sell slaves *ana kiššātim*, an expression that occurs only in §§117-118, debtors retain the right of redemption for a limited period of time, after which the slaves become the property of their creditors (cf. §118). They suggest that this transaction was something more than a mere pledge or mortgage, especially in the light of the meaning of the root verb *kašāšu* 'to overpower, have mastery over' (cf. also *kiššūtu* s. 'power', 'might'; 'totality'), which suggests that the noun denotes

---

Eichler, *Indenture at Nuzi*, pp. 81-83, who suggests that an ordinance from A-s demonstrates that such an arrangement can be made with the original creditor. I discuss this *mīšarum* edict in more detail below.

1. Cf. *CAD* 8, col. 286 (vb. *kašāšu*).

2. Driver and Miles, *Babylonian Laws*, I, pp. 212-14; cf. also Yaron, 'Redemption of Persons', pp. 157-59.

primarily mastery, control or subjection. However, Driver and Miles do not appear to be clear about whether these limitations were originally applicable in the case of the sale or surrender of a wife, son or daughter. On the one hand, they suggest that the period of redemption also applied to a wife, son or daughter in the *ana kiššātim* transaction. On the other, they suggest that since the wife, son or daughter could not be sold by the creditor, both transactions envisaged the payment of the debt through the service of the dependents. Therefore, Driver and Miles[1] suggest that both the *kiššātum* in LH §117 and the *nipûtum* who is seized in §116 worked off the debt in the creditor's house (i.e., the debtor sells only the services of any dependents). However, as we saw above, it is doubtful that LH envisaged the payment of the debt by a *nipûtum* 'distraint'.

Similarly, Szlechter[2] suggests that when a debtor 'sells' *ana kaspim* a wife, son or daughter to a creditor, the creditor would normally have the power to keep them as possessions. However, Szlechter, in contrast to Driver and Miles, suggests that in the case where debtors 'surrender' *ana kiššātim* family members the debtors would *only* have the right to redeem them for an agreed period of time, after which they would become the property of the creditor. Szlechter therefore suggests that LH §117 was written specifically to curb the power of the creditor in taking family members or certain slaves (cf. §119) of the debtor as permanent possessions.

However, Meek[3] proposes a totally different interpretation for the expression *ana kaspim* in LH §117. He suggests that this expression does not refer to the sale of the person but only to the sale of that person's capacity to work (*Arbeitskraft*)—viz., the creditor is not in possession of the person but only of the person's service.[4] Furthermore, Meek[5] suggests that the expression *ana kiššātim* refers

---

1. Driver and Miles, *Babylonian Laws*, I, pp. 210-11, 17; cf. also Eichler, *Indenture at Nuzi*, p. 83, who suggests that a *kiššātum* worked off the debt.

2. E. Szlechter, 'L'affranchissement en droit suméro-akkadien', *RIDA* 1 (1952), pp. 145-46, 162.

3. T.J. Meek, 'A New Interpretation of the Code of Hammurabi §§117-119', *JNES* 7 (1948), pp. 180-83.

4. Cf. also Cardellini, *Die biblischen 'Sklaven'-Gesetze*, p. 80, who appears to favour the position of Meek but who suggests nevertheless that debt-slaves played the role of guarantees.

5. Meek, 'Code of Hammurabi §§117-119', pp. 181-83.

to the debtor who 'has been bound over to service' *it-ta-an-di-in*,[1] and not to the surrender of the debtor's dependents. He suggests that both expressions must refer to the same type of service since the stipulation requires the same length of service. However, this interpretation is not convincing for the following reasons. First, there is no evidence to suggest that the expression *ana kaspim* should be understood to refer to anything other than an outright sale.[2] Secondly, the use of two different expressions *ana kaspim* and *ana kiššātim* in a law that stipulates the same length of service is adequately accounted for by the suggestion that the three-year release was a reform, as Szlechter correctly points out. Thirdly, both of these transactions are mentioned specifically in A-s §20, which stipulates that debtors who give themselves, their wives or their sons for *kaspim* 'money', for *kiššātim* 'surrender' or as a *mazzāzānu*-pledge were to be released. While this stipulation confirms that in practice debtors often handed themselves

---

1. Meek suggests that the verb *it-ta-an-di-in* (from the verb *nadanum* 'to give') in LH §117, l.60 is to be rendered passively (preterite/N-Stem): 'he (debtor) has been bound'. Similarly, Lambert, 'Book Review', p. 119, suggests that the verb is to be rendered reciprocally (preterite/N-Stem): 'he has bound himself'; cf. also A. Finet, *Le Code de Hammurabi: introduction, traduction et annotation* (LAPO, 6; Paris: 2nd edn, Cerf, 1983), p. 79, who suggests this verb is a (Gtn) preterite with distributive force. However, Driver and Miles, *Babylonian Laws*, I, pp. 206-207; and Kraus, *Königliche Verfügungen*, p. 266 n. 415, suggest that the verb *it-ta-an-di-in* should be rendered actively (perfect/Basic-Stem) 'he bound [them]'; cf. also TUAT I/1.56. That the latter view is to be preferred over the former two is suggested by the following observations. First, while the transcription *ittadin* is possible for the perfect/ Basic-Stem, due to the influence of the determinative *-ta-*, *ta* (*i(n)ttadin*), there is no example, as far as I am aware, that the transcription *ittadin* can be a preterite/N-Stem, since the proper form would be *innadin*, following the paradigm for the verb *iššakin* (*šakanum*; cf. paradigm 21 in K.K. Riemschneider, *Lehrbuch des Akkadischen* (Leipzig: VEB Verlag Enzyklopädie, 1984)). Second, there are examples where the protasis of a conditional sentence contains a preterite (main condition) followed by a perfect (sub-case). The second verb (perfect) is a consecutive which takes the tense of the main verb (preterite; cf. §9.1 in Riemschneider, *Lehrbuch des Akkadischen*). This construction also appears to occur in LH §117 ll.54-60, which reads: (54) *šum-ma a-wi-lam* (55) *e-ḫi-il-tum* (56) *iṣ-ba-sù-ma* [*preterite*]... (60) *it-ta-an-di-in* [*perfect*]. While this interpretation suffers from the lack of an expressed object in the second condition, the fact that the second verb (perfect) is a consecutive suggests that the object is inferred from the main clause (i.e., them—wife, son or daughter).

2. Cf. Kraus, *Ein Edikt*, p. 170.

over to creditors,[1] it also shows that debtors can give themselves over for *kaspim* or *kiššātim*. Therefore, if LH §117 envisaged the latter case (*ana kaspim*) why did it not also envisage the former (*ana kiššātim*)?[2] Fourthly, LH never refers to the forced seizure of the debtor as a *nipûtum* 'distraint', although in one OB document[3] a debtor is seized as a distraint, and as we saw above, if the debtor was not able to pay the loan the creditor could go to court and have the debtor imprisoned. Therefore, it is most likely that LH, contrary to normal practice, did not envisage either the seizure or the sale/surrender of the debtor (i.e., the head of the household) since the debtor's freedom was essential to the well-being of the family.[4]

Recapitulating, when a debtor sells *ana kaspim* 'for money' a slave to a creditor, the creditor takes absolute possession of the slave.[5] Furthermore, it is likely that in this transaction a creditor could take permanent possession of a wife, son or daughter. While a redemption clause was included in the conveyance (i.e., 'bill of sale') of several extant sale contracts (ana X KÙ.BABBAR 'for x silver')[6] and in many *šapartu* contracts (which I will discuss next), it is not clear that the same practice is envisaged in LH §§117-119. Nevertheless, it is likely

---

1. Cf. also Mendelsohn, *Slavery in the Ancient Near East*, pp. 14-16, who notes that self-sales are documented during the OB period (Rim-Sin, king of Larsa) and during the Ur III period (16); and Driver and Miles, *Babylonian Laws*, I, pp. 216-19.

2. Cf. Kraus, *Ein Edikt*, pp. 170-71, who suggests that neither expression refers to the sale of a person, or to the sale of a person's work capacity (*Arbeitskraft*), although he does not attempt to offer any explanation of his own

3. Cf. Driver and Miles, *Babylonian Laws*, I, p. 216.

4. Cf. Driver and Miles, *Babylonian Laws*, I, pp. 210, 16-17.

5. Cf. D.J. Wiseman, *The Alalakh Tablets* (Occasional publications of the British Institute of Archaeology at Ankar, 2; London: Biblical Institute of Archaeology at Ankar, 1953), Tablet 65.6f., which concerns the sale of a female slave. The text reads: (*ana kinuttūtu*): *ina andarārim ul inandar* 'In the liberty she shall not go out free'. This tablet coincides with A-s §20, which specifically exempted male and female slaves from release. Refer below to the discussion of the *mēšarum* edicts.

6. For example, see Cardellini, *Die biblischen 'Sklaven'-Gesetze*, pp. 93-101, who discusses several OB sale contracts; and B. Kienast, *Das Altassyrische Kaufvertragsrecht* (FAS, 1; Stuttgart: Franz Steiner Verlag, 1984), pp. 54-80, who discusses several OA texts that contain redemption clauses (e.g., #5A-B, 7, 8, 9, 12, 13A, 14, 16, 19, 21, 22, 28, 29); cf. also Cardellini, *Die biblischen 'Sklaven'-Gesetze*, 107-14.

that even if a redemption clause was included in the 'bill of sale' debtors often lacked the means to redeem their dependents. This is also true in the case when debtors surrendered (*ana kiššātim*) slaves, since they had only a limited period of time to redeem the slaves, after which they became the property of the creditor. Further, based upon the stipulations in LH §§117-118, it is likely that a similar transaction took place with the dependents of debtors, according to which if debtors did not redeem their dependents before the period of redemption ran out then the dependents would become the property of the creditor. While LH §117-119 probably envisaged the legal transfer of a *kiššātum* to a creditor, it should be noted that such a transaction cannot be substantiated in the extant documents. Nevertheless, according to LH the *ana kaspim* and *ana kiššātim* transactions are similar, since in both cases there was the possibility that debtors would never be able to redeem family member(s). LH §117, therefore, attempted to curb the power of the creditor in taking free persons as permanent possessions, limiting the period of service in either case (*ana kaspim* or *ana kiššātim*) to three years.[1] As I will show below, this law is very similar to the stipulations in A-s §§20-21,[2] which called for the release of debt-slaves who were sold *ana kaspim* or surrendered *ana kiššātim*. Lastly, the appearance of the release of debt-slaves in both A-s and LH §117 suggests an attempt to initiate the periodic release of debt-slaves, although, as I pointed out before, the presence of such a release in later *mîšarum* edicts after Hammurabi's reign suggests that his law was not put into practice.

The Treatment and Sale of Pledges in MAL

These laws deal with the treatment of human pledges who have either been acquired by the creditor after the foreclosure of a *šapartu* loan (A §44; G+C §7) or who are dwelling as pledges in a creditor's house

---

1. It should be noted that this law may have been a special case which had limited application. Nevertheless, I will argue that this law appears to have influenced the drafting of Exod. 21.2-6 (and Deut. 15.12-18), which envisaged the release of all debt-slaves.

2. This is noted by Bottéro, 'Désordre économique et annulation des dettes en Mésopotamie', p. 141; Korošec, 'Keilschriftrecht', pp. 117-18; Cardellini, *Die biblischen 'Sklaven'-Gesetze*, p. 80; and Kraus, *Königliche Verfügungen*, pp. 264-66, who considers LH §117 parallel to A-s §20.

(*Besitzpfand*; C §§2-3). However, in contrast to the *ḫubullûm* loan, in which a distraint was not seized until a loan was foreclosed by the debtor, in the MA *šapartu* loan contracts a *šapartu* 'pledge' was generally taken by the creditor at the commencement of a loan transaction as a substitute payment or security for a loan. Therefore, I will first discuss briefly the institution of the 'pledge' before I discuss the above laws.

The Role of the Pledge in the šapartu Loan Contracts

In a *šapartu* loan contract, the creditor took full possession of the *šapartu* 'pledge' at the beginning of the loan, as opposed to the stipulations of the *ḫubullûm* loan, under which the debtor had no obligation to return the capital but only possessed a right to redeem the pledge. The pledge, then, took on the full responsibility of the debt. After foreclosure of the loan the pledge would then become the creditor's property.[1] However, certain social and economic considerations probably forced a change in the pledging of persons, as evidenced in various laws in MAL, since they often remained in the possession of the creditors.

In the extant ancient Near Eastern documents, the pledging of movable property is rarely attested.[2] In one case, in which a large sum of silver is loaned, non-specific goods are pledged as security along with real estate and persons. While it is difficult to ascertain whether these pledges remained with the debtor or whether they were given to the creditor, due to the lack of specification the pledges were probably

1. For discussions of the function of a 'pledge' in the ancient Near East, see P. Koschaker, *Neue keilschriftliche Rechtsurkunden aus der el-Amarna-Zeit* (ASAWPHK, 5; Leipzig, 1928), pp. 96-131; H. Petschow, *Neubabylonisches Pfandrecht* (ASAW, 48; Berlin: Akademie Verlag, 1956), B. Kienast, 'Zum altbabylonischen Pfandrecht', *SZ* 83 (1966), pp. 334-38; *idem*, 'Bemerkungen zum altassyrischen Pfandrecht', *WO* 8 (1975/76), pp. 218-27; *idem*, *Das Altassyrische Kaufvertragsrecht*, pp. 77-80; cf. also Driver and Miles, *Assyrian Laws*, pp. 271-73; Korošec, 'Keilschriftrecht', pp. 194-95; Cardascia, *Les lois assyriennes*, pp. 302-303, 308-309; Eichler, *Indenture at Nuzi*, pp. 88-95; J.N. Postgate, *Fifty Neo-Assyrian Legal Documents* (Warminster: Aris & Phillips, 1976), pp. 47-54. Both Driver and Miles (p. 96) and Postgate (p. 52) explain that the word *šapartu* (*šaparum* 'to send') originally denoted a thing or person sent to the house of the creditor.

2. Cf. Postgate, *Neo-Assyrian Legal Documents*, p. 47, who mentions a rare case in which a donkey is pledged.

a *Generalhypothek*.[1] The absence of loans in which only movable property is pledged in ancient Near Eastern documents may indicate that property of this kind was not used, or that it was so used but not recorded. Postgate[2] adopts the latter explanation, pointing out that such property did not require any specific documentation to prove ownership.

On the other hand, the pledging of people is well attested in the documents of the ancient Near East. The pledged person was often a member of the debtor's family, or a slave of the household, although in some cases debtors pledged themselves.[3] According to the ancient Near Eastern documents, there were two methods by which the creditor could take possession of the human pledge. First, the pledge could be taken by the creditor at the moment the contract was completed in order to dwell and work in the creditor's house (possessory: *Besitzpfand*), most likely in order to pay the interest on the capital (*Zinsantichrese*).[4] This antichretic pledge would be released after the debtor paid the capital. Usually, no specific date of repayment of the capital is mentioned in the documents since the interest would be paid automatically by the service of the pledge. However, in other documents a specific period is mentioned at which time the capital would be paid back. If the capital was not paid at the agreed time the pledge could then become the property of the creditor. Secondly, the pledge could remain in the debtor's possession (hypothec) until the loan was foreclosed, at which time the pledge would be taken by the creditor.[5]

---

1. This mixed pledge (*Generalhypothek*) occurs in text #24 in Postgate, *Neo-Assyrian Legal Documents*, pp. 128-29. For a similar case of *Generalhypothek* (*KAJ* 66), see Eichler, *Indenture at Nuzi*, p. 89 and ns. 109, 114 .

2. Postgate, *Neo-Assyrian Legal Documents*, p. 47.

3. Cf. Driver and Miles, *Assyrian Laws*, p. 287; Kienast, 'Bemerkungen zum altassyrischen Pfandrecht', pp. 222-27; Postgate, *Neo-Assyrian Legal Documents*, pp. 48-49; Cardellini, *Die biblischen 'Sklaven'-Gesetze*, pp. 109-11; D. Arnaud, 'Humbles et superbes à Emar (Syrie) à la fin l'âge du Bronze récent', in *Mélanges bibliques et orientaux en l'honneur de M. Henri Cazelles* (ed. A. Caquot and M. Delcor; AOT, 212; Neukirchen–Vluyn: Neukirchener Verlag, 1981), pp. 11-12; and Dandamayev, *Slavery in Babylonia*, pp. 157-80, who notes that self-pledging by the debtor was considered illegal during the NB period.

4. Cf. Kienast, 'Bemerkungen zum altassyrischen Pfandrecht', p. 224; Eichler, *Indenture at Nuzi*, pp. 92-93; Postgate, *Neo-Assyrian Legal Documents*, p. 48.

5. Cf. Petschow, *Neubabylonisches Pfandrecht*, pp. 52ff.; Driver and Miles,

In both of the above cases, at the expiration of the set term the pledge is taken into possession by the creditor as payment for the loan.[1] While the hypothec is generally regarded as a later institution than the primitive *Besitzpfand*, both appear to have co-existed in most periods.[2] Furthermore, when the hypothec or *Besitzpfand* was taken by the creditor, a conveyance text ('bill of sale') was made out to record the transfer of ownership, especially when land or people were involved.[3] Nevertheless, when the pledge was a person the conveyance text often contained a redemption clause which stipulated that the debtor still had the right to redeem the pledge (*Lösungspfand*),[4] even

Assyrian Laws, p. 273; Kienast, 'Bemerkungen zum altassyrischen Pfandrecht', pp. 224-27; Postgate, *Neo-Assyrian Legal Documents*, pp. 47-53; Dandamayev, *Slavery in Babylonia*, pp. 137-40; cf. also Eichler, *Indenture at Nuzi*, pp. 88-95, who notes that the most common statement of pledging in the MA contracts is simply *ki šapartu* object PN *ukal*; e.g., 'PN (the creditor) holds/shall hold the object (real estate/person) as a pledge'. This sort of designation does not indicate whether the pledge was possessory or hypothecary, a situation that is present within many of the MA contracts (p. 89). However, as Eichler has demonstrated, in those documents that deal with the pledging of people (most of the MA documents deal with land pledges) the pledge remains in the possession of the debtor (hypothec).

1. Cf. Driver and Miles, *Assyrian Laws*, p. 272, n. 1; Eichler, *Indenture at Nuzi*, p. 89 n. 111; Postgate, *Neo-Assyrian Legal Documents*, p. 53.

2. The personal hypothec is attested during the OA, MA, and NB periods; cf. Kienast, 'Bemerkungen zum altassyrischen Pfandrecht', pp. 224-27; and Eichler, *Indenture at Nuzi*, pp. 88-95; Dandamayev, *Slavery in Babylonia*, pp. 138-39. The possessory antichretic pledge (*Besitzpfand*) is also attested during the OA, MA (especially land), NA (land and people), and NB (land and people) periods; cf. Kienast, 'Bemerkungen zum altassyrischen Pfandrecht', pp. 223-24; Eichler, *Indenture at Nuzi*, pp. 88-89; Dandamayev, *Slavery in Babylonia*, pp. 138-42; Postgate, *Neo-Assyrian Legal Documents*, pp. 51-53.

3. Cf. Postgate, *Neo-Assyrian Legal Documents*, pp. 11-55, who notes that it was essential to make out a conveyance text when transferring the ownership of persons or real estate (p. 11); cf. also Driver and Miles, *Assyrian Laws*, pp. 311-20, who discuss MAL Tablet B §6, which stipulates that that before any conveyance or transfer of land can take place a special proclamation must be given calling for any person who might hold a title to the land to come forward.

4. Such redemption clauses are attested in most periods; cf. J. Lewy, 'Old Assyrian Documents from Asia Minor (about 2000 BC)', *AHDO* 1 (1937), pp. 106-108, Yaron, 'Redemption of Persons', pp. 160-61, both of whom cite an OA document; Koschaker, *Neue keilschriftliche Rechtsurkunden*, pp. 106-107 (MA: *KAJ* 17, 28, 60, 70); Eichler, *Indenture at Nuzi*, pp. 88-95, who cites two MA documents involving people (*KAJ* 60, 17); Postgate, *Neo-Assyrian Legal*

when the pledge was sold to a third party.[1] When there was no redemption clause in the conveyance document the pledge became the permanent property of the creditor (*Verfallspfand*). Although Koschaker[2] could only find real estate pledge contracts of the *Verfallspfand* type during the MA period, he suggests that the same procedure could have been applied to personal pledges as well. He suggests that it is only by chance that such documents have not been found.[3] During the NA period, Postgate[4] suggests that pledge contracts of the *Verfallspfand* type probably applied only to slaves. However, during the NB period, Dandamayev[5] has shown that children who were used as pledges (security) could be enslaved. In one case, a boy who was taken by the creditor became a temple slave,

---

Documents, pp. 29, 53, who cites one NA document (*ARU* 631) that includes a redemption clause in a conveyance text for a slave woman (p. 29).

1. Cf. Koschaker, *Neue keilschriftliche Rechtsurkunden*, pp. 114-16; Postgate, *Neo-Assyrian Legal Documents*, p. 29.

2. Koschaker, *Neue keilschriftliche Rechtsurkunden*, pp. 102-104; cf. also Eichler, *Indenture at Nuzi*, p. 89 and ns. 109, 111; Cardascia, *Les lois assyriennes*, pp. 308-309; and Kienast, 'Bemerkungen zum altassyrischen Pfandrecht', pp. 226-27, who suggests that although immobile and human pledges (*erubātu*) are attested during the OA period, debtors most likely did not lose possession of these pledges. Cp. Mendelsohn, *Slavery in the Ancient Near East*, pp. 28-29, who suggests that *KAJ* 66 proves that personal pledges were seized by creditors as permanent property. However, it is not certain that this contract, which mentions several hypothecary pledges including a field, houses, threshing floor, wells or children of the debtors (ll. 17-22), specifically sanctions the unlimited seizure of people. Further, Postgate, *Neo-Assyrian Documents*, pp. 21, 26, 53, notes that one of the problems in ascertaining whether personal pledges became the permanent property of creditors was that a conveyance text without a redemption clause would be indistinguishable from a normal sale of slaves. It is, therefore, very hard to determine whether all personal pledges were redeemable after conveyance or whether some apparently normal sales of persons in fact represent irredeemable conveyances of pledges (p. 53). However, normal slave sales included mostly other slaves, while only a few cases of free people being sold are attested. In these cases, the circumstances surrounding the sale were exceptional (due to debt or famine) and were subject to annulment in both Babylonian and Assyrian times (i.e., *mīšarum* edicts; cf. pp. 21-22, 26).

3. Such a possibility appears to be envisaged in MAL A 44; C §3; G+C §7, which I discuss below.

4. Postgate, *Neo-Assyrian Legal Documents*, p. 53.

5. Dandamayev, *Slavery in Babylonia*, pp. 178-79.

a position from which he could not be redeemed or freed. Therefore, while permanent debt-slavery was most likely unacceptable during most periods it is clear that under certain circumstances a pledge could become the permanent possession of a creditor.[1] Nevertheless, even if a redemption clause was included in the conveyance, it was not certain that a debtor was able to redeem the family member or land.

Lastly, there are several examples in which land was pledged. In a number of MA *šapartu* loan contracts in which land was pledged, the land either remained in the possession of the debtor or was used by the creditor as an antichretic pledge. If the loan was foreclosed the land was then transferred to the creditor as a permanent possession (*Verfallspfand*).[2] In addition, there are a group of *šapartu* contracts which contain a redemption clause and also specify the creditor's right to use the pledge. In one text the land is cultivated for six years, during which time the interest for the capital is paid by the money earned from the land.[3] However, in two other texts the creditor's use of the land does not go towards the paying of the interest or the capital.[4] We may assume that in this case the creditor was taking advantage of the use of the pledged land.

MAL A §44[5]

[A §44] [40] If an Assyrian man, [41] or if an Assyrian woman, [42-43] who is dwelling in a man's house as a pledge for his value, has been taken (in discharge of the debt) up to the full value, [44] he may flog (him), he may pluck out (his hair), [45] he may bruise (and) bore his ears.

1. That creditors did not always follow legal precedent is demonstrated by the existence of pledge and distraint laws in the various ancient Near East legal collections; cf. Ziskind, 'Enslavement of the Native and Foreign Born', p. 163.

2. Cf. Koschaker, *Neue keilschriftliche Rechtsurkunden*, pp. 102-104; Kienast, 'Bemerkungen zum altassyrischen Pfandrecht', pp. 222-23; Eichler, *Indenture at Nuzi*, p. 89; J. Lewy, 'The Biblical Institution of *Derôr* in the Light of Akkadian Documents', *Eretz-Israel* 5 (1958), pp. 23-26. While the sale of property is discussed extensively in MAL, the use of land or real estate as a pledge is not mentioned. However, in LE §39 it states that if a man sells his house for a debt then whenever the creditor sells the house the debtor has the right to redeem it. Apparently, this stipulation also applied to any third parties who bought the house if the debtor could not afford to buy it at that time; cf. Yaron, *Laws of Eshnunna*, pp. 233-34; Goetze, *Laws of Eshnunna*, pp. 112-13.

3. *KAJ* 13, which is discussed by Eichler, *Indenture at Nuzi*, p. 94.

4. *KAJ* 21, 58, which are discussed by Eichler, *Indenture at Nuzi*, p. 94.

5. This translation is taken from Driver and Miles, *Assyrian Laws*, p. 413.

While LH restricts its treatment of distraints to the dependents of free-men or women, A §44 deals with the pledging and subsequent foreclosure of a free Assyrian man or woman (*aššurāyau, aššurāyitu*), generally considered members of a lower social class (plebeian), compared to the *mar awīli* of the upper class (patrician).[1] Nevertheless, according to C §3, citizens of the patrician class were also pledged, although Cardascia[2] suggests that the pledging of members of the lower social classes was more common. In A §44 it is not clear whether the Assyrian has pledged himself or whether he (or she) has been pledged by a family member. Driver and Miles suggest that the compiler was only interested in the treatment of the pledge who has been acquired by the creditor, although both options are envisaged elsewhere—i.e. the former option is envisaged in A §§39, 48 and in several Assyrian contracts, while the latter is attested in texts from Arrapha.[3]

At the end of the protasis in A §44 l.43 it states that the pledge, who was living in the house of the creditor, 'has been taken (in discharge of the debt) up to the full value'. As Driver and Miles[4] have shown, the expression *ana šīm gamir* 'for the full value' signifies that the pledge has definitely become the possession of the creditor after the debtor failed to return the amount of the loan by the agreed period. However, Cardascia[5] has pointed out correctly that it is difficult to say whether this law envisaged the permanent enslavement of the pledge (*Verfallspfand*) or whether there was a redemption clause included in the conveyance (*Lösungspfand*). Nevertheless, that a *Verfallspfand*

---

1. Driver and Miles, *Assyrian Laws*, pp. 284-85, 326-27, who follow Koschaker, note that the same distinction is found in documents from Assur, which are also discussed by Cardascia, *Les lois assyriennes*, p. 216; and Cardellini, *Die biblischen 'Sklaven'-Gesetze*, p. 197; cp. A. van Praag, *Droit matrimonial assyro-babylonien* (Amsterdam, 1945), pp. 68-70, 72, who wavers between viewing these people as either foreigners or members of a lower social class. That the Assyrian was a member of the lower social class is demonstrated by the fact that in MAL A §24 the Assyrian who harbours a fugitive wife is qualified by the expression *awīlu*. Further, in MAL C §3 the Assyrian appears in contrast to a *mar awīli*.

2. Cardascia, *Les lois assyriennes*, p. 216.

3. Cf. Driver and Miles, *Assyrian Laws*, p. 287 and n. 3; Cardascia, *Les lois assyriennes*, p. 216.

4. Driver and Miles, *Assyrian Laws*, pp. 287-88; cf. also Cardascia, *Les lois assyriennes*, p. 216.

5. Cardascia, *Les lois assyriennes*, p. 217.

contract is probably envisaged in this case is suggested by the fact that in C §3 it states that the creditor may sell an Assyrian to a foreign land, from where it would have been almost impossible to redeem him.[1] The status of the Assyrian, therefore, was probably similar to the status of a chattel-slave in LH §§117-118, who after being sold (*ana kaspim*) for a debt becomes the property of the creditor.

Lastly, this law stipulates that when a creditor takes possession of Assyrian pledges the creditor is permitted to scourge them, pluck out their hair and bruise and pierce their ears.[2] Although this sort of treatment seems harsh according to modern standards, Driver and Miles[3] note that the creditor is afforded the same rights that a husband has over his wife (cf. MAL Tablet A §59). Further, since these restrictions were legislated it follows that the creditor was not allowed to mutilate or put to death the pledge.[4]

However, Lewy[5] has proposed a slightly different interpretation for this stipulation. He writes:[6]

> ...in the Middle Assyrian legislation [A §44]...the acquisition of absolute property depends on payment of the full price: Obviously aware of the fact that, as a rule, the value of a pledge is greater than the sum owed but not paid by a defaulting debtor, the Assyrian legislator took

---

1. Cf. Driver and Miles, *Assyrian Laws*, p. 326; Cardellini, *Die biblischen 'Sklaven'-Gesetze*, p. 197; cp. Cardascia, *Les lois assyriennes*, p. 217, who suggests that if the creditor acquired the pledge through the 'courts' the creditor probably would have had to allow for the pledger's redemption; and M. David, 'Eine Bestimmung über das Verfallspfand in den mittelassyrischen Gesetzen', *BO* 9 (1952), pp. 170-71, who suggests that it is not certain that a pledge could become the permanent property of a creditor.

2. Cf. Driver and Miles, *Assyrian Laws*, p. 286; Cardascia, *Les lois assyriennes*, p. 217; Cardellini, *Die biblischen 'Sklaven'-Gesetze*, pp. 195-97. Note that in NA documents when a person is pledged (MA: *ana šaparti šakānu* 'a pledge is delivered') the verb *šakānu* 'to deliver' is replaced by the NA verb *kammusu* 'to dwell', which is the meaning intended in MAL Tablet A §§ 39, 44 . Concerning the use of the verb *kammusu*, see Postgate, *Neo-Assyrian Legal Documents*, p. 48.

3. Driver and Miles, *Assyrian Laws*, p. 286; cf. also Cardascia, *Les lois assyriennes*, p. 217; *idem*, 'Les valeurs morales dans le droit assyrien', in Harmatta and Komoróczy (eds.), *Wirtschaft und Gesellschaft*, pp. 363-72.

4. Cf. Driver and Miles, *Assyrian Laws*, p. 289, who cite the view of P. Koschaker.

5. Lewy, 'The Biblical Institution of Derôr', p. 26 and ns. 48-49.

6. Lewy, 'The Biblical Institution of Derôr', p. 26.

special care to withhold from the person in whose house an Assyrian man or woman was living as a forfeited pledge the power to inflict severe corporal punishment on him or her until payment of his or her 'full price'. By the same token, only those Assyrian men and women who had been 'taken', i.e. bought, 'at the full price' could be sold abroad [MAL C §3]. A buyer who pays the full price indicates therefore that he wishes to acquire absolute property of the object to be transferred to him, just as the seller's acceptance of the full price implies his willingness to part with his property once and for all. In other words, sales contracts relating to payment of the full price appear to concern sellers resolved not to recover their former property.

The above interpretation relies on the assumption that MAL A §44 envisages only the intent of the creditor to acquire the Assyrian pledge rather than the actual transfer of property, something that is almost impossible to demonstrate from the context of the law itself. Nevertheless, it appears that Lewy's suggestion is to be preferred over those above, since it is questionable whether creditors would harm or damage property that they would need to sell in order to reclaim their capital, as envisaged in MAL C §3. Therefore, the debtor who transferred property 'at the full price' had no right of redemption— the pledge is therefore a *Verfallspfand*.[1] A similar principle of absolute transfer apparently existed when a person, who sold property 'at the full price', did not have right of redemption. According to Westbrook,[2] the only type of land sales that included any *right* of redemption were sales that were below the full market price (cf. LE §39), which were common among people who were forced to sell their land on account of insolvency.

MAL C §§2-3[3]

[C. face: §2] 8-9 [If a man has sold] to another man for (a sum of) money
[a man] or lady by birth who is dwelling [in his house] as (security for)

---

1. Cf. also Eichler, *Indenture at Nuzi*, p. 75 n. 34, who suggests that Wiseman, *The Alalakh Tablets* *53 'seems to attest the Mesopotamian legal principle that the absolute acquisition of property depends on payment of the full price' (citing Lewy, 'The Biblical Institution of Derôr', p. 26).

2. R. Westbrook, 'The Price Factor in the Redemption of Land', *RIDA* 32 (1985/86), pp. 97-127; cp. Yaron, *Laws of Eshnunna*, pp. 232-33, who, in objection to Westbrook's thesis, notes that determining what is below 'normal' price is not so simple as it looks.

3. This translation is taken from Driver and Miles, *Assyrian Laws*, pp. 324-25.

money or as [a pledge, 10 or] has sold [any one else] who is dwelling in his house 11 (and) [charge has been brought against him], he shall forfeit his money; 12 he shall give his equivalent [according to his price] to the owner of the (person who is his) property, 13 he shall be beaten [x blows with a rod] and do labour for the king for 20 days.

[C. face: §3] 14-15 [If a man] has sold into another country for (a sum of) money [either a man] or a lady by birth [who is dwelling in his house] as (security for) money or as a pledge, 16 (and) [charge] (and) proof have been brought against him, he shall forfeit his money; 17 he shall give [his equivalent according to his price to] the owner of the (person who is his) property; 18 he shall be beaten [x blows with a rod] and do labour for the king for 40 days. 19 [If the man whom he has sold] has died in the other country, 20 [he shall pay (on principle of) a life (for a life)]. An Assyrian man or an Assyrian woman 21 [who] has been taken [at the full price] (in discharge of the debt) may be sold into another country.

The laws in MAL C §2-3, which form part of a general discussion of pledging in C + G §§1-11,[1] stipulate that a creditor was not allowed to sell a male or female patrician (*mār awīli* and *mārat awīli*)[2] who is dwelling with him *kī kaspi* 'for money' or *kī šaparti* 'as a pledge'. As long as the loan was not foreclosed the pledge remained the property of the debtor, since the creditor did not have the right to sell him or her to another man (§2) or to a foreigner (§3). However, it is not easy to establish the difference in meaning between the two expressions *kī kaspi* and *kī šaparti*. To the interpretation of these two expressions we now turn.

Driver and Miles[3] suggest that the phrase *kī šaparti* means that a person is pledged and taken into the creditor's house in order to work until the debt is paid or until he (or she) is redeemed by the debtor. Furthermore, they suggest that the expression *kī kaspi* is parallel to the phrase *ana kaspim* in LH §117, according to which a person who is sold to a creditor is released after serving three years. While they note that MAL does not stipulate a limited period of service, nevertheless they suggest that the Assyrians may also have set a limit on the period of service, since creditors could not sell pledges, and because it states that a creditor could sell an Assyrian (plebeian) to a foreign country from where redemption would be impossible.

1. Cf. Cardascia, *Les lois assyriennes*, pp. 297-315.
2. For a discussion of these expressions, see Driver and Miles, *Assyrian Laws*, pp. 324-25.
3. Driver and Miles, *Assyrian Laws*, pp. 323-24; cf. also pp. 272-73.

However, certain aspects of Driver and Miles's interpretation are not convincing, for the following reasons. First, based upon the discussion of the *šapartu* loan above, there is no indication that a *šapartu* 'pledge' dwelling with a creditor (*Besitzpfand*) worked off the entire debt, but only the interest on the capital (*Zinsantichrese*). Furthermore, G+C §7, which I will discuss in more detail below, assumes that the pledge was antichretic. Secondly, while Driver and Miles assume correctly that the presence of this stipulation at the end of C §3 concerning the sale of an Assyrian (from A §44) demonstrates that patrician pledges are redeemable, nevertheless they appear to confuse the role of a *šapartu* 'pledge', who is taken at the beginning of the debt, with the role of a *šapartu* 'pledge' who has been taken after the foreclosure of a loan (A §44).

Cardascia,[1] who has also noted the difficulties with the interpretation of Driver and Miles, has proposed two different solutions. First, he suggests that the expression *kī kaspi* can be understood to express a temporary transfer of a free person, who did not serve as security for a loan, to a creditor who used the free person's services. Cardascia suggests that this was a sort of 'business transaction' which allowed a person to realize a profit by transferring the services of one person to another. Secondly, he suggests that the expression *kī kaspi* in C §§2-3 was quite possibly understood as a synonym of the expression *kī ḥubullī* in A §48. He suggests that the stipulation in A §48, which concerns the seizure of a distraint or pledge, is similar conceptually to the taking of a *šapartu* 'pledge'. Therefore, the author of C §§2-3 viewed, 'indifféremment les cas de saisie et d'engagement: dès lors, *kī šaparti*, expression spécifique, viendrait inutilement après *kī kaspi*, expression générique'.

Recapitulating, as the above discussion shows it is not easy to establish the difference in meaning between the two expressions *kī kaspi* and *kī šaparti*. While the meaning of the expression *kī kaspi* may remain a moot point, although the suggestions offered by Cardascia appear the most cogent, it is clear nevertheless that the expression *kī šaparti* refers to the pledging of a person at the beginning of a loan, who then serves in the house of the creditor, presumably in order to pay the interest on the capital. However, it is not entirely clear why the stipulation concerning the sale of an

1. Cardascia, *Les lois assyriennes*, p. 297.

Assyrian (A §44) is appended at the end of C §3. Although Cardascia does not accept Driver and Miles's interpretation of the role of the pledge in C §2-3, he agrees nevertheless with them that the presence of the stipulation concerning the sale of Assyrians (plebeians) at the end of C §3 suggests that Assyrian law also set a limit on the period of service of pledges who have been taken after the foreclosure of a loan. Therefore, it is possible that the Assyrians, like the Babylonians, attempted to limit the power of the creditor in regards to taking possession of pledges after the foreclosure of a loan.

MAL G+C §7[1]

[G, revers (II 7-13) + C, revers (II. 1-2): §7] 7 [Si un esclave (?), un animal (?)] ou quelque bien à titre de gage [ou pour argent] 8 habite [dans la maison d'un Assy]rien et le terme est é[chu], 9 [après qui'il est éc]hu, si la créance at[teint] la valeur du bien 10 [il est acq]uis et pris. Si la créance n'at[teint] pas la valeur du bien 11 [le créancier] le fait sien et le prend; 12 [il ne] diminuera (?) [pas la valeur (du bien)] mais il dé[duira] le montant de la créance; 13 il n'y aura pas [d'intérêt (?)].

Lastly, MAL G+C §7 deals with the legitimate sale of a pledge who has become the possession of a creditor after the foreclosure of a loan. The first section shows that a slave or animal who is *wašābu kī šaparti* 'living in the capacity of a pledge' in the creditor's house can become the possession of the creditor when a loan is foreclosed. Cardascia[2] notes that, like A §44, this section does not clarify whether the pledge, who becomes the possession of the creditor, is redeemable (*Lösungspfand*) or irredeemable (*Verfallspfand*). Following the example set in the Roman Code of Justinian, which prohibited persons from becoming the permanent property of creditors, Cardascia suggests that in practice a pledge remained redeemable when the creditor acquired the pledge through the 'court' or 'justice'. Furthermore, he suggests that the pledge was irredeemable when the creditor acquired the pledge by force (i.e., self-help), something which he admits is envisaged in both A §44 and G+C §7.[3] While it is likely that the creditor often used the court to seize distraints, it is

---

1. This translation is taken from Cardascia, *Les lois assyriennes*, p. 307, who follows the restoration of David, 'Verfallspfand in den mittelassyrischen Gesetzen', pp. 170-72.

2. Cardascia, *Les lois assyriennes,* p. 308.

3. So also Cardellini, *Die biblischen 'Sklaven'-Gesetze*, p. 198.

questionable whether the drafting of a conveyance was ever influenced by the decisions of the court. Furthermore, as we have seen above, Lewy suggests that a creditor obtained complete possession of a pledge when he 'paid the full price', a consequence of which the debtor was fully aware. Nevertheless, even if a redemption clause was included in the conveyance it is not certain that the debtor would have had the means to redeem the slave or animal.

The second part of the stipulation deals with the sale of the pledge after it has become the possession of the creditor. Cardascia[1] notes that the value of the pledge may not be the same as the value of the debt. He discusses three possibilities concerning the relative value of the debt and pledge: (1) the total amount of the debt is superior to the value of the pledge; (2) the total amount of the debt is equivalent to that of the pledge; (3) the amount of the debt is less than the value of the pledge. Cardascia notes that the first (1) option is not envisaged in this law, probably because in practice a creditor usually demanded a pledge that was worth substantially more than the debt.[2] The second (2) possibility is envisaged in ll.9-10, according to which the creditor took possession of the pledge. The third (3) possibility is envisaged in ll.10-13, according to which the creditor, having sold the pledge, was required to return the balance representing the excess of the value of the pledge to the debtor. However, the creditor was not to deduct the value of the interest, since this was already paid by the service of the pledge (antichretic). If there was some dispute concerning the value of the pledge, then the debtor could probably seek a ruling in the courts (cf. C+G §§8-11).[3]

Recapitulating, the above discussions show that MAL attempted to regulate the treatment and sale of pledges. However, while it is

---

1. Cardascia, *Les lois assyriennes*, p. 309.

2. Cf. also Petschow, *Neubabylonisches Pfandrecht*, pp. 71-72; Lewy, 'The Biblical Institution of Derôr', p. 26, who suggests that the value of the pledge in MAL A §44 was substantially more than the debt; and Eichler, *Indenture at Nuzi*, p. 75 n. 34.

3. Cf. Cardascia, *Les lois assyriennes*, p. 309, who writes, 'Sans aucun doute, en pareil cas le débiteur qui s'estimait lésé ne pouvait que recourir aux tribunaux, mais cette nécessité souligne, à son égard, la rigeur du 'Verfallpfand'. Le débiteur qui a consenti pareille sûreté est exposé à devoir laisser entre les mains de son créancier, s'il ne veut pas encourir les aléas d'un procès, un gage notablement supérieur au montant de sa dette.'

possible that MAL C §§2-3 envisaged the periodic release of patrician debt-slaves, A §44 did allow creditors to take permanent possession of plebeian pledges after the foreclosure of a loan. Furthermore, G+C §7 allowed creditors to take possession of slave and animal pledges after the foreclosure of a loan, although certain provisions were made on behalf of the debtor who pledged property that was worth more than the debt.

The OB *mēšarum* Edicts

I have already pointed out that the OB *mēšarum* edicts[1] were royal proclamations that sought to release citizens from various forms of debt in order to prevent the economy from collapsing. Only three examples of such edicts have survived, the most complete of which is the edict of Ammi-saduqa, which was published and extensively commented on by Kraus[2] in 1958.[3] In 1965 Kraus[4] published a fragment of a *mīšarum* edict proclaimed by Samsu-iluna, and in 1984 he published a second and more exhaustive study of the OB *mēšarum*

---

1. For discussions about the OB *mīšarum* edict, see Kraus, *Ein Edikt*; idem, 'Der "Palast", Produzent und Unternehmer im Königreiche Babylon nach Hammurabi (ca. 1750–1600 v. Chr.)', in Lipiński (ed.), *State and Temple Economy*, pp. 423-34; idem, *Königliche Verfügungen*; Bottéro, 'Désordre économique et annulation des dettes en Mésopotamie', pp. 113-64; Finkelstein, 'Ammisaduqa's Edict', pp. 91-104; idem, 'Some New Misharum Material and its Implication', in *Studies in Honor of Benno Landsberger on His Seventieth Birthday, April 21, 1965* (The Oriental Institute of the University of Chicago Assyriological Studies, 16; Chicago: University of Chicago Press, 1965), pp. 233-46; idem, 'Edict of Ammisaduqa's: A New Text', *RA* 63 (1969), pp. 45-64; Edzard, 'Social Reformen', pp. 145-56; N.P. Lemche, 'Andurārum and Mīšarum: Comments on the Problem of Social Edicts and their Application in the ancient Near East', *JNES* 38 (1979), pp. 11-22; G. Komoróczy 'Zur Frage der Periodizität der altbabylonischen *MĪŠARUM*-Erlässe', in Dandamayev *et al.* (eds.), *Societies and Languages*, pp. 196-205; H. Petschow, 'Gesetze', *Reallexikon der Assyriologie*, III (ed. G. Ebeling and M. Meissner; Berlin, 1970), cols. 269-76.

2. Kraus, *Ein Edikt*; cf. also Bottéro, 'Désordre économique et annulation des dettes en Mésopotamie', pp. 113-64, who has commented on various aspects of Ammisaduqa's edict.

3. In 1969 Finkelstein, 'Edict of Ammisaduqa's: A New Text', pp. 45-64, published a duplicate of A-s.

4. Kraus, 'Ein Edikt des Königs Samsu-iluna von Babylon', *AS* 16 (1965), pp. 225-31.

edicts, including a discussion of ancient allusions and references to these edicts from southern Mesopotamia, the Diyala region, Mari, Hana, Assyria, Syria and Elam.[1] In this work Kraus suggests that a cuneiform tablet originally published by Langdon in 1914, which was originally thought to have been a copy of A-s, is actually an example of an edict of an unknown king (presumably from Babylon).

The *mēšarum* edicts are written records of oral acts declared by several OB kings during their first regnal year and at some other occasions later during their reign.[2] While Finkelstein[3] suggests that these edicts were declared at fairly regular and predictable intervals, the consensus of scholarly opinion[4] is that these edicts, while occurring frequently during the reigns of many OB kings, did not occur at predictable intervals but only during times when drastic economic measures were called for. That these measures were often enacted attests to the economic turmoil of the time and the temporary effectiveness of the measures, not to the predictability of the edicts.[5]

The function of these edicts, however, still remains a matter of debate. For example, Kraus[6] suggests that the *mīšarum*-act was probably an oral decree and must therefore be distinguished from the *mēšarum*-edicts, which he suggests probably served as written guides for enforcement of the *mīšarum*-act. However, we have already seen

---

1. Kraus, *Königliche Verfügungen*, pp.16-110 (chs. ii-vi).

2. Cf. Kraus, *Ein Edikt*, pp. 224-39; *idem*, 'Ein Edikt des Königs Samsu-iluna von Babylon', p. 229; *idem*, *Königliche Verfügungen*, pp. 19-109; Finkelstein, 'Some New Misharum Material and its Implication', pp. 233-46. For example, Rim-Sin enacted at least three edicts (26th, 35th, 41st years of his reign); Hammurabi enacted four (1st, 12th, 20th, 30th); Samsuiluna (1st, 8th); Ammiditana (1st, 20th); Ammi-saduqa (1st, 10th).

3. Finkelstein, 'Some New Misharum Material and its Implication', p. 245; cf. also M. Weinfeld, 'Sabbatical Year and Jubilee in the Pentateuch: Laws and their ancient Near Eastern Background', in *The Law in the Bible and in its Environment* (ed. T. Veijola; Publications of the Finnish Exegetical Society, 51; Göttingen: Vandenhoeck & Ruprecht, 1990), pp. 58-59 and n. 84.

4. Cf. Westbrook, 'Jubilee Laws', pp. 220-21; Komoróczy, 'Zur Frage der Periodizität der altbabylonischen *MĪŠARUM*-Erlässe', pp. 196-205.

5. Cf. Bottéro, 'Désordre économique et annulation des dettes en Mésopotamie', pp. 113-64; Westbrook, 'Jubilee Laws', pp. 217-18; Komoróczy, 'Zur Frage der Periodizität der altbabylonischen *MĪŠARUM*-Erlässe', pp. 198-201.

6. Kraus, *Ein Edikt*, pp. 243-47.

that Finkelstein[1] suggests that these edicts may have been copied for their own sake as a type of literary genre. While the function of these edicts, like the function of the legal collections, may remain a moot point, it is clear that the *mēšarum*-acts were carried out in order to prevent the collapse and ruin of the economy and the state.[2]

In the preamble to A-s we find a declaration which reads:[3]

> dub-pí [...] *ša-mi-am* [...] *i-nu-ma [šar-rum mi-ša-ra-am a-na ma-tim iš-[ku-nu]*
> The tablet which contains the decree imposed upon the country to be heard at the time when the king established justice [a *mīšarum*] for the land.

I have already pointed out that the expression *mēšarum šakānum* 'to establish justice' was a distinctive feature of many of the Mesopotamian reforms and legal collections, occurring, for example, in the legal collections of Ur-Nammu and Lipit-Ishtar (Sumerian equivalent: níg.si.sá gar). A similar expression occurs in the reform of Urukagina (ama.gi₄ e-gar) and in LH §117 (*andurāram šakānum*), which stipulates the periodic release of debt-slaves.[4] While Kraus referred to the *mēšarum* edicts as *Erlässe* 'edicts' in his previous study of them (1954), he has since referred to both legal collections and *mēšarum* edicts as *Rechtsakte* 'legal acts', since both use the phrase 'to establish justice' (1984).[5] However, Lambert[6] notes that the use of term *Rechtsakte* 'serves to obscure the real differences between

---

1. Finkelstein, 'Ammiṣaduqa's Edict', p. 92.

2. Cf. Bottéro, 'Désordre économique et annulation des dettes en Mésopotamie', pp. 153-55; R. Westbrook, 'Jubilee Laws', pp. 217-18; G. Komoróczy, 'Zu den Eigentumsverhältnissen in der altbabylonischen Zeit: Das Problem der Privatwirtschaft', in Lipiński (ed.), *State and Temple Economy*, pp. 411-22, esp. 20; H. Olivier, 'The Effectiveness of the Old Babylonian Mēšarum Decree', *JNSL* 12 (1984), pp. 107-13.

3. This reconstruction is found in Kraus, *Königliche Verfügungen*, pp. 167-168, whose translation reads: 'Tafel *des/der* [...] den Hörenden [...,] als [der König Gerechtigkeit] für das Land wiederhergestellt hatte'.

4. For a discussion of the etymology, use and relationship of the two terms *mīšaru* (= Sumerian níg.si.sá) and *andurāru* (= Sumerian ama.ar.gi₄ [or ama.gi₄], see *CAD* 5/2, cols. 116-19; 1: 115-17; Lewy, 'The Biblical Institution of Derôr', pp. 27-29; Lemche, 'Andurārum and Mīšarum', pp. 11-22; Kraus, *Ein Edikt*, pp. 224-47; *idem*, *Königliche Verfügungen*, pp. 3-14.

5. Cf. Kraus, *Königliche Verfügungen*, pp. 3-15.

6. Lambert, 'Book Review', p. 119.

codes and edicts and the use of one phrase to refer to both does not imply that as legal institutions the two categories are really one'. Lastly, Kraus[1] suggests that the clause 'because the king has established a *mīšarum* in the land', which occurs in the preamble and throughout the edict, was used as a formula to indicate which provisions were meant to have effect only at the time of the announcement of the edict.

Ammi-saduqa's Edict contains 22 sections that regulated various aspects of the state, temple and 'private' economies. In several of these stipulations various types of debts, taxes and rent were annulled. Although A-s does not stipulate the release of land sold on account of debt, Finkelstein[2] has shown that certain deeds of sale and other types of contracts relating to real estate were directly affected by the declaration of the *mēšarum*-acts that effected the retention of title to purchased immobile property (e.g., BM 80318; cf. also *VAB* 5 no. 273[3]). While a discussion of all the stipulations found in A-s is beyond the scope of my discussion,[4] I will briefly discuss §20-21, which contain the regulations concerning the freeing of debt-slaves. The two sections read:[5]

> §20: If a liability had bound a free man from Numhia, a free man from Emut-balum, a free man from Ida-maraz, a free man from Uruk, a free man from Isin, a free man from Kusura, a free man from Malgum, and (consequently) the free man had pledged himself, his wife or (his children) for silver into bondage or as a pledge—in the event the King again brought law and order back to the land, he is free, his freedom is once again established.

1. Kraus, *Ein Edikt*, pp. 183-85.

2. Finkelstein, 'Some New Misharum Material and its Implication', pp. 233-46; cf. also Lewy, 'The Biblical Institution of Derôr', pp. 23-29; Westbrook, 'Jubilee Laws', p. 217; Lemche, 'Andurārum and Mīšarum', pp. 17-19; Olivier, 'Old Babylonian Mēšarum Decree', p. 109.

3. This OB text from the reign of Ammisaduqa is discussed by Olivier, 'Old Babylonian Mēšarum Decree', pp. 109-13, who demonstrates that 'the *mēšarum* did affect the normal procedure of the drafting of contracts whereby creditors attempted to circumvent the implications in their business-dealings of an impending *mēšarum*' (pp. 109-10).

4. For the most recent and exhaustive study of these stipulations, see Kraus, *Königliche Verfügungen*, pp. 184-288.

5. Both sections are taken from Kraus, *Königliche Verfügungen*, pp. 180-83.

3. *The Legal Background to Debt-Slavery in Mesopotamia* 89

§21: If someone from a position of slavery, who is house-borne of a free man from Numhia, a free man from Emut-balum, a free man from Idamaraz, a free man from Uruk, a free man from Isin, a free man from Kisura, a free man from Malgum, is sold for silver or is given into bondage or has been left as a pledge, his freedom is not restored again.

Scholars have noted that the stipulation in A-s §20 is similar (Bottéro, Korošec, Cardellini)[1] or parallel (Kraus)[2] to the stipulation found in LH §117. Kraus, in particular, attempts to illustrate how LH §117 (ll.54-67) is parallel to A-s §20 (ll.25-35) by placing the two legislations side by side:

LH §117	A-s §20
54. *šum-ma a-wi-lam*	25. *[šum-ma* du]mu *nu-um-ħi-a*
	...
55. *e-ħi-il-tum* 56. *iṣ-ba-zu-ma*	28. *... i-il-tum i-il-šu-ma*
57. *dam-zu* dumu-*šu ù* dumu.	29. *[pa-ga-a]r-šu aš-ša-az-zu*
	munus-*zu* 30. [XXX]X
58. *a-na* kù.babbar *id-di-in*	*a-na* kù.babbar
59. *ùlu a-na ki-iš-a-tim*	*a-na k[i-iš-š]a-tim*
60. *it-ta-an-di-in*	31. *[ù-lu a-na ma-az-z]a-za-ni*
61. mu 3.kam 62.*é ša-a-a-ma-ni-šu-* 32. [XXX}	
nu	
63. *ù ka-ši-ši-šu-nu*	*[aš-šum šar-rum m]i-ša-ra-am*
64. *i-ip-pé-šu i-na ri-bu-tim*	33. *[a-na ma-tim išk]u-nu*
65. *ša-at-tim*	34. *[uš-šu]-ur*
66. *an-du-ra-ar-šu-nu*	*[a]n-d[u-ra-a]r-šu*
67. *iš-ša=ak-ka-an*	35. *[ša]-ki-[i]n*

This comparison strengthens my previous suggestion that the stipulation in LH §117 was an attempt by Hammurabi to release debt-slaves periodically, something that was accomplished less periodically through the *mēšarum* edicts.[3] That §20 was meant to have only a

---

1. Cf. Bottéro, 'Désordre économique et annulation des dettes en Mésopotamie', p. 141; Korošec, 'Keilschriftrecht', pp. 117-18; Cardellini, *Die biblischen 'Sklaven' -Gesetze*, p. 80; and Kraus, *Königliche Verfügungen*, pp. 265-66.

2. Cf. Kraus, *Königliche Verfügungen*, pp. 264-66.

3. Cf. H. Klengel, 'Die Palastwirtschaft in *Alalaħ*', in Lipiński (ed.), *State and Temple Economy*, p. 446, who suggests that those examples in which king Ammitakum 'released' debtors from paying the interest on their loans (KÙ.BABBAR *ul uṣṣab ul idda/urar* 'The money bears no interest or security[?]'; cf. Wiseman, *The Alalakh Tablets* *29-*31) were similar to the *andurārum*-decrees in LH §117 and A-s §20. The loans referred to in these texts, and elsewhere in *The*

limited effect is demonstrated by the appearance of the formula
'because the king has instituted the *mīšarum* in the land', which we
saw above probably demonstrates the limited duration of this
particular decree. Furthermore, A-s §20 limits the release to certain
areas of the country, while LH §117 was meant to be administered
throughout Babylonia.

Section 20 stipulated the release of citizens who were either sold for
money (*ana kaspim* = kù.babbar), surrendered (*ana kiššātim*) or
given over as a pledge (*ana mazzāzāni*) to a creditor. We have already
seen that the first two conditions are found in LH §§117-119, which
deal with a debtor who has sold or surrendered family members in
order to pay a defaulted loan, while the last condition is found in
several OB contracts (parallel to the Nuzi *tidennūtu* contracts). Kraus[1]
notes that it is curious that this stipulation should only refer to these
three forms of 'debt-slavery', a problem that he notes 'is currently
beyond our knowledge or understanding'. While we have already seen
that it is difficult to discern the difference between the first two
conditions, it is also difficult to understand why the first two
conditions occur alongside the last, since a *mazzāzānu*-pledge was
taken at the beginning of a loan. While Kraus[2] considers the problem
moot, Eichler[3] suggests that the *mazzāzānu*-pledge was taken by a
third party who has given a debtor a loan to pay an antecedent debt,
similar to the transactions *ana kaspim* and *ana kiššātum*.

While §20 stipulates the release of free-citizens, §21 exempts male
or female (a *geme* or an *arad*)[4] 'houseborn' slaves (*wilid bītim*) from
such a release (cf. also LH §118). Kraus[5] notes that although §21 does

---

Alalakh Tablets are *mazzazānūtu* contracts in which the debtor and (or) family
members enter the creditor's house as pledges in order to work off the interest. The
so-called *andurārum*-decrees in *The Alalakh Tablets* *29-*31 suggest that the debtor
and/or family members were no longer required to serve in the creditor's house.
Cp. Eichler, *Indenture at Nuzi*, p. 73, who suggests that the debtor and/or family
members serve in the new creditor's house as a pledge(s).

1. Kraus, *Königliche Verfügungen*, pp. 277-78.
2. Kraus, *Königliche Verfügungen*, p. 277.
3, Eichler, *Indenture at Nuzi*, pp. 82-83.
4. For a discussion of the use of these two terms as references to male and female
slaves, see I.J. Gelb, 'Terms for Slaves in Ancient Mesopotamia', in Dandamayev *et
al.* (eds.), *Societies and Languages*, pp. 81-98.
5. Kraus, *Königliche Verfügungen*, pp. 283-84. He suggests, therefore, that the

not begin with stating the reasons why a debtor has been forced to sell, surrender, or pawn a slave, he suggests that it is clear that the reader would understand that the reason is the same as that described at the beginning of §20—viz., the debtor has defaulted on a loan. The expression *wilid bītim* is generally considered to refer to 'houseborn'[1] chattel-slaves. Further, Kraus notes that such slaves held little prospect of freedom unless their masters released them, a prospect extended to free-citizen debt-slaves through the declaration of *mēšarum* edicts. He suggests, therefore, that the expression *wilid bītim*, in addition to describing the background (or origin) of these chattel-slaves, describes their legal position.[2] That is, for any sale contract that designates a slave as a *wilid bītim*, there is an implicit guarantee that the buyer/seller will not lose a slave in the event that a *mēšarum* edict is declared.

Lastly, while the *mēšarum* edicts with their declarations of release (*andurārum*) for the whole land are no longer declared after the OB period, limited declarations of release were made by various kings during other periods. For example, during the Kassite period the so-called *kidinnūtum*, which sometimes parallels *andurārum*, apparently declared a city (rather than individual citizens) free from corvée work, levy and perhaps debt, although it should be noted that there is a lack of any specific references to debt-slaves in these decrees.[3]

gap after part B VI 1 in §21 must have contained a short passage that is not contained in §20, but he does not venture to say what this might have been.

1. Cf. Mendelsohn, *Slavery in the Ancient Near East*, pp. 57-58; Kraus, *Ein Edikt*, p. 173; Finkelstein, 'Ammiṣaduqa's Edict', p. 99; C. Wilcke, 'Zu den spät-altbabylonischen Kaufverträgen aus Nordbabylonien', *WO* 8 (1975/76), pp. 271-79. Finkelstein suggests that the wilid bîtim belonged to a class of 'houseborn' chattel-slaves who were different from the 'Subartu' chattel-slaves who were bought at market. He suggests a parallel can be found in Gen. 17.12-13: יליד בית and ומקנת־כסף; cf. also Wilcke (p. 271) and Mendelson (p. 57).

2. Kraus, *Königliche Verfügungen*, p. 283.

3. Cf. D.J. Wiseman, *Nebuchadrezzar and Babylon: The Schweich Lectures 1983* (London: The British Academy, 2nd edn, 1985), p. 79 n. 97; H. Reviv, 'Kidinnu: Observations on Privileges of Mesopotamian Cities', *JESHO* 31 (1988), pp. 286-98; cf. also M. Weinfeld, ' "Justice and Righteousness" in Ancient Israel Against the Background of "Social Reforms" in the Ancient Near East', in *Mesopotamien und seine Nachbarn. Politische und kulturelle Wechselbeziehungen im Alten Vorderasien vom 4. bis 1. Jahrtausend v. Chr. Teil 1 & 2* (ed. H.J. Nissen and J. Renger; BBVO, 1; Berlin: Dietrich Reimer Verlag, 1982), p. 493.

Further, Nuzi kings often issued a *šūdūtum* 'public proclamation' (= *andurārum*) which called for the release of debt-slaves and property.[1] Finally, during the NA period several texts mention the declaration of an *andura–rum*, which called for the release of debt-slaves and property.[2]

The Nuzi tidennūtu Loan and ḫābiru Service Contracts

Although these loan and service contracts[3] do not appear in any of the legal collections, they have been used by some scholars to help elucidate the meaning of the manumission laws in Exod. 21.2-6; Deut. 15.12-18. The first Nuzi *tidennūtu* transaction was published by Scheil in 1918.[4] Based on this single document Scheil concluded that the text was a lease contract. However, as more *tidennūtu* contracts were discovered there were more views about the nature of these contracts. One of the most recent and most comprehensive treatments of these loan transactions is presented by Eichler,[5] who has suggested that the *tidennūtu* contracts exhibit the same basic scheme by which two contracting parties exchange certain property—i.e., PN receives

1. Cf. Eichler, *Indenture at Nuzi*, pp. 32-34; M. Müller, 'Sozial- und wirtschaftspolitische Erlässe im Lande Arrapha', in *Beiträge zur sozialen Struktur des Alten Vorderasien* (ed. H. Klengel; SGKAO, 1; Berlin: Akademie-Verlag, 1971), pp. 53-60; Lemche, 'Andurārum and Mīšarum', p. 19; Weinfeld, ' "Justice and Righteousness" ', p. 496.

2. Cf. Postgate, *Fifty Neo-Assyrian Legal Documents*, pp. 21-22; Lemche, 'Andurārum and Mīšarum', pp. 20-21; Weinfeld, ' "Justice and Righteousness" ', p. 493.

3. The *tidennūtu* loan contract is similar to the OB *mazzazānūtu* loan transaction mentioned in A-s §§20-21. The latter contract is discussed at length by Eichler, *Indenture at Nuzi*, pp. 49-88. Cf. also H. Hirsch, 'Akkadische (altassyrisch) *mazzāzum* "Pfand, Verpfändung" ', *Wiener ZKM* 62 (1969), pp. 52-53, who has identified a *mazzāzum* loan (= OB *mazzazānūtu*) in two OA letters in which the *mazzazu*-pledge rendered service in lieu of interest, which is the same as the OB *mazzazānu*-pledge (Eichler cites this reference on pp. 49-50 n. 7).

4. For a discussion of the views of Scheil and others, see Eichler, *Indenture at Nuzi*, pp. 7-9; Korošec, 'Keilschriftrecht', pp. 169-73; Cardellini, *Die biblischen 'Sklaven'-Gesetze*, pp. 180-82.

5. Eichler, *Indenture at Nuzi*, p. 12; cf. also Cardellini, *Die biblischen 'Sklaven'-Gesetze*, pp. 180-83; and W.F. Leemans, 'Quelques Remarques à Propos d'une TIDDENNŪTU Étude sur PERSONNELLE À NUZU', *JESHO* 19 (1976), pp. 95-101.

certain property from PN$_2$; PN$_2$, in turn, receives a person or persons from PN. When PN returns the given property, PN reclaims the person or persons from PN$_2$. In many of these contracts the time for repayment is of an indefinite duration, while in others there is a fixed time limit. The duration of the contract can range from one year (after harvest) to 50 years, although in most of the contracts in which a large sum of money is exchanged (30–180 shekels of silver) the duration of the contract is indefinite. In both of these types of contracts the exchanged person is usually the borrower or a member of the borrower's family.[1]

Upon close examination of these contracts, Eichler suggests that the service given by the exchanged person is antichretic. However, the person is not a 'pledge'—i.e., not mere security for the loan, since the debtor retains responsibility for the debt. Furthermore, the pledge is considered a hired hand and not a slave. Therefore, Eichler[2] concludes: 'The institution of personal *tidennūtu* seems to be governed by a concept of personal debt liability, although it preserves the older contractual form of a substitute payment pledge.' Furthermore, the institution of the personal *tidennūtu* represents not only an antichretic security but also a type of indentured servitude. It would appear that this sort of loan transaction allowed Nuzi landlords to secure a long-term labour force, which would be superior to holding slaves since the creditor is protected if anything should happen to the pledge.[3]

The *tidennūtu* contracts have often been compared with the Nuzi *ḫāpiru* service contracts, both of which were forms of indentured servitude.[4] The Nuzi *ḫabiru*, a group of foreign 'immigrants' whom I

1. Cf. Eichler, *Indenture at Nuzi*, p. 18, who shows that in 25 of the 52 transactions the borrower is exchanged, while in 18 cases it is the borrower's son.

2. Eichler, *Indenture at Nuzi*, pp. 43-44. Thus the debtor assumes the liability in case of the absence, death, or disappearance of the pledge (p. 44). When the debtor pledges himself and dies the debt passes to one of his sons or to a guarantor (*māḫiṣ pūti*) (pp. 28-29).

3. Cf. Eichler, *Indenture at Nuzi*, pp. 45-47. In one of the *tidennūtu* transactions, the creditor is Teḫib-tilla, son of Puḫi-šenni, who was one of the most economically influential people in Nuzi. He owned vast real estate and he was in need of obtaining a labour force to work his land (p. 46).

4. Cf. J. Lewy, 'Ḫābirū and Hebrews', *HUCA* 14 (1939), pp. 590-91; Paul, *Book of the Covenant*, p. 48 n. 2; E. Cassin in J. Bottéro, *Le problème des ḫabiru à la 4e recontre assyriologique internationale* (CahSA, 12; Paris: Imprimerie

will discuss in more detail in Chapter 6, sometimes entered into a type of 'indentured servitude' in which service was exchanged for the necessities of life. Documents from Nuzi demonstrate that both individual ḫabiru men or women (sometimes accompanied by their families) entered into this type of contractual agreement according to which no money exchanged hands and the servants were expected to remain with the lord as long as they lived, although the contracts make it clear that the ḫabiru entered 'of their own free will' into service as 'slaves' (ana ardūti/amtūti/wardūti).[1] The ḫabiru, though, were allowed to leave their service if they met one of three conditions: (1) supplying a substitute;[2] (2) paying a certain amount of

Nationale, 1954), pp. 65-69; B.L. Eichler, Indenture at Nuzi, p. 47; Cardellini, Die biblischen 'Sklaven'-Gesetze, pp. 186-87.

1. For a discussion of the ana ardūti/amtūti contracts, see Cardellini, Die biblischen 'Sklaven'-Gesetze, pp. 184-87; M.B. Rowton, 'The Topological Factor in the "ḫapiru" Problem', in Studies in Honor of Benno Landsberger on His Seventieth Birthday, April 21, 1965 (The Oriental Institute of the University of Chicago Assyriological Studies, 16; Chicago: University of Chicago Press, 1965), pp. 375-87; Paul, Book of the Covenant, pp. 45-52; Bottéro, Le problème des ḫabiru, pp. 43-65; idem, 'Habiru', in Reallexikon der Assyriologie, IV (ed. G. Ebeling and M. Meissner; Berlin, 1972), pp. 14-27; E. Cassin in Bottéro, Le problème des ḫabiru, pp. 65-70; idem, 'Nouveaux documents sur les Habiru', JA 246 (1958), pp. 225-36; H. Cazelles, 'Book Review of M. Greenberg, Hab/piru"', BO 13 (1956), pp. 149-51; M. Greenberg, The Hab/piru (AOS, 39; New Haven: American Oriental Society, 1955), pp. 23-32, 65-70; Mendelsohn, Slavery in the Ancient Near East, pp. 16-18; Lewy, 'Ḫābirū and Hebrews', pp. 587-623; idem, 'A New Parallel between Ḫābiru and Hebrews', pp. 47-58; A. Saarisalo, 'New Kirkuk Documents Relating to Slaves', StudOr 5 (1934), pp. 61-65; E. Chiera, 'Ḫabiru and Hebrews', AJSL 49 (1933), pp. 115-24; E. Chiera and E.A. Speiser, 'Selected "Kirkuk" Documents', JAOS 47 (1927), pp. 36-60.

2. Cf. JEN V, 448 (= Greenberg, The Ḫab/piru, Text #41 = Bottéro, Le problème des ḫabiru, Text #54): 'If ever Adad-rabî should leave the house of Teḫip-tilla he shall give 1 man of Lullu as his substitute' (lines 8-12); JEN V, 463 (= Greenberg, The Ḫab/piru, Text #42 = Bottéro, Le problème des ḫabiru, Text #52): 'If Nan-Teshup should infringe (the agreement) and leave the house of T. he must compensate T. with his substitute, (a man) as able as he' (lines 6-10); JEN V, 458 (= Greenberg, The Ḫab/piru, Text #43 = Bottéro, Le problème des ḫabiru, Text #49) : 'If Warad-Kūbi should infringe (the agreement) and leave the house of T. he must give T. (as) his substitute 1 robust man' (lines 6-10); JEN V, 456 (= Greenberg, The Ḫab/piru, Text #59 = Bottéro, Le problème des ḫabiru, Text #65): 'If ever Attilamu

money;[1] (3) incurring a severe injury or penalty.[2] While it appears that the *ḫabiru* could end their service before the death of their lord by meeting one of the previous conditions,[3] Greenberg[4] suggests that

stays away from the place of T.'s son a scribe (as) his substitute he shall give to T.'s son, and then he may go' (lines 17-23).

1. Cf. JEN V, 460 (= Greenberg, *The Ḫab/piru*, Text #44 = Bottéro, *Le problème des ḫabiru*, Text #51): '[...]ḫaya, a ḫapīru, made himself enter into service to T., son of Puḫi-šenni. [If...]ḫaya should infringe (the agreement) [x minas] of silver and [x minas] of gold he must pay to Teḫipitil]la' (lines 1-7); JAOS 55 pl. i-ii (= Greenberg, *The Ḫab/piru*, Text #48 = Bottéro, *Le problème des ḫabiru*, Text #63): 'If the women infringe (the agreement) and say: "We are not maid-servants", a tenfold mina of gold they shall pay' (lines 40-42); JEN VI, 613 (= Greenberg, *The Ḫab/piru*, Text #60 = Bottéro, *Le problème des ḫabiru*, Text #66d): 'If *now* Attilammu stays away, 10 minas of silver and 10 minas of gold he shall pay' (lines 15-18); JEN V, 446 (= Greenberg, *The Ḫab/piru*, Text #62 = Bottéro, *Le problème des ḫabiru*, Text #66c): 'If [Washkabiy]a [...] anything and say [...T. [...] [...x] minas of gold he shall pay [T.]' (lines 5-11).

2. Cf. JEN V, 452 (= Chiera and Speiser, 'Kirkuk', p. 8 = Greenberg, *The Ḫab/piru*, Text #45 = Bottéro, *Le problème des ḫabiru*, Text #61): 'If Sinbālti should infringe (the agreement) and go into another [house] T. may put out both eyes of Sinbālti and sell her for a price' (lines 5-9); JEN V, 449 (= Greenberg, *The Ḫab/piru*, Text #58): 'If Waḫuluki should infringe (the agreement), leave the house of T., and say thus: 'I am not a maid-servant, and my children are not servants,' then T. may put out the eyes of and her offspring and sell them for a price' (lines 5-14); JEN V, 462 (= Greenberg, *The Ḫab/piru*, Text #61 = Bottéro, *Le problème des ḫabiru*, Text #66a): 'If they infringe (the agreement), and leave the house of T., he may do to them as he pleases' (lines 8-12); JEN V, 457 (= Greenberg, *The Ḫab/piru*, Text #63 = Bottéro, *Le problème des ḫabiru*, Text #66b): 'If , Iliutum, [Sin-iddina] and Adad-mi-ilu should infringe (the agreement) and say to T.: 'We are not man- nor maid-servants', then T. may put out their eyes and sell them for a price' (lines 7-13).

3. Cf. Cassin in Bottéro, *Le problème des ḫabiru*, pp. 65-69; Cardellini, *Die biblischen 'Sklaven'-Gesetze*, p. 186.

4. Greenberg, *The Ḫab/piru*, pp. 26, 31. M. Greenberg bases his interpretation on JEN VI, 613 (= Greenberg, *The Ḫab/piru*, Text #60 = Bottéro, *Le problème des ḫabiru*, Text #66d) which reads: 'Attilammu, son of A[...], an Assyrian, entered into the house of Teḫip-tilla, son of Puḫi-šenni as a servant. As long as T. lives Attilammu [shall serve him]. When T. dies, Attilammu shall give the son of T. a scribe (as) his substitute; [then he may go]. And T. shall give Attilammu food and clothing. If *now* Attilammu stays away, 10 minas of silver and 10 minas of gold he shall pay.' M. Greenberg suggests that this document represents a complete contract upon which the other Nuzi service contracts are fashioned. He arranges the above clauses as follows:

condition (1) referred only to cases in which *ḫabiru* individuals or families wanted to leave after the death of their lords, while conditions (2) and (3) referred to cases in which the *ḫabiru* wanted to leave before the death of their lords. As Greenberg correctly points out, while it is possible that the *ḫabiru* could supply a substitute, it is highly questionable whether the *ḫabiru* could meet the financial conditions or would wish to receive severe treatment in order to leave the service of their lord.[1] Therefore, he concludes that the extravagant penalties (conditions 2 and 3) must have been intended chiefly to ensure that the *ḫabiru* remained in the service of their lords until their death. That these people held a status higher than that of chattel-slaves, though, is confirmed by three contracts[2] that state that only after desertion will the *ḫabiru* be sold—viz., reduced to the status of chattel-slaves.

While the Nuzi *tidennūtu* contract was a form of indentured servitude, Eichler[3] has noted correctly nevertheless that a comparative study of this and the Nuzi *ḫabiru* service contracts reveal that they reflect different institutions. For example, the status of a *tidennu* was higher than that of the *ḫabiru* who entered into *ana ardūti/ amtūti/*

a. Declaration of 'entrance' into the service of T.
b. Conditions of service, as regards,
    (1) time limit of obligatory service (the lifetime of T.);
    (2) return for service (food and clothing);
    (3) severance from service (permitted upon furnishing a substitute to the son of T.)
c. Penalty for breach of contract [specifically, of b (1)] (prohibitive fine of 10 gold and 10 silver minas.

1. Cf. also Lewy, 'Ḫābirū and Hebrews', p. 608 n. 108.
2. Cf. JEN V, 449 lines 5-14 (= Greenberg, *The Ḫab/piru*, Text #58 = Bottéro, *Le problème des ḫabiru,* Text #62); JEN V, 452 lines 5-9 (= Greenberg, *The Ḫab/piru*, Text #45 = Bottéro, *Le problème des ḫabiru,* Text #61); JEN V, 457 lines 11-13 (= Greenberg, *The Ḫab/piru*, Text #63 = Bottéro, *Le problème des ḫabiru,* Text #66b). Cf. also JEN V, 448 lines 13b-15 (= Greenberg, *The Ḫab/piru*, Text #41 = Bottéro, *Le problème des ḫabiru,* Text #54) which is badly damaged and the reconstructed section reads: 'If Adad-rabî [...] steals [anything from the house], his [master shall treat him] as a slave'; JEN V, 455 lines 8-15 (= Greenberg, *The Ḫab/piru*, Text #46 = Bottéro, *Le problème des ḫabiru,* Text #56): "Ma–r-Ishtar, a *ḫapīru* of the land of Akkad, gave his son, Zilgenuri for service to T. Thus : 'If I withdraw my son Zilgenuri I will give 10 slaves to T.'; cf. also Greenberg, *The Ḫab/piru,* 67-70.
3. Eichler, *Indenture at Nuzi,* p. 47; cf. also Cassin in Bottéro, *Le problème des ḫabiru,* pp. 65-69; Greenberg, *The Ḫab/piru,* pp. 23-32, 65-70.

wardūti contracts. This can be attributed to the fact that the *tidennu* was either a slave or dependent of a citizen who secured a loan (or sometimes the citizen himself), while the *ḥabiru* were immigrants[1] who were forced to enter less than favourable contracts in order to secure the necessities of life.[2]

Summary and Conclusions

To sum up, in this chapter I have examined the various laws, royal decrees, loan transactions and service contracts that may have a particular bearing on the interpretation of the biblical manumission laws. I began this survey with a discussion of the laws concerning the distraint and voluntary surrender or sale of dependents in LH §§114-116, 117-119. The former laws are pertinent to the discussion of the so-called משה 'pledge' which appears in the discussion of the Sabbatical year release in Deut. 15.1-3 (Chapter 7), and to the discussion of the slave law in Exod. 21.20-21 (Chapter 6), while the latter laws are pertinent to the discussion of the biblical manumission laws in Exod. 21.2-6 and Deut. 15.12-18 (Chapters 6 and 7). In my discussion of these laws in LH, I noted that §§114-116 concern the taking of a *nipûtum* 'distraint' or 'pledge' when a *ḥubullûm* loan was foreclosed. The *ḥubullûm* loan was usually given to farmers who used the money or grain to sow their land for the following harvest. In this type of transaction a pledge was not taken by the creditor at the commencement of a loan, but only after the loan was foreclosed. Although there is some question about the role of the *nipûtum*, I concluded that this sort of pledge was probably taken by the creditor in order to compel the debtor to pay the debt. Furthermore, I noted that creditors were not allowed to illtreat their pledges, since pledges remained the property of the debtors, and the creditors were prevented from taking pledges that were deemed essential to the

---

1. The *ḥabiru* are referred to as foreigners in JEN V, 458 (= Greenberg, *The Ḥab/piru*, Text #43 ; Greenberg, *The Ḥab/piru*, Text #48 = Bottéro, *Le problème des ḥabiru*, Text #63); JEN V, 462; JEN V, 446; JEN VI, 613; HSS 14, 49; HSS 13, 152; HSS 16, 438; HSS 16, 396; JEN V, 455 (= Greenberg, *The Ḥab/piru*, Text #40 = Bottéro, *Le problème des ḥabiru*, Text #56).

2. For discussions on how the *ḥabiru*, who entered into *ana ardūti/ amt'ti* contracts, were maltreated, see Cardellini, *Die biblischen 'Sklaven'-Gesetze*, pp. 186-87; Mendelsohn, *Slavery in the Ancient Near East*, p. 18.

existence of the debtors and the debtor's family, including the debtors themselves.

The laws in LH §§117-119, however, concern the sale of dependents by debtors who were not able to pay back a foreclosed *ḫubullûm* loan. I noted that these laws envisaged two types of sale transactions: *ana kaspim* 'for money' and *ana kiššātim* 'into control' or 'bondage'. While there is much confusion over the meaning of these two transactions, I concluded the the former transaction probably envisaged the absolute transfer of a dependent from the seller to the buyer, while the latter transaction probably envisaged the surrender of a dependent from the seller to the buyer, although the debtor had a right to redeem the dependent for an agreed period of time, after which he or she was transferred to the creditor. Furthermore, since LH §117 stipulated that a dependent who was sold either *ana kaspim* or *ana kiššātim* was to be released after three years' service, I concluded that this law attempted to curb the power of the creditor in taking free persons as permanent possessions.

Secondly, I discussed the laws concerning the treatment and sale of a *šapartu* 'pledge' in MAL A §44; C §§2-3; and G+C §7. The discussion of these laws is pertinent to the discussion of the function of mobile and immobile pledges in relation to the the Sabbatical year release in Deut. 15.1-3 and the manumission law in Deut. 15.12-18 (Chapter 7), as well as the stipulations regarding the 'sale' of land in Lev. 25 (Chapter 8). These laws in MAL deal with the treatment of human pledges who have been either acquired by the creditor after the foreclosure of a *šapartu* loan (A §44; G+C §7) or who are dwelling as pledges in a creditor's house (C §§2-3). However, in contrast to the *ḫubullûm* loan, in the *šapartu* loan contracts a pledge was generally taken by the creditor at the commencement of a loan transaction (although the *Besitzpfand* is attested in most periods) as a substitute payment or security for the loan. While the pledging of movable property is rarely attested, the pledging of both persons and land is well attested during most periods in the ancient Near East. A pledge who was taken by the creditor at the commencement of the loan performed antichretic services which most likely went toward the payment of the interest on the capital. The pledge would therefore be released once the debtor paid the capital. While most documents do not indicate when a loan was to be repaid, there are some that do set a specific period of repayment. In the latter case, if the debtor did not repay the loan by the agreed period the creditor took possession of the pledge (*Verfallspfand*), although in many conveyances a redemption clause was included (*Lösungspfand*). The *Verfallspfand* case is envisaged in MAL A §44; G+C §7, in which lower-class Assyrians, or slaves, animals or any other types of pledges became the possession of the creditor. However, we observed that MAL C §§2-3, which concern the treatment of patrician pledges who are dwelling in a creditor's house, probably did envisage the absolute transfer of such pledges to the creditor. It is possible therefore that the Assyrians, like the Babylonians, attempted to limit the power of a creditor in regards to taking possession of pledges after the foreclosure of a loan.

Thirdly, I discussed A-s, which is the most complete example of an OB *mīšarum* edict. The *mēšarum* edicts, which were declared by several OB kings in order to prevent the economy of their kingdoms from collapsing, contained various stipulations which annulled various types of debts, taxes and rents, the most important of which are those that concern the release of land and debt-slaves. These edicts are particularly relevant to the discussion of the Jubilee year in Leviticus 25, which contains stipulations concerning the release of both land and debt-slaves (Chapter 8). Although A-s does not stipulate the release of land sold on account of debt, various documents, especially those from Hana, demonstrate that such land releases were also provided for in the *mēšarum* edicts. However, A-s §20 does stipulate the release of debt-slaves who were sold *ana kaspim* or *ana kiššātim* or *ana mazzāzāni*. I argued that this stipulation is parallel to LH §117, which suggests that LH §117 was an attempt by Hammurabi to release debt-slaves periodically, something which was accomplished less periodically through the *mēšarum* edicts.

Lastly, I discussed the Nuzi *tidennūtu* loan transactions and the *ḫabiru* service contracts, both of which envisaged a sort of indentured servitude. Both of these institutions have been compared with the biblical manumission laws in Exod. 21.2-6 and Deut. 15.12-18 (Chapters 6 and 7). However, while these two forms of indentured servitude have often been compared with each other, we have seen that they nevertheless reflect different institutions. For example, the status of a *tidennu*, who provided antichretic services in the house of a creditor, was higher than that of the *ḫabiru* who entered into service contracts with the citizens of Nuzi. This can be attributed to the fact that the *tidennu* was either a slave or dependent of a citizen (or the citizen him- or herself) who secured a loan, while the *ḫabiru* were immigrants who were forced to enter less than favourable contracts in order to secure the necessities of life.

Chapter 4

THE SOCIAL BACKGROUND TO DEBT-SLAVERY IN ISRAEL

The biblical accounts portraying the history of the patriarchs, the Exodus and the Settlement of Israel have often been considered not to portray accurately these early periods of Israelite history. This view is best exemplified in the recent historical works of Soggin[1] and Garbini,[2] who begin their discussion of Israelite history with the monarchy, since they do not consider the biblical account of the earlier periods as a reliable historical record. However, Hallo,[3] who notes correctly that the study of Mesopotamian history relies on various literary sources, some of which are no more 'worthy' than the biblical historical record, suggests that the historical era of Israel begins with Israel's oppression in Egypt (Exod. 1). A more moderate view, however, is held by Malamat,[4] who suggests that the historical era begins with the Settlement of Israel in Canaan. In the following brief discussion of the formation of the state of Israel I will also begin

1. J.A. Soggin, *A History of Israel: From the Beginings to the Bar Kochba Revolt, AD 135* (London: SCM Press, 1985).

2. G. Garbini, *History and Ideology in Ancient Israel* (London: SCM Press, 1988); cf. also H. Reviv, 'History', *EncJud*, VIII, col. 613; G.E. Mendenhall, 'Ancient Israel's Hyphenated History', in *Palestine in Transition: The Emergence of Ancient Israel* (ed. D.N. Freedman and D.F. Graf; SWBAS, 2; Sheffield: Almond Press, 1983), p. 95.

3. W.W. Hallo, 'Biblical History in its Near Eastern Setting: The Contextual Approach', in *Scripture in Context: Essays on the Comparative Method* (ed. C.D. Evans, W.W. Hallo and J.B. White; PTMS, 34; Pittsburgh: Pickwick Press, 1980), pp. 1-26.

4. A. Malamat, 'The Proto-History of Israel: A Study in Method', in *The Word of the Lord Shall Go Forth: Essays in Honor of David Noel Freedman in Celebration of His Sixtieth Birthday* (ed. C.L. Meyers and M. O'Connor; ASORSVS, 1; Winona Lake, IN: Eisenbrauns, 1983), pp. 303-13.

with the Settlement period, a period that continues to be the focal point of much scholarly discussion.[1]

The Formation of the State of Israel

Recent reconstructions of the Settlement of Israel have relied on two important archaeological finds. First, several archaeological surveys of the highlands of Canaan, beginning with Aharoni's survey of the Upper Galilee in the 1950s have shown that there was a great increase in the number of new village settlements (mostly unwalled) during the Early Iron Age (ca. 1200–1000 BCE).[2] To date some three hundred Israelite settlements have been discovered in the hill country of Ephraim–Manasseh, Benjamin–Judah, Northern Galilee and the Negev. Secondly, scholars now generally agree that the Stele of Merneptah,[3] which refers specifically to Israel, has demonstrated

1. For a concise discussion of this very important area of scholarship, see K.W. Whitelam, 'Israel's Traditions of Origin: Reclaiming the Land', *JSOT* 44 (1989), pp. 19-42.

2. For a survey of these archaeological finds, see I. Finkelstein, *The Archaeology of the Israelite Settlement* (Jerusalem: Israel Exploration Society, 1988), pp. 25-112; M. Kochavi, 'The Israelite Settlement in Canaan in the Light of Archeaological Surveys', in *Biblical Archaeology Today: Proceedings of the International Congress on Biblical Archaeology, Jerusalem, April 1984* (ed. J. Amitai; Jerusalem: Israel Exploration Society, 1985), pp. 54-60; A. Mazar, 'The Israelite Settlement in Canaan in the Light of Archaeological Excavations', in Amitai (ed.), *Biblical Archaeology Today*, pp. 61-71; J.A. Callaway, 'Respondents: Session II: Archaeology, History and Bible The Israelite Settlement in Canaan: A Case Study', in Amitai (ed.), *Biblical Archaeology Today*, pp. 72-77; G.W. Ahlström, *Who Were the Israelites?* (Winona Lake, IN: Eisenbrauns, 1986), pp. 25-36; Coote and Whitelam, *The Emergence of Early Israel*, pp. 119-27; Stager, 'The Archaeology of the Family in Ancient Israel', pp. 3-4; Y. Aharoni, *The Archaeology of the Holy Land: From the Prehistoric Beginnings to the End of the First Temple Period* (London: SCM Press, 1982).

3. Cf. H. Engel, 'Die Siegesstele des Merenptah', *Bib* 60 (1979), pp. 373-99; L.E. Stager, 'Merneptah, Israel and the Sea Peoples: New Light on an Old Relief', *Eretz-Israel* 18 (1985), pp. 56-64; G.W. Ahlström and D. Edelman, 'Merneptah's Israel', *JNES* 44 (1985), pp. 59-61. Refer also to F. Yurco, '3,200-Year-Old Picture of Israelites Found in Egypt', *BARev* 16 (1990), pp. 20-38, who has identified one of the battle reliefs on the western outer wall of the Cour de la Cachette in the Karnak temple in Egypt as the Israelite battle scene described on the Merneptah Stele; cp. A.F. Rainey, 'Rainey's Challenge', *BARev* 17 (1991), pp. 56-60, 93,

conclusively that Israel was a political and military entity in Canaan at ca. (1228) 1208 BCE, although they are not in agreement whether this reference to Israel refers to the 12 tribes,[1] to a few or a single tribal group[2] or even to a geographical area.[3] However, the structure of the stele, in which Israel is mentioned in parallel with other important political states, suggests that the Israel was considered an important political and military power even during its early history.[4] Nevertheless, there is still no consensus concerning the origin or manner of the settlement of the Israelites. To date, three main views

who, while in agreement with Yurco's thesis, nevertheless suggests that Israel is depicted in a different relief. For Yurco's reply to Rainey's challenge, see 'Yurco's Response', *BARev* 16 (1991), p. 61.

1. Cf. Malamat, 'The Proto-History of Israel: A Study in Method', p. 305; S. Herrmann, 'Basic Factors of Israelite Settlement in Canaan', in Amitai (ed.), *Biblical Archaeology Today*, p. 49; L.E. Stager, 'Respondents: Session II: Archaeology, History and Bible. The Israelite Settlement in Canaan: A Case Study', in Amitai (ed.), *Biblical Archaeology Today*, p. 86; N.K. Gottwald, 'The Israelite Settlement as a Social Revolutionary Movement', in Amitai (ed.), *Biblical Archaeology Today*, p. 43; Z. Kallai, 'Organizational and Administrative Frameworks in the Kingdom of David and Solomon', in *Proceedings of the Sixth World Congress of Jewish Studies, Jerusalem 1973* (Jerusalem, 1973), p. 219.

2. Cf. Malamat, 'The Proto-History of Israel: A Study in Method', p. 305, who suggests that the name 'Israel' may refer to the house of Joseph; cf. also N.P. Lemche, *Ancient Israel: A New History of Israelite Society* (TBS, 5; Sheffield: JSOT Press, 1987), pp. 88-89, 103, who suggests that the stele refers to the tribes of Ephraim, Manasseh, and perhaps Benjamin. This view conforms with the settlement areas that have been excavated so far, although it should be borne in mind that these surveys are still very limited. Lastly, refer to Rainey, 'Rainey's Challenge', p. 93, who writes: '. . . I do not mean to say that the "Israel" of the Merneptah Stele necessarily includes or is equivalent of the 12-tribe nation depicted in the Bible. Some of the later tribes arrived in Canaan from different directions and perhaps at different times. However, the Merneptah Stele leaves no doubt that an ethnic group called "Israel" did exist in 1207 BCE.'

3. Cf. Ahlström and Edelman, 'Merneptah's Israel', pp. 59-61; Ahlström, *Who Were the Israelites?*, pp. 39-43; cp. Rainey, 'Rainey's Challenge', pp. 60, 93.

4. Cf. B. Halpern, *The Emergence of Israel in Canaan* (SBLMS, 29; Chico, CA: Scholars Press, 1983), pp. 181-82; and Kallai, 'Organizational and Administrative Frameworks', pp. 213-20, who suggests that the existence of the 12 tribes at the outset of the monarchical period can only be explained by the presence of these tribes during Israel's entrance into Canaan; cf. also L.E. Stager, The Song of Deborah: Why Some Tribes Answered the Call and Others Did Not', *BARev* 15 (1989), pp. 51-64; Yurco, 'Yurco's Response', p. 61.

have been proposed for the origin and settlement of the Israelites.[1]

First, there are scholars who suggest that the Iron Age settlers were new nomadic immigrants who either entered Canaan in around 1200 BCE or who had a long contact with the Canaanites before they settled in the highlands. The former view is held by proponents of the 'conquest model'[2] and 'nomadic infiltration model'[3]. The latter view is held by Fritz,[4] who suggests that the Iron Age settlers were nomads who migrated into Canaan before 1500 BCE, after which they adopted many aspects of the Canaanite culture (e.g., symbiosis) before they eventually settled in the highlands. Similarly, Callaway[5] suggests that the Iron Age settlers were newcomers to Canaan, but proposes that they were not nomads but farmers and herders who brought their

1. For a critique of these viewpoints and their advocates, see W.H. Stiebing, *Out of the Desert? Archaeology and the Exodus/Conquest Narratives* (Buffalo, NY: Prometheus, 1989); and J.J. Bimson, 'The Origins of Israel in Canaan: An Examination of Recent Theories', *Themelios* 15 (1989), pp. 4-15; *idem*, 'Merenptah's Israel and Recent Theories of Israelite Origins', *JSOT* 49 (1991), pp. 3-29.

2. The 'conquest model' suggests that the numerous accounts of the destruction of Canaanite cities found in Joshua largely agrees with the historical facts. For example, see W.F. Albright, 'Archaeology and the Date of the Hebrew Conquest of Palestine', *BASOR* 58 (1935), pp. 10-18; *idem*, 'The Israelite Conquest of Palestine in the Light of Archaeology', *BASOR* 74 (1939), pp. 11-23; G.E. Wright, *Biblical Archaeology* (Philadelphia: Westminster Press, 2nd edn, 1962); J. Bright, *A History of Israel* (Philadelphia: Westminster Press, 3rd edn, 1981); *idem*, *Early Israel in Recent History Writing: A Study in Method* (London: SCM Press, 1956).

3. The 'nomadic infiltration model' suggests that the biblical account of 'conquest' in Joshua is inaccurate and that the invasion of Palestine was in reality a gradual infiltration of nomads who originated outside the country but who in the course of time became settled in Palestine, a situation reflected in the accounts of Judges 1 and elsewhere in Joshua. For example, see A. Alt, 'Erwägungen über die Landnahme der Israeliten in Palästina', in *Kleine Schriften zur Geschichte des Volkes Israel*, I (Munich: Beck, 1959) pp. 126-75 = 'The Settlement of the Israelites in Palestine', in *Essays on Old Testament History and Religion* (Oxford: Oxford University Press, 1966), pp. 133-69; M. Noth, *The History of Israel* (Oxford: Basil Blackwell, 1960).

4. V. Fritz, 'The Israelite "Conquest" in the Light of Recent Excavations at Khirbet el-Meshash', *BASOR* 241 (1981), pp. 61-73; 'Conquest or Settlement? The Early Iron Age in Palestine', *BA* 50 (1987), pp. 84-100.

5. J.A. Callaway, 'Excavating Ai (et-Tell): 1964–1972', *BA* 39 (1976), pp. 18-30; 'Israelite Settlement in Canaan', pp. 72-77.

sedentary life with them. Both of these scholars suggest that the
entrance of these people into Canaan was marked by a peaceful
'infiltration' rather than conquest, although Fritz acknowledges that
some of the Late Bronze Age destruction of Canaanite cities may be
attributed to the Israelites. However, it appears that the 'conquest
model', as illustrated in the book of Joshua, can no longer be dated
during the early Iron Age, as suggested by Albright, since many of
the cities purported to be destroyed by Joshua were already destroyed
by 1200 BCE. Nevertheless, a revised version of the 'conquest model'
has recently been proposed by Bimson,[1] who suggests that the
conquest should be dated to the time of the fall of the Canaanite cities
during the Middle Bronze Age. His version of the 'conquest model'
coincides with the above views that the Israelites had a long period of
contact with the Canaanites before they settled in the highlands.[2]

Secondly, Finkelstein[3] suggests that the Iron Age settlers were
mainly Canaanite nomads/pastoralists who were once part of the
sedentarized populations of the surrounding city-states. These

1. J.J. Bimson, *Redating the Exodus and Conquest* (Sheffield: Almond Press,
2nd edn, 1981); *idem*, 'Redating the Exodus—The Debate Goes On: A Reply to
Baruch Halpern's "Radical Exodus Redating Fatally Fawed" ', *BARev* 14 (1988),
pp. 52-55; *idem*, 'Merenptah's Israel and Recent Theories of Israelite Origins',
pp. 3-29; J.J. Bimson and D. Livingston, 'Redating the Exodus', *BARev* 13
(1987), pp. 40-53, 66-68.

2. Cp. Lemche, *Ancient Israel*, pp. 110-11, who thinks that a date of 1425 BCE
for the Israelite conquest of Canaan is unlikely, since there is no mention of Israel
until 1200 BCE. However, this argument from silence is not convincing, particularly
if one recognizes that the so-called conquest of Canaan did not come to fruition until
the time of Saul and David. The fact that Israel adopted many aspects of Canaanite
culture suggests that the Israelites were in Canaan for a relatively long period of time,
perhaps as nomadic groups who stayed on the fringes of Canaanite city-states. Cf.
Bimson's reply to Lemche in 'Merenptah's Israel and Recent Theories of Israelite
Origins', pp. 15-16, 24-25. More critical comments come from Rainey, 'Rainey's
Challenge', p. 60, who considers Bimson's thesis to be an exercise in 'science
fiction'; and Halpern, 'Radical Exodus Redating Fatally Flawed', pp. 56-61; cf.
Bimson's reply in 'Redating the Exodus', pp. 52-55.

3. I. Finkelstein, 'Respondents: Session II: Archaeology, History and Bible The
Israelite Settlement in Canaan: A Case Study', in Amitai (ed.), *Biblical Archaeology
Today*, pp. 80-83; *idem*, *The Archaeology of the Israelite Settlement*; cf. also
G.W. Ahlström, 'Giloh: A Judahite or Canaanite Settlement', *IEJ* 34 (1984),
pp. 170-72; *idem*, *Who Were the Israelites?*, pp. 11-24; Coote and Whitelam, *The
Emergence of Early Israel*, pp. 125-26.

sedentary Canaanites dropped out of the city-states during the Late Bronze Age (1550–1200 BCE), during which several cities were destroyed, and became nomads/pastoralists, but then re-sedentarized during the early Iron Age when they settled in the highlands.

Thirdly, there are scholars who suggest that the Iron Age settlers were composed of both new nomadic immigrants and indigenous Canaanite peasant groups who were once part of the sedentarized populations of the surrounding city-states. This view is held by the proponents of the 'rebellion model',[1] who suggest that these Israelite and Canaanite groups rebelled against the Canaanite city-states.

The fact that there has yet to be a consensus reached concerning the origin and manner of settlement of the Israelites in Canaan is due, in part, to the difficulty in distinguishing between Israelite and Canaanite

---

1. The 'rebellion model', which represents a significant departure from the first two models, was first proposed by G.E. Mendenhall, 'The Hebrew Conquest of Palestine', in *Biblical Archaeology Reader*, III (ed. D.N. Freedman and F. Campbell, Jr; Garden City, NY: Doubleday, 1970), pp. 100-20, who suggests that the conquest of Israel was not an immigration or invasion of nomads but a 'peasant's revolt' based upon a cultural and ideological revolution; cf. also *idem*, *The Tenth Generation: The Origins of the Biblical Tradition* (Baltimore: The John Hopkins University Press, 1973), pp. 24-26; *idem*, 'Ancient Israel's Hyphenated History', p. 92. The key to the solidarity between the Hebrews and the other 'stateless' social units that withdrew from or rebelled against the Canaanites was achieved through a common adherence to the Yahwistic religion, which was anti-Canaanite in nature. Mendenhall's views are taken up and expanded by N.K. Gottwald, *The Tribes of Yahweh: A Sociology of the Religion of Liberated Israel 1250–1050 BCE* (London: SCM Press, 1979), pp. 323-27, esp. 325, who also suggests that the nomadic origins of Israel should be rejected. However, he stresses the political rather than ideological nature of the 'revolt', which was accomplished through a process known as 'retribalization' (i.e., a rejection of the Canaanite system by returning to a primitive and egalitarian tribal social system). However, Mendenhall, 'Ancient Israel's Hyphenated History', pp. 91-102, has made it clear that he does not agree with various views of Gottwald's, particularly regarding 'retribalization' and 'egalitarianism'. Cf. also M.L. Chaney, 'Ancient Palestinian Peasant Movements and the Formation of Premonarchic Israel', in *Palestine in Transition: The Emergence of Ancient Israel* (ed. D.N. Freedman and D.F. Graf; SWBAS, 2; Sheffield: Almond Press, 1983), pp. 39-90; *idem*, 'Systemic Study of the Israelite Monarchy', *Semeia* 37 (1986), pp. 53-76; R. Boling, *The Early Biblical Community in Transjordan* (SWBAS, 6; Sheffield: Almond Press, 1988), who have proposed important refinements to the 'revolt model'.

settlements, since it is now known that the three- or four-room house, 'collared rim jar' and plastered cisterns, features that were often attributed only to the Israelites, were most likely adopted from the Canaanites.[1] Nevertheless, Coote and Whitelam,[2] who have attempted to clarify certain aspects of the manner of the Israelite Settlement, suggest that the settlement of the highlands was probably prompted by the significant decrease in trade that occurred during the Late Bronze IIB Age (1300–1200 BCE). Furthermore, they suggest that this economic decline, as evidenced by the destruction of several Late Bronze Age cities, gave rise to an increase in highland agricultural settlements. While the invention of terracing, which allowed farmers to plant crops in the highlands, is often considered to be the impetus behind the settlement of the highlands, Frick,[3] in a private correspondence with Edelstein, suggests that there is evidence that terracing was in use during the Intermediate Bronze Age (2200–1950 BCE).

Therefore, the steady decline of the Canaanite city-states during the Late Bronze period probably allowed populations to settle peacefully in the highlands, as demonstrated by the appearance of a significant number of new unfortified settlements. This opinion is also shared by Kochavi,[4] who notes that the first Israelite settlements occurred in areas where there were no Canaanite cities. It is the peaceful aspect of these highland settlements that has prompted Kochavi and other archaeologists, such as Stager, Callaway and others[5] to suggest that

1. Cf. Stager, 'The Archaeology of the Family in Ancient Israel', pp. 10-11, 16; A. Mazar, 'The Israelite Settlement in Canaan', pp. 66-68; Callaway, 'Israelite Settlement in Canaan', pp. 75-76; Coote and Whitelam, *The Emergence of Early Israel*, pp. 122-27; Ahlström, *Who Were the Israelites?*, p. 28; F. Braemer, *L'architecture domestique du Levant à l'age du fer: protohistoire du Levant* (ERC, 8; Paris: A.D.P.F., 1982), pp. 103-105; Finkelstein, *The Archaeology of the Israelite Settlement*, pp. 337-38.

2. Coote and Whitelam, *The Emergence of Early Israel*; idem, 'The Emergence of Israel', pp. 107-47; cp. Stiebing, *Out of the Desert? Archaeology and the Exodus/Conquest Narratives*, p. 187, who suggests that the emergence of Israel in Canaan was due to the effects of prolonged drought and famine.

3. Frick, *The Formation of the State in Ancient Israel*, p. 131.

4. Kochavi, 'The Israelite Settlement in Canaan', pp. 54-60.

5. Stager, 'Israelite Settlement in Canaan', p. 85; Callaway, 'Israelite Settlement in Canaan', pp. 72-77; Cf. J.M. Miller, 'The Israelite Occupation of Canaan', in *Israelite and Judaean History* (OTL; ed. J.H. Hayes and J.M. Miller; London: SCM

there is no evidence of a revolt as suggested by proponents of the 'revolt model'. However, while it may be difficult to demonstrate that a rebellion occurred, the economic decline of Canaan during this period suggests that the Israelite settlers could have been either immigrants who entered the land during this period or earlier, or displaced Canaanite urban populations.[1] Nevertheless, archaeological surveys have shown that a significant *new* population did arise within Canaan which cannot be explained solely by the effects of economic decline or revolt,[2] although these Israelites adopted much of the Canaanite culture and were to an extent reliant upon the Canaanite populations for economic support.[3] However, it is difficult to tell to

---

Press, 1977), pp. 213-79; *idem*, 'Israelite History', in *The Hebrew Bible and its Modern Interpreters* (ed. D.A. Knight and G.M. Tucker; SBLI; Philadelphia: Fortress Press; Chico, CA: Scholars Press, 1985), pp. 10-12; A.J. Hauser, 'Israel's Conquest of Palestine: A Peasant's Rebellion?', *JSOT* 7 (1978), pp. 2-19; *idem*, 'Response to Thompson and Mendenhall', *JSOT* 7 (1978), pp. 35-36; *idem*, 'The Revolutionary Origins of Ancient Israel: A Response to Gottwald', *JSOT* 8 (1978), pp. 46-49; A.F. Rainey, 'Rainey's Challenge', p. 60; and Finkelstein, *The Archaeology of the Israelite Settlement*, pp. 306-14, who presents various archaeological arguments against the 'rebellion model'.

   1. Cf. H.N. Rösel, 'Die Entstehung Israels, Evolution oder Revolution?', *BN* 59 (1991), pp. 28-32, who writes: 'Das Verhältnis von Kanaan und Israel hat sich als von dialektischer Art erwiesen. Mit ihm verkaüpft sind die Gegensätze von Evolution und Revolution. Nur wenn diese Dialektik begriffen und kein Element in einseit iger Weise herausgestellt wird, kann der Versuch, Israels Enstehung und sein Wesen zu verstehen, mit Aussicht auf Erfolg unternommen werden.'

   2. Cf. Stager, 'The Archaeology of the Family in Ancient Israel', pp. 3-4; cp. Coote and Whitelam, *The Emergence of Early Israel*, p. 133; and D.C. Hopkins, *The Highlands of Canaan: Agricultural Life in the Early Iron Age* (SWBAS, 3; Sheffield: Almond Press, 1985), pp. 152-57, who note that making estimations of populations is hazardous.

   3. It is no longer expedient to regard pastoralists/nomads as wandering peoples who had no contact with urban areas, since it has been shown that these groups did not live in isolation, and that they moved easily in and out of urban areas depending on the political and economic climate; cf. Lemche, *Early Israel*, pp. 198-201; Gelb, 'Household and Family in Early Mesopotamia', pp. 3-4; M.B. Rowton, 'Enclosed Nomadism', *JESHO* 17 (1974), pp. 1-30; Stager, 'The Israelite Settlement in Canaan', p. 85; A. Kempenski, 'Discussion: Session II: Archaeology, History and Bible. The Israelite Settlement in Canaan: A Case Study', in Amitai (ed.), *Biblical Archaeology Today*, p. 90; A. Malamat, 'Mari and Early Israel', p. 240; Fritz, 'Conquest or Settlement?', pp. 84-100; A. Kahan, 'Economic History', *EncJud*,

what extent early Israel was composed of Israelites who migrated from outside Canaan.[1] Nevertheless, the Stele of Merneptah suggests that much more credence should be given to the biblical view of the Israelites as non-Canaanite tribal groups who eventually settled in Canaan.[2]

While the origin of the Israelites remains a moot point, it is clear that Israel eventually developed into a national state under the leadership of Saul, David[3] and Solomon, whose military actions repelled the threat of the imperial Philistines in the highlands,[4] and allowed the Israelites to settle into the lowlands of Canaan. The formation of the national state of Israel, like the formation of the Mesopotamian and Canaanite states, must be seen as a long process that involved both environmental and social factors.[5] However, as

XVI, col. 1268. Furthermore, the Israelites, who eventually settled in the highlands, probably shared a 'symbiotic' relationship (or adaption) with the Canaanites, borrowing various aspects of their culture and relying on them for economic support; cf. Stager, 'The Israelite Settlement in Canaan', p. 85; Kempenski, 'The Israelite Settlement in Canaan', p. 90; Fritz, 'Conquest or Settlement?', pp. 84-100.

1. Cf. Finkelstein, *The Archaeology of the Israelite Settlement*, p. 348, who, although he accepts that there were Israelites who entered Canaan from Egypt, nevertheless suggests that the vast majority of people who settled in the hill country must have been indigenous Canaanites who dropped out of the city-states in the Late Bronze period.

2. Cf. Herrmann, 'Israelite Settlement in Canaan', p. 49, who notes that the stele connects Israel with the Ephraimite hill country, a view substantiated in the book of Judges; cf. also Fritz, 'Conquest or Settlement?', p. 99, who suggests that the 'song of Deborah' in Judges 5 depicts an accurate historical account which demonstrates that Israel was in Canaan at the end of the Late Bronze Age.

3. Cf. Frick, *The Formation of the State in Ancient Israel*, pp. 51-97; Coote and Whitelam, *The Emergence of Early Israel*, pp. 150, 61; C. Hauer, 'From Alt to Anthropology: The Rise of the Israelite State', *JSOT* 36 (1986), pp. 3-15; J.W. Rogerson, 'Was Early Israel a Segmentary Society?', *JSOT* 36 (1986), pp. 17-26; J. Flanagan, 'Chiefs in Israel', *JSOT* 20 (1981), pp. 47-73; Whitelam, *The Just King*, pp. 71-89, all of whom suggest that Israel went through an intermediate stage of development—'chiefdom'—under the leadership of Saul and David before it became a national state in the latter part of the reign of David.

4. Cf. Bright, *A History of Israel*, p. 185; Soggin, *A History of Israel*, p. 49.

5. Cf. Frick, *The Formation of the State in Ancient Israel*, pp. 194-96, who likens the formation of Mesopotamian city-states to the formation of the Israelite state; Coote and Whitelam, *The Emergence of Early Israel*, pp. 164-66; Hauer, 'From Alt to Anthropology', pp. 3-10; Lemche, *Ancient Israel*, pp. 131-35;

Stager[1] correctly points out, with 'few exceptions throughout Mediterranean history, it has been the highlanders beyond the coastal plains who overcame political fragmentation (so endemic to the cosmopolitan city-states [of Canaan]) to create much larger polities'. The social organization of pre-monarchic and monarchic Israel, like that in Mesopotamia and elsewhere in the ancient Near East, was most likely based on the lineage system, a system that has been used to discuss various aspects of Israel's social and political structures.[2]

S. Talmon, 'The Rule of the King', in *King, Cult and Calendar in Ancient Israel: Collected Studies* (Jerusalem: Magnes, 1986), pp. 53-67. Cf. also I. Finkelstein, 'The Emergence of the Monarchy of Israel: The Environmental and Socio-economic Aspects', *JSOT* 44 (1989), pp. 43-74, who provides a critique of the above views in the light of archaeological and socio-economic findings. Cp. E. Neufeld, 'The Emergence of a Royal-Urban Society in Ancient Israel', *HUCA* 31 (1960), p. 37; Herrmann, *A History of Israel*, p. 132; J. Bright, *A History of Israel*, p. 187; B. Halpern, *The Constitution of the Monarchy in Israel* (HSM, 25; Chico, CA: Scholars Press, 1981), pp. 246-49.

1. Stager, 'The Archaeology of the Family in Ancient Israel', p. 5. For discussions concerning the history of Canaan, see T.E. Levy, 'That Chalcolithic Period', *BA* 49 (1986), pp. 83-109; S. Richard, 'The Early Bronze Age: The Rise and Collapse of Urbanism', *BA* 50 (1987), pp. 22-43; W.G. Dever, 'The Middle Bronze Age: The Zenith of the Urban Canaanite Era', *BA* 50 (1987), pp. 149-77.

2. For discussions of the genealogical lists in the OT, see A. Malamat, 'Tribal Societies: Biblical Genealogies and African Lineage Systems', *Archives européenes de Sociologie* 14 (1973), pp. 126-36 and Wilson, *Genealogy and History*. For discussions of the early social structure of Israel, see F.I. Andersen, 'Israelite Kinship Terminology and Social Structure', *BT* 20 (1969), pp. 29-39; de Geus, *The Tribes of Israel*; Gottwald, *The Tribes of Yahweh*; and Lemche, *Early Israel*; *idem*, *Ancient Israel*, pp. 92-102. For discussion of law and judicial authority in early Israel, see R.R. Wilson, 'Enforcing the Covenant: The Mechanisms of Judicial Authority in Early Israel', in *The Quest for the Kingdom of God: Studies in Honor of G.E. Mendenhall* (ed. H.B. Huffmon, F.A. Spina and A.R.W. Green; Winona Lake, IN: Eisenbrauns, 1983), pp. 59-76; *idem*, 'Israel's Judicial System in the Preexilic Period', *JQR* 74 (1983), pp. 229-48; and E. Bellefontaine, 'Customary Law and Chieftainship: Judicial Aspects of 2 Samuel 14: 4-21', *JSOT* 38 (1987), pp. 47-72. For discussions of the development of the state of Israel, see Frick, *The Formation of the State in Ancient Israel*; Rogerson, 'Was Early Israel a Segmentary Society?', pp. 17-26; and Hauer, 'From Alt to Anthropology', pp. 3-15. For a discussion of the anti-monarchical texts in the OT, see F. Crüsemann, *Der Widerstand gegen das Königtum: Die antiköniglichen Texte des Alten Testamentes und der Kampf um der frühen israelitischen Staat* (WMANT, 49; Neukirchen–Vluyn: Neukirchener Verlag, 1978). Cp. Lemche, *Early Israel*, pp. 219-23; and D. Fiensy,

While scholars continue to debate the dating cf the various literary strata that illustrate the society and social structure of pre-monarchic and monarchic Israel, I am in agreement with Frick in the view that, 'at least for the most part, such passages point to a knowledge on the part of the several editors of the various stages of sociocultural evolution, as well as something of the implications of these changes for the society of which they were a part'.[1]

During the Pre-Monarchic period Israelite tribes, like their ancient Near Eastern counterparts, were responsible for the protection of the social and territorial rights of the local inhabitants.[2] Furthermore, Malamat[3] and Milgrom[4] suggest that the Sumerian assembly of free adults is similar to the Israelite 'assembly' or 'council' (i.e., the קהל/עדה cf. Exod. 12.3, 21; Num. 8.7; 14.1-4; 31.26, 28, 43; Josh. 22.13), which were collective bodies of self-government in pre-monarchic Israel. These 'popular' secular assemblies, as well as related sacral institutions, continued to exert political and constitutional

---

'Using the Nuer Culture of Africa in Understanding the Old Testament: An Evaluation', *JSOT* 38 (1987), pp. 73-83, both of whom question the validity of such discussions.

1. Frick, *The Formation of the State in Ancient Israel*, p. 73; cf. also Halpern, *The Emergence of Israel in Canaan*, p. 239, who suggests that the biblical accounts of pre-monarchic Israel are fairly accurate; and Chaney, 'Systemic Study of the Israelite Monarchy', pp. 57-58, who suggests that the Deuteronomistic Historian and the Chronicler preserve information about the 'materiality' of Israel, and that the prophetic and legal texts address socioeconomic and technoenvironmental realities. Cp. Lemche, *Early Israel*, p. 274, who does not accept that references to political organizations in the Priestly data of the Tetrateuch date to the pre-monarchic period, although he uses these texts to demonstrate the social structure of early Israel; cf. also *idem, Ancient Israel*, pp. 119-24, where Lemche is equally pessimistic about the historical reliability of the Deuteronomistic history.

2. Cf. Gottwald, *The Tribes of Israel*, pp. 293-337.

3. A. Malamat, 'Kingship and Council in Israel and Sumer: A Parallel', *JNES* 22 (1963), pp. 247-51.

4. Milgrom, 'Political and Social Structure of Pre-Monarchic Israel', pp. 2, 11. Milgrom notes that terms referring to the political organization 'assembly of all free male adults' can be found in Sumerian, Akkadian, Hittite, Phoenician, Ugaritic, Latin and finally in the two Hebrew terms קהל/עדה, which Milgrom understands to be synonymous. Whether or not one agrees with Milgrom that these two terms are synonymous is not important. What is important is that one of these terms, עדה, does refer to an assembly composed of all free male adults which is a political association developed from the coalition of the 12 Israelite tribes.

pressure upon the king (c.f. 1 Sam. 8.1-22; 10.25; 1 Kgs 12.1-15; 2 Kgs 23.1-3).[1] Similarly, McKenzie,[2] Wilson[3] and Bellafontaine[4] have shown that much of early Israel's judicial organization was derived from its kinship structure, although the judicial authority of the kinship groups was gradually subsumed under the monarchical judicial systems of David, Solomon and Jehoshaphat (cf. 2 Chron. 19.4-11).[5]

While the formation of the Israelite state, like those in the rest of the ancient Near East, brought significant improvements to the lives of the Israelites, during the process of centralization tribal authority was weakened and social stratification increased,[6] although there is no evidence of the extensive state sector households that we find in Mesopotamia. Furthermore, the ownership of patrimonial land (נחלה) remained an important institution of the private sector during the Monarchic period and later (cf. 2 Samuel 14; 1 Kgs 21.1-19; Ruth),[7]

---

1. Cf. N.E. Andreasen, 'The Role of the Queen Mother in Israelite Society', *CBQ* 45 (1983), pp. 179-94; Z. Ben-Barak, 'The Mizpah Covenant (1S 10.25)—the Source of the Israelite Monarchy', *ZAW* 91 (1979), pp. 30-43; Halpern, *The Constitution of the Monarchy in Israel*, pp. 175-216, esp. 214-16; Gottwald, *Tribes of Yahweh*, p. 143; H. Tadmor, '"The People" and the Kingship in Ancient Israel: The Role of the Political Institutions in the Biblical Period', *JWH* 11 (1968), pp. 46-68; S. Talmon, 'Kingship and the Ideology of the State', in *King, Cult and Calendar in Ancient Israel: Collected Studies* (Jerusalem: Magnes, 1986), pp. 21-25; *idem*, 'The Rule of the King', pp. 53-67; Wiseman, 'Law and Order in Old Testament Times', pp. 12-13.

2. J.L. McKenzie, 'The Elders in the Old Testament', *Bib* 40 (1959), pp. 522-40.

3. Wilson, 'Judicial Authority in Early Israel', pp. 59-75; 'Israel's Judicial System in the Preexilic Period', pp. 229-48.

4. Bellefontaine, 'Customary Law and Chieftainship', pp. 4-21.

5. According to Ezek. 16.40; 17.17; 23.3, 46-47; Ezra 10.12; Neh. 8.2, the judicial sentence of death by stoning was executed by the קהל/עדה 'assembly' during the pre- and post-exilic periods. For comparative discussions of the pre-monarchic and monarchic judicial systems, see Whitelam, *The Just King*, pp. 39-71; J.A. Dearman, *Property Rights in the Eighth-Century Prophets: The Conflict and its Background* (SBLDS, 106; Atlanta: Scholars Press, 1988), pp. 78-107.

6. Cf. Neufeld, 'The Emergence of a Royal-Urban Society in Ancient Israel', pp. 41-53.

7. Cf. Malamat, 'Mari and the Bible', pp. 147-50; *idem*, 'Pre-Monarchical Social Institutions in Israel', pp. 172-76; S.E. Loewenstamm, 'נחלה', *Encyclopedia Biblica: Thesaurus Rerum Biblicarum Alphabetico Ordine Digestus*, XIX (Hebrew)

although with the increase in centralization debt-slavery and the alienation of land increased (cf. 2 Kgs 4.1-7; Neh. 5.1-13; Isa. 5.8; Jer. 34.8-16; Mic. 2.1-2; Amos 8.5).[1] In the following discussion I will examine the composition of the state and private sector households and those factors that contributed to the increase in debt-slavery and land loss among the Israelite free citizens.

Composition of the State and Private Sector Households

State Sector Households

While there is sufficient documentary evidence with which to reconstruct the composition of the state households of Mesopotamia, there is very little evidence with which to reconstruct the composition of the temple and palace households of the united and divided kingdoms of Israel, although archaeological finds and various biblical accounts do give some indication of the various administrative offices created by David and Solomon and the extent and composition of their palace economies.[2] Despite this paucity of evidence, scholars generally agree that the monarchies of David and Solomon closely resembled the bureaucratic complexities often associated with Mesopotamian city-states.[3] The Israelite state, like the Mesopotamian states, provided funds from which the state could protect the community in emergencies, such as war,[4] and fund large-scale projects that were

(ed. H. Tadmor; Jerusalem: Bialik Institute, 1968), cols. 815-16; E. Lipiński, 'נחלה', *ThWat*, V, cols. 341-60; T.J. Lewis, 'The Ancestral Estate (נחלת אלהים) in 2 Samuel 14:16', *JBL* 110 (1991), pp. 597-612; Chaney, 'Systemic Study of the Israelite Monarchy', pp. 61-62; Silver, *Prophets and Markets*, pp. 73-74; de Vaux, *Ancient Israel*, pp. 72, 176; Halpern, *The Emergence of Israel*, p. 211.

1. Cf. Dearman, *Property Rights in the Eighth-Century Prophets*; and R.H. Lowery, *The Reforming Kings: Cult and Society in First Temple Judah* (JSOTSup, 120; Sheffield: JSOT Press, 1991), pp. 54-61.

2. The lists of the court officials of David and Solomon are found in 2 Sam 8.15-18 = 1 Chron. 18.14-17; 20.23-26; 1 Kgs 4.1-6. For a discussion of these offices, see Soggin, *A History of Israel*, pp. 60-64; Bright, *A History of Israel*, pp. 205-207; Herrmann, *A History of Israel*, pp. 160-62; T.D.N. Mettinger, *Solomonic State Officials* (ConBot, 5; Lund, 1971).

3. Cf. de Vaux, *Ancient Israel*, p. 68; Hauer, 'From Alt to Anthropology', p. 6; cf. also *idem*, 'The Economics of National Security in Solomonic Israel', *JSOT* 18 (1980), pp. 63-73; *idem*, 'David and the Levites', *JSOT* 23 (1982), pp. 33-54.

4. Cf. N. Na'aman, 'The List of David's Officers (šālišîm)', *VT* 38 (1988),

beyond the means of the individual, such as building the Temple of
Jerusalem.

The palace households. According to the biblical accounts, the
economic activities of the palace under the administrations of David
and Solomon included olive and grape cultivation, animal husbandry
and other assorted 'industries'. Furthermore, the palace also
controlled a significant share of international trade due to its strategic
position in the Middle East. For example, according to 1 Chron.
27.25-31, David owned various properties, including vineyards and
olive groves; animals, including cattle, camels, donkeys and sheep; and
storehouses, all of which were maintained by various overseers. In
addition to these overseers, there was also an overseer in charge of the
workers who tilled the soil (v. 26).[1] While there is no mention of an
official who was in charge of David's property, de Vaux,[2] Mettinger[3]
and Gottwald[4] suggest that Ahishar, who was an official 'over the
king's house' during Solomon's reign (1 Kgs 4.1-6), was actually in
charge of the king's household (i.e., his properties).[5]

The Crown properties of David were probably obtained from the
conquered lowlands of Canaan, although David may have bought
other properties which he added to his holdings (cf. 2 Sam. 24.24).[6]

pp. 71-79, who suggests that the existence of a professional army, which is
indicative of city- and national states, is attested during the reign of David.

1. Cf. Dearman, *Property Rights in the Eighth-Century Prophets*, p. 113.

2. De Vaux, *Ancient Israel*, p. 125.

3. Mettinger, *Solomonic State Officials*, pp.73-79.

4. N.K. Gottwald, 'The Participation of Free Agrarians in the Introduction of
Monarchy to Ancient Israel: An Application of H.A. Landsberger's Framework for
the Analysis of Peasant Movements', *Semeia* 37 (1986), p. 84.

5. Cp. S.C. Layton, 'The Steward in Ancient Israel: A Study of Hebrew ('A—
ŠER) 'AL-HABBAYIT in its Near Eastern Setting', *JBL* 109 (1990), pp. 635-37,
641-48, who suggests that the *original* sphere of activity of the אשר על־בית '(the
one) over the house' in 1 Kings 4 was relegated only to the palace household,
although he acknowledges that in later times this royal administrative office expanded
to include all of the king's property.

6. There is no reason to assume that the royal properties of David and Solomon
were obtained from the community, since they could easily have obtained them from
the conquered territories, although once the settlement of the lowlands was complete
competition for land undoubtedly increased, particularly during the period of the
divided state when the territories of the north and south were significantly decreased.

Solomon also added to the Crown properties, some of which are perhaps described in Eccl. 2.4-7 (?), through conquest and the bestowal of gifts (cf. 1 Kgs 9.16). However, it is unclear what type of labour was used to maintain the various Crown properties. There are four possible sources of labour: (1) conscripts/slaves; (2) tenants who rent royal land; (3) semi-free citizens; and (4) clients who are given royal land in exchange for service.

1. Dearman[1] suggests that agricultural workers who worked the palace properties were conscripted Israelite labour, based upon 1 Sam. 8.12, in which Samuel tells the people that the future king will appoint people to plow and reap his harvest, and make war materials such as weapons and equipment for his chariots. If, as Talmon[2] suggests, the rules contained in 1 Sam. 8.4-22 were part of the ordinances contained in the so-called book 'The Rule of the King' (1 Sam. 10.25), then the king had the authority to use Israelite labour in his various households. According to 1 Kgs 5.13-15 Solomon conscripted (lit. ויעל מס...מס 'and he raised up forced labourers') 30,000 Israelites to work in the Lebanon in order to help with the building of the Temple of Jerusalem.[3] He sent three groups of 10,000 men in one-month relays, each of which worked for a month and returned home for two months. However, there is no indication that Israelite corvées were

Cf. Chaney, 'Systemic Study of the Israelite Monarchy', p. 72, who suggests that most of the land-owning Israelites remained in the highlands; cf. also L.E. Stager, 'Archaeology', *IDBSup*, p. 13.

1. Dearman, *Property Rights in the Eighth-Century Prophets*, p. 113.
2. Talmon, 'Kingship and the Ideology of the State', pp. 21-25; 'The Rule of the King', pp. 53-67.
3. Cf. Soggin, *A History of Israel*, p. 84; Bright, *A History of Israel*, p. 230; Herrmann, *A History of Israel*, p. 190; de Vaux, *Ancient Israel*, pp. 133-36; M. Noth, *Könige I: Teilband* (BKAT, 9.1; Neukirchen–Vluyn: Neukirchener Verlag, 1968), pp. 92, 216-18. There is a question, however, whether the corvée was levied against both the north and south, since 1 Kgs 4.7-19 speaks only about the division of Israel into 12 districts. Soggin (pp. 82-83) and Herrmann (pp. 177-78) suggest that only the north was subject to tax and the corvée. However, Noth suggests that Solomon levied corvées from both the north and south. Furthermore, Bright (pp. 221-22 and n. 91) and de Vaux (pp. 135-36) suggest that Josh. 15.21-61, which divides Judah into 12 districts, reflects a system that goes back to the time of Solomon, although he dates this text to the time of Jehoshaphat; cf. F.M. Cross and G.E. Wright, 'The Boundary and Province Lists of the Kingdom of Judah', *JBL* 75 (1956), pp. 202-26.

used for duties other than building projects during the reigns of Solomon and Asa (cf. 1 Kgs 15.22),[1] although it is clear that the principal reason why Israel seceded from Judah was the institution of the corvée, which Rehoboam was intent on maintaining.[2] It is likely, as Borowski[3] points out, that the people were concerned that the continued use of corvées, which seriously disturbed agricultural cultivation within Israel, would begin to cause them to lose their land because they could not adequately maintain it. It is also possible that the reaction of the Israelites was due to the corvée levy, which may have been limited to the districts of Israel, rather than Judah, although it is questionable whether Solomon could have afforded to exempt the prosperous south from duties to the king (e.g., corvée service and taxes).[4] However, according to a letter dating to the time of Josiah (ca. 630 BCE), Albright[5] and Gibson[6] suggest that there is a reference to a

---

1. In 1 Kgs 15.22, the term סבל 'burdensome labour' is used instead of the term מס. The term סבל is also used in 11.28 in reference to Jeroboam, who was in charge of forced labour under Solomon. Cf. Mettinger, *Solomonic State Officials*, pp. 128-39, who suggests that the term סבל is a north Israelite synonym for מס.

2. A similar situation occurred during the NA period, when Shalmaneser V, the king of Assyria, attempted to impose forced labour in the ancient capital Ashur. As a result of this action an insurrection took place and Sargon II became king, declaring freedom from certain taxes and obligations to the people of Ashur and elsewhere; cf. Saggs, *The Might That Was Assyria*, p. 92.

3. O. Borowski, *Agriculture in Iron Age Israel: The Evidence from Archaeology and the Bible* (Winona Lake, IN: Eisenbrauns, 1987), p. 9; cf. also Chaney, 'Systemic Study of the Israelite Monarchy', p. 69; Gottwald, 'The Participation of Free Agrarians in the Introduction of Monarchy', p. 85; Bright, *A History of Israel*, p. 223; and Soggin, *A History of Israel*, pp. 60-61, 84, who suggests that the two cases of rebellion against David (2 Sam. 15-19, 20) were probably due to 'tribal' conflicts over forced labour and conscriptions (cf. 2 Sam. 12.31).

4. This point is put forward cogently by Gottwald, 'The Participation of Free Agrarians in the Introduction of Monarchy', p. 86.

5. *ANESTP*, p. 568.

6. J.C.L. Gibson, *Textbook of Syrian Semitic Inscriptions* (Oxford: Clarendon Press, 1971), pp. 26-30. Gibson notes that this letter may refer to either tenant farmers who had to deliver quotas to the fort or to a conscript corvée employed for a period in order to help stock the fort with grain. He prefers the latter view since the worker appears to be destitute or nearly so. The letter reads: (1) The attention of my lord the commandant is drawn to (2) the complaint of his servant. (3) As for your servant—your servant was harvesting at (4) חצר אסם 'village of storing or the granary'; and your servant had reaped (5) and measured and stored (grain) for the

royal corvée of men who were working in fields under the supervision of a military foreman. If this interpretation is correct, we have confirmation that Israelite corvées were used to maintain Crown lands during the time of Josiah. The fact that the biblical record does not record the use of corvées in Judah during the reign of Josiah suggests that it is possible that corvées were used on the Crown lands and other palace projects and industries before the time of Josiah, although by the time of Josiah other sources of labour, such as foreign captives, were less numerous than during the time of Solomon.[1]

According to 1 Kgs 5.15 and 2 Chron. 2.17-18, Solomon also used foreign labour in the building of the Temple of Jerusalem and other state projects.[2] These labourers are probably the same foreign labourers mentioned in 1 Kgs 9.20-21 (= 2 Chron. 8.7-8; cf. also Josh. 16.10 = Judg. 1.28-36), which states that Solomon levied מס־עבד 'a slaving labour-band' from all the foreigners who still lived in Canaan. This passage also states that while Solomon used foreigners as מס־עבד he did not make slaves of the Israelites (v. 22a: מבני ישראל לא־נתן שלמה עבד). Soggin[3] suggests that the expression מס־עבד also

days agreed before (6) stopping. After your servant had measured his (quota of) grain and (7) put it in store for the days agreed, along came Hashabiah son of Shobai, (8) and appropriated your servant's garment. After I had measured (9) my (quota of) grain over the aforementioned days, he appropriated your servant's garment. (10) But all my comrades can testify on my behalf, the ones who were reaping beside me in the heat (11) (of the sun), my comrades can bear witness that it was as I say—I am not guilty of any (12) (crime. So please return) my garment, that I may be given satisfaction—It is the commandant's place to return (13) (his servant's garment, and to show) mercy to him. (14) (If you have paid attention to the complaint of) your servant, then you will not keep silent, but (15)...

1. Cf. Kahan, 'Economic History', col. 1269; cf. also I. Mendelsohn, 'Slavery in the Old Testament', *IDB*, IV, p. 389; C.A. Fontela, 'La esclavitud a través la Biblia', *EstBíb* 43 (1985), pp. 238-42, both of whom suggest that Israelite corvées were employed in the construction of roads, fortresses and temples; helped to maintain crown lands; and worked in palace factories.

2. Cf. Elat, 'The Monarchy and the Development of Trade in Ancient Israel', p. 535, who suggests that the overseer called Obil, who was in charge of raising camels in David's household, was probably an Arab (1 Chron. 27.30). It is likely, therefore, that this aspect of the palace economy was run by foreigners paid by the palace. Furthermore, the palace's international trade was run by foreign merchants, which suggests that foreigners played an important role in the palace households.

3. Soggin, *A History of Israel*, p. 83.

refers to the Israelite corvée mentioned in 1 Kgs 5.13, which contradicts the claim in 1 Kgs 5.13-15 that Solomon did not use Israelites as 'slaves'. In this passage both conscripted Israelites and foreigners are mentioned. However, following the suggestion of North[1] and others,[2] it seems preferable to understand the expression מס־עבד as a type of service that was fundamentally different from the service rendered by the Israelite corvées, for the following reasons. First, the expression מס־עבד is used elsewhere in reference to Issachar (Gen. 49.15), and in reference to the Canaanites who are made to serve the Israelites (Josh. 16.10; 1 Kgs 9.21). That the Israelites were not to be treated as 'slaves', a reference that is not found in any connection with the Israelite corvées, is a reflection back upon Israel's forced service in Egypt under the שרי מסם 'gang overseers' (Exod. 1.11).[3] Secondly, the fact that the Israelites were meant to work only for limited periods of time, so that they could still attend to their own lands or businesses, is in direct contrast to the foreign conscripts, who most likely worked full-time, since no limitation of service is mentioned in their case. Therefore, these foreign slave labourers either worked for longer periods of time or they (more likely) became the permanent possessions of the king (e.g., semi-free), a status that parallels that of the Israelites in Egypt.[4] Lastly, chattel-

---

1. R. North, 'מס', *ThWat*, IV, cols. 1007-1008.

2. Cf. Bright, *A History of Israel*, p. 222; Noth, *Könige I*, pp. 92, 216-18; de Vaux, *Ancient Israel*, p. 141; Mendelsohn, *Slavery in the Ancient Near East*, pp. 97-98; *idem*, 'On Corvée Labor in Ancient Canaan and Israel', *BASOR* 167 (1962), pp. 31-35; cf. also Herrmann, *A History of Israel*, p. 184 n. 26, who appears to adopt the position of Noth. Cp. A.F. Rainey, 'מס־עבד', *Encyclopedia Biblica: Thesaurus Rerum Biblicarum Alphabetico Ordine Digestus*, V (Hebrew) (ed. H. Tadmor; Jerusalem: Bialik Institute, 1968), cols. 55-56; *idem*, 'Compulsory Labour Gangs in Ancient Israel', *IEJ* 20 (1970), pp. 191-202, who suggests that the expressions מס and מס־עבד are equivalent, since the term עבד was added as a kind of official gloss.

3. Although Soggin, *A History of Israel*, p. 83, argues that the term עבד was added to the term מס in order to clarify that labour service is meant, since this term means 'tax' in later and modern Hebrew, this argument is not convincing because only the term מס is used in reference to Israelite corvées.

4. Cf. Noth, *Könige I*, pp. 216-18, who suggests that the foreigners who were conscripted were either slaves or members of the semi-free populations of the Canaanite city-states; cf. also Mendelsohn, *Slavery in the Ancient Near East*, pp. 95-98; Fontela, 'La esclavitud', p. 101; Kahan, 'Economic History', col. 1269.

slaves, most of whom were captured or bought, were used by both the palace and temple (cf. Lev. 21.11; Numb. 31.32-47; Deut. 20.10-14; 21.10; Josh. 9.23-27; Judg. 5.30; Ezek. 44.7-9; Ezra 2.43-58; 8.20; Neh. 7.46-60; 11.3).[1]

2. We saw above in Chapter 2 that Mesopotamian palace Crown lands were often rented out to people. However, while this may have been a source of labour for the palace household, there is no indication in the biblical sources or elsewhere that the renting of Crown property was ever practiced in Israel.

3. Furthermore, we saw in Chapter 2 that semi-free citizens, who either sought refuge or were 'coerced' into service, accounted for the majority of labour in the temple households of Mesopotamia. However, it is doubtful that a semi-free class existed during the reign of David or Solomon, although there is some suggestion that Israelite peasants did maintain lands acquired by officials who owned or controlled large land holdings during the eighth century. I will discuss this possibility in greater detail below.

4. Dearman[2] notes that Mephibosheth, the son of Jonathan, was given a land grant from David, thus making him a patron or client of the royal court (cf. 2 Sam. 9.1-13). This practice is similar to that found in Egypt, Ugarit, Alalakh and Assyria, where clients of the king were given property or other concessions in return for service. Stager[3] notes that Israelite kings most likely employed many clients (i.e., stewards, soldiers and priests) who entered the service of the king due to the reduction of patrimony into smaller and smaller plots of land, and to the difficulty some males had in establishing themselves as heads of households. It is possible, therefore, that Israelite kings employed a group of clients who were given land in order to supply the palace with commodities (cf. 2 Sam. 14.30; 16.1-4; 19.31-40).[4] However, contrary to the view of Whitelam[5] that the king was generally able to seize private land and distribute it to his supporters (cf. 1 Sam 8.14), there is no evidence that this was ever practised

---

1. Cf. Mendelsohn, *Slavery in the Ancient Near East*, pp. 96-97, 105-106.

2. Dearman, *Property Rights in the Eighth-Century Prophets*, pp. 117-23, esp. 20-21; cf. also Whitelam, *The Just King*, p. 173.

3. Stager, 'The Archaeology of the Family in Ancient Israel', pp. 24-28.

4. For the discussion of the possible existence of a large population of semi-free clients in Israel, see in Chapter 6 (מכאן).

5. Whitelam, *The Just King*, p. 173.

during the period of the United and Divided Monarchy.[1]

As the above discussion shows, there were many possible sources of labour that David and Solomon could have used for the maintenance of the Crown properties. The most likely sources, though, would have been the foreign state 'slaves', clients and perhaps national conscripted labour. However, it is difficult to determine whether the palace agricultural households approached the size and significance of the Mesopotamian state agricultural households.

That agricultural produce was an important commodity of the palace is suggested by the royal storehouses located in various cities,[2] and the commercial activities of Solomon, who traded agricultural goods in return for various resources that were used for his extensive building programme (cf. 1 Kgs 5.10-25).[3] While this suggests that Solomon either owned or controlled a significant amount of agricultural land, it is not clear whether these goods, or the money to purchase these goods, were generated by the palace agricultural households.[4] On the one hand, as we saw in the discussion of the control of trade within the state sector of the Mesopotamian states in Chapter 2, consolidation of land ownership increased as the role of trade increased. While the consolidation of land ownership may have been one of the aims of Solomon's administration, although there is little evidence to demonstrate this, I will argue below that it is clear

1. Cf. Gottwald, 'Free Agrarians in the Introduction of Monarchy', p. 81; Mettinger, *Solomonic State Officials*, pp. 80-85; A. Alt, 'Der Anteil des Königtums an der sozialen Entwicklung in den Reichen Israel und Juda', in *Kleine Schriften zur Geschichte des Volkes Israel*, II (Munich: Beck, 1959), pp. 361-64, who suggest that land grants were not confiscated from private citizens but were issued from royal properties obtained primarily through conquest. Even if the king had some rights over community land, according to the so-called 'Rule of the King' it is doubtful that the Israelite public and kinship leadership would have permitted such actions, particularly in view of the turmoil caused by the institution of the corvée.

2. Cf. Aharoni, *The Archaeology of the Land of Israel*, pp. 222-25, who notes that storehouses used for the storing of agricultural products have been found at Megiddo, dating to the time of Solomon (cf. 1 Kgs 9.19; 2 Chron. 11.11; 14.6 (Hebrew v. 5)).

3. Cf. Elat, 'Trade in Ancient Israel', pp. 537-38; Soggin, *A History of Israel*, pp. 77-79; Bright, *A History of Israel*, pp. 214-216.

4. Cf. Gottwald, 'The Participation of Free Agrarians in the Introduction of Monarchy', p. 81, who suggests that David accrued funds largely through the cultivation of crown land.

that such consolidation was the aim of some state officials in later administrations. On the other hand, Solomon received agricultural goods or money from other sources, including taxes he imposed on those who used his trade routes (cf. 2 Chron. 9.14, 21-24), and the 12 districts of Israel (and Judah?),[1] which were responsible for supplying provisions to the king and his household (cf. 1 Kgs 4.7-19). It is possible, therefore, that these sources of money and produce, particularly the taxes imposed upon the people,[2] accounted for a significant amount of the surpluses that Solomon used for his court and for his building programme. Furthermore, it is possible that agriculture played a less significant role in the palace economy than trade and various related 'industries', which remained vital to the economic survival of the divided kingdom.

As we saw above, trade was an important part of the economy of the palace. Both David and Solomon were aware of the strategic position Israel maintained in relation to the important international trade routes of the Middle East that ran through the territory of Israel.[3] One of the more important employees of the palace household who was involved in trading was the merchant, who played an active

1. I have already noted above that it is uncertain whether Solomon levied taxes only from the north, or from both the north and south. Cf. D.B. Redford, 'Studies in Relations between Palestine and Egypt during the First Millennium BC: I: The Taxation Systems of Solomon', in *Studies on the Ancient Palestinian World Presented to Professor F.V. Winnett on the Occasion of his Retirement 1 July 1971* (ed. J.W. Wevers and D.B. Redford; TSTS, 2; Toronto: University of Toronto Press, 1972), pp. 141-56, who suggests that this system of taxation was probably based on contemporary Egyptian models, according to which taxes for the state and temple were raised as well as levies for the boarder garrisons; cf. also Soggin, *A History of Israel*, pp. 81-82.

2. Cf. Chaney, 'Systemic Study of the Israelite Monarchy', p. 69, who suggests that the Israelite farmers supplied agricultural products to the palace of Solomon in the form of tax in order to pay for the building of the temple and in order to provide food for the court. Further, he suggests that the tax collectors demanded more of their production each year; cf. also Gottwald, 'The Participation of Free Agrarians in the Introduction of Monarchy', pp. 84-86.

3. For a discussion of the development of trade under David and Solomon, see Elat, 'Trade in Ancient Israel', pp. 529-41; Kahan, 'Economic History', cols. 1267-69; Soggin, *A History of Israel*, pp. 77-80; Bright, *A History of Israel*, pp. 214-17.

role throughout the history of Israel.[1] In Hebrew the most common term for merchant was כנעני—'Canaanite', which suggests that trading was a Canaanite occupation, although it is likely that Israelite officials also engaged in this commercial activity (cf. Isa. 23.8; Ezek. 17.4; Zeph. 1.11; Prov. 31.24).[2] Other terms for traders and merchants, which are found in the narratives concerning Solomon, include מאנשי התרים—'the people of the emissaries', מסחר הרכלים—'the trade of the merchants' (1 Kgs 10.15) and סחרי המלך—'the traders of the king' (1 Kgs 10.28). However, while it is unclear whether these merchants worked exclusively for the palace or were active in the private sector during Solomon's reign, references to merchants in the prophets suggest that they did engage in private enterprise at that time (cf. Zeph. 1.11; Hos. 12.8 [Hebrew v. 9]).

Despite the economic successes of Solomon, the latter part of his reign was marked by economic[3] and political turmoil which eventually led to the division of the kingdom in 922 BCE. While Solomon's reign brought significant wealth and power to Israel, it also put economic pressure on its free citizens, who were subject to taxation and corvée service. Furthermore, as Gottwald[4] suggests, it is likely that the rich land-owning elite, many of whom were probably connected with the palace, were able to improve their economic position through the acquisition of property that was lost on account of debt, although there is little documentary evidence to demonstrate this. Although there is little indication of the impact the division of the

1. Cf. Elat, 'Trade in Ancient Israel', pp. 529-31; Bright, *A History of Israel*, p. 216.

2. Cf. Kahan, 'Economic History', col. 1269, who suggests that Israelites participated in mercantile occupations up to the period of the divided kingdom, during which Canaanites took over mercantile occupations. Although Kahan bases his view on the use of the term 'Canaanite' in later biblical passages, it is difficult to demonstrate that such a transition took place solely on the use of the term 'Canaanite'. Cp. de Vaux, *Ancient Israel*, pp. 78-79; Elat, 'Trade in Ancient Israel', pp. 529-31, both of whom suggest that foreigners handled the mercantile occupations while Israelites engaged in small businesses.

3. Cf. Soggin, *A History of Israel*, pp. 79-80, who questions Solomon's economic success; and Bright, *A History of Israel*, pp. 220-21, who suggests that Solomon's costs, such as his ambitious building programme, outstripped his capital.

4. Gottwald, 'The Participation of Free Agrarians in the Introduction of Monarchy', pp. 85-86; cf. also Chaney, 'Systemic Study of the Israelite Monarchy', pp. 68-70; Lemche, *Ancient Israel*, pp. 148-53.

kingdom had on the so-called agricultural households of Judah and Israel, it is certain that both kingdoms experienced various phases of economic prosperity and decline attributed to their tentative control over land and trade routes. In the following discussion I will look specifically at the period of the Omride dynasty and the eighth century, during which there was a marked increase in the oppression of free citizens.

During the reigns of Omri (876–869 BCE) and Ahab (869–850 BCE) in Israel, and the reign of Jehoshaphat (873–849 BCE) in Judah, both kingdoms were able to secure important trade routes which resulted in economic prosperity.[1] This period of prosperity is highlighted by an extensive building programme in Israel and significant legal reforms in Judah that replaced customary law with royally appointed judges (cf. 2 Chron. 19.4-11; cf. also Exod. 18.13-27; Deut. 1.9-17). While the centralization of judicial authority under Jehoshaphat can be seen as an attempt by the king to diminish the role of the tribal groups, it is likely that this reform was carried out in order to root out injustice.[2] However, on the negative side the position of the small free citizen landowners probably deteriorated in the face of creditors (cf. 2 Kgs 4.1), and a drought that occurred in Ahab's reign probably forced many small landowners to lose their land (cf. 1 Kgs 17).[3] Furthermore, Chaney[4] suggests that both the Omride building programme, which required the citizens to serve in corvées, and the extensive military campaign of Ahab put extreme economic pressure on the citizens of Israel. This tended to favour the position of the rich landowners, who

---

1. Cf. Elat, 'Trade in Ancient Israel', pp. 542-43.
2. Cf. Dearman, *Property Rights in the Eighth-Century Prophets*, pp. 93-101; Whitelam, *The Just King*, pp. 185-206; Bright, *A History of Israel*, pp. 251-52. Cp. Soggin, *A History of Israel*, p. 212, who suggests that little can be said about this 'reform' since 'it is impossible to establish whether or not the Chronicler was using ancient traditions about the events.' However, Whitelam has shown that despite the exclusion of this reform in the Deuteronomic history, the reform is historical and reflects the significant changes in the administration of justice that took place between the time of the death of Solomon and that of the eighth-century prophets (pp. 185-90).
3. Cf. Bright, *A History of Israel*, pp. 244-45.
4. Chaney, 'Systemic Study of the Israelite Monarchy', pp. 71-72; cf. also Lemche, *Ancient Israel*, p. 149.

increased their holdings through the acquisition of property lost on account of debt.

One example that is often cited to illustrate the injustice of these times is the appropriation of Naboth's vineyard by Ahab (cf. 1 Kgs 21.1-20). While Ahab offered to buy Naboth's vineyard or exchange it for a better one, Naboth refused, stating, 'the Lord forbid me that I should give you the inheritance of my fathers [נחלת אבתי]' (v. 3). In order to obtain Naboth's vineyard Ahab frames Naboth for false witness and has him executed. While it is likely that this incident demonstrates that, in principle, Israelite land was non-transferable (cf. Lev. 25.13-34),[1] Andersen,[2] Whitelam,[3] and Dearman[4] suggest that in reality land was transferable, although there must have been community pressure to prevent this. Similarly, the principle of non-transferable land is probably attested in Mari and Ugarit, although this principle was circumvented by fictitious adoptions and meaningless contractual statements. Therefore, while a similar circumvention of legal principles probably occurred in Israel during this time, it is difficult to determine whether this was accomplished by circumventing known laws or customs, by disobeying or ignoring accepted legal principles (i.e., *Bodenrecht*), or by some other means.[5]

---

1. Cf. A. Rofé, 'The Vineyard of Naboth: the Origin and Message of the Story', *VT* 38 (1988), p. 90. Both Alt, 'Der Anteil des Königtums', pp. 349-65 and G. von Rad, 'The Promised Land and Yahweh's Land in the Hexateuch', in *The Problem of the Hexateuch and Other Essays* (New York: McGraw-Hill, 1966), pp. 79-93; *idem, Old Testament Theology*, I (New York: Harper & Row, 1965), pp. 296-305, suggest that property was inalienable in Israel based on the view that Yahweh was the ultimate owner of all property (cf. Lev. 25.23; Mic. 2.2b), a concept that von Rad suggests is understood as part of the *Leitmotive* of the entire Hexateuch. While it is likely that this principle originated in early Israel, the date of the Jubilee legislation, which contains laws regulating the sale of land, remains unclear.

2. F.I. Andersen, 'The Socio-Juridical Background of the Naboth Incident', *JBL* 85 (1966) pp. 46-57.

3. Whitelam, *The Just King*, pp. 170-81.

4. Dearman, *Property Rights in the Eighth-Century Prophets*, pp. 62-77; cf. also T.L. Thompson, *The Historicity of the Patriarchal Narratives: The Quest for the Historical Abraham* (BZAW, 133; Berlin: de Gruyter, 1974), p. 211.

5. Cf. Halpern, *The Constitution of the Monarchy in Israel*, pp. 175-76, who notes that it is possible that Ahab was not empowered to expropriate land, and that the assembly who condemned Naboth was guilty of complicity as suggested by the

During the reigns of Jehoash/Jeroboam II of Israel (802–786/786–746 BCE) and Amaziah/Uzziah of Judah (800–783/783–742 BCE), the borders of Israel and Judah were extended to the limits attained under David and Solomon.[1] Valuable trade routes were re-opened and both states experienced a period of prosperity. However, the prophets Amos and Hosea make it clear that during this period the small farmers of Israel and Judah were particularly vulnerable to the wealthy private and state sector landowners who made them debt-slaves and obtained their property (cf. Amos 2.6-8; 5.8-12; Hos. 4.2; 5.10; 12.7-8 [Hebrew vv. 8-9]).[2] Amos, in particular, condemns the activities of officials. For example, he writes:

2.8b וויין ענושים ישתו ביח אלהידם

And wine in exaction (ענש) they drink in the house of God.

5.11a לכן בושסכם על־דל

ומשאת־בר תקחו ממנו

Because you place exactions (בושסכם) on the poor

And take grain tribute from him.

Regarding the interpretation of these two passages, Lang[3] suggests that Amos 2.8b may refer to exactions taken from debtors or tenants, and that Amos 5.11a should read: 'Because you make tenants out of the weak, and take tribute of corn from him',[4] based on the view that the *hapax legomenon* בושסכם is a veiled reference to the common Akkadian idiom *šabašu šibša ina eqli* which Wolff[5] and Coote[6]

---

narrator (1 Kgs 21.13); cf. also Lowery, *The Reforming Kings*, p. 57; K. Baltzer, 'Naboths Weinberg (1 Kön 21); der Konflikt zwischen israelitischem und kanaanäischem Bodenrecht', *WD* 8 (1965), pp. 73-88, who suggests that Naboth would have lost his civil rights if he sold his land.

1. For a brief social, economic and historical survey of this period, see P.J. King, 'The Eighth, The Greatest of the Centuries?', *JBL* 108 (1989), pp. 3-15.

2. Cf. Dearman, *Property Rights in the Eighth-Century Prophets*, pp. 18-57; 132-47; Sicre, *La justicia social en los profetas de Israel*, pp. 87-189; Silver, *Prophets and Markets*, pp. 111-18; Lang, 'Peasant Poverty in Biblical Israel', pp. 47-63; Bright, *A History of Israel*, pp. 259-63; Saggs, *The Might That Was Assyria*, p. 82.

3. Lang, 'Peasant Poverty in Biblical Israel', pp. 50-59.

4. Cf. also J. Mays, *Amos* (OTL; Philadelphia: Westminster Press, 1969), p. 90

5. H.W. Wolff, *Amos and Joel* (Hermeneia; Philadelphia: Fortress Press, 1977), p. 230.

6. Coote, *Amos Among the Prophets*, pp. 31-32.

suggest should be rendered 'to take rent from a field'. Therefore, Lang suggests that both references in Amos 2.8b and 5.11a refer to debts and rent taken from tenants who resided on the officials' prebendal domain.

However, Dearman[1] notes correctly that tenant farming does not have a clear reference elsewhere in the Old Testament and probably was not a common practice in Israel. He also suggests that the reference to exaction in Amos 2.8 refers to some kind of tax, following the use of the term in 2 Kgs 23.33, which refers to forced tribute.[2] Furthermore, in reference to Amos 5.11a he notes that the Akkadian verb *šābašu* and its cognate accusative *šibšu* referred to regular taxes collected by local officials during the NA period. This practice of taxation was often susceptible to graft and corruption, a situation that has strong parallels with the biblical accounts. It is therefore most likely that Amos 5.11a refers to a system of taxation that was used by the local state officials in order to increase their wealth and acquire the land of poor citizens for their own use.[3] It is nevertheless possible that tenants worked on the lands obtained by officials, although the above references in Amos most likely do not refer to such a practice.

The formation of latifundia or plantations allowed the rich to market more valuable crops, such as wine and olive oil, rather than the less valuable crops and herds which were vital to the existence of

1. Dearman, *Property Rights in the Eighth-Century Prophets*, pp. 28-31; cf. also Mettinger, *Solomonic State Officials*, p. 87. There is no evidence that the king gave significant amounts of prebendal land to officials, especially since it is unlikely that the king had the judicial power to secure private land for his own use.

2. Cf. Dearman, *Property Rights in the Eighth-Century Prophets*, pp. 117-223 and 18-33, who notes that the Samaria Ostraca, which contains a group of at least 65 dockets recording shipments of oil and wine received by the royal court, probably date to the reign of Jeroboam and appear to indicate either a system of taxation or a system of land-grants. While the latter option has its parallel in Egypt, Ugarit, Alalakh and Assyria, it is more likely that these dockets refer to a system of taxation that was patterned after Solomon's 12 districts.

3. Cf. also K. Koch, 'Die Entstehung der sozialen Kritik bei den Propheten', in *Probleme Biblischer Theologie* (ed. H.W. Wolff; Munich: Chr. Kaiser Verlag, 1971), pp. 146-47; and M. Fendler, 'Zur Sozialkritik des Amos', *EvT* 33 (1973), pp. 37-38, both of whom are cited in Dearman, *Property Rights in the Eighth-Century Prophets*, pp. 29-30.

Israelite agricultural households.[1] However, as Gottwald[2] suggests, this process of latifundiation probably began during the reign of Solomon, when valuable crops were already in demand at the palace or for export (cf. Prov. 22.7). While excessive taxation is one of the possible causes for debt-slavery and the alienation of land, it is also most likely that the control of resources and lending by the ruling elite, which included both state officials and private landowners, caused many small farmers to sell their dependents and themselves into debt-slavery, and eventually to sell their land (i.e., *Rentenkapitalismus*).[3] Similar activities are illustrated clearly in Amos 8.4-6, which reads:

> 4 Hear this, you who trample the needy, to do away with the humble of the land,
> 5 saying, 'When will the new moon pass by, So that we may sell grain, And the Sabbath that we may open the wheat [market], To make the *ephah* smaller and the shekel bigger, And to cheat with balances of deception,
> 6 So as to buy the helpless for silver, And the needy for a pair of sandals, And [that] we may see the refuse of the wheat?'

1. Cf. Hopkins, *The Highlands of Canaan*, pp. 274-75; Chaney, 'Systemic Study of the Israelite Monarchy', pp. 72-73; Silver, *Prophets and Markets*, pp. 73-77; Coote, *Amos Among the Prophets*, p. 34; cf. also Sicre, *La justicia social en los profetas de Israel*, pp. 76-77. Cf. also Saggs, *The Might That Was Assyria*, p. 134; and Dearman, *Property Rights in the Eighth-Century Prophets*, p. 127, both of whom note that the activity of the Israelite officials in regard to the acquisition of land is paralleled in Assyria during the NA period.

2. Gottwald, 'The Participation of Free Agrarians in the Introduction of Monarchy', pp. 85-86.

3. Cf. Sicre, *La justicia social en los profetas de Israel*, p. 82; O. Loretz, 'Die prophetische Kritik des Rentenkapitalismus', *UF* 7 (1975), pp. 271-78; Coote, *Amos Among the Prophets*, pp. 29-32; Dearman, *Property Rights in the Eighth-Century Prophets*, pp. 386-87. Cp. Lowery, *The Reforming Kings*, pp. 49-50, concerning his reservation about using the term 'rent-capitalism' to describe Israel's monarchic economy. His point is well taken in that we should be careful not to compare what was basically a 'mode-of-production' economy with modern-day capitalist economies, although it nevertheless should be borne in mind that the side-effects of the two systems are similar. That is, means of production (land etc.) is consolidated, although this only adversely affects present-day agricultural based third-world economies. This is particularly true for countries such as India and many South American countries where various forms of debt-slavery still exist.

These verses most likely describe how merchant speculators sold wheat at high prices to the poor by using short measures and false scales (cf. also Prov. 11.26). Furthermore, these verses most likely describe how such speculation and dishonesty lead to the sale of the poor as debt-slaves (cf. also Amos 2.6-8).[1] Similarly, Hosea condemns the activity of the merchant who used false scales and oppressed (עשק) the people (Hos. 12.8 [Hebrew v. 9]).

After the fall of Samaria in 722–721 BCE, the kingdom of Judah, under the reign of Ahaz (735–715 BCE), became a vassal state of the Assyrian empire.[2] The loss of trade routes and the tribute demanded by Assyria seriously taxed the palace economy of Judah, although wealth and prosperity continued to persist in many towns. However, as Isaiah and Micah observed, large landowners often made debt-slaves out of the poor farmers and dispossessed them of their land, much as they did in Israel (cf. Isa. 3.13-15; 5.8; Mic. 2.1-9).[3] For example, Micah writes in Chapter 2:[4]

> 1 Woe to those who scheme iniquity, Who work out evil in their beds!
> In the light of the morning they do it, For it is in their power of their hands.
> 2 They covet fields and then seize (them) [וגזלו], And houses, and take (them) away.
> And they oppress [ועשקו] a man and his house, A man and his inheritance.

Furthermore, the reign of Ahaz is distinguished by a significant increase in syncretism, which was to continue under the reign of Manasseh (687/686–642 BCE). However, during the reigns of

---

1. Cf. Sicre, *La justicia social en los profetas de Israel*, pp. 136-41; L. Epsztein, *Social Justice in the Ancient Near East*, p. 96; Coote, *Amos Among the Prophets*, pp. 93-94; Lang, 'Peasant Poverty in Biblical Israel', pp. 58-59.

2. Cf. Bright, *A History of Israel*, pp. 276-78; Saggs, *The Might That Was Assyria*, pp. 91-92.

3. Cf. Dearman, *Property Rights in the Eighth-Century Prophets*, pp. 37-52; Sicre, *La justicia social en los profetas de Israel*, pp. 191-312, esp. 262-64.

4. For a discussion of these verses, see especially Sicre, *La justicia social en los profetas de Israel*, pp. 253-62; and Westbrook, *Studies in Biblical and Cuneiform Law*, pp. 35-38, who notes that the verbs גזל and עשק are used as similar technical terms for abuse: גזל is used where property was taken away from the victim (cf. Gen. 31.311; Job 24.9) and עשק was used where the victim was denied his legal due (cf. Lev. 19.13).

Hezekiah (715–687/686 BCE) and Josiah (640–609 BCE),[1] important cultic and legal reforms were carried out, although no matter how significantly these reforms improved the position of the Israelite citizens it is clear that in subsequent periods they would again be victims of the wealthy private and state landowners.

The temple households. While various aspects of the Israelite cult were in existence during the Pre-Monarchic period, such as the local shrines and priestly judicial authority, there is no conclusive evidence for the existence of anything resembling temple households during this period. While Milgrom[2] suggests that the plans for the Levitical cities are practical and date from the Settlement period (cf. Joshua 20–21), scholars generally suggest that these cities did not come into existence until the united monarchy or later, during which the temple came under the supervision of the palace.[3] Nevertheless, since the Levitical cities were to provide land and revenue for the Levites who did not have a share in patrimony (cf. Lev. 25.32-33; Num. 35.1-5), and to provide a place of refuge for murderers (cf. Num. 35.6-34), it is likely that these two functions were implemented in some fashion before the actual construction of the cities.[4] As Milgrom[5] has noted,

---

1. For an excellent treatment of this period of Israelite history, see Lowery, *The Reforming Kings*, pp. 142-68 (Hezekiah), pp. 190-209 (Josiah).

2. Cf. J. Milgrom, 'The Levitical Town: An Exercise in Realistic Planning', *JJS* 33 (1982), pp. 185-88; cf. also de Vaux, *Ancient Israel*, pp. 366-67, who considers the Levitical cities a 'utopian' concept based on ancient documents.

3. For the view that the Levitical cities date to the united monarchy, see W.F. Albright, 'The List of Levitical Cities', in *Louis Ginzberg Jubilee*, I (New York, 1945), pp. 49-73; B. Mazar, 'The Cities of the Priests and of the Levites', in *Congress Volume* (VTSup, 7; Leiden: Brill, 1957), pp. 193-205; Mettinger, *Solomonic State Officials*, pp. 97-99; Z. Kallai, 'The System of Levitic Cities: A Historical-Geographical Study in Biblical Historiography' (Hebrew), *Zion* 45 (1980), pp. 13-34. For the view that they date to the time of Jehoshaphat, or Hezekiah, or Josiah, see M. Haran, 'Studies in the Account of the Levitical Cities', *JBL* 80 (1961), pp. 45-54; A. Cody, *A History of the Old Testament Priesthood* (AnBib, 35; Rome: Pontifical Biblical Institute, 1969), pp. 159-61; Soggin, *A History of Israel*, pp. 151-53; R. Boling, 'Levitical Cities: Archaeology and Texts', in *Biblical and Related Studies Presented to Samuel Iwry* (ed. A. Kort and S. Mirschauser; Winona Lake, IN: Eisenbrauns, 1985), pp. 23-32.

4. Cf. Boling, 'Levitical Cities: Archaeology and Texts', pp. 23-32.

5. Milgrom, 'The Levitical Town: An Exercise in Realistic Planning', p. 188.

the layout of these cities, many of which were located in the valleys, and their pastoral emphasis, all point to an early date for these city plans, since it was unreasonable to hope that these cities could be built once Israel had settled in the lowlands, or to expect the Levites to live exclusively on a pastoral economy. Lastly, as we saw above, the temple also employed the use of chattel-slaves who were either bought by the priests or donated by the palace (cf. Lev. 22.11; Ezra 2.43-58; 8.20; Neh. 7.46-60).[1] Nevertheless, unlike the Mesopotamian temples, the size or economic importance of the Levitical cities remains a moot point.

Private Sector Households

The primary source of information about the Israelite private sector households is found in the Old Testament, although archaeological and ethnographic studies have helped to clarify both the structure of the dwellings and aspects of everyday life of the Israelites. Three kinship groups can be discerned in the Old Testament: בית אב 'father's house', משפחה 'clan', and מטה, שבט 'tribe'. In the following discussion I will examine the בית אב and משפחה, since both kinship groups are either alluded or referred to in the manumission laws (e.g., the term משפחה occurs in Lev. 25.10, 41, 45, 47, 49).

The בת אב. The expression בית אב refers to the smallest Israelite social unit, which is usually understood to refer to an extended-type family whose members reside within the same residence.[2] However, scholars

---

1. Two expressions, נתינים 'temple servants' and בני עבדי שלמה 'sons of the servants of Solomon', are found in the books of Ezra and Nehemiah. Both terms probably refer to the מס־עבד who were levied from the Canaanites; cf. North, 'מס', col. 1009; cf. also D. Kidner, *Ezra and Nehemiah* (TOTC; Leicester: Inter-Varsity Press, 1979), pp. 40-41, who suggests that the term נתינים refers to both the Levites and foreigners; F.C. Fensham, *The Books of Ezra and Nehemiah* (NICOT; Grand Rapids: Eerdmans, 1982), pp. 54-55, who suggests that the נתינים were subordinate to the Levites, since the Levites are mentioned before the נתינים, and that they included foreign slaves; D.J.A. Clines, *Ezra, Nehemiah, Esther* (NCBC; Grand Rapids: Eerdmans, 1984), p. 56, who suggests that the נתינים were slaves; cf. also H.G.M. Williamson, *Ezra and Nehemiah* (WBC, 16; Waco, TX: Word Books, 1985), pp. 35ff. Cp. A. Levine, 'The Netînîm', *JBL* 82 (1963), pp. 207-12, who suggests that the נתינים were free foreigners who belonged to guilds.

2. For example, see Gottwald, *The Tribes of Yahweh*, pp. 285-92; de Geus, *The Tribes of Israel*, p. 134; de Vaux, *Ancient Israel*, p. 39; G.J. Wenham, *Numbers:*

have also noted that the expression בית אב, as well as the other social terms used within Israel, has a wider semantic meaning than 'family'. For example, Weinfeld,[1] Rogerson,[2] and Mendenhall[3] have observed that the expressions בית אב and משפחה are interchangeable. Weinfeld[4] notes too that the flexible use of terms in connection with social institutions is characteristic of the entire area of Mesopotamia and Syria-Palestine, particularly in the Amarna letters from the second half of the second millennium BCE. A more accurate understanding of this important term has been provided by Lemche,[5] who has recently examined the use of the expression בית אב in the Old Testament. He suggests that the term בית אב, while it can refer to extended families, can also refer to both a nuclear family and a proper lineage. Similarly, Gottwald[6] suggests that a בית אב refers to an extended family that resides in a single 'residential unit' (cf. Judg. 17–18). This residential unit, he suggests, contained from fifty to one hundred individuals, who were presumably housed in a cluster of individual nuclear dwellings. Although Gottwald identifies this family unit as an 'extended family', it is probably best to understand this kinship group

---

An Introduction and Commentary (TOTC; Downers Grove, IL: IVP, 1981), p. 58; Halpern, *The Emergence of Israel in Canaan*, p. 211.

1. M. Weinfeld, 'Congregation', *EncJud*, V, cols. 893-95.

2. Rogerson, *Anthropology and the Old Testament*, pp. 93-95.

3. Mendenhall, 'Ancient Israel's Hyphenated History', p. 93; cf. also A.F. Rainey, 'Family', *EncJud*, VI, col. 1164; J.E. Hartley, 'Father's House; Father's Household', *ISBE*, II, p. 286; G. Wyper, 'Clan', *ISBE*, II, p. 716.

4. Weinfeld, 'Congregation', p. 894; cf. also Rogerson, *Anthropology and the Old Testament*, p. 95 and n. 25, who refers to T. Nöldeke, 'Review of R. Smith's *Kinship and Marriage*', *ZDMG* 40 (1886), pp. 158, 175-76, who observes that Arabic kinship terms are also imprecise (i.e. *qabîla, batn, fāḫiḏ,* which can refer to tribes or to divisions within tribes).

5. Lemche, *Early Israel*, pp. 245-59. The results of this study have also been employed in his more recent historical work, *Ancient Israel*. Cf. also J. Scharbert, '*Bēyt 'āb* als soziologische Größe im Alten Testament', in *Von Kanaan bis Kerala: Festschrift für Prof. Mag. Dr. Dr. J.P.M. van der Ploeg O.P* (ed. W.C. Delsman, J.T. Nelis, J.R.T.M. Peters, W.H.Ph. Römer and A.S. van der Woude; AOT, 211; Neukirchen-Vluyn: Verlag Butson & Berker Kevelaer, 1982), pp. 213-38, who arrives at similar conclusions.

6. Gottwald, *The Tribes of Yahweh*, pp. 285-92; cf. also C.J.H. Wright, *God's People in God's Land: Family, Land, and Property in the Old Testament* (Grand Rapids: Eerdmans; London: Paternoster Press, 1990), pp. 53-55.

as a proper lineage, which was composed of either several spatially distinct nuclear houses or multiple family compounds.[1]

That the typical Israelite household was nuclear in form is confirmed by both archaeological and ethnographic studies, both of which have examined ancient and modern settlements.[2] During the Settlement period nuclear dwellings were either spatially distinct farmhouses, containing three of four rooms, or were grouped together to form multiple family compounds.[3] Multiple family compounds, which contain two or three independent or linked nuclear dwellings, characterized the social organization of Raddana Ai, and Meshash. While Shiloh[4] suggests that the average nuclear family

1. Cf. Stager, 'The Archaeology of the Family in Ancient Israel', p. 22; Lemche, *Early Israel*, pp. 248-49; cp. Scharbert, '*Bēyt 'āb* als soziologische Größe im Alten Testament', p. 235, who suggests that the 'extended family' 'ist die grundlegende Gemeinschaft'.

2. Cf. Y. Yadin, 'Excavations at Hazor (1955-1958)', in *Biblical Archaeology Reader*, II (ed. G.E. Wright and D.N. Freedman; Garden City, NY: Doubleday, 1964), pp. 93-100; W.F. Albright, *The Archaeology of Palestine and the Bible* (Cambridge, MA: American Schools of Oriental Research, 3rd edn, 1974), pp. 115-16; Y. Shiloh, 'The Four-Room-House—Its Situation and Function in the Israelite City', *IEJ* 20 (1970), pp. 180-90; *idem*, 'The Four-Space House—The Israelite House Type' (Hebrew), *Eretz-Israel* 11 (1973), pp. 277-85; F.S. Frick, 'Religion and Sociopolitical Structure in Early Israel: An Ethno-Archaeological Approach', in *Society of Biblical Literature Seminar Papers 1979* (Missoula, MT: Scholars Press, 1979), pp. 243-44; Lemche, *Early Israel*, p. 248; *idem*, *Ancient Israel*, p. 93; Stager, 'The Archaeology of the Family in Ancient Israel', pp. 11-23; D.C. Hopkins, 'Life on the Land: The Subsistence Struggles of Early Israel', *BA* 50 (1987), p. 172; and C.H.J. de Geus, 'The Profile of an Israelite City' *BA* 49 (1986), pp. 224-27, who suggests that the standard four-room Israelite house contained more than one floor: the courtyard may have contained hearths and ovens; the ground floor may have contained either servants' quarters or stables; the second floor may have contained the family quarters; cf. also Wilson, 'Judicial Authority in Early Israel', pp. 62-63; *idem*, *Sociological Approaches*, pp. 39-41. Cp. de Vaux, *Ancient Israel*, p. 72, who acknowledges the view that the typical Israelite house contained four rooms but who, nevertheless, maintains that the typical Israelite household was an extended type.

3. Cf. Stager, 'The Archaeology of the Family in Ancient Israel', pp. 17-18.

4. Y. Shiloh, 'The Population of Iron Age Palestine', *BASOR* 239 (1980), pp. 25-35; cf. also Lemche, *Ancient Israel*, p. 93, who suggests that the nuclear household contained six or seven individuals.

contained eight members, Stager[1] suggests that each nuclear dwelling contained, on average, four members during the Settlement period. Furthermore, Stager[2] notes that the multiple family compound, which came under the authority of the *pater familias*, was probably the ideal type of household organization, since it was more capable of holding on to its patrimony and was able to meet essential labour needs. However, due to segmentation and demographic constraints, these patrilocal residences were in the minority.[3] The fact that these residences dominate certain sites, while the nuclear residence dominates others, suggests that demographic constraints played an important role in the highland settlements.[4] Stager[5] suggests that both the single and multiple nuclear structures were linked into larger kinship groups (lineages) based upon their residential propinquity and the various biblical references to Israelite 'folk society'.

However, despite the fact that various studies confirm the presence of nuclear families and lineages in early Israel, the Old Testament appears to say very little about either, particularly in the patriarchal narratives.[6] Nevertheless, Lemche suggests that the existence of the

1. Stager, 'The Archaeology of the Family in Ancient Israel', pp. 18, 21. Based upon a personal communication with Israel Finkelstein, Stager notes that nuclear families only approached an average of eight persons during modern times after the introduction of penicillin.

2. Stager, 'The Archaeology of the Family in Ancient Israel', p. 20.

3. Cf. Stager, 'The Archaeology of the Family in Ancient Israel', p. 20, who cites E.A. Wrigly, *Population and History* (New York: McGraw-Hill, 1969), pp. 131-33, and L.K. Berkner, 'The Stem Family and the Developmental Cycle of the Peasant Household: An Eighteenth-Century Austrian Example', *AHR* 77 (1972), p. 407 and n.25, notes that under pre-modern conditions families including three generations probably accounted for less than 30 per cent of families, and extended or multiple families perhaps constituted no more than half of the population at any particular moment. This figure approximates that given by Gulick, *The Middle East: An Anthropological Perspective*, pp. 128-30, who suggests that in the Middle East extended families account for about 10 per cent of all households. See above, my discussion in Chapter 2.

4. This ecological factor may also have been one of the reasons for the existence of a strong sense of kinship among Israelites, which continued throughout Israel's history.

5. Stager, 'The Archaeology of the Family in Ancient Israel', pp. 20-22.

6. Cf. Heltzer, *The Rural Community in Ancient Ugarit*, pp. 96-102, who has observed that Ugaritic families in most cases were nuclear families, although there is

lineage can be demonstrated in some of the narratives of the Old Testament. For example, he notes that in Gen. 18.19 the expression ביתו אחריו refers to Abraham's lineage, that is, not to the grandchildren of the still-living Abraham, but to his descendents, that is, his lineage, which implies the nation of Israel.[1] In other instances Lemche suggests that the term בית אב can be ambiguous; it can refer to either a lineage or to an extended family. For example, in Gen. 12.1 Abraham is told to abandon his מולדת 'relatives' and his בית אב. In this context the term בית אב could be rendered both 'family' and 'lineage'.[2] While this sort of reasoning can be considered circular, the fact that archaeological and ethnographic studies have already demonstrated the existence of lineage kinship groups in much of the ancient Near East makes Lemche's suggestions more likely.[3]

However, Lemche[4] admits that it is more difficult to demonstrate from the Old Testament that the term בית אב can refer to a nuclear family. The clearest example of the existence of nuclear families is found in Gen. 34.19, 26, but this refers to Canaanite families. Shechem, who is unmarried in Gen. 34.19, lives in his father's house,

---

evidence that extended families existed in Ugarit as well.

1. Lemche, *Early Israel*, p. 251; cf. also Wilson, 'Judicial Authority in Early Israel', p. 67; de Vaux, *Ancient Israel*, pp. 20-21; Weinfeld, 'Congregation', col. 894; Scharbert, '*Bēyt 'āb* als soziologische Größe im Alten Testament', p. 235.

2. Lemche, *Early Israel*, p. 252. Lemche also writes, 'Gen 20:13 refers to Abraham's absence from his בית אב. In this case Abraham is described as wandering about in a foreign land with his family. Thus in this context it would be most appropriate to take בית אב to refer to his lineage' (p. 252, n. 24).

3. Lemche, *Early Israel*, pp. 246-47; cf. also J. Pedersen, *Israel: Its Life and Culture*, I–II (London: Oxford University Press, 1926), pp. 47-60, who suggests that the borderline between Israel's kinship terms 'tribe', 'family' (which is the clan) and 'father's house' was fluid. Lemche notes correctly that Pedersen appears to understand the clan/family as a lineage that has strong links with the father's house. Lemche therefore translates Pedersen's words: 'Sometimes we come across the word "family", where, according to the system, we should expect "father's house"' as ' "Sometimes [we] discover the word "lineage" where the system would lead us to expect "father's house"'.

4. Lemche, *Early Israel*, p. 253. Gottwald, *The Tribes of Israel*, p. 286, suggests that a בית אב can consist of a few individuals, which further suggests that the house is a nuclear type. Therefore, Lemche (p. 249) suggests that Gottwald's analysis shows that Israel possessed both nuclear families, extended families and lineages, and that all three were referred to by the expression בית אב.

but in Gen. 34.26, when Shechem is married, it states that Dinah (Shechem's wife) is removed from *Shechem's* house. This suggests that the newly-married Shechem formed his own household.[1] Nevertheless, Lemche admits that in the Old Testament the emphasis is on the extended rather than the nuclear family, though he attributes this phenomenon to the fact that the Old Testament tends to deal with characters who are great men.

Lastly, Lemche[2] suggests that in the book of Genesis, where extended families are normally assumed, the term בית אב may refer to neolocal residences under the protection and authority of the *pater familias*.[3] Lemche notes that the existence of neolocal residences is not out of the question when one considers that Esau abandoned the house of Jacob after his marriage (Gen. 26.34-35; 36.1), and that in the book of Ruth Elimelech took Naomi, his wife, with him to Moab. Furthermore, he writes: [4]

> In Gen 45.10-11 Jacob's family is described as an extended family consisting of fathers, sons, and sons' wives, while in Gen 45.18 we apparently have to do with Jacob's family on the one hand and on the other the nuclear families of his various sons, understood as independent units. It is possible that a number of passages in the OT in which the extended family appears in reality have to do with nuclear families, although the tradents of those materials have described them as if the familial fellowship has not come to an end.

It is possible that the extended family, which is often mentioned in the patriarchal narratives, was actually housed in multiple family compounds (or tents) rather than in a single dwelling (or tent). These multiple dwellings would still come under the protection and authority of the *pater familias* and they would also be susceptible to segmentation, as in the case of Esau who left the house of Jacob.

The משפחה. The term משפחה has traditionally been understood to refer to the clan (or proper lineage) which is thought to occupy the middle

1. Cf. Lemche, *Early Israel*, pp. 253-58, for other examples of apparent nuclear families in the patriarchal and settlement narratives.
2. Lemche, *Early Israel*, p. 258.
3. Cf. Wilson, 'Judicial Authority in Early Israel', p. 62, who notes that at the lowest levels of social structure, judicial authority resided in the *pater familias* (cf. Genesis 31 and 38).
4. Lemche, *Early Israel*, p. 258.

position of the social hierarchy of Israel. However, Rogerson,[1] Mendenhall,[2] and Lemche[3] have observed that the term משפחה can refer to other social units than 'clan', such as בית אב 'father's house'. Lemche has pointed out correctly that scholars tend to be vague about the specific nature and definition of the clan in ancient Israel,[4] due, no doubt, to the fact that the term משפחה occurs mostly in genealogical lists and in other places where the exact composition or nature of the clan is not discussed (or is assumed).[5]

In his own study, Lemche,[6] who follows the views of Pedersen[7] and de Vaux,[8] both of whom note that the term בית אב could refer to higher kinship groups such as the משפחה, notes that the term משפחה appears to be synonymous with the term בית אב in passages in which both terms occur and in passages where the term משפחה occurs on its own. For example, he[9] notes that the terms משפחה and בית אב appear in parallel in Gen. 24.38, 40, where the order of the terms are reversed. The verses read: (v. 38) 'but you shall go to my father's house (בית אב), and to my relatives (משפחה), and take a wife for my son'; (v. 40) '. . . and you will take a wife for my son from my relative (משפחה) and from my father's house (בית אב)'. Lemche admits, though, that this parallelism is not conclusive for

---

1. Rogerson, *Anthropology and the Old Testament*, pp. 93-95.

2. Mendenhall, 'Ancient Israel's Hyphenated History', p. 93.

3. Lemche, *Early Israel*, pp. 245-59.

4. For example, see Wyper, 'Clan', p. 716, who notes that the boundaries between social groups is unclear; Hartley, 'Father's House; Father's Household', p. 286, who notes that the relationship between father's house and family (משפחה) is vague; Rainey, 'Family', col. 1166, who suggests that the משפחה is a 'family [בית אב] in the larger sense'; Wenham, *Numbers*, p. 58, who suggests that the משפחה is 'the main social unit, intermediate in size between a tribe and the father's house'.

5. The term משפחה occurs approximately 300 times in the Old Testament. However, the term occurs mostly in the genealogical and census lists: e.g., the term occurs 18 times in Numbers 1; 14 times in Numbers 3; 13 times in Numbers 4; 92 times in Numbers 26 (total 137 times); 41 times in Josh. 13-21.

6. Lemche, *Early Israel*, pp. 260-68.

7. Pedersen, *Israel*, I–II, p. 53, writes that 'Unless special emphasis is laid on the idea of the household, institution, the two words [i.e., משפחה, בית אב] are rather used indiscriminately'.

8. De Vaux, *Ancient Israel*, pp. 20-21, suggests that the בית אב 'family' was the same group as the 'clan' משפחה.

9. Lemche, *Early Israel*, p. 263.

demonstrating that the two terms are synonymous.[1] Lemche[2] also points out that in three other passages the term בית אב is left out where it would normally be expected. For example, in Deut. 29.15ff. the social units which are envisaged as potentially falling away into apostasy are a man or a woman, a משפחה, or a tribe. The level בית אב 'father's house' is left out. This is also the case in 1 Sam. 9.21, where Saul describes himself as a Benjaminite from a משפחה among the משפחות of Benjamin. Lastly, 1 Sam. 10.21 describes the casting of lots to determine who is to be king in Israel. This procedure is the same as that described in Josh. 7.14ff., which shows that the lot-casting order falls to the tribe, בית אב ,משפחה, and man. In 1 Sam. 10.21, though, the lot falls on the tribe of Benjamin, then on the משפחה of Matri, and finally on Saul. Again, the level 'father's house' is left out. Lemche suggests that while the absence of the term בית אב in the above passages can be explained by the desire for brevity, it is just as likely that in these passages the term משפחה represents the same level as do בית אב and משפחה in Josh. 7.14. Lemche therefore proposes the following hypothesis: [3]

> If the latter assumption is correct, then it will have been possible to refer to any of several levels within Israelite social structure as a משפחה. I have shown above how בית אב is used of the steps leading from the family to the lineage; thus it would be possible to formulate a hypothesis to the effect that משפחה covers the areas of [proper] lineage and the maximal lineage.

Lastly, Lemche suggests that marriages between families and lineages were arranged within the clan (endogamous), although other conditions may have forced some marriages to be made outside the clan (exogamous).[4] This view is supported by the fact that the Old Testament always describes Israel within the compass of a single genealogical system.[5]

1. Cf. Rogerson, *Anthropology in the Old Testament*, p. 94, who notes that in Exod. 6.14 ff. the terms בית אב and משפחה seem to be interchangeable.
2. Lemche, *Early Israel*, p. 264.
3. Cf. Lemche, *Early Israel*, pp. 264, 265-68, where Lemche notes a similar inconsistency in the use of the two terms בית אב and משפחה in the census lists contained in the book of Numbers.
4. Cf. Lemche, *Early Israel*, pp. 224-31; cf. also Rogerson, 'Was Early Israel a Segmentary Society?', p. 19; Rainey, 'Family', col. 1166; Wyper, 'Clan', p. 716.
5. Cf. Lemche, *Early Israel*, p. 264; cp. C.R. Taber, 'Kinship and Family',

Recapitulating, the above discussion attempts to show that the term
משפחה can refer to a proper lineage or to a maximal lineage/clan.
Thus the meaning of the term משפחה appears to overlap the meaning
of the term בית אב which can refer to an individual nuclear or
extended family and to a proper lineage. According to semantic
terminology, the expression בית אב can be described as an *overlapping
synonym* of משפחה. Based on the fluidity that exists between these
social terms, it is clear that Israelite society was characterized by a
strong sense of kinship between social groupings.[1] The fact that
kinship groups in the sedentary societies of the ancient Near East
dwelled together in groups suggests that the בית אב (e.g., single
family, multiple family, lineage) and the משפחה (e.g., lineage,
maximal lineage) also lived in the same locality (i.e., village or town),
although each family was probably economically independent.[2] This
sort of social structure helped facilitate the co-operative social,
economic and political support required by the individual members or
families of the higher kinship groups, particularly regarding the
protection of coparcenary rights on property.[3] However, with the
increase of centralization and the resultant social stratification, it is
likely that the economic and political assistance of higher kinship
groups could no longer prevent the sale of dependents and land on
account of insolvency, a trend that also occurred in the city-states of
Mesopotamia.[4] Therefore, incidents of debt-slavery and land loss
increased during the Monarchic period. However, as I argued in
Chapter 2, although tribes eventually disintegrate under the influence

IDBSup, pp. 523-24; and Rogerson, *Anthropology in the Old Testament*, p. 97.

1. Cf. D.I. Block, 'Israel's House: Reflections on the use of בית שראל in the Old
Testament in the Light of its Ancient Near Eastern Environment', *JETS* 28 (1985),
pp. 257-75, who suggests that the kinship term 'house of Israel' (house-
Geographical Name; cf. also 'house of Esau', which is a designation for Edom in
Obadiah 18) assumes a nation that is essentially an ethnic unity. This usage is not
attested in Phoenician, Akkadian and Aramaic texts. Cf. also Pedersen, *Israel*, I–II,
pp. 48-50.

2. Cf. Lemche, *Early Israel*, p. 269; *idem, Ancient Israel*, p. 95; Pedersen,
Israel, I–II, pp. 34-35; de Geus, *The Tribes of Israel*, p. 138; Halpern, *The
Emergence of Israel in Canaan*, pp. 109, 117.

3. Cf. Dearman, *Property Rights in the Eighth-Century Prophets*, pp. 73-77;
Mendenhall, 'Ancient Israel's Hyphenated History', p. 93; Lemche, *Early Israel*,
p. 269.

4. Dearman, *Property Rights in the Eighth-Century Prophets*, pp. 73-77.

of the state, the lower kinship groupings (minimal and proper lineage) do not disintegrate.

Social Stratification in Israel

As the above discussions show, with the advent of the monarchy and its respective state controlled economy social stratification increased, particularly during the eighth century BCE and later. However, due to the lack of documentary evidence it remains unclear when social stratification began in Israel, although as Coote and Whitelam[1] suggest, social stratification was most likely already in evidence in early Israel as separate village communities underwent an ongoing economic diversification, a process that allowed some to take advantage of their relative position to trade routes. The clearest example of a socio-economically stratified community was Tel Masos, which Frick[2] suggests supported a ranked society during pre-monarchic Israel. The developing rich landowners, who likely held some authoritative position in their communities, retained and improved their economic position during the Monarchic period.[3]

However, during the early Monarchic period there was an active suppression of social stratification by both the secular and sacral league authorities, who continued to exert pressure on the king

---

1. Coote and Whitelam, *The Emergence of Early Israel*, pp. 154-59; 'The Emergence of Israel', pp. 135-38.

2. Cf. Frick, *The Formation of the State in Ancient Israel*, pp. 159-69; cf. also Stager, 'The Archaeology of the Family in Ancient Israel', pp. 18-23, who notes that such sites as Ai, Raddana and Tel Masos show evidence of social stratification. Cp. Finkelstein, *The Archaeology of the Israelite Settlement*, pp. 41-46, who suggests that this site, which is completely unlike the Israelite settlements in the hill country and valley itself, does not fit into the framework of Israelite Settlement, although he suggests that the mixed population of the site may have included a few 'Israelite' families (p. 46).

3. Coote and Whitelam, *The Emergence of Early Israel*, pp. 157-58; 'The Emergence of Israel', pp. 137-38, suggest that the biblical accounts of the 'judges' and town and village elders are the clearest examples of rich people who held authoritative positions. It is most likely that these people became part of the royal court, just as they did in Mesopotamia, from which position they could remain active in trade and acquire property.

throughout the period (cf. 1 Sam 8; 10.17-27; 11.12).[1] Nevertheless
the history of Israel is characterized by various periods of increased
social stratification, although it is likely that Israel did not develop
into as highly a stratified society as those in the states of Mesopotamia
and Canaan.[2] Therefore, only two social classes can be clearly
distinguished in Israel: (1) free citizens; (2) chattel-slaves. However, it
is likely that some segments of the foreign population that were used
as labour by the Israelite kings occupied a social position equivalent to
that of semi-free citizens.

The first (1) category includes priests, nobility, officials, merchants
and the kinship families who owned land or some other means of
production.[3] The second (2) category includes the foreign captives
(and 'slave' levies) who were utilized in the palace households and
chattel-slaves who were used by both the state and private sector
households.

The biblical accounts of the Monarchic period attest to the existence
of both debt-slaves and the alienation of land in Israel, particularly
during the eighth century BCE and later. The existence of debt-slaves
and landless people may be attributed on the one hand to the burden of
taxation, and on the other to the growing monopoly the rich
landowning elite held over resources. Once this dependency was
established the small landowners were often forced into procuring
loans which probably involved high interest rates. While there are
biblical laws which prohibit Israelites from exacting interest from one
another (poor Israelite?; cf. Exod. 22.25 [Hebrew v. 24]; Deut. 23.19-

1. Cf. Halpern, *The Constitution of the Monarchy in Israel*, pp. 246-49; Coote
and Whitelam, *The Emergence of Early Israel*, pp. 154-59.

2. Cf. Coote and Whitelam, *The Emergence of Early Israel*, pp. 154-59;
N.K. Gottwald, 'Two Models for the Origins of Ancient Israel: Social Revolution or
Frontier Development', in *The Quest for the Kingdom of God: Studies in Honor of
G.E. Mendenhall* (ed. H.B. Huffmon, F.A. Spina and A.R.W. Green; Winona
Lake, IN: Eisenbrauns, 1983), pp. 17-19; *idem*, 'Early Israel and the Canaanite
Socio-economic System', in *Palestine in Transition: The Emergence of Ancient Israel*
(ed. D.N. Freedman and D.F. Graf; SWBAS, 2; Sheffield: Almond Press, 1983)
p. 35; de Vaux, *Ancient Israel*, pp. 164-65.

3. As I suggested above, there was probably a client population that performed
services for the king in exchange for land or allowances, although there is no way of
telling how large this group might have been. For discussions of the various terms
used to designate the various free citizens in Israel, see de Vaux, *Ancient Israel*,
pp. 69-79; Sicre, *La justicia social en los profetas de Israel*, pp. 57-60.

20), it is likely that these provisions were ignored by many of the money-lenders during the eighth century BCE and later.[1] Israelite small farmers, like those in Mesopotamia, were therefore often hard-pressed to pay back their loans. Many of these small landowners, who were forced to engage in subsistence farming, were forced to sell or surrender dependents into debt-slavery. Furthermore, they were eventually forced to sell themselves and their land (means of production). Debt-slavery in Israel, as in Mesopotamia, demonstrates the mobility that existed between the free and unfree classes, since in many cases people were not able to redeem their dependents (cf. 2 Kgs 4.1; Jer. 34.8-16). While it is unclear what happened to those families who were forced to sell all of their land, it is possible that they became tenants (or peasants) who worked land owned by the large landowners, particularly during the eighth century BCE.

The relationship that the Israelite landed elite often had with the free citizens was most likely one of exploitation, which was also evident in the societies of Mesopotamia and Canaan.[2] While this exploitation is particularly evident in the writings of the prophets of the eighth century BCE, it is likely that the ruling elite were exploiting the free citizens as early as the reign of Solomon. This exploitation probably accounted for much of the latifundia that developed during the united and divided monarchy.[3]

According to the various biblical accounts and laws pertaining to chattel-slaves, their position was similar to those attested in Mesopotamia and elsewhere. For example, there are various laws that suggest chattel-slaves attained the status of free citizens, much as those chattel-slave laws in LH discussed in Chapter 2 (cf. Lev. 19.20-22; Deut. 21.10-14; 23.15-16). These slaves, however, must be differentiated from the foreign captives and conscripts who worked for the various palace households and industries, since, like their Mesopotamian counterparts, they probably were often harshly treated. Furthermore, there was a clear distinction between chattel- and debt-slaves, since chattel-slaves most likely did not have individual rights to

---

1. I discuss these biblical laws in more detail in Chapter 7.
2. Cf. Dever, 'The Middle Bronze Age', pp. 163-65.
3. Cf. Chaney, 'Systemic Study of the Israelite Monarchy', pp. 55-56, who follows Lenski, *Power and Privilege*, suggests that the ruling elite of Israel controlled up to half or more of the goods and services during the eighth century.

redemption (cf. Lev 25.44-45). However, while there is a clear distinction made between chattel- and debt-slaves in the ancient Near Eastern legal collections, in which the term *wardum* is never used to designate debt-slaves, in the Old Testament legal corpora the term עבד 'slave' is used to designate both chattel- and debt-slaves. Therefore, it is often difficult to distinguish between chattel- and debt-slaves in the biblical legal corpora, particularly in the Covenant Code, in which chattel slaves appear to be afforded rights normally afforded to free citizens.

Summary and Conclusions

To sum up, I have examined the social and economic structures of pre-monarchic and monarchic Israel in an attempt to gain a better understanding of the way in which slavery (both debt-and chattel-slavery) and the alienation of land developed and increased. As the above examination has shown, the rise of debt-slavery and the alienation of land in Israel, as in Mesopotamia, can be attributed to insolvency among free citizens that was caused by various interrelated socio-economic factors, including taxation, the monopoly of resources and services among the state and private elite (i.e., rent capitalism), high interest loans and the economic and political collapse of higher kinship groups. That the development of debt-slavery and the alienation of land were similar in each of these societies can be attributed to the similarity in the kinship structure of the various tribal societies that made up the population of these agrarian states and the development of these tribal groups into state societies.[1]

---

1. Cf. Lemche, *Early Israel*, pp. 268-69; and Mendenhall, 'Ancient Israel's Hyphenated History', pp. 92-93. Contra Gottwald, *Tribes of Yahweh*, pp. 228-341, who regards Israel as a unique 'egalitarian' tribal society that was organized from non-tribally organized Canaanites in order to establish a different political system from that of the Canaanites. The conception that there was a fundamental difference in the social structure of people who lived in rural areas (nomads, peasant farmers) and in cities (large landowners, priests, palace and temple officials, merchants and so on) is not well founded. For example, see Gelb, 'Household and Family in Early Mesopotamia', pp. 3-4; W.F. Leemans, 'The Pattern of Settlement in the Babylonian Countryside', in Dandamayev *et al.* (eds.), *Societies and Languages*, pp. 245-49; Lemche, *Early Israel*, pp. 198-201; Frick, *The City in Ancient Israel*, pp. 91-97; N.E. Andreasen, 'Town and Country in the Old

In response to the abuse of economic and political power of the landed elite, Mesopotamian rulers established various reforms and laws in order to deal with the increasing problems of debt-slavery and the alienation of land.[1] These legal reforms, particularly the OB *mēšarum* edicts, sought to correct the economic crises that resulted when the economy of the ruling elite and large private landowners disrupted the economy and welfare of free citizens, most of whom were small farmers. The release of both debt-slaves and alienated land is attested during various periods, although such releases are most evident during the OB period. For example, we noted in Chapter 3 that at Mari and Ugarit there was an attempt to regulate the sale of patrimonial land, although it is clear that such provisions did not prevent the permanent alienation of such lands. Furthermore, certain legal collections allowed for the redemption of people and property sold on account of debt (cf. LH §116-117; LE §39), although it is unclear whether such laws were enforced. Similarly, Israelite legal collections allowed for the release of debt-slaves and the redemption and release of land sold on account of debt (cf. Exod. 21.2-6; Deut. 15.12-18; Lev. 25). While the date of these laws remains unclear it is generally acknowledged that some sort of *Bodenrecht*, which was responsible for much of the conflict between kinship groups and the state,[2] existed in early Israel in order to protect patrimonial land, although it is unclear whether this 'law' took the form of actual legal prescriptions that were upheld by the political influence of the local assemblies and kings or whether it represented the traditional law of kinship groups who tried to prevent the loss of patrimonial land through mutual co-operation.[3] Nevertheless, on the basis of my

Testament', *Enc* 42 (1981), pp. 259-75; R.R. Wilson, 'The City in the Old Testament', in *Civitas: Religious Interpretations of the City* (ed. P.S. Hawkins; SPSH; Atlanta: Scholars Press, 1986), pp. 3-14

1. Cf. Westbrook, *Studies in Biblical and Cuneiform Law*, pp. 9-38, esp. 9-15.

2. Cf. A.E. Hill and G.A. Herion, 'Functional Yahwism and Social Control in the Early Israelite Monarchy', *JETS* 29 (1986), pp. 277-84; J.L. McKenzie, 'The Sack of Israel', in *The Quest for the Kingdom of God: Studies in Honor of G.E. Mendenhall* (ed. H.B. Huffmon, F.A. Spina and A.R.W. Green; Winona Lake, IN: Eisenbrauns, 1983), pp. 25-34.

3. Cf. Dearman, *Property Rights in the Eighth Century Prophets*, pp. 62-77, who notes that it is clear that both legal prescriptions and traditional law were practiced in many ancient Near Eastern states.

examination of the social background to debt-slavery in Israel, the biblical manumission laws may have been relevant for the Settlement period, during which social stratification was already in evidence, and particularly for the Monarchic period during which social stratification greatly increased.

Chapter 5

OLD TESTAMENT LAWS DEALING WITH CHATTEL- AND DEBT-SLAVES

In my discussion of the debt- and chattel-slave laws in Chapter 3, we saw that in the ancient Near East debt-slaves were not identified with foreign chattel-slaves. For example, according to LH §117 if a loan was foreclosed and dependents were sold or surrendered to a creditor (who may or may not be the original creditor) as debt-slaves, they were released after three years' service. These laws demonstrate that citizens who became debt-slaves were not to be regarded as the property of their creditors—viz., the creditor has only purchased the service or capacity for work (*Arbeitskraft*) of his debt-slaves. While certain rights pertaining to debt-slaves were also in special cases extended to chattel-slaves (e.g., LH §119), the latter were always regarded as the property of their owners. This attitude is also reflected in the *mēšarum* acts, which proclaimed the release of debt-slaves and their estranged property but not the release of chattel-slaves.[1]

Furthermore, it is most likely that chattel-slaves were treated more harshly than debt-slaves, although there are various laws in LH that afforded certain rights to chattel-slaves (e.g., §§170-171) and prevented excessive penalties from being imposed upon them by their masters (i.e., §282).[2] It is also clear that the position of chattel-slaves

1. Cf. Ziskind, 'Enslavement of the Native and Foreign Born', pp. 159-62.
2. Mendelsohn, *Slavery in the Ancient Near East*, p. 123, suggests that a slave is not considered chattel in LH §282, which prescribes that an owner may cut off the ear of a slave who denies his non-free status; cf. also P. Heinisch, *Das Buch Exodus: übersetzt und erklärt* (DHSAT, 1.2; Bonn: Peter Hanstein, 1934), p. 170. However, this law appears to be a reform in contradistinction to the general practice according to which an owner, without recourse to a court ruling, may mutilate his slave in whatever manner he chooses (cf. Driver and Miles, *Babylonian Laws*, I, pp. 489-90 and n. 3). This practice is attested in the Sumerian Laws (BC 7) and in private documents from the OB and MA periods.

improved during the OB period and later, since they often engaged in various businesses and attained high positions in society, although they remained the property of their owners. Nevertheless, one of the most important features of the cuneiform chattel-slave laws is that they did not deal with the treatment or injury of slaves by their owners, since chattel-slaves were considered to be the property of their owners.[1] It is clear from many OB and MA private documents that owners could 'mutilate' their slaves, although if owners killed their slaves or seriously injured their slaves this would mean that the owners would suffer a financial loss. Therefore, owners would be reluctant to injure slaves seriously, even though to do so was not generally considered an illegal act. Furthermore, the fact that MAL A §44; C §§2–3 set limits on the way in which owners could treat debt-slaves also confirms that on occasion chattel-slaves received harsh treatment (i.e., mistreatment, mutilation, and death).[2] I concluded, therefore, that it is likely that the compilers of both LH and MAL did not employ the term *wardum* 'slave' of debt-slaves in order to make it clear that a debt-slave was not to be identified with or treated like a chattel-slave.[3]

The biblical legal collections also consider chattel-slaves as the property of their owners (cf. Lev. 25.44-45), although some laws appear to afford rights to chattel-slaves normally afforded to free citizens.[4] While various laws show a special concern for the well-being of a slave, there is nevertheless some confusion as to whom these slave laws apply, since the term עבד 'slave', and similar terms, are employed in most of the slave laws of the Old Testament. That is,

1. LH §282 is an exception because the court was involved in the ruling regarding the status of the slave. In most cases an owner would have power over his own chattel-slave in regard to treatment or punishment (e.g., self-help).

2. This case deals with 'Assyrian' debt-slaves who were plebeians, compared to the patrician or *mar awīli* who is dealt with in MAL C §§ 2–3. The fact that limits were placed on the type of treatment an owner could exercise over his plebeian slaves suggests that no such treatment could be allowed in the case of patricians. Refer above to my discussion of these laws in Chapter 3.

3. Cf. Struve, 'Disintergration of the Slave Societies', p. 55; Ziskind, 'Enslavement of the Native and Foreign Born', p. 164.

4. Cf. Boecker, *Law and the Administration of Justice*, p. 162; S.M. Paul, *Book of the Covenant*, p. 69; Driver and Miles, *Babylonian Laws,* I, p. 408; M. David, 'The Codex Hammurabi and its Relation to the Provision of Law in Exodus', *OTS* 7 (1950), pp. 161-62.

do these slave laws apply exclusively to foreign chattel-slaves, or to Israelite debt-slaves, or to both types of slaves?[1] The cases in which it is particularly difficult to determine whether chattel- and/or debt-slaves are referred to are found in the laws concerning assault in the Covenant Code (i.e., Exod. 21.20-21, 26-27, 28-32). It is therefore important to attempt to discover whether the biblical legal compilers distinguished the chattel-slave laws from the debt-slave laws, particularly those in the Covenant Code, because the interpretation of the debt-slave laws Exod. 21.2-6, 7-11 has been influenced by the interpretation of the slave laws in Exod. 21.20-21, 26-27.

A Survey of the Slave Laws in the Pentateuch

The treatment of slaves in the Pentateuch is discussed in many different legal stipulations which can be categorized according to the following topics.

1.	Manumission (male slave)	Exod. 21/2-6; Lev. 25.39-42, 47-55.
2.	Marriage and Manumission (female slave)	Exod. 21.7-11 (אמה); Deut. 21.10-14
3.	Sex outside marriage	Lev. 19.20-22 (שפחה)
4.	Coveting	Exod. 20.17 = Deut. 5.21
5.	Assault	Exod. 21.20-21, 26-27, 32
6.	Sabbath	Exod. 20.10 = Deut. 5.14
7.	Sabbatical Year	Lev. 25.6
8.	Offerings	Deut. 12.12, 18
9.	Feasts	Deut. 16.11 (Feast of Weeks), 14 (Feast of Booths)
10.	Misc.	Lev. 25.44-45 (note on permanent slavery עבד & אמה); Deut. 23.15-16 (escaped slaves)

The reference to foreign slaves in Lev. 25.44-45 indicates clearly that these slaves were the permanent property of their owners. However, while the chattel-slave laws in LH, for example, were generally not concerned with the treatment of slaves by their owners, the majority of the biblical slave laws do refer to the fair treatment of slaves by

---

1. This ambiguity is also noted by Jackson, 'Biblical Laws of Slavery: a Comparative Approach', p. 96.

their owners. For example, the manumission laws in Exodus, Leviticus and Deuteronomy stipulated the release of Hebrew and/or Israelite debt-slaves who were released after a six- (Exod. 21.2-6; Deut. 15.12-18) or 49-year (Lev. 25.39-42) period of service.[1] While scholars generally agree that these laws do not refer to chattel-slaves, since these slaves were released after six or 49 years' service, several other laws allowed slaves to participate in many of the Israelite cultic observances (cf. Exod. 20.10, 17; Deut. 5.14, 21; Lev. 25.6; Deut. 12.12, 18; 16.11, 14; cf. also Exod. 12.42-51). It is therefore possible that these latter laws referred to both chattel- and debt-slaves. Furthermore, it is difficult to determine whether the slave laws in Exod. 21.20-21, 26-27, which concern the assault of slaves, refer to chattel-slaves or Hebrew and/or Israelite debt-slaves, since the term עבד[2] is used to designate both types of slaves.[3]

While it is clear that the legal reforms contained in both LH and MAL attempted to make a clear distinction between chattel- and debt-slaves, the question remains whether the biblical laws also sought to make a similar distinction. I will attempt to answer this difficult question by looking specifically at the slave law in Exod. 21.20-21 (and 21.26-27) which remains a *crux interpretum* in the discussion of the relationship between the debt-slave laws in Exod. 21.2-11 and the remaining slave laws in the Covenant Code and elsewhere in the Old Testament. To this discussion we now turn.

Exegesis of Exodus 21.20-21 (and 26-27)

Exodus 21. 20-21

20   וכי־יכה איש את־עבדו או את־אמתו בשבט ומת תחת ידו נקם ינקם:

21   אך אם־יום או יומים יעמד לא יקם כי כספו הוא:

---

1. Scholars are not in agreement over the identification of the Hebrew debt-slave in Exod 21.2-6. I will discuss this in greater detail in Chapter 6.

2. Note, however, that the terms שפחה and אמה are also used to designate women slaves in certain cases, particularly in laws regarding marriage and sexual offenses (cf. Exod. 21.7-11; Lev. 19.20-22), but also in Lev. 25.44-45 which deals generally with foreign chattel-slaves (אמה and עבד).

3. This problem is also dealt with by Cardellini, *Die biblischen 'Sklaven'-Gesetze*, pp. 258-68, 343-47; and Boecker, *Law and the Administration of Justice*, p. 170.

20 And if a man strikes his male or female slave with a rod and dies under his hand, he shall suffer vengeance.

21 If, however, within a day or two he gets up, no vengeance shall be taken; for he is his property.

This case deals with a man who strikes (יכה) his slave with a rod (wooden?; cf. Num. 35.18), which is usually understood to be the normal method used for the punishment of slaves (and also children; cf. Prov. 10.13; 13.24).[1] If the slave dies 'as a direct result' of the beating (lit., 'under his hand' תחת ידו),[2] then נקם ינקם; 'vengeance shall be taken' against the owner. However, if the slave gets up within or survives a day or two, then לא יקם 'no vengeance shall be taken'. Scholars generally have been divided over whether this law refers to foreign chattel-slaves or Hebrew debt-slaves. This lack of a consensus of opinion is due to two difficult exegetical problems: (1) does the expression נקם ינקם—lit. 'he shall suffer vengeance'—refer to the death penalty or does it refer to a lighter penalty?; (2) what is the meaning of the explanatory motivation clause כי כספו הוא—'for he is his money'?

The interpretation of the slave law in Exod. 21.20-21 has been determined mainly by the way in which scholars have understood the first exegetical problem. On the one hand, many scholars[3] suggest that

1. Cf. F.C. Fensham, 'Das nicht-haftbar-sein im Bundesbuch im Lichte der altorientalischer Rechtstexte', *JNSL* 8 (1980), p. 25; S.R. Driver, *The Book of Exodus: With Introduction and Notes* (CBSC; Cambridge: Cambridge University Press, 1911), p. 218; Paul, *Book of the Covenant*, p. 69 n. 3; H. Cazelles, *Études sur le code de l'alliance* (Paris: Letouzey et Ané, 1946), p. 54; M. Greenberg, 'More Reflections on Biblical Criminal Law', in *Studies in Bible 1986* (ed. S. Japhet; Scripta Hierosolymitana, 31; Jerusalem: Magnes, 1986), p. 11; H.W. Wolff, 'Master and Slaves: On Overcoming Class-Struggle in the Old Testament', *Int* 27 (1973), p. 267; cf. also Ibn Ezra and Ramban, *ad. loc.*

2. Cf. W.H. Gispen, *Exodus* (BSC; Grand Rapids: Zondervan, 1982), p. 212; Paul, *Book of the Covenant*, p. 69; U. Cassuto, *A Commentary on the Book of Exodus* (Jerusalem: Magnes, 1976), p. 273; Ramban, *ad. loc.*

3. For example, see A.H. McNeile, *The Book of Exodus: With Introduction and Notes. With Commentary* (London: Methuen, 1908), p. 129; B.S. Childs, *The Book of Exodus: A Critical, Theological Commentary* (Philadelphia: Westminster Press, 1974), p. 471; Driver, *Exodus*, p. 218; A. Dillmann, *Die Bücher Exodus und Leviticus* (KH, 12; Leipzig: S. Hirzel, 2nd edn, 1880), p. 231; B. Baentsch, *Exodus-Leviticus-Numeri übersetzt und erklärt* (HKAT, 1.2; Göttingen: Vandenhoeck & Ruprecht, 1903), p. 195; H. Holzinger, *Exodus erklärt* (KHAT;

the expression נקם ינקם in v. 20 does not refer to the death penalty but to a lighter penalty that is left to the decision of the judge (e.g., Dillmann, Driver, Childs) or to the sanctuary (e.g., Baentsch, Driver). Furthermore, these scholars, such as McNeile, Driver and Childs, suggest that this slave law refers to chattel-slaves since in the case of a freeman (or debt-slave) the law would demand capital punishment.[1]

For example, McNeile[2] writes: 'The killing of a slave was not a capital offence. The code is based upon the principle of just requital; and the death of a free man would be a disproportionate requital for that of a slave, who was only a piece of property.' Furthermore, McNeile suggests that if the slave survived a day or two (v. 21) then the owner intended only to punish his slave. The motivation clause in v. 21b therefore explains that no further punishment is required since the owner has already inflicted punishment on himself by losing his property (lit., כסף—'money'). Lastly, he suggests that the motivation clause was inserted in order to make a legal distinction between intentional (v. 20) and unintentional (v. 21) homicide.

Further, Driver,[3] who follows the exegesis of Dillmann,[4] suggests that the expression נקם ינקם probably does not refer to the death penalty for the following two reasons: (1) the expression מות יומת (cf. vv. 12, 15, 16, 17) would have been used if the death penalty was meant; (2) vv. 21 (cf. 19f.), 26-27 (cf. 23ff.) and v. 32 (cf. 28ff.) show a marked difference between a slave and a freeman.

Lastly, Childs[5] notes that the expression נקם ינקם is rather vague and cannot be identified with the death penalty *per se*, and that the

---

Tübingen: Mohr, 1900), p. 85; D. Patrick, *Old Testament Law* (London: SCM Press, 1985), p. 75; F.C. Fensham, *Exodus: De Prediking van het Oude Testament* (Nijkerk: G.F. Callenbach B.V., 2nd edn, 1977), pp. 154-55; idem, 'Das nicht-haftbar-sein,' pp. 23-25; A. Clamer, *L'Exode* (La Sainte Bible, 1.2; Paris, 1956), p. 191; J.P. Hyatt, *Exodus* (NCBC; Grand Rapids: Eerdmans; London: Morgan & Scott, 1971), p. 233; Jackson, 'Reflections on Biblical Criminal Law', p. 45.

1. Cp. Holzinger, *Exodus*, p. 85, who writes, 'Warum die Bestimmung nur für Sklaven und Sklavinnen nichthebräischer Herkunft gelten soll (Dillmann 256), ist nicht ersichtlich; bei denen wurden höchstens noch weniger Umstände gemacht.'

2. McNeile, *Exodus*, p. 129.

3. Driver, *Exodus*, p. 218.

4. Dillmann, *Exodus*, p. 231.

5. Childs, *Exodus*, pp. 471-72.

punishment would be left to the discretion of the judge. Childs substantiates his interpretation of the phrase נקם ינקם by appealing to the use of the motivation clause in v. 21. He writes: [1]

> Any doubt as to whether a different standard from that for a free citizen was applied is removed by the final motivation clause. The master is fully exonerated from injuring his slave 'because he is his property'. It is sad to realize that this verse continued to provide a warrant for the 'biblical teaching' on slavery throughout the middle of the nineteenth century in the United States.

However, in contrast to Driver, Childs notes that the slave law in vv. 26-27, which prescribes the release of a slave whose eye or tooth is knocked out, seeks to prevent the mistreatment of slaves by putting them on a level with freemen, since the slave is no longer treated as property. Therefore, he agrees that this law stands in contrast with the slave law in vv. 20-21 which regards the slave as the property of his owner. Childs explains this disparity by suggesting that the slave law in vv. 20-21 is a pre-talion law that is older than the talion laws connected to the stipulations in v. 12 and vv. 24-25. Childs follows the views of Diamond,[2] who suggests that the talion principle (*ius talionis*; i.e., literal retaliation) represents an advanced stage in ancient Near Eastern jurisprudence which can be traced to LH and LE. Furthermore, Diamond[3] suggests that the talionic principle is a later addition to the Covenant Code, although Childs[4] suggests that the principle of talion probably included the concept of compensation from the outset. However, the principle of compensation did not

---

1. Childs, *Exodus*, p. 471.
2. A.S. Diamond, 'An Eye for and Eye', *Iraq* 19 (1957), pp. 151-55; cf. also Epsztein, *Social Justice in the Ancient Near East*, pp. 6-7; Paul, *Book of the Covenant*, pp. 75-76; Finkelstein, 'Ammisaduqa's Edict', p. 98; B.S. Jackson, *Theft in Early Jewish Law* (Oxford: Clarendon Press, 1972), p. 153; *idem*, 'The Problem of Exodus 21: 22-25 (IUS TALIONIS)', in *Essays in Jewish and Comparative Legal History* (SJLA, 10; Leiden: Brill, 1975), pp. 101-102.
3. Diamond, 'An Eye for an Eye', p. 153; cf. also Jackson, 'The Problem of Exodus 21.22-25', pp. 99-107, esp. 99-102, whose reconstruction of the *Urgesetz* in Exod 21.12-25 is similar to that of Childs.
4. Childs, *Exodus*, p. 472. Childs follows the view of Daube, *Studies in Biblical Law* (Cambridge: Cambridge University Press, 1947), pp. 102-47; cf. also Boecker, *Law and the Administration of Justice*, pp. 174-75; cp. Jackson, 'Problems of Exodus 21.22-25', pp. 102-107.

extend to cases involving homicide, except in the case of the goring ox (cf. Num. 35.31; cp. Exod. 21.29-30).[1] Childs therefore regards the slave law in vv. 26-27, which prescribes compensation for the loss of an eye or tooth, as a 'new Hebrew stamp on old material'.

On the other hand, many scholars[2] suggest that the expression נקם ינקם refers to the death penalty, although they are generally divided over whether this law refers to foreign chattel-slaves or to Hebrew debt-slaves. Furthermore, these scholars are divided over the method by which the death penalty is administered—viz., is it the court/temple that administers the penalty (e.g., in the case of a foreign chattel-slave) or the relatives of the slave (e.g., in the case of an Israelite debt-slave; גאל הדם; cf. Num. 35.19ff.)?

For example, Cassuto[3] and Paul[4] suggest that the expression נקם ינקם

---

1. For discussions concerning the apparent discrepancy between Exod. 21.30, which allows ransom, and Num. 35.31-32, which forbids ransom in cases of homicide, see Paul, *Book of the Covenant*, pp. 81-82; M. Greenberg, 'Some Postulates of Biblical Criminal Law', in *Yehezkel Kaufman Jubilee Volume* (ed. M. Haran; Jerusalem: Magnes, 1960), p. 20 n. 119; A. Phillips, 'Another Look at Murder', *JJS* 28 (1977), p. 26f.; cf. also Daube, *Studies in Biblical Law*, pp. 106-108; R. Yaron, 'The Goring Ox', *ILR* 1 (1966), pp. 396-406.

2. For example, see Cardellini, *Die biblischen 'Sklaven'-Gesetze*, p. 260; Liedke, *Gestalt und Bezeichnung*, p. 48; M. Noth, *Exodus: A Commentary* (OTL; London: SCM Press, 1962), p. 181; Cassuto, *Exodus*, p. 273; Cole, *Exodus*, pp. 168-69; Boecker, *Law and the Administration of Justice*, pp. 160-63; Paul, *Book of the Covenant*, pp. 69-70; David, 'The Codex Hammurabi', p. 162; Cazelles, *Code de l'alliance*, p. 54; Wolff, 'Master and Slaves', p. 267; Pedersen, *Israel*, I-II, p. 402; J.P.M. van der Ploeg, 'Slavery in the Old Testament', in *Congress Volume, Uppsala 1971* (VTSup, 22; Leiden: Brill, 1972), p. 80; L. Katzoff, 'Slavery in the Bible', *Dor le Dor* 10 (1982), p. 205; M. Greenberg, 'Crimes and Punishments', *IDB*, I, p. 738; *idem*, 'More Reflections', pp. 12-14; Gispen, *Exodus*, p. 212; A. Phillips, *Ancient Israel's Criminal Law: A New Approach to the Decalogue* (Oxford: Basil Blackwell, 1970), pp. 87-88; Heinisch, *Exodus*, p. 170; Mendelsohn, *Slavery in the Ancient Near East*, pp. 123, 143; *idem*, 'Slavery in the Old Testament', p. 388; J.L. Saalschütz, *Das Mosaische Recht nebst den vervollständigenden thalmudisch-rabbinischen Bestimmungen für Bibelforscher, Juristen und Staatsmänner* (Berlin: Carl Heymann, 3rd edn, 1853), pp. 539-42; Wright, *God's People in God's Land*, pp. 241-42.

3. Cassuto, *Exodus*, p. 273.

4. Paul, *Book of the Covenant*, p. 69; cf. also Heinisch, *Exodus*, p. 170; Mendelsohn, *Slavery in the Ancient Near East*, p. 123; and F. Horst, *Gottes Recht: Gesammelte Studien zum Recht im Alten Testament* (Theologische Bücherei

refers to capital punishment, which represents an important innovation in the treatment of chattel-slaves. This opinion is also shared by Cole[1] and Gispen,[2] who suggest that the expression נקם ינקם refers to capital punishment since the slave law in vv. 26-27 also advocates a humanitarian approach to slaves. In addition, these scholars agree that the motivation clause in v. 21 makes it clear that the death of the slave was an accident which does not demand any penalty since the owner has already received material punishment through the loss of his slave. While Cassuto, Cole and Gispen do not specify who would administer the death penalty in the event of the death of the slave (v. 20), Greenberg[3] and Paul[4] suggest that a foreign slave would 'be avenged' by Israelite justice, although they do not elaborate upon how this would be accomplished.

However, while Boecker also suggests that this law refers to a chattel-slave and suggests that the expression נקם ינקם refers to the death penalty, he finds the use of the motivation clause in v. 21 especially puzzling. For example, he writes: [5]

> If this [the motivation] is taken literally, the remaining prescriptions are not only superfluous but unintelligible. If the slave was regarded as no more than a possession without personal rights, as the end of v. 21 regards him, his owner could do with him as he liked.

He thus concludes, along with Jepsen,[6] that the motivation clause in v. 21 is a later addition. However, he follows the majority of scholars in asserting that the motivation clause sought to differentiate between intentional and unintentional homicide, although he does not agree with Noth[7] and Childs that the entire law is older than that in

---

Neudrucke und Berichte aus dem 20. Jahrhundert, 12; Munich: Chr. Kaiser Verlag, 1961), p. 274, who regards the slave law in Exod. 21.20 as a surprising addition to the participial laws on homicide in vv. 12-13.

1. Cole, *Exodus*, pp. 168-69.
2. Gispen, *Exodus*, p. 212.
3. Greenberg, 'Crimes and Punishments', p. 738.
4. Paul, *Book of the Covenant*, p. 70 and n. 2.
5. Boecker, *Law and the Administration of Justice*, p. 161.
6. A. Jepsen, *Untersuchungen zum Bundesbuch* (Wissenschaftliche MANT, 41; Neukirchen–Vluyn: Neukirchener Verlag, 1927), pp. 32-33; cf. also Jackson, 'Biblical Laws of Slavery: a Comparative Approach', p. 95.
7. Noth, *Exodus*, p. 181; cf. also Wolff, 'Master and Slaves', p. 267, who also argues that the law in Exod. 21.20-21 is older than the law in 21.26-27 since the

vv. 26-27 (and 21.7-11). As we saw above, this is the usual interpretation posited for this motivation clause, although other scholars, such as Cassuto, Paul and Cole, do not appear to recognize the difficulty the motivation clause presents to the interpretation of the other slave laws found in Exodus 21. Lastly, Boecker suggests that the expression נקם ינקם refers to blood vengeance that was carried out by either the family or by the legal assembly acting on behalf of the family (i.e., blood vengeance executed by the גאל הדם 'blood avenger'; cf. Num. 35.19ff.), although he does not pursue this aspect of the law further, since he regards the fact that a penalty is provided for as the most important feature of this law.

David,[1] however, suggests that since the death penalty is prescribed in Exod. 21.20-21 the term עבד refers to Hebrew debt-slaves rather than foreign chattel-slaves. Therefore, according to David, the act of 'revenge' would be administered by the relatives of the slave's family (cf. Num. 35.16-28). This view is also advocated by Liedke,[2] who further points out that while it is possible for the family of a Hebrew debt-slave to exact blood vengeance (נקם), it is unimaginable to think that the family of a chattel-slave, who was a foreign captive, would be able to exact blood vengeance on behalf of their family member.

While David and Liedke suggest that this law refers to Hebrew debt-slaves because of the method of punishment, Cardellini[3] suggests that this law refers to Hebrew debt-slaves based on his comparison of Exod. 21.20-21, 26-27, 32 to the similar slave laws occuring in LH §116 and LE §§23/24. I will discuss Cardellini's study in more detail below in a separate excursus. Lastly, Couroyer,[4] Mendelsohn,[5] and others[6] suggest that this law applies equally to Israelite debt-slaves and

---

motivation clause in v. 21 reinforces the old idea of an owner's property rights.

1. David, 'Codex Hammurabi', p. 162.
2. Liedke, *Gestalt und Bezeichnung*, p. 48; cf. also Cazelles, *Code de l'alliance*, p. 54; and Pedersen, *Israel*, I-II, p. 402. Liedke, however, notes that while it is the גאל who executes the blood-feud, it is the court (elders) that approves or imposes the execution. I deal with this institution in more detail below.
3. Cardellini, *Die biblischen 'Sklaven'–Gesetze*, pp. 260, 63, 65-68; cf. also Westbrook, *Studies in Biblical and Cuneiform Law*, pp. 89-101.
4. B. Couroyer, *L'Exode* (Bible de Jerusalem; Paris, 3rd edn, 1968), p. 102.
5. Mendelsohn, 'Slavery in the Old Testament', p. 388.
6. Cf. Greenberg, 'More Reflections', p. 14; H.H. Cohn, 'Slavery', *EncJud*, XXIV, col. 1655; Saalschütz, *Mosaisches Recht*, pp. 697-717.

foreign chattel-slaves, since the law makes no distinction between the two types of slaves.

The Meaning of the Expression נקם ינקם

In the above discussion we saw that scholars have been divided over how to interpret the expression נקם ינקם. Similar divisions over the interpretation of this expression are found in several early translations of the Old Testament—w מת יומת, ℭ (Onkelos), and *Pešiṭṭà* דן 'to be judged'[1]—and in the Mekilta and commentaries of some Medieval rabbinic commentators,[2] who also debated whether the phrase referred to the death penalty or punishment. While scholars[3] agree that the root נקם is part of the legal terminology of the Old Testament, few have discussed the legal and social background to the practice of vengeance, which can be traced back to the administration of justice among kin groups in the ancient Near East. Therefore, in the following discussion I will briefly discuss the legal development of the practice of vengeance in the ancient Near East and Israel (as illustrated in the Old Testament) before I discuss the meaning of the term נקם in the Old Testament and in the legal stipulation in Exod. 21.20-21.

The socio-legal background to vengeance in the ancient Near East and Israel. In two separate articles, McKeating[4] has discussed the legal development of the practice of vengeance within the ancient Near East and Israel, especially in regard to the law of homicide. Drawing upon

1. The Targum and *Pešiṭṭa–* usually render נקם as *pera'*; cf. van der Ploeg, 'Slavery and the Old Testament', p. 79.
2. Cf. Mekilta, *ad. loc.*; Rashi, *ad. loc.*; and Ramban, *ad. loc.*
3. For example, see Mendenhall, *The Tenth Generation*, pp. 69-104, who is refuted by W.T. Pitard, Amarna *ekēmu* and Hebrew *nāqam*', *Maarav* 3 (1982), pp. 5-25; cf. also G. Sauer, 'נקם', *Theologisches Handwörterbuch zum Alten Testament*, II (ed. E. Jenni and C. Westermann; Munich: Chr. Kaiser Verlag, 1976), cols. 106-109; H. McKeating, The Development of the Law of Homicide in Ancient Israel', *VT* 25 (1975), pp. 46-53; *idem*, 'Vengeance is Mine: A Study of the Pursuit of Vengeance in the Old Testament', *ExpTim* 74 (1962–63), pp. 239-45; W.J. Harrelson, 'Vengeance', *IDB*, I, pp. 748-49; H. Shmidman, 'Vengeance', *EncJud*, XVI, col. 93.
4. McKeating, 'Homicide in Ancient Israel', pp. 46-56; *idem*, 'Vengeance is Mine', pp. 239-45; cf. also the more recent discussion of customary law by Bellefontaine, 'Customary Law and Chieftainship', pp. 51-55.

the comparative studies of law of Diamond[1] and Seagle,[2] McKeating[3] notes that before the advent of state government, kin groups were responsible for the discipline of their members. When an offence was committed by a member of one kin group against another, compensation would be demanded by the offended kin group. Compensation would be set according to the damage done; e.g., compensation (or recompense) might be paid in money or other movable assets, or in persons who might be handed over either for slaughter or for use as slaves.

In the Old Testament, one can perhaps see in the reference to Lamech's vindictiveness in Gen. 4.23-24 how vengeance was considered the accepted form of justice during the Patriarchal period. In v. 23 Lamech tells Adah and Zillah that he has killed a man for wounding him and a boy for striking him. Furthermore, he tells them in v. 24 that if Cain is avenged sevenfold (שבעתים יקם־קין), then he will be avenged seventy-sevenfold. McKeating[4] notes that this example of vengeance, which clearly goes beyond the requirement of 'just recompense', does not represent what normally would occur under established clan law. Further examples of such abuse can be found in Genesis 32–33, where Jacob expects Esau to take vengeance upon him and his family (cf. Gen. 32.6-8; 33.8-11),[5] and in Genesis 34, where the sons of Jacob take vengeance upon the Shechemites for the rape of Dinah by killing all the males of the city.[6] Although the term נקם is not found in these latter two passages, they, nonetheless, demonstrate that vengeance was administered by kin groups without any recourse to local courts or councils, which is what we would expect in similar societies of the ancient Near East that have not come under the control of the temple or city-state.[7]

However, once a society becomes centralized under a state government, the offence is thought of as being against society as a whole

1. A.S. Diamond, *Comparative Study of Primitive Law* (London, 1965).
2. W. Seagle, *Quest for Law* (New York: Knopf, 1941).
3. McKeating, 'Homicide in Ancient Israel', pp. 46-48.
4. McKeating, 'Homicide in Ancient Israel', p. 49.
5. Cf. McKeating, 'Vengeance is Mine', p. 239.
6. Cf. McKeating, 'Homicide in Ancient Israel', pp. 48-49.
7. These passages also suggest that vengeance was administered within different levels of the lineage; e.g. individual families בית אב as well as larger units such as the משפחה; cf. Bellefontaine, 'Customary Law and Chieftainship', pp. 49-51.

and compensation is replaced by punishment, which is determined by the courts. This new development may occur either under the rule of a temple or king, although sacral crimes eventually became secularized when the state took over the administration of the temple.[1] Nevertheless, McKeating acknowledges that this administrative transition may take generations to occur.[2] Furthermore, he notes that some offences may remain under the jurisdiction of kin groups while other offences have already come under the jurisdiction of the state.[3] This is particularly true for cases of homicide, since the practice of blood vengeance remained operative in the city-state societies of the ancient Near East and in Israel (cf. 1 Sam. 14.7; 2 Sam. 3.30)[4].

During Israel's Settlement period it is likely that vengeance no longer came under the authority of individual kin groups, but rather came under the broader control of the tribes under the sacral authority of God. For example, in Numbers 31 vengeance that is executed by Israel upon the Midianites is sanctioned by God. This vengeance is also declared as the Lord's vengeance upon Midian, because the Midianites tried to seduce Israel away from God

---

1. Cf. also J.R. Porter, *The Extended Family in the Old Testament* (OPSEA, 6; London: Edutext, 1967), p. 8; Bellefontaine, 'Customary Law and Chieftainship', p. 54.

2. Cf. K.S. Newman, *Law and Economic Organization: A Comparative Study of Pre-industrial Societies* (Cambridge: Cambridge University Press, 1983), p. 115, who suggests that due to the range of legal complexities that exist across different societies there are eight possible types of legal systems ranging from the simplest to the most complex: (1) Self- or kin-based redress; (2) Advisor systems; (3) Mediator systems; (4) Elders' councils; (5) Restricted councils; (6) Chieftainships; (7) Paramount chieftainships; (8) State-level legal systems; cf. also the discussion in Bellefontaine, 'Customary Law and Chieftainship', pp. 56-58.

3. Cf. also L. Pošpisil, 'Legal Levels and Multiplicity of Legal Systems in Human Societies', *JCR* 11 (1967), pp. 24-25; Bellefontaine, 'Customary Law and Chieftainship', p. 52.

4. Cf. H. Schulz, *Das Todesrecht im Alten Testament: Studien zur Rechtsform der Mot-jumat-Sätze* (BZAW, 114; Berlin: Töpelmann, 1969), pp. 113-27; A. Phillips, 'Prophecy and Law', in *Israel's Prophetic Heritage: Essays in Honour of Peter R. Ackroyd* (ed. R. Coggins, A. Phillips and M. Knibb; Cambridge: Cambridge University Press, 1982), p. 230; E. Gerstenberger, *Wesen und Herkunft des 'Apodiktischen Rechts'* (WMANT, 20; Neukirchen–Vluyn: Neukirchener Verlag, 1965), pp. 107-108, 143-44; Bellefontaine, 'Customary Law and Chieftainship', p. 54.

(cf. Num. 25.1-13). Therefore, the vengeance that is carried out by the Israelites against the Midianites is carried out because of the Midianites' disobedience towards God's commands.[1] Furthermore, when Joshua takes vengeance upon the Amorites he does so with God's sanction and assistance (cf. Josh. 10.12-13; cf. also Judg. 11.36).[2]

Lastly, during Israel's Monarchic period various disputes, including crimes involving assault and homicide, came under the jurisdiction of the courts and temple. Nevertheless, in the Covenant Code, which probably dates back to or was operative in limited ways during the Settlement period (cf. Exod. 21.12-14, 18, 22, 30; 22.8, 9 [Hebrew vv. 7, 8]),[3] laws concerning assault, homicide and theft came under the jurisdiction of the courts, although biblical legislation acknowledges that God is also an active participant in the administration of justice (cf. Exod. 21.6, 13-14; 22.11 [Hebrew v. 10]). Both McKeating[4] and Greenberg[5] note that, although the cultic law of sanctuary (cf. Exod. 21.12-14; Num. 35; Deut. 19) was in operation during the early Monarchic period (cf. 1 Kgs 1.50-53; 2.28-34), the law in Exod. 21.13, which refers to the altar as a place of refuge for murderers, most probably reflects the usage of an even earlier period. Furthermore, a relative of the slain person was required to execute blood vengeance, although this practice, which was a remnant of 'clan'-law, was regulated by the court. Therefore, while it is likely that certain crimes came under the jurisdiction of the courts during the Settlement period, centralization of power and administration did not occur until the Monarchic period, although during this latter

---

1. Cf. Wenham, *Numbers*, p. 210, who suggests that the Midianites' seduction was tantamount to adultery, which carried the death penalty (cf. Lev. 20.10; Deut. 22.22).

2. Cf. McKeating, 'Vengeance is Mine', pp. 239-40.

3. For example, see Patrick, *Old Testament Law*, p. 65; L. Horst, 'Bundesbuch', *RGG*, I, col. 1524; E. Nielsen, *The Ten Commandments in New Perspective* (SBTSS, 7; London: SCM Press, 1968), pp. 77-78; Noth, *Exodus*, p. 174; Boecker, *Law and the Administration of Justice*, pp. 141-44; von Rad, *Old Testament Theology*, I, pp. 15-35; Jepsen, *Bundesbuch*, pp. 101-102; Lemche, 'The Hebrew Slave', pp. 130-34 and n. 3.

4. McKeating, 'Homicide in Ancient Israel', p. 53.

5. M. Greenberg, 'The Biblical Conception of Asylum', *JBL* 78 (1959), pp. 125-32.

period God is also understood to participate along with the judges when judgment is rendered (cf. 2 Chron. 19.4-11).[1]

The meaning of the term נקם in the Old Testament. In the Old Testament the root נקם occurs 79 times: the verb נקם occurs 35 times; the masculine substantive נקם occurs 17 times; and the feminine substantive נקמה occurs 27 times.[2] Surprisingly, the root נקם only occurs in two legal stipulations (cf. Exod. 21.20-21; Lev. 19.18), and in a handful of passages in which individuals take vengeance upon their enemies.[3] Elsewhere, in the majority of cases vengeance is taken either by Israel upon her enemies[4] or by God upon disobedient nations.[5]

However, if we compare the way in which vengeance was supposed to be administered among kin groups and under the administration of the state in the ancient Near East with the way in which vengeance is administered in the Old Testament, we can observe some interesting differences. For example, we saw in the above section that the reference to Lamech's vindictiveness in Gen. 4.23-24 demonstrates how vengeance could be abused by an individual member of a clan. However, such vindictiveness is also exhibited in the case of Cain, whom God promises to avenge sevenfold if he is slain (cf. Gen. 4.15). Furthermore, Samson executes vengeance against the Philistines for the death of his wife (cf. Judg. 15.7) and for the loss of his eyes (cf. Judg. 16.28). In these two cases Samson kills many Philistines which, on the surface, seems to reflect the abuse of clan-law. Both McKeating[6] and Pitard[7] concur that these two passages represent acts

---

1. Cf. Bellefontaine, 'Customary Law and Chieftainship', pp. 55-58.
2. For a thorough breakdown of the occurrences of the root נקם in the OT, see Sauer, 'נקם', cols. 106-109; J. Licht, 'נקמה', *Encyclopedia Biblica. Thesaurus Rerum Biblicarum Alphabetico Ordine Digestus*, V (Hebrew) (ed. H. Tadmor; Jerusalem: Bialik Institute, 1968), cols. 917-21; Pitard, 'Amarna *ekēmu* and Hebrew *nāqam*', pp. 16-25.
3. Cf. Judg. 15.7; 16.28; 1 Sam. 14.24; 24.13; Prov. 6.34; cf. also Sauer, 'נקם', col. 108.
4. Cf. Num. 31.2-3; Josh. 10.13; Judg. 11.36; Esther 8.13.
5. Cf. Lev. 26.25 and Ezek. 24.8 (Israel); Deut. 32.35, 41, 43; Isa. 34.8; 47.3; Ezek. 25.12ff.; Mic. 5.14.
6. McKeating, 'Vengeance is Mine', p. 239.
7. Pitard, 'Amarna *ekēmu* and Hebrew *nāqam*', p. 17.

of 'revenge' which are not to be considered proper acts. Clearly, Samson's vengeance in these two cases exceeds the demand for 'just recompense', which is regarded by both McKeating and Pitard to be the basic meaning of the term נקם. However, one must not overlook the fact that, according to the biblical narrative, Samson's revenge is possible only with the help of God, who endows him with special strength. This suggests clearly that Samson's acts were not 'illegal'.

Similarly, the term נקם is used to refer to the vengeance which the Israelites, under the protection of God, execute upon their enemies during battles (cf. Num. 31.2-3; Josh. 10.12-13; Judg. 11.36). In these passages the total destruction of the enemy is envisaged. Moreover, in the prophetic oracles God pronounces his judgement and vengeance upon those nations who have disobeyed Him (cf. Deut. 32.41-43; Isa. 34.8; Jer. 51.34-37) and who have sinned or committed crimes against Israel (cf. Ezek. 25.1-7, 8-11, 12-14, 15-17).[1] In these passages the total annihilation of God's enemies is also envisaged (cf. Isa. 47.3; Jer. 9.11), which suggests that God's vengeance is as severe as the vengeance that Israel executed upon her enemies (cf. Nah. 1.2-6). God also promises to execute vengeance upon Israel if she breaks His covenant (cf. Lev. 26.23-26; cf. also Jer. 5.9 = 5.29 = 9.8; Ezek. 9.4-10; cp. Gen. 4.15).

However, vengeance was never sanctioned as a means for settling disputes between Israelites. For example, the legal stipulation in Lev. 19.18, which is connected with the love command in v. 17, prohibits an Israelite from taking vengeance upon or bearing a grudge against his neighbour.[2] McKeating, therefore, suggests that while to exact vengeance is regarded as just (cf. Prov. 6.24), not to exact it is a virtue. This ideal might also be the motive behind the actions of David when he spares the life of Saul, who tried to kill him. Instead of taking Saul's life David decides to spare him, leaving the execution of vengeance to God (cf. 1 Sam. 24.1-7; 26.1-25). David also spares the life of Shimei even though the sons of Zeruiah demand that he be put

---

1. Cf. Pitard, 'Amarna *ekēmu* and Hebrew *nāqam*', pp. 16-17, who lists 14 passages in which the term deals with actual legal situations: Exod. 21.20-21; Lev. 26.25; Deut. 32.35-43; Judg. 11.36; 1 Sam. 24.13; Isa. 1.24; 34.8; 59.15-19; Jer. 5.9 = 5.29 = 9.8; 20.10-12; 51.34-37; Ezek. 25.13-14,16-17; Ps. 94.1.

2. Cf. Riesener, *Der Stamm* עבד, p. 124; Elliger, *Leviticus*, pp. 341-42; cf. also Rashi, *ad. loc.*; and J.L. Kugel, 'On Hidden Hatred and Open Reproach: Early Exegesis of Leviticus 19: 17', *HTR* 80 (1987), pp. 60-61.

to death (cf. 2 Sam 19.16-23).[1] These passages, then, suggest that the execution of vengeance was not applicable within the covenant community, although God Himself took the role of avenger in certain cases (cf. 2 Sam. 22.48; Jer. 15.15 and 20.10-12).

Nevertheless, scholars generally regard the execution of a murderer by the blood-avenger (lit. 'redeemer of blood' גאל הדם) as an act of blood vengeance, which they trace to the penalty stipulated in Exod. 21.20-21. For example, Pitard[2] suggests that the root נקם refers to the punishment given to a wrongdoer who has been found guilty of a crime, or to the damages or recompense awarded to the victim of the crime. Moreover, he suggests that this recompense or vengeance must be seen as a just recompense or payment for a crime, which is exactly what is called for in *lex talionis*,[3] and not simply as brutal revenge.[4] However, while this definition may be true for the way in which 'vengeance' was administered under the jurisdiction of the courts (i.e., מות יומת), although the term נקם is not used in these contexts except in Exod. 21.20-21, it does not appear to apply to the way in which the term is generally employed when it refers to the divine vengeance which either Israel or God executes upon enemies. In these cases the death penalty is enacted in both capital and non-capital offenses. Furthermore, this penalty is often extended to people not immediately involved in the offense, which contrasts clearly with the accepted view of vengeance as the 'just recompense' of a crime administered by kin groups or city-state governments.[5]

---

1. Cf. also 2 Sam. 18.5; 19.1-5, according to which David spares the life of Absalom, although it is understandable that a father would want to spare the life of his son (cp. 2 Sam. 18.6-8).

2. Pitard, 'Amarna *ekēmu* and Hebrew *nāqam*', p. 17. Pitard lists 24 passages which reflect the idea of 'just recompense' for a crime: Num. 31.2-3; Josh. 10. 12–13; 1 Sam. 14.24; 18.25; 2 Sam. 4.8; 2 Kgs 9.7; Isa. 35.4; 47.3; 61.1-4; 63.4; Jer. 15. 15; 46.10; 50.15, 28; 51.6,11; Ezek. 24.8; Mic. 5.14; Nah. 1.2; Ps. 18.48 = 2 Sam. 22.48; Ps. 58.11; 79.10; 99.8; 149.7; Esther 8.13.

3. Cf. also W. W. Eichrodt, *Theology of the Old Testament*, II (Philadelphia: Westminster Press, 1967), pp. 423-24; Harrelson, 'Vengeance', p. 748; Shmidman, 'Vengeance', col. 93; G.E. Mendenhall, 'Ancient Oriental and Biblical Law', *BA* 17 (1954), p. 29.

4. Contra Mendenhall, *The Tenth Generation*, p. 748; 'God of Vengeance, Shine Forth', *WB* 45 (1948), p. 38.

5. There are only a few cases in the Old Testament where improper revenge and vindictiveness are mentioned: Lev. 19.18; Jer. 20.10; Ezek. 25.12,15; Prov. 6.34;

As the above discussion shows, on the basis of the use of the term נקם in the Old Testament the expression נקם ינקם in Exod. 21.20 should be rendered 'he shall suffer vengeance', which elsewhere always includes the idea of the death penalty.[1] That the death penalty was

---

cf. Harrelson, 'Vengeance', p. 748; Shmidman, 'Vengeance', col. 93; cp. Pitard, 'Amarna *ekēmu* and Hebrew *nāqam*', p. 17, who lists 11 passages: Gen. 4.15, 24; Lev. 19.18; Judg. 15.7; 16.28; Jer. 20.10; Ezek. 25.12, 15; Ps. 44.17; Prov. 6.34; Lam. 3.60.

1.   Contra McNeile, *Exodus*, p. 129; Driver, *Exodus*, p. 218; Childs, *Exodus*, pp. 471-72; van der Ploeg, 'Slavery in the Old Testament', p. 80. As I pointed out above, Childs does not think that the expression נקם ינקם refers to the death penalty, since the term נקם in Exod. 21.20 cannot be identified with the death penalty referred to in v. 12 or with the talion principle enunciated in vv. 24-25, under which a slave is released when his or her owner puts out an eye or a tooth (vv. 26-27). Therefore, Childs posits a different meaning for the term נקם by appealing to the existence of pre-talion laws which antedate the usage of the term נקם elsewhere in the Old Testament. However, Childs' argument is not convincing for the following reasons. First, his argument that the slave law in vv. 20-21 prescribes a different standard (pre-talion) from that in vv. 26-27 appears to be circular. This is his argument: (1) the expression נקם ינקם does not refer to the death penalty but to a lighter punishment; (2) the motivation clause in v. 21 fully exonerates the master from injuring his slave 'because he is his property'; (3) since slaves in this law are not treated the same as in vv. 26-27 (and elsewhere) this law must be dated to a period earlier than the rest of the talion laws. Step (1) in the argument is assumed, it is not proven, and step (2) is used to prove/substantiate step (1), which is clearly circular: i.e., the meaning of נקם ינקם follows *a priori* from Childs' interpretation of the motivation clause in v. 21. This type of circular reasoning is also evident in the argumentation of both McNeile and Driver. Secondly, Childs' argument that Exod. 21.20-21 represents a pre-talionic law is not convincing, since even if one accepts that the talionic principle is a late interpolation to the laws of assault in the Covenant Code, it is unlikely that that any so-called pre-talion law would remain unaltered once the talionic principle had been inserted into the discussion. This is particularly true for cases of homicide which clearly require the death penalty in all of the biblical laws on homicide. For cogent arguments against the view that the talion principle in Exod. 21.23-25 is a late deuteronomic redaction, see S.E. Loewenstamm, 'Exodus XXI 22-25', *VT* 27 (1977), pp. 352-60; cf. also the comments of Daube, *Studies on Biblical Law*, pp. 106-109; and W.G. Lambert, 'Interchange of Ideas Between Southern Mesopotamia and Syria-Palestine as Seen in Literature', in *Mesopotamien und seine Nachbarn: Politische und kulturelle Wechselbeziehungen im Alten Vorderasien vom 4. bis 1. Jahrtausend v. Chr. Teil 1* (ed. H.J. Nissen and J. Renger; BBVO, 1; Berlin: Dietrich Reimer Verlag, 1982), p. 313, who suggests that *lex talionis* is an Amorite innovation belonging to the 'law of the desert',

prescribed for an owner who killed a slave is consonant with the principle 'life for life' stipulated in Exod. 21.12 that scholars generally trace to the principle laid down in the source P, Gen. 9.5-6.[1] However, while I contend that Exod. 21.20 prescribes the death penalty, I propose nevertheless that the term נקם should not be identified with the legal principle 'just recompense', since this term refers to actions that rise above and beyond this legal principle. Moreover, this idea of vengeance should not be confused with the notion of blood vengeance, which clearly reflected the judicial activity of just recompense (i.e., מות יומת).[2] The question still remains, then, to what penalty does the expression נקם ינקם refer? To this question I now turn.

The execution of blood vengeance in Exodus 21.20. While I have argued that the penalty for killing a slave was most likely death, there remains the difficult problem of understanding how and by whom the penalty was administered, which also has some bearing on the problem concerning the identification of the עבד in Exod. 21.20-21, 26-27. That the expression נקם ינקם refers specifically to the institution of blood vengeance was first proposed by Merz[3] who has been followed more recently by David,[4] Liedke[5] and the majority of modern scholars.[6] The practice of blood vengeance by the blood avenger גאל הדם (cf. Num. 35.19, 25, 27) is also suggested in Exod. 21.12 (cf. v. 13 which refers obliquely to the cities of refuge), 21.30 and in 22.2 (Hebrew v. 1). As I already noted above, blood vengeance

---

although he suggests that that *lex talionis* was not a fundamental principle of early law (contra Driver and Miles, *Babylonian Laws*, I, p. 408).

1. Cf. Greenberg, 'The Biblical Conception of Asylum', pp. 128f.; *idem*, 'Some Postulates of Biblical Criminal Law', pp. 15-16; Wenham, *Leviticus*, p. 283; Paul, *Book of the Covenant*, p. 61; Driver, *Exodus*, p. 215.

2. Cf. also Westbrook, *Studies in Biblical and Cuneiform Law*, pp. 92-99, who arrives at similar conclusions.

3. E. Merz, *Die Blutrache bei den Israeliten* (Leipzig, 1916).

4. David, 'The Codex Hammurabi', p. 162.

5. Liedke, *Gestalt und Bezeichnung*, p. 48.

6. Cf. M. Greenberg, 'Avenger of Blood', *IDB*, I, p. 321; F. Horst, *Gottes Recht*, pp. 274-75; Noth, *Exodus*, p. 181; Cazelles, *Code de l'alliance*, p. 54; Boecker, *Law and the Administration of Justice*, p. 162; McKeating, 'Homicide in Ancient Israel', pp. 49ff.

was originally an institution of 'clan-law', which was practised outside the jurisdiction of the state and which sometimes resulted in an escalation of violence (cf. Gen. 4.23-24; 34; Judg. 19–21). In the OB period Hammurabi drafted several laws in order to regulate the practice of blood vengeance, although he was never altogether successful in abolishing blood vengeance carried out by kin groups.[1] Biblical scholars generally agree that at some stage in the early history of Israel the institution of blood vengeance was also regulated by the court and temple, which intervened in cases of homicide.[2] In addition,

---

1. Cf. Driver and Miles, *Babylonian Laws*, I, pp. 314-15; cf. also M.T. Roth, 'Homicide in the Neo-Assyrian Period', in *Language, Literature, and History: Philological and Historical Studies Presented to Erica Reiner* (ed. F. Rochberg-Halton; AOS, 67; New Haven: American Oriental Society, 1987), pp. 351-65, who notes that while the government authority takes an interest in cases of homicide, it nonetheless does not directly interfere with the proceedings (e.g., compensation or self-help and vengeance).

2. Cf. Liedke, *Gestalt und Bezeichnung*, p. 48; Boecker, *Law and the Administration of Justice*, p. 162; Greenberg, 'Biblical Conception of Asylum'; McKeating, 'Homicide in Ancient Israel', pp. 65-66; Childs, *Exodus*, p. 470; Patrick, *Old Testament Law*, pp. 72-74, all of whom date the court regulation of blood vengeance to an early period. Cf. also L. Stulman, 'Encroachment in Deuteronomy: An Analysis of the Social World of the D Code', *JBL* 109 (1990), pp. 624-26. Cp. Noth, *Exodus*, p. 181; and H.G. Reventlow, *Gebot und Predigt im Dekalog* (Gütersloh, 1962), pp. 72ff., both of whom suggest that blood vengeance began automatically after the crime, which suggests that blood vengeance was not demanded by law. However, see Bellefontaine, 'Customary Law and Chieftainship', p. 53, who notes that even under customary law, which includes self-help, blood vengeance operated under the approval or direction of the community. Lastly, see Phillips, *Ancient Israel's Criminal Law*, pp. 87-88, 102-104; *idem*, 'Another Look at Murder', pp. 112-113, who suggests that blood vengeance, which was carried out by a relative of the slain person, did not exist in Israel. He suggests that the formula מות יומת referred to the execution of a killer by an official of the court who is called the גאל הדם. However, in Exod. 21.20-21 Phillips suggests that the expression נקם ינקם refers to the private execution of blood vengeance, which was normally prohibited. He contends that the reason why blood vengeance is allowed in this case is that slaves did not exist during the time of the composition of the original legislation concerning murder. Cf. also Fensham, *Exodus*, pp. 154-55, who suggests that blood vengeance was not permitted in Israel. However, he also suggests that blood vengeance could not have been prescribed in Exod. 21.20, nor in the case of a Hebrew slave. He therefore suggests that the expression נקם ינקם refers to punishment that was administered by the authorities of the community.

Merz and others[1] have noted that blood vengeance in Israel was individualized according to the talion principle, under which compensation was allowed in the case of the goring ox (Exod. 21.30), although this case must be seen as an exception in the law of homicide (cf. Num. 35.32). Furthermore, Boecker[2] and Mendenhall[3] note that the talion principle also prevented the practice of blood vengeance from escalating into uncontrollable violence (cf. Gen. 4.23-24).

However, I have already argued above that the biblical understanding of vengeance was not necessarily consonant with the legal idea of vengeance or 'just recompense' that was administered by kin groups and state governments alike. Moreover, it is most likely that the practice of blood vengeance and *lex talionis* (Exod. 21.23-25),[4] which are often viewed as similar penalties, are not consonant with the way in which the term נקם is generally used in the Old Testament. As we saw above, the term נקם is not used in connection with the legal execution of blood vengeance except in Exod. 21.20-21, the interpretation of which is not entirely clear. Furthermore, the term נקם always envisages the death of the offender for the offence, as well as the death of people who are not directly associated with the offence. Therefore, while I am in general agreement with scholars who suggest that the expression נקם ינקם points to the institution of blood vengeance, I suggest nevertheless that this expression is not to be identified with the *normal* legal administration of justice as exemplified in the expression מות יומת, which clearly refers to the institution of blood vengeance in cases of homicide (cf. Exod. 21.12; Num. 35.16-18, 21), but rather that this expression is a veiled reference to divine vengeance as executed either by those who were endowed with God's authority (e.g., judges or priests) or by God himself. Furthermore, I suggest that this penalty is more applicable to the case of the death of a chattel-slave rather than that of a Hebrew debt-slave for the following reasons.

First, although there is no problem with associating the practice of

---

1. Cf. Cassuto, *Exodus*, pp. 275-78; Jackson, 'The Problem of Exodus 21: 22-25 (IUS TALIONIS)', pp. 101-102; Boecker, *Law and the Administration of Justice*, pp. 174-75.
2. Boecker, *Law and the Administration of Justice*, p. 174.
3. Mendenhall, 'Ancient Oriental and Biblical Law', pp. 18-19.
4. Cf. also Cazelles, *Code de l'alliance*, p. 54; G. Te. Stroete, *Exodus* (DBHOT, I/II; Roermond: J.J. Romen en Zonen, 1966), p. 170.

blood vengeance with the case in which a Hebrew debt-slave is killed, we saw that Liedke suggests that it is inconceivable that a chattel-slave would be extended the right of blood vengeance since the family would have to be active participants in the execution. However, if the death of a Hebrew debt-slave is envisaged in this case, why does the expression נקם ינקם occur rather than the more usual expression מות יומת? Furthermore, would not the death of an Israelite citizen, including a Hebrew debt-slave, be included under the general stipulation concerning homicide in Exod. 21.12-13? It seems likely that relatives of the debt-slave would be able either to execute blood vengeance or go to the court to demand that a judgement be given for the death of their kin (cp. LH §116).

Secondly, contrary to Liedke's view, there is nothing in the text to suggest that the court could not intervene in the case of a chattel-slave who has no one to act as blood avenger.[1] Mendenhall[2] notes correctly that there would probably be no one who would convene the court or make the necessary indictment of murder when a chattel-slave was killed by his or her owner. He suggests, nonetheless, that the expression נקם ינקם was used in order to demonstrate that the 'executive authority of Yahweh Himself is the basis for community action against the slave-owner'. Therefore, the responsibility for bringing this case to the attention of the court rested with the community (cf. Deut. 21.1-9).[3] Furthermore, Mendenhall suggests

---

1. Cf. Paul, *Book of the Covenant*, p. 70 and n. 2 who cites Greenberg, 'Crimes and Punishments', p. 738, who acknowledges that if the slave is a Hebrew debt-slave then blood vengeance would be executed, but if the slave is a chattel-slave then the owner would be executed by Israelite justice.

2. Mendenhall, *The Tenth Generation*, pp. 90-91; cf. also Saalschütz, *Das Mosaische Recht*, p. 540.

3. This view is also advocated by Fensham, 'Das nicht-haftbar-sein', p. 24; *idem*, 'Widow, Orphan and the Poor in Ancient Near Eastern Legal and Wisdom Literature', *JNES* 21 (1962), p. 135; cf. also Greenberg, 'More Reflections', p. 14; *idem, Biblical Prose Prayer: A Window to the Popular Religion of Ancient Israel* (Berkeley: University of California Press, 1983), p. 13, who suggests that the expression מות יומת is used for 'normal' execution while the expression נקם ינקם indicates an extraordinary procedure invoked on behalf of a foreign slave. However, Greenberg also suggests that this extraordinary procedure could extend to Israelite debt-slaves, since they might not have family in the neighborhood of their death. Nevertheless, such a possibility would exist in any case of murder involving Israelites (cf. Num. 35.25-27, which suggests that the 'blood-avenger' was often

that if the covenant community failed to take action against the owner who kills a slave then the guilt for the death of the slave fell upon them, which would then make them subject to the wrath of God (cf. Deut. 7.9-11).

Lastly, the death of a chattel-slave might easily go undetected, since if the beating was done in private the owner could cover up the crime. And since there would most likely be no family members present to question their kin's disappearance, there would be no one to report the crime to the proper authorities.[1] Therefore, the use of the unique expression נקם ינקם also suggests that God himself will execute vengeance against the owner if the crime goes undetected by the court or community.[2] That God acts on the behalf of the oppressed, who generally have little or no legal representation, is clearly enunciated in Exod. 22.22-24 (Hebrew vv. 21-23), which reads:

> 22 You shall not afflict any widow or orphan.
>
> 23 If you afflict him at all; if he does cry out to Me, I will surely hear his cry;
>
> 24 and My anger will be kindled, and I will kill you with the sword; and your wives shall become widows and your children fatherless.

Since the widow and orphan are susceptible to oppression,[3] God himself is understood to execute judgement with the sword against their oppressors.[4] The active participation of God in the administra-

---

required to follow or chase an assailant to a city of refuge).

1. Cf. J. Renger, 'Wrongdoing and its Sanctions. On "Criminal" and "Civil" Law in the Old Babylonian Period', *JESHO* 20 (1977), p. 73, who notes that during the OB period crimes were prosecuted only at the complaint of the injured party.

2. In Lev. 20.17-21 there are a group of sexual laws which prescribe penalties for crimes which would be committed in private. The idea behind the penalties in these laws is the same; that God will carry out the penalties even if the crime goes undetected by the community or court. I would like to thank Jacob Milgrom who proivded his insight into these laws during a graduate seminar I attended at Berkeley during spring semester, 1993.

3. Cf. D.E. Gowan, 'Wealth and Poverty in the Old Testament: The Case of the Widow, the Orphan, and the Sojourner', *Int* 41 (1987), pp. 349-53.

4. Cf. also Ibn Ezra, who has this to say about the change from plural to singular in Exod. 22.21 (English v. 22): 'The text first states: "You shall not afflict"—in the plural and then switches to "if *thou* afflict him". For whoever sees a person afflicting an orphan or widow and does not succour them, he is also accounted an afflictor. Now the punishment meted out when one is guilty of afflicting and no one intervenes applies to all; for this reason the text continues: My wrath shall burn and I will kill

tion and execution of justice is a common feature throughout the Covenant Code (cf. 21.6, 13; 22.11, 27 [Hebrew vv. 10, 26]), particularly in those laws that deal with people who often fail to receive proper legal representation. This feature also has its corollary within certain Sumerian hymns which speak about the protection of the oppressed, and in several of the prologues to the ancient Near Eastern law collections where the king also promises to protect the oppressed.[1]

Recapitulating, it is most likely that the expression נקם ינקם, which only occurs here in biblical law, was used in Exod. 21.20-21 in order to rouse the conscience of the judge or community to dispense strict recompense since the slave has no representation within the community.[2] If the community or the court failed to prosecute the

---

you—all of you.' This text is found in N. Leibowitz, *Studies in Shemot (Exodus): Part II Mishpatim—Pekudei (Exodus 21,1 to end)* (Jerusalem: The World Sionist Organization, 1981), p. 39.

1. Cf. Kramer, 'Aspects of Mesopotamian Society', pp. 5-6, who cites a Sumerian hymn concerning the city Nippur, which was the main seat of the worship of Enlil. In contrast to other Mesopotamian cities, such as Lagash, which frequently oppressed the poor and helpless, Nippur, under the direction of Enlil, abolished all forms of oppression and upheld divine judgment. Furthermore, such abuses were also condemned by certain kings, who wrote about the oppressed in the prefaces to legal collections (e.g. see the preface to the legal collections of Urnammu, Lipitishtar and Hammurabi). While Lagash was known for its oppression, the so-called 'reforms' of Urukagina did, in fact, address the plight of the widows and orphans; cf. Cooper, *Sumerian and Akkadian Royal Inscriptions*, I, pp. 70ff. Cf. also Fensham, 'Widow, Orphan, and the Poor', pp. 129-39; and J.D. Levenson, 'Poverty and the State in Biblical Thought', *Jud* 25 (1976), pp. 234-36; cf. also Cardellini, *Die biblischen 'Sklaven'—Gesetze*, p. 266, who traces the humanitarian aspect of the protection of slaves in Exod. 21.20-21 to the Sumerian literature.

2. Cf. P.D. Hanson, 'Conflict in Ancient Israel and Its Resolution', in *Understanding the Word: Essays in Honour of B.W. Anderson* (ed. J.T. Butler, E.W. Conrad and B.C. Ollenburger; JSOTSup, 37; Sheffield: JSOT Press, 1985), pp. 185-205, who notes that God acts as a divine protector of the oppressed and that as a result God provokes the community into similar actions; J.T. Willis, 'Old Testament Foundations of Social Justice', *ResQ* 18 (1975), pp. 69-70, who suggests that 'one cannot be "like God" in his attitude and action unless he devotes his life to advocating and promoting social justice and to doing all he can to oppose and stop social injustices'; cf. also Saalschütz, *Mosaische Recht*, p. 539, who writes, 'Jedenfalls hebt der nur dies einzige Mal im Mos. Strafrechte vorkommende Ausdruck, gewissermassen noch schärfer wie im vorhergehenden Gesetze, die

guilty party, then they became accountable for the crime. As Gordon[1] points out correctly, while the execution of justice was expressed in the literature of the ancient Near East as the moral duty of rulers, in Israel this duty was extended to the entire community. Moreover, it might be difficult to find out about the death of a chattel-slave, since an owner could easily hide the body or cover up the crime. Therefore, the expression נקם ינקם also suggests that God himself will execute vengeance against the owner if he is not discovered by the community.[2]

The Meaning of the Motivation Clause כי כספו הוא

While the motivation clause 'for he is his money' in v. 21b still presents difficult interpretative problems, the majority of scholars nevertheless interpret this explanatory motivation clause as an attempt by the legislator (original or later redactor) to make a legal distinction between intentional homicide (e.g., murder) and unintentional homicide (e.g., manslaughter or accidental homicide). According to this view, if the slave survives a day or two then the owner did not intend to kill this slave. Thus the owner is not punished, since the loss of property is considered to be adequate punishment.

However, as we saw above, this interpretation poses conceptual problems which have been recognized by scholars such as Childs, who does not discuss the view that the motivation clause distinguished between intentional and unintentional homicide. He suggests, rather, that the motivation clause substantiates his view that this slave law does not consider slaves as human but as property which owners can treat as they like, which is contrary to the view exhibited in the so-called talion law in Exod. 21.26-27. In addition, Boecker, who takes

Verpflichtung der Richter hervor, hier strenge Gerechtigkeit walten zu lassen (um so mehr da kein Goël für den fremden Sklaven auftrat).'

1. C.H. Gordon, 'The Ugaritic Texts: Half a Century of Research', in Amitai (ed.), *Biblical Archaeology Today*, p. 495.

2. Cf. McKeating, 'Homicide in the Old Testament', pp. 52-53; *idem*, 'Vengeance is Mine', p. 244, who suggests that God is the universal גאל who ensures that justice is administered when others fail to act; cf. also Greenberg, 'Crimes and Punishments', p. 741.

an opposite position to Childs in his view of Exod. 21.20-21, is uncomfortable with the use of the motivation clause, which seems to be in conflict with v. 20 and the stipulations in 21.26-27. He is concerned that the motivation clause gives the impression that the owner might illtreat a slave as long as the slave is not killed or murdered. That is, if an owner could beat a slave to the point of death and not be punished, then the owner could easily illtreat a slave in more subtle ways without threat of punishment. This view seems to be at odds with the regulation in 21.26-27, which demonstrates that a slave who received a permanent injury from an owner is set free. Boecker, nonetheless, concedes that the only possible explanation for the presence of the motivation clause is that it is a late addition that was meant to distinguish between intentional and unintentional homicide.[1] While both Childs and Boecker arrive at similar interpretations, they nevertheless raise some important questions regarding the interpretation of the Exod. 21.20-21. To these questions we now turn.

For example, if the motivation clause distinguishes between intentional and unintentional homicide, why are the regulations concerning accidental homicide not applied in this law (cf. 21.13)? If the owner was subject to the death penalty in the first case (v. 20), why is the owner not also subject to the same consequences placed upon a person who accidentally kills a person? It clearly states in Num. 35.22-25, which is already alluded to in Exod. 21.13, that in the case of accidental homicide the slayer is required to seek asylum in one of the cities of refuge (or altar in Exod. 21.14) when the blood avenger is in pursuit. In this case, the law still demands 'just recompense', which is apparently satisfied in the event of the death of the high priest (cf. Num. 35.28).[2] Although I have argued that there would be no one to execute blood vengeance on behalf of a chattel-slave, which might have some bearing on why asylum is not mentioned in Exod. 21.21, the court would probably still require the owner to seek asylum at

---

1. Cp. D. Daube, 'Direct and Indirect Causation in Biblical Law', *VT* 11 (1961), pp. 248-49, who adopts a slightly different interpretation of this motivation clause.

2. Cf. Wenham, *Numbers*, p. 238, who notes that both murder and manslaughter require atonement: murder by the execution of the murderer and manslaughter through the natural demise of the high priest.

some stage of the legal proceedings. Furthermore, in the light of the general opinion among scholars that the motivation clause is a later addition, it is unlikely that a later redactor would not be aware of the difficulty created by inserting a motivation clause into this law which does not do more to clarify the penalty.

Furthermore, there is reason to doubt that the death of a slave in v. 21 was an accident or that it was an act of manslaughter (e.g., an act of sudden rage). While there is no doubt that the death of the slave in v. 20 was due to the beating given by the owner, even though the rod was used to punish disobedient slaves and children, this right does not extend to inflicting bodily harm which may result in serious injury or death. For example, Num. 35.16-18 stipulates that if someone is killed with either an iron object, a stone in the hand or a wooden object in the hand, then the slayer is considered a murderer even though the intention may not have been to kill (cf. Exod. 21.18-19).[1] Therefore, an owner who disciplines a slave is clearly in danger of being convicted of murder if the slave is killed with a wooden rod. However, if an owner can be considered a murderer in v. 20 then it is unlikely that if the slave survives a day or two that death was due to an accident, since these circumstances logically follow and depend on the circumstances described in v. 20.[2] Furthermore, the laws of homicide in Numbers 35 do not make such a fine distinction—in both cases (v. 20 and v. 21) the owner would be guilty of committing murder. Therefore, it is unlikely that the case in Exod 21.20-21 is making a legal distinction between murder and accidental homicide.

Lastly, while some scholars[3] assume nevertheless that this law makes a distinction between murder and manslaughter, the discussions on homicide in Numbers 35 and Deuteronomy 19 appear not to make

---

1. Cf. Patrick, *Old Testament Law*, pp. 73,75, who suggests that v. 18 does not envisage a premeditated attack, but who nevertheless suggests that if the man had died then the assailant would have been prosecuted as a murderer.

2. Cf. also Westbrook, *Studies in Biblical and Cuneiform Law*, p. 99, who suggests that 'the rationale actually provided by the text [v. 21] appears to relate neither to intention nor to causation but to an irrelevant factor...'.

3. Cf. Gispen, *Exodus*, p. 212; Driver, *Exodus*, p. 218, who suggest that the owner intended to kill his slave in v. 20 (e.g., murder), but that in v. 21 he did not intend to kill him, but only to punish/correct him (e.g., manslaughter); cf. also Childs, *Exodus*, p. 471, who considers the slave law in vv. 20-21 and the general law on homicide in v. 12 as cases of manslaughter.

a modern legal distinction between *murder* (i.e., homicide committed intentionally) and *manslaughter* (i.e., homicide that is the result of recklessness or violent outburst).[1] According to the stipulations in Numbers 35, the only distinction that is made is a simple one between non-criminal homicide (e.g., accidental homicide; cf. Num. 35.22-23; cp. Deut. 19.4-5) and criminal homicide (i.e., manslaughter, murder and so on; cf. Num. 35.16-18, 20-21; cp. Deut. 19.11-13).[2] While the Anglo-American codes classify homicide as two or more separate crimes, the biblical laws sanction the death penalty for all forms of homicide, although in cases of non-criminal homicide the slayer is allowed to seek asylum in a city of refuge.[3] Therefore, it is unlikely

1. The term *homicide* is generally used for one human being being killed by another. The expression *criminal homicide* refers to homicide that is not regarded as justified or excusable. For example, homicide due to an accident is considered to be an excusable offense. However, while 'mercy killing' is considered excusable in some European countries it is considered a criminal homicide in Britain and the USA. The Anglo-American codes classify homicide into two or more separate crimes, which we will adopt in our own discussion:

> (1) *murder*, which is defined as homicide committed intentionally, although there are some interesting distinctions—felony murders in Britian are confined to only a few serious crimes—malice aforethought also includes acts of extreme recklessness—transferred intent refers to the case where one intends to kill a person but kills another by mistake;
> (2) *manslaughter*, which is homicide committed as the result of recklessness or violent emotional outburst—reckless homicide is penalized more seriously in European codes. Cf. 'Homicide', *Encyclopedia Britannica Micropaedia*, V (Chicago: Helen Hemingway Benton, 15th edn, 1982), p. 104.

2. Cp. Josh. 20.3, which has been rendered by the NASB as: 'that the manslayer who kills any person unintentionally (בשגגה), without premeditation (בבלי־דעת) and did not hate him beforehand', which suggests that accidental homicide included manslaughter. However, Deut. 19.4-5, from which Josh. 20.3 is probably dependent (note the similar use of בבלי־דעת), clearly makes a distinction between accidental homicide (v. 5) and any other type of criminal homicide. The expression בבלי־דעת in Deut. 19.4 is rendered 'unintentional'; i.e. accidental. Thus the expression בבלי־דעת in Josh 20.3 should also be rendered 'unintentional' (i.e. accidental), which makes the term בשגגה, which is in apposition to the expression בבלי־דעת, a synonym; cf. BDB, pp. 395, 993; Driver, *Deuteronomy*, p. 231; cf. also N. Kiuchi, *The Purification Offering in the Priestly Literature: Its Meaning and Function* (JSOTSup, 56; Sheffield: JSOT Press, 1987), pp. 25-31; cp. J. Milgrom, 'The Cultic שגגה and its Influence in Psalms and Job', in *Studies in Cultic Theology and Terminology* (SJLA, 36; Leiden: Brill, 1983), pp. 124-26 and n. 18.

3. Cf. Driver and Miles, *Babylonian Laws*, I, pp. 314-17.

that the motivation clause in Exod. 21.21b sought to differentiate between murder and manslaughter or between manslaughter and accidental homicide, since the penalty for all these crimes is the same.[1]

While the above discussion shows clearly that there are serious problems with the way in which the motivation clause in v. 21 has been interpreted, I suggest nevertheless that there is another way in which the motivation clause in v. 21 can be interpreted that avoids the aforementioned difficulties. Daube[2] has already noted that the slave law in Exod. 21.20-21 is closely associated with the law in 21.19-20, both of which deal with a similar problem—viz., where to draw the limit of imputing consequences in the case of assault. Furthermore, both laws are similar in content and in the relationship between the cases envisaged in the two laws. For example, the law in Exod. 21.18-19 deals with assault that does not lead to death, although it is understood that, in the event of death, the assailant would be put to death (cf. 21.12; cf. also Num. 35.17, which discusses assault with a stone).[3] The case in Exod. 21.20 deals with assault that leads to death, although the manner of the assault is similar to that in v. 18—viz., the owner strikes the slave with a rod (cf. Num. 35.18, which, incidentally, follows the discussion of assault with a stone). However, in v. 19 the assailant is required to take care of the injured person until he is completely healed,[4] compared with v. 21 which

1. Cp. B.S. Jackson, 'Legal Drafting in the Ancient Near East in the Light of Modern Theories of Cognitive Development', in *Mélanges à la Mémoire de Marcel-Henri Prévost: Droit biblique-Interprétation rabbinique Communautés et Société* (PULII; Paris: Presses Universitaires de France, 1982), pp. 65-66 and n. 104; and Paul, *Book of the Covenant*, p. 70, who suggests that v. 20 envisages the intentional or unintentional killing of a slave, but suggests that v. 21 refers to non-homicidal killing of a slave. However, according to modern legal terminology, to suggest that the death of the slave in v. 21 is non-homicidal is to say that no death occurred. The death in v. 21 is still homicidal. The question still remains, then, whether the death was due to a criminal or non-criminal act, which is also envisaged in v. 20 (e.g. intentional or unintentional).

2. Daube, 'Direct and Indirect Causation in Biblical Law', p. 248; cf. also Greenberg, 'More Reflections', p. 11.

3. Cf. Driver, *Exodus*, p. 217; Gispen, *Exodus*, p. 220; Patrick, *Old Testament Law*, p. 75.

4. Cf. LH §206; HL §10 and the discussion of these parallels in Paul, *Book of the Covenant*, p. 68; F.C. Fensham, 'Exodus XXI 18:19 in the Light of Hittite Law 10', *VT* 10 (1960), pp. 333-35.

apparently envisages the death of a slave.

Traditionally, scholars have understood Exod. 21.21 to refer to the death of the slave. Verse 21 reads:

אך אם־יום או יומים יעמד לא יקם כי כספו הוא:

> If, however, within a day or two he survives, he is not to be punished; for he is his property.

Nevertheless, this is not the only way in which this verse can be rendered. The more literal rendering for the verb יעמד is 'he stands'.[1] Verse 21 can therefore be rendered: [2]

> If, however, within a day or two he gets up [out of bed], he is not to be punished for he is his property.

This rendering is preferred over the traditional one for the following reasons. First, although the rendering 'survive' can be substantiated from the LXX reading εαν δε διαβωση 'and if he survives' (cf. New Testament βιοω 'to live'), the verb עמד is not rendered 'survive' elsewhere in the Old Testament.[3] If the legislator had wished to indicate that the slave only survived or recovered for a day or two then he could have used a different verb that conveyed the proper meaning clearly, such as חיה (cf. Num. 21.8, 9; Josh. 5.8; 2 Kgs 1.2; 8.8, 9; 20.7). Second, the idea that the slave only survived a day or two and then died is inferred from the context of v. 21 and not from the literal meaning of the expression אם־יום או יומים יעמד, which does not necessarily indicate that the slave died after a day or two.

Therefore, I suggest that the verb עמד indicates that the slave was able to stand or get up after a few days, which is the same legal requirement made in v. 19 of the previous case. Verse 19 reads:

אם־יקום והתהלך בחוץ על־משענתו ...

> If he gets up and walks around outside on his staff...

---

1. Cf. Ramban, *ad. loc.*

2. Cf. the New International Version of the Bible, which renders the Hebrew, 'but he is not to be punished if the slave gets up after a day or two, since the slave is his property.'

3. The only text in which the idea of 'survival' is expressed is Jer. 32.14, which reads: ונתתם בכלי־חרש למען יעמדו ימים רבים 'and put them [deeds] in an earthenware jar in order that they may stand a long time'. However, the use of the verb עמד in this text does not sufficiently demonstrate that the term should be rendered 'survive' in Exod. 21.21.

That v. 21 is not as specific about the recovery of the slave as v. 19 is about the free-man can be attributed to the tendency of the legislator or compiler not to repeat legal circumstances already referred to in a previous case (cf. Exod. 21.31, 32).[1] Moreover, the imprecise nature of v. 21 explains why the verb עמד is used instead of the verb קם, because there was no need to repeat that the slave must get up out of bed and walk about; it was only necessary to indicate that the slave had recovered enough to be able to stand or get up [out of bed] (which is synonymous to the verb קם[2] in v. 19). Furthermore, the phrase יום או יומים 'in a day or two' likely designates an imprecise amount of time, which also suggests that the stipulation in v. 21 applies if the slave eventually gets up [out of bed].[3]

Therefore, according to my interpretation, v. 21 envisages the recovery of the slave,[4] which is parallel to the situation already envisaged in 21.19. Moreover, v. 21 stipulates that if the slave gets up then no vengeance (i.e., retaliation or 'just recompense') is taken against the owner, which is parallel to v. 19 which also states that if the injured person is able to get up then the assailant is exempt from punishment (ונקה המכה 'he who struck him shall go unpunished'). While it is not entirely clear whether the two verbs נקה/נקם refer to

---

1. Cf. also B.S. Jackson, 'Unpublished Text of the Speaker's Lectures in Biblical Studies, University of Oxford, 1983–86', IX.3, who writes: 'we do find elsewhere [in the Mishpatim] a carrying over of some aspects of the situation described in the protasis of the first clause of a paragraph into the protasis of subsidiary clauses.'

2. The verb עמד is sometimes used instead of the verb קם to refer to someone or something rising from a lying or sitting position; cf. Josh. 3.13 ויעמדו נד אחד (parallel to v. 16 ויעמדו המים...קמו נד-אחד); Ezra 2.63 = Neh. 7.65; 8.5; Job 29.8 וישישים קמו עמדו (cf. also Gen. 43.15); Ps. 106.30; cf. also Dan. 8.22-23; 11.2-3, which refers to a king arising on the scene = קם.

3. Cf. Cardascia, *Les lois assyriennes*, p. 146; S.E. Loewenstamm, 'The Phrase "X (or) X plus one" in Biblical and Old Oriental Laws,' *Bibl* 53 (1972), p. 543; cp. R. Yaron, 'The Middle Assyrian Laws and the Bible: Review of G. Cardascia, *Les lois assyriennes*', *Bib* 51 (1970), p. 553; and B.S. Jackson, 'Two Or Three Witnesses', in *Essays in Jewish and Comparative Legal History* (SJLA, 10; Leiden: Brill, 1975), pp. 160-61, who envisages the possibility that the formula 'X or X plus one' may mean 'more than X', 'at least X', 'X or more' and so on, but who, nonetheless, prefers to interpret it to mean 'for a day or more', which coincides with his interpretation that v. 21 deals with the death of a slave.

4. This possibility appears also to be envisaged by G.H. Davies, *Exodus* (TBC; London: SCM Press, 1967), pp. 177-78; and Patrick, *Old Testament Law*, p. 76.

the death penalty or to some other, lighter penalty (note that both verbs only occur once in the book of Exodus), it is sufficient for my discussion to note that both verbs are used in a similar way, which further suggests that the cases are parallel.

Lastly, I suggest that, contrary to the consensus of scholarly opinion, the motivation clause in v. 21b does not differentiate between intentional and unintentional homicide, but rather, following the context of v. 19 which stipulates that the assailant is required to take care of the injured person, I suggest that the explanatory motivation clause is used to explain that, since the slave is the property of the owner, the responsibility for taking care of the slave naturally falls upon the owner 'for he is his money'.[1] This interpretation coincides with the view of slaves found elsewhere in the biblical laws and also avoids the contextual problems that arise from the other interpretations that have been proposed for this law.[2] That the slave law in Exod. 21.20-21 should closely follow the discussion of assault in vv. 18-19 is supported by the fact that in the discussion of assault in the Covenant Code the other slave laws closely follow the previous legal case.[3]

Therefore, the biblical law in Exod. 21.20-21 not only prohibits mistreatment against chattel-slaves, but this law also stresses that

1. Cf. Davies, *Exodus*, pp. 177-78, who suggests that the motivation clause explains that no further punishment is required since the owner has lost the use of his slave. While this interpretation is possible it does not follow the context of the previous law in vv. 18-19 upon which the law in vv. 20-21 is based.

2. Contra Jackson, 'Speaker's Lectures in Biblical Studies', IX.1-16, who suggests that the law in vv. 18-19 originally read: 'When men quarrel and one strikes the other with a stone or with his fist and the man does not die but keeps his bed, he shall only pay for the loss of his time, and he shall have him thoroughly healed. If the man rises again and walks abroad with his staff [and then dies], he that struck him shall be clear'. (IX.3). Jackson emends the law in vv. 18-19 in order to make it coincide with the discussion in vv. 20-21. I, however, do not see much merit in such attempts to emend the text in order to reconcile apparent inconsistencies, since this method often leads to a great amount of speculation concerning the structure of the *Urgesetze*.

3. For example, see vv. 26-27, which follow the discussion of assault that contains the talion formula (vv. 22-25), and v. 32, which follows the discussion concerning the death of a man or women who is gored by an ox; cf. Ibn Ezra, *ad. loc.*, who notes that laws concerning slaves occur at key points in each legal discussion.

wnership is a responsibility that requires owners to treat their slaves like fellow members of the covenant community. This view is consonant with the other laws in the Old Testament, which also guaranteed that slaves were able to share the rights and privileges extended to Israelites (cf. Gen. 17.12-13; Exod. 12.44; Lev. 25.6; Deut. 12.18; 16.11, 14).[1] Furthermore, we can now place the discussion of assault of slaves in Exod. 21.20-21, 26-27 within the larger context of the discussion of assault in Exod. 21.12-28. While the two laws in vv. 18-19 and vv. 20-21 deal with cases of assault where permanent injury does not occur, the laws in vv. 23-25 and vv. 26-27 discuss cases where some sort of permanent injury does occur (cf. also a similar juxtaposing of laws concerning assault in HL §§1-2, 7-8[2]).[3] Thus in the case where a slave loses an eye or a tooth, which might result from the same sort of 'beating' envisaged in v. 20, the injured slave is allowed to go free. This suggests that owners only have the right to keep slaves and take care of them until they are healed when no permanent injury results. Viewed together, these laws demonstrate the radical nature of the biblical slave laws concerning assault, which place chattel-slaves on a level with freemen.[4]

1. Cf. Mendelsohn, *Slavery in the Ancient Near East*, pp. 34-74; F. Steiner, 'Enslavement and the Early Hebrew Lineage System', *Man* 54 (1954), p. 74. This principle is enunciated clearly in Deut. 23.15-16 (Hebrew vv. 16-17), which stipulates that a runaway slave who seeks refuge in Israel is not to be returned to his master nor is he to be mistreated by any Israelite. This law is striking in that it goes against the parity and suzerainty treaties of the ancient Near East, which made provisions for the extradition of various fugitives from one country to another (cf. *ANET*, 200-201, 203-204); cf. P.C. Craigie, *The Book of Deuteronomy* (NICOT; Grand Rapids: Eerdmans, 1977), pp. 300-301; G. von Rad, *Studies in Deuteronomy* (SBT, 9; London: SCM Press, 1953), p. 147; *idem, Deuteronomy: A Commentary* (OTL; Philadelphia: Westminster Press, 1966), p. 264; cp. Weinfeld, *Deuteronomy*, p. 272 and n. 5.

2. In HL §§1-2, 3-4; 7-8, the law concerning the slaying of a free man in anger (§1) is followed by the same law concerning a chattel-slave (§2), and the law concerning the blinding or the knocking out of teeth of a free man (§7) is followed by the same law concerning a chattel-slave (§8).

3. Cf. Jackson, 'The Problem of Exodus 21.22-25', pp. 93-94, 106.

4. This view is consonant with the way in which the גר 'alien' is treated in the Covenant Code and elsewhere. See C. van Houten, *The Alien in Israelite Law* (JSOTSup, 107; Sheffield: JSOT Press, 1991), pp. 45-67.

Excursus: Cardellini's Analysis of the Slave Laws in the
Covenant Code

While the above discussion shows that the slave laws in Exod. 21.20-
21, 26-27, 32 refer to chattel-slaves, it is expedient nevertheless to
take a closer look at Cardellini's[1] extensive discussion of ancient Near
Eastern slavery, in which he suggests that these slave laws refer to
Hebrew debt-slaves, except for v. 32 which clearly refers to a chattel-
slave (*echte-Sklaven*). Furthermore, he suggests that these laws, which
are based upon the older cuneiform tradition that referred to chattel-
slaves, have been reworked in order to make them applicable to
Hebrew debt-slaves, although there still remains in the received text a
visible link between the older legal material, which shares similarities
with some ancient Near Eastern legal stipulations, and the new
reworking (*Bearbeitung*). Cardellini provides three main lines of
argument in favour of the view that these laws refer exclusively to
Hebrew debt-slaves. To these arguments we now turn.

First, Cardellini,[2] in his attempt to demonstrates the ways in which
these biblical laws afforded rights to slaves not present in the
cuneiform tradition, notes that in Exod. 21.20-21, 26-27 it is the
owner who is guilty of maltreating slaves, while in the cuneiform laws
the only laws that deal with the mistreatment of slaves concern cases
where a slave is assaulted by someone other than an owner (cf. LH
§§199, 201, 213, 219). Furthermore, he notes that the motivation
clause in v. 21 establishes a legal distinction between intentional and
unintentional homicide, something that would never have been
considered in the case of a chattel-slave in the cuneiform tradition.

However, these distinctions between the biblical and cuneiform laws
do not necessarily argue against the view that the biblical laws in
Exod. 21.20-21, 26-27 refer to chattel-slaves, for the following
reasons. First, Cardellini does not take into account the fact that, as a
whole, the biblical laws protect chattel-slaves from mistreatment

---

1. Cardellini, *Die biblischen 'Sklaven'–Gesetze*, pp. 265-68, 343-47; cf. also
Jackson, 'Speaker's Lectures in Biblical Studies', IX.13; *idem*, 'Biblical Laws of
Slavery: a Comparative Approach', pp. 86-101; and Westbrook, *Studies in Biblical
and Cuneiform Laws*, pp. 89-101, who also suggest that Exod. 21.20-21, 26-27
refer to debt-slaves.

2. Cardellini, *Die biblischen 'Sklaven'–Gesetze*, pp. 265-66.

cf. Exod. 20.10, 17 = Deut. 5.14, 21; Lev. 19.20-22; 25.6; Deut.
6.11, 14; 21.10-14; 25.15-16).[1] Secondly, the identification of the
slave in 21.21 as the 'money' or 'property' of the owner indicates a
relationship common between chattel-slaves and their owners[2] but not
between debt-slaves and their creditors. We already saw in Chapter 3
that in the cuneiform tradition debt-slaves were not to be regarded as
the property of their creditors, since the creditor has only purchased
the service or capacity for work (*Arbeitskraft*) of the debt-slaves.[3] In
fact, Cardellini[4] acknowledges that this reference in Exod. 21.21 is to
chattel-slaves, but suggests nevertheless that this reference is a
remnant of the older law which has been reworked. However, this
explanation is not very convincing, since it is unlikely that a later
redactor would retain such an archaic reference when elsewhere in the
Old Testament (cf. also Exod. 21.32) it clearly refers to chattel-slaves.
Moreover, it is unlikely that the motivation clause in v. 21, which
scholars generally consider to be a later addition, would contain such
a clear reference to chattel-slaves in a law concerning Hebrew debt-
slaves.[5]

Secondly, Cardellini[6] notes the similar use of vocabulary in the
manumission laws of Hebrew debt-slaves and the law in Exod. 21.26-
27 as illustrated below.

---

1. There is some question, though, whether all these laws refer exclusively to
chattel-slaves and not also to Hebrew debt-slaves.

2. Cf. Exod. 11.44 (איש מקנה-כסף) and Lev. 22.11 (יקנה נפש קנין כספו), which
refer to chattel-slaves as property bought with money. Cf. also Jackson, 'Biblical
Laws of Slavery: a Comparative Approach', p. 95, who considers the motivation
clause in v. 21 as an addition to the text, since it clearly envisages permanent
slavery.

3. This view is also advocated by Riesener, *Der Stamm* עבד, pp. 1, 130; cf. also
Rashi, *ad. loc.*

4. Cardellini, *Die biblischen 'Sklaven'–Gesetze*, pp. 265-66.

5. Cp. Jackson, 'Speaker's Lectures in Biblical Studies', IX.15-16, who
suggests that a later redactor inserted the motivation clause thinking that the law
referred to chattel-slaves rather than Hebrew debt-slaves. He also suggests that the
term עברי in v. 2 was inserted at a later stage.

6. Cardellini, *Die biblischen 'Sklaven'–Gesetze*, pp. 345-46.

Exod. 21.2b	Exod. 21.26b,27b	Deut. 15.12b	Jer. 34.9,10,11,14,16
יצא (Qal) = לחפשי	שלח (Piel) = = לחפשי	שלח (Piel) = = חפשי	שלח (Piel) [ם]חפשי

On the basis of the similarity in vocabulary and syntactical structure in these passages, Cardellini suggests that the formula ל)חפשי שלח refers specifically to the manumission of Hebrew debt-slaves. However, similar terms are commonly used to refer to release and freedom in the Old Testament; i.e., the noun חפשה in Lev. 19.20 refers to the release of a female chattel-slave (שפחה), and the verb שלחתה (שלח) 'you shall let her go' in Deut. 21.14 refers to the release of a foreign captive who is taken by an Israelite in battle in order to become his wife (cf. also the law of divorce in Deut. 21.1, 3, 4, where the verb שלח is used to describe the 'sending out' of the wife from the husband's house (ושלחה מביתו; Job 3.19; Isa. 58.6). Therefore, the so-called manumission formula + (ל)חפשי שלח could easily have been used to indicate the release of a chattel-slave, especially since the release of a chattel-slave is consonant with the view that these slaves were entitled to rights normally attributed to Israelite citizens.

Thirdly, Cardellini[2] compares the slave law in Exod. 21.20-21 with the ancient Near Eastern laws concerning the assault on a distraint (*nipûtum*) by a creditor in a *ḫubullûm* loan (i.e., LH §116; LE §§23/24). As we saw in Chapter 3, LH §116 stipulates that if a distraint (who is legally seized) dies in the house of a creditor who strikes or ill-treats the distraint, the creditor shall be convicted. If the distraint is the son of the debtor then the creditor's son is put to death (vicarious retribution), but if the distraint is a slave of the debtor then the creditor pays 1/3 maneh of silver. Similarly, the law in LE §§23/24 stipulates that if a distraint (who is illegally seized) is killed in the house of the creditor then the creditor is punished. If the distraint is a slave of the debtor the creditor replaces two slaves for

---

1. Cf. also Jackson, 'Biblical Laws of Slavery: a Comparative Approach', p. 96.
2. Cardellini, *Die biblischen 'Sklaven'–Gesetze*, pp. 260, 66, 68, 344; cf. also Boecker, *Law and the Administration of Justice*, p. 162, who compares LH §116 to Exod. 21.20-21; and Jackson, 'Speaker's Lectures in Biblical Studies', IX.13-15; Westbrook, *Studies in Biblical and Cuneiform Law*, pp. 89-100, esp. 90-92, 100, both of whom compare LH §115-116 and LE §23-24 to Exod. 21.20-21.

the one, but if the wife or son of the debtor is killed then the creditor is killed according to the principle of *lex talionis*.[1]

Cardellini suggests that the biblical law in Exod. 21.20-21 is based upon the legal tradition present in these two cuneiform laws, both of which sanction the death penalty when a distraint (free-man) is killed in the house of a creditor. However, this comparison is not convincing, for the following reasons. First, while the biblical law envisages a specific crime (i.e., assault with a rod), the two cuneiform laws envisage a variety of different types of assault that lead to the death of a distraint. While the biblical law probably envisaged the death of a slave who was being disciplined, it is doubtful that a creditor, who could distrain one or more of the debtor's dependents, would be allowed to illtreat or assault them, since they are not the creditor's property but belong to the debtor.[2] Secondly, while the law in LH §117 is similar to the law in Exod. 21.2-6, it nevertheless does not deal with the taking of distraints or with any case of assault but, rather, it deals only with the manumission of debt-slaves. Cardellini therefore does not demonstrate sufficiently why the law in Exod. 21.20-21 should deal with the taking of distraints while the previous law in 21.2-6, which he suggests is closely connected with the law in 21.20-21, deals only with the sale or surrender of debt-slaves. The law in Exod. 21.20-21 does not state clearly that the slave is a distraint, but rather it states that the slave is the 'money' of the owner. Therefore, the biblical law most likely envisages a slave who is the property of the owner not a distraint who is detained by a creditor in order to compel the debtor to pay a loan.[3]

Therefore, these two cuneiform laws have very little in common with the law in Exod. 21.20-21 except that they sanction the death penalty, although for completely different reasons.[4] Moreover,

1. Cf. Yaron, *Laws of Eshnunna*, pp. 173-75.

2. Cf. MAL A §44.

3. The same criticisms also apply to Westbrook, *Studies in Biblical and Cuneiform Law*, pp. 90-91, in his analysis of Exod. 21.20-21.

4. Cf. also Jackson, 'Speaker's Lectures in Biblical Studies', IX.15, who suggests that this biblical law refers to debt-slaves, and that the cuneiform tradition, particularly LH §116, where the creditor is not allowed to illtreat or beat his distraint, is more humane than the biblical tradition, since biblical law only punishes the 'owner' if he kills his distraint. Furthermore, Jackson suggests that even if the law in Exod. 21.20-21 refers only to chattel-slaves the law in LH §116 still affords debt-

although the comparative analysis of biblical and cuneiform laws can help to clarify the meaning of certain biblical laws, such as the debt-slave laws in Exod. 21.2-11 and so on, Cardellini's analysis of Exod. 21.20-21 and the two cuneiform laws in LH §116 and LE §§23/24 fails, since these laws deal with totally different legal cases.[1]

The Use of 'Slave' Terminology in the Pentateuch

As a result of my investigation of the slave laws in Exod. 21.20-21, 26-27, I have concluded that chattel-slaves were afforded certain legal rights normally afforded to Israelite citizens. Particular penalties were enacted in the laws concerning assault in the case of chattel-slaves because they were not able to participate in the normal procedures of talion—viz., they could not negotiate compensation in cases of injury or institute blood vengeance in the case of homicide. This innovative view of the treatment of slaves is consonant with the other laws that deal with chattel-slaves. This conclusion, however, makes it more difficult to discern whether many of the biblical slave laws deal with foreign chattel-slaves or Israelite debt-slaves, since these laws use common terms for slaves (e.g., עבד and so on). Nevertheless, despite the fact that the biblical slave laws use similar terminology, there is a particular way in which the biblical legislator(s) differentiated between chattel- and debt-slaves, which, as we saw above, is clearly

slaves with protection not afforded to Hebrew debt-slaves. However, these arguments are not convincing for the following reasons. First, it is better to understand the laws in Exod. 21.20-21, 26-27 as referring to chattel-slaves, since the opposite view creates too many exegetical and conceptual difficulties which can only be solved by positing a complicated history of redaction. Secondly, that LH §116 protected the debt-slave more rigorously than the biblical debt-slave laws is an argument from silence, since the biblical laws never deal with the treatment of distraints; they, in fact, are never referred to in any of the legal stipulations. Moreover, the biblical laws that deal with debt-slavery refer only to rights of manumission—the legislator(s) apparently saw no need to protect the distraint from abuse since the death penalty is already guaranteed in Exod. 21.12-14. Lastly, Jackson himself points out in a previous lecture that the ancient codes in general, and the Mishpatim in particular, tend not to be 'comprehensive' (VII.4).

1. Cf. R. Yaron, 'Jewish Law and Other Legal Systems of Antiquity', *JSS* 4 (1959), pp. 308-31, who warns against the tendency among scholars to conclude that a certain biblical law is dependent upon another cuneiform law; cf. also the comments of Driver and Miles, *Babylonian Laws*, I, p. 408.

evident in the debt-slave laws in LH and MAL, which did not employ terms that normally designated chattel-slaves in order that a distinction could be made between the two classes of slaves.

While Couroyer suggests that Exod. 21.20-21 applied equally to Israelite debt-slaves and foreign chattel-slaves, since the law attempts to make no distinction between these two types of slaves, the debt-slave law in Exod. 21.2-6 does use terminology that is different from that used in the other slave laws in the Covenant Code. In v. 2 we find the expression עבד עברי 'Hebrew slave', which clearly limits the application of this law to Hebrews. While it is not certain to what class of people the term עברי 'Hebrew' refers, it is sufficient enough for my present discussion to demonstrate that this designation qualifies the meaning of the term עברי.[1] This designation does not appear elsewhere in the Covenant Code, which suggests that the term עברי is used to differentiate the laws concerning Hebrew debt-slaves from other slave laws in the Covenant Code that do not use this term.[2] While it is possible that the term עבד, and similar slave terms, can refer to both Hebrew debt-slaves and foreign chattel-slaves, I have shown that the laws in 21.20-21, 26-27 refer only to chattel-slaves, since the law in vv. 20-21 gives reference to procedures and terminology that is reminiscent of chattel-slavery rather than debt-slavery, and both laws prescribe penalties that are different from those prescribed for Israelites. Furthermore, while it is also possible that the law in Exod. 20.10, 17 refers to both chattel- and debt-slaves, the fact that this law refers to coveting suggests that these slaves are the property of the owner. Lastly, it is also possible that the law of the sabbath refers to both chattel- and debt-slaves, although there is no reason to suppose that debt-slaves are referred to here.

Similarly, the designation עברי 'Hebrew' is found in the manumission law in Deut. 15.12-18 but not in the other slave laws in the book of Deuteronomy, which suggests that those laws that do not employ the term 'Hebrew' apply specifically to chattel-slaves.[3] It is

---

1. I discuss this term in greater detail in Chapter 6.

2. This view is also held by I. Rapaport, 'The Origins of Hebrew Law', *PEQ* 73 (1941), pp. 162-63; and Ramban, *Exod.*, 21.20. The term עברי, however, is not found in the law in Exod. 21.7-11. Nevertheless, it is clear that this law refers to a Hebrew debt-slave since it is closely connected with the law in vv. 2-6; cp. Ramban, *ad. loc.*

3. This supports the view that the slave law in Deut. 23.15-16 (Hebrew vv. 16-

clear that the law in Deut. 21.10-14 refers to a female captive. Furthermore, it is most likely that Deut. 5.21, which is parallel to Exod. 20.17, refers to chattel-slaves, since this law deals with coveting. However, it is possible that the various laws that allow slaves to participate in cultic festivals refer to both chattel- and debt-slaves (cf. Deut. 12.12, 18; 16.11, 14). However, it is likely that debt-slaves would join their own families in the observance of the major festivals. Furthermore, the purpose of these laws was to allow chattel-slaves to participate in the covenant (cf. Exod. 12.44, 48), a privilege which was naturally extended to all Israelites, including debt-slaves.[1] Lastly, the law in Deut. 23.15-16 (Hebrew vv. 16-17), which stipulates that any runaway slaves who seek refuge in Israel are not to be returned to their masters nor to be mistreated by any Israelite, possibly refers to both chattel- and debt-slaves. However, it is doubtful that a debt-slave who was being maltreated would have no other option than to flee. It is more likely that this law refers only to chattel-slaves who would have little recourse but to run away if they were being maltreated by their owners.

However, while the term 'Hebrew' is not employed in the manumission law in Lev. 25.35-44, 47-55, I will argue in Chapter 8 that this law is different from those found in Exodus and Deuteronomy. Nevertheless, except for the sabbath law in Lev. 25.6, the rest of the slave laws clearly refer to chattel-slaves (cf. Lev. 19.20-22; 25.44-45).

Summary and Conclusions

To sum up, I have examined the slave law in Exod. 21.20-21 in an attempt to determine whether the biblical laws differentiate between chattel- and debt-slaves. As the above examination has shown, the biblical writers most likely differentiated between chattel- and debt-slaves, although it is often difficult to see a marked difference between the legal treatment of these two classes of slaves, since chattel-slaves

17) referred to foreign chattel-slaves. Contra Weinfeld, *Deuteronomy*, p. 272 and n. 5.

1. Contra Phillips, *Ancient Israel's Criminal Law*, pp. 73-74, who suggested that a Hebrew debt-slave lost his status as a member of the covenant community, although he appears to retract his earlier view in 'The Laws of Slavery: Exod 21.2-11', p. 57; cf. also Baltzer, 'Naboth's Weinberg', pp. 73-78.

were afforded rights extended to members of the covenant community. While it is possible that some of the biblical slave laws refer to both chattel- and debt-slaves, the term עברי was most likely employed in order to differentiate between these two classes of slaves. The context of several of the slave laws clearly reflects the legal status of chattel-slaves rather than debt-slaves. Therefore, when the term עבד and similar terms are used on their own they refer specifically to chattel-slaves. However, when the term עבד is qualified by the designation עברי, as in Exod. 21.2 and Deut. 15.12, the resultant expression עבד עברי refers specifically to debt-slaves. Therefore, there is no sufficient evidence with which to suggest, as Cardellini does, that the debt-slave law in Exod. 21.2-6 should be categorized along with the other slave laws in Exod. 21.20-21, 26-27, which refer to chattel-slaves.

However, while it is a temptation to suggest that the biblical chattel-slave laws were more humane then their cuneiform counterparts,[1] it should be pointed out that the reforms undertaken by those authors or compilers of the laws concerning chattel-slaves in the Book of the Covenant and elsewhere in the Pentateuch are similar to the various reforms found in LH and elsewhere regarding the status and treatment of chattel-slaves. Nevertheless, the biblical laws are far more radical in their approach, since the purpose of many of these laws was to extend to chattel-slaves rights that were afforded to members of the covenant community. Therefore, while chattel-slaves were considered the property of Israelites, this principle of ownership did not permit owners to subject their slaves to mistreatment, but to extend to them every right due to a covenant member. Therefore, while it is inaccurate to suggest that the biblical slave laws are more humane than the cuneiform slave laws, it is nevertheless a fact that the various ancient Near Eastern laws concerning the assault of chattel-slaves generally considered a citizen's rights of ownership to override generally the concern for the safety or protection of chattel-slaves.

---

1. Cf. Cardellini, *Die biblischen 'Sklaven'–Gesetze*, p. 265; and Paul, *Book of the Covenant*, p. 69, who suggest that those biblical slave laws that stipulated penalties for the mistreatment of slaves by their owners are an important advance in the humane treatment of slaves compared with the slave laws found in the other ancient Near Eastern law collections which do not even deal with such cases.

Chapter 6

THE MANUMISSION LAWS OF EXODUS 21.2-6, 7-11

In Chapter 4 we saw that chattel-slaves were afforded rights normally afforded to Israelite citizens, since despite the difference in their class they both belonged to the covenant community. Therefore, it is often difficult to determine whether some of the biblical slave laws refer to chattel- and/or debt-slaves, although I argued that the term עברי was most likely employed by the legal compilers in order to distinguish between debt- and chattel-slaves. Nevertheless, while scholars are in general agreement that the two manumission laws in Exod. 21.2-6, 7-11 envisage the sale of people on account of insolvency, a general consensus has yet to be reached concerning the meaning of the law in vv. 2-6, which is the focal point the following discussion. This state of affairs is due primarily to the difficulty in determining the relationship of this biblical regulation to the parallel terms, laws, and customs of the ancient Near East. To this discussion we now turn.

The Setting, Form and Structure of Exodus 21.2-6, 7-11

Setting

The debt-slave laws in Exod. 21.2-6, 7-11 occur within the so-called Covenant Code, which is the oldest biblical legal collection.[1] Like the other legal collections of the ancient Near East (e.g. LH, LE, HL), the Covenant Code does not follow any modern legal conventions in arranging its regulations.[2] Several attempts have been made to

---

1. Cf. Boecker, *Law and the Administration of Justice*, pp. 135-44; Paul, *Book of the Covenant*, pp. 43-45; Patrick, *Old Testament Law*, pp. 63-66; cp. F. Crüsemann, 'Das Bundesbuch—Historischer Ort und Institutioneller Hintergrund', *Congress Volume, Jerusalem 1986* (ed. J.A. Emerton; VTSup, 40; Leiden: Brill, 1988), pp. 27-41.
2. For a discussion of the structure of the various ancient Near Eastern legal

discover the reasoning behind the order of the regulations in the first section of the Covenant Code (i.e. the casuistic laws in 21.2–22.15 [Hebrew 21.2–22.14]) and, in particular, the reasons for placing the debt-slave laws at the head of this collection.[1] For example, Cassuto[2] and Paul[3] have noted that the slave laws in vv. 2-11 are structurally parallel to the introduction to the Decalogue, in which the release of

collections, see H. Petschow, 'Zur Systematik und Gesetzestechnik im Codex Hammurabi', *ZA* 23 (1965), pp. 146-72; R. Haase, 'Zur Systematik der zweiten Tafel der hethitischen Gesetze', *RIDA* 8 (1960), pp. 51-54; E. Otto, *Rechtsgeschichte der Redaktionen im Kodex Eshnunna und in 'Bundesbuch'* (OBO, 85; Göttingen: Vandenhoeck & Ruprecht, 1989), pp. 9-14; S.A. Kaufman, 'The Structure of the Deuteronomic Law', *Maarav* 1.2 (1978–79), p. 115; G. Braulik, 'Die Abfolge der Gesetze in Deuteronomium 12-26 und der Dekalog', in *Das Deuteronomium: Entstehung, Gestalt und Botschaft [Deuteronomy, Origin Form and Message]* (ed. N. Lohfink; BETL, 68; Leuven: Leuven University Press, 1985), pp. 257-58. Both Petschow and Haase suggest that the ancient Near Eastern legal collections imposed three kinds of structures on previously existing independent materials: (1) the gathering into separate collections of cultic, moral and civil laws (cf. also B. Landsberger, 'Die babylonischen Termini für Gesetz und Recht', in *Symbolae ad iura orientis antiqui pertinentes Paulo Koschaker dedicatae* [SDOAP, 2; Leiden: Brill, 1939], pp. 219-34; Paul, *Book of the Covenant*, pp. 8-9, 37); (2) the framing of the impersonal legal corpus by a first person, nonjuridical, largely historical section (cf. also Paul, *Book of the Covenant*, pp. 11-42); (3) a traditional organization of content (e.g. Petschow for LH and Haase for HL). Similarly, Kaufman suggests that there are three interacting principles of arrangement in ancient Near Eastern legal collections: (1) laws, possibly of many different origins, are grouped together according to general topics; (2) within each topical unit the laws are arranged according to observable principles of priority; (3) the individual laws are arranged according to the ancient Near Eastern method of concatenation of ideas, key words and phrases, and similar motifs so as to form what for the ancient eye and ear were smooth transitions between subunits and, frequently, between the various topical units themselves (cf. also Paul, *Book of the Covenant*, p. 106).

1. Cf. L. Waterman, 'Pre-Israelite Laws in the Book of the Covenant', *AJSL* 38 (1921), pp. 36-54; Cazelles, *Code de l'alliance*, p. 156; C.M. Carmichael, 'A Singular Method of Codification of Law in the Mishpatim', *ZAW* 84 (1972), pp. 19-25; cf. also the historical survey in B.S. Childs, *Exodus*, pp. 459-60; cp. J.I. Durham, *Exodus* (WBC, 3; Waco, TX: Word Books, 1987), p. 315 who finds the many attempts to discover an underlying organization to the Covenant Code generally unconvincing.

2. Cassuto, *Exodus*, p. 266.

3. Paul, *Book of the Covenant*, pp. 106-107; cf. also Jackson, 'Some Literary Features of the Mishpatim', pp. 237-38; Boecker, *Law and the Administration of Justice*, p. 156.

Israel from Egypt occupies a special place (Exod. 20.2; cf. also 19.1, 4; 23.9, 15), especially since the verb יצא which is used in Exod. 21.2b to refer to the release of debt-slaves—'but on the seventh *he shall go out* (יצא) as a free man'—occurs in Exod. 20.2—'I am the Lord your God, *who brought you* (הוצאתיך) out of the land of Egypt, out of the house of slaves'.[1] As I will argue in Chapters 7 and 8, the release of Israel from Egypt also plays an important role in the manumission laws of Deut. 15.12-18 and Lev. 25.39-54, in which specific references to this release are found.[2] Similarly, Phillips[3] deals only with the final form of the Covenant Code, although he suggests that the debt-slave laws stand at the beginning of the Covenant Code because they pertain to Israelite debt-slaves while the other slave laws in this collection pertain to all types of slaves (i.e. foreign chattel-slaves and Israelite debt-slaves). While I concur with the view that the debt-slave laws were placed at the head of the Covenant Code in order to differentiate them from the other slave laws in the Covenant Code, I have argued nevertheless that the latter slave laws refer only to chattel-slaves.

However, other scholars have suggested that the final order of the laws within the casuistic section of the Covenant Code have undergone some rearrangement by the final compiler, although they too suggest that there were theological reasons for placing the debt-slave laws at the head of this legal collection. For example, van der Ploeg[4] suggests that the debt-slave laws in Exod. 21.2-11 were placed here because great importance was attached to the liberation of slaves. Furthermore, he suggests that the slave laws were added to the Covenant Code at a later stage, because v. 2 is formulated in the second person rather than in the third person,[5] and because these slave laws do not seem to belong with the unified section of laws in Exod. 21.12–22.15 (Hebrew

---

1. Cf. Gispen, *Exodus*, pp. 1-2, 206.

2. Cf. Weinfeld, 'Justice and Righteousness', p. 510, who notes that while the Holiness Code concludes with laws of release, the Covenant Code opens with the law of release.

3. Phillips, 'The Laws of Slavery: Exod 21.2-11', p. 61.

4. J.P.M. van der Ploeg, 'Studies in Hebrew Law. II. The Style of the Laws', *CBQ* 12 (1950), pp. 425-26; *idem*, 'Slavery in the Old Testament', p. 81.

5. Van der Ploeg follows both Alt, 'The Origin of Israelite Law', p. 93 and n. 28, who amends תקנה to ימכר in order to coincide with Deut 15.12 and Lev 25.39, and Jepsen, *Bundesbuch*, p. 56, who amends תקנה to יקנה'.

21.2–22.14). However, regarding van der Ploeg's former argument, both Paul[1] and Lemche[2] note correctly that the second-person formulation in v. 2 appears to be influenced by the second-person address in v. 1, which links the personal introduction to the Covenant Code to the impersonally formulated regulations. Furthermore, regarding van der Ploeg's latter argument, it is no longer expedient to determine the unity of legal collections based on the difference in form and origin of individual regulations, since mixed formulations occur in various ancient Near Eastern legal and non-legal collections.[3] Therefore, while the debt-slave laws may have been placed at the head of the Covenant Code in order to make a theological statement, it does not necessarily follow that this occurred at a later stage than the compilation of the rest of the Covenant Code (at least Exod. 21.12–22.15 [Hebrew 21.2–22.14]).[4]

1. Paul, *Book of the Covenant*, p. 46 and n. 7.

2. Lemche, 'The Hebrew Slave', p. 136.

3. For a discussion of the antiquity of the 'if-you' formulations in biblical law, see H.W. Gilmer, *The If-You Form in Israelite Law* (SBLDS, 15; Missoula, MT: Scholars Press, 1975), pp. 19-61, 126-53; Gevirtz, 'Problem of the Origins of Hebrew Law', p. 157; Yaron, *Laws of Eshnunna*, pp. 59-60; R.A.F. MacKenzie, 'The Formal Aspect of Ancient Near Eastern Law', in *The Seed of Wisdom* (ed. W.S. McCullough; Toronto: University of Toronto Press, 1964), pp. 31-44, esp. 39-42; Liedke, *Gestalt und Bezeichnung*, pp. 101-200, esp. 107, 126-35; V. Wagner, *Rechtssätze in gebundener Sprache und Rechtssatzreihen im israelitischen Recht* (BZAW, 127; Berlin: de Gruyter, 1972), pp. 51-69; cf. also Jackson, 'Legal Drafting in the Ancient Near East', pp. 56-57; Paul, *Book of the Covenant*, pp. 27-42, 112-24, esp. 115-16; Boecker, *Law and the Administration of Justice*, p. 156; Patrick, *Old Testament Law*, p. 66; Durham, *Exodus*, p. 316; M. Weinfeld, 'The Origin of Apodictic Law: An Overlooked Source', *VT* 23 (1973) p. 68 n. 4.

4. Cp. E. Otto, *Wandel der Rechtbegründungen in der Gesellschaftsgeschichte des antiken Israel: Eine Rechtsgeschichte des 'Bundesbuches' Ex xx, 22–xxiii, 13* (StudBib, 3; Leiden: Brill, 1988), who provides one of the latest redaction-critical analyses of the Covenant Code. In his structural analysis of the pre-deuteronomic form of the Covenant Code, Otto discerns two chiastic original structures: (1) 21.2–22.26 [Hebrew v. 25]; (2) 22.28 [Hebrew v. 27]–23.12 (pp. 5-11). Otto further suggests that the former section originally contained four separate collections (21.2-11; 21.12-17; 21.18-32; 21.33–22.14 [Hebrew v. 13]) which, in turn, exhibit a two-stage redaction from casuistic laws of restitution (21.33-36; 22.4-5, 9-14 [Hebrew vv. 3-4, 8-13]) to laws of sanctions (21.37-22.3, 6-8 [Hebrew vv. 2, 5-7]) that contain systematic laws sanctioned by the cult and are directed towards larger social units than the family (בֵּיתׇאָב?). Otto then suggests that a final redaction can be traced

Similarly, Kaufman[1] suggests that the debt-slave laws were placed at the head of the Covenant Code because the theologian-legislator wanted to make a statement about the worth of slaves as human beings. Although similar humanitarian statements occur in vv. 26-27, Kaufman suggests that this regulation, and those regulations in vv. 20-21, 32, are inconsistent with the view that slaves should be treated as persons and therefore that these verses belong to the earlier form of the Covenant Code. Furthermore, he suggests that the debt-slave laws originally belonged somewhere before the discussion of 'deposits' in Exod. 22.7-15 (Hebrew vv. 6-14), following the order of discussion in LH §117-127 in which the debt-slave laws are followed by a short discussion of deposits. Kaufman follows Wagner,[2] who attempts to demonstrate that the arrangement of laws in LH is echoed

to the Jerusalem priesthood, who added additional uncollected laws (20.24-26; 22.15-16 [Hebrew v. 15]; 22.17-19a [Hebrew vv. 16-18a]; 22.20-26 [Hebrew vv. 19-25]) to form the first original section 21.2–22.26 [Hebrew v. 25]. These stages of redaction are attributed to social changes during which family-based law was limited or qualified by the monarchic and cultic legal system. During this transition subsistence farming was replaced by a surplus economy and clan-based society (egalitarian) was replaced by social stratification (pp. 12-44). While it is beyond the scope of my present study to engage in a thorough critique of Otto's impressive work, I would nevertheless like to comment on two major points. First, while it is clear that the Covenant Code underwent some sort of redaction, it seems to me that to base this redaction on a rather simplistic view of what social changes occurred within Israel is misguided, since it ignores the ancient Near Eastern legal tradition, upon which the Covenant Code is based, which had already undergone an extensive transition from 'family'-based (e.g. self-help) to government- and cult-sanctioned laws. It is therefore natural that the compiler(s) of the Covenant Code would already be aware of such legal transitions, which, by the way, are never clear cut, since family-based law continued to influence legal proceedings, particularly in cases of homicide, throughout the history of the ancient Near East. I develop this view further below in this chapter. Secondly, Otto also assumes that there was a gradual shift from family/clan-law to government/cultic law, based on the change from a clan-based to a stratified social structure, a process that I have already shown to be evident in early Israel. Furthermore, it is not evident that the cultic laws in the Covenant Code should be attributed to the work of the so-called Jerusalem priesthood, particularly since these laws often exhibit very archaic legal elements.

1. Kaufman, 'The Structure of Deuteronomic Law', pp. 116-17.
2. V. Wagner, 'Zur Systematik in dem Codex Ex 21:2-22:16', *ZAW* 81 (1969), pp. 176-82; cf. Kaufman, 'The Structure of Deuteronomic Law', p. 116 and n. 50, who appears to follow Wagner's conclusions.

in the Covenant Code, although, as I will show below, Kaufman's conclusions are very different from those of Wagner. Nevertheless, Kaufman's argument concerning the positioning of these slave laws is not convincing, because it is most likely that the slave laws in Exod. 21.20-21, 26-27 refer to chattel-slaves who received rights similar to those afforded to Israelite citizens.

Lastly, Wagner,[1] who follows the important work of Petschow,[2] compares the topical structure of the first part of the Covenant Code (i.e. Exod. 21.2–22.16 [Hebrew 21.2–22.15]) to the topical structure of certain sections of LH.[3] In his analysis, Wagner organizes the regulations of the first part of the Covenant Code under three topical headings:

1. Slaves—§1–§2 (Exod. 21.2-11)[4]
2. Bodily injuries—§4–§8 (Exod. 21.18-32)
3. Liability in connection with agricultural and trade work—§9–§16 (Exod. 21.33-22.7; 22.9-14 [Hebrew 21.33–22.6; 22.8-13]).

Wagner notes that there appears to be no logical connection between the discussion of debt-slavery in vv. 2-11 and bodily injuries in vv. 18-32. However, he observes a similar connection between legal discussions in LH, where the discussion of the length of service of

---

1. Wagner, 'Zur Systematik', pp. 176-82; cf. also Paul, *Book of the Covenant*, p. 107 n. 1; Boecker, *Law and the Administration of Justice*, pp. 138-39; Childs, *Exodus*, p. 459; W.M. Clark, 'Law', in *Old Testament Form Criticism* (ed. J.H. Hayes; San Antonio, TX: Trinity University Press, 1974), pp. 116-17; Cardellini, *Die biblischen 'Sklaven'-Gesetze*, p. 242.

2. Petschow, 'Zur Systematik und Gesetzestechnik im Codex Hammurabi', pp. 146-72. Petschow suggests that LH follows a traditional organization of content: (a) slavery; (b) bodily injury; (c) commerce and wages; (d) family law. Cf. also *idem*, 'Zur "Systematik" in den Gesetzen von Eschnunna', in *Symbolae juridicae et historicae M. David dedicatae*, II (ed. J.A. Ankum, R. Feenstra and W.F. Leemans; IOA; Leiden: Brill, 1968), pp. 131-43; Boecker, *Law and the Administration of Justice*, pp. 138-39; Clark, 'Law', pp. 116-17; Cardellini, *Die biblischen 'Sklaven'-Gesetze*, p. 242.

3. A more recent work on the structure of LH, LE and the Covenant Code has been produced by Otto, *Rechtsgeschichte der Redaktionen im Kodex Eshnunna und in 'Bundesbuch'*. Unfortunately this work did not come to my notice until just before I submitted my present work for publication. I hope to comment on this work at some future date.

4. For a discussion of the position of the 'altar law' within the Covenant Code, see Childs, *Exodus*, pp. 464-67.

debt-slaves in §117 is followed by the discussion of 'deposits' in §§120-126, 'marriage and family' in §§127-194 and 'bodily injuries' in §§195-225. He suggests, therefore, that the compiler of the Covenant Code had access to a *Schultradition* which he developed only so far, choosing to eliminate the discussion of 'marriage' and 'family' from his own compilation. He also suggests that the discussion of 'family' and 'marriage' might have originally been discussed but in the process of redaction was removed when vv. 12-17 were inserted. That the compiler of the Covenant Code had access to a *Schultradition* is further demonstrated by the following observations.

First, several regulations that occur in the first part of the Covenant Code are similar to regulations that occur in LH §§117-225. For example, several scholars[1] note that LH §117 is similar to Exod. 21.2-6, since they both prescribe a periodic release of debt-slaves. The laws in LH §§196–201 regulate the *talionic* principle 'eye for eye, tooth for tooth' for the *awīlum*, *muškênum* and *(w)ardum*, which is also found in the *talionic* 'formula' in Exod. 21.23,[2] and in the regulations concerning slaves in vv. 26-27, although the biblical regulations[3] in vv. 26-27 concern owners striking their own slaves, compared to LH §199, which concerns one person striking another's slave.[4] The law in LH §206 concerns the striking of one person by another, who must then pay the surgeon for costs, which is similar to the law found in

1. For example, see Cardellini, *Die biblischen 'Sklaven'-Gesetze*, pp. 245-46; Riesener, *Der Stamm עבד*, pp. 128-29; Heinisch, *Exodus*, p. 164; Fensham, *Exodus*, p. 147; North, *Sociology of the Biblical Jubilee*, pp. 59-60; I. Mendelsohn, 'The Conditional Sale into Slavery of Free-Born Daughters in Nuzi and the Law of Ex. 21:7-11', *JAOS* 55 (1935), p. 194; *idem*, *Slavery in the Ancient Near East*, pp. 85-86; *idem*, 'Slavery in the Old Testament', p. 388; Cazelles, *Code de l'alliance*, p. 150; Boecker, *Law and the Administration of Justice*, pp. 158-59; Lemche, 'The Hebrew Slave', p. 136; van der Ploeg, 'Slavery in the Old Testament', p. 81; Stroete, *Exodus*, p. 167; Hyatt, *Exodus*, p. 228; Driver, *Exodus*, pp. 210, 421; A. Phillips, 'The Laws of Slavery: Exod 21:2-11', p. 65 n. 23; Horst, *Gottes Recht*, p. 94; P. Heinisch, 'Das Sklavenrecht in Israel und Alten Orient', *SCath* 11 (1934–35), pp. 284-85.

2. Cf. Lambert, 'Interchange of Ideas', pp. 311-13.

3. Cf. Paul, *Book of the Covenant*, p. 78 and n. 4.

4. Cf. J.P. van der Westhuizen, 'A comparative study of the related laws in Babylonian and Biblical legal texts (verbal connotations)', *Semitics* 10 (1989), p. 53, who notes a verbal similarity between Exod. 21.26-27, LH §199, LE §42.

Exod. 21.18-19 (cf. also HL §10).[1] The laws in LH §§209-214 concern the striking of a pregnant woman, which is found in Exod. 21.22-23 (cf. also HL §§17-18; MAL A §§21, 50-52).[2] Lastly, the case of the 'goring ox' occurs in LH §§250-252 (cf. also LE §§54-55) and in Exod. 21.28-32, although the former is found in the section concerning 'agricultural work', 'deposits' and 'hire' in LH §§228-277.[3] However, while there is some correspondence between the organization of these two legal discussions, the fact that some material that is found in LH has been left out of the Covenant Code (i.e. 'deposits', and 'marriage' and 'family') deserves further explanation. While the Covenant Code does not treat in detail regulations concerning 'marriage' and 'family', the debt-slave regulations in Exod. 21.2-11 do include considerations of such issues, something that is absent in LH §117. However, it is difficult to demonstrate, as Wagner suggests, that regulations concerning 'marriage' and 'family' originally appeared where Exod. 21.12-17 now stands, especially when some of the regulations in vv. 12-17, which form an integral part of the discussion of 'bodily injuries',[4] are similar to those found in LH §§225 (cf. LH §195 and Exod 21.15; LH §§206-208 and Exod. 21.12-13[5]). Furthermore, although there is no treatment of 'deposits' between the discussions in Exod. 21.2-11 and vv. 18ff., as in LH §§120-126, the Covenant Code does nevertheless treat 'deposit' and 'hire' in 22.5-15 (Hebrew vv. 4-14), which is also treated more extensively in LH §§228-277. While Kaufman's suggestion that Exod. 21.2-11 originally belonged next to the discussion of deposits is possible, Wagner's view, that these laws originally belonged at the head of the Covenant Code, is more convincing since his discussion of the order of the regulations in the Book of the Covenant is much more extensive and covers far more topical boundaries.

Secondly, in the Covenant Code there are two stipulations, parallels to which occur only in LH. First, as we saw above, LH §117 is similar to Exod. 21.2-6 in that it prescribes the release of debt-slaves after a fixed period of time. Moreover, the periodic release of debt-slaves

---

1. Cf. Paul, *Book of the Covenant*, pp. 68-69.
2. Cf. Paul, *Book of the Covenant*, pp. 70-73.
3. Cf. Boecker, *Law and the Administration of Justice*, pp. 163-64.
4. Cf. Paul, *Book of the Covenant*, pp. 61-67; D. Patrick, *Old Testament Law*, pp. 72-75.
5. Cf. Paul, *Book of the Covenant*, pp. 62-64.

that is prescribed in LH §117 and Exod. 21.2-6 is not found elsewhere in ancient Near Eastern legal collections.[1] I have already argued in Chapter 3 that LH §117 was most likely the by-product of the royal *mēšarum* edicts of Hammurabi during the OB period. Furthermore, I will argue below that a similar tradition most likely existed in Israel which was responsible for the various manumission regulations in the Old Testament (i.e. Exod. 21.2-6; Deut. 15.12-18; Lev. 25.39-55). Secondly, Lambert[2] has noted that the principle of *talion* in LH §§196-201, 218, 229-230 was an innovation of Hammurabi that was not tied to the earlier Sumerian and Akkadian legal traditions, which prescribed monetary fines for bodily injury. Outside Mesopotamia only Israelite law offers 'life for life, eye for eye, tooth for tooth, hand for hand, foot for foot' (Exod. 21.23-25). Lambert notes that the appearance of the pair 'eye-tooth', which is found elsewhere only in LH §§196-201, suggests an oral diction of great antiquity, probably an Amorite legal tradition from which both Hammurabi and the Israelite legal compilers drew.[3] Therefore, it is very unlikely that two unique regulations would occur in two different legal collections, both of which exhibit similar topical organization, without there being a common legal source or tradition behind these regulations. Nevertheless, whether the compiler of the Book of the Covenant had access only to an Amorite legal tradition that is evident in LH, or to a copy of LH itself, remains a moot point.[4]

1. Cf. LI §14, which appears to provide for the release of a debtor once he has given services equivalent to twice the amount of his debt. Similar types of manumission appear to be attested in texts from Alalakh and Ugarit that are cited in J.J. Rabinowitz, 'Manumission of Slaves in Roman Law and Oriental Law', *JNES* 20 (1960), pp. 42-45; and B. Maarsingh, *Onderzoek naar de ethiek van de wetten in Deuteronomium* (J.M. van Amstel, 1961), pp. 100-101. The text from Alalakh reads: 'as from this day forth, Niqmepa, the king, son of Idrimi, has released Qabi to (be a) mariannu. As the sons of mariannu-men of the citystate of Alalakh (are), so also are Qabia and his grandsons in perpetuity'. In this text the term 'mariannu' appears to refer to a free man.

2. Lambert, 'Interchange of Ideas', pp. 311-13; cf. also Yaron, *Laws of Eshnunna*, p. 93.

3. Cp. David, 'Codex Hammurabi', pp. 176-77.

4. Cf. Lambert, 'Interchange of Ideas', p. 312, who suggests that the Israelite compiler did not have access to LH since no fragments of these laws have yet been found in the West. However, according to Numbers 21 and Judg. 11.12-28, early Israel did have contact with Amorites who controlled the territory from the valley of

Recapitulating, that the compiler of the Covenant Code drew upon common ancient Near Eastern legal traditions is accepted by most scholars.[1] Therefore, Wagner's suggestion that the compiler of the Covenant Code drew upon a common *Schultradition* similar to that found in LH §117-119 is likely, since both Exod. 21.2-32 and LH §§117-225 contain similar laws and exhibit similar structures.[2] Moreover, the fact that two regulations in the Covenant Code are found elsewhere only in LH within the same sections noted by Wagner suggests that it is most likely that both compilers drew upon similar traditions, particularly regarding the manumission law in LH §117. I will discuss the similarities that exist between Exod. 21.2-6 and LH §117 in a later discussion. Furthermore, the placement of the debt-slave laws in Exod. 21.2-11 at the beginning of the Covenant Code, along with the placement of the slave laws in the ensuing discussions

Arnon to Mount Sion (Hermon; cf. Deut. 4.46-48 and the discussion in Boling, *The Early Biblical Community in Transjordan*, pp. 41-52). These Amorites may have had access to a copy of LH. Furthermore, a number of scholars suggest that such a cuneiform legal tradition existed in Canaan during Israel's Settlement period although no extant legal collections have been discovered; cf. Paul, *Book of the Covenant*, pp. 104-105 and n. 1, 116-18; Hyatt, *Exodus*, pp. 220-24; Durham, *Exodus*, p. 317. Further, Cazelles, *Code de l'alliance*, pp. 168-83, suggests that the draftsman of the Covenant Code (i.e. Moses) came in contact with various legal traditions while in Egypt. Lastly, based upon the close relationship between cuneiform material and the patriarchal narratives, many scholars have suggested that the legal traditions in the Covenant Code might have been part of the cultural heritage from the patriarchal sojourn in Haran and Palestine before the Settlement period; cf. Paul, *Book of the Covenant*, p. 104; Durham, *Exodus*, p. 317; R. Kilian, *Literarische und formgeschichtliche Untersuchung des Heiligkeitsgesetzes* (BBB, 19; Bonn: Peter Hanstein, 1963), pp. 2-3; J.J. Stamm and M.E. Andrew, *The Ten Commandments in Recent Research* (SBTSS, 2; London: SCM Press, 1967), p. 36; Bright, *A History of Israel*, p. 89; cf. also R. Westbrook, '1 Samuel 1:8', *JBL* 109 (1990), pp. 14-15, who notes that the use of the figure 10 in 1 Sam. 1.8 probably stems from its use in OB adoptions texts from Sippar and Mari.

1. Cf. Boecker, *Law and the Administration of Justice*, pp. 163-64; van der Westhuizen, 'A comparative study of the related laws in Babylonian and Biblical legal texts', pp. 56-57; cf. also J. Barr, 'Biblical Law and the Question of Natural Theology', in *The Law in the Bible and in its Environment* (ed. T. Veijola; Publications of the Finnish Exegetical Society, 51; Göttingen: Vandenhoeck & Ruprecht, 1990), pp. 10-11.

2. That the biblical compiler was aware of LH §117 is also supported by Deut. 15.18, which mentions that the service of a debt-slave was worth twice that of a hired hand (i.e. three years).

of assault, has resulted in a chiastic structure that is illustrated below.[1]

A			Exod. 21.2-11	Release of male and female debt-slaves
	B		Exod. 21.12-17	Capital provisions
		Ca	Exod. 21.18-19	Assault on a pregnant woman
		Cb	Exod. 21.20-21	Assault on one's own chattel-slave
		Ca'	Exod. 21.22-23	Assault on a pregnant woman
	B'		Exod. 21.24-25	Talionic provisions
A'			Exod. 21.26-27	Release of male and female chattel-slaves

The above chiastic structure illustrates clearly the significant position the slave laws hold within every major legal discussion in Exodus 21. Furthermore, both the discussion of the release of debt-slaves (vv. 2-11) and of chattel-slaves (vv. 26-27) provide a clear connection to the historical remembrance of Israel's escape from Egypt found in the introduction to the Covenant Code (Exod. 20.2) and subsequent legal discussions (cf. Exod. 22.21 [Hebrew v. 20]; 23.9, 15). This historical motivation is an integral part of Yahweh's covenant with Israel.[2]

Form

The debt-slave law in Exod. 21.2-6 is conditionally formulated ('when/if' form: casuistic), containing a main case (כי in v. 2) followed by four subordinate or secondary cases (אם in vv. 3a, 3b, 4, and ואם in v. 5).[3] The main conditional כי clause, which contains a

---

1. A slightly different structure has also been observed by Jackson, 'Some Literary Features of the Mishpatim', pp. 240-41, although he suggests that the laws in 21.20-21.26-27 refer to Israelite debt-slaves; cf. also *idem*, 'Biblical Laws of Slavery: a Comparative Approach', pp. 95-97; cp. Otto, *Rechtgeschichte der Redaktionen im Kodex Eshnunna und in 'Bundesbuch'*, p. 7; *idem*, *Wandel der Rechtbegründungen in der Gesellschaftsgeschichte des antiken Israel:*, p. 27.

2. Cf. B.S. Jackson, 'The Ceremonial and the Judicial: Biblical Law as Sign and Symbol', *JSOT* 30 (1984), p. 43, who writes: 'Why for example, do we find slave laws at the beginning of the mishpatim, when on several occasions the mishpatim returns to the theme of the slave? Is the arrangement here designed to reinforce the message that this is a covenant being offered to a group of people only recently released from slavery in Egypt?'; cf. also R. Rendtorff, ' "Covenant" as a Structuring Concept in Genesis and Exodus', *JBL* 108 (1989), pp. 388-90, 393.

3. I have adopted the descriptive terminology proposed by R. Sonsino, *Motive Clauses in Hebrew Law: Biblical Forms and Near Eastern Parallels* (SBLDS, 45; Chico, CA: Scholars Press, 1980), in which he discerns two basic groups of legal formulations: I. *Laws in the Conditional Form*, which include A. 'when/if' form

second-person verb in the protasis and a third-person verb in the apodosis, is mixed in form.[1] The relationship of the secondary cases to the main case is illustrated below.[2]

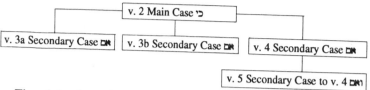

The debt-slave law in Exod. 21.7-11 is also conditionally formulated, containing a main case (וכי in v. 7) followed by four subordinate or secondary cases (אם in vv. 8, 10 and ואם in vv. 9, 11). The relationship of the secondary cases to the main case is illustrated below.[3]

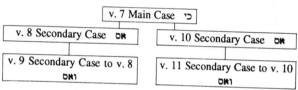

The formulation of these manumission laws, apart from the mixed form in v. 2, is very similar to the majority of the conditional (casuistic) laws found in Exod. 21-22. Furthermore, Patrick[4] has noted that conditional (casuistic) formulations can be divided into two

(1) third person (parallel to Alt's casuistic law) (2) second person (3) mixed forms B. relative form (1) third person (2) mixed forms C. participial forms II. *Laws in the Unconditional Form* (parallel to Alt's apodictic law) A. direct address (1) positive commands (a) perceptive imperfect (second person) (b) imperative (c) infinitive absolute (2) negative commands B) third-person jussive (1) positive commands (2) negative commands.

1. A similar construction also occurs in Deut. 22.23-24; 25.11-12 where the protasis is formulated in the third person and the apodosis is formulated in the second person; cf. Sonsino, *Motive Clauses*, p. 21; Liedke, *Gestalt und Bezeichnung*, pp. 34-39.

2. Cf. Liedke, *Gestalt und Bezeichnung*, p. 33; and the *Mekilta, ad. loc.*; contra Cassuto, *Exodus*, p. 267, who suggests that v. 5 is subordinate to both vv. 3 and 4.

3. Cf. Liedke, *Gestalt und Bezeichnung*, p. 32.

4. Patrick, *Old Testament Law*, pp. 23-24, 69-70; *idem*, 'Casuistic Law Governing Primary Rights and Duties', *JBL* 92 (1973), pp. 180-84; cf. also Boecker, *Law and the Administration of Justice*, p. 152.

categories based upon their content. The first category is called *primary law*, according to which the protasis describes a legal relationship while the apodosis prescribes the terms of the relationship. The second category is called *remedial law*, according to which the protasis describes the case while the apodosis sets out the legal remedy (compensation and/or punishment). In the Covenant Code the majority of conditional laws belong to the second category (cf. Exod. 21.18-19, 20-21, 22-25, 26-27, etc.). However, the two manumission laws in Exod. 21.2-11 belong to the first category, since the legal relationship of the two debt-slaves is set forth in the protases while the terms of the relationship are discussed in the apodoses.[1] For example, regarding the first law, v. 2 sets the length of service; vv. 3-4 describe the rights of the slave and master at the conclusion of the legal relation; vv. 5-6 describe the conditions and procedures necessary to nullify the slave's right to freedom; and v. 7 describes the new relation that exists between slave and master as a result of the ceremony described in vv. 5-6. Regarding the second law, v. 7 describes the length of service; vv. 8-10 set forth the duties of the one who has purchased the אמה; and v. 11 states the conditions under which an אמה should be set free.

Structure

As the above discussion shows, the debt-slave laws in Exod. 21.2-6, 7-11 are formulated similarly and they contain similar stipulations.[2] Furthermore, Zakovitch[3] has revealed an unusual structure in these two laws based upon the literary pattern 'three-four' (three plus one) which is found in the narrative and legal portions of the Old Testament and other ancient Near Eastern writings. The structure for Exod. 21.2-6, 7-11 is illustrated below.

---

1. Cf. Patrick, *Old Testament Law*, pp. 69-70; Boecker, *Law and the Administration of Justice*, p. 152. That these laws are different in tone from the other casuistic regulations in the Covenant Code has been noted by Cazelles, *Code de l'alliance*, p. 117; Liedke, *Gestalt und Bezeichnung*, pp. 51-52.

2. Cf. also Wagner, 'Zur Systematik', p. 177.

3. Y. Zakovitch, *'For Three . . . and for Four': The Pattern for the Numerical Sequence Three-Four in the Bible* Hebrew (Jerusalem: Makor, 1979), pp. xxv-xxvi, 450-53; cp. A. Schenker, 'Affranchissement d'une esclave selon Ex 21,7-11', *Bib* 69 (1988), pp. 547-56.

וכי־ימכר איש את־בתו לאמה ⁷
לא תצא כצאת העבדים

אם־רעה בעיני אדניה אשר־לו יעדה ⁸   I
והפדה לעם נכרי לא־ימשל למכרה
בבגדו־בה

ואם־לבנו ייעדנה ⁹   II
כמשפט הבנות יעשה־לה

אם־אחרת יקח־לו ¹⁰   III
שארה כסותה ועׄנתה לא יגרע

ואם־שלש־אלה לא יעשה לה ¹¹   IV
ויצאה חנם אין כסף

² כי תקנה עבד עברי שש שנים יעבד
ובשבעית יצא לחפשי חנם

³ אם־בגפו יבא   I
בגפו יצא

אם־בעל אשה הוא   II
ויצאה אשתו עמו

⁴ אם־אדניו יתן־לו אשה וילדה   III
לו בנים או בנות
האשה וילדיה תהיה לאדניה
והוא יצא בגפו

⁵ ואם־אמר יאמר העבד אהבתי   IV
את־אדני את־אשתי ואת־בני
לא אצא חפשי

⁶ והגיׄשו אדניו אל־האלהים
והגישו אל־הדלת או אל־המזוזה
ורצע אדניו את־אזנו במרצע
ועבדו לעלם

In his analysis Zakovitch notes that both laws start with a general principle (v. 2, 7), followed by four sub-sections (vv. 3-6, 8-11). In each law the fourth sub-section (IV) deals with an exceptional occurrence that does not fit in with the general principle—viz., the male slave chooses to remain with his master rather than going free in the seventh year, and the female slave goes out without payment when her lord does not fulfil his contractual obligations to her (i.e. Exod. 21.8-10). Moreover, the fourth section (IV) of each law forms a chiastic structure with the two general principles in vv. 2, 7:

⁷
IV ¹¹   לא תצא כצאת העבדים   ובשבעית יצא לחפשי חנם ²
ויצאה חנם   לא אצא ⁵ IV

The male slave goes out free without payment in v. 2, as does the female slave in section IV; the female slave does not go out free in v. 7, nor does the male slave, who chooses to stay with his master in section IV.

The above analysis demonstrates that the two debt-slave laws in Exod. 21.2-6, 7-11 were juxtaposed in such a fashion that resulted in the creation of an intricate literary structure. It is most likely, therefore, that such an elaborate literary structure was mainly the work of a single compiler.

Exegesis of Exodus 21.2-6

Exodus 21.2: The Identity of the עבד עברי

‫² כי תקנה עבד עברי שש שנים יעבד ובשבעת יצא לחפשי חנם:‬

2 If you acquire a Hebrew slave, he shall serve for six years; but on the
seventh he shall go out as a free man without payment.

Scholars are in general agreement that this slave law envisaged the
sale of people on account of insolvency,[1] although the exact identity of
the עבד עברי remains in dispute because scholars have not been able to
agree on the relationship between the biblical עברי(ם) 'Hebrew(s)',
who are mentioned in several biblical historical and legal texts, and
the *ḫabiru* who are mentioned in several cuneiform documents from
Mesopotamia to Egypt via Asia Minor, Syria and Palestine in the
period between 2000 and 1200 BCE. Nevertheless, there are a number
of scholars who argue that the term עברי in Exod. 21.2 refers to a
ḫabiru-type slave who was forced to enter into indentured servitude.
However, as I will attempt to show below, scholars who make this
comparison have not only misunderstood the identity of the *ḫabiru*,
but have also wrongly compared the biblical law in Exod. 21.2-6 with
the *ḫabiru* service contracts.

The ḫabiru. References to the *ḫabiru* were first found in the Amarna
letters (EA) discovered in 1888[2]. In EA the *ḫabiru* (often written with

---

1. Cf. Greenberg, 'More Reflections on Biblical Criminal Law', p. 5; and
Westbrook, *Studies in Biblical and Cuneiform Law*, pp. 125-26, both of whom
suggest that this law also envisaged the case in which a thief is sold for insolvency
(cf. Exod. 22.3). I discuss this interpretation below under the section *Exod 21.2-4
and the manumission law in LH §117.*

2. For a review of the history of research concerning the *ḫabiru* problem and
bibliography, see H.H. Rowley, *From Joseph to Joshua: Biblical Traditions in the
Light of Archaeology* (SLBA, 1948; London: The British Academy, 1950), pp. 3-
56, esp. 3-8, 39-56; Bottéro, *Le problème des Ḫabiru*, pp. v-xxii; *idem*, 'Les
habiru, les nomades et les sédentaires', in *Seminar: Nomads and Sedentary People*
(ed. J.S. Castillo; Mexico City, 1981), pp. 14-27; Greenberg, *The Ḫab/piru*, pp. 3-
12; *idem*, 'Hab/piru and Hebrews', in *Patriarchs* (ed. B. Mazar; WHJP, 2;
Jerusalem, 1970), pp. 188-200, 279-81; M. Weippert, *The Settlement of the
Israelite Tribes in Palestine*; Rowton, 'The "Ḫapiru" Problem', pp. 375-87; *idem*,
'The Problem of the *'Apiru-'Ibrîm*', pp. 13-20; de Geus, *The Tribes of Israel*,
pp. 182-83 nn. 236-43; Chaney, 'Ancient Palestinian Peasant Movements', pp. 52-

the Sumerian logogram SA.GAZ[1]) generally referred to rebels who were a source of trouble and rebellion against Egyptian authority in many Canaanite city-states. Based on the etymological resemblance between the terms *ḫabiru(ū)* and עברי(ם), the proximity of their location and the chronological relationship between Amarna and the settlement of the Israelites in Canaan, many scholars suggested that the two terms referred to the same ethnic group. However, after the subsequent discovery of other ancient Near Eastern documents from Boghazköi, Nuzi, Ras-Shamra and so on, this view was eventually modified.[2] It was evident from these latter documents that the term *ḫabiru* was used over a wide region of the ancient Near East in reference to people of various ethnic origins (e.g. Akk. SA.GAZ/*ḫapiru* (Sumer, Alishar, Mari, Alalakh, Nuzi, El Amarna, Boghazköi, Ras Shamra); Ugaritic *'pr(m)*; Egyptian *'pr(.w)*). Therefore, despite recent attempts by some scholars to revert to the older view that the term *ḫabiru* was primarily or originally an ethnic designation,[3] the majority of modern scholars suggest that the term is an appellation representing a certain social (and political) element.[4]

57; O. Loretz, *Habiru-Hebräer: Eine soziolinguistische Studie über die Herkunft des Gentiliciums 'bri vom Appellativum habiru* (BZAW, 160; Berlin: de Gruyter, 1984), pp. 1-88; N. Na'aman, '*Ḥabiru* and Hebrews: The Transfer of a Social Term to the Literary Sphere', *JNES* 45 (1986), pp. 271-88; Ahlström, *Who Were the Israelites?*, pp. 11-18; D.N. Freedman and B.E. Willoughby, 'עברי', *ThWAT*, V, cols. 1041-46.

1. Cf. *CAD* 6: col. 85 and the discussion in Greenberg, *The Ḥab/piru*, pp. 85-91.

2. Most of the relevant documents can be found in Bottéro, *Le problème des Ḥabiru*; Greenberg, *The Ḥab/piru*; and *CAD* 6: cols. 84-85.

3. Cf. R. de Vaux, *The Early History of Israel*. I. *To the Exodus and Covenant of Sinai* (London: Darton, Longman & Todd, 1978), pp. 105-12, who suggests that the term *ḫabiru* originally was an ethnic term; cf. also M.C. Astour, 'Habiru', *IDBSup*, pp. 382-85; and de Geus, *The Tribes of Israel*, p. 182 n. 237. For a critical treatment of de Vaux's analysis, see P.W. Coxon, 'Review of de Vaux's *The Early History of Israel*', *JSOT* 11 (1979), pp. 72-76. For general critical treatments of the ethnic understanding of *habiru*, see Weippert, *The Settlements of Israelite Tribes*, p. 70; de Geus, *The Tribes of Israel*, pp. 182-83; Rowton, 'Problem of the *'Apiru-'Ibrim*', p. 17; Mendenhall, *Tenth Generation*, pp. 122-24.

4. Cf. *CAD* 6: cols. 84-85; Bottéro, *Le problème des ḥabiru*; *idem*, 'Habiru', pp. 14-27; J. Lewy, 'The Biblical Term "Hebrew"', pp. 8-9; Rowton, 'Problem of the *'Apiru-'Ibrîm*', pp. 13-20; *idem*, 'The "Ḥapiru" Problem', pp. 375-87; Chaney, 'Ancient Palestinian Peasant Movements', p. 53; Rowley, *From Joseph to Joshua*,

However, it is clear from the usage of the term ḫabiru between the first half of the eighteenth century to the twelfth and eleventh centuries BCE that it underwent a transition in meaning from its primary meaning 'migrant' or 'alien' during the earlier periods to the more derogatory meaning 'rebel' found in EA. In the following discussion I will briefly summarize the anthropological, ethnographical and documentary research that has helped to clarify this transition in meaning of the term ḫabiru.

Rowton,[1] for example, has shown that the ḫabiru were composed of the poorest tribal elements who were forced, on account of wars, disasters, famine, debt,[2] heavy taxes, prolonged military service and so on, to break away from their tribes and society in order to find somewhere else to support their family. Furthermore, Bottéro,[3] contrary to earlier views, has shown that these people, who included a wide variety of peoples including semi-nomads, pastoralists, farmers and city dwellers, were mostly displaced from the sedentary urban and rural populations of the ancient Near East.[4] Although these tribal

p. 52; Lemche, *Early Israel*, pp. 420-32; E.A. Speiser, 'Nuzi', *IDB*, III, p. 574; Mendenhall, *Tenth Generation*, p. 122.

1. Rowton, 'Problem of the *'Apiru-'Ibrîm'*, p. 14; cf. also M. Liverani, 'Il fuoruscitismo in Siria nella tarda età del bronzo', *RevSI* 77 (1965), pp. 315-36; Na'aman, 'Ḫabiru and Hebrews', p. 272; Renger, 'Flucht as soziales Problem', pp. 178-79.

2. Cf. Liverani, 'Il fuoruscitismo in Siria', pp. 317-19, who has suggested that debt-slavery, in particular, led to the appearance of many ḫabiru.

3. J. Bottéro, 'Entre nomades et sédentaires: les Ḫabiru', *Dialogues d'histoire ancienne* 6 (1980), pp. 89-107; *idem*, 'Les Ḫabiru, les nomades et les sédentaires', pp. 96-99; cf. also Na'aman, 'Ḫabiru and Hebrews', p. 273.

4. Cp. M.B. Rowton, 'Dimorphic Structure and Topology', *OrAnt* 15 (1976), pp. 17-31; *idem*, 'Dimorphic Structure and the Parasocial Element', pp. 181-98, who suggests that the process of tribal disintegration was confined to the non-urban areas — he suggests that society can be divided into two sectors: tribal (non-urban) and urban (non-tribal). He calls this social model 'Dimorphic Scoiety'. However, I have already pointed out in Chapter 2 that ancient Near Eastern societies were not as monolithic as it once was thought. Furthermore, the model of 'dimorphic society' has been largely criticized for its tendency to oversimplify the intergration between urban and non-urban society, since it does not allow for the possibility that real intergration can exist between these two social elements. For a critique of M.B. Rowton's work, see Kamp and Yoffee, 'Ethnicity in Ancient Western Asia', pp. 92-99, esp. 92-94; Loretz, *Hebräer-Habiru*, pp. 71-78.

groups often maintained a strong ethnic identity, during difficult times urban and rural tribal populations would break away in order to survive. These break-away groups of ḥabiru, who often migrated in non-tribally organized bands under the control of a single ruler,[1] sometimes turned to brigandage, which was indicative also of small and poor tribes or tribal splinter groups who were not able to assert their claim to land.[2] This behaviour, though, was not indicative of the majority of the ḥabiru populations, who either eventually re-integrated into the rural or urban tribal elements of a sedentary society or who might have formed the nucleus of a new tribe.[3] While it is evident that some of the ḥabiru were absorbed into the lower social classes of the kingdoms in which they eventually settled, especially in Nuzi where they often became indentured servants,[4] Na'aman[5] suggests that the term ḥabiru should be defined more narrowly to include only the 'act of migration' and not any specific social status that the ḥabiru obtained in their migration and eventual re-integration into sedentary society.[6]

1. Cf. Bottéro, 'Les Ḥabiru', p. 94; *idem*, 'Ḥabiru', p. 26; cf. also Na'aman, 'Ḥabiru and Hebrews', p. 273.

2. Cf. Rowton, 'Dimporphic Structure and the Parasocial Element', p. 193; cf. also Lemche, *Early Israel*, p. 421.

3. Cf. Greenberg, *The Ḥap/biru*, pp. 86-88; Bottéro, 'Les Ḥabiru', pp. 93-106; Rowton, 'Dimporphic Structure and the Parasocial Element', p. 194; cf. also Na'aman, 'Ḥabiru and Hebrews', p. 273; Lemche, *Early Israel*, p. 421.

4. Cf. Greenberg, *The Ḥap/biru*, p. 86; Weippert, *The Settlement of the Israelite Tribes in Palestine*, pp. 67-69; Na'aman, 'Ḥabiru and Hebrews', p. 273. For example, at Alishar (Greenberg Text #12 = Bottéro Text #5) the Ḥabiru belonged to the palace of *Shalaḥshuwe*; they were state dependents at Larsa (Greenberg Text #4-11, 20 = Bottéro Text #13-15, 12, 9, 11, 16); they were soldiers under various local rulers at Mari (Greenberg Text #13-14 = Bottéro Text #18-19); they were garrison troops at Boghazköi (Greenberg Text #120 = Bottéro Text #72); they were dependents of individuals at Nuzi (Greenberg Text #32-50 = Bottéro Text #55, 50, 58, 66, 65, 57, 65, 56, 54, 52, 49, 51, 61, 60, 63, 59, [Greenberg Text #50 not in Bottéro]); were dependents of the palace or temple at Nuzi (Greenberg Text #51-57 = Bottéro Text #64, [Greenberg Text #52 not in Bottéro, Greenberg Text #53 not in Bottéro]), 68-69; were organized into local military units in Alalakh (Greenberg Text #24-26, 29-30 = [Greenberg Text #24 not in Bottéro], Bottéro Text #41, [Greenberg Text #26 not in Bottéro], Bottéro Text #43, [Greenberg Text #30 not in Bottéro]), and in Palestine (Greenberg Text #97 = Bottéro Text #132).

5. Na'aman, 'Ḥabiru and Hebrews', pp. 273-75.

6. Contra Lewy, 'The Biblical Term "Hebrew"', p. 9, who suggests that the

Lastly, there was a significant development in the usage of the appellation *ḫabiru* in EA, in which the term is used as a derogatory appellation for 'rebels' against Egyptian authority.[1] Although the use of the term *ḫabiru* presupposes the actual presence of *ḫabiru* -bands, which were a major cause of disturbance in Canaan, the term became a designation for any group including defecting Canaanite citizens who opposed Egyptian rule.[2] Eventually, though, the term *ḫabiru* disappears at the beginning of the first millennium BCE.[3]

Recapitulating, the term *ḫabiru* was sometimes a social designation for foreign immigrants who attempted to assimilate into the various states of the ancient Near East. Scholars have therefore defined the term *ḫabiru* as 'refugees', 'immigrants', 'aliens', 'displaced people' and so on.[4] Furthermore, while there is a tendency to associate the term *ḫabiru* with lower social classes, it is more likely that this term

---

term *ḫabiru* refers specifically to 'aliens' who were not afforded the civil rights of the ruling classes. Cf. Astour, 'Habiru', p. 383, who notes that no legal discrimination of foreigners is attested in any city-state of Mesopotamia or Syria during the second millennium. Furthermore, as we saw in Chapter 1, indigenous free citizens were often forced to enter into a type of indentured servitude (e.g. *tidennūtu* service contracts from Nuzi) or into the service of the state or temple households.

1. Cf. Greenberg, *The Ḫap/biru*, pp. 70-72; Bottéro, *Le problème des Ḫabiru*, pp. 85-118; E.F. Campbell, 'The Amarna Letters and the Amarna Period', *BA* 23 (1960), p. 15; Weippert, *The Settlement of the Israelite Tribes in Palestine*, pp. 71-74; Mendenhall, *Tenth Generation*, pp. 122-35; M. Liverani, 'Farsi Ḫabiru', *VicOr* 2 (1979), p. 71; Na'aman, 'Habiru and Hebrews', pp. 275-78; Lemche, *Early Israel*, p. 421; Chaney, 'Ancient Palestinian Peasant Movements', pp. 72-83; J.M. Halligan, 'The Role of the Peasant in the Amarna Period', in *Palestine in Transition: The Emergence of Ancient Israel* (ed. D.N. Freedman and D.F. Graf; SWBAS, 2; Sheffield: Almond Press, 1983), pp. 21-22.

2. Cf. K. Koch, 'Die Hebräer vom Auszug aus Ägypten bis zum Grossreich Davids', *VT* 19 (1969), pp. 37-38; Liverani, 'Farsi Ḫabiru', pp. 65-77; Na'aman, 'Habiru and Hebrews', p. 276; Halligan, 'The Role of the Peasant in the Amarna Period', pp. 21-22.

3. Cf. Rowton, 'Problem of the *'Apiru-'Ibrîm*', p. 16, who suggests that the term *ḫabiru* was replaced by the ethnic term 'Sutean' which evolved into a social ethnonym; cf. also Na'aman, 'Habiru and Hebrews', p. 286; Chaney, 'Ancient Palestinian Peasant Movements', p. 57.

4. Cf. Bottéro, *Le problème des Ḫabiru*, pp. 191-98; cf. also Liverani, 'Il fuoruscitismo in Siria', p. 317; Na'aman, 'Habiru and Hebrews', p. 275; Lewy, 'The Biblical Term "Hebrew"', pp. 8-9; Lemche, *Early Israel*, pp. 420-32; *idem*, *Ancient Israel*, p. 86.

conveyed the idea of the 'act of migration' only, rather than any
specific social status the *ḥabiru* may have obtained in their migration
and eventual assimilation into sedentary society. Lastly, while the term
ḥabiru refers to both foreign and domestic rebels in EA, this usage
must be understood as a later development of the term *ḥabiru* .

The (ם)עברי *and the* ḥabiru. While the majority of biblical scholars no
longer suggest that the two terms *ḥabiru* and (ם)עברי refer to the same
ethnic group, they suggest nevertheless that these two terms are
somehow related. Scholars have generally opted for one of two
interpretations. First, there are scholars who suggest that the term
(ם)עברי 'Hebrew' is an ethnic rather than social designation, although
while some deny any connection between the two terms *ḥabiru* and
(ם)עברי others admit the possibility that the two terms are
etymologically related but not semantically similar.[1] Second, there are
scholars who suggest that the term (ם)עברי 'Hebrew' is etymologically
related and semantically similar to the term *ḥabiru*, although the term

---

1. For example, see R. Borger, 'Das Problem der 'apiru ('*ḥabiru*')', *ZDPV* 74
(1958), pp. 121-32; H.A. Landsberger in Bottéro, *Le problème des Ḥabiru*, p. 161;
Rapaport, 'The Origins of Hebrew Law', pp. 158-67; Fensham, *Exodus*, p. 146;
Loretz, *Habiru-Hebräer*, pp. 181-90; Freedman and Willoughby, 'עברי', cols.
1054-56; Cardellini, *Die biblischen 'Sklaven'-Gesetze*, p. 247 n. 30; Riesener, *Der
Stamm* עבד, pp. 115-35, esp. 115-25; A. Levy-Feldblum, 'The Law of the Hebrew
Slave. . . ', Hebrew *BM* 31 (1985–86), pp. 348-59; J. Van Seters, *Abraham in
History and Tradition* (New Haven and London: Yale University Press, 1975),
pp. 54-58; E. Lipiński, "Apīrū et Hébreux', *BO* 42 (1985), pp. 562-67; Phillips,
'The Laws of Slavery: Exodus 21.2-11', pp. 63-64 n. 16; Otto, *Wandel der
Rechtbegründungen in der Gesellschaftsgeschichte des antiken Israel*, pp. 34-37.
Recently, both Riesener and Loretz have employed descriptive semantics (i.e.
synchronic as opposed to diachronic method) in their studies of the use of the term
(ם)עברי in the Old Testament. It is my contention that these studies hold the most
promise for resolving the problem of the meaning of the term (ם)עברי. However,
while Riesener suggests that the term (ם)עברי is an ethnic designation which has an
entirely different origin than *ḥabiru* (cf. also Borger, Freedman and Willoughby, and
Van Seters), Loretz suggests that the term (ם)עברי is a late degenerate archaism of
the earlier *ḥabiru* (cf. also Lipiński, Otto). While Loretz suggests that the term
(ם)עברי is a 'social ethnonym', he gets around the problem of assigning a social
meaning to the term by dating all the occurrences of (ם)עברי to the exilic or post-exilic
periods.

עברי(ם) was originally a social designation that later became an ethnic designation for Israelites.[1]

While a critique of these two interpretations is beyond the scope of my present discussion, it is only necessary to point out that scholars who adopt the latter view suggest nevertheless that some biblical references to the עברי(ם) are clearly ethnic designations for Israelites.[2] These scholars suggest that those passages, in which the term עברי(ם) is deemed to be semantically similar to the cuneiform term *ḫabiru*, exhibit strong legal and/or social parallels to similar texts that refer to the *ḫabiru*. This is particularly true for the law in Exod. 21.2-6, which, as we saw above, many scholars[3] suggest is parallel to the Nuzian *ḫabiru* service and loan contracts. To these so-called parallels we now turn.

---

1. For example, see M.P. Gray, 'The Ḫâbirū-Hebrew Problem in the Light of the Source Material Available at Present', *HUCA* 29 (1958), pp. 173-88, 193-96; Liverani, 'Il fuoruscitismo in Siria', p. 334; *idem*, 'Review of R. de Vaux, History of Ancient Israel I-II', *OrAnt* 15 (1976), p. 151; H. Cazelles, 'Hebreu, ubru et hapiru', *Syria* 35 (1958), pp. 198-217; *idem*, 'The Hebrews', in *People in Old Testament Times* (ed. D.J. Wiseman; Oxford: Clarendon Press, 1973), pp. 1-3, 21-24; Mendenhall, *Tenth Generation*, pp. 135-38; Gottwald, *The Tribes of Yahweh*, pp. 417-25, 493-97; Rowton, 'Problem of the *'Apiru-'Ibrîm*', pp. 13-20; Koch, 'Die Hebräer', pp. 68-71; Lemche, *Early Israel*, pp. 420-32; *idem*, 'The Hebrew and the Seven Year Cycle', *BibN* 25 (1984), pp. 65-75; *idem*, '"Hebrew" as a National Name for Israel', *ST* 33 (1979), pp. 1-23; de Vaux, *Early History of Israel*, p. 213; C.H. Weir, 'Nuzi', in *Archaeology and Old Testament Study* (ed. D.W. Thomas; Oxford: Clarendon Press, 1967), p. 78.

2. Cf. Greenberg, '*Ḫab/piru* and Hebrews', p. 198, who writes: 'no scriptural passage gives explicit ground for extending the scope of עברי beyond Israelites'.

3. For example, see Paul, *Book of the Covenant*, pp. 45-53; Ellison, 'The Hebrew Slave', pp. 30-35; Wright, 'What Happened Every Seven Years II', pp. 193-201, esp. p. 196 and n. 12; Weippert, *The Settlement of the Israelite Tribes in Palestine*, pp. 85-87; Rowton, 'Problem of the *'Apiru-'Ibrîm*', p. 19; Lewy, 'Ḫabiru und Hebräer', pp. 738-46, 825-33; *idem*, 'Ḫâbirū and Hebrews', pp. 587-623; *idem*, 'A New Parallel between Ḫâbirū and Hebrews', pp. 47-58; Gray, 'The *Ḫâbirū*-Hebrew Problem', pp. 182-85; F.F. Bruce, 'Tell el-Amarna', in Thomas (ed.), *Archaeology and Old Testament Study*, pp. 11-14; J. Gray, 'Ugarit', in Thomas (ed.), *Archaeology and Old Testament Study*, p. 157; Weir, 'Nuzi', p. 78; Mendenhall, *Tenth Generation*, p. 90 n. 60; de Vaux, *The Early History of Israel*, p. 215; C.H. Gordon, 'Biblical Customs and the Nuzi Tablets', *BA* 3 (1940), pp. 1-12; Lemche, 'The Hebrew Slave', pp. 129-44.

The (ם)עברי and the Nuzi service and loan contracts. While several scholars have suggested that the Nuzian service contracts are similar to the debt-slave law in Exod. 21.2-6, Paul,[1] who follows the work of Lewy,[2] presents the most recent and exhaustive attempt to compare these two institutions. In the following discussion I will examine seven main comparisons.

1. Paul[3] suggests that the עבד עברי in Exod. 21.2 is probably a *ḫabiru*-type 'slave' based upon the so-called parallel Nuzian service and loan contracts, although he notes that the עבד עברי in Deut. 15.12 clearly refers to an Israelite. However, Paul does not explain how Exod. 21.2-6, which apparently refers to the *ḫabiru* service contracts, was later used in Deut. 15.12-18 to refer to Israelite debt-slaves. Furthermore, as Na'aman correctly points out, in Nuzi the *ḫabiru* were immigrants who entered into service contracts with Nuzian citizens, while the biblical law in Deut. 15.12-18 refers to Israelites who are sold to fellow Israelites. Therefore, Lewy,[4] who may have been aware of the difficulty in equating the Nuzian *ḫabiru* with Israelites, suggests that both Exod. 21.2-6 and Deut. 15.12-18 refer to aliens, although this view is not held by the majority of scholars.[5] In addition, as Phillips[6] correctly points out, from a comparativist's

1. Paul, *Book of the Covenant*, pp. 45-53.
2. Lewy, 'Ḫabiru und Hebräer', pp. 738-46, 825-33; 'Ḫabirū and Hebrews', pp. 587-623; 'A New Parallel between Ḫâbirū and Hebrews', pp. 47-58.
3. Paul, *Book of the Covenant*, pp. 45-47; cf. also Weippert, *The Settlement of the Israelite Tribes in Palestine*, p. 85; Horst, *Gottes Recht*, p. 97.
4. Lewy, 'The Biblical Term "Hebrew"', pp. 3-4; cf. also Gray, 'The Ḫâbirū-Hebrew Problem', pp. 182-85; J. Weingreen, 'Saul and the Habirū', in *Fourth World Congress of Jewish Studies*, I (Jerusalem, 1967), pp. 63-66; and Wright, 'What Happened Every Seven Years, II', pp. 195-201, who also suggests that Exod. 21.2-6 and Deut. 15.12-18 refer to a 'landless and rootless substratum of society who lived by selling their services to Israelite households' (p. 199), while Lev. 25.9-55 refers to Israelites who retained legal ownership of their land; cf. also *idem*, *God's People in God's Land*, pp. 251-59, esp. 253-55. However, as Lemche, 'The Hebrew Slave', pp. 137-38, points out, this view is not accepted by the majority of scholars.
5. Cf. Lemche, 'The Hebrew Slave', pp. 136-44, who concludes that the עבד עברי in Exod. 21.2 refers to a *ḫabiru* who may or may not be an Israelite. This uncertainty is due to Lemche's view that the first part of the Book of the Covenant was of Canaanite origin but that the later law in Deut. 15.12-18 deals only with Israelites.
6. Phillips, 'The Laws of Slavery: Exodus 21.2-11', p. 55. For the view that the

viewpoint the addition of עבד to עברי is tautologous, although such an addition would not be tautologous if עברי were used as an ethnic designation.[1] In fact, while Paul[2] favours the view that the debt-slave law in Exod. 21.2-6 is parallel to the Nuzian service contracts, he points out nevertheless that the term ḫabiru is never used as a gentilic in the cuneiform tradition. Lastly, that the עבד עברי is an ethnic designation in Exod. 21.2 is further suggested by the law concerning the sale of a free Israelite daughter in Exod. 21.7-11,[3] which, as we saw above, is carefully juxtaposed to the law in vv. 2-6.

2. Paul[4] suggests that the verb חקנה 'juridically means to acquire as one's own property'. While he notes that no money was exchanged when Nuzians acquired ḫabiru, he fails to mention that nowhere in the service contracts is there any reference to the ḫabiru being sold for anything. As Cardellini[5] correctly points out, the ḫabiru commence their service with a lord without having to be sold (i.e. *ana ardūti/amtūti/wardūti*).[6] If the compiler had wanted to make it clear that Exod. 21.2-6 referred to this type of service contract he would have used a verb other than קנה, which is generally used to refer to the act of 'buying',[7] especially in Lev. 22.11 (כי־יקנה נפש קנין כספו) and 25.44-45 (תקנו עבד ואמה), both of which clearly refer to the purchase of chattel-slaves. Furthermore, we saw in Chapter 3 that the ḫabiru exchanged their service for the necessities of life. Although the biblical law defines the legal relationship of the עבד עברי in the

---

phrase עבד עברי is a proleptic expression; viz., a 'Hebrew' only becomes a 'slave' after he is bought, see A. Alt, 'Die Ursprünge des Israelitischen rechts', p. 291 n. 2; Noth, *Exodus*, p. 177; Lemche, 'The Hebrew Slave', pp. 135, 38, 143-44; *idem*, '"Hebrew" as a National Name for Israel', pp. 10, 20.

1. Cp. Wright, 'What Happened Every Seven Years, II', p. 196, who suggests that if the term עברי is an ethnic designation then the phrase אחיך העברי או העברייה in Deut. 15.12 would be tautologous. Refer to the discussion of Deut. 15.12a in Chapter 7.

2. Paul, *Book of the Covenant*, p. 45.

3. Refer below to my discussion of Exod. 21.7-11.

4. Paul, *Book of the Covenant*, p. 46.

5. Cardellini, *Die biblischen 'Sklaven'-Gesetze*, pp. 247 n. 30, 186.

6. Cf. Lewy, 'Ḫabirū and Hebrews', p. 594, who also points out that in no Nuzian service contract is a purchase price paid.

7. Cf. Gen. 25.10; 33.19 (purchase of a field); 39.4 (Joseph bought by Potiphar) 47.22, 23 (purchase of land and burial place); Lev. 25.28, 30, 50 (infinitive used to refer to 'buyers' of land).

protases and sets forth the terms of this legal relationship in the
apodoses (i.e. primary law), there is no reference to the necessities of
life, but rather the conditions of the debt-slave's release are most
clearly set forth. Cardellini[1] correctly notes that in the Nuzi service
contracts there is no clause that sets the period of service of the
ḥabiru. The *ḥabiru* were expected to remain with the lord as long as
they lived. Paul[2] suggests nevertheless that the six-year maximum
service is a major reform of the Nuzi service contracts. However, as
Phillips[3] correctly points out, Paul does not offer any explanation as
to why the compiler(s) of the Book of the Covenant should want to
undertake such a reform. Surely, limiting the period of service of the
ḥabiru would only make it more difficult for the *ḥabiru* to find a place
to maintain themselves and their families.[4] Perhaps a periodic release
would be helpful if the *ḥabiru* were maltreated, but as we have seen in
Chapter 5 such treatment is condemned in the biblical legal corpora.
Moreover, the best solution would be to allow the *ḥabiru* to buy their
freedom or find replacements, something that is already stipulated in
many of the Nuzi service contracts but not in the biblical legislation.

3. Paul[5] compares the Hebrew adjective חפשׁי with the social
designation *ḥupšu*, which he notes generally refers to a member of the
lower social classes. He suggests, therefore, that the biblical term חפשׁי
refers to the state of 'belonging to the class of freedmen'. While Paul

1. Cardellini, *Die biblischen 'Sklaven'-Gesetze*, p. 247 n. 30.
2. Paul, *Book of the Covenant*, p. 47.
3. Phillips, 'The Laws of Slavery: Exodus 21.2-11', p. 54.
4. Cp. Lewy, 'Ḥabiru and Hebrews', pp. 608-10, who suggests that since a
date at which a Nuzian service contract was entered is found on some contracts it is
likely that these contracts were concluded after a set time. He thus suggests that these
contracts are parallel to the release prescribed in the biblical legislation. However,
this suggestion is not convincing for the following reasons. First, the fact that a date
is found in certain contracts does not prove that these contracts were concluded after
a set time. Secondly, there is no reason why a Nuzian service contract would
prescribe a set period of service since it was in the interest of servants to remain with
their lords until which time they could sustain themselves and their family. I have
already noted in Chapter 3 that in reality servants who engaged in a *tidennūtu* loan or
ḥabiru service contract most likely were not allowed to leave before the death of their
lords; cp. Lewy, 'Ḥabiru and Hebrews', p. 608 n. 108.
5. Paul, *Book of the Covenant*, p. 47; cf. also Alt, 'The Origin of Israelite Law',
p. 95 and n. 33; W.F. Albright, 'Canaanite *ḥapši* and Hebrew *ḥofši* Again', *JPOS*
6 (1926), p. 107.

does not define the social position of the Hebrew *ḫupšu* precisely, Wright[1] suggests that the released Hebrew in Exod. 21.2-6 and Deut. 15.12-18 is someone who does not hold any legal title to land and is therefore forced to sell his or her services to Israelite households. Similarly, Lemche[2] suggests that the released Hebrew in Exod. 21.2-6 either enters into a 'client' relationship with his former master or with the city-state in which his or her former master belonged. However, Lemche suggests that Deut. 15.12-18 is different in that it treats manumission as complete *restitutio*—viz., the deuteronomist no longer understood the term חפשי as a social designation.[3]

As in the case of the interpretation of the term עברי(ם), Wright's and Lemche's views are dependent upon both the so-called social and legal parallels that exist between the *ḫupšu* and the חפשי, and the apparent semantic change that has occurred in the term חפשי during the composition of the Old Testament—viz., from a social designation referring to a member of a lower social class to its 'secondary' and more general designation *'Freigelassener'*.

The term *ḫupšu* occurs in many second-millennium documents from Babylon, Nuzi, Alalakh, Ugarit (*ḫb/pt*) and Amarna.[4] While scholars are in general agreement that the *ḫupšu* were members of a lower social class, they have not been able to agree upon a more precise definition.[5] For example, while Albright[6] has referred to the *ḫupšu* as 'serfs', Mendelsohn[7] has suggested that they resemble the 'free proletariat' who are comparable to the Roman *coloni* 'tied tenant farmers'. Similarly, Landsberger[8] suggests that the term *ḫupšu* covers

---

1. Wright, 'What Happened Every Seven Years, II', pp 195-201; *God's People in God's Land*, pp. 253-54, 256-57.

2. N.P. Lemche, 'חפשי in 1 Samuel xvii 25', *VT* 24 (1974), pp. 373-74; 'The Hebrew and the Seven Year Cycle', pp. 72-75; *Ancient Israel*, p. 88.

3. Cf. also O. Loretz, 'Die hebräischen Termini *ḤPŠJ* "Freigelassen, Freigellassner" und *ḤPŠH* "Freilassung"', *UF* 9 (1977), p. 164.

4. Cf. *CAD* 6: cols. 241-42; N. Lohfink, 'חפשי', *ThWAT*, III, cols. 123-28.

5. Cf. Lemche, 'The Hebrew Slave', pp. 140-41; Halligan, 'The Role of the Peasant in the Amarna Period', p. 20; Chaney, 'Ancient Palestinian Peasant Movements', p. 74 n. 31.

6. Albright, 'Canaanite *ḫapši* and Hebrew *ḥofši* Again', pp. 106-108; 'New Canaanite Historical and Mythological Data', *BASOR* 63 (1936), pp. 23-32.

7. I. Mendelsohn, 'The Canaanite Term for "Free Proletarian"', *BASOR* 83 (1941), pp. 36-39; 'New Light on the *Ḫupšu*', *BASOR* 139 (1955), pp. 9-11.

8. H.A. Landsberger, 'Peasant Unrest: Themes and Variations', in *Rural Protest:*

the continuum of 'all low-status cultivators' who constitute a large majority of any agrarian society. These peasants owned small rural plots and were subject to corvée and military service. However, Heltzer[1] and Gottwald[2] doubt that feudalism is the best model for understanding Syro-Palestinian social organization. They suggest, instead, that the *ḫupšu* were a group of court clients who performed military (e.g. ERÍN.MEŠ/ ERIM.MEŠ *ḫupšu* in EA, Alalakh and Assyria),[3] craft (e.g. LÚ.MEŠ U ŠBAR.MEŠ *ḫu-up-šu* weavers in Nuzi), and professional duties.[4]

In the Old Testament[5] the verb חפש and the feminine noun חפשה occur only in Lev. 19.20, which reads:

20 ואיש כי־ישכב את־אשה שכבת־זרע והוא שפחה נחרפת לאיש
והפדה לא נפדתה או חפשה לא נתן־לה בקרת תהיה לא
יומתו כי־לא חפשה:

20 And if a man lies carnally with a woman who is a slave acquired for *another* man, but who has in no way been redeemed nor given her freedom חפשה, there shall be punishment; they shall not be put to death because she was not free חפשה (a freed-woman).

Similarly, the adjective חפשי is used in reference to the manumission of slaves in Exod. 21.2, 5, 26, 27; Deut. 15.12, 13, 18; and Jer. 34.9,

---

Peasant Movements and Social Change (ed. H.A. Landsberger; New York: Barnes & Noble, 1973), pp. 6-18; cf. also Chaney, 'Ancient Palestinian Peasant Movements', p. 74 n. 31.

1. M. Heltzer, 'Problems of the Social History of Syria in the Late Bronze Age', in *La Siria nel Tardo Bronzo*, IX (ed. M. Liverani; Rome: Orientis Antiqui Collectio, 1968), pp. 31-46.

2. Gottwald, 'Early Israel and the Canaanite Socio-economic System', pp. 25-37.

3. Cf. also W.A. Ward, 'Two Unrecognized *ḫupšu*-Mercenaries in Egyptian Texts', *UF* 12 (1980), pp. 441-42.

4. Cf. also Lemche, 'The Hebrew Slave', pp. 140-41; Chaney, 'Ancient Palestinian Peasant Movements', p. 62; cp. J. Gray, 'Feudalism in Ugarit and Early Israel', *ZAW* 64 (1952), p. 55, who notes that the *ḫupšu* were a class set apart for military service, but associates them with the feudal system.

5. For a discussion of the term חפשי see Lohfink, 'חפשי', cols. 123-28; T. von Willi, 'Die Freiheit Israels: Philologische Notizen zu den Wurzeln *ḥpš*, *ʿzb* und *drr*', in *Beiträge zur alttestamentlichen Theologie: Festschrift W. Zimmerli zum 70. Geburtstag* (ed. H. Donner, R. Hanhart and R. Smend; Göttingen: Vandenhoeck & Ruprecht, 1977), pp. 533-38; O. Loretz, 'Ugaritisch—Hebräisch *ḤB/PT, B T ḤpTT—HPŠJ, BJT HḤPŠJ/WT*', *UF* 8 (1976), pp. 129-31; *idem*, 'Die hebräischen Termini HPŠJ', pp. 163-67; *idem, Habiru-Hebräer*, pp. 253-63.

10, 11, 14, 16. In Isa. 58.6 the term is used in reference to the release of the oppressed: שלח רצוצים חפשים 'to let oppressed ones go free'. In Job 3.19 it is used symbolically in reference to those who are cut off from Yahweh's remembrance—עבד חפשי מאדניו 'a slave is free from his lord'—while in 39.5 it is used in reference to the release of a donkey. Lastly, the term חפשי is found in 1 Sam. 17.25, where it is generally understood to refer to the exemption from taxes or corvées.

However, there are no Old Testament passages that give explicit grounds for rendering the term חפשי as a designation of a lower social class. In fact, scholars are in agreement that the term חפשי is not used as a social designation in Job 3.19; 39.5; Ps. 88.6; or Isa. 58.6. Furthermore, both Loretz[1] and Fensham[2] suggest that the term חפשי is not used as a social designation in the Old Testament, but as a term referring to a free citizen. That the above view is to be preferred over the views of Paul, Wright and Lemche, who suggest that the biblical term חפשי in Exod. 21.2 is used as a social designation parallel to the term *ḫupšu*, is supported by the following observations.

First, neither Paul nor Wright demonstrates that the biblical term חפשי in Exod. 21.2 is parallel to the cuneiform *ḫupšu*. As Lohfink,[3] Willi,[4] Rainey[5] and Phillips[6] correctly point out, there is no textual or historical evidence that the lower social class represented by the term *ḫupšu* ever existed during the various periods of Israelite history. Lemche's view that the released 'Hebrew' in Exod. 21.2-6 enters into either a 'client' relationship with his former master or with the city-state to which his former master belonged, which is dependent on his interpretation of the adjective חפשי as a social designation in 1 Sam.

---

1. Loretz, 'Ugaritisch—Hebräisch *ḤB/PT, BT ḤpTT—ḤPŠJ, BJT ḤḤPŠJ/WT*' pp. 129-31; 'Die hebraïschen Termini ḤPŠJ', pp. 163-67; *Habiru-Hebräer* pp. 253-63.

2. F.C. Fensham, 'Note on Keret in CTA 14.90-103a', *JNSL* 8 (1980), p. 35.

3. Lohfink, 'חפשי', col. 125. Note, however, that Lohfink suggests that the חפשי of Exod. 21.2-6 *originally* referred to a lower social group, although he can find no evidence for the existence of such a lower class within Israel.

4. Von Willi, 'Die Freiheit Israels', p. 534 n. 13.

5. A.F. Rainey, 'Institutions: Family, Civil, and Military', in *Ras Shamra Parallels: Texts from Ugarit and the Hebrew Bible,* II (ed. L.R. Fisher, D.E. Smith and S. Rummel; AnOr, 50; Rome: Biblical Institute Press, 1975), pp. 92, 103-104.

6. Phillips, 'The Laws of Slavery: Exod 21.2-11', p. 55; cf. also Loretz, *Habiru-Hebräer*, p. 259.

17.25, has been refuted by the majority of scholars,[1] who have noted that there is little or no textual grounds for Lemche's interpretation since there are no other texts within the Old Testament that suggest that the term חפשי ever referred to clients of the king, although we did note in Chapter 4 that Israelite kings did employ clients.[2] Lastly, Lemche's view that the deuteronomist no longer understood the term חפשי as a social designation in Deut. 15.12 is not convincing, since he does not explain how a law which supposedly stipulates the release of foreign indentured servants evolved into a manumission law stipulating the release of Israelite citizens, which he admits is very similar to the manumission law in LH §117.[3]

Secondly, Paul, Wright and Lemche assume that the *ḥupšu*/חפשי are somehow related to the עברי/*ḥabiru*. However, if the biblical law in Exod. 21.2-6 is a later reflex of the Nuzian *ḥabiru* contracts it is difficult to understand why their release should be likened to the status of the *ḥupšu*, who are never mentioned in the *ḥabiru* service contracts. As we saw above, the *ḥupšu* were citizens who belonged to a lower social order, while the *ḥabiru* were foreign immigrants who eventually integrated within the social structure of the country in which they settled. While there is the possibility that some *ḥabiru* joined the ranks of the *ḥupšu*, it is not clear that a *ḥabiru* who left the service of a Nuzi citizen would automatically become a member of the *ḥupšu*. Furthermore, there are texts that mention that the *ḥupšu*

---

1. Cf. von Willi, 'Die Freiheit Israels', p. 536; Loretz, *Habiru-Hebräer*, p. 259; and P.K. McCarter, *I Samuel: A New Translation with Introduction, Notes and Commentary* (AB; Garden City, NY: Doubleday, 1980), p. 304, who suggests that a closer parallel is noted by Rainey, 'Institutions', p. 104. Rainey notes that the Akkadian adjective *zaki* is found in RS 16:250: 21-22 to describe an emancipated slave, and in RS 16:269: 14-16, which describes a soldier, who because of a brave deed at arms has been granted freedom by the king from service to the palace. McCarter suggests that the latter text offers a striking parallel to the offer made by Saul. Cf. also R.W. Klein, *I Samuel* (WC, 10; Waco, TX: Word Books, 1983), p. 178; de Vaux, *Ancient Israel*, p. 80; H.P. Smith, *The Book of Samuel* (ICC; Edinburgh: T. & T. Clark, 1977), p. 158; R.P. Gordon, *1 & 2 Samuel: A Commentary* (Exeter: Paternoster Press, 1986), p. 156.
2. Cf. B.S. Jackson, 'Unpublished text of Speaker's Lectures in Biblical Studies, Lecture VII: Slavery', pp. 16-17 who notes that while the *ḥupšu* were bound to serve in some capacity for the state (e.g. soldier, craftsman, labourer) the term חפשי is used in 1 Sam. 17.25 to describe *freedom* from such obligations.
3. Lemche, 'The Hebrew Slave', p. 139.

joined the ranks of the *ḥabiru*, not *vice versa*. For example, EA 118: 21-39 reads:[1]

> Furthermore, hostility is strong against me. There is no sustenance for the *amēlūtme*š *ḥu-ub-ši*, and indeed, they have deserted to the sons of Abdi-Ashirta, and to Sidon and Beruta. Indeed, the sons of Abdi-Ashirta are hostile toward the king, and Sidon and Beruta are no longer the king's. Send a commissioner to take them! Let not a city be abandoned that it fall away from you! Indeed, if the *amēlūtme*š *ḥu-ub-ši* desert, then the GAZ [*ḥabiru*] will seize the city.

Therefore, it is questionable whether the *ḥupšu* were ever identified with the Nuzian *ḥabiru* or that the Nuzian *ḥupšu* ever entered into *ḥabiru*-service contracts.

4. Paul[2] suggests that the term חנם, which is found in the final clause in Exod. 21.2—ובשבעת יצא לחפשי חנם 'but on the seventh he shall go out as a free man *without payment*', indicates that the released debt-slave does not have to pay for his release nor provide a replacement upon leaving. The first point seems to be correct, but the second unproven. For example, in the Old Testament the term חנם is used in reference to 'working for no pay' (cf. Gen. 29.15; Jer. 22.13); 'paying no money for something' (cf. Exod. 21.11; Num. 11.5; 2 Sam. 24.24 = 1 Chron. 21.24); and 'fearing God for nothing' (cf. Job 1.9). Therefore, it is most likely that this term indicates that the released debt-slave does not have to pay for his release. However, the term חנם is not used elsewhere in the Old Testament in reference to the requirement that an indentured servant must supply a replacement before leaving the service of his or her lord. Moreover, the Nuzi

---

1. Cp. the translation of EA 118.21-39 in W.L. Moran, *Les Lettres d'El-Amarna* (LAPO; Paris: Cerf, 1987), which reads: 'En outre, la guerre [cont]re moi est rude aussi *n'y a-t-il* plus de vivres [pour] les paysans. Vois, [il]s sont [partis] chez les fils de 'Abdi-Aširta, à Si<do>n, et Beyrouth. Puisque les fils de 'Abdi-Aširta sont nostiles au roi, et puisque Sidon e<t> Beyrouth n'appartiennent (plus) au roi, envoie le commisaire pour le (re)prende, a fin que je n'abandonne pas la ville et que je ne parte pas chez toi. Vois, si le paysans partent, le 'Apiru s'empareront de la ville.' Cf. also EA 117: 89-94 (= Greenberg, *The Ḥap/biru*, Text #86 = Bottéro, *Le problème des Ḥabiru*; Text #118), and the discussion in Chaney, 'Ancient Palestinian Peasant Movements', pp. 72-83, esp. 75-76; A. Altman, 'The Revolutions in Byblos and Amurru During the Amarna Period and their Social Background', in *Bar-Ilan in History* (Ramat-Gan, 1978), pp. 10-24.

2. Paul, *Book of the Covenant*, p. 47.

ervice contracts state clearly that the *ḫabiru* must provide a
replacement if they wish to leave the service of their lord. Therefore,
f the biblical stipulation had this sort of requirement in mind the
compiler would have stated it more clearly, especially since this
requirement is attested only in the Nuzi service contracts. Finally, if
we follow Greenberg[1] in his suggestion that the Nuzi service contracts
differentiated between the release of the *ḫabiru* during their lifetime
(e.g. monetary payment) or after the death of their lords (e.g.
replacement), then the biblical law is ambiguous since it does not
differentiate between these two different types of release. Paul's
suggestion, therefore, that the term חנם refers to the exemption from
supplying a replacement cannot be substantiated from the Old
Testament, but is based on the assumption that this law is parallel to
the Nuzi service contracts.

5. Paul suggests that the verbs יבא and יצא are legal terms for
'entering' and 'leaving' the slave status. He suggests too that the
Akkadian verb *erēbu* is the 'interdialectal' functional equivalent of יבא
and the verb *waṣû* is the etymological and functional equivalent of יצא.
These two Akkadian verbs are attested in both Nuzi service contracts
and *tidennūtu* contracts. While Cardellini[2] follows Paul in his
suggestion that this aspect of the biblical law is parallel to the Nuzi
stipulations, he fails to note that the Nuzi *tidennūtu* contracts were
negotiated between Nuzian citizens but *not* the *ḫabiru*. This
terminology is employed in many different types of service and loan
contracts (which employ an antichretic pledge), a phenomenon that we
would expect to find in documents that treat similar contractual
agreements (e.g. the OB *mazzazānūtu* contracts). Therefore, the use of
similar terminology does not demonstrate that the biblical law refers
specifically to the Nuzi service contracts, especially in the light of
Paul's generally unconvincing so-called Nuzi parallels.

6. Paul suggests that an exact parallel to the biblical provision to
give a debt-slave a wife in Exod. 21.4 is found in JEN VI, 610, both
of which read:

אם־אדניו יתן־לו אשה וילדה־לו בים או בנות האשה וילדיה תהיה 4
לאדניה והוא יצא בנפו:

1. Greenberg, *The Ḫab/piru*, pp. 26, 31. Refer to the discussion above in
Chapter 3.
2. Cardellini, *Die biblischen 'Sklaven'-Gesetze*, p. 247 n. 30.

4 If his master gives him a wife, and she bears him sons or daughters, the wife and her children shall belong to her master, and he shall go out by himself.

The tongue of Zini, son of Sin-iddina spoke thus before witnesses: 'I made myself enter for service into [the house of Ennamat]ti. And [Ennamati] has given [m]e [1] talent 5 minas of copper, 7 mi[nas of lead. . .] *sheep*, (and) a full [. . .] wool. [N] as a wife he has given me.' As long as Ennamati lives Zini shall serve him. When Ennamati dies, he shall serve Takku. If Zini infringes (the agreement) and leaves the house of Takku, his wife, his offspring, 1 talent 5 [mi]nas of copper, 7 minas of lead [. . .] *sheep*, 1 [. . .] ? ? Zini must give (back) to Takku; then he may leave.

Cardellini[1] notes correctly that there is great similarity between these Nuzian and biblical stipulations. However, that the children of such marriages (in which an owner gives one of his female chattel slaves to a man) remain the property of the owner is characteristic of chattel-slavery in general.[2] Therefore, although the Nuzi document bears a striking resemblance to the biblical stipulation this parallel does not demonstrate that the biblical law is parallel to the Nuzi service contracts. Presumably, such a 'marriage' could be entered into by anyone who happens to be in the service of a man who owns female chattel-slaves. I will discuss this biblical stipulation in more detail below.

7. Paul[3] suggests that the formal declaration to remain a slave for life in Exod. 21.5 is similar to a declaration found in a Nuzi *tidennūtu* contract.[4]

ואם־אמר יאמר העבד אהבתי את־אדני את־אשתי ואת־בני לא אצא חפשי

But if the slave says, 'I love my master, my wife, and my children; I will not go out as a free man

---

1. Cardellini, *Die biblischen 'Sklaven'-Gesetze*, p. 247 n. 30.

2. Cf. Paul, *Book of the Covenant*, p. 49 n. 5, who acknowledges this very fact; cf. also Koschaker, *Neue keilschriftliche Rechtssurkunden*, p. 83; *idem* 'Fratriarchat, Hausgemeinschaft und Mutterrecht in Keilschrift-rechten', ZA 41 (1933), p. 18; Saarisalo, 'New Kirkuk Documents Relating to Slaves', pp. 24-26.

3. Paul, *Book of the Covenant*, p. 49 and n. 2.

4. Cf. R.H. Pfeiffer and E.A. Speiser, *One Hundred New Selected Nuzi Text* (AASOR, 16; New Haven: American Schools of Oriental Research, 1936), p. 88 no. 29; Eichler, *Indenture at Nuzi*, pp. 129-30 no. 37.

ù ra-ma-ni-ma ra-ma-ni i-na še-er-še-er-ri-ti i-it-ta-an-ni
So of my own free will I have cast myself in chains (i.e. bondage)

Paul therefore suggests that the Hebrew verb אהב has legal overtones that suggests that the slave's declaration does not reflect his true feelings.[1] However, Paul incorrectly compares the *tidennūtu* contracts, which were negotiated between Nuzian citizens, with the Nuzi service contracts which were undertaken by the foreign *ḫabiru*. As we saw above, there is no correspondence between the *tidennūtu* contracts and the sale of a 'Hebrew slave' in Exod. 21.2. While the Nuzi declaration may be construed to refer to permanent bondage in cases where the term of the loan was 50 years, it is clear that such a declaration would not signify a change in status from a temporary slave to a permanent one in most of the extant *tidennūtu* contracts.

Recapitulating, the above discussion shows that there is little correspondence between the debt-slave law in Exod. 21.2-6 and the Nuzian service and loan contracts. As Phillips[2] correctly points out, comparative analyses, such as the one attempted by Paul, 'place too much reliance on apparent resemblances at the expense of essential differences in the societies from which they [the laws and customs] emanate and which, if recognized, would have rendered any attempt at comparison suspect'. Moreover, Paul, Rowton, Wright and others have determined the semantic value of the biblical terms עברי(ם) and חפשי largely by etymological discussions rather than by current usage, which is by far the best method for determining the semantic value of

---

1. However, Paul cites Akkadian texts, which do not deal with slavery, in support of his assertion that the expression אהבתי is a legal term; cf. also Childs, *Exodus*, p. 468, who apparently follows Paul. He writes: 'The term "love" should not be romanticized. Still there is a recognition by the law that a subjective factor can decisively alter the legal situation.'

2. Cf. Phillips, 'The Laws of Slavery: Exodus 21:2-11', pp. 54-55; cf. also R. Yaron, 'Jewish Law and Other Legal Systems', pp. 308-31; H. Ringgren, 'Israel's Place Among the Religions of the Ancient Near East', in *Studies in the Religion of Ancient Israel* (VTSup, 23; Leiden: Brill, 1972), pp. 1-8; S. Talmon, 'The "Comparative Method" in Biblical Interpretation—Principles and Problems', *VTSup* 29 (1978), pp. 320-56; Jackson, 'Reflections on Biblical Criminal Law', pp. 32-34.

biblical terms.[1] Therefore, it is most likely that the term עברי in Exod. 21.2-6 refers to Israelite debt-slaves.

Exod. 21.2-4 and the Manumission Law in LH §117

Exod. 21.2-4

2 כי תקנה עבד עברי שש שנים יעבד ובשבעת יצא לחפשי חנם:

3 אם־בנפו יבא בנפו יצא אם־בעל אשה הוא ויצאה אשתו עמו:

4 אם־אדניו יתן־לו אשה וילדה־לו בים או בנות האשה וילדיה תהיה לאדניה והוא יצא בנפו:

2 If you acquire a Hebrew slave, he shall serve for six years; but on the seventh he shall go out as a free man without payment.

3 If he comes by himself, he shall go out by himself; if he is the husband of a wife, then his wife shall go out with him.

4 If his master gives him a wife, and she bears him sons or daughters, the wife and her children shall belong to her master, and he shall go out by himself.

We saw above that the debt-slave law in Exod. 21.2-6 is similar to the manumission law in LH §117. While various scholars have also noted this similarity, no systematic comparison of these laws has been attempted. Therefore, in the following discussion I will compare the manumission law in Exod. 21.2-4 with the manumission law in LH §117, drawing upon many of the social and legal observations I made in Chapters 2 and 3.

1. Exod. 21.2 envisages the sale of a person, which is similar to the law in LH §117 which envisages the surrender or sale of a dependent (i.e. wife, son or daughter) in order to meet the obligation of a defaulted loan.[2] While it is evident from the use of the verb קנה in

---

1. Cf. J. Barr, *The Semantics of Biblical Language* (Oxford: Oxford University Press, 1961), pp. 107-60; M. Silva, *Biblical Words and their Meaning: An Introduction to Lexical Semantics* (Grand Rapids: Zondervan, 1983), pp. 17-32, 35-51.

2. Cf. also Loretz, *Habiru-Hebräer*, pp. 137-38, who writes: 'In diesem Zusammenhang [concerning the use of קנה in Exod. 21.2] dürfte zu beachten sein, daß in KH §117 das Eintreten in die Schuldknechtschaft mit *ana kaspim nadānu* "verkaufen" umschrieben wird. Daß es sich jedoch hierbei nicht um ein endgültiges Verkaufen ohne zeitliche Begrenzung handelt, wird im Kontext von KH §117 eindeutig festgelegt. Wir können so wenigstens davon ausgehen, daß Dtn 15,12 eindeutig die Rechtsmaterie der Schuldknechtschaft vorliegt und diese auch auch in Ex 21,2 nicht ausgeschlossen ist, sondern mindestens als einer der Gründe in Betracht zu ziehen ist, aus denen ein *'brî* "Hebräer" in die Sklaverei geraten konnte.'

Exod. 21.2 that this biblical law does not envisage any particular type of transaction, it is nevertheless likely that this transaction is similar to the first type of transaction dealt with in LH §117—*ana kaspim*, which was commonly used for the sale of various items, including houses and slaves. However, while it is likely that the biblical law envisaged the complete transfer of a person, a redemption clause might have been included, especially in cases in which the person was not sold at the 'full price'. Nevertheless, both the biblical and Babylonian manumission laws (including the *mēšarum* edicts) were drafted because in many cases people did not have the means to redeem relatives who were sold on account of insolvency.

Furthermore, Greenberg[1] suggests that the law in Exod. 21.2 also envisaged the sale of a thief who was not able to make restitution for the theft (Cf. Exod. 22.3 [Hebrew v. 2]). Similarly, Westbrook[2] suggests that the thief in Exod. 22.3 was sold (נמכר) to the person from whom the thief stole, although Jackson,[3] who follows the interpretation of Falk,[4] suggests that the verb נמכר in this context should be rendered 'he shall be handed over'. The thief therefore became the slave of the victim. Nevertheless, while these views are possible the text does not indicate to whom the thief was sold or handed over. While the thief may have been sold as a slave to a third party in order to provide restitution for the victim, it is also possible that this stipulation refers to a different penalty. For example, we saw in Chapter 3 that the verb *kašāšu* (s. pl. noun *kiššātu*) can also be used to refer to services exacted from a thief by the court in order to provide restitution to the victim. It is rather interesting that one of the texts that illustrates this practice comes from Eshnunna,[5] since the law in LE §13 is very similar to the law in Exod. 22.2-3 (Hebrew vv. 1-2).[6] Therefore, it is likely that Israelite law stipulated that the court

---

1. Greenberg, 'More Reflections on Biblical Criminal Law', p. 5.
2. Westbrook, *Studies in Biblical and Cuneiform Law*, pp. 125-26.
3. Jackson, *Theft in Early Jewish Law*, pp. 140-44.
4. Z.W. Falk, 'Hebrew Legal Terms II', *JSS* 12 (1967), pp. 241-44.
5. Cf. *CAD* 8.286: 'they seized PN (a slave) in the act of stealing and the judges of Neributu exacted services (*ik-šu-šu-ma*) (from him) for PN2, the owner of the stolen goods, but PN went to Eshnunna and declared (the merchant of my town has the right of ownership over me)' 'the judges asked PN whether he had committed the theft in Neributu and (whether) they had exacted services from him (PN confirmed this before the judges).'
6. LE §13 reads: 'A man, who will be seized in the house of a *muškenum*, in the

kašāšu = מכר 'exact services' from a thief who was not able to make restitution for what was stolen.[1]

2. The law in LH §117 most likely envisaged the defaulting of an agricultural loan which was probably due at the end of the harvest (i.e. a one-year loan). Similarly, it is likely that the law in Exod. 21.2-6 (and Deut. 15.12-18) envisages the sale of persons caused by the defaulting on an agricultural loan. That this law envisages the defaulting of an agricultural loan is supported by the many references to agriculture found in the Covenant Code (cf. Exod. 21.28-32, 33-34, 35-36; 22.1 [Hebrew 21.37], 5-6; 23.10-11). However, Wright,[2] Riesener[3] and Kaufman[4] suggest that the law in Exod. 21.2-6 refers to a landless alien (Wright?)[5] or Israelite (Riesener, Kaufman) who is forced to sell himself because he can no longer maintain himself. However, this interpretation is not convincing, for the following reasons. First, I have already noted above that it does not make much sense to release landless people, since they would most likely only be forced to find support in another household.[6] Secondly, the only evidence that suggests that Exod. 21.2 refers to landless people (or aliens) is the Nuzian service contracts which I have shown to be unconvincing. Thirdly, I noted in Chapter 4 that, while it is clear that

house, in broad daylight, shall weigh out 10 shekels silver. (He) who will be seized at night in the house—he shall die, he shall not live.'

1. LH §117 does not envisage the surrender of a thief, since in LH §8 a thief who is unable to make restitution is put to death.

2. Wright, 'What Happened Every Seven Years II', pp. 195-201.

3. Riesener, *Der Stamm* עבד, p. 125.

4. Kaufman, 'Social Welfare Systems of Ancient Israel'. pp. 277-86; cf. also E. Lipiński, 'L' "esclave hébreu"', *VT* 26 (1975), pp. 121-22, who suggests that the status of the Hebrew slave was identical to that of the 'Assyrien' who is mentioned in MAL A §44.

5. Wright, 'What Happened Every Seven Years, II', pp. 196, 199-200. Wright appears to suggest that Exod. 21.2-6 originally referred to landless aliens who were forced to seek service in an Israelite household, while Deut. 15.12-18 refers to landless Israelites, since by the time the deuteronomist drafted this law Israelites no longer could hold on to their patrimony. Cp. *God's People in God's Land*, pp. 254-55, in which Wright appears now to suggest that the term עברי refers to both an alien and Israelite landless class in both Exod. 21.2-6 and Deut. 15.12-18.

6. It is possible, though, that while in the service of a household a 'debt-slave' could learn a trade that would enable him or her to earn a livelihood once released. But this would be the exception rather than the rule.

during the Monarchic period Israelites were often forced to sell all of their land, the biblical legal corpora stresses the importance of the maintenance of patrimony among the Israelites (*Bodenrecht*), since Yahweh was the ultimate owner of the land—the people were Yahweh's *Nutzniesser* in the promised land (cf. Lev. 25.23).[1] The presence of a *Bodenrecht* makes it very unlikely that the law in Exod. 21.2-6 refers to landless Israelites, especially since this regulation occurs in the Covenant Code which belongs to the narrative depicting Yahweh's covenant with his people.[2]

3. LH §117 refers specifically to the sale of a dependent of a debtor. Similarly, I suggest that Exod. 21.2-6 (and Deut. 15.12-18) envisaged cases in which the head of a family, who likely belonged to a nuclear or multiple or extended household, defaulted on his agricultural loan and sold his son (or his son and his wife) in order to pay this loan. It is likely that the amount received from the sale of this dependent was equivalent to the price paid for a chattel-slave. The original debt would then be extinguished with the money obtained by this sale.[3] This situation is similar to that envisaged in Exod. 21.7-11, in which a

---

1. Cf. W. Brueggemann, 'On Land-losing and Land-receiving', *Dialog* 19 (1980), pp. 166-73; Wright, *God's People in God's Land*, chs. 1–4.

2. This point is further elaborated on by C.J.H. Wright, 'The Israelite Household and the Decalogue: The Social Background and Significance of some Commandments', *TynBul* 30 (1979), pp. 101-24, who asks why the Ten Commandments, which contain general moral obligations, occur at the precise foundation of the Israelite nation as a covenant people? He writes: 'I want to suggest that, for at least some of the social commandments, the answer lies in the nature of the socio-economic grounding of the covenant relationship. The relationship between Israel and Yahweh was not merely a conceptualized, spiritual entity. It was very deeply rooted in the concrete circumstances of Israel's life—social, economic and political. The primary symbol of this was the land, and its primary locus of tangible realization of the privileges and responsibilities of the covenant relationship was the family. My intention is that the fifth (parents), seventh (adultery), eighth (stealing) and tenth (coveting) commandments should be seen within their specifically Israelite context, as designed to protect, externally and internally, the household-plus-land units upon which the covenant relationship, humanly speaking, rested' (p. 102). It seems that these observations should also hold true for the manumission law in Exod. 21.2-6, which is also intimately connected to the foundation of the Israelite nation as a covenant people. Wright, however, does not place this law within a specifically Israelite context, according to which this law can also be seen to protect the household-plus-land units.

3. Cf. Driver and Miles, *Babylonian Laws*, I, p. 219 n. 2.

father is forced to sell his daughter as a wife or concubine, although, as I will show below, this law envisages a different type of sale than that envisaged in LH §117.

While the above discussion suggests that Exod. 21.2-6 envisages the sale of dependents, Wright[1] and Mendelsohn,[2] both of whom note the similarity between Exod. 21.2-6 and LH §117, suggest that this law nevertheless envisages the sale of the debtor himself. However, this view is not convincing, for the following reasons. First, while in practice the head of a nuclear, multiple or extended household could be subject to arrest or sale by a creditor, LH §117 most likely does not envisage the sale of the head of the household. Secondly, as Mendelsohn[3] himself points out, cases of self-sale among natives is only attested during periods of extreme economic crisis, such as the crisis that occurred during the reign of Rim-Sin (OB period; cf. YOS 5,132; 8,17; 8,31), although from the time of Hammurabi onwards self-sale is rarely attested.[4] However, as we saw above in Chapter 3, the sale of dependents was very common in the ancient Near East. Although Mendelsohn notes correctly that the Nuzian service contracts envisage a kind of self-sale although the two contracts are very different, I have shown that these service contracts bear little resemblance to the biblical manumission law in Exod. 21.2-6. Thirdly, cases of self-sale, which included the sale of entire families, was most likely facilitated by the loss of means of production (e.g. loss of land), a condition that is not envisaged in LH §117 (nor in Exod. 21.2-6). While this condition is envisaged in Lev. 25.39-54, which I will discuss in more detail in Chapter 8, it is my contention that this law deals with a much more serious type of insolvency than that envisaged in Exod. 21.2-6 (or Deut. 15.12-18). Fourthly, I observed in Chapter 2 that LH placed stringent restrictions on the taking of a distraint or pledge which was deemed essential to the existence of the debtor. Therefore, I suggested that LH §117 most likely did not envisage the sale of head of a household, since he was probably deemed essential to the existence of the family. Similarly, the biblical legal corpora placed stringent restrictions upon the taking of a pledge (cf. Deut. 24.6, 12-

---

1. Wright, 'What Happened Every Seven Years, II', p. 196.
2. Mendelsohn, *Slavery in the Ancient Near East*, pp. 18, 89.
3. Mendelsohn, *Slavery in the Ancient Near East*, pp. 14-16.
4. Cf. Cardellini, *Die biblischen 'Sklaven'-Gesetze*, pp. 94-95.

13). I will examine these regulations in more detail in Chapter 7. Therefore, it is doubtful that Exod. 21.2-6 envisaged the sale of the head of a household on account of debt, especially since the loss of the head of a nuclear family, which is the most common type of family in the ancient Near East, would leave the family without adequate leadership and would seriously decrease the labour force of the family. Although the biblical law does envisage the sale of a married man (Exod. 21.3b), which suggests that the debtor is the head of the household, it is nevertheless likely that this is a reference to a dependent of a multiple or extended household, especially since no children are mentioned in this stipulation. This would account for the secondary position of this condition in v. 3, since these households were less common than nuclear households.

Several scholars have noted that the manumission laws in Exod. 21.2-6 and Deut. 15.12-18 are similar to the law in LH §117, since they both limit the service of a debt-slave. In both cases the amount of money received for the sale of a person is repaid by the service of the debt-slave. This is made clear in Exod. 21.2b by the use of the expression חנם 'without payment', which most likely refers to the exemption of paying money to the creditor upon the debt-slave's release, since the debt has been paid by the service of the debt-slave. Although these laws stipulate different periods of service they both attempted to prevent debt-slaves from becoming the permanent property of their owners—both laws envisaged only the sale of the capacity of work of a debt-slave (*Arbeitskraft*).[1] That such stipulations are found only in these two legal collections strongly suggests that both laws have similar purposes. However, the seventh-year release in the biblical law needs further clarification.

Scholars[2] generally agree that the seventh-year release is somehow

---

1. Contra Noordtzij, *Leviticus*, p. 259; Porter, *Leviticus*, p. 205; Cohen, 'Slavery', col. 1655; Saalschütz, *Mosaisches Recht*, pp. 697-717.

2. For example, see Dillmann, *Exodus*, p. 226; Driver, *Exodus*, p. 210; Heinisch, *Exodus*, p. 164; Cassuto, *Exodus*, pp. 190-91; Noth, *Exodus*, p. 185; North, *Sociology of the Biblical Jubilee*, p. 184; Fensham, *Exodus*, p. 147; Cole, *Exodus*, p. 165; Craigie, *Deuteronomy*, p. 238; Cardellini, *Die biblischen 'Sklaven'-Gesetze*, p. 246. Contra Lemche, 'The Hebrew Slave', pp. 129-44; *idem*, 'The Manumission of Slaves', pp. 43-45; *idem*, 'The Hebrew and the Seven Year Cycle', pp. 70-71, who, in his attempt to demonstrate that the debt-slave law in Exod. 21.2-6 does not contain any Israelite institutions, suggests that the seven-year release is not associated with the Sabbath or Sabbatical year but rather understands

associated with the Sabbath (cf. Exod. 20.8-10; Deut. 5.12-13) and Fallow or Sabbatical year (cf. Exod. 23.10-11; Deut. 15.1-3; Lev. 25.1-7), although the release was not simultaneous or identical with the Fallow year in Exod. 23.10-11.[1] Further, the Sabbatical year in Deut. 15.1-3 is closely associated with the manumission law in Deut. 15.12-18, both of which I will examine in Chapter 7. Lastly, the Fallow or Sabbatical year is connected to the Jubilee year in Lev. 25.8-17 (and also with the debt-slave law in vv. 39-54), both of which I will examine in Chapter 7. The Sabbath and Fallow-Sabbatical years were based on religious rather than economic considerations. That the biblical legislation probably reflected more of a concern for religious continuity than practical application can be substantiated by comparing the average mean price of chattel-slaves with the amount of money a debt-slave would earn in six years (assuming that the service of a debt-slave was similar to that of a hired worker[2]). As Wenham[3] shows, the price of chattel-slaves can be gleaned from the valuations given for males and females in Lev. 25.2-8. Thus a male aged between 5 and 20 years cost 20 shekels, while a female of the same age cost 10 shekels. Further, a male aged between 20 and 60 years cost 50 shekels, while a female of the same age was 30. Assuming that a debt-slave was between the ages of 5 and 60 (although a dependent would rarely be

the number '7' as a round number indicating no precise date of manumission. However, this suggestion is totally unconvincing.

1. For example, see Dillmann, *Exodus*, p. 226; Driver, *Exodus*, p. 210; Heinisch, *Exodus*, p. 164; J. Morgenstern, Covenant Code II', *HUCA* 7 (1930), pp. 40-41; Clamer, *Exodus*, p. 187; Gispen, *Exodus*, p. 206; Cardellini, *Die biblischen 'Sklaven'-Gesetze*, p. 245 n. 21; Phillips, 'The Laws of Slavery: Exodus 21:2-11', pp. 57-59. Contra Fensham, *Exodus*, p. 147, who suggests that the seventh-year release is associated with the Sabbatical year. However, there is no textual evidence that the debt-slave release in Exod. 21.2 was associated with the Sabbatical year. Further, such a universal release is not very practical, since a creditor would be unlikely to purchase the service of a debt-slave close to the end of a Sabbatical year cycle, since he could acquire another for the same price at the beginning of a Sabbatical year cycle. Finally, it is clear that LH §117 did not envisage a universal release. Such universal releases are, however, evident in both the *mēšarum* edicts and the debt-slave law in Lev. 25.39-54 which I will discuss in Chapter 8.

2. Cf. Driver and Miles, *Babylonian Laws*, I, p. 217.

3. G.J. Wenham, 'Leviticus 27:2-8 and the Price of Slaves', *ZAW* 90 (1978), pp. 264-65; *Leviticus*, p. 338.

above the age of 40) the average price would be 35 shekels for a male and 15 shekels for a female—the mean average for both would be 25 shekels.[1] This mean average is similar to the mean average prices set in LH §§116, 214, 252 (20 shekels), in Ugarit (40 shekels) and in Syria (30 shekels) (fourteenth century BCE).[2]

Unfortunately, we do not have any records that indicate the rate of pay for a hired man in Israel. Nevertheless, based on LH, whose valuations for slaves is similar to those in biblical legislation, the rate of pay for free workers ranged from 6 to 11 shekels per year, although extant OB contracts show that pay ranged from 10 to 14 shekels per year.[3] Assuming that the average was about 12 shekels per year,[4] it would take about three years to work off the debt. While this figure reflects the amount of service required in LH §117, the Israelite debt-slave is required to work about twice as long. This calculation is probably very nearly accurate since according to the motivation clause in Deut. 15.18ab the debt-slave's service was likely worth twice as that of much as a hired hand.[5] Verse 18a reads:

---

1. Although Exod. 21.2-6 does not mention the sale of a woman I suggest that this law nevertheless presupposes such a sale. See below the discussion of Exod. 21.7-11.

2. Cf. Mendelsohn, *Slavery in the Ancient Near East*, pp. 117-20. That the biblical prices reflect the price of chattel-slaves during the first and second millennium is suggested by Wenham, 'Leviticus 27.2-8 and the Price of Slaves', p. 264. The price of slaves greatly increased during the Persian NB and NA periods (Mendelsohn, pp. 117-18).

3. Cf. Driver and Miles, *Babylonian Laws*, I, pp. 469-78; H. Farber, 'A Price and Wage Study for North Babylonia during the Old Babylonian Period', *JESHO* 21 (1978), pp. 1-51.

4. Cf. Mendelsohn, *Slavery in the Ancient Near East*, p. 118; de Vaux, *Ancient Israel*, p. 76, who suggest that the average wage for a hired man in the Chaldean and in the Persian periods was 12 shekels per year.

5. Cf. Zakovitch, *'For Three . . . and for Four'*, pp. xxv-xxvi; and Mendelsohn, 'Slavery in the Old Testament', p. 388; *idem, Slavery in the Ancient Near East*, pp. 32-33, who suggest that this verse indicates that the biblical compiler was aware of LH §117. Cf. also A. Phillips, 'Double for all her Sins', *ZAW* 82 (1982), pp. 130-32; and *idem*, 'The Laws of Slavery: Exodus 21:2-11', p. 65 n. 28, who notes that LI §14 also prescribes service that is worth twice as much as the incurred debt. Cp. von Rad, *Deuteronomy*, p. 108; Craigie, *Deuteronomy*, p. 239 n. 17, and Mayes, *Deuteronomy*, pp. 252-53; all of whom suggest that the the term משנה should be rendered 'equivalent to' (cf. NEB) based on the use of *mištannu* in texts from Alalakh (see M. Tsevat, 'Alalakhiana', *HUCA* 29 [1958],

לא־יקשה בעינך בשלחך אתו חפשי מעמך כי משנה
שכר שכיר עבדך שש שנים

Do not consider it hardship to let your servant free, because his service
has been worth twice as much as that of a hired hand.

Recapitulating, the above discussion shows that the debt-slave law in
Exod. 21.2-6 is very similar to the law found in LH §117, both of
which prevented debt-slaves, who were the dependents of defaulting
debtors, from becoming the permanent property of creditors. I have
argued that this interpretation is to be preferred over those that
attempt to compare this biblical law with the Nuzian service and loan
contracts. However, as we saw above, this biblical law does contain
stipulations that are unique to the biblical legal collection, the most
important of which is the stipulation that allows a Hebrew debt-slave
to become the permanent servant of his or her owner. To this unique
stipulation we now turn.

Exod. 21.5-6: The Procedure for Entering into Permanent Slavery

5 ואם־אמר יאמר העבד אהבתי את־אדני את־אשתי ואת־בני לא אצא חפשי:
6 והגישו אדניו אל־האלהים והגישו אל־הדלת או אל־המזוזה
ורצע אדניו את־אזנו במרצע ועבדו לעלם:

5 And if the slave says, 'I love my lord, my wife, and my children, I will
not go out free,'
6 then the lord shall bring him to God and bring him to the door or
doorpost, and the lord shall pierce his ear with a rod, and he shall serve
him forever.

As we saw above, the secondary case in vv. 5-6 (ואם) is subordinate
to v. 4, which discusses the situation when the lord gives his debt-
slave a wife. The conditional half of v. 5 contains the slave's
declaration to remain with his lord and family, while the contingent
actions, which outline what the lord is to do when his slave declares
that he does not want to go out free, are found in v. 6. The expression
ואם־אמר יאמר העבד in v. 5a contains the construction inf. absolute +

pp. 109-26). Cf. also Japhet, 'The Relationship between the Legal Corpora', p. 83
n. 59, who notes that a consensus of opinion has not been reached. Lastly, refer to
J.M. Lindenberger, 'How Much for a Hebrew Slave? The Meaning of *MIŠNEH* in
Deuteronomy 15:18', *JBL* 110 (1991), pp. 479-82, who suggests that *mištannu* is
not a Semitic word, and that the expression משנה שכר שכיר is not a legal term at all
(cf. LI §14, which is not specific about the amount of compensation), although he
concludes that this Hebrew expression has the sense of 'double'.

imperfect which is also found in many of the laws of the Covenant Code (in the protasis: 21.5; 22.3, 11, 16, 22; 23.22; and the apodosis: 21.12, 19, 20, 28). This construction is probably used in v. 5 in order to emphasize the importance of the condition in relation to the consequences listed in v. 6.[1] Thus the slave must be willing to declare that he wishes to revoke his freedom in order that he can become a permanent slave. Further, v. 5 clarifies that the reason why the slave wishes to become a permanent slave is that he loves his lord, his wife and children. As Cardellini[2] and Lohfink[3] correctly point out, this provision is unique to the biblical corpora. However, Paul has compared the slave's declaration (v. 5) and the two rituals in v. 6 with similar practices found at Nuzi. Furthermore, there is some question concerning the intentions of a slave who wishes to remain in servitude. To these important issues we now turn.

The meaning of the slave's declaration in Exod. 21.5. In v. 5 the slave declares:

אהבתי את־אדני את־אשתי ואת־בני לא אצא חפשי

I love my lord, my wife, and my children, I will not go out free.

According to this declaration, the reason(s) why the debt-slave wishes to remain in servitude is because he loves his lord, wife, and his children. While several scholars have accepted the plain meaning of this declaration,[4] Childs,[5] who notes the apparent harshness of the stipulation in v. 4 which does not permit the slave's wife to leave with her husband, concludes that the love that the slave has for his master should not be romanticized. Similarly, Daube[6] suggests that the time

---

1. Cf. GKC §113o; and Driver, *Exodus*, pp. 210-11. Driver therefore suggests that the translation 'plainly' in v. 5 (RSV, NIV, NASB) should be omitted, since it inadequately represents the idiomatic use of the inf. abs. in the expression of a condition.

2. Cardellini, *Die biblischen 'Sklaven'-Gesetze*, p. 248 n. 30.

3. Lohfink, 'חפשׁי', col. 127.

4. Cf. Noth, *Exodus*, p. 178; Durham, *Exodus*, p. 311; Gispen, *Exodus*, pp. 206-207; Holzinger, *Exodus*, p. 82; Heinisch, *Exodus*, p. 164; Cassuto, *Exodus*, p. 267; G. Beer and K. Galling, *Exodus* (HKAT, 1.3; Tübingen: Mohr, 1939), p. 108.

5. Childs, *Exodus*, p. 468.

6. D. Daube, *The Exodus Pattern in the Bible* (ASSt, 2; London: Faber & Faber, 1963), p. 48.

when Pharaoh used the Israelite women and children as hostages to guarantee that the Israelite men would not escape (Exod. 10.9-10) is parallel to the so-called attempt by a lord to keep his slave in his service by keeping his wife and children. However, these interpretations are not convincing, since this law sets forth the rights of both the slave and master (primary law). Thus the lord has the right to keep both the wife, whom he has given to his slave, and also the children, since it is likely that the wife was a chattel-slave who remained the property of the lord.[1] While this aspect of the law appears harsh it merely reflects a legal right held by any owner of female chattel-slaves. The law also states that the slave has the right to remain in servitude in order to stay with his wife. However, since the law clearly sets forth the rights of both parties it is unlikely that the lord has given his debt-slave a wife in order to 'trick' him into staying. It is more likely that the slave has taken a wife with the intention of remaining in his lord's household as a permanent slave. Therefore, the wording of the declaration is significant, since it clearly shows that the slave's love for his lord was the principal reason for remaining, although the offer of a wife may have been an added incentive for the debt-slave to remain in his owner's service.[2]

This latter incentive may be explained by the fact that crop yields were often dependent upon the amount of available labour there was, particularly in the highlands where Israelite farmers were forced to engage in intensive agriculture which demanded more labour than did similar farmers in the lowlands.[3] As I have noted in Chapter 4, the size of an Israelite nuclear household during the Settlement period probably numbered around four members. Therefore, more prosperous farmers who could afford to buy a debt-slave(s) were able to increase their yields by employing more labour. A similar strategy can be found in the narrative in Genesis 29–31, in which Jacob is forced to work in Laban's household for seven years in order to

---

1. Cf. also Jackson, 'Some Literary Features of the Mishpatim', pp. 235-36; Durham, *Exodus*, p. 311; Cole, *Exodus*, p. 165; Baentsch, *Exod-Lev-Num*, p. 189; and Boecker, *Administration of Justice*, p. 159, who compares this marriage to the Roman *contubernium* which allowed a male slave to enter into marriage with a female slave, since a slave did not have the right to enter into a marriage.

2. Cf. Beer and Galling, *Exodus*, p. 108.

3. Cf. Hopkins, *The Highlands of Canaan*, pp. 42-52, 213-61, and esp. 265-75.

marry his daughter Rachel. Laban, however, deceives Jacob by giving him Leah, thus forcing him to work an additional seven years in order to marry Rachel. This narrative demonstrates that the head of a household could attempt to secure male labour by offering his daughter as a wife in return for service. Therefore, the woman whom the owner gave to his debt-slave in Exod. 21.4 could have been his own daughter who remained with him if the debt-slave left his service. The fact that the law in Exod. 21.4 only refers to the woman as an אשה leaves the identity of the woman unclear. While legal parallels make it likely that the woman is a chattel-slave, it is nevertheless possible that this stipulation refers to the daughter of the owner, who gives her as a wife in order to secure the labour of his debt-slave, especially since Jacob released himself from his service to Laban in the seventh year (Gen. 31.41)—the year in which a debt-slave is manumitted in Exod. 21.2. Although the number 'seven' is ubiquitous both in the law and narrative of the Pentateuch, the fact that it is only used in connection with service in Genesis 29–31 and the debt-slave laws in Exodus and Deuteronomy (Jer. 34) more than suggests that the law in Exodus may have the background of Genesis 29–31 in mind.

The above interpretations are therefore to be preferred over that of Childs and Daube, since they have the advantage of removing the supposed harshness of the stipulation in v. 4,[1] and treat the slave's declaration as a sincere request[2] reflecting his true feelings towards both his master and his wife and children. That the state of permanent servitude was only entered into when the debt-slave loved his lord is consonant with the other laws which vigorously protected the rights of slaves and the oppressed (cf. esp. Deut. 23.15-16 [Hebrew vv. 16-17]), which stipulates that runaway slaves are to receive refuge). While the declaration in v. 5 demonstrates that the principal reason for remaining a slave was the attachments the debt-slave has formed

---

1. Cp. Patrick, *Old Testament Law*, p. 113; Noth, *Exodus*, p. 177; Driver, *Deuteronomy*, pp. 182-83; von Rad, *Deuteronomy*, p. 107; all of whom suggest that the deuteronomist repealed this stipulation in Deut. 15.12-18 on account of its unhumanitarian disposition.

2. Cf. Holzinger, *Exodus*, p. 82; Heinisch, *Exodus*, p. 164; and Durham, *Exodus*, p. 311, who note that one of the reasons why the slave does not wish to leave is that he loves his wife and children; they nevertheless do not attempt to minimize the slave's love for his lord.

with his lord, there have been two other important suggestions made concerning the nature of this declaration. To these suggestions we now turn.

First, several commentators suggest that another reason why the slave would choose to remain a slave has to do with his prospects as a free man. Noth,[1] for example, notes that a slave could possibly do better as a slave than as a free man. Similarly, Hyatt,[2] Daube,[3] Clements,[4] Cole,[5] Phillips[6] and Heinisch[7] suggest that many slaves would prefer to face slavery than the possibility of poverty even though free. Lastly, Keil[8] suggests that in certain circumstances releasing a slave may be an act of cruelty rather than of love, for a slave may not have the means to support himself once he is released. While the above suggestions are certainly possible, especially since Deut. 15.16 appears to suggest that one of the reasons why the slave wishes to remain is that he is well off with his lord (ואתדביתך כי־טוב לו עמך), a qualification must be made. There is nothing in the context of Exod. 21.2-6, or Deut 15.12-18 for that matter, to suggest that fear of poverty or destitution is the reason the slave does not wish to go out free. If such considerations were paramount, why would the law in Deut. 15.12-18 retain the provision to remain a slave when it stipulates that released slaves must be provided for upon release? Surely, if poverty was the principal reason for remaining a slave, then the deuteronomist would have left out this provision.[9] Therefore, while it is possible that one of the reasons a slave would choose to

1. Noth, *Exodus*, p. 178
2. Hyatt, *Exodus*, p. 229.
3. Daube, *The Exodus Pattern*, p. 49.
4. R.E. Clements, *Exodus* (CBC; Cambridge: Cambridge University Press, 1972), pp. 132-33.
5. Cole, *Exodus*, p. 166.
6. A. Phillips, 'Some Aspects of Family Law in Pre-Exilic Israel', *VT* 23 (1973), p. 357; 'The Laws of Slavery', p. 51.
7. Heinisch, *Exodus*, p. 164.
8. Keil, *Pentateuch*, p. 373; cf. also Craigie, *Deuteronomy*, pp. 238 n. 12, 239 n. 15.
9. Cf. Clements, *Exodus*, pp. 132-33; and Mayes, *Deuteronomy*, p. 249, both of whom suggest that Deut. 15.13-14 represented an attempt to help a released debt-slave establish himself as a free citizen by providing provisions, but who nevertheless do not explain why the deuteronomist has retained the provision to remain a slave.

remain in servitude was fear of destitution, it is clear that the slave's declaration must demonstrate that he chooses to remain because he has formed a close relationship to his lord, not because he has no other choice.[1] Furthermore, in most cases dependents would return to their family, where their labour would be needed in order to prevent their families from falling into debt again.[2]

Secondly, that the slave's declaration in v. 5 is a formal request that may have some legal connotations has been suggested by Dillmann,[3] McNeile[4] and Gispen[5]. Similarly, Paul has observed the legal connotations of the slave's declaration, although we have already seen above that his comparison of the biblical declaration with the declaration made by a *tidennu* in a Nuzi *tidennūtu* contract is unconvincing. Nevertheless, this does not mean that the slave's declaration is not a formal request, for I will argue below that the declaration in v. 5 was probably an oath that was ratified in the ceremony in v. 6b. What I am suggesting at the present moment, though, is that the slave's declaration or oath is sincere and reflected his feelings for his master and wife accurately. There is no suggestion that the slave has been compelled to declare his 'allegiance' to his lord in order to meet some legal requirement so that he might stay with his wife and children.

The meaning of the two rituals in Exod. 21.6. Verse 6 stipulates what the lord is to do when his slave declares that he does not wish to go out free:

והגישו אדניו אל־האלהים והגישו אל־הדלת או אל־המזוזה
ורצע אדניו את־אזנו במרצע ועבדו לעלם:

then the lord shall bring him to God and bring him to the door or doorpost, and the lord shall pierce his ear with a rod, and he shall serve him forever.

---

1. Cp. Craigie, *Deuteronomy*, p. 239 n. 15, who suggests that a blind debt-slave might have preferred to remain in a household. However, it is difficult to envisage a blind debt-slave since he would probably not be able to work.

2. The fact that labour was often very important to the Israelites suggests that the slave who decides to become a permanent slave came from an extended household, since the survival of such a household may not have depended on the release of one dependent.

3. Dillmann, *Exodus*, p. 26.

4. McNeile, *Exodus*, p. 127.

5. Gispen, *Exodus*, p. 207.

The term האלהים is a *crux interpretum* and has been interpreted to mean either (1) household gods (Penates); (2) 'judges'; or (3) God (who is located in the sanctuary).

1. האלהים = *household gods (Penates)*. Many scholars suggest that the term האלהים probably refers to the Penates or household gods that were placed by the door of houses (cf. Gen. 3.5).[1] Although Driver[2] notes that the term האלהים might refer to 'God' (i.e. the slave is taken to the sanctuary), he nevertheless suggests that the second clause refers to the door or doorpost of the lord's house, since it is reasonable that the ceremony for binding a slave to the lord's household would take place at his house.[3] Furthermore, Driver suggests that the first clause cannot refer to the sanctuary but must refer also to the lord's house, since the two clauses are closely connected (*waw copulative*).[4] The

1. For those who suggest that the term אלהים in Exod. 21.6 refers to housegods, see Paul, *Book of the Covenant*, pp. 50 and ns. 4-5, 51 and ns. 1-4; Phillips, *Ancient Israel's Criminal Law*, pp. 60-61, 74-75; *idem*, 'Some Aspects of Family Law in Pre-Exilic Israel', p. 357; *idem*, 'The Laws of Slavery: Exodus 21:2-11', p. 52; Driver, *Exodus*, p. 211; A.E. Draffkorn, '*Ilâni*/Elohim', *JBL* 76 (1957), pp. 216-24; Beer and Galling, *Exodus*, p. 108; Baentsch, *Exod-Lev-Num*, p. 190; C.H. Gordon, *The World of the Old Testament* (Garden City, NY: Doubleday, 2nd edn, 1958), p. 129; *idem*, 'אלהים in its Reputed Meaning of Rulers, Judges', *JBL* 54 (1935), pp. 134-44; *idem*, 'Parallèles nouziens aux lois et coutumes de l'Ancien Testament', *RB* 49 (1935), pp. 34-41; *idem*, 'The Study of Jacob and Laban in the Light of the Nuzi Tablets', *BASOR* 66 (1937), pp. 25-27; *idem*, 'Biblical Customs and the Nuzi Tablets', pp. 5-6; B.D. Eerdmans, 'The Book of the Covenant and the Decalogue', *ExpTim* 8 (1919), p. 136.

2. Driver, *Exodus*, p. 211.

3. Cf. also A.B. Ehrlich, *Randglossen zur hebräischen Bibel*, I (Leipzig, 1908), p. 348, who writes: 'Die Türe ist derjenige Teil des Hauses, der nicht vermieden werden kann. Darum soll die hier vorgeschriebene Operation an der Türe und den Pfosten vollzogen werden, damit der Sklave, aus eingehend, durch den Anblick der daran zurückgelasseneb Spuren der Durchbohrung an die Liebe und den Gehorsam erinnert wird, die er seinem Herrn geschworen.'

4. Cf. GKC §§104 d-g, 154a. Cp. Gispen, *Exodus*, p. 207, who notes the possibility of Driver's view but rejects it nevertheless, since he suggests that the actions took place before God in the sanctuary. Cp. Driver, *Deuteronomy*, p. 184, who writes: 'In Ex. 21⁶ (see above) the slave is to be brought "unto God", i.e. to the sanctuary at which judgement is administered, and then led (probably by the judge) to the door or the door-post (whether of the sanctuary, or of his master's house, is not clearly expressed), where the ceremony symbolizing his perpetual servitude is

ceremony in v. 6 therefore has the symbolic effect of bringing the slave into a relation of dependence on the gods of his lord's family, and of admitting the slave to the full 'religious privileges' of the family.[1] However, as I will argue below, it is not necessary to suggest that the initial or subsequent ritual took place at the lord's house. Nevertheless, Driver's interpretation has remained an influential one ever since the discovery of adoption texts from Nuzi which illustrate the legal and social functions of the Ilani or household gods. To a discussion of these texts we now turn.

In 1957 Draffkorn[2] published a comprehensive study in which she compared the Ilani of Nuzi with the אלהים/תרפים of the Old Testament, particularly Exod. 21.6 and 22.7-10 (Hebrew vv. 6-10). Her study is based upon the examination of several Nuzi adoption texts, particularly Gadd 51,[3] which reads:

> Tablet of adoption, whereby Naswa, son of Aršenni, has adopted Wullu, son of Buhišenni. So long as Naswa is alive, Wullu will give him food and clothing, and when Naswa [the adopter] is dead, Wullu [the adopter] will give him a burial. If there be a son of Naswa, he shall divide [the estate] equally with Wullu, and the gods of Naswa the son of Naswa shall take. But if there be no son of Naswa then Wullu shall take also the gods of Naswa. Also he has given his daughter Nuhuia to Wullu to wife; if Wullu shall take another wife he shall vacate the lands and houses of Naswa. Whoever infringes [the agreement] shall pay in full one mina of silver and one of gold.

On the basis of this text and others like it, Draffkorn suggests that one of the main functions that the Ilani performed at Nuzi was that they were used as symbols of the right of property (e.g. inheritance).[4] She suggests that in domestic law the Ilani were passed on to the son as a symbolic title to the family property. This usage has particular relevance for the interpretation of Genesis 31, which concerns

performed by his master'. These comments date to 1901, which is earlier than his revised view found in his commentary on Exodus (1911).

1. Cf. Baentsch, *Exod-Lev-Num*, p. 190.

2. Draffkorn, '*Ilâni*/Elohim', pp. 216-24.

3. C.J. Gadd, 'Tablets from Kirkuk', *RA* 23 (1926), p. 127 no. 5. Draffkorn, '*Ilâni*/Elohim', pp. 220-22, also examines Gadd 5 and HSS XIV 108, both of which demonstrate that the eldest sons are given the household gods.

4. The other main function of the Ilani, which is not pertinent to the present discussion, is that persons would swear an oath before the Ilani when the judges did not have enough evidence to determine a verdict.

Rachel's theft of the אלהים/תרפים from Laban,[1] and of the term האלהים in Exod. 21.6. Draffkorn suggests that the term האלהים in Exod. 21.6 refers to the Ilani, and that the ceremony before the Ilani/האלהים symbolically makes the slave a member of the lord's household, and, in so doing, he becomes part of the family estate. Furthermore, she also dismisses the view that the term האלהים refers to 'God', since this term is used in Exod. 22.8 (Hebrew v. 7) with the plural verb (ירשיען). She thus suggests that the term האלהים in 22.8 (Hebrew v. 7) refers to the communal Ilani which witness the oaths in cases where there is insufficient evidence to determine a verdict.

Similarly, Paul[2] suggests that the term האלהים referred originally to the Ilani and that the ceremony in Exod. 21.6 brought the slave within the family estate, and, on the basis of Ur III and OB documents which illustrate that symbols of deities were stationed near the doors of chapels and alongside houses, he suggests that it is possible that the האלהים were stationed by the doors of private houses. Furthermore, Paul and Phillips[3] have followed Draffkorn in asserting that the references to האלהים in Exodus 21–22 (21.6; 22.7, 8 [Hebrew vv. 6, 7]) refer to the Ilani of Nuzi,[4] although it should be pointed out that

---

1. Cf. the earlier works of E.A. Speiser, *Mesopotamian Origins* (Philadelphia: University of Pennsylvania; London: Oxford University Press, 1930), p. 162; and Gordon, 'The Study of Jacob and Laban in the Light of the Nuzi Tablets', p. 26; *idem*, 'Paralléles nouziens aux lois', pp. 35-36; *idem*, 'Biblical Customs and the Nuzi Tablets', pp. 5-7; *idem*, 'The Patriarchal Narratives', *JNES* 13 (1954), p. 56; *idem*, *Adventures in the Near East* (London: Phoenix House, 1957), pp. 119-20, both of whom suggest that inheritance was guaranteed by the possession of the אלהים/תרפים, although while they suggest that possession of these gods made Jacob heir to Laban's property, Draffkorn suggests that Rachel was heir. The former view has been adopted by many scholars; cf. C.H. Gordon, 'Erēbu Marriage', in *Studies on the Civilization and Culture of Nuzi and the Hurrians* (ed. M.A. Morrison and D.I. Owen; Winona Lake, IN: Eisenbrauns, 1981), pp. 155-60; *idem*, 'On Making Other Gods', in *Biblical and Related Studies Presented to Samuel Iwry* (ed. A. Kort and S. Mirschauser; Winona Lake, IN: Eisenbrauns, 1985), p. 78.

2. Paul, *Book of the Covenant*, pp. 50-51 and ns. 2-3. Cf. Judg. 18.14, which states that the תרפים were stationed in the house.

3. Phillips, *Ancient Israel's Criminal Law*, pp. 136-37, also cites the plural verb ירשיען as evidence that האלהים refers to the תרפים (p. 136); cf. also H.C. Brichto, 'Kin, Cult, Land and Afterlife–A Biblical Complex', *HUCA* 44 (1973), p. 46 n. 74.

4. Cf. also K. Seybold, 'תרפים', *Theologisches Handwörterbuch zum Alten*

the use of the plural verb in Exod. 22.8 (Hebrew v. 7) does not necessarily demonstrate that an identical meaning should be accepted for the other occurrences of the term האלהים.

Nevertheless, regarding the interpretation of Gadd 51 and the term האלהים, Greenberg,[1] who has been followed recently by several scholars,[2] presents substantial arguments against Draffkorn's interpretation. He has argued that the household gods in Gadd 51 and texts like it do not actually refer to symbols of inheritance but refer to the position of *pater familias* (or perhaps head of the household),[3] since when the property is divided between Wullu (adopted son) and the son of Našwi, the household gods are not divided as well but go with the son of Našwi. Similarly, Thompson concurs with Greenberg's conclusion that the household gods are not symbols of inheritance, although he offers a slightly different view of the role of the Ilani. He writes.[4]

> ... the bequeathal of the household gods does not determine who is to be the *pater familias*. Rather, the household gods are given to that son. In this respect, the possession of the gods does not have legal significance in its own right, and is to be compared with the possession of a family heirloom; it is secondary to the inheritance.

Recapitulating, although the Ilani did perform various functions

---

Testament, II (ed. E. Jenni and C. Westermann; Munich: Chr. Kaiser Verlag, 1976), col. 1058.

1. M. Greenberg, 'Another Look at Rachel's Theft of the Teraphim', *JBL* 81 (1962), pp. 239-48.

2. Cf. S. Greengus, 'Sisterhood Adoption at Nuzi and the "Wife-Sister" in Genesis', *HUCA* 46 (1975), p. 5 n. 3; J. Huehnergard, 'Biblical Notes on some New Akkadian Texts from Emar (Syria)', *CBQ* 47 (1985), pp. 428-34; M.J. Selman, 'Comparative Customs and the Patriarchal Age', in *Essays on the Patriarchal Narratives* (ed. A.R. Millard and D.J. Wiseman; Leicester: Inter-Varsity Press, 1980), pp. 101, 110, 132 n. 60; E. Cassin, 'Une querelle de famille', in Morrison and Owen (eds.), *Civilization and Culture of Nuzi and the Hurrians*, pp. 37-46; K. Deller, 'Die Hausgötter der Familie Sukrija S. Huja', in Morrison and Owen (eds.), *Civilization and Culture of Nuzi and the Hurrians*, pp. 47-76; M.A. Morrison, 'The Jacob and Laban Narrative in Light of Near Eastern Sources', *BA* 46 (1983), pp. 155-64, esp. 161-62; Thompson, *Historicity of the Patriarchal Narratives*, pp. 261-80.

3. This view is also considered by both Gordon, *The World of the Old Testament*, p. 129 and Draffkorn, *'Ilâni/Elohim'*, pp. 221-22.

4. Thompson, *Historicity of the Patriarchal Narratives*, p. 278.

within the home, temple and court,[1] Draffkorn's argument that the household gods were employed in the domestic law of Exod. 21.6 as symbols of inheritance cannot be substantiated from the Nuzi contract Gadd 51. There is also no evidence in the Old Testament that such a use of household gods ever existed in Israel.[2] Nevertheless, while it possible that the term האלהים in Exod. 21.6 referred to some non-legal use of the Ilani who were often found within the home, temple and court, one must wonder why the more common term תרפים was not employed instead of the less common term האלהים. Furthermore, it is difficult to imagine what function, other than the legal functions proposed by Driver and Draffkorn, these symbols performed that were relevant to the ceremony in Exod. 21.6. Lastly, it is difficult to explain why a reference to idols should appear in Exod. 21.6 (and 22.8 [Hebrew v. 7]), since Exod. 20.4-5 expressly forbids the making or worship of idols.

2. האלהים = *judges*. Ehrlich[3] suggests that the use of the plural verb in Exod. 22.8 (Hebrew v. 7) indicates that the term האלהים in Exod. 21.6 refers to judges.[4] As we saw above, it is possible that the slave was taken to a place where his oath or formal declaration in v. 5 was ratified. Therefore, it is possible that judges would have officiated at such a ceremony. However, the term האלהים in Exod. 21.6 most likely does not refer directly to judges, for the following reasons.[5]

---

1. Cf. Greenberg, 'Rachel's Theft of the Teraphim', p. 248; Paul, *Book of the Covenant*, p. 51.

2. The use of this term in Judg. 17.1-5; 18.17, 18, 20; 1 Sam. 19.13, 16 appears to fit Greenberg's, rather than Draffkorn's, explanation of the function of the תרפים.

3. Ehrlich, *Randglossen*, I, p. 350. Ehrlich (p. 348) also suggests that if the term האלהים was meant to refer to either God or to the Penates then the verse would have read הגישׁ אדניו לפני האלהים instead of הגישׁ אדניו אל־האלהים. However, while the Hiphil verb נגשׁ + the preposition אל is not used with God as object, the Qal is used with God as object in Ezek. 44.13. Further, the Hiphil verb נגשׁ + the preposition לפני is not used with God. The use of the preposition אל, therefore, appears to indicate general motion towards rather than referring to presence before (לפני).

4. Cf. also Rashi and Ibn Ezra, *ad. loc.*

5. Based on the use of the term אלהים in Exod. 21.6; 22.6ff., several scholars have suggested that in 1 Sam. 2.25; Judg. 5.8; and Ps. 82.1, 6 the term אלהים should be rendered as 'judges'; cf. HALAT 1.51. For 1 Sam. 2.25, see McCarter, *I Samuel*, p. 84; cp. Keil, *Pentateuch*, p. 38; E.F. Ward, 'Superstition and Judgement: Archaic Methods of Finding a Verdict', ZAW 89 (1977), pp. 1-19,

First, Driver[1] notes that while the term האלהים has been rendered 'judge(s)' by the Targum and Peshitta, this rendering is only a paraphrase; 'for though God, in cases such as the present, may be conceived as acting through a judge, as His representative or mouthpiece, that does not make "Elohim" *mean* judge, or judges.'[2] Secondly, Driver, Dillmann[3] and Gispen[4] correctly point out that the term (ה)אלהים is used with plural verbs elsewhere in the Old Testament (Cf. Gen. 20.13; 35.7: note that in each case the Samaritan Pentateuch has a singular verb[5]).[6] Thirdly, if the compiler of this law had wished to indicate that judges or priests were meant by the term then he would have used another term that clearly referred to judges, such as פללים[7] which is found in Exod. 21.19. Therefore, while judges

---

H.W. Hertzberg, *I and II Samuel* (OTL; London: SCM Press, 1964), p. 36. For Judg. 5.8, see G.F. Moore, *Judges* (ICC; Edinburgh: T. & T. Clark, 1895), pp. 145-47; R. Boling, *Judges* (AB; Garden City, NY: Doubleday, 1981), p. 102; cp. D.N. Freedman, *Studies in Ancient Yahwistic Poetry* (Missoula, MT: Scholars Press, 1975), and J.A. Soggin, *Judges* (OTL; Philadelphia: Westminster Press, 1981), pp. 86-87; both of whom adopt the position of P.C. Craigie, 'Some Further Notes on the Song of Deborah', *VT* 22 (1972), pp. 349-53; and D. Cundall, *Judges* (TOTC; Leicester: Inter-Varsity Press, 1968), p. 95. For Ps. 82.1.6, see M. Dahood, *Psalms, Vol 2* (AB; Garden City, NY: Doubleday, 1968), pp. 268-69, who renders the term אלהים as 'God'.

1. Driver, *Exodus*, p. 211.

2. Cf. also Gordon, 'אלהים in its Reputed Meaning of Rulers, Judges', p. 41, who dismisses the rendering 'judges' on the basis that it is a late interpretation of the Targum Onkelos.

3. Dillmann, *Exodus*, p. 236.

4. Gispen, *Exodus*, pp. 218-19.

5. Gen. 20.13: 𝔐 = והתעו; 𝔴 = התעה; Gen. 35.7: 𝔐 = נגלו; 𝔴𝔊𝔖 = נגלה

6. Cf. also O. Loretz, 'Exodus 21,6; 22,8 und angebliche Nuzi-Parallelen', *Bibl* 41 (1960), pp. 170-71 n. 3, who suggests that the plural verb ירשיעך may be a singular form because: (1) the Masoretic vocalization does not always deserve preference; (2) the vocalization of the Samaritan Pentateuch points to a singular (ירשיעו; cf. also Cazelles, *Code de l'alliance*, p. 69, who suggests that the use of the plural verb is a particular stylization of the redactor); 3) the verb can be a *nun energeticum* (cf. GKC §58i). However, Gispen, *Exodus*, p. 218 and Dillmann, *Exodus*, p. 236, note correctly that the Samaritan reading is doubtful. Therefore, it is preferable to retain the Masoretic Text reading where the verb is a *nun paragogicum* (cf. GKC §47 m).

7. In Exod. 21.19 the term פללים is often translated as 'judges'; cf. HALAT 3: 880-881. Cp. Cazelles, *Code de l'alliance*; p. 69; and Liedke, *Gestalt und Bezeichnung*, pp. 44-45, both of whom suggest that the term פללים probably refers

might have presided over the ceremony in v. 6 there is no sufficient evidence to suggest that the term הָאֱלֹהִים refers directly to judges.

3. הָאֱלֹהִים = *court, sanctuary, God.* Cassuto,[1] who follows the interpretation of the Mekilta, suggests that the term הָאֱלֹהִים refers to the court or sanctuary where the slave was brought and where his ear was bored. However, he arrives at this interpretation because he suggests that the term הָאֱלֹהִים originally referred to the idols who stood in the court of justice and remained a stereotyped term signifying the place of the court. However, scholars have not been convinced by Cassuto's suggestion since he offers no evidence to support his interpretation.

The majority of scholars, though, render the term literally as 'God' who resides in the sanctuary.[2] According to this interpretation, the slave was brought to the sanctuary in order to make a declaration under oath to remain a slave in his lord's house.[3] That such a declaration would be carried out at the sanctuary is illustrated by many ancient Near Eastern laws and documents which record that disputes and other legal cases were often brought to the temple where the parties involved gave an oath before their god(s).[4] For example,

to priests who arbitrate between the parties.

1. Cassuto, *Exodus*, p. 267.

2. For example, see Driver, *Deuteronomy*, p. 184; Z.W. Falk, 'Exodus XXI:6', *VT* 9 (1959), pp. 86-88; North, *Sociology of the Biblical Jubilee*, p. 154; Gispen, *Exodus*, pp. 218-19; Boecker, *Law and the Administration of Justice*, p. 159; Hyatt, *Exodus*, p. 229; McNeile, *Exodus*, p. 127; Lemche, 'The Hebrew Slave', p. 142 n. 61; Loretz, 'Nuzi-Parallelen', pp. 168ff.; Weinfeld, *Deuteronomy*, p. 233; J. Reider, *Deuteronomy with Commentary* (Philadelphia: The Jewish Publication Society of America, 1937), pp. 154-55; Heinisch, *Exodus*, pp. 164-65; Durham, *Exodus*, p. 321; Fontela, 'La esclavitud', p. 251.

3. Cf. Dillmann, *Exodus*, p. 226; McNeile, *Exodus*, p. 127; Keil, *Pentateuch*, p. 130; Reider, *Deuteronomy*, pp. 154-55; Gispen, *Exodus*, p. 207; Durham, *Exodus*, p. 321.

4. Cf. Z.W. Falk, 'Exodus XXI:6', pp. 86-87, who notes that slaves in Babylon were often released after participating in a ceremony at the temple of the sun-god Šamaš. He suggests that these analogies suggest that God was concerned with the manumission of slaves, especially in light of God's redemption of Israel from Egypt, and that the ceremony in Exod. 21.5-6 thus took place in the sanctuary. Cf. also Driver and Miles, *The Babylonian Laws*, I, pp. 225-26, 292-309, who note that slaves often participated in religious ceremonies in which they had their brows cleansed and then turned and faced the sunrise or an emblem or image of the god

Loretz,[1] who follows Fensham,[2] notes that legal decisions often required that an oath be given in the temple. Such an example can be found in LE §37, which reads:[3]

> If the house of the man was plundered, (and) with the goods of the deposit(or), which he had given to him, loss of the owner of the house was incurred—the owner of the house shall in the house (B: in the door) of Tispak swear to him by god: 'Together with thy goods my goods were (B: verily) lost, I have not done evil and/fraud.' He shall swear to him, and he shall have nothing upon him.

This law is similar to the law of deposit in Exod. 22.8-9 [Hebrew vv. 7-8], which also requires that an oath be sworn before האלהים, which also likely refers to the sanctuary.[4] Even though the law in Exod. 22.8-9 [Hebrew vv. 7-8] deals with theft, this law and the ceremony in Exod. 21.6 do share one thing in common: in both passages an oath was likely given before האלהים. It is most likely, then, that the declaration of the slave in Exod. 21.5 was a declaratory[5] (a simple declaration given before God) or voluntary obligatory oath[6]

Šamaš. In Greece, manumission included dedication of the slave to the gods.

1. Loretz, 'Nuzi-Parallelen', pp. 167-75.

2. F.C. Fensham, 'New Light on Exodus 21:6 and 22:7 from the Laws of Eshnunna', *JBL* 78 (1959), pp. 160-61.

3. Cf. Yaron, *The Laws of Eshnunna*, pp. 130-31; cf. also Loretz, 'Nuzi-Parallelen', p. 169, who compares Exod. 21.6 with Jer. 26.10 and cites an Assur inscription which reads: 'Als das Treppentor des Assur-Tempels, meines Herrn, das gegenüber dem (Tempel-) Tore des Gotteseides und dem Tor der göttichen Richter (sich befindet)'.

4. Cf. Paul, *Book of the Covenant*, pp. 90-91; Hyatt, *Exodus*, op. 238; M. Greenberg, 'Oath', *EncJud*, XXII, col. 1297; and Exod. 22.10, which is probably parallel to 22.8-9 and which states that the oath is given 'before Yahweh'. Cf. also J. Milgrom, 'The Paradox of the Red Cow (NUM. XIX)', *VT* 31 (1983), pp. 62-72 = *Studies in Cultic Theology and Terminology* (SJLA, 36; Leiden: Brill, 1983), p. 89 n. 311, who notes that Exod. 22.7-9 (Hebrew vv. 6-8) is parallel to 22.10-13 (Hebrew vv. 9-12); contra Phillips, *Criminal Law*, who argues that 22.8-9 (Hebrew vv. 7-8) concerns a trial by ordeal.

5. Cf. Driver and Miles, *Babylonian Laws*, I, pp. 198, 467-68, who note that a declaratory oath is attested in LH §§23, 106-107, 120, 126, 240, 266, 281. This oath was a simple declaration done before a god(s): e.g. LH §23 reads: 'If the robber is not caught, the man who has been robbed shall formally declare whatever he has lost before a god, and the city and the mayor in whose territory or district the robbery has been committed shall replace whatever he has lost for him.'

6. Greenberg, 'Oath', col. 1297, states that an voluntary obligatory oath bound

(an oath which bound a person to a particular action) that would require the same ratification before God as the exculpatory oath[1] in Exod. 22.8, 9 (Hebrew vv. 7, 8) (an oath which a man made before God in order to declare his innocence). In the Old Testament, as well as other ancient Near Eastern documents, there are no external legal sanctions for oaths, since punishment for false oaths is in the hands of God 'who will not hold guiltless one who swears falsely by His name' (Exod. 20.7; cf. also Exod. 22.8 [Hebrew v. 7]).[2] Therefore, the slave's declaration probably was a personal oath which was ratified before God, who would punish the slave if he did not keep his oath (cf. 1 Sam. 14.36ff.; 2 Sam. 21.1-2; 1 Kgs 16.34).

Therefore, it is most likely that the debt-slave was taken to 'God' in the sanctuary in order to reaffirm his oath to remain a slave. However, it is not obvious that the ceremony in v. 6b, which describes the boring of the slave's ear, also took place at the sanctuary. We already saw above that Driver suggests that the ceremony in v. 6b took place at the lord's house, since the two actions in v. 6a-b occurred at almost the same time. However, a more convincing interpretation has been proposed by Loretz,[3] who, noting that the two actions in v. 6a-b occur almost concurrently, suggests that the *waw* in the second clause is a *waw explicativum*.[4] Verse 6 would thus read: 'Dann führt ihn sein Herr vor Gott, d.h. er führt ihn zur Tür (des Haikal), bzw. zum Türpfosten (des Haikal)'.[5]

Recapitulating, the above discussion shows that when a debt-slave declares that he does not wish to go out free (v. 5), he must then be

the taker to do or not to do something (cf. Lev. 5.4). Cp. Milgrom, 'The Paradox of the Red Cow (NUM. XIX)', p. 89 n. 311, who claims that biblical law knows only of exculpatory oaths.

1. Cf. Driver and Miles, *Babylonian Laws*, I, pp. 412-13, 423, who note that in LH an exculpatory oath is required when someone who is alleged to be guilty exculpates himself by the oath 'by the life of a god(s)' within or at the door of a temple, and before a shrine. Cf. also Yaron, *The Laws of Eshnunna*, pp. 250-51; and Greenberg, 'Oath', col. 1297, who states that the exculpatory oath in the Old Testament was given in similar circumstances to that in LH, and that the oath was also given at the sanctuary.

2. Cf. Greenberg, 'Oath', col. 1297; Falk, 'Exodus XXI:6', p. 88.

3. Loretz, 'Nuzi-Parallelen', pp. 168-69; cf. also Cazelles, *Code de l'alliance*, p. 147.

4. Cf. GKC §154 n.b; HALAT 245, 5.

5. Cf. Loretz, 'Nuzi-Parallelen', p. 169.

brought before God in the sanctuary in order to reaffirm his oath
(v. 6a), after which his ear is bored against the door of the sanctuary
(v. 6b).[1] That the latter ceremony took place at the sanctuary is
further demonstrated by the fact that both contingent actions in v. 6a-
b most likely took place almost concurrently (note the use of the verb
והגישו in v. 6a-b). Furthermore, since Exod. 21.6 does not specify
where the ceremony was to take place it is likely that the expression
אל־האלהים was meant to identify clearly the place where the two
ceremonies were to take place (i.e. the sanctuary). Lastly, I also
concur with Loretz that v. 6b is an explanatory gloss of v. 6a.
However, it is not clear whether priests or judges would officiate at
the ceremony (cf. Deut. 1.16; 17.8-9),[2] or if the ceremony involved
only the slave and lord.[3] While the term האלהים indicates that the oath
was given before God, it does not necessarily indicate whether anyone
officiated at the ceremony. Phillips[4] suggests that this ceremony is an
example of 'family law', according to which the debt-slave's change in
status was accomplished without any recourse to the courts. He
suggests, too, that there was no need for witnesses or court action
because the debt-slave had no rights since he was his lord's property—
viz., this was a private matter between the debt-slave and his lord.
However, Phillips's interpretation is not convincing, since he fails to
distinguish between the status of a chattel-slave, who is the property of

1. Cf. Deut. 23.18 (Hebrew v. 19), which refers to the sanctuary as the 'house of
the Lord'; and 1 Sam. 1.9; 3.15, which describe that the sanctuary has a door and a
doorpost.

2. There appears to be some confusion as to who presided over legal disputes, as
well as confusion over where such disputes were settled. According to Exod. 18.19-
27, Moses selected leaders of thousands, of hundreds, of fifties and of tens to judge
legal matters. However, major disputes were handled by Moses himself (v. 22).
However, Deuteronomy identifies these leaders as 'judges' (Deut. 1.16), 'judges'
and 'officers' in Deut. 15.18. More difficult cases were to be referred to the
sanctuary where the 'priest' or 'judge' would determine the verdict. In addition to the
sanctuary, the 'city gate' (Amos 5.10; Ruth 4.1; Dan. 2.39), and the palm tree of
Deborah (Judg. 4.5), are cited as places where legal disputes could be brought; cf.
W.J. Harrelson, 'Court of Law', *IDB*, I, p. 713.

3. Cf. Liedke, *Gestalt und Bezeichnung*, pp. 44-45; Cazelles, *Code de l'alliance*,
ad. loc., both of whom argue that Exod. 21.6, 22 (פללים); 22.6ff. probably refer to
priests.

4. Phillips, 'Some Aspects of Family Law in Pre-Exilic Israel', p. 357; 'The
Laws of Slavery: Exodus 21:2-11', pp. 51-52.

an owner (cf. Exod. 21.20-21), and the debt-slave, who was not considered the property of an owner.[1] Furthermore, Phillips's interpretation rests on the assertion that the term האלהים refers to the household gods. As I have argued above, this interpretation is the least convincing of the interpretations that have been discussed. Therefore, since priests or judges were usually present when oaths or evidence were given in disputes at the sanctuary or temple (cf. Exod. 22.8 [Hebrew v. 7], which appears to assume the presence of priests or judges), it is most likely that the ceremony in Exod. 21.6 was no different. Lastly, contrary to Driver's suggestion that the latter ceremony took place at the lord's house since it is reasonable that the ceremony for binding a slave to the lord's household would take place at his house, it is my contention that it is not necessary that the debt-slave's ear be bored at the lord's house since the *main* significance of both of the ceremonies in v. 6 was to solemnize the slave's oath before God and not necessarily to emphasize the attachment to the lord's house.[2]

The status of the permanent slave. Lastly, it remains for me to discuss the status of the debt-slave who agrees to serve 'forever' (ועבדו לעלם). While the rabbinic commentators, in an attempt to reconcile the law in Exod. 21.2-6 with the slave law in Lev. 25.39-54, suggested that a Hebrew slave who serves 'forever' was released during the jubilee, the scholarly consensus is that a slave who becomes a permanent slave served in this capacity for life. This suggests that such a slave was

---

1. Note that Phillips, 'Some Aspects of Family Law', p. 357; 'The Laws of Slavery: Exodus 21:2-11', pp. 53-54, accepts the standard view that the slave in Exod. 21.2-6 was a debt-slave and not a chattel-slave.

2. Contra Falk, 'Exodus XXI:6', p. 88; Driver, *Exodus*, p. 211; Thompson, *Deuteronomy*, p. 191. Cf. North, *Sociology of the Biblical Jubilee*, p. 154, who interprets the boring of the ear as a suitable warning to the slave of the solemnity of the step he has taken. Note that the view that regards the ear as a symbol of obedience (cf. Ps. 40.6; LH §282) makes better sense if the ceremony in Exod. 21.5-6 symbolizes the ratification of the slave's oath. Cf. also N. Leibowitz, *Studies in Shemot I*, pp. 290, 298, who notes that only by a special ceremony before God can a Hebrew revoke his right to be a free man and serve a human master for life. Under God's order the Hebrews were to be servants only unto Him (cf. also Exod. 4.23, 3.12, where the 'service' of Egyptian bondage is replaced by the 'service of God' on the mountain).

similar to a chattel-slave, since such a slave served for life. Similarly, Mendelsohn,[1] who notes that chattel-slaves were often marked for identification, suggests that a tag might have been attached to the debt-slave's ear indicating ownership of the slave. In the ancient Near East chattel-slaves were often marked so that they could be identified. For example, in the OB and MA periods chattel-slaves were shaved, in contrast to free men who wore their hair long and grew beards and moustaches.[2] Furthermore, chattel-slaves often received a slave-mark (*abbuttum*) which appeared on various parts of the body.[3]

However, in certain cases a chattel-slave did not receive any mark. For example, in LH §146 a chattel-slave girl who bears children for the husband of a *nadîtûm* 'priestess' was not required to have a slave-mark. In Exod. 21.2-6 there is nothing in the context that suggests that a slave who voluntarily becomes a permanent slave should be required to be marked like a chattel-slave. On the contrary, this Israelite has voluntarily bound himself to his master. Therefore there would be no reason to mark such a slave. Furthermore, there was no requirement in the ancient Near East that indentured servants, such as the *ḫabiru*, were ever required to be marked. Therefore, it is most likely that the two ceremonies in Exod. 21.6 were symbolic acts which ratified the slave's entrance into the lord's household. Thus it is likely that the bored ear was left to heal.[4]

Furthermore, it is questionable whether the expression ועבדו לעלם refers to the service of a chattel-slave. For example, the term עבד can refer to various types of service, including service rendered by hired labourers or king's attendants. Furthermore, Craigie[5] notes that the expression עבד עולם also occurs in the Ugaritic literature, in which the expression does not seem to have any derogatory implications (cf. *CTA* 14.II.55). Therefore, it is likely that the expression ועבדו לעלם referred to a type of service which legally bound the debt-slave to the

---

1. Mendelsohn, 'Slavery in the Old Testament', p. 385.
2. Cf. Driver and Miles, *Babylonian Laws*, I, pp. 306-309.
3. Cf. Cardellini, *Die biblischen 'Sklaven'-Gesetze*, p. 101.
4. Cf. Hyatt, *Exodus*, p. 229; A-G. Barrois, *Manuel d'archéologie biblique*, II Paris: Picard, 1953), pp. 2, 212, both of whom suggest that the hole would soon become almost invisible; cf. also North, *Sociology of the Biblical Jubilee*, p. 154 n. 3, who states that the evidence for tatooing of slaves (cf. LH §§226-227) is not conclusive (cf. Gen. 4.15; Isa. 44.5; 49.16; Ezek. 9.4).
5. Craigie, *Deuteronomy*, p. 239 and n. 16.

owner but which should not be compared to the status of a chattel-slave. However, the law does not go any further in defining the status of an עבד עולם.

Exegesis of Exodus 21.7-11

Exod. 21.7-11

7 וכי־ימכר איש את־בתו לאמה לא תצא כצאת העבדים:

8 אם־רעה בעיני אדניה אשר [Qere לו]־לא יעדה והפדה לעם נכרי לא־ימשל למכרה בבגדו־בה:

9 ואם־לבנו ייעדנה כמשפט הבנות יעשה־לה:

10 אם־אחרת יקח־לו שארה כסותה וענתה לא ינרע:

11 ואם־שלש־אלה לא יעשה לה ויצאה חנם אין כסף:

7 And if a man sells his daughter as an אמה, she is not to go out free as the male slaves go out.

8 If she is displeasing in the eyes of her lord who designated her for himself, then he shall let her be redeemed. He does not have the authority to sell her to a foreign family because of his dealing treacherously with her.

9 And if he designates her for his son, he shall deal with her according to the custom of daughters.

10 If he takes to himself another woman, he may not reduce her food, her clothing, or her conjugal rights.

11 And if he will not do these three *things* for her, then she shall go out for nothing, without *payment of* money.

We noted above that this law is conditionally formulated, containing a main case (v. 7) followed by four subordinate or secondary cases (vv. 8, 9, 10, 11). Furthermore, we noted that this law is carefully juxtaposed to the preceding law in Exod. 21.2-6, which has resulted in an intricate literary structure. However, scholars are not in agreement about how to delimit these two laws. For example, Noth[1] suggests that the female אמה in vv. 7-11 is identical to the female slave who is referred to in v. 4. He suggests, therefore, that the law in vv. 2-6 is much older than the law in vv. 7-11, which attempted to improve the position of Israelite slaves. Similarly, Phillips[2] suggests that the service of an אמה was similar to that of a chattel slave—viz., the אמה became the possession of her lord. However, Phillips, unlike Noth,

---

1. Noth, *Exodus*, p. 178; cf. also Heinisch, 'Das Sklavenrecht in Israel und Alten Orient', p. 277.
2. Phillips, 'The Laws of Slavery: Exodus 21:2-11', pp. 59-60.

does not identify the אמה in vv. 7-11 with the female slave in v. 4, but rather he compares the אמה with the עבד עברי in v. 2. Phillips suggests that the law in vv. 7-11 is related closely to the former law in vv. 2-6, although while v. 2 stipulates the release of an עבד עברי in the seventh year, vv. 7-11 sought to treat humanely a female אמה who was used by her lord as a concubine or wife. He suggests, therefore, that this practice was later abandoned in Deut. 15.12-18, which stipulates the release of both male and female slaves in the seventh year. However, the above two views of the relationship between the laws in vv. 7-11 and vv. 2-6 are not convincing, for the following reasons.

First, regarding Noth's interpretation, we have already seen that the literary structure of vv. 2-11, which shows various legal and literary connections between the two manumission laws, makes it unlikely that the law in vv. 7-11 is older than the law in vv. 2-6. Furthermore, why would a compiler, who carefully juxtaposed these two laws, bring together two laws representing such diverse social attitudes?[1]

Secondly, regarding Phillips's interpretation, there is no indication that the law in vv. 7-11 envisaged the same sort of sale transaction envisaged in vv. 2-6, since the two verbs קנה and מכר are used elsewhere in the Old Testament to refer to various types of sale transactions.[2] Furthermore, while only Deut. 15.12-18 mentions specifically the sale of both male and female Israelites for household or other non-sexual labour, it is nevertheless most likely that the author or compiler of the debt-slave laws in the Covenant Code was also aware of this sort of sale transaction, especially since such non-sexual sales were very common in the rest of the ancient Near East.[3] While I will discuss whether Deut. 15.12-18 abandoned the practice illustrated in Exod. 21.7-11 below (in Chapter 7), the question remains why the law in Exod. 21.2-6 did not discuss the sale of female slaves for household or non-sexual labour. Following the analysis of

1. Cf. also Phillips, 'The Laws of Slavery: Exodus 21:2-11', p. 59; Jackson, 'Lecture VIII', p. 15.

2. For example, see the use of מכר in Gen. 25.31, 33; Exod. 21.35, 37; Deut. 14.21; 22.24; Lev. 25.16; Neh. 10.32; Prov. 31.24; and קנה in Gen. 47.20, 22; 50.13; Lev. 27.24.

3. Cf. Jackson, 'Some Literary Features of the Mishpatim', p. 235, who notes that the evidence of the ancient Near East suggests that women were more frequently sold as debt-slaves by members of their own family than were men.

both Zakovitch[1] and Jackson,[2] I suggest that the answer lies in the literary structure of Exod. 21.2-6, 7-11, in which the law of the male debt-slave in vv. 2-6 is carefully juxtaposed with the law of the female אמה in vv. 7-11. In these two slave laws the release and marital rights of both slaves are carefully juxtaposed, since they differ in each case. While the marriage of a male debt-slave does not affect his release, the female אמה is released only if her lord or husband does not fulfil his part of the marriage contract. This emphasis accounts for the relatively incomplete discussion of the sale of dependents in Exod. 21.2-6 as compared to that in Deut. 15.12-18, which I will discuss in more detail in Chapter 7.

That Exod. 21.7-11 deals with a particular type of marriage contract, as opposed to a more general sale contract for household or non-sexual labour, is demonstrated by the existence of extant Nuzi contracts entitled *ṭuppi mārtūti ù kallatūti* 'Tablet of daughtership and daughter-in-law-ship'.[3] Paul[4] explains that these contracts allowed a man who adopted a girl to marry her himself or give her in marriage to one of his sons or slaves, or to another man outside the purchaser's household. The girl, however, does not have any right to inheritance—she remains under the jurisdiction of her adopter or designated husband(s). Paul notes correctly that various conditions in these contracts are different from the biblical law in Exod. 21.7-11, since the biblical law bestows certain rights not found in the Nuzi contracts—for example, the girl is no longer considered a type of property that can be passed from one husband to the next; she is considered a free maiden or daughter if she is designated for the purchaser's son (v. 9).[5] Furthermore, as Thompson correctly points out:[6]

> The relationship established by this agreement [from Nuzi] was widely known throughout the Near East. We find this practice reflected in the texts and laws of the Old Babylonian period, in the Middle Assyrian Law

1. Zakovitch, *'For Three . . . and for Four'*, pp. xxv-xxvi, 450-53.
2. Jackson, 'Some Literary Features of the Mishpatim', pp. 235-41.
3. Cf. Mendelsohn, 'The Law of Exodus 21:7-11', pp. 190-95; Paul, *Book of the Covenant*, pp. 52-61, esp. 52-53.
4. Paul, *Book of the Covenant*, pp. 52-53; cf. also Mendelsohn, 'The Law of Exodus 21:7-11', pp. 190-95.
5. Cf. also Riesener, *Der Stamm* עבד, pp. 123, 129.
6. Thompson, *Historicity of the Patriarchal Narratives*, pp. 230-31.

code [§§30, 33], in a text dated to the Cassite period (c. 1342), as well as in Ugaritic tablets and the Old Testament [esp. Exod 21.7-11]. The contracts of this type from Nuzi are quite numerous and show a wider variety of intention than those found elsewhere. Nevertheless, there seems to be no reason to see the development of this legal form at Nuzi as significantly different from its development elsewhere in the ancient Near East. This type of contract is particularly close to the adoption of daughter, but without the right of inheritance. However, the emphasis on the *terḥatu*, as well as on the conditions under which the girl can be given in marriage by the adopter, mark this as a type of adoption that can have quite limited purposes. There are wide variations of intentions in these contracts ranging from the establishment of a relationship fully comparable to that of a real daughter to a relationship that is close to but not entirely equal to slavery [e.g. some of the contracts from Nuzi].

Therefore, while it is evident that the biblical law in Exod. 21.7-11 esembles the Nuzi contracts in that both appear to refer to the sale of laughters as slave-wives, it is equally evident that the biblical law also esembles other ancient Near Eastern adoption contracts which :stablished a relationship fully comparable to that of a real daughter v. 9).[1] However, the exact position of the אמה can only be letermined by a closer examination of the stipulations in Exod. 21.8-I 1. To a discussion of these stipulations we now turn.

The first secondary case in v. 8 has been interpreted in various ways due to the difficulty in rendering the clause אשר־לא יעדה (Kethibh), which I have rendered above as אשר־לו יעדה (Qere). The 'ormer rendering is adopted by only a few scholars,[2] including

---

1. For example, a Cassite text dated to the 21st year of Kurigalzu, which is cited ×y Thompson, *Historicity of the Patriarchal Narratives*, pp. 231-32 n. 154, reads: [*Ina-Uruk-rîšat*] die Tochter des [. . .]-*muššallim*, hatte keine Tochter; deshalb ıdoptierte sie die *Etirtum* die Tochter des *Ninirta-mušallim*. 7 sekel Gold gab sie. Sei ːs, daß sie sie einem Manne geben will, sei es, daß sie sie zur Hierodulenschaft »estimmt, (jedenfalls) darf sie sie nicht zur ihrer Magd machen. Macht sie sie zu ihrer Magd, so soll sie in ihr Vaterhaus fortgehen. Solange *Ina-Uruk-rîšat* lebt, soll ℥tirtum ihr Ehrfurcht erweisen. Stirbt *Ina-Uruk-rîšat* so soll *Etirtum* als ihre Tochter hr Wasser spenden. Sagt *Ina-Uruk-rîšat* '(du bist) nicht meine Tochter' so geht sie ᵈes Silbers, das sie besitzt (?) verlustig. Sagt *Etirtum* "(du bist) nicht meine Mutter", ːo wird sie zur Magd gemacht'.

2. Cf. J.G. Murphy, *A Critical and Exegetical Commentary on the Book of Exodus* (Andover, MA: Waren F. Draper, 1868), pp. 249-50; Clements, *Exodus*, p. 131.

Carmichael,[1] who notes that the latter reading poses certain contextual problems, since 'this ruling in the case of a master's taking a concubine would contradict the final ruling (v. 11), where a master must uphold the rights of a concubine he has taken and, if he fails, must release her without payment and not give her to be ransomed as in vs. 8'. This apparent contextual problem appears to be noted by the New English Bible which, following the Peshitta, emends יעדה to ידעה—viz., 'If her master has not had intercourse with her...'.[2] However, it is not evident that v. 8 assumes that the marriage has already been consummated (i.e. intercourse has taken place) as envisaged by Carmichael and the New English Bible. On the contrary, as Paul[3] has noted correctly, the verb יעד 'to designate' is most likely a technical term designating this particular type of marriage contract, not the actual act of marriage. That v. 8 does not refer to the consummation of marriage is further demonstrated by the protasis in the same verse which provides for the redemption of the girl if the contract is broken, since, as Carmichael suggests, it is unlikely that the family of the girl would have to provide redemption in this case— viz., the girl could no longer be sold as a virgin. Lastly, as Beer,[4] Driver[5] and Zakovitch[6] note correctly, the reading אשר־לו יעדה is to be preferred over the reading אשר־לא יעדה because the former reading is parallel or in balance with the clause ואם־לבנו ייעדנה in v. 9, which refers to the lord's son. Therefore, following the majority of scholars, it is best to emend לא to לו following the LXX, Vg and Targ.

If the lord was not pleased with the girl, whom he designated for himself, then והפדה לעם נכרי לא־ימשל למכרה בבגדו־בה 'he shall let her be redeemed. He does not have the authority to sell her to a foreign family because of his dealing treacherously with her.' While it is clear that if the lord breaks his contract to marry the girl he is to allow her to be redeemed by a member of her family,[7] it is not so clear to

---

1. C.M. Carmichael, *The Laws of Deuteronomy* (Ithaca/London: Cornell University Press, 1974), pp. 57-59.

2. Cf. also Clements, *Exodus*, p. 131.

3. Paul, *Book of the Covenant*, p. 52; cf. also Davies, *Exodus*, p. 176.

4. Beer and Galling, *Exodus*, pp. 108-109.

5. Driver, *Exodus*, p. 213.

6. Zakovitch, *'For Three . . . and for Four'*, p. 451.

7. It is possible, as David, 'The Manumission of Slaves under Zedekiah', p. 68 n. 19; and Phillips, 'The Laws of Slavery: Exodus 21:2-11', p. 60, suggest, that

whom the lord is not allowed to sell the girl. The expression עם נכרי, which is rendered literally as 'foreign people', has been interpreted to refer to anyone outside the girl's nuclear family,[1] or outside the lord's nuclear family,[2] or outside the covenant community of Israel.[3] While all three interpretations are possible, it appears from the context that the first option is preferable, since it is likely that the contract allowed the lord or purchaser to designate the girl only to himself or to his son, as the law itself envisages.[4] Lastly, the motivation clause בבגדו־בה 'on account of his dealing treacherously with her' provides the explanation as to why the lord was not able to sell the girl to anyone other than a member of her family. The key to the interpretation of this motivation clause is found in the use of the verb בגד, about which Erlandsson writes:[5]

> The verb expresses the unstable relationship of man to an existing established regulation, and can be translated 'to act faithlessly (treacherously).' It is used when the OT writer wants to say that a man does not honor an agreement, or commits adultery, or breaks a covenant or some other ordinance by God.

The range of the usage of this verb includes: (1) faithlessness in marriage (i.e. adultery, which is also used as a reference to Israel's faithlessness to God; cf. Jer. 3.20; 9.2 [Hebrew v. 1]; Mal. 2.10ff.); (2) transgression against God's covenant (cf. 1 Sam. 14.33; Jer. 3.21; Ps. 78.57; Mal. 2.10ff.); (3) those who live contrary to created order (cf. Prov. 2.22; 11.6; 21.18); and (4) the breaking or violation of human agreements or treaties (cf. Judg. 9.23; Lam. 1.2; Isa. 21.2;

---

the redeemer was not restricted to the girl's father or near kinsmen (cf. Lev. 25.48-54).

1. Cf. Jepsen, *Bundesbuch*, p. 2; Cazelles, *Code de l'alliance*, pp. 48-49.

2. Cf. Cassuto, *Exodus*, p. 268; Paul, *Book of the Covenant*, p. 54; Mendelsohn, 'Slavery in the Old Testament', p. 384.

3. Cf. Baentsch, *Exod-Lev-Num*, p. 190; Beer and Galling, *Exodus*, p. 108; Heinisch, *Exodus*, p. 166; Noth, *Exodus*, p. 179; J. Hoftijzer, 'EX. xxi 8', *VT* 7 (1957), p. 391; Boecker, *Law and the Administration of Justice*, p. 160.

4. Cf. Mendelson, *Slavery in the Ancient Near East*, pp. 54-55; *idem*, 'The Law of Exodus 21:7-11', pp. 192-93 and n. 11; Phillips, 'The Laws of Slavery: Exodus 21:2-11', p. 60, both of whom suggest that this limitation prevented the girl from being sold as a prostitute, which is envisaged in some of the Nuzi adoption texts.

5. S. Erlandsson, 'בגד', *ThWat*, I, col. 511; cf. also M.A. Klopfenstein, 'בגד', *Theologisches Handwörterbuch zum Alten Testament*, I (ed. E. Jenni and C. Westermann; Munich: Chr. Kaiser Verlag, 1971), col. 262.

33.1). While Erlandsson notes that the use of the verb בגד in Exod. 21.8 conforms to the first range of usage (1), Paul,[1] who suggests that this verb is an interdialectal functional equivalent of the Akkadian verb *nabalkutu* 'to break an agreement', suggests that the motivation clause refers to the breaking of the 'marriage' contract that the lord negotiated with the girl's father. This view conforms with usage (4) above, according to which the motivation clause בבגדו־בה can be rendered 'because he has severed/broken his relationship/agreement with her'. While Erlandsson's interpretation emphasizes the transgression of a relationship, which is apparent in the use of the verb בגד in reference to Israel's faithlessness to God, Paul's interpretation emphasizes the breaking of an objective legal ordinance or contract. It would appear, then, that both views should be adopted, although, as Klopfenstein[2] points out correctly, while the verb בגד 'treulos handeln' can be used in reference to both relationships and laws, Exod. 21.8 appears to emphasize the more objective aspect of law rather than the subjective aspect of relationships.

The second secondary case in Exod. 21.9-10 deals with the legal obligations of the lord who designates the girl for his son. Noth,[3] Phillips[4] and Gispen[5] suggest that this condition causally follows from the main condition in v. 8—viz., the girl is not redeemed and the lord designates her to his son. However, it is possible, as Zakovitch[6] suggests (Gispen also notes this possibility), that v. 8 is a new independent case—viz., from the beginning the lord designates the girl for his son. In view of the fact that v. 8 makes it clear that if the lord does not marry the girl himself he breaks the agreement with the girl, it is unlikely that the agreement allowed the lord, who was unhappy with the girl, to designate her to his son. Neither is it likely that the lord would keep her despite his disapproval of her, as it is envisaged in v. 10, since the family would most likely redeem her.[7]

---

1. Paul, *Book of the Covenant*, p. 54 and n. 7.
2. Klopfenstein, 'בגד', col. 262.
3. Noth, *Exodus*, p. 179.
4. Phillips, 'The Laws of Slavery: Exodus 21:2-11', p. 60.
5. Gispen, *Exodus*, p. 209-10.
6. Zakovitch, *'For Three . . . and for Four'*, p. 451.
7. Cp. Patrick, *Old Testament Law*, p. 71, who suggests that it would be difficult for a father, who sold his daughter under financial duress, to redeem his daughter. However, it is likely that the girl could be redeemed by any member of the

In this respect the biblical law is unlike the Nuzi adoption contracts, which often allowed purchasers to designate or sell girls to whomever they wished. That the girls were not treated as property, which is evident in the Nuzi texts, is further demonstrated by the expression כמשפט הבנות יעשהדלה—literally 'according to the rights of daughters', which Paul[1] notes is most likely a technical phrase meaning 'to treat as a free(-born) woman'. While both Cardellini[2] and Riesener[3] concur with this view, they suggest nevertheless that the girl was bought as a concubine (slave) in vv. 8-10. However, neither adequately explains why the stipulation in v. 9 should bestow upon a girl a free-born status when she is designated for the lord's son but not if she is designated for the lord. While the girl is called an אמה in v. 7, this designation should not be confused with its use in other contexts, in which it is used to refer to chattel-slaves (cf. Exod. 20.10; 21.20, 26, 27, 32; 23.12), nor in certain narratives in which it is used in conjunction with the terms פילגש and שפחה, all of which can refer to maidservants or concubine slaves who bear children for men whose wives are unable to bear children (cf. Gen. 30.3 (אמה); 35.22 (פילגש); 29.29; 30.4, 7; 35.25 (שפחה); all of which are used to refer to Bilhah).[4] Therefore, although the law in Exod. 21.7-11 refers to the sale of an אמה, which can be compared with the sale of a chattel-slave or concubine, nevertheless this law should not be compared with these institutions, but rather this law should be understood as an attempt to guarantee to a girl who is sold as a wife those rights that were normally afforded to daughters who were married in the customary manner.[5]

The third secondary case in Exod. 21.10 stipulates that the lord[6]

---

father's lineage. Furthermore, the financial loss would only be temporary, since the daughter could be sold to another suitor.

1. Paul, *Book of the Covenant*, p. 55; cf. also Thompson, *The Historicity of the Patriarchal Narratives*, p. 231.

2. Cardellini, *Die biblischen 'Sklaven'-Gesetze*, pp. 255-57.

3. Riesener, *Der Stamm* עבד, p. 129.

4. For a discussion of the semantic relationship between the terms פילגש, אמה, and שפחה, see Riesener, *Der Stamm* עבד, pp. 76-83.

5. Cf. also Saalschütz, *Das Mosaische Recht*, pp. 806-807.

6. While Murphy, *Exodus*, p. 250; and Keil, *Pentateuch*, p. 132, suggest that v. 10 refers to the son, the consensus of scholarly opinion is that this verse refers to the lord. The latter view is supported by the fact that the lord is the subject of the verbs that occur in vv. 7-9. If v. 10 refers to the son, it would be necessary to

who takes another wife (polygamy) or perhaps a concubine (slave) must provide the first wife with three basic necessities: כסותה, ועונתה, שארה. Durham,[1] who follows North,[2] suggests that the three items refer to the full range of physical satisfaction (שארה), 'harem-protection' (כסותה), and the right to bear children (עונה). However, Paul has shown that several Mesopotamian legal texts demonstrate that the basic necessities of life, including food, clothing and oil, were required to be given to various dependents (cf. LE §32 (upkeep of a son given to a wet nurse); LH §178 (upkeep of a priestess); MAL §36 (upkeep of a deserted wife)). He suggests, therefore, that the term שארה refers to the girl's meat/food (cf. Mic. 3.2-3; Ps. 78.20); the term כסותה refers to her clothing; and the term עונה refers to her oil ointments, although this *hapax legomenon* is usually rendered 'her conjugal rights'. While the exact meaning of these three terms remains a moot point, both of the above scholars are in agreement that the stipulation in v. 9 demonstrates further that the girl was not sold into slavery for general purposes, but only as a wife, even if her husband then became dissatisfied with her.

Lastly, the fourth secondary case stipulates:

ואם־שלש־אלה לא יעשה לה ויצאה חנם אין כסף

And if he [the lord] does not do these three *things* for her, then she shall go out free for nothing, without *payment* of money.

While many scholars[3] suggest that this verse refers to the three necessities referred to in v. 10, Mendelsohn[4] and Zakovitch[5] suggest

---

clarify this by explicitly mentioning the son. The position of v. 10, though, is awkward, although it appears that v. 10 was placed after v. 9 in order that it is understood that v. 10 is an independent case, since it did not causally follow v. 8—viz., the lord did not keep the girl even though he was unhappy with her.

1. Durham, *Exodus*, p. 322.
2. R. North, 'Flesh, Covering, and Response, Exodus xxi 10', *VT* 5 (1955), pp. 204-206.
3. For example, see Dillmann, *Exodus*, p. 229; Cassuto, *Exodus*, p. 269; Noth, *Exodus*, p. 179; Paul, *Book of the Covenant*, p. 56; Phillips, 'The Laws of Slavery: Exodus 21:2-11', p. 60; Durham, *Exodus*, p. 322.
4. Mendelsohn, 'Slavery in the Old Testament', p. 384.
5. Zakovitch, *'For Three . . . and for Four'*, p. 452; cf. also Baentsch, *Exod-Lev-Num*, pp. 190-91; and Driver, *Exodus*, pp. 212-13, who considers Baentsch's interpretation. Cp. Dillmann, *Exodus*, p. 229, who considers this interpretation to be 'willkührlich'.

that v. 11 refers to the previous three secondary cases in vv. 8, 9, 10. The latter view is more convincing than the former, for the following reasons. First, it is unusual that the penalty for v. 10 would be expressed in another secondary case, especially since no new conditions are set forth in v. 11. Secondly, there are no penalties prescribed for the failure to comply with the stipulations in vv. 8, 9, both of which deal with the primary rights of the אמה. We already saw above that the apodosis of primary law describes the legal relationship while the apodosis prescribes the terms of the relationship. Therefore, why should a special case be made for the stipulation in v. 10 and not for the stipulations in vv. 8, 9? Lastly, as we saw in the above discussion of the structure of Exod. 21.2-6, 7-11, Zakovitch has shown that Exod. 21.5-6 and 21.11 (sub-section IV) deal with an exceptional occurrence which does not fit in with the general principle. Therefore, just as the male slave chooses to remain with his master rather than going free in the seventh year, the female slave goes out without payment (she does not have to pay for her freedom; cf. v. 8)[1] when her lord (1) fails to fulfill his contractual obligations (i.e. he does not allow her to be redeemed (v. 8);[2] (2) he fails to treat her as a daughter (v. 9); (3) he fails to provide her with the necessities of life (v. 10)). Therefore, while v. 11 is unique in that it prescribes a specific penalty for the non-observance of the stipulations in vv. 8-10, its presence can be attributed to the literary structure of Exod. 21.2-6, 7-11, in which the seventh-year release of the male debt-slave (v. 2) is parallel to the release of an אמה who is not afforded her contractual rights (v. 11).

Recapitulating, the above discussion shows that the law in Exod. 21.7-11 deals with a type of adoption or marriage contract which, although similar to the extant Nuzi adoption contracts in some respects, is more similar to other attested ancient Near Eastern laws and contracts which afforded to a girl rights equal to that of a free-woman or wife, not a concubine or slave-wife. Furthermore, I argued that while the law in Exod. 21.7-11 is closely connected to the manumission law in Exod. 21.2-6, the former law envisaged a type of

1. Cf. Saalschütz, *Das Mosaische Recht*, pp. 806-807, who suggests that Exod. 21.11 refers to a written divorce, since the girl was considered a wife.
2. Contra Cardellini, *Die biblischen 'Sklaven'-Gesetze*, pp. 255-57, who suggests that v. 11, which refers to the stipulation in v. 10, reflects the status of an Ehefrau, while v. 8 reflects the status of a Nebenfrau-Konkubine.

sale that is clearly distinct from that envisaged in Exod. 21.2-6. Whereas the law in vv. 2-6 stipulates the release of debt-slaves who performed household and other non-sexual labour, the law in vv. 7-11 attempted to protect the rights of an אמה who was sold as a wife or concubine. The release of an אמה was only stipulated when her husband failed to meet his contractual obligations to her. Lastly, I argued that although Exod. 21.2-6 does not discuss the sale of a female אמה for household or non-sexual labour, the author or compiler of the debt-slave laws in the Covenant Code was most likely aware of this sort of sale transaction, especially since such non-sexual sales were very common in the rest of the ancient Near East.

Summary and Conclusions

To sum up, I examined the various stipulations contained in the manumission law in Exod. 21.2-6 in an attempt to clarify the meaning of this law, especially in the light of the various so-called cuneiform parallels which have often been used to determine its meaning. As the above examination has shown, the biblical manumission law in Exod. 21.2-6 is similar to the cuneiform law in LH §117, both of which attempted to prevent dependents from becoming the permanent property of their creditors by stipulating a periodic release of debt-slaves.[1] The periodic release of debt-slaves, which is clearly attested in the *mēšarum* edicts, were drafted in an attempt to help preserve the social and economic solidarity of agrarian kinship groups who accounted for most of the population in the ancient Near Eastern states. Furthermore, I demonstrated that attempts by some scholars to compare the status of the עבד עברי with the cuneiform *ḫabîru* have failed, since there are few or no legal, social or semantic similarities between the expression עבד עברי and the stipulations in Exod. 21.2-6, and the various cuneiform legal and social references to the *ḫabîru*.

However, while I have demonstrated that the biblical law in Exod. 21.2-6 is very similar to the law in LH §117, I noted nevertheless that

---

1. Cp. Mendelsohn, *Slavery in the Ancient Near East*, pp. 18, 89, who suggests that the law in Exod. 21.2-6 (Deut. 15.12-18) refers to a debtor who is seized by his creditor. While this practice was common it is however not sanctioned in LH §§117-119. As I have already argued above, both LH §§117-119 and the biblical legislation attempted to prevent such wrongful seizures which jeopardized the safety of the family.

the biblical law contains stipulations not found in LH §117. For example, I noted that the biblical laws in Exod. 21.2-6, 7-11 show a special concern for the marital rights of male and female debt-slaves. In the case of a male debt-slave marriage did not affect his release, although if his owner gave him a wife she and her children stayed with her owner. However, in the case of a female אמה who was sold *into marriage*, she was only released if her owner did not fulfill his marital responsibilities. The law in Exod. 21.2-6 did not, therefore, deal with the sale of female dependents who performed only *household* or *non-sexual* labour, since the compiler wished to emphasize the marital rights of debt-slaves. Female debt-slaves who performed household or non-sexual labour are treated in Deut. 15.12-18, which I will discuss in Chapter 7.

I noted, too, that the two stipulations in Exod. 21.5-6, which envisage the permanent enslavement of an Israelite debt-slave, contain rituals which have no apparent extra-biblical parallels. The debt-slave was required to give an oath before God of his intent to remain in the service of his owner, after which his owner bored a hole through his ear in order to solemnize his intent to serve him forever. These cultic rituals were most likely required because the release of a debt-slave was closely associated with God's release of the Israelites from their bondage to the Egyptians. Therefore, any Israelite who contemplated becoming a permanent 'servant' had to declare his intention before God. However, while the status of an עבד עולם was most likely closer to the status of a free person rather than that of a chattel-slave, the biblical law says very little about the legal rights of such a 'servant'.

Chapter 7

THE MANUMISSION LAW OF DEUTERONOMY 15.12-18

While scholars agree unanimously that the manumission law in Deut. 15.12-18 is based upon the manumission law in Exod. 21.2-6, nevertheless the former law includes stipulations not found in the latter and *vice versa*. On the one hand, the law in Deut. 15.12-18 stipulates the release of female debt-slaves, as well as exhorting owners to provide their debt-slaves with provisions when they are released, both of which are absent from the law in Exod. 21.2-6. On the other, Deut. 15.12-18 omits the discussion concerning the marital rights of the male debt-slave, as well as the reference to taking debt-slaves to God's sanctuary when they wish to become permanent servants. These additions and omissions have led some scholars to suggest that the law in Deut. 15.12-18 is significantly different from that in Exod. 21.2-6.

The Setting and Form of Deuteronomy 15.12-18

Setting
The deuteronomic legal collection (Deut. 12-26), like the rest of the biblical and ancient Near Eastern legal collections, does not follow any 'modern' legal conventions in arranging its regulations. While it is beyond the scope of my present discussion to engage in a thorough analysis of the structure of the deuteronomic legal collection, I will nevertheless examine those analyses that attempt to account for the placement of the manumission law in Deut. 15.12-18 within this legal collection.

The deuteronomic legal collection, like the so-called Covenant Code, is found within a larger literary framework which has been the subject of much scholarly discussion. After Mendenhall[1] and others[2] showed that there was a relationship in form between the Hebrew covenant and the ancient Near Eastern vassal treaty, scholars such as Kline[3] and Kitchen[4] have suggested that the book of Deuteronomy follows the form of the ancient Near Eastern vassal treaty.[5] In broad outline, the treaty form of the book of Deuteronomy can be described as follows:

1. *Preamble* (1.1-5); 'These are the words which Moses addressed to all Israel...'
2. *Historical Prologue* (1.6–4.49)
3. *General Stipulations* (chs. 5–11)
4. *Specific Stipulations* (chs. 12–26)
5. *Blessings and Curses* (chs. 27–28)
6. *Witnesses* (see 30.19; 31.19; 32.1-43)

While scholars generally accept that there is some correspondence between the ancient Near Eastern vassal treaties and the book of Deuteronomy, nevertheless they are divided concerning the date of this specific form of treaty—viz., is the treaty form in the book of Deuteronomy more similar to the second-millennium 'Hittite'[6] (e.g., Kitchen, Craigie) or first-millennium vassal treaties (e.g., Frankena, Weinfeld)[7]? Furthermore, while Weinfeld[8] suggests that the book of

1. Mendenhall, 'Ancient Oriental and Biblical Law', pp. 26-46; 'Covenant Forms in Israelite Tradition', *BA* 17 (1954), pp. 50-76.

2. For example, see K. Baltzer, *The Covenant Formulary* (Oxford: Oxford University Press, 2nd edn, 1971); D.J. McCarthy, *Treaty and Covenant: A Study in Form in the Ancient Oriental Documents and the Old Testament* (AnBib, 21; Rome: Pontifical Biblical Institute, 1963).

3. M.G. Kline, *The Treaty of the Great King* (Grand Rapids: Eerdmans, 1963); *The Structure of Biblical Authority* (Grand Rapids: Eerdmans, 1972).

4. K.A. Kitchen, *Ancient Orient and Old Testament* (London: Tyndale Press, 1966), pp. 90-102; *idem*, 'Ancient Orient, "Deuteronomism" and the OT', *New Perspectives on the Old Testament* (ed. J.B. Payne; 1970), pp. 1-24; cf. also Craigie, *Deuteronomy*, pp. 18-29.

5. For a survey of the different opinions concerning the biblical and ancient Near Eastern vassal treaty form, see D.J. McCarthy, *Old Testament Covenant*.

6. Cf. D.J. Wiseman, ' "Is it Peace"—Covenant and Diplomacy', *VT* 32 (1982), pp. 311-26, esp. 311-13, who notes that the so-called Hittite vassal treaties were basically 'Mesopotamian' in form and concept.

7. R. Frankena, 'The Vassal Treaties of Esarhaddon and the Dating of Deuteronomy', *OTS* 14 (1965), pp. 122-54; Weinfeld, *Deuteronomy*, pp. 59-157.

8. Weinfeld, *Deuteronomy*, pp. 146-57.

Deuteronomy is fashioned after the first-millennium vassal treatie
nevertheless he suggests that this book is not the actual text of a vass
treaty as such. This view is also reflected in the literary analyses
Polzin,[1] who suggests that that book of Deuteronomy can be divid
into three Mosaic Addresses (1.6–4.40; 5.1b–28.68; 29.1–31.6), a
of Christensen,[2] who has suggested that the book of Deuteronon
contains an elaborate concentric structure that is based upon t
Mosaic addresses found therein.[3] Similarly, the most promisi
attempts to understand the structure of the legal collection in chapte
12–26 are based on the assertion that this legal collection is intimate
connected with the explication of the Decalogue in Deuteronomy
To these attempts we now turn.

Both Kaufman[4] and Braulik[5] suggest that the laws contained in th
legal collection are organized according to the discussion of the T
Commandments in Deuteronomy 5. In particular, both schola
maintain that the law in Deut. 15.12-18 belongs to the larg
discussion contained in 14.22–16.17, which has been organized arou
the theme of the Sabbath commandment in Deut. 5.12-15. Bo
analyses are presented below in outline form:

1. R. Polzin, *Moses and the Deuteronomist: A Literary Study of the Deuteronom
History. Part One: Deuteronomy, Joshua, Judges* (New York: Seabury, 198
pp. 25-72. Polzin places the book of Deuteronomy within the larger litera
framework of the Deuteronomistic history.

2. D.L. Christensen, 'Form and Structure in Deuteronomy 1–11', in *D
Deuteronomium: Entstehung, Gestalt und Botschaft [Deuteronomy: Origin, Fo
and Message]* (ed. N. Lohfink; BETL, 68; Leuven: Leuven University Press, 198
pp. 135-44; cf. also C.J. Labuschagne, 'Divine Speech in Deuteronomy',
Lohfink (ed.), *Das Deuteronomium*, pp. 111-26, who also sees an elaborate litera
structure to the book of Deuteronomy (and the Pentateuch as a whole) based upon
use of divine speech.

3. For recent discussions about the literary structure and dating of the book
Deuteronomy, see H.D. Preuss, *Deuteronomium* (EF, 164; Darmstadt, 198
pp. 45-74; Mayes, *Deuteronomy*, pp. 29-55; McConville, *Law and Theology
Deuteronomy*, pp. 2-7; R.E. Clements, *Deuteronomy* (Old Testament Guid
Sheffield: JSOT Press, 1989).

4. Kaufman, 'The Structure of the Deuteronomic Law', pp. 105-58.

5. Braulik, 'Die Abfolge der Gesetze in Deuteronomium 12–26', pp. 252-7
'Zur Abfolge der Gesetze in Deuteronomium 16,18–21,23: Weitere Beobachtunge
Bib 69 (1988), pp. 63-91; and more recently his collective work, *D
deuteronomischen Gesetze und der Dekalog: Studien zum Aufbau Deuteronomi
12–26* (Stuttgarter Bibelstudien, 145; Stuttgart: Katholisches Bibelwerk, 1991).

(1) Kaufman

Word IV 'Sabbath' (14.28–16.17)

   A. 14.28-29 Tithe of the third year

   B. 15.1-18 Seventh-year regulations

      B.1 15.1-11 Seventh-year remission

      B.2 15.12-18 Slave release in seventh year

   C. 15.19-23 Firstlings law

   D. 16.1-17 Pilgrimage festivals

(2) Braulik

3. 'Sabbath' Command (14.22–16.17)

      A. 14.22-15.23 'Holy Rhythm'

      A.1 14.28-29 Third- and sixth-year tithe

      A.2 15.1-6 Sabbatical-year release

      A.3 15.7-11 Lending to the poor

      A.4 15.12-18 Individual seventh-year release

      A.5 15.19-23 Firstlings law

      B. 16.1-17 Pilgrimage festivals

1. Kaufman[1] notes several significant features in the section Deut. 14.28–16.17. First, regarding the connection between the various regulations in Deut. 14.28–16.17, Kaufman observes that there is already an 'inner-biblical' connection between the Sabbath, Sabbatical release (Fallow year), and pilgrimage festivals in Exod. 23.10-14. Kaufman notes that this literary connection is strengthened further by the appearance of the motivation clause 'Remember that you were a slave in Egypt' which occurs in Deut. 5.12, 15.15, and 16.12. He notes correctly that the occurrence of this motivation clause in 5.12 seems perplexing until one notices how smoothly it fits into the context of 15.15 and 16.12. On the one hand, the motivation clause in 15.15 is connected aptly to the stipulation exhorting an owner to provide his released debt-slave liberally with provisions. On the other hand, the motivation clause in 16.12 is found at the end of the discussion concerning the observation of the feasts of Passover and of Weeks, both of which were first celebrated after God brought Israel out of Egypt (cf. 16.1).[2]

Secondly, while firstlings are already mentioned in Deut. 12.17, Kaufman suggests that the appearance of the firstling law in Deut.

---

1. Kaufman, 'The Structure of the Deuteronomic Law', pp. 128-33.

2. Cf. also McConville, *Law and Theology in Deuteronomy*, p. 85, who notes that this motivation clause follows the stipulation concerning the kind treatment of sojourners.

15.19-23 forms a perfect transition between the law of period
release and the so-called deuteronomic reform of the Passov
sacrifice.[1] For example, he notes that Ibn Ezra already observed th
the reference to the firstling not being worked in v. 19 (חעבד
בבכר שורך) recalls both the theme of the Sabbath and the release of
Israelite servant after עבדך 'working for you' (15.12, 18
Furthermore, the fact that the firstlings are eaten every ye
corresponds to the annual periodicity of the first tithe law in 14.22.[3]

Thirdly, Kaufman notes that the various regulations in Deut. 15 a
arranged according to the ancient Near Eastern socio-econom
priority system that was first discerned by Petschow,[4] who notes th
each topical discussion in LH follows the principles of socio-econom
worth—i.e., temple, state, citizen (*awīlum*), temple or Crov
dependent (*muškēnum*), slave (*wardum*). Kaufman sees these pri
ciples of socio-economic worth at work in Deut. 15—i.e., freem
(vv. 1-11)—slaves (vv. 12-18)—animals (vv. 19-23).

(2) Similarly, Braulik[5] notes several significant features in t
section Deut. 14.22–16.17, although his analysis is slightly differe
from that of Kaufman. First, while Kaufman does not include t
discussion of the yearly tithe in 14.22-27, Braulik suggests that th
regulation should be included in the 'Sabbatheiligung', since it
intimately connected with the third-year tithe. Furthermore, Brau
has noted that within the section 14.22–15.23, both the first and l
regulations refer to yearly observances. The placement of the yea
regulations at the front and back end of this section has resulted i
sort of concentric pattern: 1 yr. (14.22-27)—3 yr. and 6 yr. (14.2
29)—7 yr. (15.1-11)—7 yr. (non-cyclic: 15.12-18)—1 yr. (15.19-2

---

1. Cf. also Merendino, *Das deuteronomische Gesetz*, p. 123.
2. Cf. also McConville, *Law and Theology in Deuteronomy*, p. 95.
3. Cf. McConville, *Law and Theology in Deuteronomy*, pp. 93-94, who has a
pointed out a 'deeper' literary relationship between the firstling law and the previ
seventh-year release laws in vv. 1-11, 12-18. He suggests that the compiler
deliberately made a contrast between the treatment of Israelites and foreigners
vv. 1-18 (e.g., אח / רע and נכרי), and perfect and imperfect animals in vv. 19-
He notes that the analogies between human beings and animals are known elsewh
in the Old Testament (e.g., clean and unclean in the book of Leviticus).
4. Petschow, 'Zur Systematik und Gesetzestechnik im Codex Hammura
pp. 146-72.
5. Braulik, 'Die Abfolge der Gesetze in Deuteronomium 12–26', pp. 262-65.

Similarly, Patrick[1] has noted that the first and fourth paragraphs converge (cf. 14.23, which mentions both tithes and firstlings), while the second and third paragraphs are associated by analogy:

A–Tithe (14.22-29)
  B–Release from debt (15.1-11)
  B–Release from slavery (15.12-18)
A–Firstborn (15.19-23)

Secondly, Braulik also notes that Petschow's principles of priority are at work in the section 14.22–15.23. For example, in 14.22-27 Israelites are mentioned first while the Levites are mentioned second. In 14.28-29 the Levites are mentioned first, after which follow the lower socio-economic groups alien, orphan, and widow. In 15.1-6 a poor Israelite is mentioned, while in vv. 12-18 a Hebrew debt-slave is mentioned. Lastly, vv. 19-23 mention an Israelite family (vv. 19, 20) who is also the subject of the first discussion in 14.22-27. Braulik suggests that this link illustrates further the integrity of this entire section, although Kaufman's application of Petschow's principles of priority in Deuteronomy 15 (i.e., free man, slave, animals) seems more apparent.

Recapitulating, the above discussion shows that despite the difference in detail in the above analyses, both Kaufman and Braulik demonstrate that the section 14.22–16.17 exhibits a literary unity that was probably the product of a compiler who wanted to compare the laws contained in this section with the Sabbath Commandment. We already saw in Chapter 5 that the placement of the debt-slave laws in Exod. 21.2-6, 7-11 at the beginning of the so-called Covenant Code was partly motivated by the significance of Israel's escape from Egypt in the covenant-making process, illustrated in the narrative in Exodus 19–34. Furthermore, we saw that the literary structure of the two debt-slave laws in Exod. 21.2-6, 7-11 reflected the compiler's particular interest in the marital rights of a male עבד עברי and a female אמה. Similarly, it is most likely that the discussion of the debt-slave law in Deut. 15.12-18 has been influenced by the discussions of the other regulations contained in the section 14.22–16.17, which I will discuss in greater detail below.

---

1. Patrick, *Old Testament Law*, pp. 110-11.

Form

The slave law in Deut. 15.12-18, which basically follows the casuistic discussion in Exod. 21.2-6, is conditionally formulated. However, as Liedke[1] correctly points out, while the law in Exod. 21.2-6 contains a single casuistic complex sentence (i.e., כי followed by three subordinate אם clauses), the law in Deut. 15.12-18 contains three individual or separate casuistic sentences (v. 12 כי; v. 13 וכי; v. 16 והיה כי־). The relationship between the casuistic structure of Exod. 21.2-6 and Deut. 15.12-18 is illustrated below (bold lines indicate corresponding stipulations):

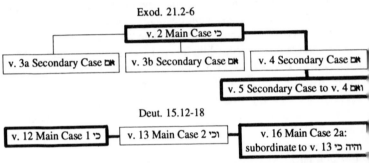

Exod. 21.2-6

| v. 2 Main Case כי |

| v. 3a Secondary Case אם | v. 3b Secondary Case אם | v. 4 Secondary Case אם |

| v. 5 Secondary Case to v. 4 ואם |

Deut. 15.12-18

| v. 12 Main Case 1 כי | v. 13 Main Case 2 וכי | v. 16 Main Case 2a: subordinate to v. 13 והיה כי |

The above illustration shows clearly that Deut. 15.12-18 does not deal with the stipulations contained in Exod. 21.3a, 3b and 5, all of which deal with the marital status and rights of the male debt-slave. While Deut. 15.12-18 has retained the main case dealing with the manumission of debt-slaves (v. 12), and the stipulation regarding a debt-slave who wishes to remain a perpetual servant (vv. 16-17), it has added a new stipulation which deals with providing released debt-slaves with provisions (vv. 13-15).

Furthermore, Deut. 15.12-18 contains motivation clauses and parenetic material which are absent from the discussion in Exod. 21.2-6. While explanatory motivation clauses are found in the Covenant Code (cf. 21.8, 21), the moral or ethical exhortations and historical references found in the motivation clauses and parenetic material in Deut. 15.15, 18 are ubiquitous in the deuteronomic legal collection and the so-called Holiness Code in Leviticus 17–26.[2] I will

---

1. Liedke, *Gestalt und Bezeichnung*, p. 32f.
2. Cf. B. Gemser, 'The Importance of the Motive Clause in Old Testament Law', in *Congress Volume, Copenhagen* (VTSup, 1; Leiden: Brill, 1953), pp. 50-6

discuss the function of these motivation clauses and parenetic material below in the exegesis of Deut 15.12-18, but before I do this I will first discuss briefly the שמטה 'release' in Deut. 15.1-11 which, as we saw above, is closely connected with the manumission law in vv. 12-18.

Excursus: The שמטה in Deuteronomy 15.1-11

Deut. 15.1-3

1 מקץ שבע־שנים תעשה שמטה:
2 וזה דבר השמטה שמוט כל־בעל משה ידו אשר ישה ברעהו
לא־יגש את־רעהו ואת־אחיו כי־קרא שמטה ליהוה:
3 את־הנכרי תגש ואשר יהיה לך את־אחיך תשמט ידך:

1 At the end of *every* seven years you shall make a release *of debts.*
2 And this is the manner of remission: each creditor shall release what he has loaned to his neighbour ; he shall not exact it of his neighbour or his brother, because the Lord's remission has been proclaimed.
3 From a foreigner you may exact *it*, but your hand shall release whatever of yours is with your brother.

Deut. 15.1-3 provides for a שמטה 'release' every seven years, during which time creditors were apparently required to release what they had loaned to their neighbours. The term שמטה 'release' or literally 'a letting drop', which comes from the verb [שמט] 'let fall, drop', is found only in Deut. 15.1f., 9; 31.10, although it is most likely that this Sabbatical release is based upon or identical with the sabbatical Fallow year regulation in Exod. 23.11 in which the verb [שמט] occurs.[1] Furthermore, it is most likely that the sabbatical Fallow year is also referred to in Lev. 25.2b-7, although the term שמטה or the verb [שמט] is not employed there. While I will discuss the relationship that exists between the various Sabbatical year regulations in more detail in Chapter 8, for the present I will examine the meaning of the Sabbatical release in Deut. 15.1-3. To this discussion we now turn.

Verse 1 begins with the second-person singular apodictic stipulation

---

S. Amsler, 'La motivation de l'éthique dans la parénèse du deutéronome', in *Beiträge zur alttestamentlichen Theologie: Festschrift W. Zimmerli zum 70. Geburtstag* (ed. H. Donner, R. Hanhart and R. Smend; Göttingen: Vandenhoeck & Ruprecht, 1977), pp. 11-22; P. Doron, 'Motive Clauses in the Laws of Deuteronomy: Their Forms, Functions, and Contents', *HAR* 2 (1978), pp. 61-77; Sonsino, *Motive Clauses*.

1. Cf. North, *Sociology of the Biblical Jubilee*, p. 188; Wright, 'What Happened Every Seven Years, I', p. 133.

מקץ שבע-שנים תעשה שממה and is followed in v. 2 by the interpretation of this stipulation וזה דבר השממה, which is framed in the third person singular. According to Horst,[1] von Rad,[2] Seitz[3] and Mayes[4] the change in number in these two verses, as well as other so-called deuteronomic additions found in Deuteronomy 15, suggests that v. 2 is a legal or secondary interpretation of the original release law in v. 1 which already applied to the release of debts (i.e., pre-deuteronomic). While the expression וזה דבר השממה indicates clearly that v. 2 is an interpretation of v. 1,[5] it is not entirely evident that v. 1 refers to a pre-deuteronomic version of the Sabbatical release of debts, especially since this stipulation is mentioned only in Deut. 15.1-11 and 31.10 (cf. also Neh. 10.32 [Hebrew v. 31]). It is just as likely that v. 1 refers to the sabbatical Fallow year mentioned in Exod. 23.10 and Lev. 25.2b-7, in which case v. 2 introduces an innovation unique to the book of Deuteronomy.[6] As Weinfeld and Wright correctly point out, Leviticus 25 is very much concerned with the commercial and financial implications of the Sabbatical year and Jubilee.[7] Therefore, if P had envisaged the שממה 'release' of debts, then the drafter of the laws in Leviticus 25 would have tacitly included this provision.[8]

---

1. Horst, *Gottes Recht*, pp. 79-80.

2. Von Rad, *Studies in Deuteronomy*, pp. 15-16; *Deuteronomy*, p. 106.

3. Seitz, *Deuteronomium*, pp. 167-68.

4. Mayes, *Deuteronomy*, pp. 247-48.

5. Cf. J.A. Thompson, *Deuteronomy: An Introduction and Commentary* (TOTC; Leicester: Inter-Varsity Press, 1974), p. 187.

6. Cp. Kaufman, 'Social Welfare Systems of Ancient Israel', pp. 283, 286 n. 21, who suggests that although the 'release' in Deuteronomy 15 is earlier than the Jubilee release in Leviticus 25, the latter release did not sanction the earlier call for the release of debts, since 'Annulments would have been rather disastrous for the priestly class, if as elsewhere in the Near East, the Temple was a major source of capital'. However, this argument is not convincing since, on the one hand, it is doubtful that the Temple in Israel engaged in extensive lending activities, and, on the other, such limitations did not discourage the OB kings from declaring the release of debts on a more frequent basis.

7. Weinfeld, *Deuteronomy*, p. 223 n. 3. Wright, 'What Happened Every Seven Years, I', p. 133.

8. Cf. Jakobson, 'Some Problems Connected with the Rise of Landed Property (Old Babylonian Period)', p. 37, who writes, 'the *mīšarum* and other related Ancient Oriental acts combine the annulment of debts with an annulment of land purchases. The kings who enacted the *mīšarum* saw clearly enough that these two social plagues were interconnected.'

The interpretation of v. 2 is complicated further by the fact that the Hebrew in this verse is difficult to render. Two main interpretations have been proposed for this difficult verse. On the one hand, Driver,[1] who follows the Massoretic Text, renders v. 2a as follows:

שמוט כל־בעל משה ידו אשר ישה ברעהו

Every possessor of a loan of his hand shall let drop that which he lendeth to his neighbour

This translation has been followed by several commentators[2] and modern translations of the Bible (e.g., AV, RSV, NASB), although they generally render the difficult expression בעל משה ידו simply as 'creditor' (literally 'the loan which his own hand has given'). However, while Ehrlich,[3] Steuernagel[4] and Dillmann[5] also follow the MT, they suggest that the term ידו is the object to the verb שמוט, following the construction חשמט ידך in v. 3. According to this view, v. 2a should be rendered 'Every creditor [literally owner of a loan] shall let drop his hand in regard to what he has loaned to his neighbour.'[6] Nevertheless, Ehrlich notes that the expression כל משא יד, which clearly connects יד with משא, is found in Neh. 10.31 (Hebrew v. 32), although he suggests that this is a 'falsche Verbindung'.[7] Nevertheless, all of the above scholars are in agreement that the object of the discussion of vv. 2-3 is the release of a loan, although they are divided over whether the release is a temporary (e.g., Driver?,

1. Driver, *Deuteronomy*, p. 175.
2. For example, see Reider, *Deuteronomy*, p. 150; von Rad, *Deuteronomy*, p. 104; J. Ridderbos, *Deuteronomy* (BSC; Grand Rapids: Zondervan, 1984), p. 180; Craigie, *Deuteronomy*, p. 234; Thompson, *Deuteronomy*, p. 187.
3. Ehrlich, *Randglossen*, II, p. 293.
4. C. Steuernagel, *Deuteronomium und Josua* (HKAT, I/3; Göttingen, 2nd edn, 1923), p. 55.
5. A. Dillmann, *Die Bücher Numeri, Deuteronomium und Joshua* (KH, 13; Leipzig: S. Hirzel, 2nd edn, 1880), p. 306.
6. This translation is also noted by Thompson, *Deuteronomy*, p. 187, although he does not indicate to whom this translation should be credited. Dillmann, *Deuteronomium*, p. 306, renders the verse as: 'Loslassen soll jeder Besitzer... sein Handdarlehen... welches er an seinem Nächsten su fordern hat'; Steuernagel, *Deuteronomium*, p. 55, renders the verse as: 'Erlassen soll jeder Gläubiger sein Handdarlehen an seinen Nächsten.'
7. Cf. also Neufeld, 'Socio-Economic Background', p. 60, who notes the parallel in Neh. 10.31 [Hebrew v. 32] and renders the expression as 'every loan' or 'what was lent out of the hand'.

Craigie) or permanent (e.g., von Rad, Thompson, Dillmann, Steuernagel) remission of a loan or debt. I will examine Craigie's interpretation in more detail below.

On the other hand, several scholars suggest that v. 2 refers to the release of a 'pledge' that is given as security for a loan. According to this interpretation the *hapax legomenon* משׁא,[1] which is rendered as 'loan' or 'Darlehen' above, should be rendered 'pledge' or 'Pfand'. For example, Horst[2] suggests that the term בעל can be rendered on its own as 'creditor'. He also suggests that the term משׁא should be rendered as a *true* Hiphil participle, from the verb [נשׁא] 'to lend', whose object is the expression ידו, according to which this expression would be rendered 'seine Hand hat beleihen lassen'. Therefore, v. 2a can be rendered: 'The creditor shall release the one who used his handshake to get a loan.' According to this interpretation, the person who is released is the debtor who was taken as a pledge by the creditor, and the expression ידו 'his handshake' signifies the agreement by which the debtor agrees to act as guarantor or security for the loan. In an attempt to demonstrate this interpretation, Horst suggests that the verb [נשׁא] refers to lending that requires the use of a human pledge as security for a loan (cf. Ps. 89.22 [Hebrew v. 23]; cf. also Neh. 5.7, 10 [n.m. משׁה]; Deut. 24.10; Prov. 22.26 [n.f משׁאה]), and that the participle נשׁא refers specifically to such pledges (cf. 1 Sam. 22.2; Isa. 24.2; Neh. 5.7). This contrasts with the use of the verb [עבט][3] in v. 8 (העבט תעביטנו 'you shall generously lend to him'), which Horst suggests refers to pledge-loan-contracts that required assorted mobile pledges (e.g., cloak; cf. Exod. 22.26-27 [Hebrew vv. 25-26]; Deut. 24.12-13).[4] While Horst's interpretation of the term משׁה is

---

1. The term משׁה comes from the verb [נשׁא] 'to lend'. The Qal participle occurs in 1 Sam. 22.2; Isa. 24.2; Neh. 5.7; the Hiphil occurs in Ps. 89.22 [Hebrew v. 23]; 1 Kgs 8.31; 2 Chron. 6.22. The masculine noun occurs in Neh. 5.7, 10; 10.32 [Hebrew v. 31]; the feminine noun occurs in construct form in Deut. 24.10; Prov. 22.26. For a recent discussion of these passages, see F.L. Hossfeld and E. Reuter, 'נשׁא', *ThWAT*, V, cols. 658-63.

2. Horst, *Gottes Recht*, pp. 79-87; cf. also H. Breit, *Die Predigt des Deuteronomisten* (Munich: Chr. Kaiser Verlag, 1933), pp. 192-94.

3. The Qal of the verb [עבט] 'to take or join a pledge' or 'to borrow' occurs in Deut. 15.6; 24.10; the Hiphil occurs in Deut. 15.6, 8; the Piel occurs in Job 2.7. The [masculine] noun עבוט occurs in Deut. 24.10, 11, 12, 13.

4. This view is accepted by Cholewiński, *Heiligkeitsgesetz und Deuteronomium*, pp. 223-24.

distinctively different from those who suggest that a loan is referred to in v. 2, he notes nevertheless that the restitution of the pledge in v. 2 is identical to the total remission of the loan or debt.

Similarly, Weil[1] suggests that the term משׁה refers to a pledge whose release is identical to the total remission of the loan or debt, although he suggests that the person pledged, in accordance with many ancient Near Eastern contracts, is a dependent of the debtor, such as his slave or one of his children. Furthermore, Weil suggests that the pledge was not handed over at the commencement of the loan transaction but after the foreclosure of the loan (i.e., distraint; cf. LH §113-116). This pledge then performed antichretic services which went towards the amortization of the debt. In contrast to Horst, Weil, who follows the accentuation of the Massoretic Text, suggests that the expression ידו refers back to בעל. Weil's interpretation appears to be followed also by North,[2] who renders v. 2 as: 'Every holder of a pledge *at his disposition* [ידו] shall release what he has received by pledge-loan-contract with his brother'. While this rendering suggests that the pledge can be a third party, as Weil proposes, North[3] suggests that the debtor himself with his family and his field is pledged. Furthermore, North suggests that the שׁמטה 'release' in Deut. 15.1-3 allowed for only the *temporary* release of the pledge(s). I will deal with this particular aspect of North's interpretation in more detail below. Lastly, North's understanding of the expression ידי is similar to that of Horst, although he suggests that it refers 'to the temporary dominion or control exercised by the holder of a pledge'. He derives this view from the so-called comparative cuneiform texts, which illustrate that pledges surrendered themselves 'into the hands' (*ina qātē*) of the creditor.[4] Similarly Wright,[5] who follows the views of both Weil and North, suggests that the pledge mentioned in Deut. 15.2 was usually land that was used by the creditor, although it could also refer to dependents whose labour paid off the debt.

---

1. H.M. Weil, 'Gage et cautionnement dans la Bible', *AHDO* 2 (1938), pp. 171-72, 186-94.

2. R. North, '*YÂD* in the Shemitta-Law', *VT* 4 (1954), pp. 196-99, esp. 199; *Sociology of the Biblical Jubilee*, pp. 186-87.

3. North, *Sociology of the Biblical Jubilee*, p. 187.

4. The preposition *ina* is usually rendered 'from'.

5. Wright, 'What Happened Every Seven Years, I', p. 136; *idem, God's People in God's Land*, pp. 171-72; cf. also Keil, *Pentateuch*, p. 369.

Lastly, Merendino,[1] Cavalleti,[2] Seitz,[3] Cholewiński,[4] Mayes[5] and Cardellini,[6] who follow the suggestion offered by *BHS*, suggest that the phrase משה את should be added after כל־בעל in v. 2a—viz. כל־בעל משה את משה ידו 'every holder of a pledge [shall release שמוט the pledge of his hand'. Furthermore, they ignore the accentuation of the Massoretic Text and suggest that the relative אשר is the subject of the next clause. Verse 2 can thus be rendered: 'every holder of pledge shall release the pledge of his hand, he who lends to his neighbour shall not exact it of his neighbour.' These scholars, like Horst and Weil, suggest that the release of a pledge was identical to the total remission of the loan or debt. Furthermore, they generally suggest that the service of the pledge, who was seized at the commencement of the loan transaction, went towards the amortization of the debt.[7] However, the above arguments, which suggest that Deut. 15.2 refers to the release of a human pledge, are not convincing for the following reasons.

First, many of the above interpretations of the role of the pledge are based on an inaccurate understanding of the ancient Near Eastern institution of pledging as illustrated in LH and many extant loan contracts. For example, we saw in Chapter 2 that pledges who were taken into the possession of the creditor at the commencement of loan transaction (*Besitzpfand*) were usually members of the debtor's family, but rarely the debtor himself, since his service was considered vital to the maintenance of his family. This view is clearly at odds with that of Horst and others, who suggest that Deut. 15.1-3 refers to the debtor who pledges himself to the creditor. Moreover, these human pledges most likely served in the house of the creditor in exchange for the payment of the interest, not the interest and capital as the majority of the above scholars suggest. In many cases human pledges remained in the possession of the debtor (hypothec) until the loan was foreclosed, after which the creditor took possession of the

1. Merendino, *Das deuteronomische Gesetz*, pp. 108-10.
2. S. Cavalletti, 'Il significato di mashsheh yad in Deuteronomy 15,2', *Antoni* 3 (1965), pp. 301-304.
3. Seitz, *Deuteronomium*, p. 168.
4. Cholewiński, *Heiligkeitsgesetz und Deuteronomium*, p. 219.
5. Mayes, *Deuteronomy*, p. 248.
6. Cardellini, *Die biblischen 'Sklaven'-Gesetze*, p. 270.
7. Cf. Mayes, *Deuteronomy*, p. 248, who does not clarify the role of the pledge

pledge. Land pledges were also used by creditors in exchange for the payment of interest, although there are examples of other types of 'land-lease' loans in which land was used by the creditor in exchange for the payment of both the interest and capital. Therefore, it is possible, as Wright suggests, that an immobile pledge, such as land, could be used by a creditor for the amortization of a debt. Nevertheless, for reasons which I will delineate below, Wright's interpretation is still not convincing.

Secondly, we also saw in Chapter 2 that creditors could seize human distraints, who were dependents of the debtor, after the foreclosure of a loan in order to compel the debtor to pay the overdue loan (e.g., LH §§113-116). This interpretation of the role of the distraint is clearly contrary to that of Weil, North and Wright, who suggest that distraints or pledges worked in the creditor's house in order to pay off the foreclosed loan.[1] Furthermore, in Chapter 2 we saw that both LH and other extant documents illustrate that the debtor could not be taken as a distraint. In fact, self-pledging was considered illegal during the NB period. Similarly, there are documents that illustrate that a creditor could not seize a debtor's dependent whose service was considered to be vital to the family. These examples also illustrate that certain people could not be distrained, since they were considered essential to the existence of the family.

Thirdly, as Boecker[2] correctly points out, the biblical pledge laws restricted the power a creditor held over a debtor. This is particularly true for the stipulations in Deut. 24.6, 10-13. Verse 6 states that a creditor was not entitled to take a mill or a millstone in pledge, since this act, in effect, would be the same as taking the life or livelihood of the debtor—viz., the acquisition of such pledges would only make it more difficult for the debtor to repay the loan. In vv. 10-13 further restrictions are imposed on the creditor, such as preventing the creditor from entering into the debtor's house in order to secure a pledge—viz., the creditor must take in pledge whatever the debtor

---

1. Weil, 'Gage et cautionnement dans la Bible', p. 171, uses LH §117 as evidence that a pledge is delivered to the creditor when the debt falls due. However, this law clearly refers to the sale or surrender of dependents, not the surrendering of pledges.

2. Boecker, *Law and the Administration of Justice*, pp. 183-84; cf. also Hossfeld and Reuter, 'נשׁא,' col. 663; Epsztein, *Social Justice in the Ancient Near East*, pp. 127-28.

brings out to him (v. 10). Furthermore, in the case of a poor man who can only give his cloak in pledge, the creditor must return the debtor's cloak each night in order that he may sleep in it (vv. 12-13). Therefore, the biblical pledge laws in Deuteronomy, like the distraint laws in LH (although these laws refer to distraints who are seized after the foreclosure of a loan), restricted the taking of pledges to those items not deemed essential to the livelihood of the debtor. The fact that Deut. 24.10-13 allowed the debtor to choose the pledge,[1] while demanding that the creditor return a cloak-pledge to the debtor at night, suggests that the biblical laws attempted to diminish the role played by a pledge or security seized at the commencement of a loan contract. Furthermore, the fact that the biblical laws do not mention the pledging of immobiles (e.g., houses, fields) and persons suggests that it is unlikely that the biblical legal collections (especially Deuteronomy) envisaged the taking of such pledges. The absence of any discussion of these pledges in biblical law is most likely due to the presence of the various biblical laws that prohibited the charging of interest on loans of accommodation (cf. Exod. 22.25; Deut. 23.19 [Hebrew v. 20]),[2] since we saw above that the service of such pledges usually went towards the payment of the interest charges (note that these stipulations appear next to each other in Exod. 22.25-27 [Hebrew vv. 24-26]). This prohibition is enunciated clearly in

---

1. Cf. Weinfeld, *Deuteronomy*, p. 289, who notes that this is an important Deuteronomic innovation.

2. Cf. North, *Sociology of the Biblical Jubilee*, pp. 176-79, 186; de Vaux, *Ancient Israel*, pp. 170-71; H. Gamoran, 'The Biblical Law against Loans on Interest', *JNES* 30 (1971), pp. 127-34; H.H. Cohen, 'Usury', *EncJud*, XXVI, cols. 27-28; Epsztein, *Social Justice in the Ancient Near East*, pp. 124-28. A.S. Kapelrud, 'נשׁך', *ThWAT*, V, cols. 665-69. North's suggestion that interest may have been charged to Israelites who were not poor finds no confirmation in biblical law. Nevertheless, it is clear that Deut. 15.1-3, 7-11 (also Lev. 25.35-38) refer to loans of accommodation that were given to poor Israelites. These laws, however, do not appear to have been observed during the Monarchic period (cf. Neh. 5.7, 12-13; Ezek. 22.12). Furthermore, during the Talmudic period, during which commercial loans were more common, various provisions, such as the *prosbul*, were made in order to circumvent the biblical usury laws; cf. H. Gamoran, 'The Talmudic Law of Mortgages in View of the Prohibition against Lending at Interest', *HUCA* 52 (1981), pp. 153-62; M. Goodman, 'The First Jewish Revolt: Social Conflict and the Problem of Debt', *JJS* 33 (1982), pp. 417-27.

Lev. 25.35-38, which, as Cholewiński[1] has shown, is parallel to Deut. 15.7-11. The restrictions that were placed upon the taking of a pledge, as well as the absence of interest charges, demonstrate that loans were meant to be 'charitable'—viz., the creditor was not able to gain any financial profit from the loan.

Lastly, that Deut. 15.1-3 did not envisage the release of an immobile or a human pledge who is secured at the commencement of a loan is demonstrated further by an examination of the context of this stipulation. While it is likely that the loan transaction referred to in v. 2 required the debtor to provide a pledge for the creditor, since v. 8 uses the verb [עבט] (העבט תעביטנו 'you shall generously lend to him') which most likely refers to pledge-loan-contracts, Horst's suggestion, that the term משה is a true Hiphil participle or that the participle נשא refers to personal pledges, is not convincing for the following reasons. For example, leaving aside the problems concerning the meaning of the term ידו 'his hand' in v. 2a,[2] it is clear that what is released in v. 3 is something that belongs to the creditor: את־הנכרי תגש ואשר יהיה לך את־אחיך תשמט ידך 'from a foreigner you may exact (it), but *whatever of yours is with your brother you shall release from your hand.*' It is difficult to understand how a pledge can be referred to in v. 3b, since it is clear that what is released in v. 3 is something that belongs to the creditor but that is in the possession of the debtor. It is much more likely that v. 3 refers to the loan (i.e., money or goods) which the creditor gave to his neighbour rather than a pledge who served in the house of the creditor. Therefore, it is more likely that the verb [נשא], like the verb [עבט], has the dual meaning 'to pledge' and 'to lend' (cf. Deut. 15.6,8). Moreover, although Horst's analysis of the use of the verb [נשא] in v. 2 and the verb [עבט] in v. 8 suggests that vv. 7-11 deal with poor (אביון; v. 7) Israelites who were able to offer only mobile pledges (e.g., cloaks; cf. Deut. 24.12-13), compared to vv. 2-3, which deals with Israelites who were able to offer human pledges, it is most likely that both sections refer to the poor Israelite farmers who were forced to seek

---

1. Cholewiński, *Heiligkeitsgesetz und Deuteronomium*, pp. 242-43.
2. I adopt the view that the phrase כל־בעל משה ידו should be rendered 'creditor', although it is also possible that the expression ידו is the object of the verb שמוט, in which case the expression בעל משה would be equivalent to the Akkadian expression *bēl ḫubullim* 'creditor' (lit. 'lord of a loan'); cf. Weinfeld, '"Justice and Righteousness"', p. 498.

maintenance from their neighbours (cf. the reference to אביון 'poor' in v. 4, which refers back to vv. 2-3, and Lev. 25.35-38, which is similar to Deut. 15.7-11).[1] Lastly, it is likely, as Weil and Neufeld[2] suggest, that Deut. 15.1-11 also envisaged other types of loans, such as loans secured without a pledge (hypothec) and loans that required the taking of a distraint after the foreclosure of a loan, although the latter distraint, contrary to the view of Weil, did not perform antichretic services but was most likely used by the creditor in order to force the debtor to pay the debt.[3] Therefore, although there is a causal relationship between the שמטה law and the manumission law in Deut. 15.12-18, nevertheless both laws refer to two completely different institutions—viz., the שמטה in vv. 1-3 refers to the release of loans while the law in vv.12-18 refers to the release of debt-slaves.

While the majority of scholars[4] are in agreement that the שמטה 'release' in Deut. 15.1-3 refers to the total remission of debts, we saw above that some scholars have suggested that this release provided for only a temporary suspension of a debt or loan. While Driver is uncertain whether the שמטה 'release' envisaged a temporary or permanent remission of loans or debts, Craigie[5] suggests that the שמטה 'release' in Deut. 15.1-3 refers only to the temporary remission of a loan during the Fallow year, since farmers would not be able to repay a loan on account of the fact that they would be unable to grow any

1. That both vv. 1-3, 7-11 refer to poor Israelite farmers is maintained by Driver, *Deuteronomy*, p. 178; Ridderbos, *Deuteronomy*, p. 181; Thompson, *Deuteronomy*, p. 186; Mayes, *Deuteronomy*, p. 247. Cf. also G. von Rad, *Deuteronomy*, p. 106, who notes that vv. 3-11 is a sermon which adds personal consideration to the apodictic stipulation in vv. 1-2.

2. Neufeld, 'Socio-Economic Background', pp. 61-62; 'Inalienability of Mobile and Immobile Pledges in the Laws of the Bible', *RIDA* 9 (1962), pp. 34-35.

3. Cf. Neufeld, 'Pledges in the Laws of the Bible', pp. 34-35; and Driver and Miles, *The Assyrian Laws*, p. 275, who suggest that 2 Kgs 4.1-7 refers to the seizure of distraints after the foreclosure of a loan. While this interpretation is possible, the fact that the widow claims that the creditor will come to take her children to be his slaves suggests that they were not distraints but hypothec pledges who became the property of the creditor.

4. For example, see von Rad, *Deuteronomy*, pp. 105-106; Neufeld, 'Socio-Economic Background', pp. 59-60; Mayes, *Deuteronomy*, p. 247; Thompson, *Deuteronomy*, p. 187; Cardellini, *Die biblischen 'Sklaven'-Gesetze*, p. 270.

5. Craigie, *Deuteronomy*, pp. 236-38.

crops during this period. However, as von Rad,[1] Phillips,[2] Lemche[3] and Epsztein[4] correctly point out, the appeal in vv. 7-11 to lend to poor Israelites, even though the שמטה might have been near, only makes sense if these verses envisaged a total discharge of loans or debts. Nevertheless, North,[5] who follows the earlier interpretation of Menes,[6] suggests that the שמטה provided for the temporary return of a pledge who worked in the creditor's house in order to pay back the loan.[7] As we saw above, North suggests that the pledge included the *debtor with his family and his field*.[8] Therefore, the שמטה allowed the debtor to earn independently for himself during one year out of seven. However, as I argued above, it is unlikely that Deut. 15.2 refers to a pledge-loan-contract that involved the taking of human distraints or pledges after the foreclosure of a loan in order to pay a foreclosed loan. Moreover, while North suggests that the Jubilee release, which provides for the release of both land and debt-slaves, is an extension and amplification of the שמטה, I will argue in Chapter 8 that these two types of release are separate and distinct types of legislation which attempted to provide for a wide range of debt-release.

That the שמטה 'release' in Deut. 15.1-3 envisaged the total remission of debts or loans is suggested further by the similarity between this

---

1. Von Rad, *Deuteronomy*, p. 106.
2. Phillips, *Ancient Israel's Criminal Law*, p. 78.
3. Lemche, 'The Manumission of Slaves', pp. 43, 45.
4. Epsztein, *Social Justice in the Ancient Near East*, p. 128.
5. North, *Sociology of the Biblical Jubilee*, pp. 186-87.
6. A. Menes, *Die vorexilischen Gesetze Israels im Zusammenhang seiner kulturgeschichtlichen Entwicklung* (BZAW, 50; Giessen, 1928), p. 80.
7. Cf. also Wright, 'What Happened Every Seven Years, I', p. 137; *idem, God's People in God's Land*, pp. 172-73; Keil, *Pentateuch*, p. 369, who suggest that Deut. 15.1-3 provided for only the temporary release of land that was pledged.
8. Cf. also E. Bellefontaine, 'A Study of Ancient Israelite Laws and their Function as Covenant Stipulations' (PhD dissertation; University of Notre Dame, 1973), p. 205, who suggests that the pledge, who was either the debtor or one of his dependents, worked in the house of the creditor in order to pay the debt.

stipulation and the stipulation found in A-s §3, which provided for the remission of non-commercial loans.[1] A-s §3 reads:[2]

> Whosoever has given barley or silver to an Akkadian or an Amorite as a loan... his document is voided (literally broken), because the king established *mīšarum* for the land, he may not collect the barley or silver on the basis of his document...

In his comparison of A-s §3 and Deut. 15.1-3, Weinfeld[3] mentions four important similarities of these stipulations. First, he notes that A-s §3, like Deut. 15.2, first mentions the proclamation about the cancellation of debts and then the warning that the creditor should not seek payment of the loan. Second, he notes that the phrase 'because the king established *mīšarum* for the land' is similar to the phrase כי־קרא שמטה ליהוה 'because the Lord's remission has been proclaimed' (Deut. 15.2), although the biblical proclamation is initiated by Yahweh rather than a king. Third, he notes that A-s §3, like Deut. 15.3, excluded foreigners from this release, and that the references to the Akkadian and Amorite in A-s §3, who are the local autochthonous citizens, are equivalent to the biblical terms אח and רע who are mentioned in Deut. 15.2—[4] לא־יגש את־רעהו ואת־אחיו. Lastly, and most importantly, Weinfeld notes that since A-s §3 refers to the *complete* cancellation of debts, it is most likely that Deut. 15.1-3, which belongs to the ancient Near Eastern tradition of remission of debts, also envisaged the complete cancellation of debts.

The above similarities between A-s §3 and Deut. 15.1-3 are particularly significant in view of the fact that the release of debt-slaves, which is dealt with in Deut. 15.12-18, is also envisaged in A-s

---

1. Cf. also H. Cazelles, 'Droit public dans le Deutéronome', in Lohfink (ed.), *Das Deuteronomium*, p. 102. That this stipulation refers to the cancellation of non-commercial loans is demonstrated in A-s §8, which states that the *mīšarum* did not apply to commercial loans.

2. This translation is provided by Weinfeld, ' "Justice and Righteousness" ', p. 497, who follows the translation of Kraus, *Königliche Verfügungen*, p. 171, which reads: 'Wer Gerste oder Silber einem Akkader oder Amurräer [als Darlehen, auf] Zins oder zur "Entgegennahme" (lit. "zerbrochen") [...]... ausgeliehen hat und (sich darüber) eine Urkunde hat ausstellen lassen—weil der König Gerechtigkeit für das Land wiederhergestellt hat, ist seine Urkunde hinfällig; Gerte oder Silber kann er nach dem Wortlaute eben der Urkunde nicht eintreiben (lassen).'

3. M. Weinfeld, ' "Justice and Righteousness" ', pp. 497-99; cf. also 'Sabbatical Year and Jubilee in the Pentateuch', p. 52.

4. Cf. also Finkelstein, 'Edict of Ammisaduqa's: A New Text', p. 53 n. 1.

§20. As we saw in Chapter 3, the stipulations in A-s §20 also appear in LH §117, which stipulates the periodic release of debt-slaves. Therefore, it is most likely that the compiler of Deuteronomy 15 carefully juxtaposed two stipulations that sought to provide for the periodic release of both non-commercial loans and debt-slaves, something that was accomplished less regularly through the declaration of the *mēšarum* edicts.

Exegesis of Deuteronomy 15.12-18

Deuteronomy 15.12a: The Identity of the העבריה *and the* העברי

Deut. 15.12

‎12 כי־ימכר לך אחיך העברי או העבריה ועבדך שש שנים ובשנה השביעת
‎תשלחנו חפשי מעמך:

12 If your brother, a Hebrew man or Hebrew woman, is sold to you, then he shall serve you six years, but in the seventh year you shall set him free from you.

One of the important innovations found in Deut. 15.12-18 is the addition of the terms אחיך 'your brother' and העבריה 'Hebrew woman'. While most scholars agree that the use of the term אח, which is ubiquitous in the book of Deuteronomy, clearly refers to Israelites, many are unclear about to which social class the designations העבריה או העברי refer. For example, Driver,[1] who is followed by several scholars,[2] notes that while the verb ימכר in Deut. 15.12, which also occurs in Lev. 25.39, can be rendered either as 'is sold' or 'sells himself', he suggests that this verb should be rendered 'he sells himself' in order to show that the העברי או העבריה were forced to sell themselves on account of destitution (cf. NEB). He suggests too that this case was exceptional, as opposed to the purchase of a Hebrew slave in Exod. 21.2, which he suggests was a matter of ordinary

---

1. Driver, *Deuteronomy*, p. 183; cf. also Ridderbos, *Deuteronomy*, p. 183 and n. 27.
2. For example, see Ridderbos, *Deuteronomy*, p. 183; Mayes, *Deuteronomy*, p. 251; Bellefontaine, 'A Study of Ancient Israelite Laws and their Function as Covenant Stipulations', p. 205; Cardellini, *Die biblischen 'Sklaven'-Gesetze*, p. 271; cf. also von Rad, *Deuteronomy*, p. 107.

occurrence. Similarly, Horst,[1] Bellefontaine[2] and Cardellini[3] suggest that the self-sale of a Hebrew man or woman in 15.12 is causally related to the pledging of an Israelite in 15.1-3—viz., if a debtor was not able to find a pledge to work off a debt (foreclosed?) he would be forced to enter into the service of a creditor or sell himself to a third party (cf. also Lev. 25.39).

However, although it is possible that the verb ימכר can be rendered reflexively, especially since this is the way it most likely should be rendered in Lev. 25.39, the context of Deut. 15.12-18 does not demand that this verb be rendered in this manner. On the contrary, the context suggests that this verb should be rendered passively 'is sold' (cf. RSV, NASB, NIV), since Deut. 15.12-18 is more similar to the law in Exod. 21.2-6 than the law in Lev. 25.39-54.[4] This interpretation is similar to that of Horst, Bellefontaine and Cardellini, except that they have misunderstood the nature of the debt-release law in Deut. 15.1-3 and have wrongly supposed that the circumstances surrounding the sale in Deut. 15.12 are similar to those envisaged in Lev. 25.39. Nevertheless, they are right in assuming that there is a causal relationship between Deut. 15.1-3 and 12-18, since the defaulting of a loan would eventually lead to the temporary or permanent enslavement of the dependent(s) of a debtor who was forced to sell them to a third party.

However, Horst,[5] Merendino,[6] Cholewiński[7] and Cardellini,[8] who have also been influenced by the relationship between Deuteronomy

---

1. Horst, *Gottes Recht*, p. 95.

2. Bellefontaine, 'A Study of Ancient Israelite Laws and their Function a Covenant Stipulations', p. 205.

3. Cardellini, *Die biblischen 'Sklaven'-Gesetze*, p. 271.

4. Cf. also Japhet, 'The Relationship Between the Legal Corpora', pp. 72-74 cp. Mayes, *Deuteronomy*, p. 251, who suggests that both translations are possible (passive, reflexive). The verb מכר occurs 16 times in the Niphal, 12 of which are clearly passive (cf. Exod. 22.2 [Hebrew v. 1]; Lev. 25.23, 34, 42, 48; 27.27, 28 Ps. 105.17; Isa. 50.1; 52.3; Neh. 5.8. This verb is usually rendered reflexively in Lev. 25.39, 47. The passages where this verb is difficult to render are Deut. 15.1 and Jer. 34.14.

5. Horst, *Gottes Recht*, p. 97.

6. Merendino, *Das deuteronomische Gesetz*, pp. 113, 124.

7. Cholewiński, *Heiligkeitsgesetz und Deuteronomium*, pp. 232 n. 53, 235.

8. Cf. also Thompson, *Deuteronomy*, p. 190, who suggests that Deut. 15.12-1 refers to a foreigner who has fallen on bad times.

15 and Leviticus 25, and by the comparison between the עברים with the *ḫabiru*, suggest that the terms העבריה and העברי refer to a lower social class of Israelites who were forced to 'sell themselves'.[1] Furthermore, Ellison,[2] Wright,[3] Riesener[4] and Kaufman[5] suggest that these terms in Deut. 15.12 refer specifically to a class of *landless* Israelites. While this view is based principally on the comparison of the biblical עברים with the cuneiform *ḫabiru*, both Wright and Kaufman also suggest that the context of Deut. 15.12-18 implies that landless Israelites are the subject of this law. On the one hand, contrary to Weippert[6] who suggests that the העברי 'Hebrew' is described as the אח 'brother' of the one who buys him, Wright[7] suggests that it is the term אח 'brother' that is being defined (i.e., limited or qualified). That is, the phrase העברי או העבריה 'a Hebrew man or Hebrew woman' is a specific qualification of the broader term אחיך 'your brother' for the purpose of indicating the Hebrew's social status. Moreover, he suggests that if the expression העברי או העבריה were used only in an ethnic sense, this expression would be tautologous. On the other hand, Kaufman[8] suggests that Deut. 15.13-14, which stipulates that an owner is to provide an 'endowment' for his released debt-slave, implies that alienated lands were not returned to their former owners at the שמטה 'release'. However, the above arguments are not convincing, for the following reasons.

First, we saw in Chapter 6 that the biblical עברים are not similar to the cuneiform *ḫabiru*. This is particularly true for the Nuzian service and loan contracts which are often used to demonstrate that the biblical manumission laws in Exod. 21.2-6 and Deut. 15.12-18 refer to Israelites who belong to a lower social class—e.g., those who do

---

1. Cf. also Thompson, *Deuteronomy*, p. 190, who suggests that Deut. 15.12-18 refers to a foreigner who has fallen on bad times.

2. Ellison, 'The Hebrew Slave', pp. 30-35.

3. Wright, 'What Happened Every Seven Years, II', pp. 196-97; *God's People in God's Land*, pp. 255-56.

4. Riesener, *Der Stamm עבד*, p. 125.

5. Kaufman, 'Social Welfare Systems of Ancient Israel', p. 282.

6. Weippert, *The Settlement of Israelite Tribes*, p. 83 n. 118; cf. also von Rad, *Deuteronomy*, p. 107; de Vaux, *Ancient Israel*, p. 83; Childs, *Exodus*, p. 468; Craigie, *Deuteronomy*, pp. 238-39; Hyatt, *Deuteronomy*, pp. 249-51.

7. Wright, 'What Happened Every Seven Years, II', p. 196; *God's People in God's Land*, p. 254.

8. Kaufman, 'Social Welfare Systems of Ancient Israel', p. 282.

not own any land. We also saw that the law in Exod. 21.2-6 was similar to the law in LH §117 which deals with the sale or surrender of dependents who belong to the head of a landed household. Therefore, on the basis of Exod. 21.2-6, it is most likely that the manumission law in Deut. 15.12-18 does not deal with landless Israelites (i.e., those without a patrimony). Moreover, as the majority of scholars suggest, the term עברי in Deut. 15.12 is used as an ethnic designation for Israelites, since it is connected with the term אחיך 'your brother' (i.e., fellow Israelite). It is extremely doubtful, as Wright suggests, that this term was used as a qualifying designation for Israelites who did not possess land. While the usage of both terms עברי and אח in Deut. 15.12 do appear to be at first sight tautologous, it is more likely that the term עברי was used in order to associate clearly this law with the law in Exod. 21.2-6 rather than the law in Lev. 25.39-54, since the literary structures of Leviticus 25 and Deuteronomy 15, including the two manumission laws in Lev. 25.39ff. and Deut. 15.12ff., are very similar in content and terminology respectively. Furthermore, contrary to the consensus of scholarly opinion, I will argue below in Chapter 8 that Lev. 25.39-54 does not deal with the type of debt-slavery that is dealt with in Exod. 21.2-6 and Deut. 15.12-18. Nevertheless, Wright is correct in noting that the term אח, which is not used in Exod. 21.2-6, has a very broad meaning. Moreover, Japhet notes correctly that the term אחיך was employed in order to emphasize that the release and provision of debt-slaves was the concern of *all* Israelites, not just their immediate kin. The term אח 'brother' is used here in its broadest meaning, as a reference to the nation of Israel or the covenant community.[1] Japhet thus concludes:[2]

> The present collection of laws [Deut 15.12-18], therefore, can be seen as an attempt to break through and broaden the tribal framework into the national, a process made possible by a broadening of the meaning of the basic concepts, and principally by conceiving of the nation as an extended family. The use of the word 'brother' in this context is one of the important means employed to achieve this goal.

---

1. Cf. O. Bächli, *Israel und die Völker: Eine Studie zum Deuteronomium* (ATANT, 41; Zurich, 1962), pp. 119, 121-23; McConville, *Law and Theology in Deuteronomy*, pp. 19, 32; M. Weinfeld, *Deuteronomy*, p. 229 and n. 5.
2. Japhet, 'The Relationship Between the Legal Corpora', p. 77.

Secondly, as Mayes[1] points out correctly, there is a natural connection between the agricultural context of the Fallow in Exod. 23.10-11 and the שמטה 'release' of debts stipulated in Deut. 15.1-3, which granted a total remission of debts for poor Israelite farmers. This is also true for the other laws contained in Deut. 14.22–16.17 which deal with various cultic laws and festivals that are connected with agricultural tithes and offerings. Moreover, there is a significant relationship between the non-release laws, that stipulated the tithing and offering of various agricultural products that were a sign of God's blessing upon Israel (15.7; 16.10, 15), and the two release laws in 15.1-11, 12-18, which stipulated that the richer segments of Israel share their agricultural products or blessings with their poorer 'brothers' (15.14). Therefore, contrary to the view of Kaufman, the fact that Deut. 15.12-18 includes a stipulation to provide released Hebrew debt-slaves with 'endowments' does not necessarily imply that these people did not possess land. It is more likely, in view of the fact that biblical law helped to prevent the permanent alienation of land (*Bodenrecht*) and that Deuteronomy frequently mentions the land that God will give to Israel as an inheritance (נחלה ; cf. Deut. 4.21, 38; 12.9; 15.4; 19.10; 20.16; 21.23; 24.4; 25.19; 26.1), that this humanitarian provision was stipulated in order to provide the released debt-slaves' families with those provisions that were helpful to poor farmers. This is particularly true for the flocks mentioned in 15.14, since they could help a poor farmer to start a new herd or strengthen an existing one. I will discuss the concept of blessing, which is one of the important innovations of Deuteronomy 15, in more detail below.

However, while the above arguments show that Deut. 15.12-18 most likely deals with the manumission of Israelite debt-slaves who are dependents of a man who was forced to sell them on account of insolvency, there still is the question about the identification of the העבריה 'Hebrew woman',[2] who, as we saw above, is not dealt with in Exod. 21.2-6. Driver,[3] who discusses the various attempts to harmonize the laws in Exod. 21.2-6, 7-11 with Deut. 15.12-18, concludes that the latter law has abrogated the stipulations concerning

---

1. Mayes, *Deuteronomy*, p. 247.
2. The term העבריה is found elsewhere only in Jer. 34.9, which appears to be dependent on the slave law in Deut. 15.12-18 and in Exod. 1.15, 16, 19; 2.7 (plural forms העברית and העבריות, which refers to Hebrew midwives (למילדת העבריה).
3. Driver, *Deuteronomy*, pp. 182-83; cf. also Thompson, *Deuteronomy*, p. 189.

the so-called Israelite debt-slave who is given to a Hebrew male deb slave (Exod. 21.4), and an Israelite daughter who is sold as a wife concubine (Exod. 21.7-11). In his discussion, Driver looks at thre attempts to harmonize the law of Exod 21.2-6, 7-11 with Deut. 15.1 18. First, he notes that Exod. 21.2 might have intended tacitly include the discussion of the העבריה 'Hebrewess'. Secondly, he note that Deut. 15.12-18 might not have abrogated the law in Exod. 21. 11. However, Driver suggests that Exod. 21.4 refers to an Israeli debt-slave (i.e., העבריה) who does not go free after six years' servic Therefore, he concludes that it is improbable that Exod. 21.2 tacit refers to the release of a female Hebrew debt-slave. Moreover, I suggests that the addition of the term העבריה would hardly have bee made in Deut. 15.12, unless some material modification had bee intended by it. Lastly, while Hengstenberg[1] suggests that Exod. 21. 11 relates only to the case of a woman who is sold into concubinag while Deut. 15.12 contemplates the case of a woman who enters into non-sexual service, Driver counters that the terms employed in Deu 15.12, 17 are too general—viz., the sale of a concubine must b included, unless the law of Deuteronomy belongs to an age fa removed from that of Exodus. Taking the latter option, Drive concludes:[2]

> No doubt the true explanation for the variation is that the law of Dt. springs from a more advanced stage of society than the law of Ex.; it thus regulates usage for an age in which the power of a father over his daughter was no longer so absolute as it had been in more primitive times, and places the two sexes on a position of equality.

However, Driver's criticism of previous harmonizing treatment like that of Hengstenberg, are unconvincing for the following reason First, as we saw in Chapter 6, the אשה mentioned in Exod. 21.4 is n a Hebrew or an Israelite debt-slave, but rather most likely a foreig chattel-slave, although I did suggest that there is the possibility tha this woman was a daughter of the lord of the עבד עברי. Moreove Phillips's[3] and Patrick's[4] suggestion that Deut. 15.12-18 abolished th

1. Hengstenberg, *Beiträge*, III, p. 439. This is cited in Driver, *Deuteronom* p. 182.
2. Driver, *Deuteronomy*, pp. 182-83.
3. Phillips, *Ancient Israel's Criminal Code*, p. 77; 'The Laws of Slavery: Exod 21:2-11', p. 56.
4. Patrick, *Old Testament Law*, p. 113.

stipulation in Exod. 21.4, which prevented a Hebrew debt-slave from taking his wife with him when he was released, is unlikely, since it is doubtful that a man's right of ownership over a chattel-slave (or a father's rights over his daughter) would ever be abrogated. The fact that the deuteronomist does not mention this transaction does not imply that he has abrogated it. Secondly, Driver uses Hengstenberg's view to suggest that Deuteronomy no longer envisaged concubinage—viz., women have attained an equal position with men. Similarly, von Rad,[1] Mayes[2] and others[3] suggest that by the time the law in Deut. 15.12-18 was composed there occurred a significant social change whereby women were on an equal footing with men. Both von Rad and Mayes note that during the Monarchic period women could inherit property (cf. 2 Kgs 8.3). On the basis of this passage, Mayes suggests that women 'held an independent position of responsibility before the law, which carried with it the possibility of being reduced through debt to slavery'. However, both Driver and Mayes assume incorrectly that the העבריה mentioned in Deut. 15.12 was a woman of independent means. As we saw in Chapter 5, Exod. 21.2, like LH §117, most likely envisaged the sale of a dependent who belonged to the debtor who was unable to pay off a loan. That Deut. 15.12 referred also to the sale of dependents is demonstrated further by the fact that this law is more similar in this respect to LH §117 than Exod. 21.2 is—viz., Deut. 15.12-18 deals with the sale of a son, daughter, and possibly a wife, although Deut. 15.16-17 could not apply to the debtor's wife. Therefore, as Hengstenberg rightly notes, Deut. 15.12 deals specifically with the sale of dependents (e.g., female chattel-slaves and daughters) who performed non-sexual labour, which was one of the most common types of slave sale transactions in the ancient Near East.[4] However, the fact that Deut. 15.12 does not refer specifically to the sale of free-born Israelite daughters does not imply

---

1. Von Rad, *Deuteronomy*, p. 107.

2. Mayes, *Deuteronomy*, p. 251.

3. Steuernagel, *Deuteronomium*, p. 110; Boecker, *Law and the Administration of Justice*, p. 181; Cardellini, *Die biblischen 'Sklaven'-Gesetze*, p. 273; Patrick, *Old Testament Law*, p. 113.

4. Cf. Jackson, 'Some Literary Features of the Mishpatim', p. 235, who correctly notes that the sale of women for household or other non-sexual labour was very common in the ancient Near East.

that Deut. 15.12-18 abrogated this provision[1].

Recapitulating, the above discussion shows that Deut. 15.12, like Exod. 21.2, deals with the release of a Hebrew debt-slave who is a dependent of a debtor who could not repay a foreclosed loan. The addition of the term העבריה in Deut. 15.12 is consistent with the discussion in LH §117, in which the sale of a son, daughter or wife is envisaged. Although a Hebrew woman is not mentioned in Exod. 21.2, it is most likely that while the compiler of this law was aware of such transactions, he chose nevertheless to direct his attention to the marital rights of male and female Hebrew debt-slaves. This special concern is clearly evident in the careful juxtaposing of vv. 2-6, 7-11. However, such concerns are not emphasized in Deut. 15.12-18, since this law concentrates on other factors, such as the debt-slave's release and his or her prerogative to become a permanent servant. Nevertheless, I concluded that although Deut. 15.12-18 does not mention the sale of a free-born Israelite daughter as a wife or concubine (Exod. 21.7-11), Deuteronomy most likely did not abrogate this institution.

Deuteronomy 15.12b: The Seventh-year Release

Deut. 15.12

12 כי־ימכר לך אחיך העברי או העבריה ועברך שש שנים ובשנה השביעת
תשלחנו חפשי מעמך:

12 If your brother, a Hebrew man or Hebrew woman, is sold to you, then he shall serve you six years, but in the seventh year you shall set him free from you.

---

1. Cf. Boecker, *Law and the Administration of Justice*, pp. 181-82; and Phillips, 'The Laws of Slavery: Exodus 21:2-11', p. 56, who suggests that the 'right of release of female slaves [in Deut. 15.12] is not to be attributed to a moral development in Israelite law which disapproved of female slaves being used for concubinage as provided by Exodus 21.8-11 [sic.]'. It should also be noted that daughters often had little freedom of choice in marital matters, although there are some cases in which women married out of love. However both methods are illustrated in pre-monarchic and monarchic texts: examples of arranged marriages include: Gen. 21.21; 24.35-58; Josh. 15.16; 1 Sam. 18.17, 19, 21, 27; 25.44; examples of 'love' marriages include: Gen. 26.34-35; 34.4; Judg. 14.2; 1 Sam. 18.20. Furthermore, husbands are often referred to as the wife's בעל 'lord' (cf. Exod. 21.3; 22.2 [Hebrew v. 1]; 2 Sam. 11.26; Prov. 12.4; the husband is also called אדני in Gen. 18.12; Judg. 19.26; Amos 4.1). Wives are also listed as the property of the head of the household in Exod. 20.17; Deut. 22.22. Cf. also the discussion of de Vaux, *Ancient Israel*, pp. 26-39.

Although the deuteronomic provision to set a male or female Hebrew debt-slave free in the seventh year is similar to that in Exod. 21.2, there are two important differences which deserve investigation. First, while Exod. 21.2 uses the expression יצא לחפשי חנם 'he shall go out as a free man without payment' in its stipulation concerning the release of a Hebrew debt-slave, Deut. 15.12 uses the expression תשלחנו חפשי מעמך 'you shall set him free from you'. Secondly, and most importantly, although most scholars[1] are in general agreement that both Exod. 21.2 and Deut. 15.12 stipulate the individual release of debt-slaves after six years' service, some scholars, who note the close association between Deut. 15.12-18 and the Sabbatical release in vv. 1-3, and who compare the seven-year release with the universal fifty-year release in Leviticus 25, suggest that Deut. 15.12 stipulates the universal release of debt-slaves during the Sabbatical year. To an investigation of these important differences we now turn.

First, a comparison of the two expressions in Exod. 21.2b and Deut. 15.12b reveals that while the Hebrew slave is the subject of the verb יצא 'he shall go' in Exod. 21.2b, the lord is the subject of the verb תשלחנו 'you shall set him (free)' in Deut. 15.12b.[2] As Weinfeld[3] notes correctly, it is most likely that the verb יצא in Exod. 21.2, 5 indicates the *right* of the slave to go free (i.e., primary law), while the verb שלח in Exod. 21.26, 27 indicates the *obligation* or *duty* of the master to manumit a slave on account of his treatment of him or her. Therefore, it is also likely that the verb שלח is used in Deut. 15.12b in order to indicate the obligation or duty of the master to release a Hebrew debt-slave, especially in the light of the fact that the master is exhorted to provide the released debt-slave with provisions in vv. 13-14 (note, though, that the verb אצא [root: יצא] occurs in v. 16). Emphasis is placed upon the master in these verses because it was

---

1. For example, see Horst, *Gottes Recht*, pp. 95-96 and n. 213; Dillmann, *Deuteronomium*, p. 309; Neufeld, 'Socio-Economic Background', p. 96; Ridderbos, *Deuteronomy*, p. 183; Gispen, *Exodus*, p. 206; Childs, *Exodus*, p. 468; Lemche, 'The Manumission of Slaves', p. 45; Westbrook, 'Jubilee Laws', p. 209; Cholewiński, *Heiligkeitsgesetz und Deuteronomium*, pp. 233-34; Cardellini, *Die biblischen 'Sklaven'-Gesetze*, p. 272 and n. 18; Wright, 'What Happened Every Seven Years, II', p. 198; Kaufman, 'The Structure of the Deuteronomic Law', pp. 282-83; Braulik, 'Die Abfolge der Gesetze in Deuteronomium 12-26', p. 263; Mekilta, *ad. loc.*

2. Cf. Seitz, *Deuteronomium*, p. 171.

3. Weinfeld, *Deuteronomy*, p. 283.

likely to be left up to him how much he gave to the released debt-slave. Therefore, as Weinfeld points out correctly, v. 12 reads more like a moral exhortation than the pronouncement of law,[1] although one must beware of relegating such humanitarian stipulations entirely to the realm of exhortation, since they form an integral part of Israelite covenantal law.[2] Lastly, this new stipulation in vv. 13-14 accounts for the missing term חנם 'without payment', which appears in Exod. 21.12, although this condition is tacitly implied in Deut. 15.12-18.

Second, there have been two major attempts to associate the 'release' in Deut. 15.1-3 with the seventh-year release in vv. 12-18. Seitz,[3] who notes that there is an intricate chiastic relationship that exists between Deut. 15.1-11, and vv. 12-18, suggests that v. 12 provided for the universal release of debt-slaves during the שמטה. However, while both Kaufman and Braulik have also noted that there is a close literary relationship between Deut. 15.1-11, 12-18, nevertheless they rightly note that there is no sufficient reason for associating the release of a debt-slave with the שמטה 'release', especially since v. 12 and v. 18 clearly refer to a fixed six years' service. Similarly, Cardellini[4] notes that there is a close association between vv. 1-3 and vv. 12-18, since both are closely connected with the concept of the Sabbath (*Sabbatgedanke*), although he notes correctly that this close association does not necessarily imply that both require the same type of universal release. Furthermore, Phillips[5] suggested that the seven-year release in Exod. 21.2 and Deut. 15.12 was performed at the so-called covenant renewal festival, which was presumably celebrated at the amphictyonic shrine (cf. Deut. 31.10-13). However, in view of Lemche's[6] criticism of Noth's amphictyonic theory, Phillips[7] no longer associates the pre-monarchic law in Exod. 21.2-6 with the so-called covenant renewal festival. He

1. Cf. also von Rad, *Studies in Deuteronomy*, 21; Carmichael, *The Laws of Deuteronomy*, 55–56.

2. Cf. McConville, *Law and Theology in Deuteronomy*, p. 93.

3. Seitz, *Deuteronomium*, pp. 167-75, esp. 171.

4. Cardellini, *Die biblischen 'Sklaven'-Gesetze*, p. 272 and n. 18.

5. Phillips, *Ancient Israel's Criminal Law*, pp. 73-75.

6. Lemche, 'The Hebrew Slave', p. 137.

7. A. Phillips, 'The Decalogue—Ancient Israel's Criminal Law', *JJS* 34 (1983), pp. 1-20; *idem*, 'The Laws of Slavery: Exodus 21:2-11', p. 58; cf. also Mayes, *Deuteronomy*, p. 250.

now suggests that Deut. 15.12-18 originally referred to the *individual* release of debt-slaves, although the deuteronomic editors understood that this law was an extension of the שמטה 'release' in vv. 1-11. Phillips, like Mayes[1] and Thompson,[2] suggests that Jer. 34.14 confirms this deuteronomic interpretation, since it uses the expression 'at the end of (every) seven years' מקץ שבע שנים, which is also found in Deut. 15.1, in its reference to the manumission of slaves in Deut. 15.12-18, although Jer. 34.8-10 does not provide for the release of debts. These scholars suggest that v. 14 pertains to the simultaneous release of debt-slaves declared by Zedekiah in vv. 8-10.[3] However, as Driver,[4] Reider,[5] Carroll[6] and Rudolph[7] note correctly, the expression מקץ שבע שנים should be rendered 'at the end of every period of seven years', which was understood to mean 'in the seventh year', from the beginning to the end of the seventh year (cf. also Deut. 14.28 מקצה שלש שנים and 26.12 בשנה השלישת שנת), since Jer. 34.14 plainly states that the people should have released their slaves in the seventh year, after serving for six years.[8] Verse 14 reads:

מקץ שבע שנים תשלחו איש את־אחיו העברי אשר־ימכר לך ועבדך שש שנים
ושלחתו חפשי מעמך ולא־שמעו אבותיכם אלי ולא הטו את־אזנם:

In the seventh year each of you shall set free his Hebrew brother, who has been sold to you and has served you six years, you shall send him out free from you; but your forefathers did not obey Me, or incline their ear to Me.

Although vv. 8-11 clearly recount that Zedekiah did proclaim a universal דרור 'release' (v. 8) of debt-slaves, since the people of Jerusalem did not release their slaves after serving six years (v. 11), there is no evidence that this particular release was based on a previous universal understanding of the debt-slave law in Deut. 15.12-

1. Mayes, *Deuteronomy*, p. 250.

2. J.A. Thompson, *The Book of Jeremiah* (NICOT; Grand Rapids: Eerdmans, 1980), pp. 611-12; contra *idem*, *Deuteronomy*, pp. 189-90.

3. Cf. also M. David, The Manumission of Slaves under Zedekiah: A Contribution to the Laws about Hebrew Slaves', *OTS* 5 (1948), p. 75.

4. Driver, *Deuteronomy*, p. 174.

5. Reider, *Deuteronomy*, pp. 148-49; cf. also Ibn Ezra and Ramban, *ad. loc.*

6. R.P. Carroll, *Jeremiah* (OTL; London: SCM Press, 1986), p. 649.

7. W. Rudolph, *Jeremia* (HKAT, 1/12; 3rd edn,1968), pp. 222-23.

8. Cf. also R.K. Harrison, *Jeremiah and Lamentations* (TOTCS; Downers Grove, IL: Inter Varsity Press, 1973), p. 147.

18.[1] It is my contention that Zedekiah, in his role as king, declared this דרור 'release' in order to re-institute the individual release of debt-slaves as provided for in the manumission laws found in both Exod. 21.2-6 and Deut. 15.12-18.[2] Similarly, Phillips[3] suggests that this release may have been a one-off event aimed at replenishing the ranks of those Judeans who were fighting the Babylonians, although he rejects this interpretation because he understands the expression מקץ שבע שנים in v. 14 as a clear statement of a universal release.

Recapitulating, the above discussion shows that although the release of a Hebrew debt-slave is expressed differently in Deut. 15.12 than in Exod. 21.2, nevertheless both laws stipulate the individual release of debt-slaves in the seventh year. Furthermore, while the release of a debt-slave is expressed from the point of view of the master in Deut. 15.12, rather than from the point of view of the debt-slave as in Exod. 21.2, nevertheless I have argued that this change is due to the deuteronomic addition in 15.13-14, which stipulates that a master was to provide a released debt-slave with provisions. To a discussion of this important innovation we now turn.

Deuteronomy 15.13-15: The Provisioning of Released Slaves

Deut 15.13-15

13 וכי־תשלחנו חפשי מעמך לא תשלחנו ריקם:
14 העניק תעניק לו מצאנך ומגרנך ומיקבך אשר ברכך יהוה אלהיך תתן־לו:
15 וזכרת כי עבד היית בארץ מצרים ויפדך יהוה אלהיך על־כן אנכי מצוך את־הדבר הזה היום:

13 And when you set him free from you, you shall not send him away empty-handed.

---

1. Cf. Rudolph, *Jeremiah*, p. 223.

2. It is, however, possible that the release proclaimed by Zedekiah extended to all Israelites, including non-dependents, since by this time many Israelites no longer owned land. Cf. also Wright, 'What Happened Every Seven Years, II', pp. 200-201; *God's People in God's Land*, p. 259, who rightly notes that the Jubilee release of land was no longer applicable during this time. However, it is not evident that the reference to Deut. 15.12 in Jer. 34.13 implies that the Deuteronomic legislation envisaged the release of landless Israelites, since I have argued above that this law most likely did not envisage the alienation of land. That the release declared by Zedekiah likely included non-dependents may have been due to the political, economic and moral changes which no longer prevented the alienation of land and the enslavement of entire families (cf. also Neh. 5).

3. Phillips, 'The Laws of Slavery: Exodus 21:2-11', p. 58.

14 You shall furnish him liberally from your flock and from your threshing floor and from your wine vat; just as the Lord your God has blessed you you shall give to him.

15 And you shall remember that you were a slave in the land of Egypt, and the Lord your God redeemed you; therefore I command you this thing today.

While the stipulation in Deut. 15.13-15 emphasizes the humanitarian aspects of the deuteronomic legislation, we already saw that this stipulation was meant to aid poor farmers by providing essential provisions for their released dependents. Furthermore, we saw that the drafting of the manumission law in Deut. 15.12-18 was influenced by its placement within the larger literary discussion found in Deut. 14.22–16.17. This influence is particularly evident in Deut. 15.14, which I will discuss below. However, there are other literary allusions upon which Deut. 15.13 draws.

In Deut. 15.13 the owner is commanded not to send his male or female slave away ריקם 'empty-handed'.[1] The adverb ריקם also occurs in the discussion of the three yearly pilgrimages in Deuteronomy 16 (cf. also Exod. 23.15; 34.20), which I will discuss later, and in Gen. 31.42 (1) and Exod. 3.21 (2), both of which depict similar circumstances to those found in Deut. 15.13-15.

1. Genesis 29–31 recounts the time when Jacob, who was under the direction of Isaac, went to Paddan-aram in order to marry one of the daughters of Laban, Jacob's mother's brother (Gen. 28.1-2). After Jacob meets Rachel, Laban's youngest daughter, he agrees to work in Laban's household for seven years in order to marry her (Gen. 29.13-20). However, after Jacob works seven years for Rachel Laban deceives Jacob by giving him Leah, his eldest daughter, instead of Rachel (Gen. 29.21-25). Jacob therefore agrees to work another seven years in order to marry Rachel (Gen. 29.26-30). However, after Jacob works seven years for Rachel, Laban persuades Jacob to remain in his service for six more years, after which Jacob secretly flees from Laban with his two wives, large flocks, servants, camels and donkeys,

---

1. The use of the adverb ריקם in the Old Testament can be categorized in the following way: (1) 'empty, empty-handed' (a) With the verb שוב 'to return': 2 Sam. 1.22; Isa. 55.11; Jer. 14.3; Ruth: 1.21; 3.17 [בוא]; (b) With the verb שלח 'to send': Gen. 31.42; Deut. 15.13; 1 Sam. 6.3; Job 22.9; (c) With the verb הלך 'to go': Exod. 3.21; (d) With the verb ראה Niphal 'to appear': Exod. 23.15; 34.20; and Deut. 16.16; (2) With the meaning 'without cause': Ps. 7.5 (Hebrew v. 4); 25.3.

all of which he was able to acquire during his service under Laban
(Gen. 30.25-43). When Laban catches up with Jacob he accuses Jacob
of deceiving him by leaving in secret. Jacob responds that he fled
because he was afraid that Laban would take his wives away (Gen.
31.31). When Laban is unable to find the missing household gods,
which Rachel secretly took from him, Jacob becomes angry and
responds by saying (Gen. 31.41-42):

> 41 These twenty years I have been in your house; I served you fourteen
> years for your two daughters, and six years for your flock, and you
> changed my wages ten times.
> 42 If the God of my father, the God of Abraham, and the fear of Isaac,
> had not been for me, *surely you would have sent me away empty-handed*
> (כי עתה ריקם שלחתני). God has seen my affliction and the toil of my
> hands, so He rendered judgement last night.

While the use of the number 'seven' is ubiquitous both in the law
and narrative of the Pentateuch, the fact that it is only used in
connection with service in Genesis 29–31 and the slave laws in Exodus
and Deuteronomy (Jeremiah 34) more than suggests that these laws
may have the background of Genesis 29–31 in mind, especially since
Jacob flees from Laban after serving him six years, the equivalent
number of years that a Hebrew debt-slave was to work before being
released. Furthermore, the verb שלח and adverb ריקם are found in
both Gen. 31.42 (עתה ריקם שלחתני) and Deut. 15.13 (לא תשלחנו ריקם),
both of which deal with the giving of provisions to persons after their
release. However, while Jacob protests that Laban would not have
given him anything, the deuteronomist stipulates that the master shall
provide the released debt-slave with provisions. It is therefore most
likely that this stipulation was influenced by the literary allusion found
in Gen. 31.42.[1]

---

1. While Carmichael, *The Laws of Deuteronomy*, pp. 86-94, does note the
association between the Deuteronomic discussion of the tithe, debt-release and
manumission laws in Deut. 14.22–16.17, he does not consider the possible literary
relationship between Genesis 29–31 and the manumission law in Deut. 15.12-18.
However, he does note elsewhere, *Women, Law, and the Genesis Traditions*
(Edinburgh: Edinburgh University Press, 1979), pp. 29-30, that many of the
traditions in the book of Genesis have been taken up by the Deuteronomist, including
the traditions concerning Leah and Rachel, although he does not apply these to the
law in Deut. 15.12-18.

2. Exod. 3.21-22 (cf. Exod. 12.35-36) is also similar to the situation in Deut. 15.12-18. Exod. 3.21-22 reads:

> 21 And I will grant this people favour in the sight of the Egyptians; and it shall be that when you go, *you will not go empty-handed* (לא תלכו ריקם).
> 22 But every woman shall ask of her neighbor and the woman who lives in her house, articles of silver and articles of gold, and clothing; and you will put them on your sons and daughters. Thus you will plunder the Egyptians.

In these verses God promises Israel that they will not go out of Egypt ריקם 'empty-handed'. While this similarity alone may not be adequate to suggest that the drafter of Deut. 15.13 drew upon the literary allusion in Exod. 3.21-22, the addition of the historical motivation clause in Deut. 15.15, which refers specifically to Israel's bondage and escape from Egypt, suggests that the deuteronomist did have Exod. 3.21-22 in mind when he composed the slave law in 15.12-18.[1] Furthermore, the verb שלח, which is used in Deut. 15.12-13, is also found in Exod. 3.20: 'So I will stretch out My hand, and strike Egypt with all My miracles which I shall do in the midst of it; and after that *he will let you go* (ישלח אתכם)'.

In Deut. 15.14 the owner is told what he should give to his released debt-slave. Verse 14 reads:

> העניק תעניק לו מצאנך ומגרנך ומיקבך אשר ברכך יהוה אלהיך תתן־לו:
> You shall furnish him liberally from your flock and from your threshing floor and from your wine vat; just as the Lord your God has blessed you you shall give to him.

This verse makes it clear that not only was the master required to give provisions to the released debt-slave, but he was to העניק תעניק 'liberally furnish' the slave just as God had blessed him. This verse, like the one before it, also contains literary allusions to a historical narrative, as well as to the legal discussions found in Deut. 14.22–16.17. First, the verb ענק 'to adorn with a necklace', 'to lay upon the neck' occurs elsewhere only in Ps. 73.6 (Qal denominative). The noun ענק 'necklace' occurs only in Judg. 8.26; Prov. 1.9 and Song 4.9. As Driver[2] and Mayes[3] note correctly, the image we get from the use of

---

1. Cf. Carmichael, *Women, Law, and the Genesis Traditions*, p. 30; *idem*, *The Laws of Deuteronomy*, p. 224; S.R. Driver, *Deuteronomy*, p. 183.

2. Driver, *Deuteronomy*, p. 183.

3. Mayes, *Deuteronomy*, p. 251

this verb is that the owner was to adorn the slave with his own possessions—literally 'to make a necklace for' (i.e., 'to honour or enrich'; cf. Prov. 1.9; Song 4.9). However, why should the deuteronomist use the unusual and rare verb ענק instead of the more common verb נתן 'to give', which is used in a similar sense in Deut. 15.9, 10, 14?[1] One possibility is that the deuteronomist is making another allusion to the release of Israel from Egypt, particularly the account in Exod. 3.22 in which God tells Israel that they will plunder the Egyptians (cf. Exod. 12.35-36). This verse reads: 'But every woman shall ask of her neighbour and the woman who lives in her house, articles of silver and articles of gold, and clothing; and *you will put them on your sons and daughters.*' Although the verb ענק is not found in this passage, nevertheless one can envisage the Israelite women placing gold and silver ornaments and chains around the necks of their children.[2] Second, as we saw above, Deut. 15.12-18 occurs within the larger discussion in 14.22–16.17, which has been organized around the discussion of the Sabbath. We saw too that the Sabbatical year release in Deut. 15.1-11, like the manumission law in vv. 12-18, attempted to meet the essential needs of poor farmers who could not sustain themselves and their families. However, a more important connection occurs in the discussion of the three yearly pilgrimages in Deuteronomy 16 and Exod. 23.14-19; 34.20-26, in which the phrase לא־יראו את־פני יהוה ריקם 'they shall not appear before Yahweh *empty-handed*' occurs (Deut. 16.16; לא־יראו פני ריקם Exod. 23.15 and 34.20).[3] In Exod. 23.15 the above phrase occurs in conjunction with the Feast of Unleavened Bread, and although there is no specific reference to what is to be brought before the Lord, Exod. 23.16 states that it is the first fruits of the land that are to be brought to the Lord. This would also appear to be the meaning in Exod. 34.20, in which the 'first fruits of the womb' are mentioned in conjunction with the

---

1. The verb העניק appears to be a functional equivalent of the verb נתן. Note the similarity between the verbal phrase נתון תתן in v. 10 and העניק תעניק in v. 14.

2. Cf. Rashi, *ad. loc.*

3. For a discussion of these pilgrimage festivals, see especially McConville, *Law and Theology in Deuteronomy*, pp. 100-23, whom I follow in this discussion. The three festivals are: (1) the Feast of Unleavened Bread (Exod. 23.15; 34.18-21; Deut. 16.1-8 in conjunction with the Passover); (2) the Feast of Weeks (In Exod. 23.16 it is called the Feast of Harvest; 34.22; Deut. 16.9-12); (3) the Feast of Booths (In Exod. 23.16; 34.22 it is called it the Feast of Ingathering; Deut. 16.13-14).

phrase 'they shall not appear before me empty-handed.' In Deut. 16.16, however, the phrase 'they shall not appear before Yahweh empty-handed' occurs in a summary statement referring to the three feasts, in which it is also mentioned that all males shall appear before the Lord three times a year (cf. Exod. 23.17; 34.23). Verse 17 expands upon this command: 'Every man shall give according to the gift of his hand, according to the *blessing* of the Lord your God which He has given you.' Thus the Israelites were commanded to appear before the Lord with their first fruits from the land which God had given them as the result of His blessing.[1] This qualification also appears in v. 10 concerning the freewill offering given during the Feast of Weeks. While these verses speak about returning the fruits of · Israel's endeavours according to the blessing of the Lord, Deut. 16.15 states that Israel is to observe these feasts because 'the Lord your God will bless you in all your produce and in all the work of your hands, so that you shall be altogether joyful.' The same motivation is found in Deut. 15.18b. Verse 18 reads:[2]

לא־יקשה בעינך בשלחך אתו חפשי מעמך כי משנה שכר שכיר עבדך
שש שנים וברכך יהוה אלהיך בכל אשר תעשה:

It shall not seem hard to you when you set him free from you, for he has given you six years double the amount of service of a hired man;[3] *so the Lord your God will bless you in whatever you do.*

As Weinfeld[4] has shown, the concept of reward (and blessing) based upon obedience lies at the core of deuteronomic literature. Moreover, McConville[5] has noted that both of the above passages appear to

---

1. Note that it is only in Deuteronomy that the first fruits are clearly associated with the possession of the land (cf. Deut. 8.1-10; 11.8-17; 15.4; 16.4, 14), while the conquest of the land is found after the discussion of the annual feasts in Exod. 23.20ff; cf. McConville, *Law and Theology in Deuteronomy*, pp. 11-13.

2. Verse 18 is a parenetic statement with its own motivation clause, 'so the Lord… '; cf. Sonsino, *Motive Clauses*, pp. 66-69, esp. 69. The position of this parenetic statement within the slave law is a matter of interest since it actually refers back to the discussion in vv. 12-15 and not to vv. 16-17! Since the parenetic statement contains the concept that Israel must obey the command in order to continue to enjoy God's blessings, it is natural that the parenetic statement refers back to vv. 12-15, since the discussion of God's blessing is found there. However, it is not clear why the parenetic statement does not come after v. 15.

3. For a discussion of the term משנה 'double', see Chapter 6.

4. Weinfeld, *Deuteronomy*, pp. 307-13, esp. 311-13.

5. McConville, *Law and Theology in Deuteronomy*, pp. 16-17.

express a causal relationship between Israel's obedience and God's blessing(s). In an attempt to illustrate this complex relationship in Deuteronomy 15, he proposes the following sequence: (1) God blesses (15.14b); (2) Israel obeys (15.15b); (3) God continues to bless (15.18b). This sequence, which illustrates the paradox between Yahweh's prior action(s) and Israel's response or obedience,[1] helps explain why Deut. 15.18 occurs at the end of the law, since although this verse is more applicable to vv. 12-15 the stipulation in vv. 16-17 was subject nevertheless to the conditions expressed in v. 18b.[2] Therefore, both Deut. 15.12-18 and Deuteronomy 16 draw upon the same paradox in the discussion of freewill offerings—viz., God will continue to bless Israel and its people as long as they continue to obey his commands, such as giving back to the Lord the first fruits of His blessing (Deuteronomy 16), and liberally providing a released slave with provisions from God's blessings.[3] It is clear, therefore, that the deuteronomist did not consider the stipulation in Deut. 15.13-15 merely as a humanitarian gesture, but as a command which was to be obeyed if Israel was to continue receiving God's blessing(s).

However, concerning the list of provisions in v. 14, Ehrlich[4] notes that while it was possible for the owner to give a released slave the first two provisions, he suggests that it is not possible for the owner to give the slave wine from his wine vat, since the slave would have to

---

1. Cf. McConville, *Law and Theology in Deuteronomy*, p. 18, who suggests that the theology of Deuteronomy can be organized around this paradox between Yahweh's prior action and Israel's response.

2. Cf. Mayes, *Deuteronomy*, p. 252, who suggests that although the position of v. 18 is awkward it nevertheless is better seen as an overall conclusion to the slave law; cp. Seitz, *Deuteronomium*, p. 172, who suggests that due to the position of v. 18, vv. 16-17 have been added at a later date.

3. Cf. also J. Halbe, ' "Gemeinschaft, die Welt Unterbricht": Grundfragen und-inhalte deuteronomischer Theologie und Überlieferungsbildung im Lichte der Ursprungsbedingungen alttestamentlichen Rechts', in Lohfink (ed.), *Das Deuteronomium*, pp. 58-60; and McConville, *Law and Theology in Deuteronomy*, pp. 12-14, who notes that in many occurrences of the verb נתן in Deuteronomy, God is the subject and the object is usually the Land, but other times it can be cities, towns (e.g. 13.12; 17.2), or the fruit of the ground, flocks and herds (26.10; 12.21). He also notes that this verb occurs in both Deuteronomy 15 and 16 in which the giving of God requires a response on the part of Israel. This idea of 'reciprocal giving' is present in the slave law in 15.12-18 in which a man 'liberally gives' to his released slave the fruits of the land that God has given him (v. 14).

4. Ehrlich, *Randglossen*, I, pp. 295-96.

drink the wine right away. While there may be some question whether this command was practicable, there is no suggestion in the text that the deuteronomist did not take this command seriously.[1] While McConville[2] observes that many of the laws in Deuteronomy may seem 'rationally indefensible' on occasion (e.g. Deut. 20.19-20; 15.12-18), nevertheless he notes rightly that these laws are more than a call to humanitarian action, since they illustrate the moral order enunciated in the book of Deuteronomy.

Moreover, although Ehrlich suggests that the list of provisions appears to be impracticable, this list may not refer specifically to what the owner actually owns but is included in order to emphasize that the master was to provide the free slave with *whatever* provisions he may have had.[3] This interpretation is clearly implied in the latter part of the verse, which reads: 'you shall give to him as the Lord your God has blessed you' (cf. also Deut. 7.13; 12.6, 17; 14.23; 16.13). Furthermore, the fact that this stipulation mentions wine implies that the released debt-slave would have somewhere to store it—viz., the released debt-slave was not a landless Israelite but a dependent who would bring the provisions to his father's property.

Lastly, in Deut. 15.15 a motivation clause referring to Israel's redemption from Egypt is found. That this historical recollection is used as a motivation to obey the manumission stipulation coincides with the literary allusions that I mentioned above, all of which deal in some way with Israel's release from Egypt. Furthermore, as Mayes[4] points out correctly, this motivation is regularly used as a motive for obedience to the law, although this motivation is particularly appropriate for the manumission law in Deut. 15.12-18 (cf. Deut. 5.15; 16.12; 24.18, 22).

Recapitulating, the above discussion shows that the stipulations concerning the provisioning of a released Hebrew debt-slave were part of a deuteronomic innovation that was motivated, on the one hand, by the historical recollection of the release of Jacob from Laban and Israel from Egypt, and on the other, by the discussions found in Deut. 14.22-16.17, particularly the requirement in 16.16 that all the

---

1. Cf. Boecker, *Law and the Administration of Justice*, pp. 182-83.
2. McConville, *Law and Theology in Deuteronomy*, 17–18.
3. Cf. Rashi, *ad. loc.*
4. Mayes, *Deuteronomy*, pp. 251-52; cf. also Daube, *Studies in Biblical Law*, pp. 49-51.

males were not to come ריקם 'empty-handed' to the three yearly
pilgrimage festivals, which is parallel to the requirement that an
owner shall liberally provide a released slave with provisions. While
this stipulation does not occur in Exod. 21.2-6, this does not suggest
that the deuteronomic law was intrinsically different from that in
Exodus.

*Deuteronomy 15.16-17: The Procedure for Entering into Permanent
Slavery*

Deut. 15.16-17

16 והיה כי־יאמר אליך לא אצא מעמך כי אהבך ואת־ביתך כי־טוב לו עמך:
17 ולקחת את־המרצע ונתתה באזנו ובדלת והיה לך עבד עולם
ואף לאמתך תעשה־כן:

16 And if he says to you, 'I do not want to go out from you, because he
loves you and your household,' since he fares well with you;
17 Then you shall take the awl and pierce it through his ear into the door,
and he shall become your slave forever. Also you shall do the same to
your female slave.

While Deut. 15.16-17 contains the essential points explicated in Exod.
21.5-6, which has been thoroughly discussed in Chapter 6, there are
some important differences which have influenced the interpretation
of the deuteronomic stipulation. For example, Deut. 15.16-17 does not
refer to the slave's love for his wife and children, although we saw
above that this omission reflects the particular emphasis that the
deuteronomist wished to convey, rather than any specific attempt to
abrogate marriages between a male debt-slave and a woman belonging
to his master. Furthermore, Deut. 15.17 includes a statement which
clarifies that a female debt-slave also had the option to become a
permanent debt-slave, although this addition merely clarifies that
which was most likely known to the compiler of Exod. 21.2-6, 7-11.
Lastly, and most importantly, the reference to the sanctuary of God in
Exod. 21.6 is not found in Deut. 15.17. To a discussion of this
important distinction we now turn.

As I already mentioned in the Introduction, the debate concerning
the date and origin of the book of Deuteronomy has been crucial in
the interpretation of several of its laws, particularly the cultic laws
that have been traced to Josiah's or Hezekiah's reform. This is
particularly true for the stipulation in Deut. 15.16-17 which has often
been cited as an example of the historical development that occurred

after the drafting of Exod. 21.5-6, since the deuteronomic stipulation apparently did not envisage the sacral rite within the sanctuary. For example, Driver[1] notes that the ceremony in Deut. 15.16-17 has a purely domestic character, which takes place entirely at the master's house. He also suggests that the deuteronomic stipulation reflects usage of a time at which the judicial ceremony enjoined in Exodus had fallen into disuse. While Driver does not explain why the ceremony in Exodus had fallen into disuse, von Rad[2] and Gispen[3] suggest that the procedure at the sanctuary lost its sacral character on account of the centralization of all cultic matters. The clearest expression of this viewpoint is found in Weinfeld's[4] treatment of Deut. 15.16-17, in which he notes that since the single sanctuary in Deuteronomy, as prescribed in ch. 12, could not perform all the functions originally discharged by the local sanctuaries, many institutions and practices were divorced from their original ties to the sanctuary in a manner that rendered them completely 'secular'. Weinfeld suggests, therefore, that the rite in Deut. 15.16-17 has been transformed into a secular one, since it was more practical in the light of the existence of a single sanctuary in Deuteronomy. This interpretation is only one argument among many that Weinfeld employs in order to show that this secularizing tendency occurs in most of the institutions and practices found in Exodus–Numbers (Priestly Source), such as the law of firstlings (15.19)[5], and the Feast of Weeks and Booths (16.9-17)[6]. While it is beyond the scope of my present discussion to examine Weinfeld's entire argumentation, nevertheless there are two important objections that can be raised against Weinfeld's interpretation of Deut. 15.16-17.

First, Weinfeld's claim that it would be impracticable to bring a slave to the central sanctuary when the slave wished to remain in service is unconvincing, since there is no reason why the debt-slave could not be brought to the so-called central sanctuary during one of the three annual feasts that are discussed in Deuteronomy 16. These religious festivals would be a suitable place at which slaves could

1. Driver, *Deuteronomy*, p. 184.
2. Von Rad, *Deuteronomy*, p. 107.
3. Gispen, *Exodus*, pp. 203 n. 6, 207 n. 8.
4. Weinfeld, *Deuteronomy*, pp. 213-14.
5. Weinfeld, *Deuteronomy*, p. 215.
6. Weinfeld, *Deuteronomy*, pp. 219-21.

present their oath before God (cf. also Exod. 23.14-17).

Secondly, it is not certain that the altar-law in Deuteronomy 12 can be traced to Josiah's or Hezekiah's reform or that this law advocates a sole sanctuary. For example, McConville[1] notes that since Josiah's reform had already begun when the book of Deuteronomy was discovered, it is likely that the altar-law (and Deuteronomy as a whole) was not used as the reform's blueprint. Furthermore, he suggests that the altar-law can be disengaged from Josiah's reform and that the altar-law does not advocate a sole sanctuary but only a pre-eminent one, tacitly allowing other, lesser altars.[2] Regarding the latter claim, McConville notes that many scholars have tried to identify the 'place'-formula in Deut. 12.5 with a single sanctuary. Wellhausen's assertion that the 'place'-formula referred to Jerusalem is still held by some scholars today.[3] However, McConville[4] notes that this view ignores the identification of the original place as Shiloh in Jer. 7.12. Furthermore, the northern sanctuaries of Shechem and Bethel also have their protagonists.[5] This continuing debate has recently centred around Noth's[6] amphictyony theory, according to which Shechem, Bethel, Gilgal and Shiloh were in succession the central sanctuary before Jerusalem. McConville notes that despite the rejection of Noth's theory, some support has remained for the view that a centralizing tendency of some sort existed in early Israel.

However, in his examination of each of the proposed central sanctuaries, McConville finds that while there there was probably an early tendency towards centralized worship, there was nothing

---

1. McConville, *Law and Theology in Deuteronomy*, p. 22.

2. McConville, *Law and Theology in Deuteronomy*, p. 29. Cf. also the discussion of Deuteronomy 12 in Ridderboss, *Deuteronomy*, pp. 12-19; G.J. Wenham, 'Deuteronomy and the Central Sanctuary', *TynBul* 22 (1971), pp. 103-18.

3. For example, see E.W. Nicholson, *Deuteronomy and Tradition* (Oxford: Basil Blackwell, 1967), pp. 94-95; R.E. Clements, *God and Temple: The Idea of the Divine Presence in Ancient Israel* (Oxford: Basil Blackwell, 1965), pp. 92-93; *idem*, 'Deuteronomy and the Jerusalem Cult Tradition', *VT* 15 (1965), pp. 303-12.

4. McConville, *Law and Theology in Deuteronomy*, p. 22.

5. For example, see H.H. Rowley, *The Worship of Israel* (London: SCM Press, 1967), p. 106 (Shechem); F. Dumermuth, 'Zur deuteronomischen Kulttheologie und ihren Voraussetzungen', pp. 69-71 (Bethel); O. Eissfeldt, 'Silo und Jerusalem', p. 146 (Shiloh).

6. M. Noth, *Das System der zwölf Stämme Israel* (BWANT, IV; Stuttgart, 1930), pp. 91-93.

approaching a single or sole sanctuary. While this centralizing tendency may have arisen out of a desire to bring all the tribes together on at least some cultic occasions (cf. Judg. 20; 1 Sam. 1–3; Josh. 22; cp. Exod. 23.14-17, which seems already to reflect a centralizing tendency), McConville[1] notes that there were other sanctuaries alongside the central ones during this period. Furthermore, while Deut. 12.5 has been interpreted to refer to a sole sanctuary, McConville suggests that scholars have misinterpreted this command. The difficulty lies in the phrase מכל־שבטיכם 'from all your tribes' (cp. Deut. 12.14). While this phrase suggests that Deut. 12.5 referred to a single sanctuary, McConville suggests that there is evidence that Deuteronomy, while requiring a pre-eminent sanctuary, did not exclude the possibility of worship elsewhere. That Deuteronomy knew of other sanctuaries is demonstrated by the presence of two laws that imply that worship was allowed elsewhere. For example, McConville[2] notes that the reference to the prohibition regarding planting a tree as an Asherah beside 'the altar of the Lord your God which you shall make' in Deut. 16.21 has been understood as a reference to other altars besides the central one, since it would have been difficult to plant a tree beside an altar that was in the central temple. While there is the possibility this law is pre-deuteronomic, McConville suggests that it is unlikely that a deuteronomic redactor would include such a law if he was anxious to press for a limitation of worship to a single sanctuary.[3] In addition, Deuteronomy 27, which states that sacrifices are to be made on Mt Ebal, in the vicinity of Shechem, assumes more than one sanctuary. Again, while this law is held to be pre-deuteronomic, the question remains why the law was included in the final form of the book.

McConville[4] concludes, therefore, that the command in Deut. 12.5 does refer to a single sanctuary but that the apparent exclusiveness of the command to seek 'the place' is coloured by the theology of Deuteronomy. He demonstrates this by looking at the verb יבחר (root: בחר) in Deut. 12.5, which is part of the choosing motif that appears throughout Deuteronomy (e.g., God chooses Israel [14.2], the king [17.15] and the priests [18.5; 21.5]). Therefore, in regards to the altar, Israel was to be distinct from the other nations in not choosing its own

1. McConville, *Law and Theology in Deuteronomy*, pp. 23-28.
2. McConville, *Law and Theology in Deuteronomy*, pp. 28-29.
3. Cp. von Rad, *Studies in Deuteronomy*, p. 18.
4. McConville, *Law and Theology in Deuteronomy*, pp. 29-40.

altar.[1] Moreover, Israel was not supposed to worship at any place that they chose, but only at the place that Yahweh would choose. Therefore, it is the notion of God's choosing that is in the foreground of the command in Deut. 12.5, not the notion of a single sanctuary.[2] Thus the other commands in Deuteronomy, which suggest that there was more than one sanctuary, do not contradict the intention of the altar-law, which did not rigidly insist upon a single sanctuary. It follows, therefore, that the altar-law cannot be used as evidence that the stipulation in Deut. 15.16-17 abolished the sacral ceremony found in Exod. 21.5-6, since it is likely that the altar-law recognized the existence of other sanctuaries.

However, Driver,[3] who criticizes Keil[4] for his attempt to harmonize the ceremony by suggesting that the ceremony in Exod. 21.5-6 is implied, says that if the deuteronomist had meant the ceremony in Deut. 15.17 to be at the sanctuary he would have stated it explicitly (cf. Deut. 17.8-9; 19.17). Reider,[5] though, notes correctly that Driver's argument is an *argumentum e silentio*. Furthermore, McConville[6] notes correctly that it is distinctive of Deuteronomy to leave out details in laws that are found in Exodus–Numbers. A good example of this can be found in the laws of the Feasts of Weeks and Booths in Deut. 16.9-17, which show some variation from legislation

---

1. McConville, *Law and Theology in Deuteronomy*, p. 31, notes that God's choosing an altar finds its closest analogy in the law of the king. He writes: 'As Israel was to be distinct from the nations in not choosing its own king, so too with the altar.'

2. Cf. McConville, *Law and Theology in Deuteronomy*, pp. 32-33, who notes that the theology of Deuteronomy often refers to singularity, such as the oneness of Israel that is reflected in Deuteronomy's reluctance to speak of divisions among Israel. Thus when the Deuteronomist 'speaks of "the place which the Lord will choose", he gives expression to his belief in the appropriateness of the idea of a single sanctuary alongside the idea of a unified people, but without feeling it necessary, or perhaps even desirable, to attempt to legislate for it'(p. 33).

3. Driver, *Deuteronomy*, p. 184.

4. Keil, *Pentateuch*, p. 372 and n. 1.

5. Reider, *Deuteronomy*, pp. 154-55.

6. McConville, *Law and Theology in Deuteronomy*, pp. 50-51, 63-66; cf. also G. Fohrer, *Introduction to the Old Testament* (London: SPCK, 1970), p. 173; and R. Rendtorff, *The Old Testament: An Introduction* (London: SCM Press, 1985), p. 154, who suggests that since only half of the regulations in the Covenant Code are taken into Deuteronomy, it is probable that they are presupposed as being known and still valid.

in other codes, and share some common themes with the laws concerning the poor and slaves in Deuteronomy 15. Bertholet,[1] Driver[2] and Weinfeld[3] note how there are differences between the deuteronomic legislation and previous legislations (Exodus, Leviticus). Bertholet,[4] for example, has concluded that since there is no mention of how much should be brought by the worshipper by way of offering at the Feast of Weeks, Deuteronomy had not yet fixed the quantities (cp. Lev. 23.17ff.). In addition, Weinfeld[5] has attributed this omission, and others, to the deliberate suppression of sacral ritual based on cult centralization. However, more recently McConville[6] has shown that the omissions in these laws are no more than a matter of imprecision, which has already been observed in many of the laws in Deuteronomy. In response to Bertholet's and Weinfeld's arguments McConville writes:[7]

> The mere absence of such details, however, compels neither of these conclusions. Once again, Deuteronomy's lack of concern for detail is sufficient explanation, and it is more satisfactory to suppose that, in the case of the Feasts of Weeks and Booths, the essential aspects of the festivals have been outlined as a framework for the habitual deuteronomic themes of blessing (vv.10, 15, 17), rejoicing (vv.11, 15), kindness to poor (vv.11, 14), and the contrast of life in the land with Egypt (v.12).

It follows, therefore, that a similar motivation accounted for the brevity of the legal discussion in Deut. 15.12-18, particularly regarding the ceremony in vv. 16-17 which enabled a debt-slave to become a permanent servant.

---

1. A. Bertholet, *Deuteronomium* (KHAT; Tübingen: Mohr, 1899), p. 52.
2. Driver, *Deuteronomy*, p. 196.
3. Weinfeld, *Deuteronomy*, pp. 219-21.
4. Bertholet, *Deuteronomium*, p. 52.
5. Weinfeld, *Deuteronomy*, p. 219. Weinfeld also notes that the laws of Feasts do not prescribe a sheaf-waving ceremony or the donation of loaves of bread and offerings of lambs, nor any allusion to the four species of flora or to the festal purpose of the booths (p. 219).
6. McConville, *Law and Theology in Deuteronomy*, pp. 110-23.
7. McConville, *Law and Theology in Deuteronomy*, p. 111.

Summary and Conclusions

To sum up, I have examined the various stipulations contained in the manumission law in Deut. 15.12-18 in an attempt to clarify the meaning of this law, especially in the light of the older manumission laws in Exod. 21.2-6, 7-11. As the above examination has shown, the biblical manumission law in Deut. 15.12-18, like the law in Exod. 21.2-6, stipulates the periodic release of debt-slaves who were the dependents of a defaulting debtor after six years service in the house of a creditor. Although this release is connected closely with the שמטה 'release' in Deut. 15.1-3, there is no adequate reason to conclude that the manumission of debt-slaves coincided with the שמטה 'release', especially since Deut. 15.12-18 states expressly that debt-slaves serve six years and be released in the seventh year.

Furthermore, although the deuteronomist has employed terminology that is not found in the manumission law in Exod. 21.2-6, such as ריקם, אח, ימכר, and so on, these additions reflect the theological intentions of the deuteronomist rather than any attempt to make fundamental changes to the older manumission law in Exod. 21.2-6. This is particularly true for the stipulation in Deut. 15.13-15, which clearly reflects the theological issues raised by the deuteronomist in Deut. 14.22–16.17.

Lastly, regarding the omission of certain stipulations in Deut. 15.12-18, although this law does not discuss the marital rights of a male Hebrew debt-slave, these omissions should not be interpreted as an attempt by the deuteronomist to repeal the earlier legislation in Exod. 21.2-6. Nor did the deuteronomist repeal the legislation concerning the sale of a free-born daughter into marriage or concubinage. These omissions, like the deuteronomic additions, reflect the theological intentions of the deuteronomist who, in addition to discussing the release of a male Hebrew debt-slave, discussed the release of a female Hebrew debt-slave who performed non-sexual duties in the house of a creditor. We saw that in this regard Deuteronomy is more similar to LH §117 than Exod. 21.2-6 is. Lastly, although Deut. 15.16-17 does not refer specifically to God's sanctuary in regard to the ceremony that allowed a Hebrew debt-slave to become a permanent servant, this omission does not necessarily suggest that the deuteronomist made this particular ceremony a secular institution, since there are other laws in Deuteronomy that appear to acknowledge more than one sanctuary. Nevertheless, even if a single sanctuary is envisaged in Deut. 15.16-17, I have noted that any slaves who wished to remain in servitude could have given their oath before God in the central sanctuary during one of the annual feasts mentioned in Deuteronomy 16.

Chapter 8

THE MANUMISSION LAWS OF LEVITICUS 25.39-43, 47-55

While the manumission laws in Lev. 25.39-55 are similar to those laws in Exodus and Deuteronomy, in that they provide for the periodic release of Israelite debt-slaves, nevertheless they remain a *crux interpretum* in the discussion of the institution of debt-slavery in Israel because these laws appear to be at odds with the laws in Exodus and Deuteronomy. For example, the fact that Leviticus 25 prescribes a fiftieth-year rather than a seventh-year release has prompted scholars, such as Reventlow,[1] to suggest that these slave laws are later additions to the older Jubilee regulations concerning the re-distribution of land (cf. Lev. 25.8-24). While it is the main purpose of my present discussion to determine the meaning of the manumission laws in Leviticus 25, nevertheless I did point out in the Introduction that in order to understand the proper significance of this law one must also examine the Sabbatical and Jubilee regulations to which these manumission laws are joined, especially since it is questionable whether the standard critical method can distinguish convincingly between the older Holiness Code regulations and the so-called additions and amplifications of the Priestly Source. To an investigation of these important regulations we now turn.

The Fallow Year (Exodus 23.10-11) and the Sabbatical Year
(Leviticus 25.2b-7)

Exod. 23.10-11

‫10 ושש שנים תזרע את־ארצך ואספת את־תבואתה:‬
‫11 והשביעת תשמטנה ונטשתה ואכלו אביני עמך ויתרם תאכל חית השדה‬
‫כן־תעשה לכרמך לזיתך:‬

---

1. Reventlow, *Heiligkeitsgesetz*, p. 136.

10 And you shall sow your land for six years and gather in its crop,
11 but [on] the seventh year you shall let it rest [literally drop] and lie Fallow, so that the needy of your people may eat; and whatever they leave the beast of the field may eat. You are to do the same with your vineyard [and] your olive grove.

Lev. 25.2b-7

2 כי תבאו אל־הארץ אשר אני נתן לכם ושבתה הארץ שבת ליהוה:
3 שש שנים תזרע שדך ושש שנים תזמר כרמך ואספת את־תבואתה:
4 ובשנה השביעת שבת שבתון יהיה לארץ שבת ליהוה שדך לא תזרע וכרמך לא תזמר:
5 את ספיח קצירך לא תקצור ואת־ענבי מירך לא תבצר שנת שבתון יהיה לארץ:
6 והיתה שבת הארץ לכם לאכלה לך ולעבדך ולאמתך ולשכירך ולתושבך הגרים עמך:
7 ולבהמתך ולחיה אשר בארצא רצך תהיה כל־תבואתה לאכל:

2 When you come into the land which I shall give you, then the land shall have a sabbath rest, a sabbath to the Lord.
3 Six years you shall sow your field, and six years you shall prune your vineyard and gather in its crop,
4 but during the seventh year the land shall have a sabbath rest, a sabbath to the Lord; you shall not sow your field not prune your vineyard.
5 [And] your harvest's aftergrowth [literally growth from spilled kernels] you shall not reap, and your grapes of untrimmed vines you shall not gather; the land shall have a Sabbatical Year.
6 And all of you shall have the sabbath [products] of the land for food; yourself, and your male and female slave[s], and your hired worker[s] and your foreign resident[s], those who live as aliens with you.
7 Even your cattle and the animals that are in your land shall have all its crops to eat.

That the Sabbatical year stipulation in Lev. 25.2-7 is dependent on the Fallow year stipulation in Exod. 23.10-11 is not generally contested.[1] This can be demonstrated, for example, by noting the verbal parallels that exist between the two passages.[2] For example, the provision to sow and harvest during the six years is nearly identical with the minor exceptions of the use of את־ארצך in Exod. 23.10 and שדך in Lev. 25.3, and the addition of the clause תזמר כרמך in Lev. 25.3, although

---

1. Cf. Wright, 'What Happened Every Seven Years, I', p. 131; Wenham, *Leviticus*, pp. 317-18; North, *Sociology of the Biblical Jubilee*, pp. 120, 133, 184-85; M. Noth, *Leviticus* (OTL; Philadelphia: Westminster Press, 1977), p. 183.
2. Cf. also Lemche, 'Manumission of Slaves', pp. 48-49.

this is understood from the clause כן־תעשה לכרמך לזיתך in Exod. 23.11.

However, while the seventh-year regulations are also similar in both passages, nonetheless they use different terminology. For example, in Exod. 23.11 it is prescribed that 'you shall let it [the land] rest and lie Fallow' תשמטנה ונטשתה, while Lev. 25.4 states that the land שבת שבתון יהיה לארץ שבת ליהוה 'shall have a sabbath rest, a sabbath to the Lord' (cf. also v. 5 where it states that שנת שבתון יהיה לארץ 'the land shall have a Sabbatical year').

Furthermore, while the motivation clause in Exod. 23.11 states that the Fallow is prescribed 'so that the needy of your people may eat; and whatever they leave the beast of the field may eat', which is humanitarian in scope, Leviticus 25 lacks any humanitarian motivation clause. Instead, the cultic significance of the Sabbatical year is accentuated, although vv. 6-7 do mention that the food that grows from the seed that falls to the ground may be used by the household, aliens and beasts of the field. The fact that the Fallow year regulation emphasizes humanitarian concerns while the Sabbatical year regulation emphasizes cultic and religious considerations has prompted scholars to suggest that the two regulations are different.

According to Wellhausen's[1] system of Israel's religious history, the Fallow year regulation in Exod. 23.10-11, which was based on agricultural and humanitarian concerns, was an early institution compared with the Sabbatical year regulation in Lev. 25.2-7, which was post-exilic since it dealt with cultic and religious considerations. However, Wellhausen's system of Israel's religious history can no longer be sustained, for the following reasons.[2] First, there are examples of seven-year cycles in the ancient Near East which already had religious and cultic associations before the similar Israelite Sabbatical year was instituted,[3] although it is not entirely clear that the

---

1. Wellhausen, *Prolegomena*, pp. 112-16; cf. also E. Ginzberg, 'Studies in the Economics of the Bible', *JQR* 22 (1932), pp. 351, 353-54.

2. Cf. N.-E. Andreasen, 'Recent Studies of the Old Testament Sabbath: Some Observations', *ZAW* 86 (1974), p. 455.

3. Cf. C.H. Gordon, 'The Biblical Sabbath, its Origin and Observance in the Ancient Near East', *Jud* 31 (1982), pp. 12-16; *idem*, 'Sabbatical Cycle or Seasonal Pattern', *Or* 22 (1953), pp. 79-81, who draws mainly upon Ugaritic material which attests to the existence of seven-year cycles of nature, including a fallow year (cf. Ugaritic texts *UT* 49.V.8f., *UT* 75.II.46, and 1 Aqht I: 42ff.); cf. also Wright, 'What Happened Every Seven Years, I', p. 129; *idem, God's People in God's*

Israelites borrowed this ancient practice from any other culture (e.g., Canaanites).[1] Nevertheless, it is doubtful whether a similar institution in Israel would have arisen from a purely humanitarian or agricultural concern.[2] Secondly, as Wright[3] observes, 'In the context of the Book of the Covenant, the Fallow year, like the rest of the requirements of the Book, was implicitly an obligation to Yahweh, so that a religious emphasis cannot have been lacking.' Thirdly, the close association of the Fallow year regulation with the sabbath command in v. 12, from which the idea of 'rest' (שבת) comes, also suggests that underneath the social or humanitarian aspect of the Fallow regulation lies the religious connotations of the sabbath institution,[4] which is also generally considered to belong to the earliest phases of Israelite religion.[5] Lastly, in Exod. 20.9-10a the sabbath, which is the day of rest referred to in Exod. 23.12 (cf. also Exod. 34.21), is called the שבת ליהוה 'sabbath to the Lord', which is also mentioned in Lev. 25.2, 4. Therefore, it is most likely that the religious emphasis found in

---

Land, p. 143; North, *Sociology of the Biblical Jubilee*, pp. 64-67; J. and H. Lewy, 'The Origin of the Week and the Oldest West Asiatic Calendar', *HUCA* 17 (1942), pp. 96-97; D.L. Lieber, 'Sabbatical Year and Jubilee', *EncJud*, XIV, cols. 576-77; Neufeld, 'Socio-Economic Background', p. 70. Contra Horst, *Gottes Recht*, pp. 213-14.

1. Cf. Hyatt, *Exodus*, p. 170; and B.Z. Wacholder, 'Sabbatical Year', *IDBSup*, p. 762, who suggests that the Sabbatical year (Exod. 23 and Lev. 25) is a uniquely Israelite institution.

2. Cf. Boecker, *Law and the Administration of Justice*, p. 91; and Kaufman, 'Social Welfare Systems of Ancient Israel', p. 280, both of whom argue that the fallow regulation is not based on agricultural considerations (e.g. to preserve soil fertility) but on cultic considerations.

3. Wright, 'What Happened Every Seven Years, I', p. 130; cf. also *idem, God's People in God's Land*, pp. 144-45; Lemche, 'Manumission of Slaves', p. 42 n. 14.

4. Cf. Noth, *Exodus*, p. 190; Nielsen, *Ten Commandments*, p. 113; Wright, 'What Happened Every Seven Years, I', p. 131; Childs, *Exodus*, p. 482; Cole, *Exodus*, p. 178; Beer and Galling, *Exodus*, p. 119; C.F. Keil, *Manual of Biblical Archæology*, II (CFTL, 35; Edinburgh: T. & T. Clark, 1888), pp. 11-12.

5. Cf. Andreasen, 'Recent Studies of the Old Testament Sabbath', pp. 455-56; Stamm and Andrew, *The Ten Commandments*, pp. 22-35; H.H. Rowley, 'Moses and the Decalogue', *BJRL* 34 (1951/52), pp. 81-118; J.P. Hyatt, 'Moses and the Ethical Decalogue', *Enc* 26 (1965), pp. 199-206; W. Kessler, 'Die literarische, historische und theologische Problematik des Dekalogs', *VT* 7 (1957), pp. 1-16; E. Lohse, 'Σαββατον', *TDNT*, VII, pp. 2-3.

Lev. 25.2-7 is not a new addition to an older humanitarian and/or agricultural principle; rather it is a detailed expression of the religious significance which itself is dependent on the earlier sabbath institution which had both social-humanitarian and religious-cultic connotations from the outset.[1]

Scholars have suggested that the Fallow year in Exod. 23.10-11, unlike the Sabbatical year in Lev. 25.2-7, was not observed simultaneously throughout the land but was observed at different times on each property. For example, Wellhausen and Menes[2] suggest that the Fallow regulation and the manumission law in Exod. 21.2-6 were connected in practice. Accordingly, they maintain that the Fallow year was not observed throughout the land simultaneously since slaves were released only in the seventh year after their purchase. Although the view that the Fallow year was connected to the slave law in Exod. 21.2-6 is not generally held today,[3] Porter[4] suggests nevertheless that the Fallow year was practical and not universal in its original form in Exod. 23.10-11 before it turned into a universal institution in Lev. 25.2-7 during the monarchy. However, after the exile the Sabbatical year was turned into a 50-year cycle since the universal Sabbatical year was not practical (this view is held by both Wellhausen and Menes).[5] Furthermore, he suggests that the original Fallow regulation, which was not universal, reflected a practical necessity in agriculture to preserve soil fertility at a time when nothing was known about crop rotation or fertilizers. Although

---

1. Cf. Wright, 'What Happened Every Seven Years, I', p. 131; *idem, God's People in God's Land*, pp. 146-47; P. Heinisch, *Das Buch Leviticus: übersetzt und erklärt* (DHSAT, 1/3; Bonn: Peter Hanstein, 1935), pp. 7, 110; contra Ginzberg, 'Studies in the Economics of the Bible', p. 354, who suggests that the Sabbatical year regulation is post-exilic since it gives a more detailed exposition than Exod. 23.10-11.

2. Menes, *Die vorexilischen Gesetze Israels*, pp. 79-83.

3. Cp. Wacholder, 'Sabbatical Year', p. 762, who suggests that in Exod. 21.2-6 the slave was to be released during the Sabbatical year, which was universal and simultaneous. However, there is no textual evidence to support the contention that the slave served only until the time of the Sabbatical year (cf. Lev. 25.40, which mentions specifically that a slave is to be released during the Jubilee, regardless of when he sold himself).

4. Porter, *Leviticus*, pp. 197-98.

5. Cf. also Borowski, *Agriculture in Iron Age Israel*, p. 145.

Ginzberg,[1] Childs,[2] North[3] and Driver[4] note that the Fallow year regulation is not explicit about how it was to be observed[5] (i.e., simultaneous universal or according to each individual preference), they suggest nevertheless that the Fallow regulation was not universal since it would be impractical for all the land to lie fallow at the same time,[6] although they do not necessarily hold to Porter's view of the evolution of the Sabbatical and Jubilee year regulations.[7] Further, Davies,[8] who does suggest that the Fallow year was simultaneous over the whole land, finds it difficult nonetheless to believe that the entire countryside remained uncultivated at the same time for a whole year. However, the view that the Fallow regulation did not apply to all fields during the same year is not convincing for the following reasons.

First, as Noth[9] has already pointed out correctly, although Exod. 23.10-11 does not make explicit whether the Fallow was universal and simultaneous or observed at different times on each property,[10] the fact that the sabbath day, which was practised by everyone on the same day, is associated with the Fallow year suggests that the Fallow year was universal and simultaneous.[11] Furthermore, the simultaneous and universal practice of the Sabbatical year is mentioned specifically in 1 Macc. 6.49, 53, which records that Judas Maccabeus was forced to give the fortress of Beth-zur to the Syrians on account of a famine

---

1. Ginzberg, 'Studies in the Economics of the Bible', pp. 353-54.

2. Childs, *Exodus*, p. 482.

3. North, *Sociology of the Biblical Jubilee*, pp. 119-20.

4. Driver, *Exodus*, p. 239; cf. also Lemche, 'The Manumission of Slaves', pp. 42-43.

5. Cf. also Patrick, *Old Testament Law*, p. 182.

6. Cf. also A. Phillips, *Deuteronomy* (Cambridge: Cambridge University Press, 1973), p. 104.

7. For example, Ginzberg, 'Studies in the Economics of the Bible', pp. 353-54, who dates both the Sabbatical and Jubilee year regulations to the post-exilic era.

8. Davies, *Exodus*, p. 188; cf. also Neufeld, 'Socio-Economic Background', p. 68.

9. Noth, *Exodus*, p. 190. Noth also points out that the association between the Fallow year and Sabbath day occurs this way only here in the Old Testament.

10. Cf. Snaith, *Leviticus and Numbers*, p. 161.

11. Cf. also Keil, *Manual of Archæology*, II, p. 13.

during a Sabbatical year (cf. also Josephus, *Ant.* xiii. 8.1.6, xiv. 10.6, xv. 1.2).[1]

Secondly, scholars who suggest that it was too impractical for early Israel to observe a universal and simultaneous Fallow/Sabbatical year are unaware of the agricultural practices that existed in Canaan during ca. 1250–1050 BCE. Contrary to Porter, who suggests that early Israel knew nothing of crop rotation or fertilizers, Hopkins[2] and Borowski[3] have demonstrated that farmers of this period and earlier used various conservation techniques in their battle to retain sufficient crop yields. Furthermore, based on the soil condition in the highlands of Canaan throughout its history of settlement, Hopkins[4] and Kaufman[5] note that if the land (discounting orchards and vineyards) was only left fallow

---

1. Cf. Wacholder, 'Sabbatical Year', p. 762, who suggests that the tithing cycles (Deut. 14.28; 26.12) presupposed the existence of the Sabbatical year since these cycles were divided into two three-year periods (note the literary connection between Deut. 14.28ff. and 15.1-2 which contains the Sabbatical year regulation; cf. also Deut. 31.10); cf. also S. Safrai, 'The Practical Implementation of the Sabbatical Year After the Restitution of the Second Temple' (Hebrew), *Tarbiz* 35 (1965–66), pp. 304-28; 36 (1966–67), pp. 1-21.

2. Hopkins, *The Highlands of Canaan*, pp. 191-210; 'Subsistence Struggles of Early Israel', pp. 149-77 and the bibliography cited therein, notes that fallowing (pp. 192-97/ 185), crop rotation (pp. 197-200), fertilization (pp. 202-208/ 185) and terracing (pp. 208-209/ 184-85) were practised widely in the ancient Near East including Israel.

3. Borowski, *Agriculture in Iron Age Israel*, pp. 8, 15-18, 143-48, notes that terracing (pp. 15-18), fallowing (pp. 144-45), organic fertilizing (pp. 145-48) and crop rotation (pp. 148-51) were practised widely in the ancient Near East including Israel.

4. Hopkins, *The Highlands of Canaan*, pp. 194, 200. Hopkins (p. 194) also cites H. Vogelstein, *Die Landwirtschaft in Palästina zum Zeit der Misnah* (Berlin: von Mayer & Müller, 1894), p. 48, who notes that the talmudic sources state that the ground must have been left fallow more frequently than one out of seven years. Hopkins (pp. 192-93) also notes that fallowing halts the decline in crop yields due to loss of soil nutrients and build-up of endemic pests and diseases. The length of a fallow depended on several factors; e.g. in the tropics, where soil nutrients are scarce, a fallow may extend for 25 years, while in the Mediterranean area, where soil nutrients are in more abundance, a short fallow is typical. Finally, a fallow is also useful in preserving soil moisture (e.g. mulching; ploughing during summer months). Lastly, Hopkins (pp. 193-95) notes that there are two types of fallow: (1) green fallow (where grain crops are rotated with leguminous pulses or grasses); and (2) bare-ground fallowing (where the ground is removed from cultivation).

5. Kaufman, 'Social Welfare Systems of Ancient Israel', p. 280.

one year out of seven then it would have been in a state of continuous or permanent cultivation which would render the land useless in a short period of time.[1] Instead, a much lower ratio of crop-to-fallow period prevailed throughout the history of the settlement of the highlands. Therefore, Hopkins[2] suggests that, based upon the Mediterranean fallow practice, the most practical system of crop management within Canaan and Israel would have been to allow for one year of fallow after one year of cultivation (i.e., biennial fallow system). In order to achieve such a fallow without disrupting the life of farmers who depended on crops for survival, an individual's land would be divided into two parts which were sown and left fallow in rotation.[3] Furthermore, it is also possible to envisage the observance of the Sabbatical year fallow alongside a biennial fallow practice. Hopkins,[4] for example, observes that a community-wide fallow every seven years would only affect half of the farmer's holdings, although production would have to be increased the year before the Sabbatical year in order to augment the production lost during the Sabbatical year. Further, he writes:[5]

1. Cp. A. Cohen, 'Leaving the Land Fallow' (Hebrew), *BM* 24 (1978), pp. 45-49, who suggests that the fallow regulation would wreck vineyards, and that this regulation was not observed before the exile since there were not enough *goyim* around who could tend the vineyards during the fallow year.

2. Hopkins, *The Highlands of Canaan*, p. 195; idem, 'The Subsistence Struggles of Early Israel', pp. 194-95; cf. also J. Feliks, 'Agricultural Methods and Implements in Ancient Erez Israel', *EncJud*, II, p. 375; L. Turkowski, 'Peasant Agriculture in the Judean Hills', *PEQ* 101 (1969), p. 102; H.J. van Wersch, 'The Agricultural Economy', *The Minnesota Messenia Expedition: Reconstructing a Bronze Age Regional Environment* (ed. W.A. McDonald and G.R. Rapp Jr; Minneapolis: University of Minnesota Press, 1972), p. 186; cp. Borowski, *Agriculture in Iron Age Israel*, pp. 144-51, who appears to favour the use of crop fertilization and crop rotation over the fallowing method.

3. Cf. Hopkins, *The Highlands of Canaan*, p. 195; Turkowski, 'Peasant Agriculture', p. 21; Vogelstein, *Die Landwirtschaft in Palästina*, p. 59. Note, however, that this does not mean that each farmer had a single large field that he could then simply divide into two equal parts. Rather, the total amount of land, which might include several distinct fields spread over a variety of settings, was divided into two parts (Hopkins, p. 195). Furthermore, it is not clear whether the inhabitants of Canaan sowed a single winter crop or a summer and winter crop. For a discussion of this problem, see Hopkins, *The Highlands of Canaan*, pp. 197-99.

4. Hopkins, *The Highlands of Canaan*, pp. 200-202.

5. Hopkins, *The Highlands of Canaan*, p. 201.

In this year previous to the Sabbatical, the farmer could increase production by eliminating the Fallow (F) of an area (P) just cropped (C). In order to compensate for this heavy use, this area would then be rested not only for the Sabbatical Year (S), but also for the subsequent year as the other half of the farm land (Q) continued in its regular biennial rotation. This is illustrated diagrammatically below.

P	C	F	C	F	C	C	S	F	C	F	C	F	C	S
Q	F	C	F	C	F	C	S	C	F	C	F	C	C	S
	1	2	3	4	5	6	7	1	2	3	4	5	6	7

It is important to point out that this theoretical system of crop rotation is not meant to give the impression that the Sabbatical year regulation would be handled matter-of-factly or that this system was actually observed by the early Israelites, although, as Hopkins notes, this system renders the Sabbatical year regulations (Exod. 23.10-11 and Lev. 25.2-7) more comprehensible and less menacing as an agricultural institution. Furthermore, Hopkins[1] suggests that the Sabbatical year institution, which would demand a mobilization of labour in order to increase pre-sabbatical year plowing, planting and gathering, is a practical way in which to create, test and maintain the necessary devices for coping with crop failure. Therefore, the Sabbatical year regulation would enforce elasticity of agricultural production and promote social cohesion, both of which would be important factors for any developing sedentary society. Lastly, there are literary allusions to doubling labour on the sixth day in Gen. 1.24-31, according to which God created both beasts and man on the sixth day, and Exod. 16.5, according to which God provided twice as much manna on the sixth day as the sons of Israel could gather daily.[2] Both of these passages may have influenced the drafting of the Sabbatical year institution.

Recapitulating, the above discussion shows that the Fallow and Sabbatical year regulations refer to the same institution that owes its origin to mainly religious and social-humanitarian concepts, although the practical agrarian aspects of a Sabbatical Fallow operating within a biennial fallow institution might also have been an important aspect of the Sabbatical year regulation.[3] Furthermore, the view that the Fallow

1. Hopkins, *The Highlands of Canaan*, p. 273.
2. These literary allusions were pointed out to me by Gordon J. Wenham.
3. Cp. Kaufman, 'Social Welfare Systems of Ancient Israel', p. 280; and Borowski, *Agriculture in Iron Age Israel*, pp. 144-45, who pays little attention to

year regulation was an early practical agrarian practice, which was observed individually on each property, as opposed to the later idealistic Sabbatical year regulation, which was meant to be observed universally/simultaneously, is without foundation in the light of the agricultural practices that existed during the early Iron Age and later.[1]

The Jubilee Year (Leviticus 25.8-12)

Lev. 25.8-12

8 וספרת לך שבע שבתת שנים שבע שנים שבע פעמים והיו לך ימי
שבע שבתת השנים תשע וארבעים שנה:

9 והעברת שופר תרועה בחדש השבעי בעשור לחדש ביום הכפרים
תעבירו שופר בכל־ארצכם:

10 וקדשתם את שנת החמשים שנה וקראתם דרור בארץ לכל־ישביה יובל
הוא תהיה לכם ושבתם איש אל־אחזתו ואיש אל־משפחתו תשבו:

11 יובל הוא שנת החמשים שנה תהיה לכם לא תזרעו ולא תקצרו
את־ספיחיה ולא תבצרו את־נזריה:

12 כי יובל הוא קדש תהיה לכם מן־השדה תאכלו את־תבואתה:

the Sabbatical year regulations and adopts the critical view that the fallow in Exod. 23.10-11 was not universal (each farmer left a seventh of his land fallow each year) and that the universal Sabbatical year was exilic or post-exilic (he regards Deut. 15.1-2, 9 as a different set of laws).

1. Cp. Wright, 'What Happened Every Seven Years, I', pp. 131-32; *idem*, *God's People in God's Land*, p. 145; and North, *Sociology of the Biblical Jubilee*, p. 119, both of whom suggest that the fallow in Exod. 23.10-11 was not simultaneous because the presence of continuous available land is more humanitarian. However, Wright, who does not wish to remove the humanitarian aspects from the Sabbatical year regulation in Leviticus 25, suggests that Leviticus added the gleaning regulations in 19.9-10 and 23.22 in order to account for the loss of available land due to the adoption of a universal-simultaneous sabbatical year in Lev. 25.2-7 (cf. also A. Noordtzij, *Leviticus* (BSC; Grand Rapids: Zondervan, 1982), p. 250, who notes that if Lev. 25.6-7 takes note even of the needs of animals, it could not deny the needs of the poor). However, the laws of gleaning in Lev. 19.9-10 and 23.22 are just two examples of the many laws in the Pentateuch that deal with the poor and oppressed which are part of the oldest legal tradition of Israel. Therefore, the fallow regulation in Exod. 23.10-11 was not meant to be an exhaustive treatment of the feeding of the poor, but like Lev. 25.2-7 it was meant to be seen as one law among many which sought to protect and provide for the oppressed. Cf. also Borowski, *Agriculture in Iron Age Israel*, p. 144, who notes that the provision in Exod. 23.10-11 could hardly sustain the poor for six years (thus the presence of other regulations in Lev. 19.19; 23.22; Deut. 14.28-29; 24.19-21), and thus this regulation was primarily meant to provide the land with rest.

8 You are also to count off seven sabbaths of years for yourself, seven times seven years, so that you have the time of the seven sabbaths of years, [namely,] 49 years.

9 You shall then sound a ram's horn abroad on the tenth day of the seventh month; on the day of atonement you shall sound a horn all through your land.

10 You shall thus consecrate the fiftieth year and proclaim a דרור through the land to all its inhabitants. It shall be a יובל for you, when each of you shall return to his own property, when each of you shall return to משפחתו.

11 You shall have the fiftieth year as a Jubilee; you shall not sow, nor reap its aftergrowth, nor gather [from] its untrimmed vines.

12 For it is a יובל; it shall be holy to you. You shall eat its crops out of the field.

While many scholars suggest that both the Sabbatical and Jubilee year regulations in Leviticus 25 have undergone a long process of redaction, I have already argued above that the Sabbatical year in Lev. 25.2-7 is based on the universal Fallow year in Exod. 21.10-11, both of which reflect practical agrarian practices. However, Porter,[1] who follows the views of Wellhausen and Menes, suggests that after the exile the Sabbatical year was turned into a 50-year Jubilee cycle, since the universal Sabbatical year was not practical. Similarly, Alt[2] suggests that the Jubilee regulations were intended to be used to restore the significance of the Sabbatical year by extending it to 50 years, since the original regulations (including the regulations in Deut. 15.1-3) could no longer be practically enforced.[3]

However, Driver[4] was correct in noting that the redistribution of land in Lev. 25.8-16 was also practised among the other ancient nations, which led him to conclude that these regulations were not idealistic and that they were probably early (and thus belonged to the Holiness Code). Furthermore, as we saw in Chapter 3, the release of land sold on account of insolvency is also attested in the *mēšarum* edicts that were regularly enacted during the OB period. Nevertheless, Driver suggests that the slave laws found in vv. 39-55 are to be attributed to the Priestly Source since this law and that in Deut. 15.12-18 could hardly have been operative at the same time—viz.,

---

1. Porter, *Leviticus*, pp. 197-98.
2. Alt, 'The Origin of Israelite Law', pp. 128-29 n. 119.
3. Cf. also de Vaux, *Ancient Israel*, pp. 175-76.
4. Driver, *Introduction*, p. 57.

Lev. 25.39-55 postdated Deut. 15.12-18. Similarly, Noth,[1] who considers the Jubilee to be of ancient origin, notes correctly that although the Jubilee regulations contain features common to the debt-slave laws in Exod. 21.2-6 and Deut. 15.12-18, and with the remission of debts in Deut. 15.1-3, the Jubilee laws uniquely deal with the restoration of rights of ownership in the land. Thus the Jubilee regulations are not merely reiterating previous legislation in a more manageable format, but, rather, they are dealing with a totally different set of regulations. However, like Driver, Noth cannot understand how the manumission laws can be dated to the same period as the other manumission laws in Exodus and Deuteronomy.

While I will attempt to reconcile the different periods of release among the various manumission laws in a later discussion, in the following discussion I will attempt to provide additional arguments in favour of both Driver's and Noth's arguments that the Jubilee regulations are part of a unified discussion of land release by examining the meaning of the terms יובל and דרור and their relationship to the historical development of Israel's social welfare system, and by examining the relationship between the Sabbatical and Jubilee years.

The Meaning of the Term יובל
The exact etymology of the term יובל is not clear,[2] although the majority of scholars take the traditional view that the term refers to a type of ram's horn (parallel to שופר).[3] Although this meaning is not

1. Noth, *Leviticus*, p. 183.
2. Cf. Lieber, 'Sabbatical Year and Jubilee', col. 576; A. van Selms, 'The Year of the Jubilee, In and Outside the Pentateuch', *OTWSA* 17–18 (1974–75), pp. 74-75; *idem*, 'Jubilee, year of', *IDBSup*, p. 496; Lemche, 'Manumission of Slaves', p. 46.
3. For example, see J. Morgenstern, 'Jubilee, Year of', *IDB*, III, p. 1001; Noth, *Leviticus*, p. 184; Pedersen, *Israel*, I–II, p. 87; Patrick, *Old Testament Law*, p. 182; Snaith, *Leviticus and Numbers*, p. 163; Dillmann, *Leviticus*, p. 609; S.R. Driver and H.A. White, *The Book of Leviticus* (PB, 3; London: James Clark, 1898), p. 99; Neufeld, 'Socio-Economic Background', p. 62 n. 4; Lieber, 'Sabbatical Year and Jubilee', p. 576; Heinisch, *Leviticus*, p. 110; Wolff, 'Masters and Slaves', p. 271; cf. also the bibliography in North, *Sociology of the Biblical Jubilee*, pp. 100-102; BDB, p. 385; Borowski, *Agriculture in Iron Age Israel*, p. 24 n. 7. Cf. also the older views of Gesenius, *Hebrew and Chaldee Lexicon*, who understands יובל as an onomatopoetic word, signifying 'a joyful sound', then applied to the 'sound of a trumpet, trumpet signal'; Saalschütz, *Mosaische Recht*,

particularly evident in Leviticus 25 (the term שופר is used in Lev. 25.9), in Exod. 19.13 a יובל 'horn' was used to signal the moment when Moses was to bring the people to the mountain; במשך היבל 'When the [ram's] horn sounds a long blast'. In Exod. 19.16, which recounts the occurrence of this event, the term שופר is used instead of the term יובל, which suggests that both terms are synonymous, although the horn that is referred to in Exodus 19 probably refers to a 'supernatural horn'. Since the additional term שופר might have been included in these contexts in order to explain the meaning of the term יובל, Noth,[1] Harrison,[2] Lieber[3] and Wenham[4] suggest that the term יובל was of ancient origin.[5]

North,[6] however, suggests that the term יובל means 'release' based on the LXX rendering αφεσις. He further suggests that the term יובל comes from the root יבל 'conduct, bear along' which, based upon the LXX, already in itself means 'release'. However, as North[7] himself points out, his 'attempt to prove that the root יבל already in itself means αφεσις has not met with acceptance'. For example, although the term יובל is not qualified by שופר in Leviticus 25, this does not necessarily indicate that the term יובל does not refer to a 'ram's horn' as it does in Exodus 19 and Joshua 6. Secondly, it is not entirely clear that the LXX has preserved the original meaning of the term יובל in

p. 159; and Keil, *Manual of Archæology*, II, pp. 15-16, who derives the term יבל from יבל 'to stream violently, with noise', and thus understands יבל to refer to the strong sounding notes of the trumpet. Accordingly, the phrase שנת יובל in Lev. 25.13 signifies the year of the sounding (of trumpets).

1. Noth, *Leviticus*, p. 183.
2. R.K. Harrison, *Leviticus* (TOTCS; Downers Grove, IL: IVP, 1980), p. 225.
3. Lieber, 'Sabbatical Year and Jubilee', col. 576.
4. Wenham, *Leviticus*, p. 319.
5. Cp. Morgenstern, 'Jubilee', p. 1001, who suggests that the ram's horn trumpets שופרות היובלים were unusual instruments which were used only during special events by the priests (i.e., theophany in Exod. 19.13 and the Jubilee year), as opposed to the ordinary שפר which was used by the people (following the Mishna). However, the fact that the term שופר is also used to describe the ram's horn used in Exod. 19.13 (see v. 16 קל שפר) and in Josh. 6.4 (see v. 4b בשופרות) does not support Morgenstern's contention that the שופרות היובלים were unusual instruments as opposed to the so-called ordinary שופר.
6. North, *Sociology of the Biblical Jubilee*, pp. 104-108; *idem*, 'יובל', *ThWAT*, III, cols. 555-56; cf. also Wenham, *Leviticus*, p. 319; Lemche, 'Manumission of Slaves', p. 50; and Ibn Ezra, *ad. loc.*
7. R. North, 'דרור', *TDOT*, III, p. 269.

Leviticus 25. For example, the LXX and Massoretic Text render Lev. 25.10 as:

10 ... καὶ διαβοησετε αφεσιν επι της γης πασιν τοις κατοικουσιν αυτην ενιαυτος αφεσεως σημασια αυτη εσται υμιν...

10 ...וקראתם דרור בארץ לכל־ישביה יובל הוא תהיה לכם...

In this verse the LXX renders the term דרור as αφεσιν, 'release', and the term יובל as αφεσεως σημασια, 'proclamation of release'. Furthermore, the LXX renders יובל as αφεσεως σημασια in vv. 11, 12 and 13 and as σημασιαν, 'proclamation', in v. 15. It is only in vv. 28, 30 and 31ff. that the LXX renders the term יובל as αφεσις, 'release'. That the term יובל is rendered αφεσεως σημασια in v. 10f. might be due to its close association with the preceding phrase וקראתם דרור = διαβοησετε αφεσιν. On the surface, the rendering αφεσεως σημασια describes the Jubilee accurately as a proclamation of release, although it does not necessarily follow that this generalization reflects the actual etymology of the term יובל accurately.

A similar development may be discerned among the OB *mēšarum* edicts where the term *andurārum*, which is cognate to the Hebrew term דרור, was used to describe specific acts of release. However, after the OB period the term *mīšarum* was no longer used to describe a royal decree but was generally used in its more common use— 'justice'.[1] During this period the term *andurārum* was used as an equivalent of *mīšarum* to describe a royal decree as well as retaining its original use of describing a specific act of release.

Therefore, it is likely that the LXX, in an attempt to describe the institution of יובל accurately, chose to render it as αφεσεως σημασια and αφεσις, thereby making it a synonym of the term דרור,[2] which

1. Cf. Kaufman, 'Social Welfare Systems of Ancient Israel', p. 279, who notes that the Hebrew term מישרים 'justice', and Akkadian *mīšarum* are undoubtedly cognate, but that it is uncertain whether the Hebrew term had the technical sense of the OB term (i.e. royal reform edict); cf. also Lemche, 'Manumission of Slaves', pp. 39-41, who suggests that that the Hebrew term did not have the technical sense of the OB term. Cp. Weinfeld, *Deuteronomy*, pp. 153-57; *idem*, ' "Justice and Righteousness" ', pp. 491-519; *idem, Justice and Righteousness in Israel and the Nations: Equality and Freedom in Ancient Israel in Light of Social Justice in the Ancient Near East* (Hebrew) (PPFBR; Jerusalem: Magnes, 1985), pp. 3-11, 45-55; Y. Bazak, 'Towards the Significance of the Pair *mišpāt û ṣedāqâ* in the Bible' (Hebrew), *BM* 32 (1986–87), pp. 135-48.

2. Note that the LXX also renders the verb שמט in Exod. 23.11, Deut. 15.3 and the

parallels the usage of the term *andurārum* in post-OB royal edicts. Furthermore, based upon the usage of the term יובל elsewhere in the Old Testament, it is most likely that this term refers to some sort of horn, although whether יובל refers to a special type of ram's horn as opposed to the so-called 'ordinary' שופר or to the sounds that come from a horn remains a moot point. Furthermore, it is likely that the term יובל is of ancient origin since the additional term שופר appears to have been included in certain contexts in order to explain the meaning of the term יובל.

The Meaning of the Term דרור

The term *andurārum* is probably the entymon, both linguistic and institutional, of the Hebrew term דרור.[1] In Chapter 3 we saw that the term *andurārum* was used to designate specific cases of release/manumission from the Neo-Sumerian to the OB period. However, in a few cases during the OB period (e.g., from the reign of Samsuiluna) and in several cases dating later than the OB period (up to the NA period), the term was used to designate a royal decree = *mīšarum*. Since the term *andurārum* has a long and complex history of usage, scholars have suggested various periods during which the term דרור, along with the institution of the יובל, originated in biblical law. Notably, Finkelstein,[2] Lewy,[3] van Selms[4] and many others[5] have

noun שמטה in Deut. 15.1, 2, 9, as ἄφεσις.

1. Cf. Lewy, 'The Biblical Institution of *Derôr*', pp. 21-31; Weinfeld, 'Sabbatical Year and Jubilee in the Pentateuch', pp. 45-46; Kaufman, 'Social Welfare Systems in Ancient Israel', p. 279; North, *Sociology of the Biblical Jubilee*, pp. 62-66; *idem*, 'דרור', p. 266; Noth, *Leviticus*, p. 187; von Willi, 'Die Freiheit Israels', pp. 543-46; Westbrook, 'Jubilee Laws', p. 216; Cholewiński, *Heiligkeitsgesetz*, p. 225 n. 38; Cazelles, 'Droit public dans le Deutéronome', p. 102.
2. Finkelstein, 'Ammiṣaduqa's Edict', pp. 101-104 and n. 19; 'Some New Misharum Material', pp. 240-43.
3. Lewy, 'The Biblical Institution of *Derôr*', pp. 29-31.
4. Van Selms, 'Jubilee', p. 497; 'The Year of the Jubilee', pp. 74-85.
5. For example, see Olivier, 'Old Babylonian *Mēšarum* Decree', pp. 107-13; Weinfeld, *Deuteronomy*, p. 153 n. 1; *idem*, '"Justice and Righteousness"', pp. 491-519; *idem*, *Justice and Righteousness in Israel and the Nations*, pp. 2-9, 43-50; Wiseman, 'Law and Order', pp. 11-14; Neufeld, 'Socio-Economic Background', pp. 56-58; Gordon, 'Parallèles nouziens aux lois', pp. 34-41; J.B. Alexander, 'A Babylonian Year of Jubilee', *JBL* 57 (1938), p. 79; M. Greenberg, 'Sabbatical Year and Jubilee: Ancient Near Eastern Legal Background', *EncJud*,

suggested that the institution of יובל, which proclaims a דרור 'release' of land and people, belongs to the Pre-Monarchic period. They base this view upon the use of the term *andurārum* in the *mēšarum* edicts and in various legal documents during the OB period, both of which employ this term for specific cases of release (of slaves and land). However, Lemche[1] suggests that the term דרור was borrowed from the NA period (contemporary with Zedekiah; cf. Jer. 34.8), since such acts of release are attested in this period and later,[2] although he admits that it is possible that the term could have been borrowed as early as the first half of the second millennium BC. Lastly, Kaufman[3] has suggested that the term דרור originally referred to royal decrees that were proclaimed by Israelite monarchs in their regnal year.

The Relationship between the Sabbatical and Jubilee Years
For many commentators the most conspicuous difficulty with the unity of Leviticus 25 is the date ascribed to the Jubilee.[4]

XIV, cols. 577-78; R.B. Sloan, Jr, *The Favorable Year of the Lord: A Study of Jubilary Theology in the Gospel of Luke* (Austin, TX: Scholars Press, 1977), p. 22 n. 31; North, *Sociology of the Biblical Jubilee*, pp. 59-69; Epsztein, *Social Justice*, pp. 133-34; Wright, 'What Happened Every Seven Years in Israel, II', p. 200; N. Sarna, 'Zedekiah's Emancipation of Slaves and the Sabbatical Year', in *Orient and Occident: Essays Presented to Cyrus H. Gordon on the Occasion of his Sixty-fifth Birthday* (ed. H.A. Hoffner, Jr; AOAT, 22; Neukirchen–Vluyn Verlag Butzon & Bencker Kevelaer, 1973), pp. 143-49; H. Gevaryahu, 'The Announcement of Freedom in Jerusalem by Nehemiah in Comparison with *Mesharum* and Social Reform in the Ancient World' (Hebrew), in *Festschrift Abraham Katz* (Jerusalem, 1969), pp. 354-87; N. Lohfink, 'The Kingdom of God and the Economy in the Bible', *Comm* 13 (1986), p. 222; J.J.M. Roberts, 'Ancient Near Eastern Environment', in *The Hebrew Bible and its Modern Interpreters* (ed. D.A. Knight and G.M. Tucker; SBLI; Philadelphia: Fortress Press; Chico, CA: Scholars Press, 1985), p. 92. Cp. Lohfink, 'The Kingdom of God', p. 222, who suggests that based on ancient Near Eastern parallels the land and contract laws in Leviticus 25 date to the 'settlement' renewed during the Exile; cp. also Neufeld, 'Socio-Economic Background', p. 117, who suggests that the Jubilee was reinstated after the division of the monarchy (circa 925 BCE).

1. Lemche, 'Andurārum and Mīšarum', p. 22.
2. Cf. also Weinfeld, '"Justice and Righteousness"', pp. 493, 499-504.
3. Kaufman, 'Social Welfare Systems in Ancient Israel', pp. 280-84.
4. For a thorough historical discussion of the literary problems connected with the Sabbatical and Jubilee institutions, see North, *Sociology of the Biblical Jubilee*, pp. 109-34; יובל', cols. 554-59.

Cardellini,[1] who sums up the contribution of various literary critics,[2] notes that vv. 8-9a and vv. 9b-12 appear to refer to two different regulations or institutions that have been brought together by a later redactor (*HG-Redaktor*); the former refers to a forty-ninth-year celebration while the latter refers to a fiftieth-year celebration on the day of atonement. Further, the two different dates suggest that two Fallow years were observed in a row which, according to Lemche,[3] de Vaux,[4] North[5] and Noordtzij,[6] would have been impractical, although Harrison[7] suggests that divine intervention was mentioned specifically in order to deal with this problem (cf. vv. 20-22). Although these problems have in part led recent scholars such as Kilian,[8] de Vaux,[9] Morgenstern,[10] Porter,[11] Gnuse,[12] Micklem[13] and Westbrook[14] to conclude that the Jubilee is an idealistic exilic or post-exilic creation, there is growing support for the view that the two dates for the Jubilee are reconcilable. In general, the view that the two dates are reconcilable has been proposed by scholars who adopt one of four different approaches.

First, in his literary analysis of the Jubilee regulations Jirku[15] has suggested that the forty-ninth year is identical with the fifieth year, following the suggestion made by Kugler that the number 50 has been reached through the Hebrew practice of inclusive counting. Similar

1. Cardellini, *Die biblischen 'Sklaven'-Gesetze*, pp. 282-83.
2. Cf. Baentsch, *Exod-Lev-Num*, p. 424; Jirku, 'Das israelitische Jobeljahr', pp. 173-74; N. Micklem, 'Leviticus', *The Interpreter's Bible*, II (New York: Abingdon Press, 1952), p. 121; Reventlow, *Heiligkeitsgesetz*, pp. 128-30; Kilian, *Heiligkeitsgesetzes*, pp. 123-25, 141-42, 148; Feucht, *Untersuchungen*, pp. 50, 72; Noth, *Leviticus*, pp. 186-87; Elliger, *Leviticus*, pp. 344-45, 347-48; Cholewiński, *Heiligkeitsgesetz*, pp. 104-106, 111-13, 224-25.
3. Lemche, 'Manumission of Slaves', p. 46.
4. De Vaux, *Ancient Israel*, pp. 175-77.
5. North, *Sociology of the Biblical Jubilee*, p. 134.
6. Noordtzij, *Leviticus*, p. 251.
7. Harrison, *Leviticus*, pp. 225-26.
8. Kilian, *Heiligkeitsgesetzes*, pp. 146-47.
9. De Vaux, *Ancient Israel*, pp. 176-77.
10. Morgenstern, 'Jubilee', p. 1002.
11. Porter, *Leviticus*, pp. 197-98.
12. Gnuse, 'Jubilee Legislation', pp. 46-48; *You Shall Not Steal*, pp. 40-45.
13. Micklem, 'Leviticus', p. 122.
14. Westbrook, 'Jubilee Laws', pp. 222-23.
15. Jirku, 'Das israelitische Jobeljahr', p. 170.

proposals have been suggested more recently in the literary analyses of Heinisch,[1] Reventlow,[2] Elliger,[3] Cardellini[4] and van Selms.[5]

Secondly, North,[6] in his sociological analysis of the Jubilee, suggests that the number 50 has been used simply in a loose sense for 49 (cf. Deut. 16.9; Lev. 23.16; cf. also Jn 20.26).[7]

Thirdly, Kaufman,[8] who notes the parallels that exist between the declaration of the יובל and the *mēšarum* edicts, suggests that the יובל was only a proclamation that occurred at the beginning of the forty-ninth year. The first year of the next יובל cycle was reckoned to be the first year of the current יובל, which meant that the next יובל would occur at the beginning of the fiftieth year. As Kaufman points out correctly, Lev. 25.20-22 states clearly that planting was forbidden for only one year.[9]

Fourthly, there have been attempts to understand the fiftieth year as an intercalary year, a short period of time inserted into the calendar year in order to bring it into time with the seasons.[10] The most viable solution has been offered by Hoenig,[11] who suggests that the יובל was a

---

1. Heinisch, *Leviticus*, p. 111.
2. Reventlow, *Heiligkeitgesetz*, p. 125.
3. Elliger, *Leviticus*, p. 352.
4. Cardellini, *Die biblischen 'Sklaven'-Gesetze*, pp. 282-83.
5. Van Selms, 'The Year of the Jubilee', p. 75.
6. North, *Sociology of the Biblical Jubilee*, pp. 109-34, esp. 129-34; 'יובל', cols. 556-57.
7. Cf. also Patrick, *Old Testament Law*, p. 182, who writes, 'There must be some trick of computation that makes this fiftieth year the same as the forty-ninth of a sabbath of sabbaths—say, counting the previous Jubilee plus the 49 years to equal the fiftieth year.'
8. Kaufman, 'Social Welfare Systems in Ancient Israel', p. 284 n. 1; cf. also Weinfeld, 'Sabbatical Year and Jubilee in the Pentateuch', pp. 39-62, esp. 40, 42-47, 58-62.
9. Further, Snaith, *Leviticus*, pp. 162-63, who is followed by Westbrook, 'Jubilee Laws', p. 222, notes that the term ספיח refers to the aftergrowth of the first fallow in Lev. 25.5 and to the second fallow in v. 11. He suggests, however, that the term סחיש should be used in v. 11 to refer to the fiftieth year fallow based on 2 Kgs 19.29; Isa. 37.30. However, it makes good sense to use the term ספיח in vv. 5,11 if one accepts that the references to both the forty-ninth and fiftieth year fallows refer to the same one-year fallow.
10. For a discussion of the various intercalary theories, see North, *Sociology of the Biblical Jubilee*, pp. 125-29; 'יובל', col. 557.
11. S.B. Hoenig, 'Sabbatical Years and the Year of Jubilee', *JQR* 59 (1969),

very short 'year' only 49 days long, intercalated in the seventh month of the forty-ninth year. This adjustment was necessary in order to bring the Jewish calendar in line with the solar year. However, such a theory requires that the Massoretic Text be amended to read 49 days instead of 49 years (Lev. 25.8).

Although it is probably a moot question which of the above suggestions offers the best solution to the problem concerning the date ascribed to the Jubilee, it is, nevertheless, clear that the text assumes that the fiftieth year was identical with the forty-ninth year.[1] Therefore, as North suggests, the יובל was no more than the seventh Sabbatical year (= שמטה) in a 'heightened' form, or, as Cardellini[2] suggests, a 'Steigerung der Sabbatidee'.[3] Furthermore, since the יובל envisages only a single fallow year, the claims that the יובל was impractical because it envisages two fallow years are no longer tenable. As I have argued above, Hopkin's system of biennial crop rotation places the institution of the universal Sabbatical/Jubilee Fallow year firmly within the realm of possibility.[4]

---

pp. 222-36; cf. also Wenham, *Leviticus*, pp. 302 n. 4, 319.

1. Cp. Keil, *Manual of Archæology*, II, pp. 14-15, who reckons that the reference to three years' yield in vv. 20-22 supposes two fallow years immediately following one another. However, according to Rashi, *ad. loc.*, the three years referred to part of the sixth, all of the seventh, and part of the eighth year (cf. v. 22, which assumes that sowing can commence during the eighth year). This suggests that the term שנה refers to agricultural periods rather than to a solar year; cf. also Wenham, *Leviticus*, p. 320 n. 12; Noth, *Leviticus*, p. 188; D. Hoffmann, *Das Buch Leviticus*, I–II (Berlin: Poppelauer, 1905–1906), p. 336.

2. Cardellini, *Die biblischen 'Sklaven'-Gesetze*, p. 283.

3. Cf. also van Selms, 'Jubilee', p. 496; contra Lemche, 'Manumission of Slaves', p. 50.

4. Contra North, *Sociology of the Biblical Jubilee*, pp. 172-74, who suggests that the Sabbatical year, and the release of land and people did not occur simultaneously and universally throughout the land. However, Lev. 25.16 clearly refers to the Jubilee as universal and simultaneous, although North considers this verse to be a gloss (p. 174); cf. Westbrook, 'Jubilee Laws', pp. 212-13. Cf. also Weinfeld, 'Sabbatical Year and Jubilee in the Pentateuch', pp. 58-59, who suggests 'that there also existed a *cyclical liberty* in Mesopotamia...the institution is undoubtedly rooted in an ancient patriarchal tendency to preserve the ancestral holding and the familial sphere of ancestry.' Weinfeld follows Finkelstein, 'Some New Misharum Material and its Implication', p. 245, in the assertion that the *mīšarum* was a cyclical institution, a view that has been shown to be suspect. Refer to the discussion of the *mēšarum* edicts in Chapter 3.

Recapitulating, the above discussion shows that the Jubilee year regulation in Lev. 25.8-12 allowed for the release of land during the seventh Sabbatical year, which most likely was a 'heightened' form of the Sabbatical year. Furthermore, the Sabbatical year in Lev. 25.2b-7 is the same as the Fallow year mentioned in Exod. 23.10-11, both of which stipulate a universal Fallow every seven years.

The Literary Structure of the Jubilee Regulations

We already saw above that the manumission laws in Lev. 25.39-55 differ greatly from those in Exod. 21.2-11 and Deut. 15.12-18. Consequently, recent research into these laws has been concerned primarily with the comparison of these different regulations, particularly Deut. 15.12-18 with Lev. 25.39-55.[1] However, such comparisons have failed to reconcile adequately the differences between these regulations without positing a radical reworking of the original regulations, something that I have already shown to be of limited value in understanding the Sabbatical and Jubilee year regulations in Leviticus 25. Nevertheless, an examination of the literary structure of Leviticus 25 can help to clarify the meaning and relationship of the Jubilee regulations and the manumission laws. To this examination we now turn.

In Chapters 6 and 7 we saw that the manumission laws in Exodus and Deuteronomy occur within two larger legal collections, the Book of the Covenant and the Deuteronomic Code, both of which share certain compositional similarities with other ancient Near Eastern legal collections. One important similarity is the observable principles of priority, which I discussed in relation to the Covenant Code in Chapter 6. For example, Petschow[2] has noted that each topical discussion in LH follows the principles of socio-economic worth (i.e., temple, state, citizen (*awīlum*), temple or Crown dependent (*muškēnum*), slave) and the primacy of contracted rights over non-contractual relationships. Similarly, Kaufman,[3] who follows the work

---

1. Cf. Cholewiński, *Heiligkeitsgesetz*, pp. 217-51; Cardellini, *Die biblischen 'Sklaven'-Gesetze*, pp. 335-56; Japhet, 'The Relationship Between the Legal Corpora', pp. 67-89.

2. Petschow, 'Zur Systematik und Gesetzestechnik im Codex Hammurabi', pp. 146-72.

3. Kaufman, 'The Deuteronomic Law', pp. 115-18.

of Petschow, has discerned a similar principle of priority in many of
the biblical laws, such as the laws concerning assault in Exod. 21.12-
36 and in Deuteronomy 15. This principle of priority can also be
discerned in the topical structure of Leviticus 25, which both
Kaufman[1] and Wenham[2] note is a complete narrative unit dealing with
a specific area of legislative concern—this literary structure is
generally indicative of the Holiness Code. The topical divisions in
Leviticus 25 are marked clearly by formal rhetorical introductions
(i.e., within a narrative framework; 'The Lord spoke to Moses') and
frequent hortatory conclusions that contain motivation clauses and
parenetic material. This sort of arrangement is illustrated clearly
below within the topical structure of Leviticus 25.

I. Rhetorical introduction (v. 1)	וידבר יהוה אל־משה
II. The Jubilee: a sabbath for the land (vv. 2-22)	
A. The Sabbatical year (vv. 2-7)	
B. The Jubilee year (vv. 8-22)	
1. Proclamation (vv. 8-12)	
2. Return to land and land returned to owner (vv. 13-16)	
C. Hortatory conclusion (v. 17)	כי אני יהוה אלהיכם
D. Parenetic excursus about the fallow (vv. 18-22)	
III. The Jubilee: and the redemption of property (vv. 23-38)	
A. Introduction: the land is Yahweh's (vv. 23-24)	
B. Sale of land due to poverty (vv. 25-28)	כי־ימוך אחיך
C. Sale of dwellings in the city (vv. 29-34)	ואיש כי
1. non-Levites (vv. 29-31)	
2. Levites (vv. 32-34)	
D. Israelites in need of support (vv. 35-37)	וכי־ימוך אחיך
E. Hortatory conclusion (v. 38)	אני יהוה אלהיכם אשר־
IV. The Jubilee: and the redemption of slaves (vv. 39-55)	
A. Man is sold to a fellow Israelite (vv. 39-43)	וכי־ימוך אחיך
B. Excursus: foreign slaves (vv. 44-46)	
C. Man is sold to a foreigner (vv. 47-54)	וכי...ומך אחיך
D. Hortatory conclusion (v. 55)	אני יהוה אלהיכם

Several observations can be made concerning the above topical
outline, which generally follows the tripartite structure already
discerned by Cholewiński[3] and others.

---

1. Kaufman, 'The Deuteronomic Law', p. 106.
2. Wenham, *Leviticus*, pp. 5-6, 300, 316.
3. Cholewiński, *Heiligkeitsgesetz*, pp. 113-15; cf. also Elliger, *Leviticus*,

First, Leviticus 25 contains three major discussions about the Jubilee: (1) It is a sabbath for the land; (2) It calls for the redemption of property; and (3) It calls for the redemption of so-called Israelite debt-slaves. The first section (1) concludes with the motivation clause כי אני יהוה אלהיכם '...I am the Lord your God' in v. 17, which also marks the end of the other two discussions (vv. 38, 55). Further, there is a parenetic excursus in vv. 18-22 concerning the hardships created by the seventh-year Fallow. The second (2) and third (3) sections contain legal discussions concerning the redemption of property and people. These two sections, in contrast with the first section, are composed of well-formulated casuistic regulations which begin with the protasis כי-ימוך אחיך (vv. 25, 35, 39 and 47 [וכי....ומך אחיך]). As I have pointed out above, this structure was noted by Reventlow, who viewed the use of this protasis as an indication that the redemption laws originally belonged to an older collection.[1]

Secondly, as Patrick,[2] North,[3] Wenham,[4] and Westbrook[5] have observed correctly, insolvency on account of debt was undoubtedly the background to the sale of land that led eventually to the enslavement of entire families. This is illustrated by the way the last two sections (vv. 25-55) are arranged according to a topical discussion which follows the principles of *successive stages of destitution* (marked by the use of the protasis כי-ימוך אחיך).[6] There are three successive stages of destitution that are dealt with in these two sections: (1) An Israelite must sell part of his land (vv. 25-34); (2) An Israelite is not able to support himself (vv. 35-38); (3a) An Israelite must be sold (with his family) to a fellow Israelite (vv. 39-43); (3b) An Israelite must be sold (with his family) to a foreigner (vv. 47-54).[7]

---

pp. 339, 347; Cardellini, *Die biblischen 'Sklaven'-Gesetze*, p. 281; Wenham, *Leviticus*, p. 316.

1. Cf. also Noth, *Leviticus*, p. 189.
2. Patrick, *Old Testament Law*, p. 183.
3. North, *Sociology of the Biblical Jubilee*, pp. 158-90.
4. Wenham, *Leviticus*, p. 317.
5. Westbrook, 'Jubilee Laws', pp. 213-14.
6. Similar structures are noted by Cardellini, *Die biblischen 'Sklaven'-Gesetze*, p. 288; and Japhet, 'The Relationship Between the Legal Corpora', p. 75; cf. also Patrick, *Old Testament Law*, p. 184, who sees a similar structure for the last two stages in vv. 35-55.
7. See also the narrative in Gen. 47.13-19, which appears to envisage similar successive stages of destitution.

It is important to point out that these successive stages of destitution must be understood from the context of the discussion, which moves from one level of destitution to another, since the protasis itself does not indicate the level of destitution.[1] Furthermore, each stage of destitution is directly related to the sale of land, which is more severe than the debts envisaged in the manumission laws in Exod. 21.2-11 and Deut. 15.12-18. As we saw above in Chapters 2 and 3, a landowner would sell part or all of his land only as a last resort, which suggests that the provisions that occur here in Lev. 25.25-55 attempted to safeguard Israelites from the worst possible forms of insolvency.

Regarding the first stage of destitution (1), an Israelite is forced to sell part of his property (vv. 25-28), or a house within a village (v. 31). According to these stipulations, a man does not actually transfer his land to the buyer but rather the buyer merely 'leases' the land, which automatically returns to the seller during the Jubilee.[2] Furthermore, the seller or one of the seller's relatives has the right of redemption over the property at any time during the period of the

---

1. It is possible that the discussion in section (1) vv. 14-16 also refers to a stage of destitution, or rather to a lack of destitution. These verses may envisage a commercial transaction that was not related to poverty similar to LH §§42-47, which envisage the renting out of land by one farmer to another. However, it is doubtful that an ordinary farmer would be in any position to rent out land in order to make a profit. It is clear that LH §§49-51, which are related to the laws in §§42-47, refer to farmers who are forced to hand over parts of their land as a pledge on account of debt. It is likely that only large landowners were in a position to rent or lease out land in order to realize a profit (cf. Driver and Miles, *Babylonian Laws*, I, p. 140). I suggest, therefore, that vv. 14-16 likely refer to some stage of destitution although the discussion does not directly refer to this (i.e., by the use of the protasis כי־ימך אחיך). It is best, therefore, to understand this discussion as a general introduction to the redemption of property which is discussed in greater detail in vv. 25ff. Further, the general reference תשבו איש אל־אחזתו 'each of you shall return to his own property' in v. 13, which probably refers to the redemption of people, is discussed in greater detail in vv. 39-41 (cf. v. 41 אל־אחזת אבתיו ישוב).

2. Cf. Boecker, *Law and the Administration of Justice*, pp. 89-90; Japhet, 'The Relationship Between the Legal Corpora', pp. 85-86; Noth, *Leviticus*, pp. 188-89; R. de Vaux, *Ancient Israel*, p. 175; Wenham, *Leviticus*, p. 320. Boecker notes that while LH contains many laws regarding the leasing of land, which presupposes that the lessor can do whatever he wishes with the land, in all of the discussions of land in the Old Testament the concept of the renting of land in biblical law does not begin to approach that of LH.

'lease' (vv. 25-26). However, houses that are located in a walled city (vv. 29-30) can only be redeemed for one year, after which they permanently pass over to the buyer, although houses belonging to Levites were redeemable since this was their only property. The latter stipulation concerning Levites demonstrates that the stipulations in vv. 25-28, 31 refer to patrimonial land, and that houses that are located in the cities refer to non-patrimonial property.[1] These stipulations also accurately reflect the settlement patterns of the majority of Israelites who settled in the highlands and lowlands of Canaan.

If a man is forced to sell part of his property, then ובא גאלו הקרב אליו וגאל את ממכר אחיו 'his redeemer who is most closely related to him must come and redeem what his brother has sold' (v. 25). Following the list of relatives who are responsible for the redemption of an Israelite who is sold to a foreigner in vv. 48-49,[2] it is likely that the גאל referred to in v. 25 would be the closest relative from either the seller's בת אב 'nuclear or extended family or proper lineage' (e.g., one of his brothers; cf. v. 48), or משפחה 'clan or lineage or maximal lineage' (cf. v. 49), who would either reside in the same town or village or come from another area (cf. Jer. 32.6-15; Ruth 4[3]). However, if his property is redeemed it is not entirely clear whether the property is automatically returned to the seller[4] or whether the ownership just reverts to someone who is a member of the seller's בת אב or משפחה.[5] In the latter case the גאל would merely take the place of the buyer until either his kin was able to redeem the property or until the Jubilee. This latter option seems more likely, since it is questionable whether a fellow kinsman could afford to provide a charitable redemption of land. If, however, no one is able to redeem the property then the seller can either buy the property back (vv. 26-27)[6]

---

1. Cf. also Westbrook, 'The Price Factor in the Redemption of Land', p. 110.

2. That the order of relationship for the redemption of a debt-slave is the same for the redemption of property is also held by R. Westbrook, 'Redemption of Land', *ILR* 6 (1971), p. 370.

3. Cf. Westbrook, 'Redemption of Land', pp. 367-75.

4. Cf. Noth, *Leviticus*, p. 189; Patrick, *Old Testament Law*, p. 183.

5. Cf. Westbrook, 'Redemption of Land', pp. 369-71; Wenham, *Leviticus*, p. 320; Japhet, 'The Relationship Between the Legal Corpora', p. 79; Bellefontaine, 'Study of Ancient Israelite Laws', p. 190; Pedersen, *Israel* , I–II, pp. 84.

6. Concerning the formulation of this provision, see Japhet, 'The Relationship

or wait until the year of Jubilee, when the property will be returned to him (v. 28). In this situation it is not clear what proportion of the seller's property is sold, but since the text envisages the possibility of him buying back the land before the Jubilee (vv. 26-27), it follows that he retains enough land in order to maintain his family and save enough currency in the process to buy back the property[1]—viz., he could make some investment or even hire out the services of himself or other members of his family.[2]

That these stipulations envisaged the sale of property on account of insolvency is demonstrated further by Westbrook's study of the redemption of land in the Bible and the ancient Near East, to which I already made reference in my discussion of MAL A §44 in Chapter 3. In this discussion we saw that both Westbrook and Lewy suggest that cuneiform law acknowledged that a buyer could only acquire a person or land as permanent property when it was sold at the 'full price'. Westbrook[3] suggests that the only type of land sales that included any *right* of redemption were sales that were below the full market price, which were common among people who were forced to sell their land on account of insolvency. The redemption price would therefore be equivalent to the sale price, even if this figure was far below the full market price. Westbrook suggests that this legal principle is most likely envisaged in LE §39, which reads:

Between the Legal Corpora', p. 79 n. 43, who writes: 'The formulation of the law as it stands appears to restrict a man's right to redeem his property to the case where he "has no one to redeem it" (Lev. 25.26). It would seem, however, that this is in fact no restriction of the right of redemption but rather a reflection of reality—for how could a man who has just been obliged to sell his property be immediately capable of redeeming it himself? The principle of the law is, then, in the emphasis on the fact that the former owner's right to redeem his property is preserved even if there is no possibility of immediate redemption.'

1. This transaction is different from the pledging of crops and land which is attested in LH §§49-51, in several Elamite documents, and in several *šapartu* contracts (refer to the discussion of the *šapartu* contracts above in Chapter 3). It was common practice for a debtor to pledge his crops or land to a creditor for a year or more without actually selling his land to the creditor. During this time the creditor would take the crops grown on the property in payment for the capital loaned plus the interest. It is possible that this practice was also followed in Israel, although it is likely that no interest was levied.

2. Cf. Ziskind, 'Legal Observations', p. 160.

3. Westbrook, 'The Price Factor in the Redemption of Land', pp. 97-127.

If a man becomes impoverished [*enēšu* 'to grow weak'] and sells his estate [literally 'house'], the day the buyer sells, the owner of the estate may redeem.

The protasis makes it clear that redemption only applies in those cases in which property is sold on account of insolvency. Furthermore, Westbrook suggests that the verb *enēšu* 'to grow weak' is the direct parallel to the Hebrew verb מוך 'to sink', 'to become poor', which occurs in the leading protasis of each level of destitution in Lev. 25.25, 35, 39. Therefore, Westbrook suggests that biblical law also was aware of the legal principles enunciated in LE §39 and elsewhere. However, Lev. 25.29 does not seem to envisage the sale of property below the full market price, since this property is not part of the seller's patrimony.[1] While it is most likely that both biblical and cuneiform law sought to protect the patrimony of citizens, Lev. 25.23 adds a theological motive to the redemption of land—all land ultimately belonged to Yahweh, who gave it to Israel as an inheritance.[2]

In the second stage of destitution (2) an Israelite no longer has sufficient means of support, which forces him to become dependent upon charitable interest-free loans to sustain him and his family (vv. 35-38). This section demonstrates that the Jubilee regulations are intimately tied to the Sabbatical year regulations that are referred to in vv. 2b-7, especially since the Sabbatical year release in Deut. 15.1-11 provided for the release of loans that are mentioned in Lev. 25.35-38. Furthermore, it is most likely, as Wenham,[3] Cardellini[4] and Japhet[5] suggest, that the Israelite still owns land but that he is no longer able to support his family from it. This condition is similar to that envisaged in vv. 23-28, except that in this case there is no גאל to redeem the seller's land nor is the seller able to support himself and his family from the sale of property, since he has already sold part of his land. Therefore, since he cannot rely on any support from his immediate kin or from any further sale of property[6] he is forced to

---

1. Cf. Yaron, *The Laws of Eshnunna*, p. 273 and n. 41.
2. Cf. Horst, *Gottes Recht*, pp. 219-20; Wright, *God's People in God's Land*, pp. 58-64.
3. Wenham, *Leviticus*, p. 322.
4. Cardellini, *Die biblischen 'Sklaven'-Gesetze*, pp. 286, 288.
5. Japhet, 'The Relationship Between the Legal Corpora', p. 75.
6. It is possible that this stage envisages the total loss of land. However, it is

rely on charitable interest-free loans with which he would likely buy seed to plant crops (i.e., agricultural loan)[1] in order to sustain his family and livestock. However, if these charitable measures did not work then he would be forced to sell all of his land and himself, as is envisaged in vv. 39-43, 47-55. To a discussion of this last level of destitution we now turn.

Exegesis of Leviticus 25.39-43, 47-55

Leviticus 25.39-43

Lev. 25.39-43

39 וכי־ימוך אחיך עמך ונמכר־לך לא־תעבד בו עבדת עבד:

40 כשכיר כתושב יהיה עמך עד־שנת היבל יעבד עמך:

41 ויצא מעמך הוא ובניו עמו ושב אל־משפחתו ואל־אחזת אבתיו ישב:

42 כי־עבדי הם אשר־הוצאתי אתם מארץ מצרים לא ימכרו ממכרת עבד:

43 לא־תרדה בו בפרך ויראת מאלהיך:

39 If your brother becomes so poor with regard to you that he is sold to you, you shall not subject him to a slave's service.

40 He shall be with you like a hired worker, or as a sojourner; until the year of Jubilee he shall serve with you.

41 Then he shall go out from you, he and his sons with him, and return to משפחתו, that he may return to the property of his forefathers.

42 For they are my slaves, whom I brought out of the land of Egypt; they must not be resold as slaves.

43 You shall not rule over him with severity, but are to fear your God.

In this third stage of destitution (3) an Israelite man, along with his family, is forced to be sold. Two cases are examined in this stage: (3a) an Israelite is sold to a fellow Israelite (vv. 39-43); and (3b) an Israelite is sold to a foreigner (vv. 47-55). As in the previous stage of destitution there is no redeemer mentioned in the first case (3a),

---

unlikely that anyone could support a family on charitable loans alone; cf. I. Cardellini, *Die biblischen 'Sklaven'-Gesetze*, p. 288. Further, since loans are the only source of support it is unlikely that a creditor, no matter how charitable he was, would give out loans if the man did not have the means to pay them back; i.e., he was able plant a crop or buy livestock in order to sustain his family and pay back the loan. Cp. Patrick, *Old Testament Law*, p. 184, who suggests that vv. 35-38 refer to a landless Israelite who must make a living by a trade, commerce, or as a day labourer. This view is certainly possible, especially in the light of the reference to the גר and תושב in v. 35, although I prefer to adopt the view that these verses refer to a poor landowner, since vv. 39-54 clearly refer to a landless Israelite.

1. Cf. Wenham, *Leviticus*, p. 322; Lohfink, 'The Kingdom of God', p. 223.

because if there were someone who could help the debtor he would
have done so when the debtor was forced to sell part of his land.[1]

Verse 39 is conditionally formulated ('when/if' form; i.e.,
casuistic), containing a single main case. The main case, which
contains the protasis וכי־ימוך אחיך עמך ונמכר־לך and the apodosis
לא־תעבד בו עבדת עבד is followed by a series of clauses (vv. 40-41)
that are subordinate to the apodosis in v. 39b.[2] Verse 40 elaborates on
the apodosis in v. 39b by explaining how the service of an Israelite
who sells himself is different from that of a chattel-slave: (a) he is to
be treated as a hired man; (b) he serves only until the Jubilee. Further,
v. 41 outlines the particulars of his release: (a) he is released with his
family; (b) he is allowed to return to his משפחה and to his property.
Lastly, vv. 42-43 contain two motivation clauses which give a
theological explanation for the release of Israelites.

In v. 39a an Israelite (literally אחיך 'your brother') is sold (נמכר) to
a fellow Israelite. The terminology used in v. 39a is very similar to
that found in Deut. 15.12. While it is not the main purpose of my
present analysis to determine the relative temporal order of the
manumission laws in Deuteronomy and Leviticus, although I have
already suggested in Chapter 7 that there is some evidence to suggest
that the law in Leviticus is earlier than that in Deuteronomy,
nevertheless it is most likely that both laws employed similar
terminology for similar theological reasons. For example, in Chapter
7 we saw that the term אחיך was employed in order to emphasize that
the release and provision of debt-slaves was to be the concern of *all*
Israelites, not just their immediate kin. Similarly, the term אח
'brother' is used here in its broadest meaning, as a reference to the
nation of Israel or the covenant community, in order to emphasize the
responsibility of the nation of Israel in the maintenance of insolvent
Israelites. This term is particularly relevant in this case, because if
there were a relative who could help a debtor who is sold he would
have done so when the debtor was forced to sell part of his land.
Furthermore, the Niphal perfect[3] verb נמכר is also found in Deut.

---

1. Cp. Yaron, 'Redemption of Persons', p. 156, who suggests that redemption
is not provided for in vv. 39-43 because of the limited scope of the provisions in
Leviticus 25.

2. For a thorough syntactical analysis of these verses, see Cardellini, *Die
biblischen 'Sklaven'-Gesetze*, pp. 287-94.

3. For a discussion of the use of the perfect in the continuation of the main

15.12, in which I rendered it passively, although we saw in this discussion that the verb can also be rendered reflexively 'he sells himself'. In Lev. 25.39 this Niphal verb is usually rendered reflexively 'he sells himself' (NASB, RSV),[1] although some translations have rendered it passively 'he is sold' (AV).[2] However, I suggest that the verb נמכר should be rendered 'he sells himself' in this context for the following reasons.[3]

First, this law clearly refers to the head of a nuclear or extended family who is forced to enter into servitude with his family (v. 41). This law is different from those manumission laws in Exodus and Deuteronomy, both of which refer to the sale of dependents by their family. I therefore argued that it was best to render the verb נמכר in Deut. 15.12 passively in order to reflect this type of transaction, since it is most likely that the head of the household would initiate such a sale, rather than some other member of his lineage or a creditor.[4]

Secondly, while it is clear that the head of the household is forced to sell himself on account of insolvency, it is not entirely clear whether he must sell himself in order to pay an antecedent debt. While this is most likely the cause of the sale of dependents in Exod. 21.2-6 and Deut. 15.12-18, it is likely that this is not the cause in Lev. 25.39. As Cardellini[5] suggests, this law envisages a man who is forced to sell himself because he has no other way to provide for himself and his family (i.e., he has lost his land and is not able to find work elsewhere). It should be pointed out that self-sale contracts were

conditional clause, see Liedke, *Gestalt und Bezeichnung*, p. 35; cf. also Japhet, 'The Relationship Between the Legal Corpora', p. 74.

1. Cf. also Patrick, *Old Testament Law*, p. 184; Wenham, *Leviticus*, pp. 315, 322; Noth, *Leviticus*, p. 182; and BDB, p. 569, which suggest that the verb מכר in Lev. 25.39, 47, 48, 50; Deut. 15.12; Jer. 34.14; and Neh. 5.8 (twice) should be rendered reflexively.

2. Cf. Elliger, *Leviticus*, pp. 358-60; Heinisch, *Leviticus*, p. 115; GKC §51; and HALAT II: 551, which suggest that Lev. 25.39; Deut. 15.12; Jer. 34.14 should be rendered passively (*verkauft werden*). However, HALAT suggests that Lev. 25.47, 48, 50; Neh. 5.8, should be rendered reflexively (*sich verkaufen*).

3. Cf. also Japhet, 'The Relationship Between the Legal Corpora', pp. 73-74.

4. Cf. Noordtzij, *Leviticus*, p. 259, who suggests that it was unlikely that a fellow Israelite was permitted to sell a countryman to another person.

5. Cardellini, *Die biblischen 'Sklaven'-Gesetze*, p. 288; cf. also Riesener, *Der Stamm* עבד, p. 124; Patrick, *Old Testament Law*, p. 184; Dillmann, *Leviticus*, p. 615.

attested as early as the Ur III.[1] Furthermore, we saw in Chapter 2 that Mesopotamian families who lost their land often become semi-free citizens in a temple or palace household. Leviticus 25.39-43, however, only envisages the sale of Israelites to private citizens since there is little evidence that the palace and temple households developed to the same extent as those in Mesopotamia. Furthermore, the purpose of the biblical legislation was to provide a haven for an Israelite family until which time their land was returned to them.

Lastly, that this law refers to the self-sale of an Israelite who has no means of production is demonstrated further by the stipulation in v. 39b, which states that he shall not be subjected to a slave's service. The particulars of the Israelite's service is outlined in v. 40, which states that he shall be like a שכיר 'hired worker' or a תושב[2] 'sojourner', and that he is to be released during the year of Jubilee, when his property is returned to him. The Israelite is compared with immigrants who must seek work in Israelite households, since many of them did not own land.[3] While I argued that scholars have incorrectly compared the service of the debt-slaves mentioned in

---

1. Cf. Mendelsohn, *Slavery in the Ancient Near East*, pp. 14-19.

2. The term תושב is used here alongside the term שכיר since it refers to those dwellers who were dependent upon the Israelites for protection and provisions; cf. Daube, *The Exodus Pattern*, pp. 24-25.

3. Cf. R. Martin-Archard, 'גור', *Theologisches Handwörterbuch zum Alten Testament*, I (ed. E. Jenni and C. Westermann; Munich: Chr. Kaiser Verlag, 1978), cols. 409-12; D. Kellermannm, 'גר', *TDOT*, II, pp. 439-49; P. Grelot, 'Le dernière étape de la rédaction sacerdotale', *VT* 6 (1956), pp. 174-89. The term תושב occurs mostly in Leviticus and is not found in Deuteronomy. Although the term תושב is often translated as 'sojourner' this term does not appear to refer to the same group of 'sojourners' to whom the term גר refers (cf. Num. 35.15). However, both groups were treated the same in regard to the humanitarian stipulations (e.g. to be sustained in need; Lev. 25.6, 35) and in cases of homicide (e.g. both are offered asylum in a city of refuge in the case of an accidental killing; Num. 35.15). In addition, the תושב was used as a hired worker (cf. Lev. 25.40). However, the תושב and people from the foreign nations (הגוים) were the only people whom Israel could acquire as permanent slaves (Lev. 25.44-45). The גר is not mentioned in this context because he was exempt from becoming a permanent slave by virtue of his membership within the congregation of Israel. This suggests that the תושב was not a member of the congregation, and thus this term was used to designate those sojourners who did not participate in the cult of Israel, while the term גר was used to refer to sojourners who participated in the cult (cf. Kellermann, 'גר', cols. 446, 448; cp. Grelot, 'Le dernière étape de la rédaction sacerdotale', p. 177).

Exod. 21.2-6 and Deut. 15.12-18 with the *ḫābiru* service contracts, which were initiated by the *ḫābiru*, such a comparison can be made with the type of sale envisaged here in Lev. 25.39-43, although it is clear that the Jubilee release of land was stipulated in order to prevent Israelite families from entering into permanent servitude. Furthermore, it is clear that this law does not envisage the type of indentured servitude normally associated with the Nuzian *ḫābiru* service contracts, but rather an Israelite was to be compared with a hired worker. To a discussion of the nature of this service we now turn.

Both Japhet[1] and Riesener[2] suggest that the creditor who buys an Israelite has only purchased the service or capacity for work (*Arbeitskraft*) of his so-called debt-slave. However, while this principle is reflected clearly in the manumission laws in Exodus and Deuteronomy, since both stipulate the release of debt-slaves, the law in Leviticus 25 makes it clear that the service of a man who sells himself should not be compared with the service of a slave, but rather with that of a hired worker. This special treatment is due to the nature of the sale that is envisaged in v. 39, since the man who seeks refuge in another household is not paying off a debt, but rather he is seeking a place to live until his land is returned to him. The regulation in Lev. 25.39-43, therefore, makes an important distinction between the nature of the work (e.g., type of work and the conditions under which it is performed) which a שכיר 'hired worker' performs and that which an עבד (i.e., debt- and chattel-slave) performs.[3] Therefore, the expression עברי, which appears in both Exod. 21.2 (with the term עבד) and Deut. 15.12, is most likely not employed in Lev. 25.39, which refers to the destitute Israelite simply as אח 'brother' (note that Deut. 15.12 uses the expression אחיך העברי 'your brother a Hebrew man'), in order that the service of a man who sells himself is not compared with the service of a dependent who is sold to pay an antecedent debt.[4]

---

1. Japhet, 'The Relationship Between the Legal Corpora', p. 84.

2. Riesener, *Der Stamm* עבד, p. 124; cf. also Noordtzij, *Leviticus*, p. 259.

3. Cf. Elliger, *Leviticus*, pp. 341-42; and Riesener, *Der Stamm* עבד, p. 124; Cholewiński, *Heiligkeitsgesetz*, pp. 236-37.

4. Cf. also Ziskind, 'Legal Observations', p. 159, who suggests that the debt-slave in Lev. 25.39 is not an עבד like the debt-slave in Exodus and Deuteronomy, but a 'civil bondman' since his service is longer. Refer also to Kaufman, 'Social Welfare Systems in Ancient Israel', p. 283, who suggests that the debt-slave is a

In contrast to both the chattel- and debt-slave, a שׂכיר 'hired worker' was entitled to certain contractual rights.[1] Although the Old Testament does not fully describe the duties and rights of the hired worker, according to the ancient Near Eastern legal collections and contracts[2] hired workers were usually contracted to do a specific task (e.g., various craftsmen such as carpenters, smiths, jewellers, etc. LH §274; ploughmen LH §§257-258; herdsmen LH §261; soldier HL §42; smith HL §160-161), although there were 'casual' or 'unskilled' workers who were employed to do various kinds of tasks (cf. LH §273; LE §§7-9, 11; HL §158-159, 177).[3] Most of the hireling laws deal in the main with the needs of an agriculture which remained the single most important part of the economy in the ancient Near East.[4] Therefore, it is most likely that the biblical law demanded that an Israelite treat his fellow countryman like a hired worker who enjoyed the contractual privilege of doing a certain task and working for a fixed number of hours per day.[5] Furthermore, he may also have been provided with other provisions, such as food, drink and clothing, depending on what

'household retainer'. Contra Wright, 'What Happened Every Seven Years in Israel, II', p. 196, who suggests that the term does not appear in Lev. 25.39 because it was a reference to landless foreigners; and Riesener, *Der Stamm* עבד, pp. 124-25, who suggests that the term את is employed in Leviticus in order to indicate that this law was more humane than the law in Exod. 21.2-6 and Deut. 15.12-18, both of which employ the term עברי.

1. For a discussion of the term שׂכיר 'hired worker' and its ancient Near Eastern context, see S. Warhaftig, 'Labor Law', *EncJud*, X, cols. 1325-30; C.H. Wolf, 'Servant', *IDB*, IV, pp. 291-92; H. Reviv, 'שׂכיר', in Tadmor (ed.), *Encyclopedia Biblica*, VIII, cols. 285-87; de Vaux, *Early Israel*, p. 76; Driver and Miles, *Babylonian Laws*, I, pp. 469-78; Yaron, *Laws of Eshnunna* (1969 edition), pp. 147-49, 167; E. Neufeld, *The Hittite Laws* (London: Luzac, 1951), pp. 157, 178; *CAD* I/1: 146-47, 151-53.

2. For a study of wages during the OB period, see Farber, 'Price and Wage Study', pp. 1-51.

3. Cf. Warhaftig, 'Labor Law', col. 1325, who notes that according to the Tosef. B.M. 7.6, a worker cannot be forced to do other jobs for which he was contracted; cf. also Wolf, 'Servant', p. 291.

4. Cf. Yaron, *Laws of Eshnunna* (1969 edition), p. 147; Driver and Miles, *Babylonian Laws*, I, pp. 469-78.

5. This is also the opinion of Ramban, *ad. loc.*; cp. Lohfink, 'Economy in the Bible', p. 223, who suggests that the debt-slave places his labour output, *and that of his family*, at the disposal of his creditor.

was customary.[1] Lastly, he was most likely provided with other benefits which were probably not provided to day labourers, such as a house and some land in which he and his family could live as a single household.[2] Israelites were therefore most likely encouraged to give to their fellow Israelites provisions and contractual rights not normally extended to those who sold themselves, or perhaps even to those who were hired as day labourers.[3] This type of arrangement is similar to the way in which the ancient Near Eastern temple and palace households maintained their semi-free citizens, although these citizens were unlikely to regain their land or freedom.

Verses 40b-41 state that an Israelite who sells himself was to serve until the Jubilee, during which he and his family ושב אל־משפחתו 'returns to his lineage' and ואל־אחזת אבתיו ישוב 'returns to the property of his forefathers'. The length of service has puzzled some commentators, since a man who was sold shortly after the Jubilee probably would not live to see the day of his release. Thus, for example, Porter[4] and Lemche[5] have suggested that a certain unreality or illusion[6] was introduced when the seventh-year release was

---

1. Cf. Driver and Miles, *Babylonian Laws*, I, p. 477, who note that in several contracts clothing, food and drink are provided by the hirer for workers engaged by him. Such allowances may also have been customary in some of the laws in LH, although these laws do not specifically mention any allowances.

2. Cf. Ellison, 'The Hebrew Slave', p. 34. The scope of this law suggests that the debt-slave's family was nuclear and not extended, since it is unlikely that any creditor would be able to provide for an extended family.

3. That the biblical legislation encouraged Israelites to extend benefits not normally extended to hired workers, is suggested by the following question: why didn't an Israelite seek employment as a hired worker instead of selling himself? Even if we accept the view of Patrick, *Old Testament Law*, p. 184, that vv. 34-37 refer to a landless Israelite who must make a living by a trade, or as a day labourer, this does not explain why vv. 39-43 call upon a fellow Israelite to treat a destitute Israelite as a hired worker, since the Israelite who sells himself was not able to support his family by making a living as a hired labourer. It is more likely, though, that an Israelite man would not be able to support his family as a hired worker, which suggests that the regulations in vv. 39-43 call upon Israelites to extend to their countrymen additional benefits, such as a house, food and so on. This is similar to the stipulations found in Deut. 15.12-18, which called upon Israelites to share their blessings (e.g., food and other commodities) with their released debt-slaves .

4. Porter, *Leviticus*, p. 205.

5. Lemche, 'The Manumission of Slaves', p. 50.

6. Cf. also de Vaux, *Ancient Israel*; Noth, *Leviticus*, p. 192; Kilian,

transferred to the Jubilee. However, these objections are not convincing, for the following reasons.

First, Israelites who sold themselves were not *required* to serve 50 years, but rather they served only from the time of their sale until the Jubilee, which means that few families served the full 50 years.

Secondly, it appears that scholars,[1] such as Porter and Lemche, have missed the main intention of the Jubilee release for they assume that the manumission laws in Lev. 25.39-43, Exod. 21.2-6, and Deut. 15.12-18 envisage the same type of debt-slavery. However, as I argued above, the regulation in Lev. 25.39-43 envisages the sale of the head of a household (and his family) because he can no longer support his family due to the loss of his patrimonial land. Therefore, the *main* point of this regulation, which is enunciated clearly in v. 41, was that patrimonial land should never be sold permanently (v. 23), but rather should be returned to the original owner (or family) during the Jubilee. As Bellefontaine[2] notes correctly, this is the most significant stipulation concerning Israel's attitude towards land (i.e., *Bodenrecht*), a principle upon which Israel's social structure was based. Furthermore, this attitude towards patrimony was also evident in Nuzi and Mari, where land could only be sold within the family, although, as we saw out in Chapter 3, this legal principle was often circumvented by fictitious 'sale-adoptions'.

Heiligkeitsgesetzes, p. 129. Cp. Gnuse, *You Shall not Steal*, p. 25, who considers the 50-year release a 'legal fiction' since a similar motif is found in some Nuzi *tidennūtu* contracts that suggest that people actually became indentured slaves. However, while there is some similarity between the *tidennūtu* contracts and Lev. 25.39-43, the *tidennūtu* contract is very different from the regulation in Leviticus 25. As we saw above in Chapter 3, the duration of the *tidennūtu* contract could range from one to 50 years, although in most of the contracts where large amounts of money were loaned the duration was left indefinite. However, in most of these contracts the person who is exchanged for the loan pays for the interest (*antichretic*) while the debtor remains accountable for the capital. Thus the 'pledge' is considered a hired hand who in the event of injury or death must be replaced by another worker. However, in the case where the duration of the loan was large the 'pledged person' became a type of indentured servant whom large Nuzi landlords obtained as long-term labour. In many of these cases it is likely that the pledge was never freed.

1. For example, see Cholewiński, *Heiligkeitsgesetz*, pp. 217-51; Japhet, 'Manumission Laws', pp. 63-89; Wenham, *Leviticus*, p. 322 n. 18; Patrick, *Old Testament Law*, p. 184; Mendelsohn, 'Slavery in the Old Testament', p. 388; Noth, *Leviticus*, p. 192.

2. Bellefontaine, 'Study of Ancient Israelite Laws', p. 181.

Although the manumission regulations in Exodus and Deuteronomy most likely reflect the concept of the *Bodenrecht*, since they would help prevent families from falling into further debt, nevertheless these laws are different from the manumission laws in Leviticus 25, since they envisaged only the sale of dependents into debt-slavery, not the entire household. In these regulations no loss of land is envisaged, which accounts for the shorter term of service, since the debt-slave only worked off a debt defaulted on by his or her family. However, the form of service that is outlined in Lev. 25.39-40, which is not really debt-slavery at all, was instituted in order that an Israelite and his family would receive adequate protection and support until such time as their land was returned to them. Seen together, the Jubilee regulations concerning the release of both land and people are very similar to the individual proclamations found in the the OB *mēšarum* edicts which stipulated the release of both people and land. Furthermore, these biblical reforms were instituted within the framework of the Sabbatical year, which proclaimed the release of lesser debts in Deut. 15.1-3. These latter reforms are also similar to the release of various debts stipulated in the *mēšarum* edicts. If we also include within this Israelite welfare system the laws concerning the release of debt-slaves in Exod. 21.2-6 and Deut. 15.12-18, both of which are very similar to the law in LH §117 (= A-s §20), the biblical legal system of debt-release sought to institute the various levels of debt-release found in the *mēšarum* edicts on a more regular basis.

Verses 42-43 contain two motivation clauses which scholars generally agree provide the theological reasoning behind the manumission regulation in vv. 39-41. Verses 42-43 read:

42 כי־עבדי הם אשר־הוצאתי אתם מארץ מצרים לא ימכרו ממכרת עבד:

For they are my slaves, whom I brought out of the land of Egypt; they must not be resold as slaves.

43 לא־תרדה בו בפרך ויראת מאלהיך:

You shall not rule over him with severity, but are to fear your God.

Concerning the first motivation clause, Daube[1] has noted that one of the most fundamental religious principles of the Hebrew religion was that during the Exodus from Egypt the Israelites underwent a significant transition from being Egypt's slaves to God's slaves (cf.

1. Daube, *The Exodus Pattern*, pp. 16-17, 44; cf. also Snaith, *Leviticus*, p. 167; Noordtzij, *Leviticus*, p. 259.

also v. 55). He notes further that the Exodus had a significant impact upon the social affairs of Israel including the legislation found in Lev. 25.39-55.[1] Similarly, Japhet[2] has pointed out that this motivation clause shows that the only 'master-servant' relationship that has any validity is between each Israelite and his God. Furthermore, she notes that the idea that an Israelite can only hire out his service and not sell his person parallels the idea that land can only be 'leased' and not sold. This single basic religious concept unites both the laws of redemption of land and slaves into a single system of social welfare.

The second motivation clause, however, presents certain problems regarding the meaning of the clause לא־תרדה בו בפרך 'you shall not rule over him with severity'. Japhet understands this clause to refer to the harsh treatment which an owner may impose on his debt-slave compared to the treatment which a hired worker receives. However, she does not define what she means by 'harsh treatment'.[3] Similarly, Snaith,[4] who follows the LXX (κατατεινω 'hold down tight') and *Vulgate* (*affligo* 'afflict'), suggests that the verb רדה 'to rule' has a much more violent meaning in v. 43. Lastly, Noth[5] suggests that the term פרך, whose precise meaning can no longer be defined, can be rendered 'forced labour' and apparently means something like 'torture'.[6] The above views make a strong contrast between the service of a chattel-slave and an Israelite who is treated like a hired worker. However, if such a strong contrast is being made, then according to v. 46, which contains the clause תרדה בו בפרך, Israelites may 'torture' or 'afflict' their own chattel-slaves, which contradicts my contention in Chapter 5 that chattel-slaves were protected from abuse in Israelite society, since they were considered members of the covenant community.[7] Furthermore, although the term פרך is used in Exod. 1.13-14 in order to describe the hard labour (בעבדה קשה v. 14)

---

1. Cf. also Noordtzij, *Leviticus*, p. 261.

2. Japhet, 'The Relationship Between the Legal Corpora', pp. 85-86.

3. Cf. also Wenham, *Leviticus*, p. 322.

4. Snaith, *Leviticus*, p. 167.

5. Noth, *Leviticus*, p. 192.

6. Cf. HALAT III: 911, where the term is rendered *Gewalttätigkeit* ('violence, outrage'), *Schinderei* ('oppressor').

7. Cf. also Noordtzij, *Leviticus*, p. 260; and Mendelsohn, 'Slavery in the Old Testament', p. 388, who notes that the fact that chattel-slaves can become the perpetual possessions of Israelites does not suggest that they are to be regarded as property at the mercy of their Hebrew masters.

that the Egyptians imposed upon the Israelites, Daube[1] notes correctly that it is uncertain whether this sort of cruelty, which was common in reference to slavery, was expressed in precisely the same way in Lev. 25.43.[2] Similarly, Snaith's contention, that the verb רדה should be rendered more harshly than its basic meaning 'to rule', is not convincing, since it rests upon his interpretation of the context of Exod. 1.13-14, rather than on the use of the verb in Leviticus 25.[3] Lastly, the motivation clause in v. 43 most likely refers back to, v. 41 which outlines the particulars of the so-called debt-slave's release. Therefore, the clause לא־תרדה בו בפרך in v. 43 probably refers to the length of service of a chattel-slave compared to that of Israelites who are released during the Jubilee. This appears to be the way in which the clause לא־תרדה בו בפרך in v. 46b is understood, since v. 46a refers to the fact that chattel-slaves can become the permanent possession (or slaves) of the Israelites. Furthermore, the use of the clause לא־תרדה בו בפרך in v. 43, which compares the service of an Israelite who sells himself with that of a hired man, likely refers to the authority that a master holds over a slave in regards to the type of work the slave does. That is, a slave could be compelled to do jobs that a hired worker had the right to refuse.[4]

Lastly, the presence of the motivation clauses in vv. 42-43, like the similar motivations that occur in Deut. 15.12-18, were meant to persuade Israelites to treat with compassion their fellow countrymen who had lost their land. While the redemption of people and land was widely practised in the ancient Near East, in many cases relatives were most likely unable to redeem their relatives. Therefore, the regulations in vv. 39-43 called upon the covenant community as a whole—thus the use of the term אחיך in v. 39—to administer

---

1. Daube, *The Exodus Pattern*, pp. 20-21.

2. Although the term פרך is used alongside the verb רדה in Ezek. 34.4, Daube, *The Exodus Pattern*, p. 21, notes that Ezekiel is speaking of the nation Israel as a whole rather than an individual as in Lev. 25.39-41.

3. The verb is found in Gen. 1.26, 28; Lev. 25.43, 46, 53; 26.17; Num. 24.19; 1 Kgs 5.4, 30; 9.23; Isa. 14.2, 6; Ezek. 29.15; 34.4; Ps. 49.15; 68.28; 72.8; 110.2; Neh. 9.28; 2 Chron. 8.10.

4. Note that the term עבדה, which is found in Lev. 25.39, 46, is also found in Exod. 1.14 to describe the type of labour to which the Israelites were subjected; cf. also Daube, *The Exodus Pattern*, p. 21. Further, the reference to service in v. 53 is not directed towards all Israelites, which suggests that the Hebrew debt-slaves in Exodus and Deuteronomy were not treated like hired-workers.

assistance to their fellow countrymen who had no other means of help.

Leviticus 25.47-55

Lev. 25.47-55

47 וכי חשיג יד גר ותושב עמך ומך אחיך עמו ונמכר לגר תושב עמך
או לעקר משפחת גר:

48 אחרי נמכר גאלה תהיה־לו אחד מאחיו יגאלנו:

49 או־דדו או בן־דדו יגאלנו או־משאר בשרו ממשפחתו יגאלנו
או־השיגה ידו וגגאל:

50 וחשב עם־קנהו משנת המכרו לו עד שנת היבל והיה כסף ממכרו במספר
שנים כימי שכיר יהיה עמו:

51 אם־עוד רבות בשנים לפיהן ישיב גאלתו מכסף מקנתו:

52 ואם־מעט נשאר בשים עד־שנת היבל וחשב־לו כפי שניו ישיב
את־גאלתו:

53 כשכיר שנה בשנה יהיה עמו לא־ירדנו בפרך לעיניך:

54 ואם־לא יגאל באלה ויצא בשנת היבל הוא ובניו עמו:

47 Now if the means of a stranger or of a sojourner with you becomes
sufficient, and a brother of yours becomes so poor with regard to him as
to sell himself to a stranger who is sojourning with you, or to descendants
of a stranger's family,

48 then he shall have redemption right after he has been sold. One of his
brothers may redeem him.,

49 or his uncle, or his uncle's son, may redeem him, or one of his blood
relatives from ממפחתו may redeem him; or if he prospers he may redeem
himself.

50 He then with his purchaser shall calculate from the year when he sold
himself to him up to the year of the Jubilee; and the price of his sale shall
correspond to the number of years. *It is* like the days of a hired man *that*
he shall be with him.

51 If there are still many years, he shall refund part of his purchase price
in proportion to them for his own redemption;

52 and if a few years remain until the year of Jubilee, he shall so calculate
with him. In proportion to his years he is to refund his redemption.

53 Like a man hired year by year he shall be with him; he shall not rule
over him with severity in your sight.

54 Even if he is not redeemed by these years, he shall still go out in the
year of Jubilee, he and his sons with him.

55 For the sons of Israel are My servants; they are My servants whom I
brought out from the land of Egypt. I am the Lord your God.

As I already noted above, these stipulations continue the legal
discussion in vv. 39-43, although in vv. 47-53 the Israelite is forced
to sell himself to a landed גר ותושב 'stranger or sojourner' who was
able to prosper in Israel. As we saw in Chapter 4, Canaanites lived

among the Israelites throughout their occupation of Canaan, some of whom, such as the merchants, most likely became very wealthy. The main case in v. 47 (וכי תשיג יד גר ותושב עמך ומך אחיך עמו ונמכר לגר תושב) is similar to that in v. 39 (וכי-ימוך אחיך עמך ונמכר-לך), although the series of clauses that follow v. 47 concern the redemption of the Israelite by one of his relatives or by himself (vv. 48-54).

As we saw above, vv. 39-43 do not envisage the redemption of an Israelite who sells himself because if there had been a relative who were able to redeem him he would have done so at an earlier stage of destitution. However, a rather strong appeal is nevertheless made for a redeemer when an Israelite is forced to sell himself to a foreigner. Therefore, the list of possible redeemers in vv. 48-49, which covers both the בת אב (e.g., minimal and proper lineage lineage—brother, uncle) and משפחה (e.g., proper and maximal lineage), most likely envisaged a wider appeal for the redemption of a kinsman than that envisaged in v. 25 (גאלו הקרב).[1]

However, while the text does not clarify whether the redeemed Israelite (and his family) is released or whether he serves within the household of his redeemer, Yaron[2] suggests that the redemption of people in the ancient Near East by relatives was likely charitable (including Lev. 25.39-55), although the extant documents do not expressly demonstrate this. However, the stipulations in Lev. 25.47-53 do not envisage the redemption of a person who is sold for a debt, rather this law envisages the type of transaction that is similar to the hiring of a worker. The amount of money involved could be substantial if the term of the servitude approached 50 years. It is questionable, therefore, whether a kinsman could provide a relative with a charitable redemption. It is more likely that the redeemed Israelite and his family lived with his relative, for whom he worked until his land was returned during the Jubilee.[3] Therefore, a special plea is

---

1. I already noted in Chapter 4 that it is debatable how large the משפחה or proper lineage was in ancient Israel. While Gottwald and Lemche suggest that a משפחה in the Pre-Monarchic period occupied a single town or village, Andersen, 'Israelite Kinship Terminology and Social Structure', pp. 29-39, suggests that a משפחה in this period contained at least 10,000 people, by a conservative estimate, which would occupy more than one town.

2. Yaron, 'Redemption of Persons', pp. 155, 167-74.

3. Cf. Daube, *The Exodus Pattern*, p. 42, who suggests that a transfer of ownership takes place (cf. Jer. 32.6-15; Ruth 2.20ff.); cf. also Neufeld, 'Socio-Economic Background', p. 76.

made for a redeemer in vv. 47-53 so that an Israelite who is forced to sell himself can work in the household of a fellow countryman, who will be more likely to treat him more favourably than a foreigner, just as the stipulations in vv. 39-43 attempt to accomplish.

Although vv. 39-43 do not mention anything about the rate of hire of an Israelite who sells himself, Noth[1] notes correctly that according to Lev. 25.50b, 53, it appears that he was to receive wages or support as if he were paid like a hired worker from year to year.[2] While I suggested that it is possible that an Israelite who sells himself to a fellow Israelite did not receive the same amount of wages as a hired worker, the stipulations in vv. 47-53 are more formal in that they clearly compare the sale of an Israelite with the wages received by a yearly worker. Furthermore, vv. 50-53 appear to stipulate that an Israelite who sells himself receives the full amount of wages or support—from the time of sale until the Jubilee—at the start of his service (vv. 50-53).[3] These stipulations appear to guarantee that an Israelite household that resided with a rich landed foreigner would be provided for until the Jubilee. This might explain why vv. 39-43 do not mention anything about the payment of wages, which would be assumed from normal practice, or why nothing is said about self-redemption (cf. v. 49), since the main purpose of self-redemption was to leave the service of a foreigner in order to enter the service of a fellow Israelite.[4]

---

1. Noth, *Leviticus*, p. 193.

2. According to Lev. 19.13 and Deut. 24.15, wages are to be paid to hired labourers before sunset, which suggests that these regulations apply particularly to day labourers. Day labourers were probably not hired on a regular basis and therefore were probably more susceptible to oppression than workers who were hired yearly (cf. also Deut. 23.25, 26 [Hebrew vv. 26, 27]). Cf. *CAD* I/1: 152, where the OB letter BIN 49.13 reads: *ana mīnim la kitti taškuna u idīwardīja tušaddina wardūa u alpūa ukullam limḫura ag-ru idīšunu lelqû* 'why do you treat me unfairly, by collecting rent from my servants? [rather], let my servants and oxen receive rations and fodder [from you], *and let my hired labor get their wages.*'

3. Cp. Porter, *Leviticus*, p. 205, and Snaith, *Leviticus*, p. 167, both of whom suggest that the debt-slave was not paid, but rather was merely treated as though he was paid. Cf. also LE §9, which shows that partial payment was made in advance for the hire of a worker during harvest; cf. Yaron, *Laws of Eshnunna* (1969 edition), p. 167.

4. Cf. Porter, *Leviticus*, p. 206; cp. Wenham, *Leviticus*, p. 322; Wright, 'What Happened Every Seven Years, II', p. 197.

Summary and Conclusions

To sum up, I have examined the various stipulations contained in the manumission laws in Lev 25.39-54 in an attempt to clarify this *crux interpretum*, especially in the light of the literary structure of the Sabbatical and Jubilee regulations to which these manumission laws are connected. As the above examination has shown, the Jubilee regulations in Leviticus 25, which have been incorporated into the institution of the Sabbatical year, stipulate both the return of land and the release of landless Israelites, both of which were sold on account of insolvency.

Concerning the former stipulation, it is clear from the topical arrangement of Leviticus 25, which follows three successive stages of destitution, that the initial responsibility for the redemption of land fell upon the lineage of the impoverished seller (vv. 23-28). If redemption could not be secured from his kinsmen then the seller would have to depend upon his own initiative to reclaim his land or wait until the Jubilee release. However, there was a good chance that if a kinsman were not able to redeem the property of his relative then the seller would fall victim to further stages of destitution. Therefore, contrary to the conclusions of some literary critics,[1] the remaining regulations, which make provisions for the lending of charitable interest-free loans (vv. 35-37) and for the fair treatment of the seller (and his family) who is forced to sell himself (vv. 39-43,47-55), are an integral part of the discussion of the Jubilee in vv. 8-34.

According to these latter stipulations, an Israelite was exhorted to take in a fellow Israelite (literally אחיך 'your brother') who was not able to support himself and his family after he was forced to sell all of his land. The term אחיך was employed in this case in order to extend the tribal concern for the maintenance of kinship groups to a national concern, according to which Israelites were to extend to *all* Israelites the sort of support normally extended to members of their own families. Furthermore, it is clear that these stipulations exceeded the requirements of the manumission laws in Exodus and Deuteronomy by stipulating that Israelites who bought fellow countrymen were to

---

1. Contra Noth, *Leviticus*, p. 191; Driver, *Introduction*, p. 57; Feucht, *Untersuchungen*, pp. 51-52, 55-57; Driver and White, *Leviticus*, p. 98; Gnuse, *You Shall not Steal*, p. 24.

treat them as hired workers. While this stipulation is not treated in depth, we argued that those who sold themselves were treated like persons who engaged in day labour, and that they most likely received additional benefits, such as housing and so forth, to which many day labourers were most likely not entitled. I therefore concluded that these stipulations exhorted Israelites to provide their landless country-men with the kind of support and protection afforded to semi-free citizens who worked for the state households in Mesopotamia and elsewhere in the ancient Near East. Furthermore, it should be noted that the biblical Jubilee regulations attempted to provide an extensive system of debt-release which was already envisaged in the OB *mēšarum* edicts.

Lastly, while scholars have generally considered the seventh-year manumission laws in Exod. 21.2-6 and Deut. 15.12-18 to be at odds with the 50-year release in Lev. 25.39, I have argued that these different dates of release reflected the severity of debt involved. The seven-year release, like the three-year release in LH §117, was stipulated in those cases in which a debtor was forced to sell a dependent in order to pay an antecedent debt. The seven years reflected, in principle, the amount of the outstanding debt, which was probably, in many cases, equivalent to the cost of planting crops for one year. However, the 50-year release of land and people, like similar types of release stipulated in the OB *mēšarum* edicts, stipulated, on the one hand, the release of patrimonial land and, on the other, people who were forced to sell all of their patrimonial land. These stipulations clearly envisaged the most serious forms of insolvency, although there was a causal relationship between this type of insolvency and that envisaged in Exodus and Deuteronomy, since the sale of dependents could eventually lead to the type of insolvency envisaged in Leviticus 25.

Chapter 9

CONCLUSIONS

In the Introduction I pointed out that although it is not my intention to determine the exact date of the biblical manumission laws, since such a task lies outside the scope of this work, nevertheless it is hoped that this investigation has led to a clarification of the relationship of these laws to each other, as well as providing a historical and interpretational framework from which to date these laws, especially in relationship to the literary sources in which they appear. In the course of my study of the biblical manumission laws in Exodus, Deuteronomy and Leviticus we saw that the differences that exist between these laws have often been interpreted as indicators of the historical development of these regulations. Usually, the laws in Exodus are considered the most primitive legislation of JE, while the laws in Deuteronomy are seen as a mid-point in the development from the primitive legislation of JE to the most sophisticated level in the Priestly Source, in which various parts of the Jubilee regulations in Leviticus 25 have been placed, including the manumission laws in Lev. 25.39-54. However, my study has contributed to the view that, although there is some evidence of a development of thought in the biblical manumission laws in Exodus and Deuteronomy, many of the so-called historical developments in Deuteronomy are of a theological nature, and as such do not alter significantly the meaning of the previous legislation in Exodus. Furthermore, I have challenged the belief that the manumission laws in Lev. 25.39-54 deal with the same type of debt-slavery as that envisaged in the manumission laws in Exodus and Deuteronomy. While this belief has generally led to the view that Lev. 25.39-54 must have abolished the law in Deut. 15.12-18 or *vice versa*, I have argued that the laws in Leviticus deal with a much more serious form of destitution than that envisaged in Exodus or Deuteronomy. These conclusions have important implications for determining the relationship between these laws as well as possible dates for their composition. Therefore, in the following discussion I will first summarize the results of my investigation of the manumission laws in Exodus (1), Deuteronomy (2), and Leviticus (3), after which I will discuss the relationship between these biblical manumission laws and possible dates of composition.

1. *Exodus 21.2-6, 7-11*

It is generally acknowledged that the manumission law in Exod. 21.2-6 is considered the oldest of the biblical manumission laws because it appears to reflect best the legal and social circumstances of various Nuzi service and loan contracts in which the term *ḫabiru* appears. For example, many scholars suggest that the terms *ḫabiru* / *ḫupšu* are etymologically related to the biblical terms עברי(ם) / חפשי, both of which are found in Exod. 21.2. However, in response to these comparative analyses I argued, on the one hand, that there is little correspondence between the debt-slave law in Exod. 21.2-6 and the Nuzi service and loan contracts, according to which homeless *ḫabiru* men, women and families served voluntarily in the houses of Nuzi citizens. On the other, I argued that the determination of the semantic value of the biblical terms עברי(ם) and חפשי is best accomplished by looking at the current usage of these terms rather than by etymological discussions. On the basis of my investigation of these terms, I concluded that the biblical term עברי(ם) was most likely used as a reference to Israelite debt-slaves, and that the term חפשי refers to the free status of the released debt-slave, not a lower social class. This conclusion was further supported by my exegesis of the slave laws in Exod. 21.2-6, 7-11. To a summary of this discussion we now turn.

First, I noted that various similarities exist between Exod. 21.2-4 and the manumission law in LH §117, having noted before that it is most likely that the compiler of the Covenant Code drew upon a common *Schultradition* similar to that found in LH §117-119, since both Exod. 21.2-32 and LH §§117-225 contain similar laws and exhibit similar structures. For example, I argued that both Exod. 21.2-6 and LH §117 referred to the release of a dependent who was sold by the head of a household who defaulted on an antecedent loan, although the biblical law envisages the release of only a male dependent while LH §117 envisages the release of male and female dependents. Nevertheless, I argued that this lack of comprehensiveness was due to the literary framework of the biblical law in Exod. 21.2-6, which is closely connected to the debt-slave law in vv. 7-11 which discusses the sale of an Israelite אמה. While these two laws have been carefully juxtaposed, I pointed out that the law in vv. 7-11 envisaged a different type of sale from that envisaged in vv. 2-6. For example, while v. 2 refers to the sale of a dependent who performed household or other non-sexual labour, v. 7 clearly refers to a type of adoption or marriage contract that was attested throughout the ancient Near East. Furthermore, while the law in vv. 2-6 stipulated that an Israelite עבד עברי was required to be released after serving six years, the law in vv. 7-11 attempted to protect the rights of an Israelite אמה, who was released only if her husband failed to meet his contractual obligations to her. Lastly, I argued that although the laws in Exod. 21.2-6, 7-11 do not make specific reference to the sale of an אמה for household or other non-sexual labour, nevertheless the compiler of these two laws was probably aware of such a transaction, since it was one of the most common types of sale transactions in the ancient Near East.

Secondly, I noted that the biblical manumission law in Exod. 21.2-6 contains stipulations that are unique to the biblical legal collection, the most important of which is the stipulation that allowed a Hebrew debt-slave to become the permanent servant of his lord. Scholars have generally understood the slave's declaration in v. 5 and the ritual in v. 6, in which the term האלהים occurs, as references to ancient legal practices which were pre-Israelite. However, I argued on the one hand that the oath in v. 5 should not be compared to the declarations made by a *tidennu* in a Nuzi *tidennūtu* contract, in which a Nuzi citizen pledges himself into the service of a fellow Nuzian, since the two oaths refer to two completely different types of contracts (i.e., sale [Exod. 21.2]; loan requiring a pledge [*tidennūtu* contract]). I concluded that the oath in v. 5 was sincere and reflected the feelings the עבד עברי had for his master and wife. On the other hand, although some scholars suggest that the term האלהים refers to household gods which were placed by the door of a house, I argued that this term most likely refers to God who is located in the sanctuary. According to the ritual in v. 6, therefore, the עבד עברי was required to confirm the oath he made to his lord before God in the sanctuary. I noted that similar declaratory oaths, which are attested in both LE and LH, were also given in the temple. The lord was then required to pierce the slave's ear in order to solemnize the slave's intent to serve the lord forever. These cultic rituals were most likely required because the release of a debt-slave was closely associated with God's release of Israel from their bondage to the Egyptians. Therefore any Israelite who contemplated becoming a permanent servant had to declare his intention before God. However, while the status of an עבד עולם was most likely closer to the status of a free person than that of a chattel-slave, nevertheless this law says very little about the legal rights of such a servant.

2. *Deuteronomy 15.12-18*

While it is generally the view of scholars that the manumission law in Deut. 15.12-18 is based upon the earlier manumission law in Exod. 21.2-6, the fact that Deuteronomy appears to abrogate various stipulations as well as instituting new innovations not found in the laws in Exod. 21.2-6, 7-11 has prompted the majority of scholars to associate this law with the so-called deuteronomic reforms and innovations of the deuteronomist during the reign of Josiah or Hezekiah. I have argued, though, that many of the so-called deuteronomic reforms and innovations in Deut. 15.12-18 can be attributed to the theological intentions of the deuteronomist rather than to any particular attempt to repeal or add to stipulations found in Exod. 21.2-6, 7-11. To a discussion of these reforms and innovations we now turn.

First, I noted that one of the most important additions to the law in Deut. 15.12-18 is the periodic release of female Hebrew debt-slaves. This addition has prompted the majority of scholars to suggest that the deuteronomist abrogated the sale of Israelite daughters as concubines which is envisaged in Exod. 21.7-11. Furthermore, they have suggested that since Deut. 15.12-18 does not refer to the marital rights of Israelite debt-slaves the deuteronomist no longer allowed a lord to control the marital rights of such slaves. We noted that much of the confusion that exists over this deuteronomic addition lies in the identification of the העבריה and the העברי in Deut. 15.12. While scholars generally suggest that these debt-slaves were non-dependents, who may or may not have owned land, I argued that this law, like that in Exod. 21.2-6, refers to the sale of dependents. Therefore, the fact that Deut. 15.12-18 refers to the release of both male and female dependents need not imply that the deuteronomist abrogated the law in Exod. 21.7-11 which envisaged the sale of an Israelite woman as a wife or concubine. This case is not dealt with in Deuteronomy 15. Furthermore, that the various marital stipulations found in Exod. 21.2-6, 7-11 are not found in Deut. 15.12-18 reflects the specific intent of the deuteronomist to discuss the release of both male and female Hebrew debt-slaves who performed non-sexual or other forms of labour in the house of a creditor. We saw that in this respect the law in Deuteronomy is more similar to LH §117 than to that in Exodus.

Secondly, I noted that the release of a Hebrew debt-slave in Deut. 15.12 is expressed differently than in Exod. 21.2. For instance, while the release of a debt-slave is expressed from the point of view of the debt-slave in Exod. 21.2, rather than from the point of view of the master in Deut. 15.12, I have shown that this change is due to the deuteronomic addition in 15.13-14, which stipulates that a master was to provide his released debt-slave with provisions. I argued that this deuteronomic innovation was motivated, on the one hand, by the historical or literary recollection of the release of Jacob from Laban and Israel from Egypt, and on the other by the discussions found in Deut. 14.22–16.17, particularly the requirement in 16.16 that all the males were not to come ריקם 'empty-handed' to the three yearly pilgrimage festivals, which is parallel to the requirement that an owner shall liberally provide his released debt-slave with provisions. While this stipulation does not occur in Exod. 21.2-6, I have argued that this fact alone does not suggest that the deuteronomic law was intrinsically different than that in Exodus. Lastly, we saw that some scholars suggest that the release of an Israelite debt-slave coincides with the Sabbatical release mentioned in Deut. 15.1-3, since both regulations are closely connected. However, while the sabbatical release of loans or debts is causally connected to the debt-release law, since defaulting on loans could eventually lead to debt-slavery, I argued that there is no evidence to connect the two releases, especially since the debt-release law clearly refers to a specific six years' service. Nevertheless, I suggested that it is significant that the deuteronomic compiler carefully juxtaposed these two stipulations, since they both sought to provide for the periodic release of both non-commercial loans and debt-slaves, something that was accomplished less regularly through the declaration of the OB *mēšarum* edicts.

Thirdly, I noted that although the ritual for entering into permanent service in Deut. 15.16-17 is based upon the ritual in Exod. 21.5-6, the former stipulation omits the reference to the male debt-slave's love for his wife and children, and the reference to the sanctuary of God. However, I concluded that the first omission merely reflects the deuteronomist's emphasis upon the rights of a female Hebrew debt-slave rather than any attempt to abrogate marriages between a male debt-slave and a woman belonging to his master, since it is doubtful that a man's right of ownership over a chattel-slave (or a father's rights over his daughter) would ever be abrogated. The second omission, though, has been associated with the centralization of the cult which occurred during the reign of Josiah or Hezekiah. The majority of scholars have suggested that the omission of any reference to God's sanctuary suggests that the ritual in Deut. 15.16-17 has been rendered completely 'secular', since it was more practical in the light of the existence of a single sanctuary in Deuteronomy. However, I argued that even if one accepts the view that Deuteronomy envisages a single central sanctuary there is no reason why the debt-slave could not be brought to this sanctuary during one of the three annual feasts that are discussed in Deuteronomy 16. These religious festivals would be a suitable place at which a slave could present his oath before God (cf. also Exod. 23.14-17). Nevertheless, I acknowledged that there is sufficient evidence to bring into question the view that Deuteronomy envisages a single sanctuary. While Deut. 15.16-17 does not refer specifically to a sanctuary, this alone does not necessarily imply that this law does not envisage one, since it has been shown that Deuteronomy often has a lack of concern for details, especially in laws that are dealt with in greater detail elsewhere in the biblical legal collections.

3. *Leviticus 25.39-54*

The interpretation of the manumission laws in Lev. 25.39-43, 47-54 has remained the *crux interpretum* to the interpretation of the biblical manumission laws. This is due, in part, to Wellhausen's view that the Deuteronomic Source is earlier than the Priestly Source, since this law, which stipulates a fiftieth-year release, appears to have abolished the previous legislation in Exod. 21.2-6 (and 7-11) and Deut. 15.12-18, both of which stipulate a seventh-year release. Furthermore, although scholars generally acknowledge that many of the laws of the Holiness Code (Lev. 17–26) date to an early period in Israel's legal history, including redemption stipulations that occur in the Jubilee year regulations in Leviticus 25, nevertheless they suggest that the Sabbatical and Jubilee year regulations, both of which are literarily connected to the manumission laws in Leviticus 25, underwent a long history of redaction which resulted in the Jubilee year replacing the Sabbatical year release. The debt-slave laws in vv. 39-54 are usually dated to this later layer of redaction in Leviticus 25.

However, my investigation of the Fallow (Exod. 23.10-11) and Sabbatical year regulations in Lev. 25.2-7 showed that both regulations refer to the same institution, which owes its origin to mainly religious and social-humanitarian concepts, although the practical agrarian aspects of a sabbatical fallow operating within a possible biennial fallow institution might also have been an important aspect of the Sabbatical year regulation. Furthermore, I argued that the view that the Fallow year regulation was an early practical agrarian practice, which was observed individually on each property, as opposed to the so-called later idealistic Sabbatical year regulation, which was meant to be observed universally/simultaneously, is without foundation in the light of agricultural practices that existed during the early Iron Age and later.

Although the Jubilee year regulation in Lev. 25.8-12, which allowed for the release of land during the seventh Sabbatical year, is often considered to be late and idealistic, we saw that the concept of the redistribution of land which was sold on account of insolvency was known as early as the OB period. Furthermore, although the date of the Jubilee is often used to discredit the unity of Leviticus 25, I argued that the text assumes that the the fiftieth year was identical with the forty-ninth year. Therefore, the Jubilee was no more than a seventh Sabbatical year in a 'heightened' form.

Nevertheless, scholars, including those who acknowledge the antiquity of the Sabbatical and Jubilee year, generally agree that the manumission laws in vv. 39-54 should be dated to a later period (e.g., exilic or post-exilic). This conclusion has been arrived at mainly by those who have been concerned primarily with the comparison of the different manumission regulations, particularly Deut. 15.12-18 with Lev. 25.39-55. However, we saw that such comparisons have failed to reconcile adequately the differences between these regulations without positing a radical reworking of the original regulations, something which I showed to be of limited value in understanding the Sabbatical and Jubilee year regulations. My own examination of the literary structure of the final form of Leviticus 25 showed that the Jubilee regulations in vv. 25-54 are arranged according to three topical discussions which follow the principles of *successive stages of destitution*: (1) An Israelite must sell part of his land (vv. 25-34); (2) An Israelite is not able to support himself (vv. 35-38); (3a) An Israelite must be sold (with his family) to a fellow Israelite (vv. 39-43); (3b) An Israelite must be sold (with his family) to a foreigner (vv. 47-54). To an examination of these successive stages of destitution we now turn.

In the first (1) stage of destitution a man who is forced to sell part of his property (vv. 25-28), or a house within a village (v. 31), does not actually transfer his land to the buyer, but rather the buyer merely 'leases' the land which automatically returns to the seller during the Jubilee. Furthermore, the seller or one of his relatives has the right of redemption over the property at any time during the period of the 'lease' (vv. 25-26). That the seller had the option to redeem his land probably demonstrates that he was forced to sell his property below the full market price, since this sort of transaction was common in the ancient Near East among people who were forced to sell their land on account of insolvency. However, a house that was located within a walled city (vv. 29-30), except for those that belonged to the Levites (vv. 25-28, 31), was not redeemable, since such a house probably did not belong to a family's patrimony. We saw that these stipulations accurately reflected the settlement patterns of the majority of Israelites who settled in the highlands and lowlands of Canaan.

In the second (2) stage of destitution an Israelite no longer has sufficient means of support which forces him to become dependent upon charitable interest-free loans to sustain him and his family (vv. 35-38). I suggested that Lev. 25.35-38 referred to a man who still owns land, which is similar to that envisaged in vv. 23-28, except that in the former case there is no redeemer available to redeem the seller's land, nor is the seller able to support himself and his family from the sale of property, since he had already sold part of his land. He is therefore forced to rely on charitable interest-free loans in order to buy seed to plant crops. However, if these measures did not work he would be forced to sell all of his land and himself (and his family) as it is envisaged in vv. 39-43, 47-55: the third (3) stage of destitution.

In this third (3) stage of destitution two cases are examined: (3a) an Israelite is sold to a fellow Israelite (vv. 39-43); and (3b) an Israelite is sold to a foreigner. As in the previous stage of destitution, there is no redeemer mentioned in the first case (3a), because if there were someone who could help the debtor he would have done so when the debtor was forced to sell part of his land. The fact that a redeemer is mentioned in vv. 47-55 was necessitated by the importance attached to this provision which stated that an Israelite who was forced to enter into the service of a non-Israelite was to be allowed to enter into the service of a fellow Israelite who would be more likely to treat favourably his poor brother. I suggested, therefore, that the list of possible redeemers in vv. 48-49, which covers both the בית אב (e.g., minimal and proper lineage) and משפחה (e.g., proper and maximal lineage), most likely envisaged a wider appeal for the redemption of a kinsman than that envisaged in v. 25, in which the expression גאלו הקרב אליו 'his redeemer who is most closely related to him' is employed.

We also saw that in Lev. 25.39-54 several special allowances were given to Israelites who were forced to sell all of their land and seek refuge in another Israelite household. For example, v. 40 makes it clear that such a person was not to be considered a chattel-slave, since he was to be treated as a hired worker who was given special contractual rights, and he was to serve only until the Jubilee. We noted that the fact that an Israelite was able to sell his service (*Arbeitskraft*), but not his person, parallels the idea that land can only be 'leased' and not sold. This single basic religious concept unites both the laws of redemption of land and slaves into a single system of social welfare. Furthermore, the Jubilee release not only guaranteed the release of the head of a household, but also the release of his family, and most importantly the release of his land. While this law is often compared with the law in Deut. 15.12-18, especially since both use similar terminology (e.g., אחיך, נמכר), I argued that the former law is very different from the latter, for the following reasons. First, Lev. 25.39 clearly refers to the sale of the head of a nuclear or extended family who is forced to enter into servitude with his family (v. 41). This is different from Exod. 21.2-6 and Deut. 15.12-18, both of which envisage the sale of only the dependents of a family. I therefore rendered the verb נמכר in Lev. 25.39 reflexively ('sold himself') rather than passively ('is sold') as I rendered it in Deut. 15.12. Secondly, while the head of the household is forced to sell himself in Lev. 25.39, which is similar to the sale of dependents in Exodus and Deuteronomy, I argued that the former sale was not due to a defaulted loan but to the man's need to find adequate protection for himself and his family, since he had no other way to provide for himself and his family. This view is supported further by the stipulation in v. 39b, which states that the man who sells himself shall not be subjected to a slave's condition of service, but treated as a hired worker. While this verse is often used in favour of the view that Lev. 25.39-54 abolished the previous manumission laws, since these laws appear to envisage a much harsher type of service, we saw that both types of laws envisaged only the sale of a person's capacity for work (*Arbeitskraft*), not the person himself. Furthermore, the fact that Lev. 25.39 does not employ the term עברי, which is found in both Exodus and Deuteronomy, suggests that the compiler of the former law wished to make it clear that this law dealt with a type of debt-slavery different from that envisaged in the latter laws. While I argued that it was incorrect to compare the service of a *ḫabiru* with the service of debt-slaves in Exodus and Deuteronomy, I noted that this comparison can be made with the type of sale envisaged in Lev. 25.39-43, although it is clear that the Jubilee release of land was stipulated in order to prevent Israelite families from entering into permanent servitude. Furthermore, although the length of service of an Israelite debt-slave could reach up to 50 years, I noted that in many cases the length of service would be less. Nevertheless, the length of service, which is much higher than that envisaged in Exodus and Deuteronomy, clearly shows that Lev. 25.39-55 envisages an entirely different type of debt-slavery than that envisaged in Exodus and Deuteronomy. I therefore argued that the main point of the debt-slave law in Leviticus 25, which is enunciated clearly in v. 41, is that patrimonial land should never be sold permanently (v. 23), but rather that it should be returned to the original owner (or family) during the year of the Jubilee (i.e., *Bodenrecht*). The theological motivations for this stipulation in vv. 42-43, like those that occur in Deut. 15.12-18, were meant to persuade Israelites to treat with compassion their fellow countrymen who had lost their land. While the redemption of people was widely practised in the ancient Near East, in many cases relatives were unable to redeem their relatives. Therefore, the regulations in vv. 39-43 called upon the covenant community as a whole—thus the use of the term אחיך in v. 39—to administer assistance to their fellow country-men who had no other means of help.

A Final Note on the Relationship Between and Dating of the Biblical Manumission Laws

While I noted that it was not my intention to determine the exact date of the different biblical manumission laws, nevertheless this study does enable me to make a few contributions to the discussion of the relationship between these laws. First, while it is clear that Deut. 15.12-18 builds upon the law in Exod. 21.2-6 by discussing important theological concerns that are emphasized in the section Deut. 14.22–16.17, such as brotherhood and blessing, the deuteronomist does not alter the laws in Exod. 21.2-6, 7-11 to such an extent as to abrogate them. This applies particularly to the marriage stipulations contained in Exod. 21.2-6, 7-11, which are absent from the discussion in Deuteronomy. Secondly, it is no longer necessary to harmonize the manumission laws in Lev. 25.39-43, 47-54 with the laws in Exodus and Deuteronomy by suggesting that the seventh-year release was applicable unless a Jubilee release came first. Nor is it necessary to suggest that the law in Lev. 25.39-54 abrogated the previous law in Deut. 15.12-18, or *vice versa*, since the law in Lev. 25.39-53 envis-ages an entirely different type of debt-slavery from that envisaged in Exodus or Deuteronomy. Therefore, it is possible that the laws in Exodus, Deuteronomy and Leviticus could have been 'operational' at the same time. Furthermore, while the relationship between the Deuteronomic Source and the Priestly Source remains a moot point, the fact that Deut. 15.1-11 provides for the release of debts or loans during the Sabbatical year, which is not found in Lev. 25.2b-7, suggests that the manumission law in Lev. 25.39-54 is prior to the laws in Deuteronomy 15, although there is no longer any sufficient reason for suggesting that one law abrogated the other. That all three laws, and their related discussions of the Sabbatical and Jubilee years, could have been understood as a single comprehensive system of social welfare legislation is further suggested by the fact that all of these regulations also appear in the OB *mēšarum* edicts.[1] This parallel alone provides a significant argument in favour of the pre-Monarchic or Monarchic dating of all of these regulations, although one must still account for their subsequent placement in the various narratives of JE, the Deuteronomic Source, and the Priestly Source. However, the task of determining the exact date (*Sitz im Leben*) of these regulations remains elusive.

For example, while scholars[2] generally date the manumission law in Exod. 21.2-6 to the pre-Monarchic period on the basis of the apparent references to 'ancient' practices in this law, such as the Nuzi service and loan contracts and the use of the term האלהים, I suggest rather that this law reflects social conditions that are more closely associated with events depicted in 2 Kgs 4.1-7 and in the eighth-century prophetic books of Amos, Isaiah and so on, during which social stratification and debt-slavery were probably at their highest levels. This point has also been noted recently by Crüsemann,[3] who suggests that the debt-slave laws in Exod. 21.2-6, 7-11 should be dated to this period. He finds it amazing how some scholars date many of the laws from the first part of the Covenant Code to the pre-Monarchic period. Similarly, Kaufman[4] dates the biblical release in Exod. 21.2-6 to the Monarchic period, during which, he suggests, kings declared royal edicts that are parallel to the OB *mēšarum* edicts.[5] However, he suggests that the law in Exod. 21.7-11 reflects the conditions of early Israel, although it is unclear how only Exod. 21.7-11 reflects the conditions of early Israel, since both laws in Exod. 21.2-6, 7-11 are

1. Refer to the excellent discussion in Weinfeld, 'Sabbatical Year and Jubilee in the Pentateuch', pp. 42-43.
2. For example, see Mendenhall, 'Ancient Oriental and Biblical Law', pp. 38-39; *idem*, 'Ancient Israel's Hyphenated History', p. 93; Childs, *Exodus*, p. 456; Gottwald, *The Tribes of Yahweh*, p. 58.
3. F. Crüsemann, 'Das Bundesbuch—Historischer Ort und Institutioneller Hintergrund', p. 2; idem, 'Der Exodus als Heiligung', in *Die Hebräische Bibel und ihre zweifache Nachgeschichte Festschrift für R. Rendtdorff zum 65. Geburstag* (ed. E. Blum, C. Macholz and E. Stegemann; Neukirchen–Vluyn: Neukirchener Verlag, 1990), pp. 128-29.
4. Kaufman, 'Social Welfare Systems of Ancient Israel', pp. 277-86.
5. Cf. also Wiseman, 'The Laws of Hammurabi Again', pp. 161-72; *idem*, 'Law and Order', pp. 11-14; Weinfeld, *Deuteronomy*, pp. 152-57; *idem*, '"Justice and Righteousness"', pp. 491-519; *idem, Justice and Righteousness in Israel and the Nations*; Whitelam, *The Just King*, pp. 216-17.

intricately juxtaposed and envisage the sale of dependents on account of insolvency. While the final composition of the Covenant Code is usually dated to the Monarchic period, scholars generally acknowledge that many of the laws contained in this legal collection probably date to the Settlement period. Therefore, while the biblical historical accounts most clearly document the existence of debt-slavery during the Monarchic period, nevertheless it should be pointed out that the biblical historical record is often too selective to allow one to determine with accuracy the social and economic conditions of the various historical periods. Furthermore, although social stratification was probably at its highest level during the eighth century and later, I did suggest that social stratification probably occurred as early as the Settlement period, during which certain communities took advantage of their proximity to trade routes. It is therefore possible that such measures as those found in Exod. 21.2-6, 7-11 were necessary as early as the Settlement period, especially since many of the early Israelite settlers engaged in subsistence farming in the highlands. Nevertheless, even if such measures were not needed or lacked the proper legal administration necessary to enforce them during the Settlement period, it is possible that these laws, along with the other laws in the first part of the Covenant Code, were composed as a sort of covenant *apologia* that were theologically expanded in the later biblical legal collections.[1]

While the date of the manumission law in Deut. 15.1-18 has been generally determined by its so-called deuteronomic reforms and innovations, I have attempted to show that such criteria are inadequate for the dating of this law, since it does not significantly alter the previous legislation found in Exod. 21.2-6, 7-11. On the basis of this alone, it is possible that Deut. 15.12-18 belongs to the *Urdeuteronomium*, rather than to a later separate stratum within the *Urdeuteronomium*. Such an explanation coincides with the present literary framework of Deuteronomy, according to which the laws in chs. 12–26 were promulgated by Moses just before Israel entered Canaan. However, the omission of any direct reference to a sanctuary in Deut. 15.16-17

---

1. Cf. F.C. Fensham, 'The Possibility of the Presence of Casuistic Legal Material at the Making of the Covenant at Sinai', *PEQ* 93 (1961), pp. 143-46; cf. also Jackson, 'The Ceremonial and the Judicial: Biblical Law as Sign and Symbol', p. 43.

could suggest that the final compilation of this law should be dated to the time of Josiah or Hezekiah, both of whom probably declared royal edicts, although this view has recently come under criticism.

While the date of the manumission laws in Lev. 25.39-43, 47-54 has generally been influenced by the views concerning the date of the Priestly Source and the Holiness Code, I have attempted to show that such criteria are inadequate for dating these manumission laws. That these laws belong to the earliest layers of the Holiness Code, along with the redemption laws in Lev. 25.8ff., which are generally considered to belong to Israel's early legal history, is suggested by the close similarities between these laws and the stipulations found in the *mēšarum* edicts, especially in A-s, which provided for the release of debt-slaves and land that was sold on account of insolvency. Furthermore, the fact that the deuteronomic release of debts and loans during the Sabbatical year (Deut. 15.1-3) appears to be an important innovation over the the Sabbatical and Jubilee regulations in Leviticus 25 suggests that these latter regulations belong to a period earlier than those in Deuteronomy, although there is no reason to suggest that Deut. 15.12-18 abrogated Lev. 25.39-54, as some scholars who date the Priestly Source prior to the Deuteronomic Source have done. As we saw above, it is possible that both of the regulations in Leviticus and Deuteronomy comprised a single welfare system which has strong parallels with the OB *mēšarum* edicts.[1] This system could have been developed at an early stage in Israel's legal history, which may account for the fact that these regulations are always seen as the promulgation of Yahweh and not a king. But they could also be dated during the Monarchic period, when some Israelite kings probably declared royal edicts.[2]

---

1. Cf. Jakobson, 'Some Problems Connected with the Rise of Landed Property (Old Babylonian Period)', p. 37, who writes: '...the *mīšarum* and other related Ancient Oriental acts combine the annulment of debts with an annulment of land purchases. The kings who enacted the *mīšarum* saw clearly enough that these two social plagues were interconnected.'

2. For the view that Israelite kings merely enforced the long tradition of Israelite law during their regnal year, in which they declared their royal edicts, see Wiseman, 'Law and Order', p. 6; cf. also N.M. Soss, 'Old Testament Law and Economic Society', *JHI* 34 (1973), pp. 323-24; Weinfeld, *Justice and Righteousness in Israel and the Nations*; Greenberg, 'More Reflections on Biblical Criminal Law', p. 3 n. 5.

BIBLIOGRAPHY

Aberbach, M., 'Mesopotamia', *EncJud*, XVI, cols. 1483-1514.

Adams, R.McC., 'Property Rights and Functional Tenure in Mesopotamian Rural Communities', in *Societies and Languages of the Ancient Near East in Honour of I.M. Diakonoff* (ed. M.A. Dandamayev, I. Gerschevitch, H. Klengel, G. Komoróczy, M.T. Larsen and J.N. Postgate; Warminster: Aris & Phillips, 1982), pp. 1-14.

Aharoni, Y., *The Archaeology of the Holy Land: From the Prehistoric Beginnings to the End of the First Temple Period* (London: SCM Press, 1982).

Ahlström, G.W., 'Giloh: A Judahite or Canaanite Settlement', *IEJ* 34 (1984), pp. 170-72.

—*Who Were the Israelites?* (Winona Lake, IN: Eisenbrauns, 1986).

Ahlström, G.W., and D. Edelman, 'Merneptah's Israel', *JNES* 44 (1985), pp. 59-61.

Albright, W.F., 'Archaeology and the Date of the Hebrew Conquest of Palestine', *BASOR* 58 (1935), pp. 10-18.

—*The Archaeology of Palestine and the Bible* (Cambridge, MA: American Schools of Oriental Research, 3rd edn, 1974).

—*The Biblical Period from Abraham to Ezra, an Historical Survey* (New York: Harper & Row, 1949).

—'The Biblical Period', in *The Jews; their History, Culture and Religion* (ed. L. Finkelstein; Philadelphia: Jewish Publication Society of America, 1960), pp. 3-69.

—'Canaanite *ḫapši* and Hebrew *ḫofši* Again', *JPOS* 6 (1926), pp. 106-108.

—'The Israelite Conquest of Palestine in the Light of Archaeology', *BASOR* 74 (1939), pp. 11-23.

—*From Stone Age to Christianity: Monotheism and the Historical Process* (Garden City, NY: Doubleday, 2nd edn, 1957).

—'The List of Levitical Cities', in *Louis Ginzberg Jubilee*, I (New York, 1945), pp. 49-73.

—'New Canaanite Historical and Mythological Data', *BASOR* 63 (1936), pp. 23-32.

Alexander, J.B., 'A Babylonian Year of Jubilee', *JBL* 57 (1938), pp. 75-79.

Allis, O.T., 'Leviticus', in *New Bible Commentary Revised* (ed. D. Guthrie, J.A. Motyer, A.M. Stibbs and D.J. Wiseman; Leicester: Inter-Varsity Press, 1970), pp. 140-67.

Alt, A., 'Der Anteil des Königtums an der sozialen Entwicklung in den Reichen Israel und Juda', in *Kleine Schriften zur Geschichte des Volkes Israel*, II (Munich: Beck, 1959), pp. 348-72.

—'Erwägungen über die Landnahme der Israeliten in Palästina', in *Kleine Schriften zur Geschichte des Volkes Israel*, I (Munich: Beck, 1959) pp. 126-75

—'The Settlement of the Israelites in Palestine', in *Essays on Old Testament History and Religion* (Oxford: Oxford University Press, 1966), pp. 133-69.

—'Festungen und Levitenorte im Land Juda', in *Kleine Schriften zur Geschichte des Volkes Israel*, II (Munich: Beck, 1959), pp. 306-15.

—'Hebräer', in *Die Religion in Geschichte und Gegenwart*, III (ed. H. Campenhausen, E. Dinkler, G. Gloege, K.E. Løgstrup and K. Galling; Munich, 1966), pp. 105-106.

—'Menschen ohne Namen', *ArOr* 18 (1950), pp. 9-24.

—'The Origin of Israelite Law', in *Essays on Old Testament History and Religion* (Oxford: Oxford University Press, 1966), pp. 79-132 (*Kleine Schriften zur Geschichte des Volkes Israel*, I [Munich: Beck, 1959], pp. 278-332).

Altman, A., 'The Revolutions in Byblos and Amurru During the Amarna Period and their Social Background', in *Bar-Ilan in History* (Ramat-Gan, 1978), pp. 3-24.

Amsler, S., 'La motivation de l'éthique dans la parénèse du deutéronome', in *Beiträge zur alttestamentlichen Theologie: Festschrift W. Zimmerli zum 70. Geburtstag* (ed. H. Donner, R. Hanhart and R. Smend; Göttingen: Vandenhoeck & Ruprecht, 1977), pp. 11-22.

Andersen, F.I., 'The Early Sumerian City-State in Recent Soviet Historiography', *AbrN* 1 (1960), pp. 53-64.

—'Israelite Kinship Terminology and Social Structure', *BT* 20 (1969), pp. 29-39.

—*The Sentence in Biblical Hebrew* (Janua Linguarum, 231; The Hague: Mouton, 1974).

—'The Socio-Juridical Background of the Naboth Incident', *JBL* 85 (1966), pp. 46-57.

Andreasen, N.-E., *The Old Testament Sabbath: A Tradition-Historical Investigation* (SBLDS, 7; Missoula, MT: Scholars Press, 1972).

—'Recent Studies of the Old Testament Sabbath: Some Observations', *ZAW* 86 (1974), pp. 453-69.

—'The Role of the Queen Mother in Israelite Society', *CBQ* 45 (1983), pp. 179-94.

—'Town and Country in the Old Testament', *Enc* 42 (1981), pp. 259-75.

Arnaud, D., 'Humbles et superbes à Emar (Syrie) à la fin l'âge du Bronze récent', in *Mélanges bibliques et orientaux en l'honneur de M. Henri Cazelles* (ed. A. Caquot and M. Delcor; AOAT, 212; Neukirchen–Vluyn: Neukirchener Verlag, 1981), pp. 1-14.

Artzi, P., '"Vox populi" in the El Amarna Tablets', *RA* 58 (1964), pp. 159-66.

Astour, M.C., 'Habiru', *IDBSup*, pp. 382-85.

Avalos, H., 'Exodus 22:9 and Akkadian Legal Formulae', *JBL* 109 (1990), pp. 116-17.

Bächli, O., *Israel und die Völker: Eine Studie zum Deuteronomium* (ATANT, 41; Zurich, 1962).

Baentsch, B., *Das Bundesbuch, Ex XX 22–XXIII 33* (Erfurt, 1892).

—*Exodus-Leviticus-Numeri übersetzt und erklärt* (HKAT, 1.2; Göttingen: Vandenhoeck & Ruprecht, 1903).

—*Das Heiligkeitsgesetz, Lev XVII–XXVI* (Erfurt, 1893).

Baltzer, K., *The Covenant Formulary* (Oxford: Oxford University Press, 2nd edn, 1971).

—'Liberation from Debt Slavery After the Exile in Second Isaiah and Nehemiah', in *Ancient Israelite Religion: Essays in Honor of Frank Moore Cross* (ed. P.D.

Miller, P.D. Hanson and S.D. McBride; Philadelphia: Fortress Press, 1987), pp. 477-84.

—'Naboths Weinberg (1 Kön 21): der Konflikt zwischen israelitischem und kanaanäischem Bodenrecht', *WD* 8 (1965), pp. 73-88.

Barr, J., 'Biblical Law and the Question of Natural Theology', in *The Law in the Bible and in its Environment* (ed. T. Veijola; Publications of the Finnish Exegetical Society, 51; Göttingen: Vandenhoeck & Ruprecht, 1990), pp. 1-22.

—*The Semantics of Biblical Language* (Oxford: Oxford University Press, 1961).

Barrois, A-G., *Manuel d'archéologie biblique*, II (Paris: Picard, 1953).

Batto, B.F., 'Land Tenure and Women at Mari', *JESHO* 23 (1980), pp. 209-39.

Bazak, Y., 'Towards the Significance of the Pair *mišpāt û ṣēdāqâ* in the Bible' (Hebrew), *BM* 32 (1986-87), pp. 135-48.

Beatie, J., *Other Cultures: Aims, Methods and Achievements in Social Anthropology* (London: Kegan & Paul, 1964).

Beer, G., and K. Galling,, *Exodus* (HKAT, 1.3; Tübingen: Mohr, 1939).

Bellefontaine, E., 'Customary Law and Chieftainship: Judicial Aspects of 2 Samuel 14: 4-21', *JSOT* 38 (1987), pp. 47-72.

—'A Study of Ancient Israelite Laws and their Function as Covenant Stipulations' (PhD dissertation; University of Notre Dame, 1973).

Ben-Barak, Z., 'The Mizpah Covenant (1S 10.25)—the Source of the Israelite Monarchy', *ZAW* 91 (1979), pp. 30-43.

Berkner, L.K., 'The Stem Family and the Developmental Cycle of the Peasant Household: An Eighteenth-Century Austrian Example', *AHR* 77 (1972), pp. 398-418.

Bernard, A., and A. Good, *Research Practices in the Study of Kinship* (ASAR, 2; London: Academic Press, 1984).

Bertholet, A., *Deuteronomium* (KHAT; Tübingen: Mohr, 1899).

Bimson, J.J., 'Merenptah's Israel and Recent Theories of Israelite Origins', *JSOT* 49 (1991), pp. 3-29.

—'The Origins of Israel in Canaan: An Examination of Recent Theories', *Themelios* 15 (1989), pp. 4-15.

—*Redating the Exodus and Conquest* (Sheffield: Almond Press, 2nd edn, 1981).

—'Redating the Exodus—The Debate Goes On: A Reply to Baruch Halpern's "Radical Exodus Redating Fatally Flawed" ', *BARev* 14 (1988), pp. 52-55.

Bimson, J.J., and D. Livingston, 'Redating the Exodus', *BARev* 13 (1987), pp. 40-53, 66-68.

Birot, M., *Lettres de Yaqqim-Addu* (Archives royales de Mari, 14; Paris, 1974).

Block, D.I., 'Israel's House: Reflections on the use of בי ישראל in the Old Testament in the Light of its Ancient Near Eastern Environment', *JETS* 28 (1985), pp. 257-75.

Bobek, H., 'Rentenkapitalismus und Entwicklung im Iran', in *Interdisziplinäre Iran-Forschung* (ed. G. Schweizer; Wiesbaden, 1979), pp. 113-24.

—'Zum Konzept des Rentenkapitalismus', *TESG* 65 (1974), pp. 73-77.

Boecker, H.J., *Law and the Administration of Justice in the Old Testament and Ancient East* (Minneapolis: Augsburg Press, 1980).

—*Redeformen des Rechtslebens im Alten Testament* (WMANT, 14; Neukirchen–Vluyn: Neukirchener Verlag, 2nd edn, 1970).

Boer, P.A.H. de, 'Some Remarks on Exodus XXI, 7-11; The Hebrew Female Slave', *OrN* (1948), pp. 162-66.

Boling, R., *The Early Biblical Community in Transjordan* (SWBAS, 6; Sheffield: Almond Press, 1988).

—*Judges* (AB; Garden City, NY: Doubleday, 1981).

—'Levitical Cities: Archaeology and Texts', in *Biblical and Related Studies Presented to Samuel Iwry* (ed. A. Kort and S. Mirschauser; Winona Lake, IN: Eisenbrauns, 1985), pp. 23-32.

Borger, R., 'Das Problem der 'apiru ('ḫabiru')', *ZDPV* 74 (1958), pp. 121-32.

Borowski, O., *Agriculture in Iron Age Israel: The Evidence from Archaeology and the Bible* (Winona Lake, IN: Eisenbrauns, 1987).

Bottéro, J., 'Le "Code" de *Ḥammūrabi*', *ADSNS* 12 (1982), pp. 409-44.

—'Désordre économique et annulation des dettes en Mésopotamie à l'époque paléobabylonienne', *JESHO* 4 (1961), pp. 113-64.

—'Entre nomades et sédentaires: les *Ḥabiru*', *Dialogues d'histoire ancienne* 6 (1980), pp. 89-107.

—'Habiru', in *Reallexikon der Assyriologie*, IV (ed. G. Ebeling and M. Meissner; Berlin: de Gruyter, 1972), pp. 14-27.

—'Les *Ḥabiru*, les nomades et les sédentaires', in *Seminar: Nomads and Sedentary People* (ed. J.S. Castillo; Mexico City, 1981), pp. 89-107.

—*Le problème des* Habiru *à la 4e recontre assyriologique internationale* (CahSA, 12; Paris: Imprimerie Nationale, 1954).

Botterweck, G.J., 'Der Sabbat im Alten Testament', *TTQ* 134 (1954), pp. 134-47; 448-57.

Braemer, F., *L'architecture domestique du Levant a l'Age du Fer: Protohistoire du Levant* (ERC, 8; Paris: A.D.P.F., 1982).

Braulik, G., 'Die Abfolge der Gesetze in Deuteronomium 12–26 und der Dekalog', in *Das Deuteronomium: Entstehung, Gestalt und Botschaft* [*Deuteronomy, Origin Form and Message*] (ed. N. Lohfink; BETL; Leuven: Leuven University Press, 1985), pp. 252-72.

—'Zur Abfolge der Gesetze in Deuteronomium 16,18–21,23: Weitere Beobachtungen', *Bib* 69 (1988), pp. 63-91.

—*Die deuteronomischen Gesetze und der Dekalog: Studien zum Aufbau Deuteronomium 12–26* (Stuttgarter Bibelstudien, 145; Stuttgart: Katholisches Bibelwerk, 1991).

Breit, H., *Die Predigt des Deuteronomisten* (Munich: Chr. Kaiser Verlag, 1933).

Brekelmans, C.H.W., 'Éléments deutéronomiques dans le Pentateuque', *RechRib* 8 (1966), pp. 77-91.

—'Die sogenannten deuteronomischen Elemente in Gen-Num; ein Beitrag zur Vorgeschichte des Deuteronomiums', in *Volume du Congrès, Genèva 1965* (VTSup, 15; Leiden: Brill, 1966), pp. 90-106.

Brichto, H.C., 'Kin, Cult, Land and Afterlife—A Biblical Complex', *HUCA* 44 (1973), pp. 1-55.

Bright, J., *Early Israel in Recent History Writing: A Study in Method* (London: SCM Press, 1956).

—*A History of Israel* (Philadelphia: Westminster Press, 3rd edn, 1981).

Brinkman, J.A., 'Forced Laborers in the Middle Babylonian Period', *JCS* 32 (1980), pp. 17-22.

—'Sex, Age, and Physical Condition Designations for Servile Laborers in the Middle Babylonian Period. A Preliminary Survey', in *ZIKIR ŠUMIM: Assyriological Studies Presented to F.R. Kraus on the Occasion of his Seventieth Birthday* (ed. G. van Driel, Th.J.H. Krispijn, M. Stol and K.R. Veenhof; NIVNO, V; Leiden: Brill, 1982).

Bruce, F.F., 'Tell el-Amarna', in *Archaeology and Old Testament Study* (ed. D.W. Thomas; Oxford: Clarendon Press, 1967).

Brueggemann, W., 'On Land-losing and Land-receiving', *Dialog* 19 (1980), pp. 166-73.

Buccellati, G., *Cities and Nations of Ancient Syria: An Essay on Political Institutions with Special Reference to the Israelite Kingdoms* (SS, 26; Rome: University of Rome, 1967).

Buis, P., *Le Deutéronome* (VS, 4; Paris: Beauchesne, 1969).

Buss, M.J., 'The Distinction between Civil and Criminal Law in Ancient Israel', in *Proceedings of the Sixth World Congress of Jewish Studies, Jerusalem 1973* (Jerusalem: Magnes, 1973).

Butz, K., 'Ur in altbabylonischer Zeit als Wirtschaftsfaktor', in *State and Temple Economy in the Ancient Near East, I, II: Proceedings of the International Conference Organized by the Katholieke Iniversiteit Leuven from the 10th to the 14th of April 1978* (ed. E. Lipiński; OLA, 5; Leuven: Dept. Oriëntalistiek, 1979), pp. 257-409.

Callaway, J.A., 'Excavating Ai (et-Tell): 1964–1972', *BA* 39 (1976), pp. 18-30.

—'Respondents: Session II: Archaeology, History and Bible. The Israelite Settlement in Canaan: A Case Study', in *Biblical Archaeology Today: Proceedings of the International Congress on Biblical Archaeology, Jerusalem, April 1984* (ed. J. Amitai; Jerusalem: Israel Exploration Society, 1985), pp. 72-77.

Campbell, E.F., 'The Amarna Letters and the Amarna Period', *BA* 23 (1960), pp. 2-22.

Cancian, F., 'Social Stratification', *ARA* 5 (1976), pp. 227-48.

Cardascia, G., 'Les droits cunéiformes', in *Histoire des institutions et des faits sociaux des origines à l'aube du Moyen Age* (ed. R. Monier, G. Cardascia and J. Imbert; Paris, 1956), pp. 17-68.

—'Droits cunéiformes et droit biblique', in *Proceedings of the Sixth World Congress of Jewish Studies Jerusalem 1973* (Jerusalem: Magnes, 1976), pp. 63-70.

—*Les lois assyriennes: Introduction, traduction, commentaire* (LAPO, 2; Paris: Cerf, 1969).

—'La transmission des sources cunéiformes', *RIDA* 7 (1960), pp. 31-50.

—'Les valeurs morales dans le droit assyrien', in *Wirtschaft und Gesellschaft im alten Vorderasien* (ed. J. Harmatta and G. Komoróczy; Budapest: Akadémiai Kiadó, 1976), pp. 363-72.

Cardellini, I., *Die biblischen 'Sklaven''-Gesetze im Lichte des keilschriftlichen Sklaven rechts: Ein Beitrag zur Tradition, Überlieferung und Redaktion der alttestamentlichen Rechtstexte* (BBB, 55; Bonn: Verlag Peter Hanstein, 1981).

Carmichael, C.M., *The Laws of Deuteronomy* (Ithaca, NY: Cornell University Press, 1974).

—'A Singular Method of Codification of Law in the Mishpatim', *ZAW* 84 (1972), pp. 19-25.

—*Women, Law, and the Genesis Traditions* (Edinburgh: Edinburgh University Press, 1979).

Carroll, R.P., *Jeremiah* (OTL; London: SCM Press, 1986).

Cassin, E., 'Nouveaux documents sur les Habiru', *JA* 246 (1958), pp. 225-36.

—'Une querelle de famille', in *Studies on the Civilization and Culture of Nuzi and the Hurrians* (ed. M.A. Morrison and D.I. Owen; Winona Lake, IN: Eisenbrauns, 1981), pp. 37-46.

Cassuto, U., *A Commentary on the Book of Exodus* (Jerusalem: Magnes, 1976).

Cavalletti, S., 'Il significato di mashsheh yad in Deuteronomy 15,2', *Anton* 31 (1965), pp. 301-304.

Cazelles, H., 'L'auteur de code de l'alliance (Exode, XX,22-XXIII,19)', *RB* 52 (1945), pp. 173-91.

—*Autour de l'Exode (Études)* (SB; Paris: J. Gabalda, 1987).

—'Book Review of M. Greenberg, *Hab/piru*" ', *BO* 13 (1956), pp. 149-51.

—'Droit public dans le Deutéronome', in *Das Deuteronomium: Entstehung, Gestalt und Botschaft [Deuteronomy, Origin Form and Message]* (ed. N. Lohfink; BETL, 68; Leuven: Leuven University Press, 1985), pp. 99-106.

—*Études sur le code de l'alliance* (Paris: Letouzey et Ané, 1946).

—'Hebreu, ubru et hapiru', *Syria* 35 (1958), pp. 198-217.

—'The Hebrews', in *People in Old Testament Times* (ed. D.J. Wiseman; Oxford: Clarendon Press, 1973), pp. 1-28.

Chaney, M.L., 'Ancient Palestinian Peasant Movements and the Formation of Premonarchic Israel', in *Palestine in Transition: The Emergence of Ancient Israel* (ed. D.N. Freedman and D.F. Graf; SWBAS, 2; Sheffield: Almond Press, 1983).

—'Systemic Study of the Israelite Monarchy', *Semeia* 37 (1986), pp. 53-76.

Chiera, E., and E.A. Speiser, 'Selected "Kirkuk" Documents', *JAOS* 47 (1927), pp. 36-60.

Chiera, E., 'Ḫabiru and Hebrews', *AJSL* 49 (1933), pp. 115-24.

Childs, B.S., *The Book of Exodus: A Critical, Theological Commentary* (Philadelphia: Westminster Press, 1974).

—'Deuteronomic Formulae of the Exodus Traditions', in *Congress Volume, Rome 1968* (VTSup, 16; Leiden: Brill, 1969), pp. 30-39.

Chirichigno, G.C., 'The Narrative Structure of Exod 21-23', *Bib* 68 (1987), pp. 457-79.

Cholewiński, S.I., *Heiligkeitsgesetz und Deuteronomium: Eine vergleichende Studie* (AnBib, 66; Rome: Biblical Institute Press, 1976).

Christensen, D.L., 'Form and Structure in Deuteronomy 1-11', in *Das Deuteronomium: Entstehung, Gestalt und Botschaft [Deuteronomy, Origin Form and Message]* (ed. N. Lohfink; BETL, 68; Leuven: Leuven University Press, 1985).

Civil, M., 'New Sumerian Law Fragments', *Assyriological Studies* 16 (1965), pp. 1-12.

Claessen, H.J., and P. Skalník, 'The Early State: Theories and Hypotheses', in *The Early State* (ed. H.J. Claessen and P. Skalník; The Hague: Mouton, 1978), pp. 3-29.

Clamer, A., *L'Exode* (La Sainte Bible, 1.2; Paris, 1956).

Clark, W.M., 'Law', in *Old Testament Form Criticism* (ed. J.H. Hayes; San Antonio, TX: Trinity University Press, 1974), pp. 99-139.

Clements, R.E., *Deuteronomy* (Old Testament Guides; Sheffield: JSOT Press, 1989).

—'Deuteronomy and the Jerusalem Cult Tradition', *VT* 15 (1965), pp. 303-12.

—*Exodus* (CBC; Cambridge: Cambridge University Press, 1972).

—*God and Temple: The Idea of the Divine Presence in Ancient Israel* (Oxford: Basil Blackwell, 1965).

Clines, D.J.A., *Ezra, Nehemiah, Esther* (NCBC; Grand Rapids: Eerdmans, 1984).

Cody, A., *A History of the Old Testament Priesthood* (AnBib, 35; Rome: Pontifical Biblical Institute, 1969).

Cohen, A., 'Leaving the Land Fallow' (Hebrew), *BM* 24 (1978), pp. 45-49.

Cohen, H.H., 'Slavery', *EncJud*, XXIV, cols. 1655-60.

—'Usury', *EncJud*, XXIV, cols. 27-33.

Cohen, R., 'Introduction', in *Origins of the State: The Anthropology of Political Evolution* (ed. R. Cohen and E.R. Service; Philadelphia: Institute for the Study of Human Issues, 1978), pp. 1-20.

—'State Origins: A Reappraisal', in *The Early State* (ed. H.J.M. Claessen and P. Skalník; The Hague: Mouton, 1978), pp. 31-75.

Cole, R.A., *Exodus: An Introduction and Commentary* (TOTC; Downers Grove, IL: Inter-Varsity Press, 1973).

Cooper, J.S., *Sumerian and Akkadian Royal Inscriptions*, I (New Haven: American Oriental Society, 1986).

Coote, R.B., and K.W. Whitelam, *The Emergence of Early Israel in Historical Perspective* (SWBAS, 5; Sheffield: Almond Press, 1987).

—'The Emergence of Israel: Social Transformation and State Formation Following the Decline in Late Bronze Age Trade', *Semeia* 37 (1986), pp. 107-47.

Coote, R.B., *Amos Among the Prophets: Composition and Theology* (Philadelphia: Fortress Press, 1981).

Couroyer, B., *L'Exode* (Bible de Jerusalem; 3rd edn, Paris: Cerf, 1968).

Coxon, P.W., 'Review of R. de Vaux's *The Early History of Israel*', *JSOT* 11 (1979), pp. 72-76.

Craigie, P.C., 'Some Further Notes on the Song of Deborah', *VT* 22 (1972), pp. 349-53.

—*The Book of Deuteronomy* (NICOT; Grand Rapids: Eerdmans, 1977).

Cross, F.M., and G.E. Wright, 'The Boundary and Province Lists of the Kingdom of Judah', *JBL* 75 (1956), pp. 202-26.

Crüsemann, F., 'Das Bundesbuch — Historischer Ort und Institutioneller Hintergrund', *Congress Volume. Jerusalem 1986* (ed. J.A. Emerton.; VTSup, 40; Leiden: E.J. Brill, 1988), pp. 27-41.

—'Der Exodus als Heiligung', *Die Hebräische Bibel und ihre zweifache Nachgeschichte Festschrift für R. Rendtorff zum 65. Geburstag* (ed. E. Blum, C. Macholz and E. Stegemann; Neukirchen–Vluyn: Neukirchener Verlag, 1990), pp. 117-29.

—*Der Widerstand gegen das Königtum: Die antiköniglichen Texte des Alten Testamentes und der Kampf um der frühen israelitischen Staat* (WMANT, 49; Neukirchen–Vluyn: Neukirchener Verlag, 1978).

Culley, R., 'Exploring New Directions', in *The Hebrew Bible and its Modern Interpreters* (ed. D.A. Knight and G.M. Tucker; SBLI; Philadelphia: Fortress Press ; Chico, CA: Scholars Press, 1985), pp. 167-200.

Cunchillos, J.L., 'Une lettre ugaritique KTU 2.17', in *Mélanges bibliques et orientaux en l'honneur de M. Henri Cazelles* (ed. A. Caquot and M. Delcor; AOAT, 212; Neukirchen–Vluyn: Neukirchener Verlag, 1981), pp. 71-78.

Cundall, D., *Judges* (TOTC; Leicester: Inter-Varsity Press, 1968).

Dahood, M., *Psalms*, I-III (AB; Garden City, NY: Doubleday, 1968).

Dandamayev, M.A., 'The Economic and Legal Character of the Slaves' Peculium in the Neo-Babylonian and Achaemenid Periods', *AbhBAW* 75 (1972), pp. 35-39.

—'The Neo-Babylonian Elders', in *Societies and Languages of the Ancient Near East in Honour of I.M. Diakonoff* (ed. M.A. Dandamayev, I. Gerschevitch, H. Klengel, G. Komoróczy, M.T. Larsen and J.N. Postgate; Warminster: Aris & Phillips, 1982), pp. 38-41.

—'Die Rolle des *tamkārum* in Babylonien im 2. und 1. Jahrtausend v.u.Z', in *Beiträge zur sozialen Struktur des Alten Vorderasien* (ed. H. Klengel; SGKAO, 1; Berlin: Akademie-Verlag, 1971), pp. 69-78.

—*Slavery in Babylonia: From Nabopolassar to Alexander the Great (626–331 BC)* (DeKalb: Northern Illinois University Press, rev. edn, 1984).

—'Social Stratification in Babylonia (7th–4th Centuries BC)', in *Wirtschaft und Gesellschaft im alten Vorderasien* (ed. J. Harmatta and G. Komoróczy; Budapest: Akadémiai Kiadó, 1976), pp. 433-44.

—'State and Temple in Babylonia in the First Millennium BC', in *State and Temple Economy in the Ancient Near East*, I, II: *Proceedings of the International Conference Organized by the Katholieke Iniversiteit Leuven from the 10th to the 14th of April 1978* (ed. E. Lipiński; OLA, 5; Leuven: Dept. Oriëntalistiek, 1979), pp. 589-96.

Daube, D., 'Direct and Indirect Causation in Biblical Law', *VT* 11 (1961), pp. 246-69.

—*The Exodus Pattern in the Bible* (ASSt, 2; London: Faber & Faber, 1963).

—*Studies in Biblical Law* (Cambridge: Cambridge University Press, 1947).

David, M., 'The Codex Hammurabi and its Relation to the Provision of Law in Exodus', *OTS* 7 (1950), pp. 149-78.

—'Eine Bestimmung über das Verfallspfand in den mittelassyrischen Gesetzen', *BO* 9 (1952), pp. 170-72.

—'The Manumission of Slaves under Zedekiah: A Contribution to the Laws about Hebrew Slaves', *OTS* 5 (1948), pp. 63-79.

Davidson, R., 'Orthodoxy and the Prophetic Word: A Study in the Relationship between Jeremiah and Deuteronomy', *VT* 14 (1964), pp. 407-16.

Davies, G.H., *Exodus* (TBC; London: SCM Press, 1967).

Dearman, J.A., *Property Rights in the Eighth-Century Prophets: The Conflict and its Background* (SBLDS, 106; Atlanta: Scholars Press, 1988).

Deller, K., 'Die Hausgötter der Familie Sukrija S. Huja', in *Studies on the Civilization and Culture of Nuzi and the Hurrians* (ed. M.A. Morrison and D.I. Owen.; Winona Lake, IN: Eisenbrauns, 1981), pp. 47-76.

Dever, W.G., 'The Middle Bronze Age: The Zenith of the Urban Canaanite Era', *BA* 50 (1987), pp. 149-77.

Diakonoff, I.M., 'Preface', in *Ancient Mesopotamia Socio-Economic History: A Collection of Studies by Soviet Scholars* (ed. I.M. Diakonoff; USSR Academy of Sciences Institute of the Peoples of Asia; Moscow: 'Nauka', 1969), pp. 8-16.

—'The Rise of the Despotic State in Ancient Mesopotamia', in *Ancient Mesopotamia Socio-Economic History. A Collection of Studies by Soviet Scholars* (ed. I.M. Diakonoff; USSR Academy of Sciences Institute of the Peoples of Asia; Moscow: 'Nauka', 1969), pp. 173-203.

—'The Rural Community in the Ancient Near East', *JESHO* 18 (1975), pp. 121-33.

—'Slaves, Helots and Serfs in Early Antiquity', in *Wirtschaft und Gesellschaft im alten Vorderasien* (ed. J. Harmatta and G. Komoróczy; Budapest: Akadémiai Kiadó, 1976), pp. 44-78.

—'Socio-Economic Classes in Babylonia and the Babylonian Concept of Social Stratification', *AbhBAW* 75 (1972), pp. 41-52.

—'Some Remarks on the "Reforms" of Urukagina', *RA* 52 (1958), pp. 1-15.

—'On the Structure of the Old Babylonian Society', in *Beiträge zur sozialen Struktur des Alten Vorderasien* (ed. H. Klengel; SGKAO, 1; Berlin: Akademie-Verlag, 1971), pp. 15-31.

Diamond, A.S., *Comparative Study of Primitive Law* (London, 1965).

—'An Eye for and Eye', *Iraq* 19 (1957), pp. 151-55.

Dillmann, A., *Die Bücher Exodus und Leviticus* (KH, 12; Leipzig: S. Hirzel, 2nd edn, 1880).

—*Die Bücher Numeri, Deuteronomium und Joshua* (KH, 13; Leipzig: S. Hirzel, 2nd edn, 1880).

Diringer, D., 'The Origins of Hebrew People', *RSO* 32 (1957), pp. 301-13.

Dole, G.E., 'Tribe as the Autonomous Unit', in *Essays on the Problem of Tribe* (ed. J. Helm; Proceedings of the 1967 Annual Spring Meeting of the American Ethnological Society; Seattle, 1968), pp. 83-100.

Doron, P., 'Motive Clauses in the Laws of Deuteronomy: Their Forms, Functions, and Contents', *HAR* 2 (1978), pp. 61-77.

Douglas, M., *Implicit Meanings* (London: Routledge & Kegan Paul, 1975).

Draffkorn, A.E., '*Ilâni*/Elohim', *JBL* 76 (1957), pp. 216-24.

Driver, G.R., and C.J. Miles, *The Assyrian Laws* (Oxford: Clarendon Press, 1935).

—*The Babylonian Laws*. I. *Legal Commentary*. II. *Transliterated Text, Translation, Philological Notes, Glossary* (Oxford: Clarendon Press, 1956).

Driver, S.R., and H.A. White, *The Book of Leviticus* (PB, 3; London: James Clark, 1898).

Driver, S.R., *The Book of Exodus: With Introduction and Notes* (CBSC; Cambridge: Cambridge University Press, 1911).

—*A Critical and Exegetical Commentary of Deuteronomy* (ICC; Edinburgh: T. & T. Clark, 1902).

—*An Introduction to the Literature of the Old Testament* (repr.; Gloucester: Peter Smith, 1972 [1897]).

Duhm, B., *Das Buch Jeremia* (KHAT, 9; Tübingen/Leipzig, 1901).

Dumermuth, F., 'Zur deuteronomischen Kulttheologie und ihren Voraussetzungen', *ZAW* 70 (1958), pp. 59-98.

Durham, J.I., *Exodus* (WBC, 3; Waco, TX: Word Books, 1987).

Durkheim, E., *De la division du travail social* (Paris, 4th edn, 1922).

Ebeling, E., 'Altassyrische Gesetze', in *Altorientalische Texte zum Alten Testament* (Berlin-Leipzig, 2nd edn, 1962), pp. 412-22.

—'Neubabylonische Gesetze', in *Altorientalische Texte zum Alten Testament* (Berlin-Leipzig, 2nd edn, 1962), pp. 422-23.

Edzard, D.O., '"Social Reformen" in Zweistromland bis ca. 1600 v. Chr.: Realität oder literarischer Topos?', in *Wirtschaft und Gesellschaft im alten Vorderasien* (ed. J. Harmatta and G. Komoróczy; Budapest: Akadémiai Kiadó, 1976), pp. 145-56.

Eerdmans, B.D., 'The Book of the Covenant and the Decalogue', *ExpTim* 8 (1919), pp. 134-38.

Ehrlich, A.B., *Randglossen zur hebräischen Bibel*, I-VII (Leipzig, 1908-14).

Eichler, B.L., *Indenture at Nuzi: The Personal* tidennutu C*ontract and its Mesopotamian Analogues* (YNER, 5; New Haven: Yale University Press, 1973).

—'Literary Structure in the Laws of Eshnunna', in *Language, Literature, and History: Philological and Historical Studies Presented to Erica Reiner* (ed. F. Rochberg-Halton; AOS, 67; New Haven: American Oriental Society, 1987), pp. 71-84.

Eichrodt, W., *Theology of the Old Testament*, II (Philadelphia: Westminster Press, 1967).

Eissfeldt, O., *The Old Testament: An Introduction* (Oxford: Basil Blackwell, 1966).

—'Silo und Jerusalem', in *Volume du Congrès, Strasbourg 1956* (VTSup, 4; Leiden: Brill, 1957), pp. 138-48.

Elat, M., 'The Monarchy and the Development of Trade in Ancient Israel', in *State and Temple Economy in the Ancient Near East. I, II. Proceedings of the International Conference Organized by the Katholieke Iniversiteit Leuven from the 10th to the 14th of April 1978* (ed. E. Lipiński; OLA, 5; Leuven: Dept. Oriëntalistiek, 1979), pp. 527-46.

—'Der *TAMKARU* in Neuassyrischen Reich', *JESHO* 30 (1987), pp. 233-54.

Elliger, K., *Leviticus* (HKAT, 4; Tübingen: Mohr, 1966).

Elliot-Binns, L.E., 'Some Problems of Holiness Code', *ZAW* 67 (1955), pp. 26-40.

Ellison, H.L., 'The Hebrew Slave; A Study in Early Israelite Society' *EvQ* 45 (1955), pp. 30-35.

Engel, H., 'Die Siegesstele des Merenptah', *Bib* 60 (1979), pp. 373-99.

Epsztein, L., *Social Justice in the Ancient Near East and the People of the Bible* (London: SCM Press, 1986).

Erlandsson, S., 'בגד', *ThWat*, I, col. 511.

Evans, G., 'Ancient Mesopotamian Assemblies', *JAOS* 78 (1958), pp. 1-11.

Falk, Z.W., 'The Deeds of Manumission of Elephantine', *JJS* 5 (1954), pp. 114-17.

—'Exodus XXI:6', *VT* 9 (1959), pp. 86-88.

—*Hebrew Law in Biblical Times. An Introduction* (Jerusalem: Wahrmann Books, 1964).

—'Hebrew Legal Terms II', *JSS* 12 (1967), pp. 241-44.

Falkenstein, A., *The Sumerian Temple City* (MANE, 1.1; Los Angeles: Undena Publications, 1974).

Farber, H., 'A Price and Wage Study for North Babylonia during the Old Babylonian Period', *JESHO* 21 (1978), pp. 1-51.

Feliks, J., 'Agricultural Methods and Implements in Ancient Erez Israel', *EncJud* II, pp. 374-82.

Fendler, M., 'Zur Sozialkritik des Amos', *EvT* 33 (1973), pp. 32-53.

Fensham, F.C., *The Books of Ezra and Nehemiah* (NICOT; Grand Rapids: Eerdmans, 1982).

—*Exodus: De Prediking van het Oude Testament* (Nijkerk: G.F. Callenbach B.V., 2nd edn, 1977).

—'Exodus XXI 18:19 in the Light of Hittite Law 10', *VT* 10 (1960), pp. 333-35.

—'New Light on Exod 21:6 and 22:7 from the Laws of Eshnunna', *JBL* 78 (1959), pp. 160-61.

—'Das nicht-haftbar-sein im Bundesbuch im Lichte der altorientalischer Rechtstexte', *JNSL* 8 (1980), pp. 17-34.

—'Note on Keret in CTA 14:90-103a', *JNSL* 8 (1980), pp. 35-47.

—'The Possibility of the Presence of Casuistic Legal Material at the Making of the Covenant at Sinai', *PEQ* 93 (1961), pp. 143-46.

—'The Role of the Lord in the Legal Sections of the Covenant Code', *VT* 26 (1969), pp. 262-74.

—'Transgression and Penalty in the Book of the Covenant', *JNSL* 5 (1977), pp. 23-41.

—'Widow, Orphan and the Poor in Ancient Near Eastern Legal and Wisdom Literature', *JNES* 21 (1962), pp. 129-39.

Feucht, C., *Untersuchungen zum Heiligkeitgesetz* (ThA, 20; Berlin: Evangelische Verlagsanstalt, 1964).

Fiensy, D., 'Using the Nuer Culture of Africa in Understanding the Old Testament: An Evaluation', *JSOT* 38 (1987), pp. 73-83.

Finet, A., *Le Code de Hammurabi: Introduction, traduction et annotation* (LAPO, 6; Paris: Cerf, 2nd edn, 1983).

—'Le "Gage" et la "sujetion" (*nipûtum* et *kiššatum*) dans les Textes de Mari et le Code de Hammurabi', *Akkadica* 8 (1978), pp 12-18.

Finkelstein, I., *The Archaeology of the Israelite Settlement* (Jerusalem: Israel Exploration Society, 1988).

—'The Emergence of the Monarchy of Israel: The Environmental and Socio-economic Aspects', *JSOT* 44 (1989), pp. 43-74.

—'Respondents: Session II: Archaeology, History and Bible. The Israelite Settlement in Canaan: A Case Study', in *Biblical Archaeology Today: Proceedings of the International Congress on Biblical Archaeology, Jerusalem, April 1984* (ed. J. Amitai; Jerusalem: Israel Exploration Society, 1985), pp. 80-83.

Finkelstein, J.J., 'Ammiṣaduqa's Edict and the Babylonian "Law Codes"', *JCS* 15 (1961), pp. 91-104.

—'Early Mesopotamia, 2500–1000 BC', in *Propaganda and Communication in World History: Volume 1 The Symbolic Instrument in Early Times* (ed. H.D. Lasswell, D. Lerner and H. Speier; Honolulu: The University Press of Hawaii, 1979), pp. 50-110.

—'Edict of Ammiṣaduqa's: A New Text', *RA* 63 (1969), pp. 45-64.

—'The Laws of Ur-Nammu', *JCS* 22 (1968–69), pp. 66-82.

—'The Ox that Gored', *TAPS* 71 (1981), pp. 5-86.

—'Some New Misharum Material and its Implication', in *Studies in Honor of Benno Landsberger on His Seventieth Birthday, April 21, 1965* (The Oriental Institute of the University of Chicago Assyriological Studies, 16; Chicago: University of Chicago Press, 1965), pp. 233-46.

—'On Some Recent Studies in Cuneiform Law', *JAOS* 90 (1970), pp. 243-256.

Fish, T., 'Aspects of Sumerian Civilisation in the Third Dynasty or Ur', *BJRL* 22 (1938), pp. 160-74.

Flanagan, J., 'Chiefs in Israel', *JSOT* 20 (1981), pp. 47-73.

Fohrer, G., *Die Hauptprobleme des Buches Ezekiel* (BZAW, 72; Berlin: de Gruyter, 1952).

—*History of Israelite Religion* (London: SPCK, 1972).

—*Introduction to the Old Testament* (London: SPCK, 1970).

Fontela, C.A., 'La esclavitud a través la Biblia', *EstBíb* 43 (1985), pp. 89-124, 237-74.

Forte, M., and E.E. Evans-Pritchard, 'Introduction', in *African Political Systems* (ed. M. Forte and E.E. Evans-Pritchard; London: Oxford University Press, 1940).

Forte, M., *Kinship and Social Order* (Chicago: Aldine, 1969).

—'The Structure of Unilineal Descent Groups', *AA* 55 (1953), pp. 17-41.

Foster, B., 'A New Look at the Sumerian Temple State', *JESHO* 24 (1981), pp. 225-41.

Frankena, R., 'The Vassal Treaties of Esarhaddon and the Dating of Deuteronomy', *OTS* 14 (1965), pp. 122-54.

Freedman, D.N., *Studies in Ancient Yahwistic Poetry* (Missoula, MT: Scholars Press, 1975).

Freedman, D.N., and B.E. Willoughby, 'עבר', *ThWAT*, V, cols. 1039-56.

Frick, F.S., *The City in Ancient Israel* (SBLDS, 36; Missoula, MT: Scholars Press, 1977).

—*The Formation of the State in Ancient Israel* (SWBAS, 4; Sheffield: Almond Press, 1985).

—'Religion and Sociopolitical Structure in Early Israel: An Ethno-Archaeological Approach', in *Society of Biblical Literature Seminar Papers 1979* (Missoula, MT: Scholars Press, 1979), pp. 233-53.

—'Social Science Methods and Theories of Significance for the Study of the Israelite Monarchy: A Critical Review Essay', *Semeia* 37 (1986), pp. 9-52.

Fried, M.H., 'The Classification of Corporate Unilineal Descent Groups', *JRAI* 87 (1957), pp. 1-29.

—*The Evolution of Political Society* (New York: Random House, 1967).

Fritz, V., 'Conquest or Settlement? The Early Iron Age in Palestine', *BA* 50 (1987), pp. 84-100.

—'The Israelite "Conquest" in the Light of Recent Excavations at Khirbet el-Meshash', *BASOR* 241 (1981), pp. 61-73.

Gadd, C.J., 'Tablets from Kirkuk', *RA* 23 (1926), pp. 49-161.

Gamoran, H., 'The Biblical Law against Loans on Interest', *JNES* 30 (1971), pp. 127-34.

—'The Talmudic Law of Mortgages in View of the Prohibition against Lending at Interest', *HUCA* 52 (1981), pp. 153-62.

Garbini, G., *History and Ideology in Ancient Israel* (London: SCM Press, 1988).

Garelli, P., and V. Nikiprowetzky, *Le Proche-Orient asiatique: Les empires mésopotamiens, Israël* (Paris, 1974).

Gelb, I.J., 'On the Alleged Temple and State Economies in Ancient Mesopotamia', in *Studi in Onore di Eduardo Volterra*, VI (Milano, 1969), pp. 137-54.

—'The Ancient Mesopotamian Ration System', *JNES* 24 (1965), pp. 230-34.

—'Approaches to the Study of Ancient Society', *JAOS* 87 (1967), pp. 1-8.

—'The Arua Institution', *RA* 66 (1972), pp. 10-13.

—'Definition and Discussion of Slavery and Serfdom', *UF* 11 (1980), pp. 283-97.
—'From Freedom to Slavery', in *Gesellschaftsklassen im Alten Zweistromland und den angrenzenden Gebeiten -XVIII: Recontre assyriologique internationale, München, 29. Juni bis 3. Juli 1970* (ed. D.O. Edzard; BAWPHKA, 75; Munich: Verlag der Bayerischen Akademie der Wissenschaften, 1972), pp. 81-92.
—'Household and Family in Early Mesopotamia', in *State and Temple Economy in the Ancient Near East.* I, II. *Proceedings of the International Conference Organized by the Katholieke Iniversiteit Leuven from the 10th to the 14th of April 1978* (ed. E. Lipiński; OLA, 5; Leuven: Dept. Oriëntalistiek, 1979), pp. 1-98.
—'An Old Babylonian List of Amorites', *JAOS* 88 (1968), pp. 39-46.
—'Prisoners of War in Early Mesopotamia', *JNES* 32 (1973), pp. 70-98.
—'Quantitative Evaluation of Slavery and Serfdom', in *Kramer Anniversary Volume* (AOAT, 25; Neukirchen–Vluyn: Neukirchener Verlag, 1976), pp. 195-207.
—'Terms for Slaves in Ancient Mesopotamia', in *Societies and Languages of the Ancient Near East in Honour of I.M. Diakonoff* (ed. M.A. Dandamayev, I. Gerschevitch, H. Klengel, G. Komoróczy, M.T. Larsen and J.N. Postgate; Warminster: Aris & Phillips, 1982), pp. 81-98.
Gemser, B., 'The Importance of the Motive Clause in Old Testament Law', in *Congress Volume, Copenhagen* (VTSup, 1; Leiden: Brill, 1953), pp. 50-66.
Gerstenberger, E., *Wesen und Herkunft des 'Apodiktischen Rechts'* (WMANT, 20; Neukirchen–Vluyn: Neukirchener Verlag, 1965).
Geus, C.H.J. de, 'The Profile of an Israelite City' *BA* 49 (1986), pp. 224-27.
—*The Tribes of Israel: An Investigation into Some of the Presuppositions of Martin Noth's Amphictyony Hypothesis* (SSN, 18; Assen, 1976).
Gevaryahu, H., 'The Announcement of Freedom in Jerusalem by Nehemiah in Comparison with *Mesharum* and Social Reform in the Ancient World' (Hebrew), *Festschrift Abraham Katz* (Jerusalem, 1969), pp. 354-87.
Gevirtz, S., 'West Semitic Curses and the Problem of the Origins of Hebrew Law', *VT* 11 (1961), pp. 137-58.
Gibson, J.C.L., *Textbook of Syrian Semitic Inscriptions* (Oxford: Clarendon Press, 1971).
Gilmer, H.W., *The If-You Form in Israelite Law* (SBLDS, 15; Missoula, MT: Scholars Press, 1975).
Ginzberg, E., 'Studies in the Economics of the Bible', *JQR* 22 (1932), pp. 343-408.
Giorgadze, G., 'Die Begriffe "freie" und "unfreie" bei den Hethitern', in *Wirtschaft und Gesellschaft im alten Vorderasien* (ed. J. Harmatta and G. Komoróczy; Budapest: Akadémiai Kiadó, 1976), pp. 299-308.
Gispen, W.H., *Exodus* (BSC; Grand Rapids: Zondervan, 1982).
Gledhill, J., and M.T. Larsen, 'The Polanyi Paradigm and a Dynamic Analysis of Archaic States', in *Theory and Explanation in Archaeology: The Southampton Conference* (ed. C. Renfrew, M.J. Rowlands and B.A. Seagraves; New York: Academic Press, 1982), pp. 197-229.
Glock, A.E., 'The Use of Ethnography in an Archaeological Research Design', in *The Quest for the Kingdom of God: Studies in Honor of G.E. Mendenhall* (ed. H.B. Huffmon, F.A. Spina and A.R.W. Green; Winona Lake, IN: Eisenbrauns, 1983), pp. 171-79.

Gnuse, R., 'Jubilee Legislation in Leviticus: Israel's Vision for Social Reform', *BTB* 15 (1985), pp. 43-48.

—*You Shall Not Steal: Community and Property in the Biblical Tradition* (Maryknoll: Orbis Books, 1985).

Goetze, A., *The Laws of Eshnunna* (AASOR, 31; New Haven: American Schools of Oriental Research, 1956).

Goodman, M., 'The First Jewish Revolt: Social Conflict and the Problem of Debt', *JJS* 33 (1982), pp. 417-27.

Gordon, C.H., *Adventures in the Near East* (London: Phoenix House, 1957).

—'Biblical Customs and the Nuzi Tablets', *BA* 3 (1940), pp. 1-12.

—'The Biblical Sabbath, its Origin and Observance in the Ancient Near East', *Jud* 31 (1982), pp. 12-16.

—'*Erēbu* Marriage', in *Studies on the Civilization and Culture of Nuzi and the Hurrians* (ed. M.A. Morrison and D.I. Owen; Winona Lake, IN: Eisenbrauns, 1981), pp. 155-60.

—'On Making Other Gods', in *Biblical and Related Studies Presented to Samuel Iwry* (ed. A. Kort and S. Mirschauser; Winona Lake, IN: Eisenbrauns, 1985), pp. 77-79.

—'אלהים in its Reputed Meaning of Rulers, Judges', *JBL* 54 (1935), pp. 134-44.

—'Parallèles nouziens aux lois et coutumes de l'Ancien Testament', *RB* 49 (1935), pp. 34-41.

—'The Patriarchal Narratives', *JNES* 13 (1954), pp. 56-59.

—'Sabbatical Cycle or Seasonal Pattern', *Or* 22 (1953), pp. 79-81.

—'The Study of Jacob and Laban in the Light of the Nuzi Tablets', *BASOR* 66 (1937), pp. 25-27.

—'The Ugaritic Texts: Half a Century of Research', in *Biblical Archaeology Today: Proceedings of the International Congress on Biblical Archaeology, Jerusalem, April 1984* (ed. J. Amitai; Jerusalem: Israel Exploration Society, 1985).

—*The World of the Old Testament* (Garden City, NY: Doubleday, 2nd edn, 1958).

Gordon, R.P., *1 & 2 Samuel: A Commentary* (Exeter: Paternoster Press, 1986).

Gottwald, N.K., 'Early Israel and the Canaanite Socio-economic System', in *Palestine in Transition: The Emergence of Ancient Israel* (ed. D.N. Freedman and D.F. Graf; SWBAS, 2; Sheffield: Almond Press, 1983), pp. 25-38.

—'The Israelite Settlement as a Social Revolutionary Movement', in *Biblical Archaeology Today: Proceedings of the International Congress on Biblical Archaeology, Jerusalem, April 1984* (ed. J. Amitai; Jerusalem: Israel Exploration Society, 1985), pp. 34-46.

—'The Participation of Free Agrarians in the Introduction of Monarchy to Ancient Israel: An Application of H.A. Landsberger's Framework for the Analysis of Peasant Movements', *Semeia* 37 (1986), pp. 76-107.

—'Sociological Method in the Study of Ancient Israel', in *Encounter with the Text: Form and History in the Hebrew Bible* (ed. M.J. Buss; Semeia Supplements; Missoula, MT: Scholars Press, 1979), pp. 69-81.

—*The Tribes of Yahweh: A Sociology of the Religion of Liberated Israel 1250–1050 BCE* (London: SCM Press, 1979).

—'Two Models for the Origins of Ancient Israel: Social Revolution or Frontier Development', in *The Quest for the Kingdom of God: Studies in Honor of G.E.*

Mendenhall (ed. H.B. Huffmon, F.A. Spina and A.R.W. Green; Winona Lake, IN: Eisenbrauns, 1983), pp. 5-24.

Gowan, D.E., 'Wealth and Poverty in the Old Testament: The Case of the Widow, the Orphan, and the Sojourner', *Int* 41 (1987), pp. 341-53.

Gray, G.B., *Numbers* (ICC; Edinburgh: T. & T. Clark, 1903).

Gray, J., 'Feudalism in Ugarit and Early Israel', *ZAW* 64 (1952), pp. 49-55.

—'Ugarit', *Archaeology and Old Testament Study* (ed. D.W. Thomas; Oxford: Clarendon Press, 1967), pp. 145-70.

Gray, M.P., 'The Ḫâbiru--Hebrew Problem in the Light of the Source Material Available at Present', *HUCA* 29 (1958), pp. 135-202.

Green, A.R.W., 'Social Stratification and Cultural Continuity at Alalakh', in *The Quest for the Kingdom of God: Studies in Honor of G.E. Mendenhall* (ed. H.B. Huffmon, F.A. Spina and A.R.W. Green; Winona Lake, IN: Eisenbrauns, 1983), pp. 181-203.

Greenberg, M.,'Another Look at Rachel's Theft of the Teraphim', *JBL* 81 (1962), pp. 239-48.

—'Avenger of Blood', *IDB*, I, p. 321.

—'The Biblical Conception of Asylum', *JBL* 78 (1959), pp. 125-32.

—*Biblical Prose Prayer: A Window to the Popular Religion of Ancient Israel* (Berkeley: University of California Press, 1983).

—'Crimes and Punishments', *IDB*, I, pp. 733-44.

—*The Hab/piru* (AOS, 39; New Haven: American Oriental Society 1955).

—'Hab/piru and Hebrews', in *Patriarchs* (ed. B. Mazar; WHJP, 2; Jerusalem: Magnes, 1970), pp. 188-200, 279-81.

—'More Reflections on Biblical Criminal Law', in *Studies in Bible 1986* (ed. S. Japhet; Scripta Hierosolymitana, 31; Jerusalem: Magnes, 1986), pp. 1-17.

—'Oath', *EncJud* XXII, cols. 1295-1302.

—'Sabbatical Year and Jubilee: Ancient Near Eastern Legal Background', *EncJud* XIV, cols. 577-78.

—'Some Postulates of Biblical Criminal Law', in *Yehezkel Kaufman Jubilee Volume* (ed. M. Haran; Jerusalem: Magnes, 1960), pp. 5-28.

Greengus, S., 'Sisterhood Adoption at Nuzi and the "Wife-Sister" in Genesis', *HUCA* 46 (1975), pp. 5-31.

Greenspahn, F.E., 'Book Review of H. Reviv, *The Elders in Ancient Israel: A Study of a Biblical Institution*', *CBQ* 47 (1985), pp. 709-11.

Grelot, P., 'Le dernière étape de la rédaction sacerdotale', *VT* 6 (1956), pp. 174-89.

Gulick, J., *The Middle East: An Anthropological Perspective* (Goodyear RAS: Pacific Palisades, 1976).

Gurney, O.R., and S.N. Kamer, 'Two Fragments of Sumerian Laws', *AS* 16 (1965), pp. 13-19.

Haase, R., *Einführung in das Studium keilschriftlicher Rechtsquellen* (Wiesbaden, 1965).

—'Zur Systematik der zweiten Tafel der hethitischen Gesetze', *RIDA* 8 (1960), pp 51-54.

Halbe, J., ' "Gemeinschaft, die Welt Unterbricht": Grundfragen und -inhalte deuteronomischer Theologie und Überlieferungsbildung im Lichte der Ursprungsbedingungen alttestamentlichen Rechts', in *Das Deuteronomium:*

Entstehung, Gestalt und Botschaft [*Deuteronomy, Origin Form and Message*] (ed. N. Lohfink; BETL, 68; Leuven: Leuven University Press, 1985), pp. 55-75.

Halligan, J.M., 'The Role of the Peasant in the Amarna Period', in *Palestine in Transition: The Emergence of Ancient Israel* (ed. D.N. Freedman and D.F. Graf, SWBAS, 2; Sheffield: Almond Press, 1983), pp. 15-24.

Hallo, W.W., 'Biblical History in its Near Eastern Setting: The Contextual Approach', in *Scripture in Context: Essays on the Comparative Method* (ed. C.D. Evans, W.W. Hallo and J.B. White; PTMS, 34; Pittsburgh: Pickwick Press, 1980), pp. 1-26.

—'God, King, and Man at Yale', in *State and Temple Economy in the Ancient Near East*. I, II. *Proceedings of the International Conference Organized by the Katholieke Iniversiteit Leuven from the 10th to the 14th of April 1978* (ed. E. Lipiński; OLA, 5; Leuven: Dept. Oriëntalistiek, 1979), pp. 99-112.

Halpern, B., *The Constitution of the Monarchy in Israel* (HSM, 25; Chico, CA: Scholars Press, 1981).

—*The Emergence of Israel in Canaan* (SBLMS, 29; Chico, CA: Scholars Press, 1983).

—'Radical Exodus Redating Fatally Flawed', *BARev* 13 (1987), pp. 56-61.

Hanson, P., 'Conflict in Ancient Israel and its Resolution', in *Understanding the Word: Essays in Honour of B.W. Anderson* (ed. J.T. Butler, E.W. Conrad and B.C. Ollenburger; JSOTSup, 37; Sheffield: JSOT Press, 1985), pp. 185-205.

Haran, M., 'Studies in the Account of the Levitical Cities', *JBL* 80 (1961), pp. 45-54.

Harrelson, W.J., 'Court of Law', *IDB*, I, p. 713.

—'Vengeance', *IDB*, I, pp. 748-749.

Harris, R., 'The Archive of the Sin Temple in Khafajah (Tutub) (Conclusion)', *JCS* 9 (1955), pp. 91-105.

—'On the Process of Secularization under Hammurabi', *JCS* 15 (1961), pp. 117-20.

Harrison, R.K., *Jeremiah and Lamentations* (TOTC; Downers Grove, IL: IVP, 1973).

—*Leviticus* (TOTC; Downers Grove, IL: IVP, 1980).

Hartley, J.E., 'Father's House; Father's Household', *ISBE*, pp. 286-87.

Hauer, C., 'From Alt to Anthropology: The Rise of the Israelite State', *JSOT* 36 (1986), pp. 3-15.

—'David and the Levites', *JSOT* 23 (1982), pp. 33-54.

—'The Economics of National Security in Solomonic Israel', *JSOT* 18 (1980), pp. 63-73.

Hauser, A.J., 'Israel's Conquest of Palestine: A Peasant's Rebellion?', *JSOT* 7 (1978), pp. 2-19.

—'Response to Thompson and Mendenhall', *JSOT* 7 (1978), pp. 35-36.

—'The Revolutionary Origins of Ancient Israel: A Response to Gottwald', *JSOT* 8 (1978), pp. 46-49.

Heinisch, P., *Das Buch Exodus: übersetzt und erklärt* (DHSAT, 1.2; Bonn: Peter Hanstein, 1934).

—*Das Buch Leviticus: übersetzt und erklärt* (DHSAT, 1.3; Bonn: Peter Hanstein, 1935).

—'Das Sklavenrecht in Israel und Alten Orient', *SCath* 11 (1934–35), pp. 276-90.

Heltzer, M., 'Mortgage of Land Property and Freeing it in Ugarit', *JESHO* 19 (1976), pp. 89-95.

—'Problems of the Social History of Syria in the Late Bronze Age', in *La Siria nel Tardo Bronzo*, IX (ed. M. Liverani; Rome: Orientis Antiqui Collectio, 1968), pp. 31-46.

—'Royal Economy in Ancient Ugarit', in *State and Temple Economy in the Ancient Near East*. I, II. *Proceedings of the International Conference Organized by the Katholieke Iniversiteit Leuven from the 10th to the 14th of April 1978* (ed. E. Lipiński; OLA, 5; Leuven: Dept. Oriëntalistiek, 1979), pp. 459-96.

—*The Rural Community in Ancient Ugarit* (Wiesbaden: Rachert, 1976).

Hengstenberg, E.W., *Beiträge zur Einleitung ins AT* (Berlin, 1831-39) = *Dissertations on the Genuineness of the Pentateuch* (Edinburgh: T. & T. Clark, 1847).

Hentschke, R., 'Erwägungen zur israelitischen Rechtgeschichte', *ThViat* 10 (1965–66), pp. 108-33.

Herion, G.A., 'The Impact of Modern and Social Science Assumptions on the Reconstruction of Israelite History', *JSOT* 34 (1986), pp. 3-33.

Herrmann, S., 'Basic Factors of Israelite Settlement in Canaan', in *Biblical Archaeology Today: Proceedings of the International Congress on Biblical Archaeology, Jerusalem April 1984* (ed. J. Amitai; Jerusalem: Israel Exploration Society, 1985), pp. 47-53.

—*A History of Israel in Old Testament Times* (London: SCM Press; rev and enlarged edn, 1981).

Hertzberg, H.W., *I and II Samuel* (OTL; London: SCM Press, 1964).

Hill, A.E., and G.A. Herion, 'Functional Yahwism and Social Control in the Early Israelite Monarchy', *JETS* 29 (1986), pp. 277-84.

Hirsch, H., 'Akkadische (altassyrisch) *mazzāzum* "Pfand, Verpfändung"', *Wiener ZKM* 62 (1969), pp. 52-61.

Hoenig, S.B., 'Sabbatical Years and the Year of Jubilee', *JQR* 59 (1969), pp. 222-36.

Hoffmann, D., *Das Buch Leviticus*, I–II (Berlin: Poppelauer, 1905–1906).

Hoftijzer, J., 'EX. xxi 8', *VT* 7 (1957), pp. 388-91.

Holzinger, H., *Exodus erklärt* (KHAT; Tübingen: Mohr, 1900).

Hopkins, D.C., *The Highlands of Canaan: Agricultural Life in the Early Iron Age* (SWBAS, 3; Sheffield: Almond Press, 1985).

—'Life on the Land: The Subsistence Struggles of Early Israel', *BA* 50 (1987), pp. 149-77.

Horst, F., 'Bundesbuch', *RGG*, cols. 1523-25.

—*Gottes Recht: Gesammelte Studien zum Recht im Alten Testament* (Theologische Bücherei Neudrucke und Berichte aus dem 20. Jahrhundert, 12; Munich: Chr. Kaiser Verlag, 1961).

Horst, L., 'Bundesbuch', in *Die Religion und Gegenwart: Handwörterbuch für Theologie und Religionswissenschaft*, I (Tübingen: Mohr, 3rd edn, 1957), col. 1524.

Hossfeld, F.L., and E. Reuter, ' מתה', *ThWAT*, V, cols. 658-63.

Houten, C. van, *The Alien in Israelite Law* (JSOTSup, 107; Sheffield: JSOT Press, 1991).

Hruška, B., 'Die innere Struktur der Reformtexte Urukaginas von Lagaš', *ArOr* 41 (1973), pp. 4-13, 104-32.

—'Die Reformstexte Urukaginas', in *Le Palais et la royauté: XIX recontre assyriologique international 1971* (Paris, 1974), pp. 151-61.

Huehnergard, J., 'Biblical Notes on some New Akkadian Texts from Emar (Syria)', *CBQ* 47 (1985), pp. 428-34.

Hurvitz, A., *A Linguistic Study of the Relationship Between the Priestly Source and the Book of Ezekiel: A New Approach to an Old Problem* (CahRB, 20; Paris: Gabalda, 1982).

—'The Evidence of Language in Dating the Priestly Code', *RB* 81 (1974), pp. 24-57.

Hyatt, J.P., *Exodus* (NCBC; Grand Rapids:Eerdmans; London: Morgan & Scott, 1971).

—'Moses and the Ethical Decalogue', *Enc* 26 (1965), pp. 199-206.

Ibn Ezra, אבן עזרא על התורה (3 vols.; Jerusalem: Mossad Harav Kook, 1977).

Jackson, B.S., and T.F. Watkins, 'Distraint in the Laws of Eshnunna and Hammurabi', in *Studi in onore di desare San Filippo*, V (ed. A. Giuffr; PFGUC, 96; Milan, 1984), pp. 409-19.

Jackson, B.S., 'Biblical Laws of Slavery: a Comparative Approach', in *Slavery and Other Forms of Unfree Labour* (ed. L. Archer; HWS; London: Routledge, 1988), pp. 86-101.

—'The Ceremonial and the Judicial: Biblical Law as Sign and Symbol', *JSOT* 30 (1984), pp. 25-50.

—'Legal Drafting in the Ancient Near East in the Light of Modern Theories of Cognitive Development', in *Mélanges à la mémoire de Marcel-Henri Prévost: Droit biblique-interprétation rabbinique communautés et société* (PULII; Paris: Presses Universitaires de France, 1982), pp. 49-66.

—'The Problem of Exodus 21: 22-25 (IUS TALIONIS)', *VT* 23 (1973), pp. 273-304 = *Essays in Jewish and Comparative Legal History* (SJLA, 10; Leiden: Brill, 1975), pp. 75-107.

—'Reflections on Biblical Criminal Law', *JJS* 24 (1973), pp.; also in *Essays in Jewish and Comparative Legal History* (SJLA, 10; Leiden: Brill, 1975), pp. 25-63.

—'Some Literary Features of the Mishpatim', in *Wünschet Jerusalem Frieden: Collected Communications to the XIIth Congress of the International Organization for the Study of the Old Testament, Jerusalem 1986* (Bern: Peter Lang, 1987), pp. 235-42.

—'Sources and Problems', in *Essays in Jewish and Comparative Legal History* (SJLA, 10; Leiden: Brill, 1975), pp. 1-24.

—*Theft in Early Jewish Law* (Oxford: Clarendon Press, 1972).

—'Two Or Three Witnesses', in *Essays in Jewish and Comparative Legal History* (SJLA, 10; Leiden: Brill, 1975), pp. 153-71.

—'Unpublished Text of the Speaker's Lectures in Biblical Studies, University of Oxford, 1983–86'.

Jacobsen, T., 'Early Political Development in Mesopotamian Assemblies', *ZA* 52 (1957), pp. 91-140.

—'Note sur le rôle de l'opinion publique dans l'ancienne Mésopotamie', *RA* 58 (1964), pp. 157-58.

—'Primitive Democracy in Ancient Mesopotamia', *JNES* 2 (1946), pp. 158-72.

Jagersma, H., *A History of Israel in the Old Testament Period* (London / Philadelphia, 1982).

Jakobson, V.A., 'Some Problems Connected with the Rise of Landed Property (Old Babylonian Period)', in *Beiträge zur sozialen Struktur des Alten Vorderasien* (ed. H. Klengel; SGKAO, 1; Berlin: Akademie-Verlag, 1971), pp. 33-37.

Jankowska, N.B., 'Communal Self-Government and the King of Arrapha', *JESHO* 12 (1968), pp. 233-82.

—'Extended Family Commune and Civil Self-Government in Arrapha in the Fifteenth–Fourteenth Century BC', in *Ancient Mesopotamia Socio-Economic History: A Collection of Studies by Soviet Scholars* (ed. I.M. Diakonoff; USSR Academy of Sciences Institute of the Peoples of Asia; Moscow: 'Nauka', 1969), pp. 235-52.

Japhet, S., 'The Relationship Between the Legal Corpora in the Pentateuch in Light of Manumission Laws', in *Studies in Bible 1986* (ed. S. Japhet.; Scripta Hierosolymitana, 31; Jerusalem: Magnes, 1986), pp. 63-89

—'מחקרים במקרא ובמורח הקרמן', 'חוקי שחרור עבדים שאלת חידש בין קבצי החוקים בוורה' (ed. שמואל א ליתמלם; Jerusalem 1984), pp. 231-48.

Jepsen, A., *Untersuchungen zum Bundesbuch* (Wissenschaftliche MANT, 41; Neukirchen–Vluyn: Neukirchener Verlag, 1927).

Jirku, A. 'Das israelitische Jobeljahr', *Reinhold-Seeberg-Festschrift II* (Leipzig, 1929), pp. 169-79.

Kahan, A., 'Economic History', *EncJud*, XVI, cols. 1266-1324.

Kallai, Z., 'Organizational and Administrative Frameworks in the Kingdom of David and Solomon', in *Proceedings of the Sixth World Congress of Jewish Studies, Jerusalem 1973* (Jerusalem: Magnes, 1973), pp. 213-20.

—'The System of Levitic Cities: A Historical-Geographical Study in Biblical Historiography' (Hebrew), *Zion* 45 (1980), pp. 13-34.

Kamp, K.A., and N. Yoffee, 'Ethnicity in Ancient Western Asia during the Early Second Millennium BC: Archaeological Assessments and Ethno-archaeological Prospectives', *BASOR* 237 (1980), pp. 85-104.

Kapelrud, A.S., 'משך', *ThWAT*, V, cols. 665-69.

Katzoff, L. 'Slavery in the Bible', *Dor le Dor* 10 (1982), pp. 204-209.

Kaufman, S.A., 'Deuteronomy 15 and Recent Research on the Dating of P', in *Das Deuteronomium: Entstehung, Gestalt und Botschaft [Deuteronomy, Origin Form and Message]* (ed. N. Lohfink; BETL, 68; Leuven: Leuven University Press, 1985), pp. 273-76.

—'A Reconstruction of the Social Welfare Systems of Ancient Israel', in *The Shelter of Elyon: Essays on Ancient Palestinian Life and Literature in Honor of G.W. Ahlström* (ed. W.B. Barrick and J.R. Spencer; JSOTSup, 31; Sheffield: JSOT Press, 1984), pp. 277-86.

—'The Structure of the Deuteronomic Law', *Maarav* 1/2 (1978–79), pp. 105-58.

Kaufmann, Y., *The Biblical Account of the Conquest of Palestine* (Jerusalem: Magnes, 1953).

—*The Religion of Israel* (London: Allen & Unwin, 1961).

Keil, C.F., *Commentary of the Old Testament in Ten Volumes. I. The Pentateuch* (repr.; Grand Rapids: Eerdmans, n.d. [1981]).

—*Manual of Biblical Archæology*, II (CFTL, 35; Edinburgh: T. & T. Clark, 1888).

Kellermann, D., 'גור', *TDOT*, II, pp. 439-49.

Kempinski, A., 'Discussion: Session II: Archaeology, History and Bible. The Israelite Settlement in Canaan: A Case Study', in *Biblical Archaeology Today: Proceedings of the International Congress on Biblical Archaeology, Jerusalem, April 1984* (ed. J. Amitai; Jerusalem: Israel Exploration Society, 1985), p. 90.

Kessler, W., 'Die literarische, historische und theologische Problematik des Dekalogs', *VT* 7 (1957), pp. 1-16.

Kidner, D., *Ezra and Nehemiah* (TOTC; Leicester: Inter-Varsity Press, 1979).

Kienast, B., *Das Altassyrische Kaufvertragsrecht* (FAS, 1; Stuttgart: Franz Steiner Verlag, 1984).

—'Bemerkungen zum altassyrischen Pfandrecht', *WO* 8 (1975/76), pp. 218-27.

—'Zum altbabylonischen Pfandrecht', *SZ* 83 (1966), pp. 334-38.

Kilian, R., *Literarische und formgeschichtliche Untersuchung des Heiligkeitsgesetzes* (BBB, 19; Bonn: Peter Hanstein, 1963).

King, P.J., 'The Eighth, The Greatest of the Centuries?', *JBL* 108 (1989), pp. 3-15.

Kitchen, K.A., *Ancient Orient and Old Testament* (London: Tyndale Press, 1966).

—'Ancient Orient, "Deuteronomism" and the OT', in *New Perspectives on the Old Testament* (ed. J.B. Payne; Waco, TX: Word Books, 1970), pp. 1-24.

Kiuchi, N., *The Purification Offering in the Priestly Literature: Its Meaning and Function* (JSOTSup, 56; Sheffield: JSOT Press, 1987).

Klein, R.W., *I Samuel* (WC, 10; Waco,TX: Word Books, 1983).

Klengel, H., 'Einige Bemerkungen zur sozialökonomischen Entwicklung in der altbabylonischen Zeit', in *Wirtschaft und Gesellschaft im alten Vorderasien* (ed. J. Harmatta and G. Komoróczy; Budapest: Akadémiai Kiadó, 1976), pp. 249-58.

—'Die Palastwirtschaft in Alalaḫ', in *State and Temple Economy in the Ancient Near East*. I, II. *Proceedings of the International Conference Organized by the Katholieke Iniversiteit Leuven from the 10th to the 14th of April 1978* (ed. E. Lipiński.; OLA, 5; Leuven: Dept. Oriëntalistiek, 1979), pp. 435-57.

Klíma, J., 'Im ewigen Banne der *muškūnum*-Problematik?', in *Wirtschaft und Gesellschaft im alten Vorderasien* (ed. J. Harmatta and G. Komoróczy; Budapest: Akadémiai Kiadó, 1976), pp. 267-74.

—'Zur gesellschaftlichen Relevanz der Hammurapischen Gesetze', in *Societies and Languages of the Ancient Near East in Honour of I.M. Diakonoff* (ed. M.A. Dandamayev, I. Gerschevitch, H. Klengel, G. Komoróczy, M.T. Larsen and J.N. Postgate; Warminster: Aris & Phillips, 1982), pp. 174-95.

—'La Perspective historique des lois hamourabiennes', in *Comptes Rendues de l'Académie des Inscriptions et Belles-Lettres* (1972), pp. 297-317.

—'Über neuer Studien auf dem Gebiete des Keilschriftrechts', *ArOr* 18 (1950), pp. 525-38.

Kline, M.G., *The Structure of Biblical Authority* (Grand Rapids: Eerdmans, 1972).

—*The Treaty of the Great King* (Grand Rapids: Eerdmans, 1963).

Klopfenstein, M.A., 'בגד', *Theologisches Handwörterbuch zum Alten Testament*, I (ed. E. Jenni and C. Westermann; Munich: Chr. Kaiser Verlag, 1971), cols. 261-64.

Klostermann, A., *Der Pentateuch*, I (Leipzig: Deichert, 1893).

Knight, D.A., 'The Understanding of "Sitz im Leben" in Form Criticism', *SBL Seminar Papers 1974*, I (Cambridge, MA: SBL, 1974), pp. 105-25.

Koch, K., 'Die Entstehung der sozialen Kritik bei den Profeten', in *Probleme Biblischer Theologie* (ed. H.W. Wolff; Munich: Chr. Kaiser Verlag, 1971), pp. 146-71.

—'Die Hebräer vom Auszug aus Ägypten bis zum Grossreich Davids', *VT* 19 (1969), pp. 37-81.

Kochavi, M., 'The Israelite Settlement in Canaan in the Light of Archeaological Surveys', in *Biblical Archaeology Today: Proceedings of the International*

Congress on Biblical Archaeology, Jerusalem, April 1984 (ed. J. Amitai.; Jerusalem: Israel Exploration Society, 1985), pp. 54-60.

Komoróczy, G., 'Zu den Eigentumsverhältnissen in der altbabylonischen Zeit: Das Problem der Privatwirtschaft', in *State and Temple Economy in the Ancient Near East.* I, II. *Proceedings of the International Conference Organized by the Katholieke Iniversiteit Leuven from the 10th to the 14th of April 1978* (ed. E. Lipiński; OLA, 5; Leuven: Dept. Oriëntalistiek, 1979), pp. 411-22.

—'Zur Frage der Periodizität der altbabylonischen *MÎŠARUM*-Erlässe', in *Societies and Languages of the Ancient Near East in Honour of I.M. Diakonoff* (ed. M.A. Dandamayev, I. Gerschevitch, H. Klengel, G. Komoróczy, M.T. Larsen and J.N. Postgate; Warminster: Aris & Phillips, 1982), pp. 196-205.

—'Work and Strike of Gods: New Light on the Divine Society in the Sumero-Akkadian Mythology', *Oikumene* 1 (1976), pp. 9-37.

Kornfeld, W., *Studien zum Heiligkeitsgesetz (Lev 17-26)* (Wien: Herder, 1952).

Korošec, V., 'Keilschriftrecht', in *Orientalisches Recht* (HOr, III; Leiden: Brill, 1964), pp. 49-219.

Koschaker, P., 'Fratriarchat, Hausgemeinschaft und Mutterrecht in Keilschrift-rechten', *ZA* 41 (1933), pp. 1-89.

—*Neue keilschriftliche Rechtssurkunden aus der el-Amarna-Zeit* (Leipzig, 1928).

Kramer, S.N., and A. Falkenstein, 'Ur-Nammu Law Code', *Or* ns 23 (1954), pp. 40-51.

Kramer, S.N., 'Aspects of Mesopotamian Society: Evidence from the Sumerian Literary Sources', in *Beiträge zur sozialen Struktur des Alten Vorderasien* (ed. H. Klengel; SGKAO, 1; Berlin: Akademie-Verlag, 1971), pp. 1-14.

—*History Begins at Sumer* (Philadelphia: University of Pennsylvania Press, 3rd edn, 1981).

—*The Sumerians: Their History, Culture and Characters* (Chicago: Chicago University Press, 1964).

—' "Vox populi" and the Sumerian Literary Documents', *RA* 58 (1964), pp. 148-56.

Kraus, F.R., *Ein Edikt des Königs Ammi-Saduqa von Babylon* (SDOAP, 5; Leiden: Brill, 1958).

—'Ein Edikt des Königs Samsu-iluna von Babylon', *AS* 16 (1965), pp. 225-31.

—*Königliche Verfügungen in altbabylonischer Zeit* (SDOAP, XI; Leiden: Brill, 1984).

—*Vom mesopotamischen der altbabylonischen Zeit und seiner Welt* (Amsterdam: Noord-hollandsche Uitgevers-Maatschappij, 1973).

—'Der "Palast", Produzent und Unternehmer im Königreiche Babylon nach Hammurabi (ca. 1750–1600 v. Chr.)', in *State and Temple Economy in the Ancient Near East.* I, II. *Proceedings of the International Conference Organized by the Katholieke Iniversiteit Leuven from the 10th to the 14th of April 1978* (ed. E. Lipiński; OLA, 5; Leuven: Dept. Oriëntalistiek, 1979), pp. 423-34.

—*Viehhaltung im altbabylonischen Lande Larsa* (MKNAW, 29.5; Amsterdam, 1966).

—'Ein zentrales Problem des altmesopotamischen Rechtes: Was ist der Codex Hammu-rabi?', *Geneva* 8 (1960), pp. 183-96.

Kugel, J.L., 'On Hidden Hatred and Open Reproach: Early Exegesis of Leviticus 19: 17', *HTR* 80 (1987), pp. 43-61.

Labuschagne, C.J., 'Divine Speech in Deuteronomy', in *Das Deuteronomium: Entstehung [Gestalt und Botschaft. Deuteronomy, Origin Form and Message]* (ed. N. Lohfink; BETL, 68; Leuven: Leuven University Press, 1985), pp. 111-26.

Lambert, M., 'L'Expansion de Lagash au temps d'Entéména', *RSO* 47 (1972), pp. 1-22.

—'Les "Réformes" d'Urukagina', *RA* 50 (1965), pp. 169-84.

Lambert, W.G., 'Book Review of F.R. Kraus *Königliche Verfügungen in altbabylonischer Zeit*', *BSO(A)S* 51 (1988), pp. 118-20.

—'Interchange of Ideas Between Southern Mesopotamia and Syria-Palestine as Seen in Literature', in *Mesopotamien und seine Nachbarn: Politische und kulturelle Wechselbeziehungen im Alten Vorderasien vom 4. bis 1. Jahrtausend v. Chr. Teil 1* (ed. H.J. Nissen and J. Renger; BBVO, 1; Berlin: Dietrich Reimer Verlag, 1982), pp. 311-16.

—'The Reading of the Name Uru.Ka.gi.na', *Or* 39 (1970), p. 41.

Landsberger, B., 'Die babylonischen Termini für Gesetz und Recht', in *Symbolae ad iura orientis antiqui pertinentes Paulo Koschaker dedicatae* (SDOAP, 2; Leiden: Brill, 1939), pp. 219-34.

—'Habiru und Lulah,h,u', *KlF* 1 (1930), pp. 321-34.

Landsberger, H.A., 'Peasant Unrest: Themes and Variations', in *Rural Protest: Peasant Movements and Social Change* (ed. H.A. Landsberger; New York: Barnes & Noble, 1973), pp. 6-18.

Lang, B., 'The Social Organization of Peasant Poverty in Biblical Israel', *JSOT* 24 (1982), pp. 47-63.

Larsen, M.T., 'Your Money or Your Life! A Portrait of an Assyrian Businessman', in *Societies and Languages of the Ancient Near East in Honour of I.M. Diakonoff* (ed. M.A. Dandamayev, I. Gerschevitch, H. Klengel, G. Komoróczy, M.T. Larsen and J.N. Postgate; Warminster: Aris & Phillips, 1982), pp. 214-44.

Larue, G.A., *Babylon and the Bible* (Grand Rapids: Zondervan, 1969).

Laslett, P., and R. Wall, *Household and Family in Past Time: Comparative Studies in the Size and Structure of the Domestic Group over the Last Three Centuries in England, France, Serbia, Japan, and Colonial North America with Further Material from Western Europe* (Cambridge: Cambridge University Press, 1972).

Layton, S.C., 'The Steward in Ancient Israel: A Study of Hebrew ('A—ŠER) 'AL-HABBAYIT in its Near Eastern Setting', *JBL* 109 (1990), pp. 633-49.

Leemans, W.F., *Foreign Trade in the Old Babylonian Period* (Leiden: Brill, 1960).

—'The Importance of Trade: Some Introductory Remarks', *Iraq* 39 (1977), pp. 2-10.

—'King Hammurabi as Judge', in *Symbolae juridicae et historicae M. David dedicatae*, II (ed. J.A. Ankum, R, Feenstra and W.F. Leemans; IOA; Leiden: Brill, 1968), pp. 107-29.

—*The Old-Babylonian Merchant: His Business and his Social Position* (SDOAP, 3; Leiden: Brill, 1950).

—'The Pattern of Settlement in the Babylonian Countryside', in *Societies and Languages of the Ancient Near East in Honour of I.M. Diakonoff* (ed. M.A. Dandamayev, I. Gerschevitch, H. Klengel, G. Komoróczy, M.T. Larsen and J.N. Postgate; Warminster: Aris & Phillips, 1982), pp. 246-49.

—'Quelques Remarques à Propos d'une *TIDDENNŪTU* Étude sur PERSONNELLE À NUZU', *JESHO* 19 (1976), pp. 95-101.

—'The Rôle of Landlease in Mesopotamia in the Early Second Millennium BC', *JESHO* 18 (1975), pp. 134-45.

Leibowitz, N., *Studies in Shemot (Exodus): Part II Mishpatim—Pekudei (Exodus 21,1 to end)* (Jerusalem: The World Sionist Organization, 1981).

Lemche, N.P., *Ancient Israel: A New History of Israelite Society* (TBS, 5; Sheffield: JSOT Press, 1987).

—'*Andurārum and Mīšarum*: Comments on the Problem of Social Edicts and their Application in the ancient Near East', *JNES* 38 (1979), pp. 11-22.

—*Early Israel: Anthropological and Historical Studies on the Israelite Society before the Monarchy* (VTSup, 37; Leiden: Brill, 1985).

—' "Hebrew" as a National Name for Israel', *ST* 33 (1979), pp. 1-23.

—'The Hebrew and the Seven Year Cycle', *BibN* 25 (1984), pp. 65-75.

—'The "Hebrew Slave": Comments on the Slave Law Ex. xxi 2-11', *VT* 25 (1975), pp. 129-44.

—'אמן in 1 Samuel xvii 25', *VT* 24 (1974), pp. 373-74.

—' "Israel in the Period of the Judges"—The Tribal League in Recent Research', *ST* 38 (1984), pp. 1-28.

—'The Manumission of Slaves—The Fallow Year—The Sabbatical Year—The Jobel Year', *VT* 26 (1976), pp. 38-59.

Lenski, G.E., *Power and Privilege: A Theory of Social Stratification* (New York: McGraw-Hill, 1966).

Levenson, J.D., 'Poverty and the State in Biblical Thought', *Jud* 25 (1976), pp. 230-41.

Levine, A., 'The *Netînîm*', *JBL* 82 (1963), pp. 207-12.

Levine, B.A., 'In Praise of the Israelite *Mišpāḥâ* Legal Themes in the Book of Ruth', in *The Quest for the Kingdom of God: Studies in Honor of G.E. Mendenhall* (ed. H.B. Huffmon, F.A. Spina and A.R.W. Green; Winona Lake, IN: Eisenbrauns, 1983), pp. 95-106.

Levine, E., 'On Intra-familial Institutions of the Bible. Book Review of D.A. Legett, *The Levirate and Goel Institutions in the Old Testament, with Special Attention to the Book of Ruth*', *Bib* 57 (1976), pp. 554-59.

Levy, T.E., 'That Chalcolithic Period', *BA* 49 (1986), pp. 83-109.

Levy-Feldblum, A., 'The Law of the Hebrew Slave...' (Hebrew), *BM* 31 (1985–86), pp. 348-59.

Lewis, T.J., 'The Ancestral Estate (נחלתאלהים) in 2 Samuel 14:16', *JBL* 110 (1991), pp. 597-612.

Lewy, J. and H., 'The Origin of the Week and the Oldest West Asiatic Calendar', *HUCA* 17 (1942), pp. 1-152.

Lewy, J., 'The Biblical Institution of *Derôr* in the Light of Akkadian Documents', *Eretz-Israel* 5 (1958), pp. 21-31.

—'*Ḥābirū* and Hebrews', *HUCA* 14 (1939), pp 587-623.

—'*Ḥabiru* und Hebräer', *OrLit* 30 (1927), cols. 738-46, 825-33.

—'A New Parallel between *Ḥhâbirū* and Hebrews', *HUCA* 15 (1940), pp. 47-58.

—'Old Assyrian Documents from Asia Minor (about 2000 BC)', *AHDO* 1 (1937), pp. 106-108.

—'Origin and Signification of the Biblical Term "Hebrew"', *HUCA* 28 (1957), pp. 2-13.

Licht, J., 'נחמה', *Encyclopedia Biblica: Thesaurus Rerum Biblicarum Alphabetico Ordine Digestus*, V (Hebrew) (ed. H. Tadmor; Jerusalem: Bialik Institute, 1968), cols. 917-21.

Lieber, D.L., 'Sabbatical Year and Jubilee', *EncJud*, XIV cols. 574-77.

Liedke, G., *Gestalt und Bezeichnung alttestamentlicher Rechtssätze. Eine form-geschichtlich-terminologische Studie* (WMANT, 39; Neukirchen–Vluyn: Neukirchener Verlag, 1971).

Lindars, B., 'The Israelite Tribes in Judges', *Studies in the Historical Books of the Old Testament* (ed. J.A. Emerton; VTSup, 30; Leiden: Brill, 1979), pp. 95-112.

Lindenberger, J.M., 'How Much for a Hebrew Slave? The Meaning of *MIŠNEH* in Deuteronomy 15:18', *JBL* 110 (1991), pp. 479-82.

Lindsey, J.E. Jr., 'Vengeance', *IDBSup*, pp. 932-37.

Lipiński, E., ''*Apīrū* et Hébreux', *BO* 42 (1985), pp. 562-67.

—'L' "esclave hébreu" ', *VT* 26 (1975), pp. 120-24.

—'נחל', *ThWAT*, V, cols. 341-60.

—'Textes juridiques et économiques araméens de l'époque sargonide', in *Wirtschaft und Gesellschaft im alten Vorderasien* (ed. J. Harmatta and G. Komoróczy; Budapest: Akadémiai Kiadó, 1976), pp. 373-84.

Liverani, M., 'Communautés de village et palais royal dans la Syrie du IIème Millénaire', *JESHO* 18 (1975), pp. 146-64.

—'Farsi *Habiru*', *VicOr* 2 (1979), pp. 65-77.

—'Il fuoruscitismo in Siria nella tarda età del bronzo', *RevSI* 77 (1965), pp. 315-36.

—'Review of R. de Vaux, History of Ancient Israel I-II', *OrAnt* 15 (1976), pp. 145-59.

Loewenstamm, S.E., 'The Phrase "X (or) X plus one" in Biblical and Old Oriental Laws', *Bib* 53 (1972), p. 543.

—'Exodus XXI 22–25', *VT* 27 (1977), pp. 352-60.

—'נחלה', *Encyclopedia Biblica: Thesaurus Rerum Biblicarum Alphabetico Ordine Digestus*, XIX Hebrew (ed. H. Tadmor; Jerusalem: Bialik Institute, 1968), cols. 815-16.

Lohfink, N., 'The Kingdom of God and the Economy in the Bible', *Comm* 13 (1986), pp. 216-31.

—'Warum wir weiter nach Israel's Anfängen fragen müssen', *DZZ* 30 (1985), pp. 173-79.

—'חרם', *ThWAT*, III, cols. 123-28, *TDOT*, V, pp. 114-18.

Löhr, M., *Das Asylwesen im Alten Testament* (Halle, 1930).

Lohse, E. Σαββατον', *TDNT*, VII, pp. 2-3.

Loretz, O. 'Ex 21,6; 22,8 und angebliche Nuzi-Parallelen', *Bib* 41 (1960), pp. 167-75.

—*Habiru-Hebräer: Eine soziolinguistische Studie über die Herkunft des Gentiliciums 'bri vom Appellativum habiru* (BZAW, 160; Berlin: de Gruyter, 1984).

—'Die hebraïschen Termini *ḤPŠJ* "Freigelassen, Freigellassner" und *ḤPŠH* "Freilassung" ', *UF* 9 (1977), pp. 163-67.

—'Zu LÚ.MEŠ SA.GAZ.ZA *a-bu-ur-ra* in den Briefen vom *Tell Ka–mid el-Lo–z*', *UF* 6 (1974), p. 486.

—'Die prophetische Kritik des Rentenkapitalismus', *UF* 7 (1975), pp. 271-78.

—'Ugaritisch—Hebräisch *ḤB/PṬ, BT ḤpṭT — ḤPŠJ, BJT ḤḤPŠJ/WT*, *UF* 8 (1976), pp. 129-31.

Lowery, R.H., *The Reforming Kings: Cult and Society in First Temple Judah* (JSOTSup, 120; Sheffield: JSOT Press, 1991).

Luke, J.T., '"Your Father Was an Amorite" (Ezek 16:3, 45): An Essay on the Amorite Problem in OT Traditions', in *The Quest for the Kingdom of God: Studies in Honor of G.E. Mendenhall* (ed. H.B. Huffmon, F.A. Spina and A.R.W. Green; Winona Lake, IN: Eisenbrauns, 1983), pp. 221-37.

Maarsingh, B., *Onderzoek naar de ethiek van de wetten in Deuteronomium* (J.M. van Amstel, 1961).

MacKenzie, R.A.F., 'The Formal Aspect of Ancient Near Eastern Law', in *The Seed of Wisdom* (ed. W.S. McCullough; Toronto: University of Toronto Press, 1964), pp. 31-44.

Malamat, A., 'Kingship and Council in Israel and Sumer: A Parallel', *JNES* 22 (1963), pp. 247-53.

—'Mari and the Bible: Some Patterns of Tribal Organization and Institutions', *JAOS* 82 (1962), pp. 143-50.

—'Mari and Early Israel', in *Biblical Archaeology Today: Proceedings of the International Congress on Biblical Archaeology, Jerusalem, April 1984* (ed. J. Amitai; Jerusalem: Israel Exploration Society, 1985), pp. 235-43.

—'Pre-Monarchical Social Institutions in Israel in the Light of Mari', in *Congress Volume, Jerusalem 1986* (ed. J.A. Emerton; VTSup, 40; Leiden: Brill, 1988), pp. 165-76.

—'The Proto-History of Israel: A Study in Method', in *The Word of the Lord Shall Go Forth. Essays in Honor of David Noel Freedman in Celebration of his Sixtieth Birthday* (ed. C.L. Meyers and M. O'Connor; ASORSVS, 1; Winona Lake, IN: Eisenbrauns, 1983), pp. 303-13.

—'Tribal Societies: Biblical Geneologies and African Lineage Systems', *Archives européenes de Sociologie* 14 (1973), pp. 126-36.

Martin-Archard, R., 'גר', *Theologisches Handwörterbuch zum Alten Testament*, I (eds. E. Jenni and C. Westermann; Munich: Chr. Kaiser Verlag, 1978), cols. 409-12.

Mayes, A.D.H. *Deuteronomy* (NCBC; Grand Rapids: Eerdmans; London: Marshall, Morgan & Scott Publishers, 1979).

Mays, J., *Amos* (OTL; Philadelphia: Westminster Press, 1969).

Mazar, A. 'The Israelite Settlement in Canaan in the Light of Archaeological Excavations', in *Biblical Archaeology Today: Proceedings of the International Congress on Biblical Archaeology Jerusalem, April 1984* (ed. J. Amitai; Jerusalem: Israel Exploration Society, 1985), pp. 61-71.

Mazar, B., 'The Cities of the Priests and of the Levites', in *Congress Volume* (VTSup, 7; Leiden: Brill, 1957), pp. 193-205.

McCarter, P.K. Jr., *I Samuel: A New Translation with Introduction, Notes and Commentary* (AB; Garden City, NY: Doubleday & Co, 1980).

McCarthy, D.J., *Old Testament Covenant: A Survey of Current Opinions* (Growing Problems in Theology; Oxford: Basil Blackwell, 1972).

—*Treaty and Covenant: A Study in Form in the Ancient Oriental Documents and the Old Testament* (AnBib, 21; Rome: Pontifical Biblical Institute, 1963).

McConville, J.G., *Law and Theology in Deuteronomy* (JSOTSup, 33; Sheffield: JSOT Press, 1984).

McKeating, H., 'The Development of the Law of Homicide in Ancient Israel', *VT* 25 (1975), pp. 46-68.

—'Vengeance is Mine: A Study of the Pursuit of Vengeance in the Old Testament', *ExpTim* 74 (1962–63), pp. 239-45.

McKenzie, J.L. 'The Elders in the Old Testament', *Bib* 40 (1959), pp. 522-40.

—'The Sack of Israel', in *The Quest for the Kingdom of God: Studies in Honor of G.E. Mendenhall* (ed. H.B. Huffmon, F.A. Spina and A.R.W. Green; Winona Lake, IN: Eisenbrauns, 1983), pp. 25-34.

McNeile, A.H., *The Book of Exodus: With Introduction and Notes. With Commentary* (London: Methuen, 1908).

Meek, T.J., 'A New Interpretation of the Code of Hammurabi §§117-119', *JNES* 7 (1948), pp. 180-83.

Meissner, B., *Babylonien und Assyrien* II (Heidelberg, 1925).

Melikichvili, G.A., 'Quelques aspects du régime socio-économique des sociétés anciennes du Proche-Orient', in *Wirtschaft und Gesellschaft im alten Vorderasien* (ed. J. Harmatta and G. Komoróczy; Budapest: Akadémiai Kiadó, 1976), pp. 79-90.

Mendelsohn, I., 'The Canaanite Term for "Free Proletarian" ', *BASOR* 83 (1941), pp. 36-39.

—'The Conditional Sale into Slavery of Free-Born Daughters in Nuzi and the Law of Exodus 21:7-11', *JAOS* 55 (1935), pp. 190-95.

—'On Corvée Labor in Ancient Canaan and Israel', *BASOR* 167 (1962), pp. 31-35.

—'New Light on the Ḫupšu', *BASOR* 139 (1955), pp. 9-11.

—*Slavery in the Ancient Near East: A Comparative Study of Slavery in Babylonia, Assyria, Syria, and Palestine from the Middle of the Third Millennium to the End of the First Millennium* (New York: Oxford University Press, 1949).

—'Slavery in the Old Testament', *IDB*, IV, pp. 383-91.

Mendenhall, G.E., 'Ancient Israel's Hyphenated History', in *Palestine in Transition: The Emergence of Ancient Israel* (ed. D.N. Freedman and D.F. Graf; SWBAS, 2; Sheffield: Almond Press, 1983), pp. 95-104.

—'Ancient Oriental and Biblical Law', *BA* 17 (1954), pp. 26-46.

—'The Census Lists of Numbers 1 and 26', *JBL* 77 (1958), pp. 52-66.

—'Covenant Forms in Israelite Tradition', *BA* 17 (1954), pp. 50-76.

—'God of Vengeance, Shine Forth', *WB* 45 (1948), pp. 37-42.

—'The Hebrew Conquest of Palestine', in *Biblical Archaeology Reader*, III (ed. D.N. Freedman and F. Campbell; Garden City, NY: Doubleday, 1970), pp. 100-120.

—*The Tenth Generation: The Origins of the Biblical Tradition* (Baltimore: The John Hopkins University Press, 1973).

Menes, A., *Die vorexilischen Gesetze Israels im Zusammenhang seiner kulturgeschichtlichen Entwicklung* (BZAW, 50; Giessen, 1928).

Merendino, R.P., *Das deuteronomische Gesetz: Eine literarkritische gattungs- und überlieferungsgeschichtliche Untersuchung zu Dt 12-16* (BBB, 31; Bonn, 1969).

Merz, E., *Die Blutrache bei den Israeliten* (Leipzig, 1916).

Mettinger, T.D.N., *Solomonic State Officials* (ConBot, 5; Lund, 1971).

Micklem, N. 'Leviticus', in *The Interpreter's Bible*, II (New York: Abingdon Press, 1952), pp. 1-134.

Middleton, J., and D. Tait, 'Introduction', in *Tribes without Rulers* (ed. J. Middleton and D. Tait; London: Routledge & Kegan Paul, 1958), pp. 1-31.

Miles, J., and O.R. Gurney, 'The Laws of Eshnunna', *ArOr* 17 (1949) pp. 174-88.

Milgrom, J., 'The Cultic מנה and its Influence in Psalms and Job', in *Studies in Cultic Theology and Terminology* (SJLA, 36; Leiden: Brill, 1983), pp. 122-31.

—'The Levitical Town: An Exercise in Realistic Planning', *JJS* 33 (1982), pp. 185-88.

—'The Paradox of the Red Cow (NUM. XIX)', *VT* 31 (1983), pp. 62-72 = *Studies in Cultic Theology and Terminology* (SJLA, 36; Leiden: Brill, 1983), pp. 85-95.

—'The Priestly Terminology and the Political and Social Structure of Pre-Monarchic Israel', *JQR* 69 (1983), pp. 65-81 = *Studies in Cultic Theology and Terminology* (SJLA, 36; Leiden: Brill, 1983), pp. 1-17.

—'You Shall not Boil a Kid in its Mother's Milk', *BibRev* 1 (1985), pp. 48-55.

Miller, J.M., 'Israelite History', in *The Hebrew Bible and its Modern Interpreters* (ed. D.A. Knight and G.M. Tucker; SBLI; Philadelphia: Fortress Press; Chico, CA: Scholars Press, 1985), pp. 1-30.

—'The Israelite Occupation of Canaan', in *Israelite and Judaean History* (OTL; ed. J.H. Hayes and J.M. Miller; London: SCM Press, 1977), pp. 213-79.

Moore, G.F., *Judges* (ICC; Edinburgh: T. & T. Clark, 1895).

Moran, W.L., *Les Lettres d'El-Amarna* (LAPO; Paris: Cerf, 1987).

Morgenstern, J., 'Covenant Code II', *HUCA* 7 (1930), pp. 19-258.

—'Jubilee, Year of', *IDB*, III, pp. 1001-1002.

Morrison, M.A., 'The Jacob and Laban Narrative in Light of Near Eastern Sources', *BA* 46 (1983), pp. 155-64.

Muilenburg, J., 'Form Criticism and Beyond', *JBL* 88 (1969), pp. 1-18.

Müller, M. 'Sozial- und wirtschaftspolitische Erlässe im Lande Arrapha', in *Beiträge zur sozialen Struktur des Alten Vorderasien* (ed. H. Klengel; SGKAO, 1; Berlin: Akademie-Verlag, 1971), pp. 53-60.

Murphy, J.G., *A Critical and Exegetical Commentary on the Book of Exodus* (Andover, MA: Waren F. Draper, 1868).

Na'aman, N., '*Habiru* and Hebrews: The Transfer of a Social Term to the Literary Sphere', *JNES* 45 (1986), pp. 271-88.

—'The List of David's Officers (*šālišīm*)', *VT* 38 (1988), pp. 71-79.

Neufeld, E., 'The Emergence of a Royal-Urban Society in Ancient Israel', *HUCA* 31 (1960), pp. 31-53.

—*The Hittite Laws* (London: Luzac, 1951).

—'Inalienability of Mobile and Immobile Pledges in the Laws of the Bible', *RIDA* 9 (1962), pp. 33-44.

—'Socio-Economic Background of *Yo–be–l* and *Šemiṭṭā*', *RSO* 33 (1958), pp. 53-124.

Newman, K.S., *Law and Economic Organization: A Comparative Study of Pre-industrial Societies* (Cambridge: Cambridge University Press, 1983).

Nicholson, E.W., *Deuteronomy and Tradition* (Oxford: Basil Blackwell, 1967).

Nielsen, E., *The Ten Commandments in New Perspective* (SBTSS, 7; London: SCM Press, 1968).

Nieuwenhuijze, C.A.O. van, *Sociology of the Middle East: A Stocktaking and Interpretation* (SPSME, 1; Leiden: Brill, 1971).

Nissen, H.J., *The Early History of the Ancient Near East, 9000–2000 BC.* (trans. E. Lutzeier; Chicago: University of Chicago Press, 1988).

—'Zur Frage der Arbeitsorganisation in Babylonien wärhend der Späturuk-Zeit', in *Wirtschaft und Gesellschaft im alten Vorderasien* (ed. J. Harmatta and G. Komoróczy; Budapest: Akadémiai Kiadó, 1976), pp. 5-14.

Nöldeke, T., 'Review of R. Smith's *Kinship and Marriage*', *ZDMG* 40 (1886), pp .158, 175-76.

Noordtzij, A., *Leviticus* (BSC; Grand Rapids: Zondervan, 1982).

—*Numbers* (BSC; Grand Rapids: Zondervan, 1983).

North, R., 'דרור', *TDOT*, III, pp. 265-69.

—'Flesh, Covering, and Response, Ex. xxi 10', *VT* 5 (1955), pp. 204-206.

—'מס', *ThWAT*, IV, cols. 1006-1009.

—*Sociology of the Biblical Jubilee* (AnBib, 4; Rome: Pontifical Biblical Institute, 1954).

—'YÂD in the Shemitta-Law', *VT* 4 (1954), pp. 196-99.

—'יובל', *ThWAT*, III, cols. 554-59.

Noth, M., *Das Buch Josua* (HKAT I, 7; Tübingen, 1953).

—*Exodus: A Commentary* (OTL; London: SCM Press, 1962).

—*The History of Israel* (Oxford: Basil Blackwell, 1960).

—*Könige I: Teilband* (BKAT, 9.1; Neukirchen–Vluyn: Neukirchener Verlag, 1968).

—*Leviticus* (OTL; Philadelphia: Westminster Press, 1977).

—*Das System der zwölf Stämme Israel* (BWANT, IV; Stuttgart, 1930).

Oded, B., *Mass Deportations and Deportees in the Neo-Assyrian Empire* (Wiesbaden: Dr Ludwig Reichert, 1979).

Oelsner, J., 'Neue Daten zur sozialen und wirtschaftlichen Situation Nuppurs in altbabylonischen Zeit', in *Wirtschaft und Gesellschaft im alten Vorderasien* (ed. J. Harmatta and G. Komoróczy; Budapest: Akadémiai Kiadó, 1976), pp. 259-66.

Oestreicher, T., *Das deuteronomische Grundgesetz* (Gütersloh Güthersloher Verlagshaus, 1923).

Olivier, H., 'The Effectiveness of the Old Babylonian *Mešarum* Decree', *JNSL* 12 (1984), pp. 107-13.

Olson, D.T., *The Death of the Old and the Birth of the New. The Framework of the Book of Numbers and the Pentateuch* (BJS, 71; Chico, CA: Scholars Press, 1985).

Oppenheim, A.L., *Ancient Mesopotamia: A Portrait of a Dead Civilization* (Chicago: University of Chicago Press, rev. edn, 1977).

—'A Bird's Eye View of Mesopotamian Economic History', in *Trade and Market in the Early Empires* (ed. K. Polanyi; Glencoe, 1957), pp. 27-37.

—'Neo-Assyrian and Neo-Babylonian Empires', in *Propaganda and Communication in World History. I. The Symbolic Instrument in Early Times* (ed. H.D. Lasswell, D. Lerner and H. Speier; Honolulu: The University Press of Hawaii, 1979), pp. 111-44.

Otto, E., *Rechtgeschichte der Redaktionen im Kodex Eshnunna und in 'Bundesbuch'* (OBO, 85; Göttingen: Vandenhoeck & Ruprecht, 1989).

—*Wandel der Rechtbegründungen in der Gesellschaftsgeschichte des antiken Israel: Eine Rechtsgeschichte des 'Bundesbuches' Ex xx, 22-xxiii, 13* (StudBib, 3; Leiden: Brill, 1988).

Owen, D.I., 'Death for Default', *MCAAS* 19 (1977), pp. 159-61.

Patai, R., 'The Structure of Endogamous Unilineal Descent Groups', *SJA* 21 (1965), pp. 325-50.

Patrick, D., 'Casuistic Law Governing Primary Rights and Duties', *JBL* 92 (1973), pp. 180-84.

—*Old Testament Law* (London: SCM Press, 1985).

Paul, S.M., *Studies in the Book of the Covenant in the Light of Cuneiform and Biblical Law* (VTSup, 18; Leiden: Brill, 1970).

Pedersen, J., *Israel: Its Life and Culture*, I–II (London: Oxford University Press, 1926).

Peterson, J.L., 'A Topographical Surface Survey of the Levitical Cities of Joshua 21 and Chronicles 6' (PhD dissertation; Evanston, Illinois: Chicago Institute for Advanced Theological Studies and Seabury-Western Theological Seminary, 1977).

Petschow, H., 'Gesetze', *Reallexikon der Assyriologie*, III (ed. G. Ebeling and M. Meissner; Berlin, 1970), cols. 269-76.

—*Neubabylonisches Pfandrecht* (ASAW, 48; Berlin: Akademie Verlag, 1956).

—'Zur "Systematik" in den Gesetzen von Eschunna', in *Symbolae juridicae et historicae M. David dedicatae*, II (ed. J.A. Ankum, R. Feenstra and W.F. Leemans; IOA; Leiden: Brill, 1968), pp. 131-43.

—'Zur Systematik und Gesetzestechnik im Codex Hammurabi', *ZA* 23 (1965), pp. 146-72.

Pfeiffer, R.H., and E.A. Speiser, *One Hundred New Selected Nuzi Texts* (AASOR, 16; New Haven: American Schools of Oriental Research, 1936).

Phillips, A., *Ancient Israel's Criminal Law: A New Approach to the Decalogue* (Oxford: Basil Blackwell, 1970).

—'Another Look at Murder', *JJS* 28 (1977), pp. 105-26.

—'The Decalogue —Ancient Israel's Criminal Law', *JJS* 34 (1983), pp. 1-20.

—*Deuteronomy* (Cambridge: Cambridge University Press, 1973).

—'Double for all her Sins', *ZAW* 82 (1982), pp. 130-32.

—'The Laws of Slavery: Exodus 21:2-11', *JSOT* 30 (1984), pp. 51-66.

—'Prophecy and Law', in *Israel's Prophetic Heritage: Essays in Honour of Peter R. Ackroyd* (ed. R. Coggins, A. Phillips and M. Knibb; Cambridge: Cambridge University Press, 1982), pp. 217-32.

—'Some Aspects of Family Law in Pre-Exilic Israel', *VT* 23 (1973), pp. 349-61.

Pitard, W.T., 'Amarna *ekēmu* and Hebrew *nāqam*', *Maarav* 3 (1982), pp. 5-25.

Ploeg, J.P.M. van der, 'Slavery in the Old Testament', in *Congress Volume, Uppsala 1971* (VTSup, 22; Leiden: Brill, 1972), pp. 72-87.

—'Studies in Hebrew Law, II: The Style of the Laws', *CBQ* 12 (1950), pp. 416-27.

—'Studies in Hebrew Law, III', *CBQ* 13 (1951), pp. 28-43.

Polzin, R., *Moses and the Deuteronomist: A Literary Study of the Deuteronomic History. Part One. Deuteronomy, Joshua, Judges* (New York: Seabury, 1980).

Porter, J.R., *The Extended Family in the Old Testament* (OPSEA, 6; London: Edutext, 1967).

—*Leviticus* (CBC; Cambridge: Cambridge University Press, 1976).

Pošpisil, L., 'Legal Levels and Multiplicity of Legal Systems in Human Societies', *JCR* 11 (1967), pp. 2-26.

Postgate, J.N., *Fifty Neo-Assyrian Legal Documents* (Warminster: Aris & Phillips, 1976).

—*The Governor's Palace Archive* (London: The British School of Archaeology in Iraq, 1973).

—'*ILKU* and Land Tenure in the Middle Assyrian Kingdom—A Second Attempt', in *Societies and Languages of the Ancient Near East in Honour of I.M. Diakonoff* (ed. M.A. Dandamayev, I. Gerschevitch, H. Klengel, G. Komoróczy, M.T. Larsen and J.N. Postgate; Warminster: Aris & Phillips, 1982), pp. 304-13.

—'Some Remarks on Conditions in the Assyrian Countryside', *JESHO* 17 (1974), pp. 225-43.

Praag, A. van., *Droit Matrimonial Assyro-Babylonien* (Amsterdam, 1945).

Preuss, H.D., *Deuteronomium* (EF, 164; Darmstadt, 1982).

Prévost, M.H., 'L'Oppression dans la Bible', in *Mélanges à la Mémoire de Marcel-Henri Prévost: Droit biblique- Interprétation rabbinique Communautés et Société* (PULII; Paris: Presses Universitaires de France, 1982), pp. 3-16.

Rabinowitz, J.J., 'Manumission of Slaves in Roman Law and Oriental Law', *JNES* 20 (1960), pp. 42-45.

Rad, G. von, *Deuteronomy: A Commentary* (OTL; Philadelphia: Westminster Press, 1966).

—*Old Testament Theology*, I-II (New York: Harper & Row, 1965).

—'The Promised Land and Yahweh's Land in the Hexateuch', in *The Problem of the Hexateuch and Other Essays* (New York: McGraw-Hill, 1966), pp. 79-93.

—*Studies in Deuteronomy* (SBT, 9; London: SCM Press, 1953).

Rainey, A.F., 'Compulsory Labour Gangs in Ancient Israel', *IEJ* 20 (1970), pp. 191-202.

—'Family', *EncJud*, VI, cols. 1164-72.

—'Institutions: Family, Civil, and Military', in *Ras Shamra Parallels: Texts from Ugarit and the Hebrew Bible*, II (ed. L.R. Fisher, D.E. Smith and S. Rummel; AnOr, 50; Rome: Biblical Institute Press, 1975), pp. 69-107.

—'מס-עבד', *Encyclopedia Biblica: Thesaurus Rerum Biblicarum Alphabetico Ordine Digestus*, V (Hebrew) (ed. H. Tadmor; Jerusalem: Bialik Institute, 1968), cols. 55-56.

—'Rainey's Challenge', *BARev* 17 (1991), pp. 56-60, 93.

Ramban [Nachmanides], *Commentary on the Torah*, 1-5 (trans. Rabbi Dr Charles B. Chavel; New York: Shilo Publishing House, 1971–76).

Rapaport, I., 'The Origins of Hebrew Law', *PEQ* 73 (1941), pp. 158-67.

Rashi, *Pentateuch with Targum Onkelos, Haphtaroth and Rashi's Commentary*, 1-5 (trans. Rev. M. Rosenbaum, Dr. A.M. Silbermann; Jerusalem: Published by the Silbermann Family, 1933).

Redford, D.B., 'Studies in Relations between Palestine and Egypt during the First Millennium BC: I: The Taxation Systems of Solomon', in *Studies on the Ancient Palestinian World Presented to Professor F.V. Winnett on the Occasion of his Retirement 1 July 1971* (ed. J.W. Wevers and D.B. Redford; TSTS, 2; Toronto: University of Toronto Press, 1972), pp. 141-56.

Redman, C.L., *The Rise of Civilization. From Early Farmers to Urban Society in the Ancient Near East* (San Francisco: W.H. Freeman, 1978).

Reider, J., *Deuteronomy with Commentary* (Philadelphia: The Jewish Publication Society of America, 1937).

Rendtorff, R. ' "Covenant" as a Structuring Concept in Genesis and Exodus', *JBL* 108 (1989), pp. 385-93.

—*The Old Testament: An Introduction* (London: SCM Press, 1985).

Renger, J., 'Flucht as soziales Problem in der altbabylonischen Gesellschaft', in *Gesellschaftsklassen im Alten Zweistromland und den angrenzenden Gebeiten -XVIII: Recontre assyriologique internationale, München, 29. Juni bis 3. Juli 1970* (ed. D.O. Edzard; BAWPHKA, 75; Munich: Verlag der Bayerischen Akademie der Wissenschaften, 1972), pp. 167-82.

—'Interaction of Temple, Palace, and "Private Enterprise" ', in *State and Temple Economy in the Ancient Near East*. I, II. *Proceedings of the International Conference Organized by the Katholieke Iniversiteit Leuven from the 10th to the 14th of April 1978* (ed. E. Lipiński; OLA, 5; Leuven: Dept. Oriëntalistiek, 1979), pp. 249-56.

—'Wrongdoing and its Sanctions: On "Criminal" and "Civil" Law in the Old Babylonian Period', *JESHO* 20 (1977), pp. 65-77.

Reventlow, H.G., *Gebot und Predigt im Dekalog* (Gütersloh: Gütersloher Verlagshaus, 1962).

—*Das Heiligkeitsgesetz formgeschichtlich untersuch* (WMANT, 6; Neukirchen–Vluyn Neukirchener Verlag, 1961).

Reviv, H., *The Elders in Ancient Israel: A Study of a Biblical Institution* (TextsS; Jerusalem: Magnes; Hebrew University Press, 1983).

—'History', *EncJud*, VIII, cols. 570-615.

—'Kidinnu: Observations on Privileges of Mesopotamian Cities', *JESHO* 31 (1988), pp. 286-98.

—'סכיר', *Encyclopedia Biblica: Thesaurus Rerum Biblicarum Alphabetico Ordine Digestus*, VIII (Hebrew) (ed. H. Tadmor; Jerusalem: Bialik Institute, 1982), cols. 285-87.

Richard, S., 'The Early Bronze Age: The Rise and Collapse of Urbanism', *BA* 50 (1987), pp. 22-43.

Ridderbos, J., *Deuteronomy* (BSC; Grand Rapids: Zondervan, 1984).

Riemschneider, K.K., *Lehrbuch des Akkadischen* (Leipzig: VEB Verlag Enzyklopädie, 1984).

Riesener, I., *Der Stamm scg im Alten Testament: Eine Wortuntersuchung unter Berücksichtigung neuerer sprachwissenschaftlicher Methoden* (BZAW, 149; Berlin: de Gruyter, 1979).

Rietzschel, G., 'Zu Jdc 5,8', *ZAW* 81 (1969), pp. 236-37.

Ringgren, H., 'Israel's Place Among the Religions of the Ancient Near East', in *Studies in the Religion of Ancient Israel* (VTSup, 23; Leiden: Brill, 1972), pp. 1-8.

Roberts, J.J.M., 'Ancient Near Eastern Environment', in *The Hebrew Bible and its Modern Interpreters* (ed. D.A. Knight and G.M. Tucker; SBLI; Philadelphia: Fortress Press; Chico, CA: Scholars Press, 1985), pp. 75-121.

Robinson, G., *The Origin and Development of the Old Testament Sabbath* (Beiträge zur biblischen Exegese und Theologie, 21; New York: Peter Lang, 1988).

Rofé, A., 'The History of the Cities of Refuge in Biblical Law', in *Studies in Bible 1986* (ed. S. Japhet; Scripta Hierosolymitana, 31; Jerusalem: Magnes, 1986), pp. 205-39.

—'The Vineyard of Naboth: the Origin and Message of the Story', *VT* 38 (1988), pp. 89-104.

Rogerson, J.W., *Anthropology and the Old Testament* (GPIT; Oxford: Basil Blackwell, 1978).

—'The Use of Sociology in Old Testament Studies', in *Congress Volume, Salamanca 1983* (ed. J.A. Emerton; VTSup 36; Leiden: Brill, 1985), pp. 245-56.

—'Was Early Israel a Segmentary Society?', *JSOT* 36 (1986), pp. 17-26.

Rösel, H.N., 'Die Entstehung Israels, Evolution oder Revolution?', *BN* 59 (1991), pp. 28-32.

Rosen, B.L., 'Some Notes on Eshnunna Laws 20 and 21 and a Legal Reform in the Law of Hammurabi', *RA* 71 (1977), pp. 35-38.

Roth, M.T., 'Homicide in the Neo-Assyrian Period', in *Language, Literature, and History: Philological and Historical Studies Presented to Erica Reiner* (ed. F. Rochberg-Halton; AOS, 67; New Haven: American Oriental Society, 1987), pp. 351-65.

Rowley, H.H., *From Joseph to Joshua: Biblical Traditions in the Light of Archaeology* (SLBA, 1948; London: The British Academy, 1950).

—'Moses and the Decalogue', *BJRL* 34 (1951–52), pp. 81-118.

—*The Worship of Israel* (London: SCM Press, 1967).

Rowton, M.B., 'Dimorphic Structure and the Parasocial Element', *JNES* 36 (1977), pp. 181-98.

—'Dimorphic Structure and the Problem of the *'Apiru-'Ibrîm'*, *JNES* 35 (1976), pp. 13-20.

—'Dimorphic Structure and Topology', *OrAnt* 15 (1976), pp. 17-31.

—'Enclosed Nomadism', *JESHO* 17 (1974), pp. 1-30.

—'The Topological Factor in the *Hapiru* Problem', in *Studies in Honor of Benno Landsberger on his Seventieth Birthday, April 21, 1965* (The Oriental Institute of the University of Chicago Assyriological Studies, 16; Chicago: University of Chicago Press, 1965), pp. 375-87.

Rudolph, W., *Jeremia* (HKAT, 1.12; 3rd edn, 1968).

Saalschütz, J.L., *Das Mosaische Recht nebst den vervollständigenden thalmudisch-rabbinischen Bestimmungen für Bibelforscher, Juristen und Staatsmänner* (Berlin: Carl Heymann, 3rd edn, 1853).

Saarisalo, A., 'New Kirkuk Documents Relating to Slaves', *StudOr* 5 (1934), pp. 61-65.

Safrai, S., 'The Practical Implementation of the Sabbatical Year After the Restitution of the Second Temple' (Hebrew), *Tarbiz* 35 (1965–66), pp. 304-28; 36 (1966–67), pp. 1-21.

Saggs, H.W.F., *The Might That Was Assyria* (Sidgwick & Jackson Great Civilizations Series; London: Sidgwick & Jackson, 1984).

San Nicoló, M., 'Das Gesetzbuch *Lipit-Ištar* II, Rechtsgeschichtliches zum Gesetzbuch', *Or* 19 (1950), pp. 111-18.

Sarna, N., 'Zedekiah's Emancipation of Slaves and the Sabbatical Year', in *Orient and Occident: Essays Presented to Cyrus H. Gordon on the Occasion of his Sixty-fifth Birthday* (ed. H.A. Hoffner Jr; AOAT, 22; Neukirchen–Vluyn: Verlag Butzon & Bencker Kevelaer, 1973), pp. 143-49.

Sasson, J.M., 'On Choosing Models for Recreating Israelite Pre-Monarchic History', *JSOT* 21 (1981), pp. 3-24.

388 Debt-Slavery in Israel and the Ancient Near East

390   Debt-Slavery in Israel and the Ancient Near East

Sauer, G., 'קנא', *Theologisches Handwörterbuch zum Alten Testament*, II (ed. E. Jenni and C. Westermann; Munich: Chr. Kaiser Verlag, 1976), cols. 106-109.

Schaeffer, H., *Hebrew Tribal Economy and the Jubilee as Illustrated in Semitic and Indo-European Village Communities* (Leipzig: Hinrichs, 1922).

—*The Social Legislation of the Primitive Semites* (repr. New York: Benjamin Blom, [1915]).

Scharbert, J., '*Bēyt 'āb* als soziologische Größe im Alten Testament', in *Von Kanaan bis Kerala: Festschrift für Prof. Mag. Dr. Dr. J.P.M. van der Ploeg O.P* (ed. W.C. Delsman, J.T. Nelis, J.R.T.M. Peters, W.H.Ph. Römer and A.S. van der Woude; AOT, 211; Neukirchen–Vluyn: Verlag Butson & Berker Kevelaer, 1982), pp. 213-38.

Schenker, A., 'Affranchissement d'une esclave selon Ex 21,7-11', *Bib* 69 (1988), pp. 547-56.

Schmid, H., *Die Gestalt des Mose: Probleme alttestamentlicher Forschung unter Berücksichtigung der Pentateuchkrise* (EF, 237; Darmstadt: Wissenschaftliche Buchgesellschaft, 1986).

Schmökel, H., ' "Biblische Du sollst"-Gebote und ihr historischer Ort', *ZSSR* 36 (1950), pp. 365-90.

Schneider, A., *Die Anfänge der Kulturwirtschaft; die sumerische Tempelstadt* (Essen, 1920).

Schultz, W., *Das Deuteronomium erklärt* (Berlin: G. Schlawitz, 1859).

Schulz, H., *Das Todesrecht im Alten Testament: Studien zur Rechtsform der Mot-jumat-Sätze* (BZAW, 114; Berlin: Töpelmann, 1969).

Schwartz, B.J., 'A Literary Study of the Slave-Girl Pericope- Leviticus 19:20-22', in *Studies in Bible 1986* (ed. S. Japhet; Scripta Hierosolymitana, 31; Jerusalem: Magnes, 1986), pp. 241-55.

Seagle, W., *Quest for Law* (New York: Knopf, 1941).

Seitz, G., *Redaktionsgeschichtliche Studien zum Deuteronomium* (BWANT, 13; Stuttgart: Kohlhammer, 1971).

Selman, M.J., 'Comparative Customs and the Patriarchal Age', in *Essays on the Patriarchal Narratives* (ed. A.R. Millard and D.J. Wiseman; Leicester: Inter-Varsity Press, 1980), pp. 93-138.

Selms, A. van, 'Jubilee, year of', *IDBSup*, pp. 496-98.

—'The Year of the Jubilee, In and Outside the Pentateuch', *OTWSA* 17–18 (1974–75), pp. 74-85.

Service, E.R., 'Classical and Modern Theories of the Origin of Government', in *Origins of the State: The Anthropology of Political Evolution* (ed. R. Cohen and E.R. Service; Philadelphia: Institute for the Study of Human Issues, 1978), pp. 21-34.

—*Origins of the State and Civilization* (New York: Norton, 1975).

—*Primitive Social Organization: An Evolutionary Perspective* (New York: Random House, 1962).

Seters, J. Van, *Abraham in History and Tradition* (New Haven: Yale University Press, 1975).

—'The Population of Iron Age Palestine in the Light of a Sample Analysis of Urban Plans, Areas, and Population Density', *BASOR* 239 (1980), pp. 25-35.

Seybold, K., 'ירפים', *Theologisches Handwörterbuch zum Alten Testament*, II (ed. E. Jenni and C. Westermann; Munich: Chr. Kaiser Verlag, 1976), cols. 1057-60.

hiloh, Y., 'The Four-Room-House—Its Situation and Function in the Israelite City', *IEJ* 20 (1970), pp. 180-90.

—'The Four-Space House—The Israelite House Type' (Hebrew), *Eretz-Israel* 11 (1973), pp. 277-85.

—'The Population of Iron Age Palestine', *BASOR* 239 (1980), pp. 25-35.

hmidman, H., 'Vengeance', *EncJud*, XVI, cols. 93-94.

icre, J.L., *'Con los Pobres de la Tierra': La justicia social en los profetas de Israel* (Madrid: Ediciones Christiandad, 1984).

iegel, B.J., 'Slavery during the Third Dynasty of Ur', *AA* ns 49/1/2 (1976 [1947]).

—'Some Methodological Considerations for a Comparative Study of Slavery', *AA* ns 49 (1976 [1947]), pp. 357-92.

ilva, M., *Biblical Words and Their Meaning: An Introduction to Lexical Semantics* (Grand Rapids: Zondervan, 1983).

ilver, M., *Economic Structures of the Ancient Near East* (London: Croom Helm, 1985).

—*Prophets and Markets: The Political Economy of Ancient Israel* (SDE; Boston: Kluwer-Nijhoff Publishing, 1983).

immons, S.D. 'Early Old Babylonian Tablets from Harmal and Elsewhere', *JCS* 14 (1960) pp. 75-87.

loan, R.B., Jr, *The Favorable Year of the Lord: A Study of Jubilary Theology in the Gospel of Luke* (Austin, TX: Scholars Press, 1977).

mith, H.P., *The Book of Samuel* (ICC; Edinburgh: T. & T. Clark, 1977).

mith, M.G., 'On Segmentary Lineage Systems', *JRAI* 86 (1956), pp. 39-80.

naith, N.H., *Leviticus and Numbers* (CB; London: Nelson, 1967).

nell, D.C. 'Ledgers and Prices: Ur III Silver Balanced Accounts' (PhD disseration, Yale University, 1975).

oden, W. von., *Herrscher im Alten Orient* (Göttingen, 1954).

—'Kleine Beiträge zum Verständnis der Gesetze Hammurabis und Bilalamas', *ArOr* 17 (1949), pp. 359-73.

oggin, J.A., *A History of Israel: From the Begings to the Bar Kochba Revolt, AD 135* (London: SCM Press, 1985).

—*Judges* (OTL; Philadelphia: Westminster Press, 1981).

ollberger, E., 'Ur-III Society: Some Unanswered Questions', in *Gesellschaftsklassen im Alten Zweistromland und den angrenzenden Gebeiten -XVIII: Recontre assyriologique internationale, München, 29. Juni bis 3. Juli 1970* (ed. D.O. Edzard; BAWPHKA, 75; Munich: Verlag der Bayerischen Akademie der Wissenschaften, 1972), pp. 185-89.

onsino, R., *Motive Clauses in Hebrew Law: Biblical Forms and Near Eastern Parallels* (SBLDS, 45; Chico, CA: Scholars Press, 1980).

oss, N.M., 'Old Testament Law and Economic Society', *JHI* 34 (1973), pp. 323-44.

peiser, E.A., 'Authority and Law in Mesopotamia', *JAOS* 17 (1954), pp. 8-15.

—'Hurrian Participation in the Civilizations of Mesopotamia, Syria, and Palestine', *JWH* 1 (1953), pp. 314-17.

—'Leviticus and the Critics', in *Oriental and Biblical Studies* (Philadelphia: University of Pennsylvania Press, 1967), pp. 123-42.

—*Mesopotamian Origins* (Philadelphia: University of Pennsylvania Press; London: Oxford University Press, 1930).

—'The muskenum', *Or* 27 (1958), pp. 19-28.

—'Nuzi', *IDB*, III, pp. 573-74.

Spina, F.A., 'Israelites as *gērîm*, "Sojourners", in Social and Historical Context', in *The Word of the Lord Shall Go Forth: Essays in Honor of David Noel Freedman i Celebration of His Sixtieth Birthday* (ed. C.L. Meyers and M. O'Connor ASORSVS, 1; Winona Lake, IN: Eisenbrauns, 1983), pp. 321-35.

Stager, L.E., 'Archaeology', *IDBSup*, pp. 11-13.

—'The Archaeology of the Family in Ancient Israel', *BASOR* 260 (1985), pp. 1-35.

—'Merneptah, Israel and the Sea Peoples: New Light on an Old Relief', *Eretz-Israel* 1 (1985), pp. 56-64.

—'Respondents: Session II: Archaeology, History and Bible. The Israelite Settlement i Canaan: A Case Study', in *Biblical Archaeology Today: Proceedings of th International Congress on Biblical Archaeology, Jerusalem, April 1984* (ed.] Amitai; Jerusalem: Israel Exploration Society, 1985), p. 85.

—'The Song of Deborah: Why Some Tribes Answered the Call and Others Did Not' *BARev* 15 (1989), pp. 51-64.

Stamm, J.J., and M.E. Andrew, *The Ten Commandments in Recent Research* (SBTSS, 2 London: SCM Press, 1967).

Steele, F.R., 'Lipit-Ishtar Law Code', *AJA* 51 (1947), pp. 138-64; 52 (1948), pp. 425 50.

Steiner, F., 'Enslavement and the Early Hebrew Lineage System', *Man* 54 (1954) pp. 73-75.

Stephens, F.J., 'Notes on Some Economic Texts of the Time of Urukagina', *RA* 4 (1955), pp. 129-36.

Steuernagel, C., *Deuteronomium und Josua* (HKAT, I.3; Göttingen, 2nd edn, 1923).

Stiebing, W.H., *Out of the Desert? Archaeology and the Exodus/Conquest Narrative* (Buffalo, NY: Prometheus, 1989).

Stol, M., 'A Cadastral Innovation by Hammurabi', in *ZIKIR ŠUMIM: Assyriologica Studies Presented to F.R. Kraus on the Occasion of his Seventieth Birthday* (ed G. van Driel, Th.J.H. Krispijn, M. Stol and K.R. Veenhof; NIVNO, V; Leiden Brill, 1982), pp. 351-58.

—*Studies in Old Babylonian History* (UNHAII, 40; Leiden: Instituut voor het Nabij Oosten Noordeindsplein, 1976).

Stolz, F. von, 'Aspekte religiöser und sozialer Ordnung im alten Israel', *ZEE* 1 (1973), pp. 145-59.

Stroete, G. Te., *Exodus* (DBHOT, I.II; Roermond: J.J. Romen en Zonen, 1966).

Struve, V.V., 'The Problem of the Genesis, Development and Disintegration of th Slave Societies in the Ancient Orient', in *Ancient Mesopotamia Socio-Economi History: A Collection of Studies by Soviet Scholars* (ed. I.M. Diakonoff; USS Academy of Sciences Institute of the Peoples of Asia; Moscow: 'Nauka', 1969) pp. 17-69.

Stulman, L., 'Encroachment in Deuteronomy: An Analysis of the Social World of th D Code', *JBL* 109 (1990), pp. 624-26.

Sturdy, J., *Numbers* (CBC; Cambridge: Cambridge University Press, 1976).

Szlechter, E., 'L'affranchissement en droit suméro-akkadien', *RIDA* 1 (1952) pp. 125-95.

—'Les anciennes codifications en Mésopotamie', *RIDA* 4 (1957), pp. 73-92.

—'Le code de *Lipit-Ištar*', *RA* 51 (1957), pp. 57-82, 177-96; 52 (1957), pp. 74-90.

—'Le code d'Ur-Nammu', *RA* 49 (1955), pp. 169-77.

—'La loi dans la Mésopotamie ancienne', *RIDA* 12 (1965), pp. 55-77.

—'Les lois d'Eshnunna', *RIDA* 25 (1978), pp. 109-219.

—'Nouveaux textes législatifs sumériens', *RA* 61 (1967), pp. 105-26.

—'A propos du code d'Ur-Nammu', *RA* 47 (1953), pp. 1-10.

—'La saisie illégale dans les lois d'*Ešnunna* et dans le code de Hammurabi', in *Studi in Onore di P. De Francisci*, I (Milano, 1956), pp. 271-81.

Taber, C.R., 'Kinship and Family', *IDBSup*, pp. 519-24.

Tadmor, H., '"The People" and the Kingship in Ancient Israel: The Role of the Political Institutions in the Biblical Period', *JWH* 11 (1968), pp. 46-68.

Talmon, S., 'The Biblical Idea of Statehood', in *The Bible World: Essays in Honor of Cyrus H. Gordon* (ed. G. Rendsburg, R. Adler, M. Arfa and N.H. Winter; New York: Ktav, 1980), pp. 239-48.

—'The "Comparative Method" in Biblical Interpretation—Principles and Problems', in *Congress Volume, Göttingen* (VTSup, 29; Leiden: Brill, 1978), pp. 320-56.

—'Kingship and the Ideology of the State', in *King, Cult and Calendar in Ancient Israel: Collected Studies* (Jerusalem: Magnes, 1986), pp. 9-39.

—'The Rule of the King', *King, Cult and Calendar in Ancient Israel: Collected Studies* (Jerusalem: Magnes, 1986), pp. 53-67.

Thiel, W., 'Erwägungen zum Alter des Heiligkeitsgesetzes', *ZAW* 81 (1969), pp. 40-73.

Thompson, J.A., *The Book of Jeremiah* (NICOT; Grand Rapids: Eerdmans, 1980).

—*Deuteronomy: An Introduction and Commentary* (TOTC; Leicester: Inter-Varsity Press, 1974).

Thompson, T.L., 'Historical Notes on "Israel's Conquest of Palestine: A Peasant's Rebellion?" ', *JSOT* 7 (1978), pp. 20-27.

—*The Historicity of the Patriarchal Narratives. The Quest for the Historical Abraham* (BZAW, 133; Berlin: de Gruyter, 1974).

Thurnwald, R., 'Sklave', in *Reallexikon der Vorgeschichte*, XII (ed. M. Ebert; Berlin, 1928), pp. 209-28.

Tsevat, M., 'Alalakhiana', *HUCA* 29 (1958), pp. 109-34.

—'The Biblical Narrative of the Foundation of Kingship in Israel' (Hebrew), *Tarbiz* 36 (1966/67), pp. 261-67.

Turkowski, L., 'Peasant Agriculture in the Judean Hills', *PEQ* 101 (1969), pp. 21-33, 101-12.

Vaux, R. de, *Ancient Israel: Its Life and Institutions* (London: Darton, Longman & Todd, 1961).

—*The Early History of Israel. I. To the Exodus and Covenant of Sinai* (London: Darton, Longman & Todd, 1978).

—'Le problème des Hapiru après quinze années', *JNES* 27 (1968), pp. 221-28.

Veenhof, K.R., 'A Deed of Manumission and Adoption from the Later Old Assyrian Period: Its Writing, Language, and Contents in Comparative Perspective', in *ZIKIR ŠUMIM: Assyriological Studies Presented to F.R. Kraus on the Occasion of his Seventieth Birthday* (ed. G. van Driel, Th.J.H. Krispijn, M. Stol and K.R. Veenhof; NIVNO, V; Leiden: Brill, 1982), pp. 359-85.

—'The Old Assyrian Merchants and their Relations with the Native Population of Anatolia', in *Mesopotamien und seine Nachbarn: Politische und kulturelle*

Wechselbeziehungen im Alten Vorderasien vom 4. bis 1. Jahrtausend v. Chr. Teil 1 & 2 (ed. H.J. Nissen and J. Renger; BBVO, 1; Berlin: Dietrich Reimer Verlag, 1982), pp. 147-60.

Vogelstein, H., *Die Landwirtschaft in Palästina zum Zeit der Misnah* (Berlin: von Mayer & Müller, 1894).

Wacholder, B.Z., 'The Calendar of Sabbatical Cycles during the Second Temple and Early Rabbinic Period', *HUCA* 44 (1973), pp. 153-96.

—'Sabbatical Year', *IDBSup*, pp. 762-63.

Wagner, V., *Rechtssätze in gebundener Sprache und Rechtssatzreihen im israelitischen Recht* (BZAW, 127; Berlin: de Gruyter, 1972).

—'Zur Systematik in dem Codex Ex 21:2-22:16', *ZAW* 81 (1969), pp. 176-82.

Waldow, H.E. von., 'Social Responsibility and Social Structure in Early Isreal', *CBQ* 32 (1970), pp. 182-204.

Ward, E.F., 'Superstition and Judgement: Archaic Methods of Finding a Verdict', *ZAW* 89 (1977), pp. 1-19.

Ward, W.A., 'Two Unrecognized Ḫupšu-Mercenaries in Egyptian Texts', *UF* 12 (1980), pp. 441-42.

Warhaftig, S., 'Labor Law', *EncJud*, X, cols. 1325-30.

Waterman, L., 'Pre-Israelite Laws in the Book of the Covenant', *AJSL* 38 (1921), pp. 36-54.

Weil, H.M., 'Gage et cautionnement dans la Bible', *AHDO* 2 (1938), pp. 171-241.

Weinfeld, M., 'Congregation', *EncJud*, V, cols. 893-95.

—'Cult Centralization in Israel in the Light of a Neo-Babylonian Analogy', *JNES* 23 (1964), pp. 202-12.

—*Deuteronomy and the Deuteronomic School* (Oxford: Oxford University Press, 1972).

—*Getting at the Roots of Wellhausen's Understanding of the Law of Israel on the 100th Anniversary of the Prolegomenon* (Jerusalem: Institute for Advanced Hebrew Studies, 1979).

—' "Justice and Righteousness" in Ancient Israel Against the Background of "Social Reforms" in the Ancient Near East', in *Mesopotamien und seine Nachbarn: Politische und kulturelle Wechselbeziehungen im Alten Vorderasien vom 4. bis 1. Jahrtausend v. Chr. Teil 1 & 2* (ed. H.J Nissen and J. Renger; BBVO, 1; Berlin: Dietrich Reimer Verlag, 1982), pp. 491-519.

—*Justice and Righteousness in Israel and the Nations: Equality and Freedom in Ancient Israel in Light of Social Justice in the Ancient Near East* (Hebrew) (PPFBR; Jerusalem: Magnes, 1985).

—'The Origin of Apodictic Law: An Overlooked Source', *VT* 23 (1973) pp. 63-75.

—'Sabbatical Year and Jubilee in the Pentateuch: Laws and their ancient Near Eastern Background', *The Law in the Bible and in its Environment* (ed. T. Veijola; Publications of the Finnish Exegetical Society, 51; Göttingen: Vandenhoeck & Ruprecht, 1990), pp. 39-62.

Weingreen, J., 'The Concepts of Retaliation and Compensation in Biblical Law', *PRIA* 76 (1976), pp. 1-11.

—'Saul and the *Habirū*', in *Fourth World Congress of Jewish Studies*, I (Jerusalem, 1967), pp 63-66.

Weippert, M., 'Abraham der Hebräer?', *Bib* 52 (1972), pp. 407-32.

—'The Israelite "Conquest" and the Evidence from Transjordan', *Symposia* (ed. F.M. Cross; Cambridge, MA, American Schools of Oriental Research, 1979), pp. 15-34.

—'Remarks on the History and Settlement in Southern Jordan during the Early Iron Age', in *Studies in the History and Archaeology of Jordan*, I (ed. A. Hadidi; Amman: Department of Antiquities, 1982), pp. 153-62.

—*The Settlement of the Israelite Tribes in Palestine* (SBTSS, 21; London: SCM Press, 1971).

Weir, C.H. Mullo, 'Nuzi', in *Archaeology and Old Testament Study* (ed. D.W. Thomas; Oxford: Clarendon Press, 1967), pp. 73-86.

Wellhausen, J., *Prolegomena to the History of Ancient Israel* (Edinburgh: T. & T. Clark, 1885).

Wenham, G.J., *The Book of Leviticus* (NICOT; Grand Rapids: Eerdmans, 1979).

—'Deuteronomy and the Central Sanctuary', *TynBul* 22 (1971), pp. 103-18.

—'Legal Forms in the Book of the Covenant', *TynBul* 22 (1971), pp. 95-102.

—'Leviticus 27:2-8 and the Price of Slaves', *ZAW* 90 (1978), pp. 264-65.

—*Numbers: An Introduction and Commentary* (TOTC; Downers Grove, IL: IVP, 1981).

Wersch, H.J. van, 'The Agricultural Economy', in *The Minnesota Messenia Expedition: Reconstructing a Bronze Age Regional Environment* (ed. W.A. McDonald and G.R. Rapp Jr; Minneapolis: University of Minnesota Press, 1972), pp. 177-87.

Westbrook, R., '1 Samuel 1:8', *JBL* 109 (1990), pp. 14-15.

—'Biblical and Cuneiform Law Codes', *RB* 92 (1985), pp. 247-64.

*—'Jubilee Laws', *ILR* 6 (1971), pp. 209-26.

*—'The Price Factor in the Redemption of Land', *RIDA* 32 (1985–86), pp. 97-127.

—*Property and the Family in Biblical Law* (JSOTSup, 113; Sheffield: JSOT Press, 1991).

*—'Redemption of Land', *ILR* 6 (1971), pp. 367-75.

—*Studies in Biblical and Cuneiform Law* (CahRB, 26; Paris: Gabalda, 1988).

Westhuizen, J.P. van der, 'A Comparative Study of the Related Laws in Babylonian and Biblical Legal Texts (verbal connotations)', *Semitics* 10 (1989), pp. 40-59.

Whitehouse, O.C., 'Servant, Slave, Slavery', *ISBE*, IV, pp. 465-67.

Whitelam, K.W., 'Israel's Traditions of Origin: Reclaiming the Land', *JSOT* 44 (1989), pp. 19-42.

—*The Just King: Monarchical Judicial Authority in Ancient Israel* (JSOTSup, 12; Sheffield: JSOT Press, 1979).

Whybray, R.N., *The Making of the Pentateuch: A Methodological Study* (JSOTSup, 53; Sheffield: JSOT Press, 1987).

Wilcke, C., 'Zu den spät-altbabylonischen Kaufverträgen aus Nordbabylonien', *WO* 8 (1975–76), pp. 254-85.

Willi, T. von, 'Die Freiheit Israels: Philologische Notizen zu den Wurzeln *ḥpš*, '*zb* und *drr*', in *Beiträge zur alttestamentlichen Theologie: Festschrift W. Zimmerli zum 70. Geburtstag* (ed. H. Donner, R. Hanhart and R. Smend; Göttingen: Vandenhoeck & Ruprecht, 1977), pp. 531-46.

Williamson, H.G.M., *Ezra and Nehemiah* (WBC, 16; Waco, TX: Word, 1985).

Willis, J.T., 'Old Testament Foundations of Social Justice', *ResQ* 18 (1975), pp. 65-87.

Wilson, R.R., 'The City in the Old Testament', in *Civitas: Religious Interpretations of the City* (ed. P.S. Hawkins; SPSH; Atlanta: Scholars Press, 1986), pp. 3-14.

—'Enforcing the Covenant: The Mechanisms of Judicial Authority in Early Israel', in *The Quest for the Kingdom of God: Studies in Honor of G.E. Mendenhall* (ed. H.B. Huffmon, F.A. Spina and A.R.W. Green; Winona Lake, IN: Eisenbrauns, 1983), pp. 59-76.

—*Genealogy and History in the Biblical World* (New Haven: Yale University Press, 1977).

—'Israel's Judicial System in the Preexilic Period', *JQR* 74 (1983), pp. 229-48.

—*Sociological Approaches to the Old Testament* (GBS; Philadelphia: Fortress Press, 1984).

Wiseman, D.J., *The Alalakh Tablets* (Occasional publications of the British Institute of Archaeology at Ankar, 2; London: Biblical Institute of Archaeology at Ankar, 1953).

—' "Is it Peace"—Covenant and Diplomacy', *VT* 32 (1982), pp. 311-26.

—'The Laws of Hammurabi Again', *JSS* 7 (1962), pp. 161-72.

—'Law and Order in Old Testament Times', *Vox Evangelica* 8 (1976), pp. 11-14.

—*Nebuchadrezzar and Babylon: The Schweich Lectures 1983* (London: The British Academy, 2nd edn, 1985).

Wolf, C.H., 'Servant', *IDB*, IV, pp. 291-92.

Wolf, E.R., *Peasants* (Englewood Cliffs, NJ: Prentice-Hall Inc., 1966).

Wolff, H.W., *Amos and Joel* (Hermeneia; Philadelphia: Fortress Press, 1977).

—'Master and Slaves: On Overcoming Class-Struggle in the Old Testament', *Int* 27 (1973), pp. 259-72.

Wright, C.J.H., *God's People in God's Land: Family, Land, and Property in the Old Testament* (Grand Rapids: Eerdmans; London: Paternoster Press, 1990).

—'The Israelite Household and the Decalogue: The Social Background and Significance of some Commandments', *TynBul* 30 (1979), pp. 101-24.

—'What Happened Every Seven Years in Israel? Old Testament Sabbatical Institutions for Land, Debts and Slaves Part I & II', *EvQ* 56 (1984), pp. 129-38, 193-201.

Wright, G.E., *Biblical Archaeology* (Philadelphia: Westminster Press, 2nd edn, 1962).

Wright, H.T., 'Recent Research on the Origin of the State', *ARA*, pp. 379-97.

—'Toward an Explanation of the Origin of the State', in *Origins of the State* (ed. R. Cohen and E.R. Service; Philadelphia: Institute for the Study of Human Issues, 1978), pp. 49-68.

Wrigly, E.A., *Population and History* (New York: McGraw-Hill, 1969).

Wyper, G., 'Clan', *ISBE*, I, p. 716.

Yadin, Y., 'Excavations at Hazor (1955–1958)', in *Biblical Archaeology Reader*, II (ed. G.E. Wright and D.N. Freedman; Garden City, NY: Doubleday, 1964), pp. 93-100.

Yaron, R., 'Biblical Law: Prolegomena', in *Jewish Law in Legal History and the Modern World* (ed. B.S. Jackson; Leiden: Brill, 1980), pp. 27-44.

—'The Goring Ox', *ILR* 1 (1966), pp. 396-406.

—'Jewish Law and Other Legal Systems of Antiquity', *JSS* 4 (1959), pp. 308-31.

—*The Laws of Eshnunna* (Jerusalem: Magnes, 1969).

—*The Laws of Eshnunna* (Jerusalem: Magnes; Leiden: Brill, 2nd edn, 1988).

—'The Middle Assyrian Laws and the Bible: Review of G. Cardascia, *Les lois assyriennes*', *Bib* 51 (1970), pp. 549-57.

—'Redemption of Persons in the Ancient Near East', *RIDA* 6 (1959), pp. 155-76.

Yoffee, N., *Explaining Trade in Ancient Western Asia* (MANE, 2.2; Los Angeles: Undena Publications, 1981).

—'On Studying Old Babylonian History: A Review Article', *JCS* 30 (1978), pp. 18-32.

Yurco, F., '3,200-Year-Old Picture of Israelites Found in Egypt', *BARev* 16 (1990), pp. 20-38.

—'Yurco's Response', *BARev* 16 (1991), p. 61.

Zakovitch, Y., *'For Three. . . and for Four': The Pattern for the Numerical Sequence Three-Four in the Bible* (Hebrew) (Jerusalem: Makor, 1979).

Ziskind, J.R., 'Legal Observations on the Enslavement of the Native and Foreign Born in the Ancient Near East in the Second and Early First Millennium BC', *Pal* 15 (1969), pp. 159-72.

INDEXES

INDEX OF REFERENCES

OLD TESTAMENT

ANCIENT NEAR EASTERN TEXTS

ANCIENT NEAR EASTERN LEGAL TEXTS

JOURNAL FOR THE STUDY OF THE OLD TESTAMENT

Supplement Series